Health and Medicine

1992

Health and Medicine

1992

The *Health and Medicine Annual* should not be used in lieu of professional
medical advice. The editors urge all readers to consult a physician
on a regular basis as part of their normal health-care routine and
to seek medical attention should symptoms arise that require
professional diagnosis or treatment.

Staff

Editorial Director
Lawrence T. Lorimer

Executive Editor
Joseph M. Castagno

Director, Annuals
Doris E. Lechner

Art Director
Tone Imset Ruccio

Editor
Lisa Holland

Photo Researcher
Lisa J. Grize

Editorial

Managing Editor	Jeffrey H. Hacker
Production Editor	Jeanne A. Schipper
Copy Editors	David M. Buskus Meghan O'Reilly LeBlanc
Proofreaders	Stephen Romanoff Patricia A. Behan
Editorial Assistants	Karen A. Fairchild Wendy M. McDougall
Chief, Photo Research	Ann Eriksen
Manager, Picture Library	Jane H. Carruth
Art Assistant	Elizabeth A. Farrington
Photo Assistant	Linda R. Kubinski
Chief Indexer	Pauline M. Sholtys
Financial Manager	Marlane L. McLean
Editorial Librarian	Charles Chang
Manager, Electronics	Cyndie L. Cooper
Production Assistant	Carol B. Cox
Staff Assistant	Audrey M. Spragg

Manufacturing

Director of Manufacturing
Joseph J. Corlett

Production Manager
Barbara L. Persan

Senior Production Manager
Christine L. Matta

Production Assistant
Gailynn French

Contributors

KIMBERLEY L. ADLER, Pharm.D., pharmacologist from the Philadelphia V.A. Medical Center
MEDICATIONS AND DRUGS

RUSS ALLEN, Free-lance writer specializing in medicine
TATTOO YOU?

JOSEPH ANTHONY, Contributor, *In Health* magazine
ANATOMY OF A HOSPITAL BILL

ROBERT BARNETT, Free-lance journalist
THE NEW FAST FOOD

EDWARD J. BENZ, JR., M.D., Professor of Internal Medicine, Chief, Section of Hematology, Yale University School of Medicine, New Haven, CT
BLOOD AND LYMPHATIC SYSTEM

BARBARA J. BERG, Contributor, *New Choices for the Best Years* magazine
I'VE GOT A HUNCH

SUE BERKMAN, Free-lance writer specializing in medicine
AS THE WORLD TURNS

EDWARD E. BONDI, M.D., Professor of Dermatology, Hospital of the University of Pennsylvania, Philadelphia
SKIN

ERIC BROWN, M.D., Medical Director of Dialysis, Department of Nephrology, Yale University School of Medicine, New Haven, CT
KIDNEYS

LINDA J. BROWN, Free-lance writer specializing in health, fitness, and environmental issues
BETWEEN A ROCK AND A HARD PLACE
ENVIRONMENT AND HEALTH

GODE DAVIS, Free-lance writer based in Salt Lake City
ABOUT BITES AND STINGS

HERBERT S. DIAMOND, M.D., Chairman, Department of Medicine, Western Pennsylvania Hospital, Pittsburgh, PA
ARTHRITIS AND RHEUMATISM

DIXIE FARLEY, Contributor, *FDA Consumer* magazine
ALIGNING EYES: STRAIGHTENING OUT STRABISMUS

BRENDAN M. FOX, M.D., Clinical Associate Professor, Department of Urology, University of Connecticut, Farmington, CT
UROLOGY

LEE GALWAY, Free-lance writer
MALADY OF THE MALADROIT

CAROLE F. GAN, Philadelphia-based free-lance writer specializing in medicine
EAR, NOSE, AND THROAT
MASSAGE: A HANDS-ON THERAPY

GLEN N. GAULTON, Ph.D., Associate Professor, Department of Pathology and Laboratory Medicine, University of Pennsylvania School of Medicine, Philadelphia, PA
IMMUNOLOGY

ABIGAIL W. GRISSOM, Free-lance writer/editor
FOOD UNDER SCRUTINY
MEDICAL TECHNOLOGY

MARIA GUGLIELMINO, M.S., R.D., Registered dietitian and exercise physiologist
NUTRITION AND DIET

MARY HAGER, Correspondent, *Newsweek*
HEALTH-CARE COSTS

HAL HIGDON, Contributor, *American Health Magazine*
CROSS OVER TO CROSS-TRAINING

LINDA HUGHEY HOLT, M.D., Chairman, Department of Obstetrics and Gynecology, Rush North Shore Hospital, Chicago, IL
WOMEN'S HEALTH

OREST HURKO, M.D., Associate Professor of Neurology, The Johns Hopkins Hospital, Baltimore, MD
BRAIN AND NERVOUS SYSTEM

ERIN HYNES, Free-lance writer based in Austin, TX
GROWING HERBS FOR HEALTHIER COOKING

KENNETH E. ISMAN, Associate Director of Engineering and Standards, National Fire Sprinkler Association, Patterson, NY
FIRE SAFETY IN THE HOME

IRA M. JACOBSON, M.D., Division of Digestive Diseases, The New York Hospital-Cornell Medical Center, New York
LIVER

JAMES F. JEKEL, M.D., M.P.H., Professor of Epidemiology and Public Health, Yale University School of Medicine, New Haven, CT
AIDS
PUBLIC HEALTH
WORLD HEALTH NEWS

KENNETH L. KALKWARF, D.D.S., M.S., Dean, The University of Texas Health Science Center at San Antonio Dental School, San Antonio, TX
TEETH AND GUMS

JENNIFER KENNEDY, M.S., Account and marketing representative with General Health, Inc.; Adjunct Professor, American University, Washington, D.C.
HOUSECALLS: FITNESS AND HEALTH

GINA KOLATA, Contributor, *The New York Times Magazine*
MENTAL GYMNASTICS

MARILYNN LARKIN, New York City-based medical and science writer
NUTRIENT THIEVES

ANDREA MALLOZZI, Free-lance writer specializing in consumer affairs
ALTERNATIVES TO TRADITIONAL SCHOOLS

THOMAS H. MAUGH II, Science writer, *Los Angeles Times*
GENETICS AND GENETIC ENGINEERING

K.F. McDONNELL, Health writer, Thomas Jefferson University, Philadelphia, PA
BONES, MUSCLES, AND JOINTS

ELIZABETH McGOWAN, Free-lance writer based in New York City
ADVENTURE TRAVEL FOR THE DISABLED

STEVEN MEIXEL, M.D., Associate Professor, Department of Family Medicine, University of Virginia, Charlottesville
HOUSECALLS: PRACTICAL NEWS TO USE

WENDY J. MEYEROFF, New York City-based free-lance medical writer
THE PROBLEMATIC PROSTATE

STEPHEN G. MINTER, Editor, *Occupational Hazards Magazine*
OCCUPATIONAL HEALTH

J. MORROW, Ph.D., Contributor, *Health* magazine
BIOFEEDBACK: WIRED FOR A MIRACLE

RICHARD L. MUELLER, M.D., Cardiovascular Center, The New York Hospital, New York, NY
HEART AND CIRCULATORY SYSTEM

SUSAN NIELSEN, Free-lance writer
TANDEMONIUM!

ROBERT C. NOBLE, M.D., Professor of Medicine, Division of Infectious Diseases, University of Kentucky College of Medicine, Lexington, KY
SEXUALLY TRANSMITTED DISEASES

MARCY O'KOON, Free-lance writer
SUICIDE IN CHANGING TIMES

MARIA LUISA PADILLA, M.D., Associate Professor of Medicine, Pulmonary Division, Mount Sinai School of Medicine, New York, NY
RESPIRATORY SYSTEM

RUTH PAPAZIAN, New York City-based free-lance writer specializing in medical and life-style topics
DAIRY AND YOUR DIET

DEVERA PINE, Free-lance writer based in New York City
WHERE DO I GO FROM HERE? TESTING POSITIVE FOR HIV

SUSAN RANDEL, Editor, *Academic American Encyclopedia*
FLEXING CORPORATE MUSCLE
SPEECH DISABILITIES IN CHILDREN

DIANA REESE, Free-lance writer specializing in dentistry
ORTHODONTICS FOR THE NEW AGE

MICHAEL X. REPKA, M.D., Wilmer Ophthalmological Institute, Johns Hopkins University School of Medicine, Baltimore, MD
EYES AND VISION

CYNTHIA PORTER RICKERT, Ph.D., Assistant Professor of Pediatrics, University of Arkansas for Medical Sciences, Little Rock, AR
CHILD DEVELOPMENT AND PSYCHOLOGY

SHARON ROMM, M.D., Free-lance writer based in Washington, D.C.
RECONSTRUCTIVE SURGERY: MORE THAN SKIN DEEP

MACE L. ROTHENBERG, M.D., Assistant Professor of Medicine, University of Texas Health Science Center at San Antonio, San Antonio, TX
CANCER

JAMES A. ROTHERHAM, Ph.D., Senior Associate, Chambers Associates, Inc., Washington, D.C.
GOVERNMENT POLICIES AND PROGRAMS

KAREN M. SANDRICK, Free-lance medical writer
HEALTH PERSONNEL AND FACILITIES

ANTHONY SCHMITZ, Contributor, *In Health* magazine
FOOD NEWS BLUES

STEPHEN A. SIEGEL, M.D., F.A.C.C., Clinical Instructor, Department of Medicine, New York University School of Medicine, New York, NY
HEART ATTACK!

MICHAEL SILVER, M.D., Medical Director, Hospital Division, Philadelphia Child Guidance Center; Clinical Assistant Professor, Department of Psychiatry, University of Pennsylvania, Philadelphia, PA
HOUSECALLS: PSYCHOLOGY

MARISE SIMONS, Contributor, *The New York Times Magazine*
LE BRAIN JOGGING

J. DOUGLAS SMITH, M.D., Clinical Director, Department of Nephrology, Yale University School of Medicine, New Haven, CT
KIDNEYS

DORI STEHLIN, Contributor, *FDA Consumer* magazine
THE CHALLENGE OF RELIEVING PAIN

MONA SUTNICK, R.D., Ph.D., Lecturer, Department of Community and Preventive Medicine, Medical College of Pennsylvania, Philadelphia, PA
HOUSECALLS: NUTRITION

JANET C. TATE, Assistant Editor, Special Reports Home Library, Whittle Communications, Knoxville, TN
CONTACT LENSES: ARE THEY FOR YOU?

JENNY TESAR, Free-lance writer
GENETIC COUNSELING

STEPHEN G. UNDERWOOD, M.D., Associate Medical Director for Admissions and Referrals, Philadelphia Child Guidance Center, Philadelphia, PA
MENTAL HEALTH

GEORGE VALKO, M.D., Instructor, Department of Family Medicine, Jefferson Medical College; Senior physician at the Jeff Care Family Practice office, Philadelphia, PA
HOUSECALLS: MEDICINE AND THE HUMAN BODY

MARVIN M. WEISBROT, R.Ph., M.B.A., Philadelphia V.A. Medical Center and the University of Pennsylvania School of Medicine, Philadelphia, PA
MEDICATIONS AND DRUGS
SUBSTANCE ABUSE

MARC E. WEKSLER, M.D., Wright Professor of Medicine, Cornell University Medical College, New York, NY
AGING

RICK WOLFF, Contributor, *Health* magazine
BIOFEEDBACK: WIRED FOR A MIRACLE

CONNIE ZUCKERMAN, J.D., Assistant Professor of Humanities in Medicine, State University of New York Health Science Center, Brooklyn, NY
BIOETHICS

Contents

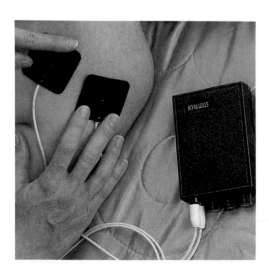

Review '92

Never before in history have people lived so long, and lived such healthy lives. At the beginning of this century, the average life expectancy of a newborn baby in the United States was about 49 years. Today a newborn's average life expectancy is over 75 years. Many factors account for the dramatic improvement, including better sanitation, the development of drugs to control infectious diseases, and new surgical techniques. Equally important has been the layperson's growing understanding of and appreciation for the importance of physical fitness and good nutrition—the realization that unlike the weather, you *can* do something about your health, and in the process not only add years to your life, but put more life into those years. Each year brings new advances. In 1991 surgeons reported the first successful transplants of the small intestine. A 52-year-old man became the world's first recipient of a fully portable heart pump. Taxol, a drug made from the bark of Pacific yew trees, has effectively treated several kinds of cancer.

Medicine has seen astonishing advances in the last decade. Unfortunately, skyrocketing health-care costs have put even the most basic medical treatment beyond the means of many Americans.

Researchers are finding ever more proof of the intimate links between physical and psychological well-being, thus aiding treatment of a range of disorders. Recent reports indicate that emotional stress increases a person's risk of getting the common cold. Mental stress also appears to increase the chances of a heart attack for people suffering from atherosclerosis (hardening of the arteries). Conversely, researchers are discovering biological bases for mental disorders. For example, they have discovered a gene that causes a type of mental retardation, as well as a gene that may predispose some people to certain psychiatric disorders and suicide.

Perhaps the area of medical research that offers the broadest potential benefits is genetic engineering, or human gene therapy. Numerous disorders, including muscular dystrophy and Alzheimer's disease, appear to have a genetic basis and thus are potential candidates for such therapy. In 1991 researchers at the National Cancer Institute (NCI) made the first attempt to treat cancer by injecting genetically altered cells into patients with advanced melanoma.

Coupled with the good news, however, is some disquieting news. AIDS has claimed the lives of more than 120,000 Americans. The incidence of cancer is soaring. Sexually transmitted diseases (STDs) are rampant among the nation's teenagers. There is a resurgence of measles, malaria, and tuberculosis—diseases once believed to be under control. The homicide rate continues to grow. Some 34.7 million Americans are without medical insurance. The nation's emergency rooms are so crowded that many patients with serious conditions leave the hospital without being treated; others wait 12 hours or more before being examined.

In the United States, wide disparities in health status and health care often exist among ethnic and economic groups. On average, the life expectancy of blacks is six years less than that of whites. Poor people are more likely than others to be exposed to high levels of lead and other toxic pollutants. Pregnant black, American Indian, Puerto Rican, and Mexican-American women are less likely than other women to receive early prenatal care. Doctors who analyzed the treatment of almost 30,000 infants in California found that sick newborns covered by insurance policies received much better medical care in hospitals than did sick newborns not covered by insurance. New studies from the American Heart Association found that strokes occur more frequently in blacks than in whites or Hispanics, and that blacks remain more physically impaired after the strokes.

Such inequities present challenges not only to the medical community, but also to political leaders. In addition, there are unresolved moral and ethical dilemmas created by medical advances: issues such as fetal-cell transplants; the use of genetic testing, prompting parents to choose between a handicapped child or aborting the fetus; a terminally ill person's right to commit suicide or to decline certain types of treatment.

Despite problems that may occasionally seem intractable, each year's advances bring hope for the future. In 1991 an orthopedic surgeon regenerated damaged cartilage in animals, using a new procedure that should lead to improved ways to repair damaged cartilage disks in human knees, and prevent or reduce the arthritis that often follows this kind of injury. Researchers used genetic-engineering techniques to treat mice born with Sly's syndrome and Duchenne's muscular dystrophy —experiments that are possible precursors to similar procedures in humans. Genetic-engineering techniques were also used to create a vaccine that protected mice against malaria— the first time that animals had been fully immunized with a human-made vaccine. It was announced that almost all of the initial group of patients with Parkinson's disease who received fetal-cell transplants showed at least minor improvements, and many were dramatically better. And in several laboratories, scientists have succeeded in growing human eye cells, leading to the possibility that it may someday be possible to replace eye tissues damaged by glaucoma.

President Bush, Congress, and the medical industry are all grappling with ways to make our health-care system fairer and less expensive.

Government officials are looking at universal health insurance and other steps that could improve the nation's health-care delivery system. Religious leaders are addressing their communities' problems with drug abuse and AIDS. Businesses are providing employees with corporate fitness centers and child-care centers.

The biggest reason for optimism, however, may well be the desire of growing numbers of ordinary people to become better informed health consumers. People are taking more responsibility for their own health. With the support of health professionals, they are placing greater emphasis on getting regular medical exams and other preventive-medicine practices. They are taking precautions against accidents at home and on the road. They are eager to improve their health through proper diet and physical fitness.

Fortunately, evidence indicates that it's never too late to change one's behavior and hence to increase one's chances of a longer, healthier life.

The Editors

Health and Medicine: Features '92

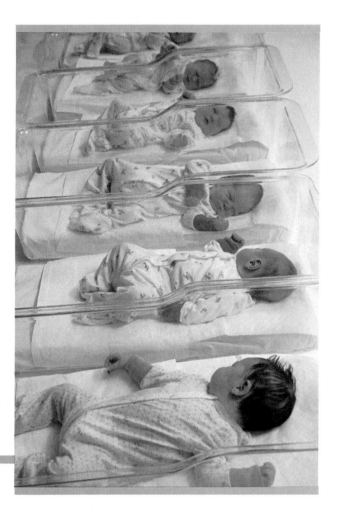

Medicine and the Human Body

New knowledge coupled with technological advances are enabling physicians to offer improved diagnoses and treatment for a host of medical problems. During 1991 the U.S. Food and Drug Administration (FDA) approved the use of alpha interferon for the treatment of hepatitis C, a viral infection that causes chronic liver inflammation and can lead to cirrhosis and cancer.

The FDA also approved didanosine (DDI) for treatment of patients with advanced AIDS who cannot tolerate or are not helped by azidothymidine (AZT), the only other approved AIDS treatment. Foscarnet was approved to combat a viral infection, cytomegalovirus retinitis, that often causes blindness in AIDS patients.

Significant new findings were reported concerning the drug enalapril, which is often used to treat high blood pressure and to alleviate symptoms of congestive heart failure. Two studies found that enalapril does more than just combat shortness of breath and other heart-failure symptoms: it actually reduces the risk of death and the need for hospitalization among people with mild or moderate heart failure. A third study found that enalapril delays the onset of heart failure among people with significant heart damage, such as that resulting from heart attacks.

Diseases of the heart and blood vessels are America's number one killer, accounting for approximately 43 percent of all deaths. The nation's second leading cause of death is cancer. And while death rates from heart disease have declined, cancer incidence and mortality rates have increased steadily. However, scientists are determining the causes of more and more types of cancer. In 1991 they detected the gene that causes colon cancer and linked a common bacterium to stomach cancer. Promising but still experimental treatments for cancer include taxol, a drug made from the bark of Pacific yew trees, and gene therapy, which involves injecting cancer patients with genetically altered cells that attack cancerous tissue.

Survival rates for the most common types of organ-transplant operations con-

See also:
Individual articles in the second half of this book, arranged in alphabetical order, for additional information.

tinued to improve. Unfortunately, the number of people awaiting transplants far exceeds the number of available organs. An estimated 25,000 Americans who die each year are suitable organ sources, but only one-sixth of them actually donate organs.

Artificial organs, or implants, are increasingly common. For example, U.S. surgeons perform more than 140,000 knee-replacement operations annually. A new computer system developed at Cornell University allows surgeons to visualize how an implant will fit and move within a particular patient before the operation is performed. This enables the surgeons to determine if a standard-design implant will be appropriate or if a customized implant is needed.

Traditionally, surgeons have limited the use of anesthetics on infants; they feared that potential harm caused by anesthesia would be greater than any pain experienced by the infants. But a study conducted on newborns undergoing heart surgery found that infants who received deep anesthesia did dramatically better than infants who received light anesthesia.

Delivery procedures for infants with spina bifida, a fairly common birth defect, were expected to change following a report that such infants are twice as likely to be severely paralyzed if they are delivered vaginally than if delivered early by Caesarean section. Another study concluded that pregnant women who take the vitamin folic acid throughout their pregnancies greatly reduce the risk of having babies with neural-tube defects, a serious problem that causes spina bifida and other types of birth defects. Because the neural tube forms within 28 days of conception, dietary vitamin supplements must begin several weeks before a pregnancy is confirmed.

Among the most painful and debilitating experiences are migraine headaches. An estimated 8 million Americans suffer from this malady. A new study found that low-income people are much more likely to have migraines than people at higher income levels. Another study involving more than 1,000 migraine sufferers found that a new drug, sumatriptan, provided significant relief within an hour. Unlike traditional drugs, sumatriptan attacks the underlying cause of the migraine: an abnormal swelling of blood vessels within the brain. Sumatriptan also relieves the nausea that typically accompanies a migraine.

Scientific insight combined with technology has been the force behind the past year's medical advances.

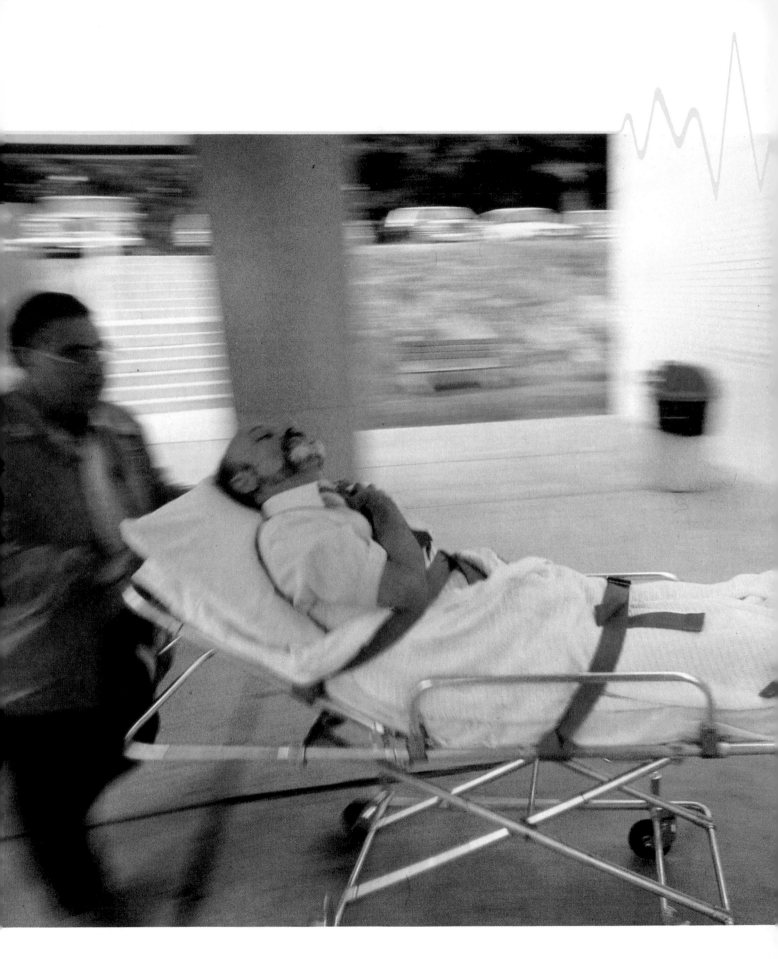

Heart Attack!

by Stephen A. Siegel, M.D.

Angie's first hint of a heart problem occurred while at work in a major New York City bank. She was having a typically stressful day as executive secretary for the vice president of consumer banking, where she dealt with customer complaints. By 10:30 A.M. she had handled 10 irate customers, smoked a half-pack of cigarettes, and had gulped her usual bagel slathered with cream cheese, washed down with three cups of coffee with cream. In anticipation of an unusually heavy workweek, she had reluctantly called her husband to cancel their weekly tennis game, which they had had to postpone too often in the past four months.

At only 47 years of age, Angie was well on her way toward becoming one of a growing number of younger women with coronary-artery disease. More than one in four Americans suffer some form of cardiovascular disease. While more men than women have heart attacks, women are twice as likely to die from them as men. And heart attack is the number one killer of American women, causing more deaths than all forms of cancer combined.

Cardiovascular disease is usually considered a rare problem in premenopausal women. But in recent years, the combination of increased cigarette smoking, hypertension, and stress in younger women has led to higher rates of cardiovascular disease. Today one in nine American women between the ages of 45 and 64 have some form of cardiovascular disease.

The Heart

Sitting in the lower chest, slightly left of center, the heart is the pump that forces oxygen- and nutrient-containing blood to all the tissues in the body. Only a bit larger than a clenched fist, the heart is able to pump 2,000 gallons of blood each day. When the body is at rest, the heart pumps an average of 70 times a minute, but in times of physical or

Most fatalities from heart attacks occur within two hours of the onset of symptoms. It is therefore essential to recognize the earliest signs of an impending attack and seek medical attention immediately.

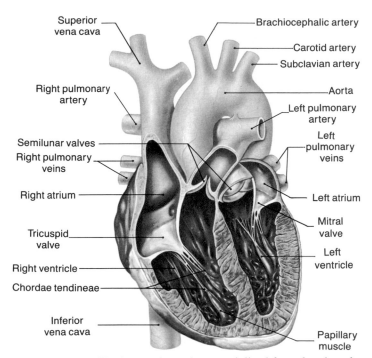

Superior vena cava

Brachiocephalic artery

Carotid artery

Subclavian artery

Right pulmonary artery

Aorta

Left pulmonary artery

Left pulmonary veins

Semilunar valves

Right pulmonary veins

Right atrium

Left atrium

Mitral valve

Tricuspid valve

Left ventricle

Right ventricle

Chordae tendineae

Inferior vena cava

Papillary muscle

The human heart is a specialized four-chambered muscle that pumps blood throughout the body. Heart attacks occur when an artery feeding oxygen-bearing blood to the heart becomes blocked.

emotional stress, this rate can nearly double. Over a span of 75 years, the heart contracts more than 3 billion times. The only time it gets to rest is in the fraction of a second between contractions.

The heart is actually two pumps that are mirror images of each other. The right side receives blood from the body and pumps it to the lungs to get replenished with oxygen. The left side of the heart receives the oxygen-rich blood from the lungs and pumps it throughout the body. The heart is also divided into four chambers. The two upper chambers, known as the atria, are thin-walled chambers that receive blood as it returns to the heart. The two lower chambers, called ventricles, have muscular walls that generate the force required to send blood off to the lungs or to the body's tissues.

Blood arriving from the body fills the right atrium and is then pushed to the right ventricle. The right ventricle expels the blood to the lungs to get replenished with oxygen. The oxygen-rich blood then returns to the left atrium of the heart and moves to the left ventricle. This ventricle has muscular

walls that are three times thicker than those of the right ventricle in order to generate the force required to send the blood on its long trip around the body and back to the heart.

A series of four valves directs the blood flow through the heart and into the major arteries that leave the heart. Each of these valves has a set of flaps that permit blood to flow in only one direction. The heart's pumping action is triggered by an electrical impulse, generated from the sinoatrial node, the body's natural pacemaker. This pacemaker causes the heart to beat at a particular rate, but this rate can change to meet the body's varying demands in response to emotional or physical factors.

Beating the Clock

Until the drenching sweats and nausea occurred, Angie believed that the pressure and burning in her chest were from her last cup of coffee. She was unaware that the inner lining, or endothelium, of one of her coronary arteries carrying fresh oxygen-rich blood to her heart was injured. Earlier that day, possibly while Angie was running to catch the subway, the damaged endothelium ruptured, exposing the deeper muscular tissue of the artery. This event triggered the body to begin to form a blood clot, or thrombosis, a natural response to any injury. This clotting response prevents us from bleeding to death with every tiny cut.

With the exposure of the inner part of the artery, special small blood cells known as *platelets* start to clump. This releases chemical mediators that cause thick bands of fibrin to form, providing the structure and glue of a blood clot. At the same time, other enzymes floating in the blood are activated to dissolve the clot. This seesaw action of clot formation and destruction had been going on for hours in Angie's coronary artery. But at 10:35 A.M. the forces of clot formation finally won. The clot blocked the blood flow inside the artery. Angie's heart muscle, which depends on that artery for nourishment, was becoming starved for oxygen, or *ischemic*. If this lack of oxygen persists long enough, *myocardial infarction* occurs, in which the heart muscle will eventually die.

Angie knew that something was wrong. The pain that she had thought was indigestion was spreading to her shoulder. When the antacids that she always kept in her desk didn't help, she called her friend in the next office. One look at Angie's pale face, rapid breathing, and obvious distress made her friend immediately call 911 for assistance.

Upon their arrival, the paramedics quickly assessed her symptoms. They started an intravenous (IV) line for medications, attached a monitor to display the electrocardiogram (ECG), which records the heartbeat, and placed an oxygen mask over her face, while at the same time whisking her to a nearby hospital. Arriving at the emergency room, the paramedics barely paused as they called out "MI" (for myocardial infarction) to the hospital clerk on the way in.

A quick medical history and a physical examination by a senior resident suggested no other medical illness that would account for Angie's symptoms: the chest pain, known as *angina;* fluid that was building up in her lungs; and the low pulse and blood pressure that made her feel so weak. The ECG revealed that there was damage in the lower, or inferior, wall of her heart. The doctors knew that the right coronary artery was blocked, and that every second that ticked by without oxygen getting through to the heart added to the extent of permanent damage.

Clot Busters

Angie was lucky that no parades, fires, or typical New York City traffic jams delayed her arrival to the emergency room. It had been less than two hours since the pressure in her chest had become severe. Permanent damage was likely to be small if the blood supply to her heart could be restored. The gathered doctors discussed injecting a spe-

Check Your Risk for Coronary-Artery Disease with This Prediction Chart

1. Find Points For Each Risk Factor

Age (If Female)		Age (If Female)		Age (If Male)		Age (If Male)		HDL-Cholesterol		Total-Cholesterol		Systolic Blood Pressure			
Age	Pts.	Age	Pts.	Age	Pts.	Age	Pts.	HDL-C	Pts.	Total-C	Pts.	SBP	Pts.	Other	Pts.
30	−12	47–48	5	30	−2	57–59	12	25–26	7	139–151	−3	98–104	−2	Cigarettes	4
31	−11	49–50	6	31	−1	60–61	14	27–29	6	152–166	−2	105–112	−1	Diabetic-male	3
32	−9	51–52	7	32–33	0	62–64	15	30–32	5	167–182	−1	113–120	0	Diabetic-female	6
33	−8	53–55	8	34	1	65–67	16	33–35	4	183–199	0	121–129	1	ECG-LVH	9
34	−6	56–60	9	35–36	2	68–70	17	36–38	3	200–219	1	130–139	2		
35	−5	61–67	10	37–38	3	71–73	18	39–42	2	220–239	2	140–149	3	0 pts for each NO	
36	−4	68–74	11	39	4	74	19	43–46	1	240–262	3	150–160	4		
37	−3			40–41	5			47–50	0	263–288	4	173–185	5		
38	−2			42–43	6			51–55	−1	289–315	5	173–185	6		
39	−1			44–45	7			56–60	−2	316–330	6				
40	0			46–47	8			61–66	−3						
41	1			48–49	9			67–73	−4						
42–43	2			50–51	10			74–80	−5						
44	3			52–54	11			81–87	−6						
45–46	4			55–56	12			88–96	−7						

2. Sum Points For All Risk Factors

_____ + _____ + _____ + _____ + _____ + _____ + _____ = _____
Age   HDL-C   Total-C   SBP   Smoker   Diabetes   ECG-LVH   Point Total

NOTE: Minus Points Subtract From Total.

3. Look Up Risk Corresponding to Point Total

4. Compare To Average 10 Year Risk

Pts.	Probability 5 Yr.	Probability 10 Yr.	Pts.	Probability 5 Yr.	Probability 10 Yr.	Pts.	Probability 5 Yr.	Probability 10 Yr.	Pts.	Probability 5 Yr.	Probability 10 Yr.	Age	Probability Women	Probability Men
≤1	<1%	<2%	10	2%	6%	19	8%	16%	28	19%	33%	30–34	<1%	3%
2	1%	2%	11	3%	6%	20	8%	18%	29	20%	36%	35–39	<1%	5%
3	1%	2%	12	3%	7%	21	9%	19%	30	22%	38%	40–44	2%	6%
4	1%	2%	13	3%	8%	22	11%	21%	31	24%	40%	45–49	5%	10%
5	1%	3%	14	4%	9%	23	12%	23%	32	25%	42%	50–54	8%	14%
6	1%	3%	15	5%	10%	24	13%	25%				55–59	12%	16%
7	1%	4%	16	5%	12%	25	14%	27%				60–64	13%	21%
8	2%	4%	17	6%	13%	26	16%	29%				65–69	9%	30%
9	2%	5%	18	7%	14%	27	17%	31%				70–74	12%	24%

Prepared by the American Heart Association with the help of William B. Kannel, M.D., Professor of Medicine and Public Health and Ralph D'Agostino, Ph.D., Head, Department of Mathematics, both at Boston University; Keaven Anderson, Ph.D., Statistician, NHLBI, Framingham Study; Daniel McGee, Ph.D., Associate Professor, University of Arizona.

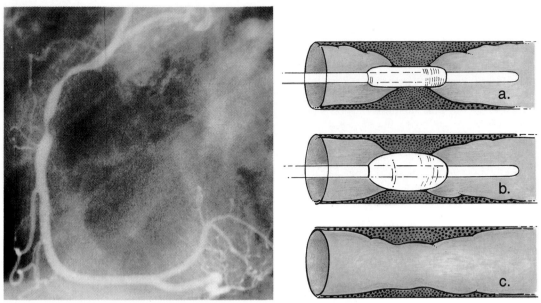

Angioplasty is a nonsurgical technique designed to widen narrowed coronary arteries (above, left). Above right, a balloon-tipped tube is inserted into the artery (A) and is inflated (B), compressing the plaque and enlarging the diameter of the artery (C).

cial "clot-busting," or thrombolytic, drug into her veins. This special drug activates the natural clot-dissolving chemicals present throughout the body. But the drug also has potential risks—it will not only dissolve blood clots in the coronary artery, but also anywhere else a clot may exist. So the needle puncture from a blood test, the irritation of the stomach lining from a small ulcer, or any clot protecting a cut or wound anywhere in the body will also dissolve. This could lead to bleeding and possibly life-threatening complications.

The doctors decided that the potential benefits for Angie from a clot-busting drug would greatly exceed any risks. Within 15 minutes of her arrival at the hospital, t-PA (tissue plasminogen activator), a genetically engineered version of the natural clot-dissolving chemical found in blood vessels, was dripping into Angie's veins. Less than three hours after the onset of her heart attack, Angie felt a short period of light-headedness, followed by a major reduction in her chest pain. The ECG revealed a profound slowing of her heart rate, followed by a series of potentially life-threatening extra beats, or *ar-*

More than 500,000 Americans die each year from heart attacks.

rhythmias, which resulted from the sudden flow of fresh blood to the damaged area. The nurse watching the ECG monitor quickly administered a drug to reduce the risk of these arrhythmias. Soon the profound abnormalities seen on earlier ECG recordings began to resolve. Additional drugs were added in another IV to reduce the ability of the body to form new clots. Angie's heart was starting to heal. She had avoided being one of the more than 500,000 people who die each year in the United States from a heart attack.

Stumbling Block

A few days after recovering from her heart attack, Angie underwent an exercise stress test on a treadmill before leaving the hospital. The t-PA had done its job dissolving the clot. However, the stress test indicated that a severe obstruction still remained. This blockage, known as *atherosclerotic plaque,* had been slowly building in her arteries for several years, and was composed of a combination of cholesterol, inflammatory cells, calcium, and blood clots. During even limited exercise, such as walking on a treadmill, this plaque prevents the artery from carrying adequate amounts of blood to supply the increased demands of the heart cells. During the stress test, Angie again developed angina and ECG abnormalities.

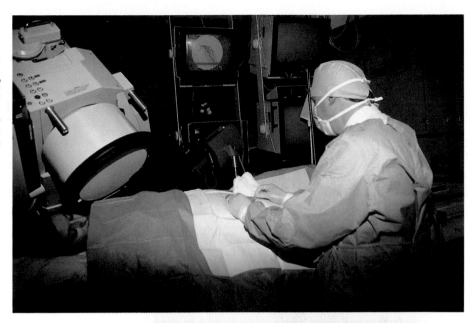

During angioplasty, a surgeon views the location of a balloon-tipped catheter (below right) on a video monitor (right). Angioplasty has come to rival coronary bypass surgery, a much more traumatic procedure.

The abnormal stress test led doctors to recommend a catheterization. After cleaning her groin area with special soaps, the cardiologist inserted a needle into an artery of her right leg. He then directed a long, thin tube, or catheter, through the artery and up to her heart. Dye was injected into the opening of the coronary arteries. As the dye flowed through the arteries, Angie was able to see her arteries appear like branches of a tree in winter, white against the dark background on a nearby monitor. Even to Angie's untrained eye, one of those artery trunks appeared extremely narrow in the middle. This was the site of the atherosclerotic plaque that had caused her heart attack. The small artery was narrowed to less than one-tenth of its usual 2- to 3-millimeter width.

The cardiologist then initiated *angioplasty,* in which another tube with a small deflated balloon was pushed through the larger catheter. The metal wire at the tip of the balloon catheter could be seen on the monitor entering the coronary artery. The doctor manipulated the wire to place the balloon in the middle of the plaque. The balloon was then inflated, appearing on the monitor as a dog bone, narrowed at the center where the plaque resisted the inflation. Angie began to develop that sick feeling in her stomach, along with the return of chest pain, as the balloon obstructed the blood flow in the artery. The balloon was then deflated to

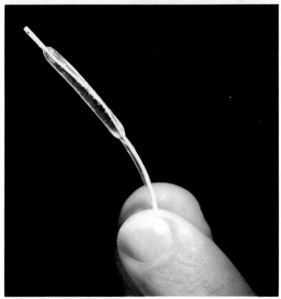

allow Angie's blood flow to the heart to return to normal. After a few minutes, the inflation was repeated. Still there was no change before signs of ischemia forced the doctor to deflate the balloon. With the third inflation, however, the narrow waist of the balloon could be seen to stretch and finally open. With repeated inflation the artery was opened to less than a 50 percent blockage. The arteries are large enough that anything less than a 75 percent blockage should not limit blood flow enough to cause angina.

Changing Life-style

Angie's brush with death spurred her to make some major life-style changes. Her first step was to kick her smoking habit, thereby reducing her risk of a second heart attack by 50 percent. (Ten years after quitting, the risk of death from heart disease for former smokers is the same as for people who never smoked.) Angie also began to change her diet to include more food low in cholesterol and saturated fats.

Often there is confusion about the relationship between cholesterol and atherosclerosis. People get cholesterol in two ways. The body—primarily the liver—produces about 1,000 mg a day. An additional 400 to 500 mg or more can come from foods derived from animals, particularly egg yolks, meat, fish, poultry, and whole-milk dairy products.

Cholesterol is carried in the bloodstream by special "carriers" called *lipoproteins*. Low-density lipoprotein (LDL) is often referred to as the "bad" cholesterol, because if too much LDL-cholesterol is circulating in the blood, it may deposit in artery walls, causing plaques that lead to atherosclerosis.

Alternatively, high-density lipoprotein (HDL) is called "good" cholesterol because it acts as a scavenger, removing deposits of cholesterol and taking them to the liver for elimination or reprocessing into necessary building blocks of cells.

Low-cholesterol, low-fat diets will reduce circulating cholesterol by affecting its metabolism in the liver and the ability of the liver to soak up cholesterol from the blood. Short periods of reduced cholesterol intake have little effect. But long-term modification of the diet over months and years will have a beneficial impact on the cholesterol profile.

As a result of her diet modifications, Angie's cholesterol fell from 270 milligrams per deciliter (mg/dl) at the time of her heart attack to 210 mg/dl. Her LDL levels had fallen from 170 to 120 mg/dl, well below the recommended level of 130 mg/dl. At the same time, she was also able to elevate her HDL cholesterol level from 35 to 60 mg/dl. Now more than 25 percent of the cholesterol in her blood was the "good" type.

Like over 46 percent of the population, Angie did not realize that she had hyperten-

Heart attack is the number one killer of American women. Regular exercise can help women of all ages control their weight and their cholesterol, and thereby decrease their risk of heart disease.

sion. This silent killer of more than 31,600 Americans a year is a major factor in heart disease, stroke, and kidney disease. Caused by the constriction of small arteries, or arterioles, hypertension causes the heart to work harder to pump blood. Over a long period of time, the overworked heart may enlarge and, as a result, may have a hard time meeting the demands placed on it. Hypertension also causes arteries and arterioles to become scarred, hardened, and less elastic, possibly leading to atherosclerosis.

Fortunately, aggressive detection programs and advances in treatment in recent years have led to a 20 percent decline in the hypertension-related death rate between 1978 and 1988. To lower her blood pressure, Angie initiated a regular exercise program. The combination of improved diet and regular exercise allowed her to lose weight, which in turn helped her lower her blood pressure. But despite her efforts, Angie's doctor didn't feel that her blood pressure was low enough. So he prescribed an antihypertensive drug that reduced her blood pressure to normal levels.

The medications that reduce blood pressure are also useful in opening, or dilating, coronary arteries. These drugs relax the muscle that wraps every artery, helping to prevent spasms that might lead to angina or recurrent damage to the endothelium. There are currently three major classes of drugs that are used to treat angina. The nitrates, such as nitroglycerin, relax the muscles in vascular walls to widen veins and arteries. Beta-blockers lower and regulate the heartbeat, which lessens the heart's work load. The calcium channel blockers dilate blood vessels by blocking the pores that let calcium ions—known to constrict vessels—into the cells of artery walls.

Surgical Options

Fortunately for Angie, the combination of life-style changes and drugs was able to control her angina enough to allow her to lead a full and active life. But for others, when medications fail, or if the blockages are so severe or numerous that they present a dangerous risk of death or heart attack, surgery may be necessary.

There are over 360,000 coronary-artery bypass operations performed each year in the United States. In this operation a cardiovascular surgeon will remove veins from the leg or arm and use them as a new conduit to direct blood flow around the blockage in the artery. Sometimes the arteries to the inner chest wall can be redirected to the coronary arteries. Although commonly performed, this procedure is still major surgery—the breastbone is sawed open, blood is redirected through a heart-lung machine while the arteries are worked on, and then the breastbone is closed using wires. Despite the intricacies of the operation, these days the risk of a serious complication or death is relatively low, less than 5 percent. And about half these operations are successfully performed on people older than 65, even those in their 90s!

If the extent of artery blockage is limited, then simpler, less-invasive techniques are possible. Angie's balloon angioplasty, which "cracks open" plaque, is one less-invasive option. Attempts to use different types of lasers to "burn away" the blockage are also being evaluated. And recently atherectomy, in which a rapidly rotating blade is used to cut away the narrowed area, has shown great promise. All of these procedures are "closed-chest" techniques that reduce the patient's complications, recovery time, and pain suffered, compared with coronary-artery bypass surgery. However, these less-invasive procedures share a relatively high rate of blockage recurrence—20 to 30 percent of arteries opened by these techniques will close again within six months.

In addition to these improved technical procedures, work is progressing on drugs that will reduce the inflammation of the artery, as well as the stickiness, or adhesiveness, of platelets. The combination of advances in surgery, less-invasive, closed-chest techniques, and medications holds great hope for reducing the 1 million deaths that occur annually in the United States as a result of heart disease.

Detection and treatment of hypertension can prevent more-serious problems from developing.

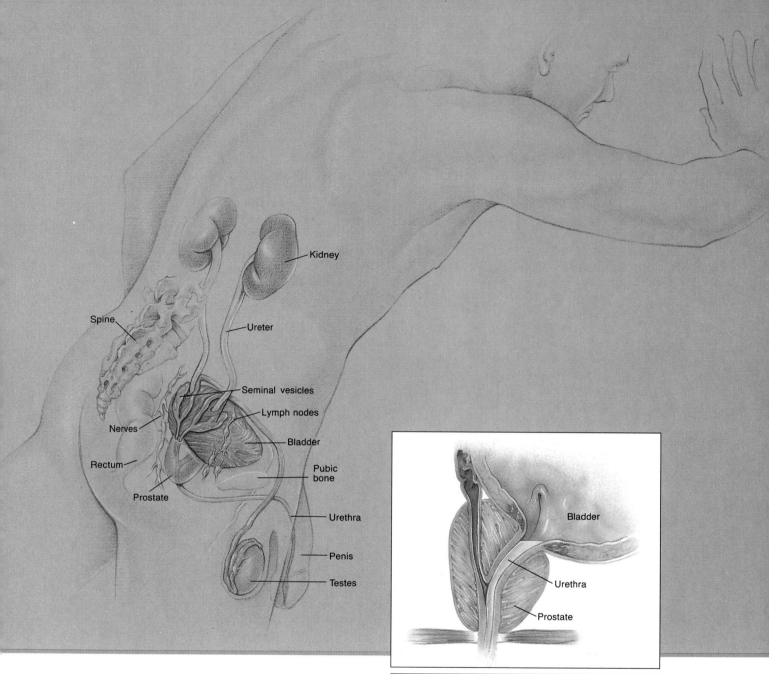

Kidney

Spine

Ureter

Seminal vesicles

Lymph nodes

Nerves

Bladder

Rectum

Pubic bone

Prostate

Urethra

Penis

Testes

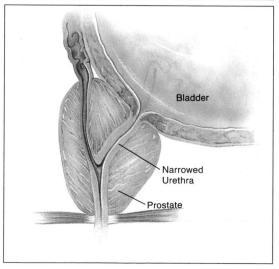

Bladder

Urethra

Prostate

Bladder

Narrowed Urethra

Prostate

THE PROBLEMATIC PROSTATE

by Wendy J. Meyeroff

It's amazing how something about the size of a walnut can cause a man so much trouble, but that's the case with one of the most—if not *the* most—troublesome parts of male anatomy: the prostate gland. Every year, hundreds of thousands of men suffer everything from mild pain to impotence because of this relatively small organ. So what exactly is it, and why does it cause all these problems?

The prostate gland is one of a man's three major sex glands, the other two being the *testicles* and the *seminal vesicles*. The prostate produces *semen,* the fluid that carries a man's sperm from the testicles. The semen is then stored in the seminal vesicles.

The prostate is located right under the bladder. The tube that empties urine from the bladder through the penis, the *urethra,* passes right through the prostate. It is the prostate's close proximity to the urethra that causes most of a man's suffering. Sometime after age 35, the prostate begins to grow. Eventually (usually after age 50), this growth starts "suffocating" the urethra, squeezing it and interfering with the proper flow of urine.

It is generally problems with urination that first alert a man that there's something wrong. The most common symptoms are an increasing number of trips to the bathroom and the need to urinate again after just 5 or 10 minutes. Other symptoms include difficulty starting or stopping urination, a feeling that the bladder is not being emptied, and, in some cases, burning urine and/or urinary-tract infection.

There are a number of conditions that can lead to urinary problems in men. In men under 40, an infection called *prostatitis* can cause an inflammation of the prostate gland and block the urine's flow. Many other urinary problems are not even related to prostate problems. Conditions in which pressure is exerted on the spinal cord, such as spina bifida, can interfere with the bladder's ability to empty properly. The sexually transmitted disease gonorrhea can also cause urination problems by producing scarring—and thus narrowing—of the urethra. Finally, antihistamines or decongestants may sometimes cause acute urinary blockage. Effective treatment relies on proper diagnosis. For this reason, a man who finds himself with any of the aforementioned symptoms should consult a urologist, a doctor who specializes in diagnosing and treating problems of the urinary system, as soon as possible.

In men 50 or older, urinary problems generally lead back to the prostate. One common ailment, *benign prostatic hyperplasia* (BPH), is a fancy way of saying the prostate has enlarged enough to cause problems. The specific cause of BPH is unknown, although hormonal activity is strongly suspected. Over 75 percent of men over 50 are affected with this problem. Another problem is prostate cancer. Although not as pervasive (it affects 1 out of 11 American men), it is far more dangerous than BPH: out of 132,000 men afflicted each year, 34,000 die.

In trying to pinpoint the cause of prostate cancer, researchers have found that race seems to be one factor. No one knows why, but black Americans have the world's highest rate of prostate cancer. Diet may also play some sort of role. Carolyn Clifford, Ph.D., of the National Cancer Institute's (NCI's) Diet and Cancer Branch notes that some epidemiological studies have linked high dietary fat with increased risk of prostate cancer.

Prostate problems plague thousands of men each year.

A recent report from Johns Hopkins University Medical School indicates that, as in breast cancer among women, family history plays a strong role in determining the chance of prostate cancer in men. In a study of 690 men who already had prostate cancer, 15 percent were found to have a brother or father with the disease. The number of affected relatives increased the risk: men with one affected relative were twice as likely to develop prostate cancer, while those with three or more family members affected had *11 times* the risk!

The walnut-sized prostate gland lies between the pubic bone and the rectum (facing page). The urethra, the tube which carries urine from the bladder, passes through the prostate (upper inset); an enlarged prostate constricts the urethra (lower inset), interfering with urine flow.

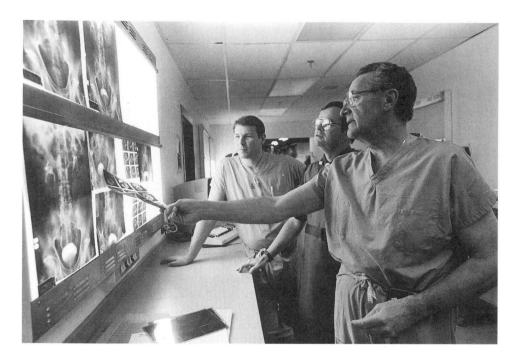

When the prostate is enlarged, doctors often prescribe various imaging procedures and study the results (left) before making a final diagnosis.

If a tumor is suspected, a needle biopsy (opposite) may be used to determine whether the tumor is malignant or benign. In such a biopsy, a thin needle, guided by ultrasound, is used to remove tissue samples.

Diagnosis

Early diagnosis to determine if prostate enlargement is due to a serious problem or simply normal aging is critical to survival. To diagnose prostate problems, experts agree that there are now two procedures that every man over 50 should undergo annually. The first, called a *digital rectal exam,* has been used for years, and is simply a matter of the doctor inserting his gloved finger in the patient's rectum to examine the size and shape of the prostate.

The second is a new blood test that looks for elevated levels of a protein called *prostate-specific antigen* (PSA). PSA is produced exclusively by the prostate gland. Levels apparently rise when cancer or some other prostate problem is present. Besides early detection, PSA is being used to determine how far prostate cancer has progressed (which in turn determines the choice of treatment), and how well the diseased prostate is responding to treatment.

It should be emphasized that a PSA-positive test is not a death sentence. Many men live with prostate cancer without even knowing it. The NCI notes that in autopsies of men 75 and older, 80 percent had prostate cancer! What is important is to know how advanced the cancer is. Further tests, particularly a *transrectal ultrasonography* (an ultrasound of the prostate area) and a biopsy (a tissue sample), help make that determination.

Choosing Therapy

Doctors also consider the following questions before determining a course of treatment:

• *Is there any sign of infection?*

• *Is there any back pain?* If so, the kidneys may be involved.

• *Can the bladder empty completely?* In a test called *urodynamics,* the bladder is filled with water. Then the doctor measures how well the patient holds his water, and the flow rate upon urination.

• *How uncomfortable is the patient?* Some men hardly notice a problem, even with a highly enlarged prostate. If the growth seems benign and the man is only mildly inconvenienced, the "grin-and-bear-it" solution is often suggested. Changing certain habits may help to ease demand on the bladder and decrease the urge to urinate. Specifically, cutting down on or eliminating alcohol (a diuretic) and stimulants (such as caffeine), and, as mentioned earlier, not using antihistamines and decongestants are the steps usually recommended.

• *How old is the patient?* Few doctors will recommend surgery, even if the prostate is cancerous, to a patient who is extremely elderly or feeble.

BPH Treatment Options

For the BPH patient for whom surgery is deemed too risky, or for those who are uncomfortable enough to want relief (but not so

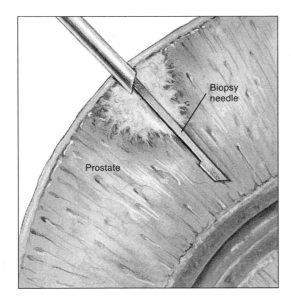

Biopsy needle

Prostate

uncomfortable that surgery can't wait), drugs are offering hope of at least temporary relief. Generally, however, once drug therapy is discontinued, the symptoms return. Among the most promising drugs are:

• *Hytrin:* Currently approved by the Food and Drug Administration (FDA) only for treating hypertension, Hytrin relaxes blood-vessel muscles so that blood flows more smoothly. In BPH, this same relaxing effect seems to open the neck of the bladder, allowing smoother urine flow.

• *Proscar:* This medication inhibits the production of an enzyme that seems to spur prostate growth. Although not yet approved by the FDA, Proscar looks very promising: in clinical studies, it increases urine flow in up to 71 percent of patients.

Today, however, the most common procedure for treating prostate enlargement is *transurethral resection of the prostate* (TURP), used in treating both BPH and early prostate cancer. The 90-minute operation involves inserting a hollow tube called a catheter into and through the urethra, and scraping away excess prostatic tissue. The catheter remains in the patient to drain urine from the bladder into a collection bag. The catheter is generally removed before the patient is released from the hospital. Over 400,000 TURPs are performed each year.

Doctors are now seriously reevaluating the procedure's effectiveness—for several reasons. While no one argues against surgery being recommended when an enlarged prostate causes major problems—such as infection, bleeding, or a total inability to urinate—doctors now recognize that only 25 percent of the men on whom TURPs are performed each year experience such symptoms. Even more important, the procedure produces several less-than-pleasant side effects.

One side effect, experienced by approximately 70 to 90 percent of TURP patients, is retrograde ejaculation. This means that semen leaks backward into the bladder. The fluid harmlessly flushes out during urination, and some couples even enjoy the fact that retrograde ejaculation makes lovemaking "less messy." However, there is one definite negative: this side effect renders a man infertile.

Other TURP problems, though rare, are distasteful enough to make many men seek other answers. Somewhat less than 1 percent of TURP patients end up suffering incontinence, or loss of bladder control. Of even more concern to most men is the fact that up to 6 percent of those who undergo the procedure become impotent. Despite all the potential problems, the procedure offers no guarantees that a man is cured: approximately 15 to 20 percent of those treated through TURP are back for further scrapings within eight years.

The only currently approved surgical alternative to TURP is *balloon dilatation,* but it is generally out of favor among surgeons. The inflation of a small balloon inside the urethra clears a path as the balloon expands. The procedure takes only 10 minutes and can be done on an outpatient basis. Unfortunately, the effect is only short-term: most patients have to be re-treated within two years. Also, because the procedure doesn't remove any tissue, it doesn't allow the surgeon to check for prostate cancer.

It's no wonder, therefore, that scientists have been searching for other answers. Among the exciting options now being explored are the following:

• *USA* (ultrasonic aspiration). Ultrasound waves lacerate the tissue and suck it out. As in TURP, the removed tissue can be checked for signs of cancer. Two-year post-operative studies at Pennsylvania Hospital in Philadelphia seem promising: only *15 percent* of patients experienced retrograde ejaculation, and some 5 percent reported erection impairment.

• *TULIP*. The Lahey Clinic in Massachusetts reports real promise with this procedure, an acronym for Transurethral Ultrasound-guided, Laser-Induced Prostatectomy. A laser cuts away excess tissue in only 15 minutes; there is no bleeding, no reported problems with incontinence or impotence, and less than *1 percent* chance of retrograde ejaculation. The patient stays in the hospital overnight, and a different type of catheter, more comfortable and effective than that used in TURP, is inserted into the bladder near the pubic bone for about a week for drainage.

• *Prostatron*. In this procedure, microwaves heat the prostate through a catheter, causing the gland to shrink, resulting in increased urine flow. Some estimates indicate that the one-hour procedure, currently being tested at Rush-Presbyterian Hospital in Chicago and four other centers nation-

In a procedure abbreviated TURP, a catheter is inserted into and through the urethra, and excess prostatic tissue is scraped away.

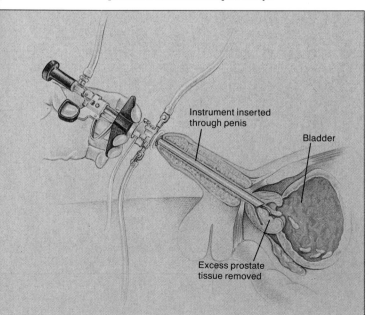

Instrument inserted through penis

Bladder

Excess prostate tissue removed

wide, might replace up to 40 percent of current TURPs.

• *Intraurethral Stent*. This is a permanent urethral implant that essentially serves as a "tunnel" for the urine. Studies at the Mayo Clinic in Minnesota indicate that the intraurethral stent can be implanted in less than 15 minutes on an outpatient basis under local or regional anesthesia. It causes no problems with bleeding, incontinence, or impotence, though there may be a few weeks of irritation during urination.

Current research focuses on the aforementioned procedures in terms of treating BPH, mainly because so many more men suffer from, or are likely to develop, that problem. However, just as TURPs are already used in excising very small cancers, eventually many of the other experimental procedures mentioned above may also be applied to that end. (Microwaves, for example, are already being tested on cancer in Europe.)

Cancer Treatment

Current options for fighting prostate cancer include surgery, radiation therapy, hormone therapy, and chemotherapy, each of which may be used alone or in combination with another treatment. How far the disease has progressed plays a key role in determining the type of therapy plan selected.

• *Radical prostatectomy* is the surgical removal of the prostate. This procedure works best when the cancer is still in the early stages, confined to a small area. The *retropubic* technique involves removing the cancer through the lower abdomen, while the *perineal* technique approaches the cancer through the perineum, the area between the scrotum and anus. The perineal approach requires less operating time, which can be an advantage for patients with heart conditions. However, it doesn't allow the surgeon access to the lymph nodes, to which the cancer may have spread. At Johns Hopkins a new retropubic technique is allowing surgeons to remove a wider margin of tumors while offering greater reassurance of preserving potency. It also shows an impressive local recurrence rate of only 4 percent after five years.

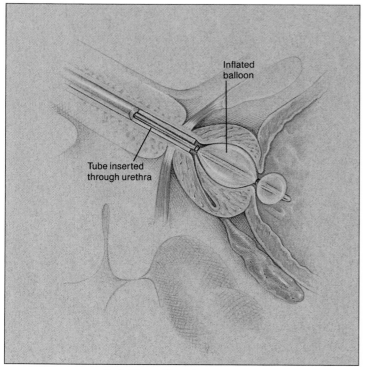

In balloon dilatation, a balloon is inflated to push prostate tissue away from the urethra. The beneficial effects generally last only a few years.

• *Radiation therapy* is best used when the cancer is localized; this treatment can cure cancer in its early stages. The radiation may be administered externally, by machine, or by implanting tiny radioactive seeds directly into the tumor (a process called *interstitial radiation therapy*). Side effects of this treatment include nausea, fatigue, and skin reactions. External treatments often cause a gradual loss of sexual potency.

• *Hormone therapy* is used when the cancer has already spread beyond the prostate. It is intended to reduce testosterone, a male sex hormone that seems to spur cancer growth. In one method, the testicles, the glands that produce testosterone, are surgically removed in a procedure called an *orchiectomy*. Most men know it better as castration, and, for obvious reasons, they are not anxious to submit to the procedure when other options suffice.

In *estrogen therapy*, female sex hormone (estrogen) is administered (usually in pill form) to reduce the production of testosterone. The disadvantages of this option

are the hormone's "feminizing" effects, such as enlargement of the breasts and water retention, though these seem to reverse when therapy is discontinued. Other side effects include nausea, vomiting, and increased risk of heart problems.

• *Luteinizing Hormone-Releasing Hormone (LHRH) agonists:* Lupron, which is either injected daily or injected once a month under the skin to release slowly, and Zoladex, given only in monthly time-release form. This newer procedure seems to avoid the side effects of estrogen therapy, though it may cause a temporary rise in other cancer symptoms, such as bone pain. These symptoms may be treated with aspirin alone, or in combination with *antiandrogen therapy,* which also blocks male hormonal activity. The latter is recommended only in combination with LHRH, and it brings its own set of side effects, including diarrhea, nausea, and vomiting.

• *Chemotherapy* is generally recommended only when prostate cancer has spread throughout the body. There are many drugs used in chemotherapy, some used in combination, but all have numerous side effects, since they invade healthy cells as well as diseased ones. Hair loss (which grows back after therapy is completed), nausea, vomiting, and interference with blood clotting are just a few of the complications arising from chemotherapy.

Because sexual function is so often impaired or even destroyed in prostate treatment (particularly surgery), much of today's research is focusing on ways to preserve potency. At Johns Hopkins, experimental nerve grafts on mice have restored the animals' ability to have erections. This research leads to speculation that in the future, doctors who have cut the nearby nerves during prostatectomy may be able to restore sexual function through nerve grafts.

Finally, all men who have had prostate problems, whether benign or cancerous, must see their doctor regularly (every six months or annually). It is crucial to keep track of the condition's current status and to monitor the effectiveness of any ongoing treatment.

Where do I go from here? Testing positive for HIV

by Devera Pine

When L.A. Lakers star Magic Johnson announced last year that he was HIV-positive, he brought the AIDS epidemic glaringly to the attention of mainstream America. AIDS centers around the country reported a surge in the demand for AIDS tests; at the same time, AIDS hot lines lit up with callers requesting information on the deadly disease. Magic's announcement drove home the fact that although AIDS has been a recognized killer for more than a decade now, it still remains a deep mystery to a large segment of society. Many people know some of the basic facts about AIDS, but they remain bewildered when it comes to the physical and emotional implications of the disease. Just what does it mean to be HIV-positive? And what does the future hold for Magic Johnson and for the estimated 1 million other Americans who are HIV-positive?

AIDS and HIV: The Basics

AIDS (acquired immune deficiency syndrome) is caused by HIV (human immunodeficiency virus). The disease attacks the body's immune system, destroying the cells that fight off invading bacteria and viruses. Without this protection, a variety of serious infections can take hold in the body.

Like other viruses, HIV comes in several strains. In the United States, the most common strain is HIV-1. HIV-2, often found in Africa, is responsible for only 20 AIDS cases in the United States, according to the Centers for Disease Control (CDC). HIV is transmitted via body fluids such as blood and semen: sex, sharing infected needles during intravenous drug use, transfusions, and organ transplants can all pass on the virus. A woman may also transmit the virus to her baby during pregnancy or via breast-feeding. Although AIDS was first noticed in this country in homosexual men and intravenous drug users, Magic Johnson's case pointedly illustrates that heterosexuals and, indeed, *anyone* can become infected.

An estimated 1 million Americans have acquired HIV and the numbers are growing.

Precautions such as using condoms during intercourse can reduce (but *not* eliminate) the risk of contracting AIDS.

If you're at risk for AIDS, there are two tests commonly used to screen for the HIV virus: the ELISA (enzyme-linked immunosorbent assay) and the Western blot tests, both of which search for the presence of HIV antibodies in the bloodstream produced in response to the virus. Once a person is infected with HIV, it takes six to eight weeks for antibodies to the virus to appear in the bloodstream. During this period an HIV test may come back negative. Therefore, a diagnosis of HIV-positive is confirmed only when two successive ELISAs and one Western blot test give positive results. Although there were some problems with false-positive and false-negative results when these tests were first developed, according to the CDC, the assays are now more than 99 percent accurate. Between 20 million and 25 million HIV tests are performed each year, mostly by blood banks and plasma centers.

Myth vs. Fact

One common misconception about AIDS is the belief that once a person has tested HIV-positive, he or she will immediately fall ill. While the disease seems to progress quite rapidly in children, in adults an HIV infection occurs in several stages. In the six to eight weeks that it takes for antibodies to develop after the initial infection, some people experience brief but mild symptoms, including fever, headache, fatigue, and swollen glands. Once antibodies develop, an "incubation" period, often symptom-free, occurs. According to one study, the average length of this symptom-free period is 11 years, says Jay Dobkin, M.D., director of the AIDS Program at Columbia-Presbyterian Medical Center in New York City.

For instance, Ron, a 37-year-old computer programmer, first learned that he was HIV-positive two years ago. In spite of a few persistent colds and one bout of pneumonia, so far Ron has remained basically healthy since getting the bad news.

As the immune system becomes increasingly damaged, early signs of illness begin to appear, including loss of appetite; weight loss; fatigue; swollen lymph nodes in the neck, armpits, and groin; night sweats; fever and chills; persistent diarrhea; a persistent cough; and lingering infections. Some people whose immune systems are seriously damaged experience AIDS-related complex, or ARC. Symptoms of this condition include fungal infections of the mouth, throat, skin, and mucous membranes; severe and constant viral infections (herpes, for instance); fevers; fatigue; and headaches.

The final stage of an HIV infection is AIDS. At this point, opportunistic diseases take advantage of the severely weakened immune system. Common opportunistic infections include *Pneumocystis carinii* pneumonia (PCP), Kaposi's sarcoma (a type of skin cancer), and toxoplasmosis, a parasitic infection, often of the brain and nervous system. Because the immune system is so damaged at this stage, these infections are eventually fatal.

AIDS: The Numbers

Since the Centers for Disease Control (CDC) first began keeping records on AIDS in 1981, there have been 202,921 full-blown cases in this country. Of that number, over 133,000 people have died. In America, AIDS is more common among men: according to the CDC, 181,696 males have had the disease, as opposed to 21,225 females. An estimated 3,400 children have also been infected.

The CDC estimates that 56 percent of all cases of AIDS have occurred in men who have had sex with other men (regardless of whether they are primarily heterosexual, bisexual, or homosexual); 19 percent occurred in intravenous-drug users. An estimated 6 percent of all cases occurred in heterosexuals; 2 percent occurred in individuals who have received transfusions of blood or blood components, or tissue transplants; 1 percent occurred in hemophiliacs. The remaining cases are the result of multiple modes of exposure to the HIV.

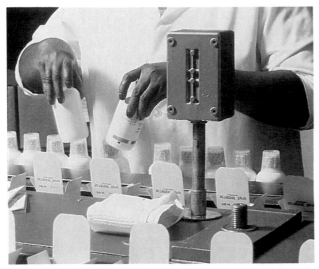

Researchers (above) hope to develop a drug that will neutralize HIV. In the meantime, people who have HIV can find some encouragement in the life of Elizabeth Glaser (right), who remains healthy, active, and upbeat 10 years after testing positive.

New Hope

People who are HIV-positive are now surviving longer than ever, thanks to several new drugs that appear to slow the course of the virus. Ron, for instance, takes the drug AZT (azidothymidine); the drug DDI (dideoxyinosine), which the Food and Drug Administration (FDA) approved last year for patients who can't tolerate AZT, also seems to help slow the disease. Other drugs now being tested also offer hope: a drug that inhibits a gene on the HIV virus; and interleukin 2, which may rebuild the immune system. Both drugs are now currently in clinical trials. (For information about enrolling in an experimental drug-treatment program, call 1-800-TRIALS-A or call the American Foundation for AIDS Research at 212-682-7440. Also see the other hot-line numbers on page 34.)

New treatments for the diseases that affect HIV-positive people also have had a big impact on the survival and quality of life of AIDS sufferers, says Dr. Dobkin. "When we counsel patients who have tested positive, we tell them that it may take a long time—they really can't start acting as if they're on their last legs. On the other hand, they have to assume that they're infected and infectious. They have to modify their behavior."

Part of that behavior modification, for instance, means understanding—and following—the principles of safe sex. A person who is HIV-positive also cannot donate blood or organs. For women who are HIV-positive, pregnancy is a big issue: not only can they pass the virus on to a fetus, pregnancy can worsen the mother's HIV infection. Other life-style changes involve common sense—although there is no systematic data indicating the effect of exercise, nutrition, and alcohol use on the disease, it probably wouldn't hurt to quit smoking, eat right, exercise regularly, and forgo alcohol and other drugs, says Dr. Dobkin. Interestingly, many physicians were surprised by Magic Johnson's decision to give up professional basketball, since it's not clear that strenuous exercise has an effect on the course of the disease.

Bertram Schaffner, M.D., psychiatrist and cochairman of the New York District Branch of the American Psychiatric Committee on AIDS, also advises that anyone diagnosed

HIV-positive should arrange for good medical care—if you can't afford the drugs, you may be able to get them for free under certain government programs—and get their legal affairs in order by, for instance, making a will.

A Helping Hand

If you're the friend, spouse, lover, or relative of someone who has just been diagnosed as HIV-positive, chances are that you, too, will experience shock, fear, and a sense of powerlessness, says Bertram Schaffner, M.D., psychiatrist and cochairman of the New York District Branch of the American Psychiatric Committee on AIDS. But your support can help a loved one who is HIV-positive through a difficult adjustment. Dr. Schaffner suggests taking these two steps:

—Learn as much as you can. "Getting educated about AIDS is one of the first things a friend, wife, or lover should do," he says. "Knowledge helps." When Francine's hemophiliac son was diagnosed positive, for instance, Francine headed to her county medical society to search the library for information. She also contacted the local hemophilia society, as well as several toll-free AIDS hot lines. She now keeps track of the latest experimental treatments for her son.

—Join a support group. Contact your city's AIDS service organization for a reference to an appropriate group in your area: Francine, for instance, joined a group for parents whose children have AIDS. She found that sharing her fears and angers with other parents gave her the strength she needed to support her son.

—Be a friend. Motivate your HIV-infected friend or relative to stay healthy; make sure he or she eats properly, gets enough rest, and follows through with medical treatment.

The Emotional Side

Although an HIV infection may not always have an immediate physical impact, it does have immediate emotional repercussions. Although reactions vary according to individual backgrounds and personalities, most people are shocked. "The immediate feeling is that you've been given a death sentence," says Dr. Schaffner. "There's an uncertainty over how soon you will die and what kind of death you will have—whether it will be painful or repulsive, for instance."

Many people also feel disgraced and isolated. They fear being abandoned by their friends and family, being fired from their jobs, or losing their health insurance. They are afraid that having the disease will reveal something about their life-styles that they have sought to keep secret. For all of these reasons, the urge to commit suicide is, at

Most people are shocked to learn they have tested HIV-positive. Numerous support groups help people get through the initial period of uncertainty.

On The Job

Given the stigma of AIDS and the rising costs of health care, many people with HIV fear losing both their jobs and their health insurance. Unfortunately, in many cases their fears are well-grounded: there are no federal laws that protect people who are HIV-positive from this type of discrimination. Instead, the laws vary from state to state. Check with your state insurance commissioner to learn about the laws in your state; or call the Occupational Safety and Health Administration (both numbers should be in the phone book).

AIDS Information Numbers

The following phone numbers can provide more information about AIDS:

National AIDS hot line: 1-800-342-AIDS
Gives referrals, answers questions, can provide information on treatment program test sites. Open 24 hours.

National AIDS Clearinghouse: 1-800-458-5231
Provides general information, information on clinical trials, publications, and business and workplace information. Open Monday through Friday 9 AM to 7 PM Eastern Standard time.

Clinical Trials Information Service: 1-800-TRIALS-A
Provides information on clinical trials of experimental drugs. Open Monday through Friday 9 AM to 7 PM Eastern Standard time.

Project Inform: 1-800-822-7422
Provides treatment and disease information to people with HIV. Open 10 AM to 4 PM Pacific time Monday through Friday; 10 AM to 1 PM Saturday.

American Foundation for AIDS Research: 212-682-7440
Provides information on clinical trials of experimental drugs.

first, strong. "There's a great feeling of powerlessness and helplessness," says Dr. Schaffner. Suicidal impulses generally ease up as people learn what they *can* do to help themselves.

After the initial shock, a person with HIV may experience feelings ranging from panic, anger, surrender, and depression to, sometimes, eventual resignation and acceptance. Again, the exact reactions depend on the particular individual involved: Paul, a 26-year-old hemophiliac, cannot overcome his anger. He and his wife were about to start a family when he learned that he was HIV-positive, having contracted the virus from an infected blood transfusion. Paul says he feels cheated and disillusioned with life. He also worries that he may have infected his wife (so far she has tested negative).

Paul coped with his feelings by withdrawing: he divorced his wife, quit his job, and began traveling about the country, supporting himself with odd jobs. Although he remains in touch with his mother, Francine, he cannot bring himself to call his ex-wife.

Ron, on the other hand, turned to his friends and family for support, visiting his parents in Oklahoma for the first time in 10 years and talking to his friends about his changing emotions. He found solace from the support of the people closest to him. Ron also joined a support group for people who are HIV-positive.

In fact, says Dr. Schaffner, support groups are one of the most effective ways for HIV-positive people to get counseling—the groups are affordable and helpful. "People find out that they're not alone; they can talk with others who have been through it," he says. Every major city in the United States now has at least one AIDS organization that can point you toward a support group. There are also support groups for the care givers, families, and friends of people with AIDS. (Check your local phone book or our sidebar on hot-line numbers.)

In the end the right combination of treatments and emotional support can help a person who is HIV-positive come to realize that, as Dr. Schaffner puts it, "it's not a sentence of death—it's a question of learning how to live with what you have left to live."

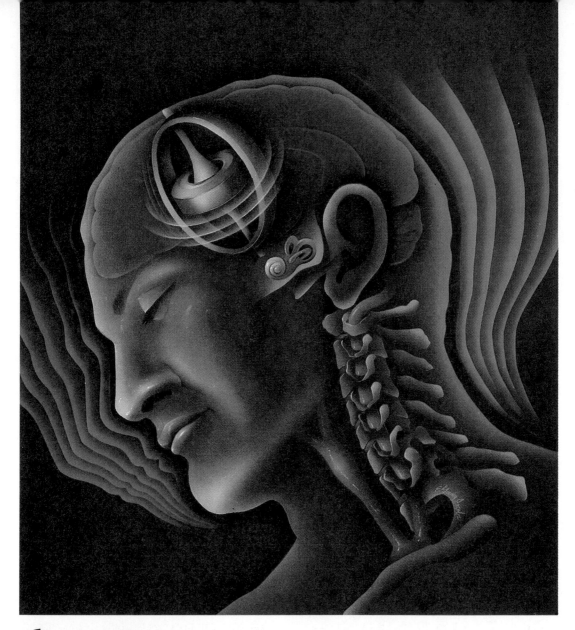

As the WORLD TURNS

by Sue Berkman

At the height of his career, a 31-year-old baseball superstar signs a five-year, $5.7 million contract. Then, inexplicably, in his first nine games, he strikes out 14 times and commits five errors at first base. He sits out the rest of the season on the disabled list.

A 70-year-old widow moves into a new apartment on New Year's Day. One week later she falls down in her kitchen and frac-

tures her hip in three places. She spends the rest of the year in a nursing home.

A 21-year-old journalism graduate takes a job in a prestigious New York City advertising agency. After three months of daily panic attacks, she quits. She spends the next 25 years a virtual prisoner in her apartment.

What links these seemingly dissimilar individuals is a condition called *vertigo.* From the Latin root meaning "to turn," vertigo

In Hitchcock's 1958 thriller Vertigo, *the hero, portrayed by Jimmy Stewart, above, was plagued by a dizzying fear of heights.*

sufferers most often use the word *dizziness* to describe the sensations they experience. But the disconcerting set of symptoms may also include a perception of spinning, rocking, tilting, light-headedness, loss of balance, disorientation, fear of falling, and, very frequently, nausea and vomiting.

It is not uncommon. According to the Vestibular Disorders Association in Portland, Oregon, more than 5 million Americans visit their doctor each year for vertigo; an estimated 10 percent of them are severely disabled by the time they get there.

In the past, vertigo sufferers were victims in the truest sense of the word—at the mercy of a condition so debilitating and po-tentially dangerous that they could not lead normal lives. Today the picture is considerably brighter: drugs and dietary changes can often control the attacks. And, with training and practice, the human brain can be retaught to keep the body in balance.

Illusion of Motion

For Nick Esasky, first baseman for the Atlanta Braves, the disability could have ended his career. In an interview with *Sports Illustrated,* Esasky described the feeling like this: "I was having problems reacting. I didn't feel coordinated. It was like I was in slow motion, and everything else was still moving very quickly around me."

The illusion of motion is the hallmark of true vertigo. "A portion of the nervous system is stimulated, and it responds by creating a sense of motion when there is no motion," says Martin A. Samuels, M.D., associate professor of neurology at Harvard Medical School. "Some people experience themselves as moving while the world stays still; others feel as though the world is moving relative to them."

The problem starts in the vestibular system, an area within the bone behind the eardrum and in front of the cochlea. About the size of an olive, the vestibular system is an intricate network of canals, sacs, chambers, hair cells, and nerve endings—a network that, along with eyes, ears, muscles, joints, and skin, sends signals to the brain telling it how the body is moving and reminding it which way is up.

There are two key motion sensors in the vestibular system. The first is composed of three fluid-filled semicircular canals lined with sensory cells, called *hair cells,* that have the ability to detect rotation. With the body's most minute movement, the fluid surges through the canals, stimulating the sensory cells to flash signals to numerous sites, including the 12 muscles of the eyes, the cerebellum (the part of the brain that coordinates all the messages to the brain), and the nerves that control muscle movement.

Two sacs in the vestibular system also have the ability to detect up-and-down and back-and-forth motion. One, the *saccule,* reacts to vertical motion (such as an elevator), while the other, the *utricle,* reacts to horizontal motion (such as a train). Each sac contains calcium granules, called *otoliths,* or "ear dust," floating in a gel. When these granules move, they stimulate sensory cells to signal the brain.

The balance system is well protected within the inner ear. But if the inner ear is disturbed by injury, infection, or loss of blood supply, the otoliths sometimes float free from their sac and land on the sensor in one of the semicircular canals that normally sense rotation. The brain then thinks that the head is rotating when it is only turning from side to side or moving forward.

That's what happened when elderly Elaine Cole turned from the stove to answer the telephone on the wall of her kitchen before falling and injuring her hip. The way she

tells it, the world upended: "I felt like I was standing on my head with my kitchen spinning all around me. It only lasted for a couple of minutes, but I was so terrified that I didn't even know that I was badly injured until the dizziness stopped."

Causes of Vertigo

Not every episode of dizziness heralds vertigo. Some sensations of motion—following a ride on a carousel, for instance, where the balance system has adjusted to whirling and must readjust to standing still—can even be pleasurable. But if there is no obvious reason for the sensation of motion, or if it persists for a long period of time, or disappears and reoccurs many times, there is likely to be a physical explanation.

While Elaine Cole feared the worst after her kitchen episode, she was relieved to learn that the cause was actually benign positional vertigo (BPV), which commonly affects older people. The topsy-turvy sensation is brought on by placing the head in certain positions, such as lying down with the left ear on the pillow or tilting the head back to look straight up. BPV is the most common form seen by doctors, and, as the name implies, it is not life-threatening. But

Anatomy of Balance

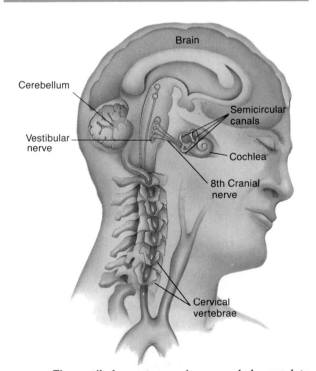

The vestibular system, or inner ear, helps regulate balance in conjunction with information from the eyes and sensory nerves in the skin, muscles, and joints. It consists of three fluid-filled semicircular canals, which help detect body rotation, and the vestibular nerve, which helps a person recognize his or her position, even in the dark or when swimming underwater.

Although separate nerves, the vestibular nerve for balance and the cochlear nerve for hearing together are called the eighth cranial nerve. Since these nerves are intertwined, damage to one is likely to affect the other.

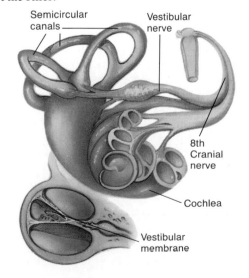

because people come to dread the spinning sensation, BPV is anything but an innocuous condition.

A viral infection is another possible cause of vertigo. *Labyrinthitis,* a viral infection of the ear, or vestibular neuronitis, which affects the nerve, are two common culprits. "These are unpleasant and somewhat debilitating for a couple of weeks, but tend to go away on their own," says Dr. Samuels.

Reversible vertigo can also be caused by many drugs—including sedatives, tranquilizers, and even aspirin. Reducing the drug dosage, stopping it altogether, or substituting another medication may help solve the problem.

Ménière's disease, on the other hand, can cause permanent problems. Named after French physician Prosper Ménière, who first described it in 1861, the disease seems to result from the accumulation of a fluid called endolymph within the inner ear, the balance center.

A brain tumor is the least common cause of vertigo—and the one that most people think of first. Two types of tumors can cause vertigo: the most common are benign tumors of the eighth cranial nerve, which carries both hearing and balance information to the brain stem. Known as acoustic neuromas, or *schwannomas,* these tumors are slow-growing and usually can be surgically removed. They don't spread, as cancerous tumors do, but they can inflict nerve damage and affect hearing if they are not found and removed early enough. Cancerous brain tumors are much rarer—but life-threatening. Each year, some 15,000 new cases are detected in this country, and some 11,000 people with brain cancer die annually.

Balance is maintained by a complex interaction of the inner ear, brain and spinal cord, eyes, joints, sensory receptors, and muscles.

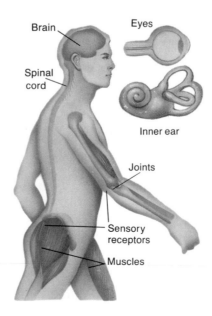

Brain
Spinal cord
Eyes
Inner ear
Joints
Sensory receptors
Muscles

Diagnosis of vertigo depends heavily on the patient's account of his or her symptoms and on physical findings. "There's no single diagnosis and no single treatment," says Abraham Eviatar, M.D., professor and chief of otolaryngology at the Albert Einstein College of Medicine in the Bronx, New York.

The consultation with a physician usually begins with lots of questions for the patient: When was the first dizziness experience? How long did it last? What are you generally doing when it happens? Is the room spinning around? Are *you* spinning around? Do you have pain or ringing in one or both ears, nausea, or headache?

An ear, nose, and throat examination will be followed by a battery of tests, including a hearing test to check for involvement of the inner ear or auditory nerve; a CAT (computerized axial tomography) scan to look for a disruption in the anatomy of the brain, possibly from a tumor, multiple sclerosis, or some abnormality in an artery; or an EEG (electroencephalogram) to test for brain seizures.

If these tests turn up normal results, the testing may proceed to one or more high-tech diagnostic studies:

Electronystagmography (ENG): measures eye movement and may indicate that vestibular damage is causing *nystagmus,* a rapid side-to-side motion of the eyes;

Brain-stem audio-evoked responses (BAER): measure brain waves when a person is exposed to sound, and may indicate abnormalities in the vestibular system;

Computerized posturography: measures the systems that help maintain balance, and indicates the degree of impairment.

Mistaken Identity

Often a physician doesn't recognize the symptoms of vertigo from a patient's description. "There's no real language for dizziness," says Dr. Eviatar.

Vertigo sufferer Nick Esasky of the Atlanta Braves undergoes training to make him less sensitive to the nausea and fatigue that accompany dizziness.

"Doctors sometimes find it difficult to discuss something in such vague terms as patients are apt to use in talking about their feelings of disequilibrium."

Consequently, patients are sometimes dismissed as "hypochondriac." And because their dizziness doesn't cause any changes in appearance, they can't even convince friends that something is wrong. Yet they are afraid to drive, unable to go to work, and wary of venturing outside their homes.

Andrea Rexton knows all about that outcome. Early in her career as an advertising copywriter, she was plagued with episodes of dizziness while she walked on busy midtown Manhattan streets. It finally got to a point that she had to quit her job and she stopped going outside.

Desperate about the situation, Rexton started seeing a psychiatrist, who assured her that it was an emotional problem that she would have to work out through psychoanalysis. "Twenty-five years later, I happened to read an article about someone with my exact symptoms who was diagnosed with an inner-ear disturbance. That's what mine was, too —a vestibular dysfunction."

Feet Firmly on the Ground

According to Jeffrey Kramer, M.D., director of the Dizziness and Balance Center in Wilmette, Illinois, a majority of those who complain of dizziness are told that they have to live with it. That's what Nick Esasky started to hear through his consultations with dozens of specialists.

By the time the Atlanta Braves' Esasky reached Kramer's center, defining the cause of the vertigo seemed less important than finding a cure. In Esasky's case, his inner ear was nonfunctional, and doctors could not determine what the damage was, so there was no way to repair it. A cure meant overcoming the debilitating symptoms. "We set up a program for him that retrained his balance system," says Dr. Kramer. The program involved exercises that made him less sensitive to the nausea and fatigue that accompany dizziness.

Elaine Cole's broken hip made it impossible for her to carry out an exercise regimen; drugs and a change in diet, however, enabled her to overcome vertigo symptoms.

Doctors can now choose from more than 20 drugs, such as Antivert, Dramamine, and Phenergan. These drugs do have side effects, including drowsiness and a dry mouth, but, says Dr. Eviatar, "for a lot of people, they do the trick."

So, for some, does a change in diet. Most doctors put vertigo patients on low-salt diets to decrease pressure in their inner ears. Others have become convinced that regulating blood-glucose levels may be just as important. But since dietary restrictions are often difficult to follow diligently, few doctors rely on dietary changes alone.

In some cases, structural damage is detectable; when vertigo is caused by a leak in the membrane of the inner ear, surgery *can* produce a cure.

Once Andrea Rexton discovered that her vertigo really had a physiological basis, she felt incredible relief. "I could finally tell myself that I wasn't crazy—that I had an illness, and that it had a name," she says.

For more information, contact the Vestibular Disorders Association, 1015 N.W. 22nd Ave., D230, Portland, OR 97210-3079; 503-229-7705.

Reconstructive surgery owes many of its astonishing advances to the ability to culture human skin.

RECONSTRUCTIVE SURGERY:
more than skin-deep

by Sharon Romm, M.D.

Dr. Snyder, a Midwest plastic surgeon, has a full operating schedule. His first case is Tanya R., a three-year-old who suffered burns over most of her body last year. Today Dr. Snyder will remove the badly scarred skin on her cheek and replace it with undamaged skin from her neck. He will then operate on Susan L., a 61-year-old woman with breast cancer. After the general surgeon in the operating room next door has removed the cancerous breast, Dr. Snyder will create a breast mound to match the size and shape of Susan's healthy breast. And finally he will re-create a nipple for Sally T., a young woman who has already had several stages of breast reconstruction following cancer.

Dr. Snyder does not work miracles. Like thousands of plastic surgeons around the country, he is just a physician who is well-trained in the state-of-the-art techniques of reconstructive surgery.

The American Society of Plastic and Reconstructive Surgeons reports that in 1990, 1.25 million patients had restorative surgery. Men and women of all ages had operations to correct birth defects and deformities caused by cancer, burns, and other accidents. Operations were not necessary by most standards: life could go on even with a scar or a missing breast. Yet patients, wishing to appear normal, often chose risky surgery in hopes of improving their self-esteem and quality of life.

For centuries, plastic surgeons have been performing reconstructive repair on every part of the human body. Indeed, ever since ancient Roman surgeons first mended a torn ear, physicians have sought new techniques for repair and reconstruction. These days, top surgeons team with laboratory scientists to develop new and more-effective reconstruction techniques. Although progress has often been slow, recent advances offer the prospect of better lives to more patients than ever before.

Scars

Scars are lifetime reminders of accidents and operations. No matter how carefully the surgeon repairs a wound, a scar is inevitable. And no matter how much the scar is coaxed and massaged, nothing can make it less ugly. Scientists do not know exactly why scars form or what makes some patients produce worse scars than others, but they are finding better ways of treating them.

All scars are not the same. A soft, flat, narrow scar may not be pretty, but, except for the fact that it never goes away, such a scar causes little trouble and requires no treatment. On the other hand, hypertrophic scars are thick, raised, and painful, and often grow larger than the original wound. If located near a joint, these scars can severely limit movement. Hypertrophic scars can form after any skin trauma, such as a burn or surgical incision. Black, Asian, and young patients are especially prone to these types of scars, although whites and the elderly are by no means immune.

Reducing or camouflaging hypertrophic scars is very difficult. Once the scar forms, it cannot be cut away without an even larger scar growing in its place. Doctors use several different procedures, depending upon the scar's size and location.

Compression Therapy: Soon after injury the patient is outfitted with an elastic garment—gloves, masks, or suits, depending on the scar's location—fitted as tight as a second skin to prevent a scar from thickening. Terribly hot and uncomfortable, these garments are worn around the clock and are removed only for washing. The garment must be used for at least a year to show any benefit at all.

Steroids: Small scars (less than an inch or two long) might improve when rubbed with steroid cream. Doctors sometimes inject steroids directly into larger scars—an often painful treatment. Unfortunately, too much steroid produces dangerous and unpleasant side effects. Although steroid injections often help, they can turn both scar and surrounding skin purple and paper-thin.

Silicone-gel bandages: Bandages of silicone gel—made from the same material found in breast implants and artificial joints—have emerged as a potentially more effective and pleasant means of hypertrophic-scar cor-

Many of the reconstruction techniques considered routine in the United States are virtually unknown in the Third World. To help remedy this situation, an organization called Doctors Without Borders now arranges for American physicians to travel abroad and operate on children with various problems. The Latin American boy at left has just had a serious harelip corrected.

rection. Surgeons at Washington University in St. Louis wrapped new scars with silicone bandages for half a day at a time. They found that this gentle treatment worked better than compression therapy to prevent scars from becoming thick and hard. The bandages are completely painless and produce no side effect worse than an occasional mild rash. Although silicone bandages have not yet been used widely, they show promise of liberating patients from their elastic prisons.

Burns

Every year nearly 2 million Americans suffer burn injuries. More than 60,000 men, women, and children are hurt seriously enough to require care in specialized burn centers. Almost all hospitalized victims need skin grafts to heal their wounds.

A burn wound must be closed at all costs. An open wound weeps vital body fluids and protein, leaving the patient prone to life-threatening infection. Ideally, the wound should be covered with the patient's own skin, but this is not always possible: there may not be enough undamaged skin to use as

a graft, or the patient may simply be too weak to endure an operation. Surgeons frequently must rely on temporary measures like cadaver skin or synthetic dressings. But each of these alternatives has drawbacks: cadaver skin carries the risk of AIDS and hepatitis, and, in addition, the body soon rejects it; synthetic dressings are poor barriers against harmful bacteria.

Since the patient's own skin is the gold standard, so to speak, of wound coverage, scientists have devised a clever way of making a speck of unburned skin go a very long way. By using sophisticated laboratory-culture techniques, a postage-stamp-sized patch of undamaged skin can grow, in just three weeks, to 10,000 times its original size!

In the technique, doctors remove a small piece of the patient's unburned skin and place it in a flask of nutrient-rich fluid that keeps the skin cells alive. Under laboratory conditions, the cells rapidly multiply and divide. After a week the first batch of new skin is ready to be cut into squares the size of a handkerchief. The squares are then wrapped

For burn victims, hydrotherapy helps prevent dehydration and maintain skin elasticity. Great advances have been made using skin grafts (below, prior to application, and bottom, in place).

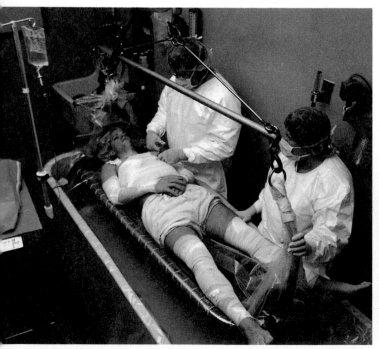

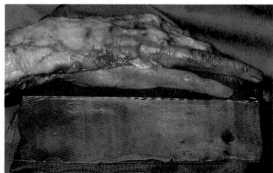

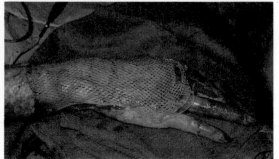

carefully and shipped to the burn center or hospital for grafting onto the waiting patient.

In less than a decade, skin cultured in commercial laboratories has become standard therapy. Skin culture proved its worth in 1984, when doctors at Boston's Shriners Burns Institute saved the lives of two badly burned boys, ages 5 and 7. Thanks to grafting with cultured skin, the technique used to save these boys' lives is available today for burn victims around the world.

Although a boon to burn treatment, cultured skin is still far more fragile than the patient's own skin. Normal skin is composed of two layers: delicate epidermis on the surface and leathery dermis underneath; cultured skin consists entirely of epidermis. Providing cultured skin with a sturdy dermis would make it the perfect substitute.

In 1991 researchers worked on toughening cultured skin. If they can create a dermis, they can eliminate the tendency of cultured skin to blister and slide off the wound area. Scientists have had some success with manufacturing dermis using a laboratory technique that joins the patient's own cells to a synthetic chemical scaffold.

Another solution to the problem of skin slippage and fragility is also being pursued. Scientists cover the burn wound with Integra, an artificial skin in which the epidermis is made from polysiloxane polymer, and the dermis from collagen, a type of protein taken from cows, which is then combined with the chemical glycosaminoglycan chondroitin-6-sulfate. After a week the epidermal layer is peeled off, and the artificial dermis remains behind as a solid base for a graft of cultured skin. Although the final word is not yet in, this technique, as well as skin culture, looks promising in saving the lives of patients who, a few years ago, were almost sure to die of their massive burns.

Birthmarks

Three out of every 1,000 children born today have a red birthmark. Most marks are too small to be noticed, but many are large enough to cover much of a child's face, neck, or limbs. Called by their scientific name *hemangiomata*—meaning malformed blood vessels—or by the more common name

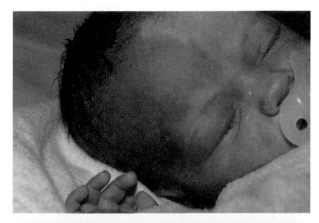

Using lasers, doctors can remove even a facial port-wine-stain birthmark (top) so that virtually no trace of a scar remains (above).

"port-wine stains," these painless marks often tamper with children's self-esteem, especially when they become victim to the taunts of their peers.

Less frequently, hemangiomata injure more than just the psyche. Blood vessels of larger varieties of birthmarks can erupt through the skin and cause frightening episodes of bleeding. Blood vessels can also grow inward, damaging bones and muscles. They may even penetrate the brain to cause seizures or blindness.

Many treatments have been tried, but few can reliably erase birthmarks. Results are usually less than satisfactory when port-wine stains are cut away and the area is reconstructed with a thin skin graft from the hip or a thicker flap of nearby healthy skin and fat. The resulting color match is never precise, and the scars at the junction of the graft and the normal skin are unsightly. Results of tattooing the port-wine stain are inconsistent; freezing the port-wine stain does not work; and camouflage makeup is only a temporary solution.

Lasers, introduced in the past decade to erase port-wine stains, are the best treatment to date. The laser's color specificity is key to the successful elimination of birthmarks. When a laser beam is aimed at hemoglobin (the chemical that makes a blood cell red), it destroys the cell. The blood vessel carrying the red cell shrivels and disappears, yet the surrounding skin is untouched.

In theory, lasers should work perfectly; in reality, lasers can cause problems. The carbon-dioxide laser occasionally leaves scars and turns skin dark. The argon and copper-vapor lasers carry less risk of scarring, but are less effective in eliminating the birthmark.

A new laser on the market shows great promise. Made by the Candela Laser Corporation of Massachusetts, this machine emits a pulse of yellow light that is absorbed exclusively by the red blood vessels of the skin. Because this laser's pulse is so brief—360 millionths of a second—the heat it generates is confined completely to the target. Treatments are relatively painless, results are good, and scarring rarely occurs.

Depending on the birthmark's size, children need up to 10 15-minute sessions with the laser, a small price to pay to eliminate a source of lifelong trouble.

Fetal Surgery

Can doctors operate without a scar? The answer is yes . . . as long as the patient has not yet been born! Through animal experimentation, surgeons have learned that fetal skin has a remarkable capacity to heal; even more amazing, fetal surgical incisions leave no trace of a scar.

Collagen, the main ingredient in scar tissue, behaves differently depending on the age of the person. While adult collagen makes scars, fetal collagen does not. And the younger the fetus, the more perfect and unmarred is the healing.

If an operation could be performed before birth, surgeons reasoned, babies with life-threatening defects would have a better chance of survival. History was made in 1989, when surgeon Michael Harrison operated on a "patient" still in his mother's womb. Ultrasound, a popular diagnostic technique now routine in prenatal care, had detected that the unborn baby had a hole in his diaphragm—the muscular barrier between chest and belly—that stopped

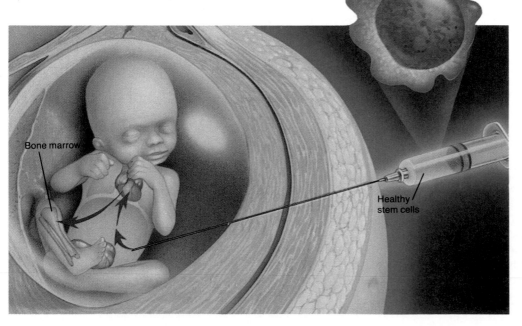

Medicine is advancing to the point where fetuses with life-threatening conditions can be treated before birth. Researchers think that some blood diseases could be avoided by injecting healthy stem cells into the fetus' bone marrow. Since the fetal immune system has not developed enough to reject the donor cells, they are accepted as part of the fetus. The new stem cells should be able to produce healthy red blood cells.

Bone marrow

Healthy stem cells

normal development of his lungs. Harrison closed the hole with a fabric patch so the baby, born just a bit before schedule, could breathe without any trouble at all.

Plastic surgeons have a twofold interest in fetal surgery. It may provide a solution to the problems of wound healing. And even with extensive fetal flaws, there would be no telltale sign that skin, bones, and muscles had been rearranged. The virtually seamless repair would divorce the child from a lifetime stigma.

In particular, fetal surgery would greatly help the 1 in 750 children born with clefts—splits in the lip, palate, or, in severe cases, the skin and bones of the cheek, forehead, or chin. Fernando Ortiz-Monasterio, a plastic surgeon in Mexico City, has now successfully accomplished intrauterine cleft-lip repairs in monkeys; other physicians have performed the same operation on mice. The surgery itself is very difficult: fetal tissue has the consistency of grape jelly, so cutting and sewing is a challenge to even the best technician. Also, not all experimental mothers and babies survive this surgery. But for the surviving animals, the results were just what the doctor ordered. After delivery by cesarean section, there was no trace of a scar.

A fetal hernia can cause lung damage. Doctors repairing it must make an incision through the mother and rotate the tiny patient into position.

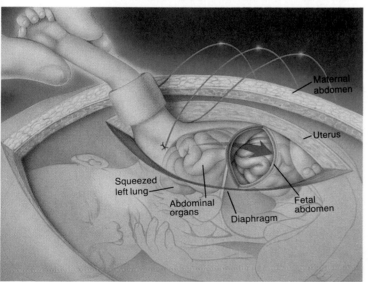

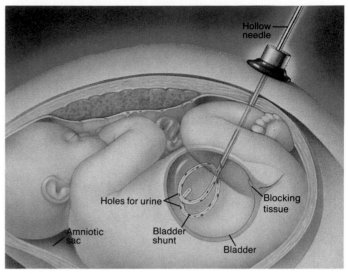

Doctors have successfully tested a fetal bladder shunt. The shunt is implanted in a fetus suffering from a blocked bladder.

The time has not yet arrived for surgery on humans. Too many technical problems need to be solved, and there are pressing ethical issues that must be addressed. Yet, remembering that heart transplants and spaceflight were once a dream, it is not impossible that the future holds the first operation to correct a cleft in a human still in his or her mother's womb.

Breast Reconstruction

Breast cancer strikes one out of every nine women today. Some patients are treated by removal of the cancerous lump, followed by radiation or chemotherapy. But most women have a mastectomy, or amputation, of the diseased breast. Last year, according to the American Society of Plastic and Reconstructive Surgeons, over 42,000 women opted for breast reconstruction either at the time of cancer surgery or during the months that followed.

Although no surgical technique can duplicate a lost breast, most techniques can provide the patient with a chest mound similar to the remaining breast in size and shape. Although all restorative operations leave unattractive scars, when wearing street clothes or even swimwear, mastectomy or reconstruction is undetectable.

One-quarter of the women who choose reconstruction elect to have the new breast made from their own tissue. The surgeon moves a chunk of back or belly muscle, con-

Breast Implants

Three-quarters of all breast-reconstruction patients elect to have a silicone implant—the same used for women having breast enlargement—placed underneath their chest-wall muscles. In the past year, the media have resounded with charges that silicone implants cause cancer. The two million American women who already have implants have expressed concern that they carry a time bomb in their chests; some have even demanded that their implants be removed. In bowing to public pressure, one major manufacturer has taken a popular implant from the market until the controversy is resolved.

Scientific studies have shown that laboratory rats develop a rare type of tumor called *fibrosarcoma* when any foreign material, such as cellophane, metal, or silicone, is inserted beneath the skin. But this tumor is different from carcinomas, the cancers that typically grow in women's breasts.

Many surgeons defend their continued use of silicone implants. Even if silicone leaks, they maintain, it poses no danger. Patients with silicone pacemakers or artificial finger joints, as well as diabetics who take insulin from a silicone-coated syringe, are exposed to far greater concentrations of silicone than are women with breast implants.

This year another type of popular implant was permanently removed from the market. This device's cover, polyurethane, was particularly effective in preventing capsular contracture, the firm, leathery layer that the body produces in response to the presence of any foreign substance. Unfortunately, the polyurethane was found to disintegrate into the chemical 2,4-diaminotoluene, known as TDA. This chemical has been found to produce liver cancer in laboratory rats.

Silicone implants are also suspected of causing lupus and scleroderma, rare connective-tissue diseases that damage the victim's skin, blood vessels, and internal

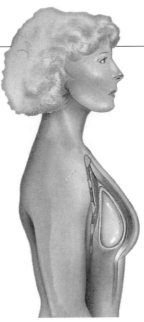

Women who have undergone mastectomies now have a variety of reconstruction options available to them. Silicone implants (left), while they recreate the shape of the breast, have come under close FDA scrutiny.

The popular "expander" method of reconstruction substitutes saline solution for silicone. In this method, injections of saline (below) stretch the chest skin until the reconstructed breast is the desired size.

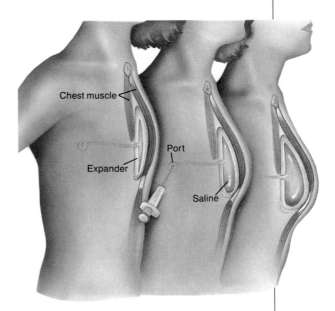

Chest muscle

Expander

Port

Saline

organs. Despite the findings of a task force of plastic surgeons, epidemiologists, and arthritis specialists who decided that there was no cause for alarm, in January the Food and Drug Administration (FDA) declared a moratorium on silicone implants until new implant-safety studies could be examined. For those women who already have these implants, the FDA encourages them to bring any problems to the immediate attention of their physician.

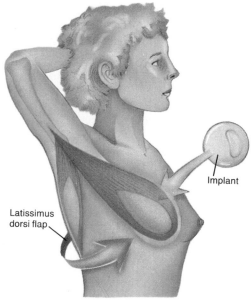

In a latissimus dorsi muscle flap, a portion of back muscle and skin is placed over the chest area. An implant is then inserted under the flap.

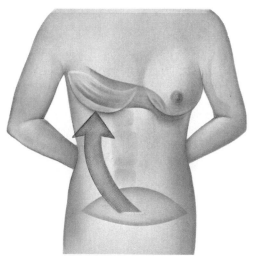

By using abdominal skin and tissue to create a new breast, a rectus abdominis muscle flap combines a "tummy tuck" with reconstruction.

nected by its blood vessels and covered by skin, onto the chest wall. By trimming and sewing, this tissue is tailored into a breast shape. A finishing touch is often building a nipple from the patient's own skin.

This technique offers the advantage of avoiding the use of synthetic materials to rebuild the breast. But surgery can be long, and

several operations may be needed. Complications from this surgery can be serious, and recovery is usually lengthy.

Recently surgeons introduced several variations of creating a breast from available tissue from the patient's own body. They build a breast mound from a wedge of buttock consisting of skin, fat, and muscle. After this tissue is removed, its blood flow is restored by attaching its arteries and veins to blood vessels on the patient's chest or armpit. In another new procedure, plastic surgeons create a breast from skin and fat from the patient's thigh. Both techniques, though innovative, are used only in special cases when no other alternative is available and the patient is ideally suited for such radical surgery.

The Psychology of Reconstruction

Every patient having reconstructive surgery has the same wish: to look normal. Absolute beauty is rarely the goal. No one wants to have the scars, marks, or assymetries that make him or her look different from the rest of society. Patients as a whole are much more willing to settle for improvement than to demand perfection. They often feel lucky to have survived their cancer or accident, and are grateful to be rid of some of the evidence of deformity.

All patients opting for reconstructive surgery are brave. They are willing to endure considerable discomfort and inconvenience to attain a goal that is often uncertain. There is no guarantee that an operation will be successful and the results satisfactory.

Certain attitudes are more compatible with success than others. Patients are more likely to appreciate their results if expectations before surgery are reasonable. In addition, the outcome of an operation undertaken to please a spouse, relative, or friend stands less of a chance of success than surgery done only to please the person having it.

The patient and surgeon work as a team. They are bonded together until the various operations have accomplished as much improvement as possible, and until the patient is satisfied with his or her results. And, thanks to the combined efforts of scientists and surgeons, better results can be offered to patients with each passing year.

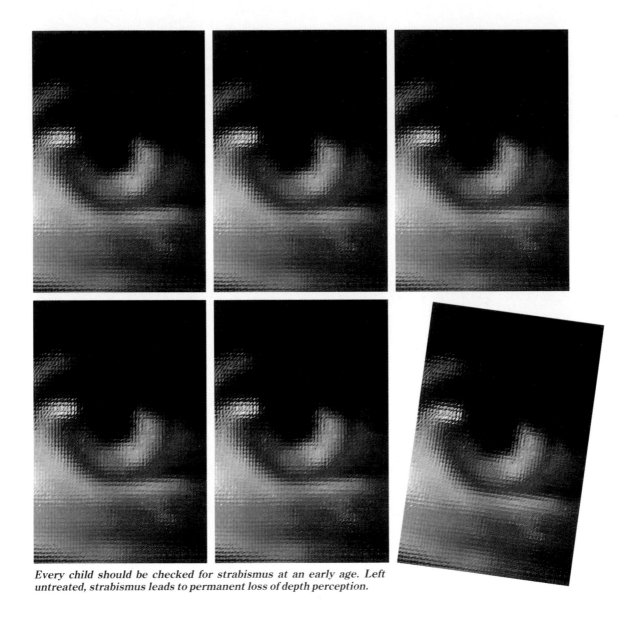

Every child should be checked for strabismus at an early age. Left untreated, strabismus leads to permanent loss of depth perception.

ALIGNING EYES:
STRAIGHTENING OUT STRABISMUS

by Dixie Farley

Strabismus affects approximately 4 percent of U.S. children under age 6. In some, strabismus occurs as crossed eyes. In others, it may manifest itself as eyes that turn out, up, or down. Its name can be traced to the Greek word *strabismos,* to look obliquely or with unstraight eyes; some use the terms "squint" and "lazy eye." Strabismus can disable sight in one eye, yet leave the other with 20/20 vision. Strabismus can be acquired from diverse causes at any age, and there are more than a dozen variations.

Sight: A Team Effort.

Healthy eyes move together to send similar images along the optic nerve to the brain for fusion into a single three-dimensional picture at the brain-vision junction, or visual cortex. Toward this end, six muscles attached to the outside of each eye contract and relax to move the eyes in perfect synchronization, permitting fusion, or binocular vision, across a large area of the visual field.

Strabismic eyes, on the other hand, do not move in unison. A muscle may pull too weakly or too strongly against its opposing muscle, creating an imbalance that causes one eye to drift from parallel alignment with its mate; more than one pair of muscles may be imbalanced.

Since each eye fixates on an object at a different point in space, the images received by the brain are dissimilar. The brain is unable to fuse the dissimilar images, resulting in double vision, a very disturbing condition. To avoid this disturbance, the brain may suppress vision in the deviating eye, allowing clear sight to develop solely in the straight eye. Decreased vision in the suppressed eye is called amblyopia. Prolonged amblyopia causes a loss in three-dimensional viewing and depth perception.

The resulting "squint" or turn usually is constant, but may be intermittent and may occur in only one eye or alternate between the two eyes. Vision in people with alternating strabismus generally remains good in each eye individually.

While strabismus clearly stems from muscle imbalance, the causes of such imbalance are not all completely understood.

"There's a strong genetic influence, but there are also many anatomic and neuromuscular reasons," says ophthalmologist John F. O'Neill, M.D., director of the Pediatric Ophthalmology and Strabismus Service at Georgetown University's Center for Sight in Washington, D.C.

Strabismus can be associated with many conditions that cause poor vision in one or both eyes—for example, cataract, Down syndrome, thyroid disease, eye tumor, damage to the fetal central nervous system from toxoplasmosis (a parasitic infection that can pass from the mother during pregnancy), or damage to a nerve supplying the eye muscle (perhaps from birth trauma).

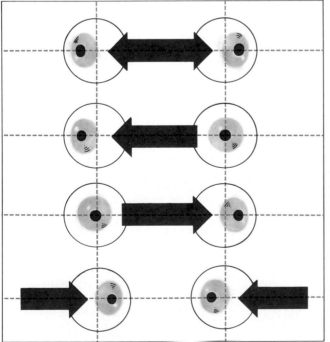

Types of eye misalignments are (left, from top): both eyes turning out; the right eye turning out; the left eye turning out; and both eyes turning in. To avoid double vision (below), the brain may suppress vision in one of the eyes.

Is It Strabismus?

"The first thing we do in examining children is to assess their vision, to determine the degree of visual attentiveness in each eye separately," O'Neill says. "We observe the child's ability to fixate on an object, and then we test how well each eye alone, and both eyes together, can follow that object in different directions and at different distances."

Many techniques are used to check the alignment and movement of the eyes to test for strabismus.

A quick screening method is the Hirschberg corneal-reflex test, says Walter Sloane, M.D., an ophthalmologist with the Food and Drug Administration's (FDA's) Center for Devices and Radiological Health, which regulates medical devices, including those used to test and treat the eye. The examiner directs an examining light onto the child's cornea as the child looks at the light. In normal eyes, the light reflection appears in the center of both pupils. An eye that reflects light from a different place may be strabismic and should be further examined, Sloane says.

Another corneal-reflex test is the Krimsky method. It compares the location of the reflected examining light in each pupil; again, light reflections that are dissimilar indicate strabismus. Prisms placed over one or both eyes align the reflections to estimate the amount of the turn.

The alternate-cover test quickly spots misalignment. "The examiner rapidly covers and uncovers each eye, shifting back and forth from one eye to the other like a windshield wiper," Sloane says. "If the child has a deviation, the eye will immediately move as the cover is shifted to the uncovered eye."

The cover-uncover test differentiates serious types of strabismus called tropias from latent drifts called phorias, which seldom require any treatment.

"The brain immediately overcomes a phoria drift," Sloane says. "So when the drift is a phoria, we see movement immediately after the eye is uncovered as it responds to control by the brain.

"But when the eye with tropia is covered, it becomes unhooked from the brain's control so that it drifts—in any direction—and remains turned in that position when uncovered until we cover its fellow eye, which has been staring at the object. When the fellow eye is covered, the turned eye is reconnected to the brain. The turned eye then moves to fixate on the object, as if to say, " 'Oops, I was facing the wrong direction.' "

One new method, a "preferential looking technique," uses Teller acuity cards. These devices are similar to educational flash cards, but instead of letters or numbers, they have black-and-white stripes ranging in patterns from very broad to very narrow, simulating large to small pictures or letters.

"Vision is gauged," O'Neill says, "by how attentively a child, even a baby, looks at each pattern."

Best Chance to See

Prompt attention to correcting eye misalignment will provide the most satisfactory outcome of treatment. Indeed, if some cases of strabismus are left untreated until age six, permanent visual impairment can result.

Corrective eyeglasses can help children as young as six months of age. They're most effective when there is significant farsightedness and the eyes turn in, and they're the only therapy needed in about a third of those patients whose eyes turn in. Prisms incorporated in eyeglasses may relieve double vision in some older patients.

An infant with crossed eyes (below) should be examined by an ophthalmologist. Only medical intervention can correct the condition (bottom).

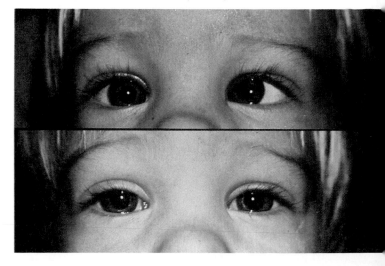

To force use of a "lazy" eye while preserving vision in the preferred eye, patching is very effective.

Surgery Can Help

Some 60,000 to 80,000 operations are performed each year to correct strabismus. When the eyes turn out, up, or down, correction usually requires surgery. Sometimes a second operation is required. With current knowledge and techniques, it's uncommon for a patient (about 1 in 20) to need a third operation, O'Neill says. The need for further corrective surgery, he says, depends on the stability of the muscle system and the degree of muscle response (over- or underresponse) to the surgical adjustment.

By weakening or strengthening an eye muscle (or muscles), strabismus surgery alters the muscular pull on the afflicted eye in order to align its movements with the other eye. The ophthalmologist can weaken or strengthen a muscle function by repositioning the muscle on the outside of the eye (never cutting into the eyeball), and also can strengthen a muscle by cutting out (resecting) a small piece of its tendon. Techniques with adjustable sutures allow additional muscle repositioning within the first day following surgery.

New Treatments

Following a number of years of investigations, the FDA, in December 1989, licensed a therapy for strabismus patients age 12 and older: Oculinum, an injectable form of sterile, purified *Botulinum* toxin, type A.

Oculinum is injected into an eye-turning muscle outside the eye, through an electromyographic needle that guides placement by recording the muscle's electrical activity. Anesthetic eye drops generally are used before the injection.

The toxin "turns off" the muscle by paralyzing it. Scientists theorize the paralysis affects muscle pairs by causing the injected muscle to lengthen, thus prompting the opposing muscle to shorten.

About half of patients require repeated treatments. In a recent study of 677 patients, 55 percent showed improvement six months later. Correction may be permanent, pro-

Eyeglasses can help children as young as six months of age. They are the only therapy needed in about one-third of patients whose eyes turn in.

vided the injected muscle is paralyzed well enough and long enough, and the opposing muscle is intact.

Another new therapy may benefit patients who acquire crossed eyes after the age of six months. It involves the use of eyeglasses overlaid with thin plastic prisms.

In September 1990, the University of Iowa Hospitals and Clinics in Iowa City announced the results of a six-year study led by William Scott, M.D., in which 14 medical centers tested the efficacy of treatment with prism eyeglasses before surgery in patients who had had no previous eye surgery.

"By knowing the exact prism power that corrects the misalignment," Scott says, "we can more accurately determine the surgical adjustment needed on the eye muscles, thus reducing the possible need for additional surgery." The eyes of about 83 percent of patients who used the special eyeglasses were straightened by the surgery, compared with 72 percent of patients without them.

Appropriate management offers strabismus patients the best possible circumstances for improvement.

"The key most often is early detection and treatment," says Georgetown's O'Neill. "Without proper care, strabismus in an infant or in a child early in life will generally get worse, not better. Children do not outgrow strabismus when the eyes truly are 'crossed.' "

A child who seems to be developing speech difficulties can benefit from an early evaluation. A certified speech-language therapist can help define the problem and suggest treatment options.

Speech Disabilities In Children

by Susan Randel

"Don't ask me what my name is, because I can't say it," announces six-year-old Curtis, who cannot properly pronounce his S and Z sounds.

Six-year-old Sandy is frustrated by her severe stutter: "I can't say what I want."

A child may not always speak clearly when he or she first learns to talk. Most often he or she mispronounces sounds or trips over word fragments. A certain amount of such misarticulation, or *disfluency,* is considered a normal part of the process of learning to speak. Fortunately, most children outgrow these problems. But for some the difficulties continue as they get older. These children, like Curtis and Sandy, have a speech or language disability.

Speech disabilities have a number of causes. *Organic* disabilities are caused by hearing impairment, muscular-coordination problems, or physical deformities such as cleft palate. *Functional* disabilities include problems such as stuttering and articulation errors. The causes of these problems are often unknown.

Functional speech disabilities usually appear between the ages of two and seven, as the child is learning to talk. Because most children outgrow speech problems, parents in the past were often told by their pediatricians to take a "wait-and-see" approach. As researchers in the field have learned more about the nature of speech disabilities, however, this recommendation has changed.

Parents concerned about the way their child speaks are now advised to get an early evaluation by a speech-language pathologist. This evaluation is useful on two counts: if there is a problem, an intervention program can be started; if the pathologist does not feel intervention is necessary at the time, the parents and therapist will have this information to compare with a later evaluation should the problems continue.

Stuttering

Stuttering is the problem most people think of when discussing speech disabilities. Typically, a stuttering person repeats the initial sound of a word, and extends vowel sounds in the middle of the word. Often accompanying this problem is blocking—opening the mouth, but not being able to get the sound to come out—accompanied by grimacing. A stutter can range from mild, with only the occasional repetition, to severe, with constant repetition of sounds, vowel elongation, and facial grimacing.

It is difficult to distinguish between the normal disfluency of a small child struggling to get the words out as fast as possible, and the disfluency of a child at risk for developing a stutter. Initially, a stutter is virtually indistinguishable from the normal disfluencies of a child learning to talk, says Barry Guitar, Ph.D., professor of communication science and disorders at the University of Vermont in Burlington. However, as the stutter develops, it follows characteristically distinct speech patterns. Parents may have to listen closely to differentiate between normal disfluencies and a stutter.

"Mommy Mommy, I-I want want a c-c-cookie now," says the child with normal disfluency. He or she will often repeat whole words or phrases, usually no more than one or two times. These repetitions are rhythmic, use the normal vowel sound, and occur in no more than 9 out of every 100 words. All the while the child's speech keeps going through the repeats and stumblings.

The speech pattern for a child at risk for stuttering is noticeably different, as in "Muh-muh-muh-Mommy, I waaaant a cuh-cuh-cookie nnnnnow." He or she may repeat sounds or syllables of words, prolong a sound, or break up the word. The repetitions usually occur at least three times, with an "uh" sound often substituted for the normal vowel sound in the word. The child may use a broken rhythm for these repetitions, and may open his or her mouth to speak, but with no sound coming forth. In a child likely to develop a stutter, there are usually 10 or more disfluencies per every 100 words.

Furthermore, the effortless stumble of a child who cannot get the words out fast enough is of less concern than the child who notices and is self-conscious of stumbling. The latter child may be more at risk for developing a stutter.

Theories abound on the cause of stuttering. In the past, people who stuttered were thought to have psychological conflicts that caused the speech problems. This idea has been discredited somewhat, although psychological factors are still believed to play a role in some cases, as when a child suddenly starts stuttering after the birth of a sibling or at a time of family turbulence. Present work focuses on physiological causes. One theory is based on a lack of coordination between phonation (the ability to make the sounds of speech), articulation (pronouncing the words clearly), and respiration.

Stuttering is three times more common in boys than girls.

Stuttering can run in families, and some children seem to have a predisposition for it. The condition is three times more common in boys than girls. Experts believe that stuttering may have a genetic component.

Articulation Problems

Articulation problems can cause great discomfort for a child who is not being understood when speaking, and untold embarrassment to a child who is a target of teasing from other children because of the way he or she sounds. The major types of articulation errors are *deleting, substituting,* and *adding* or *distorting* sounds to the point where the child is hardly intelligible. *Residual distortions,* such as a lisp, or a *lateral distortion,* described as a slushy sound (like Elmer Fudd or Daffy Duck), are separate categories

Speech and language time line.

Age	Behavior
Newborn	Crying and noncrying sounds may be observed.
0–3 months	Responds to human voice. Coos. Makes pleasure sounds, different cries for different needs. Makes vocal response to speech of others.
4–6 months	Babbles strings of consonants. Shows pitch variation. Vocalizes to toys. Imitates sounds.
6 months	Varies volume, pitch, and rate of vocalization. Vocalizes pleasure and displeasure.
7 months –1 year	Vocal play. Distinct intonation patterns. Imitates coughs, hisses. Imitates gestures and tone quality of adult speech. Tongue clicks, "raspberries," and social gestures. Imitates adult speech if sounds are in the repertoire. Imitates inflections, rhythms, facial expressions. Speaks one or more words. Practices words that are in vocabulary with inflection.
1–2 years	Uses single words to name objects, gain attention, or obtain information. Puts together two words toward the end of this age range. Asks questions. Vocabulary increases every month.
2–3 years	Has word for almost everything. Sentence length increases to at least three words. Speech understandable to parents. Asks for objects by naming them.
3–4 years	The child asks *many* questions. Uses more complex sentence forms. Recounts stories in recent past due to growth of short-term memory. Speech becomes intelligible to people outside the family. There are only a few sound errors (*r, l, th, s*).

Source: American Speech-Language Hearing Association

of articulation errors. These types of articulation problems do not dramatically affect intelligibility in most cases.

There are a number of possible causes of articulation problems. Some children may have fluctuations in hearing level resulting from repeated middle-ear infections (*otitis media*); if the ear never clears between bouts of infection, the child may not be hearing properly at a critical point in learning to speak. A slower rate of maturation may also contribute to articulation errors.

There may also be a learning-process breakdown associated with these problems. Children with speech-sound errors also make frequent grammatical errors and experience comprehension problems. These children may continue to have language problems throughout their education, even after the articulation problems are resolved.

Taking Steps

Any very small child can be difficult to understand. Parents should be aware, however, that children should *not always* be difficult to understand. If parents find their child hard to understand, or if they notice a pronounced disfluency, an evaluation by a speech-language therapist could help.

Before taking this step, however, parents can take a number of steps at home to help the child. For starters, says Barry Guitar, slow down the pace of speech in the house. All children benefit from having their parents talk slowly; slower speech can serve as an important preventive measure for the child who is at risk for stuttering. Parents should also set aside a certain time of day to spend with the child, talking slowly while letting the child direct the play.

If the child appears to be stuttering, and struggling or physically tensing as he or she tries to talk, parents should acknowledge that it is O.K. to struggle with words sometimes, and that everyone has trouble talking at times. If the struggling continues after six weeks of setting aside time to talk slowly, the parents might wish to consider meeting with a speech-language pathologist. Most researchers feel that early intervention is the most effective way to treat stuttering.

According to Guitar, the speech therapist's actions depend upon the severity of the child's problem. If the child is hardly aware of any disfluency, the therapist may work to make the speech environment more easygoing, thereby reducing stress and slowing

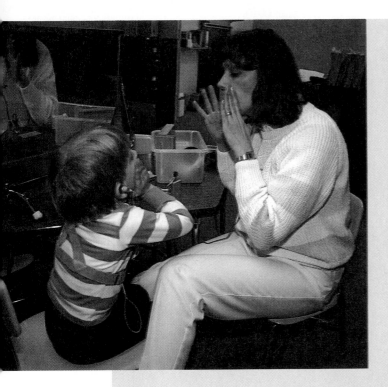

About 40 percent of organic speech disorders are due to hearing impairment. Neurological disease accounts for another 10 percent, while the remaining 50 percent of cases stem from Down syndrome, cleft lip, and a range of other conditions.

Organic Speech Disabilities

According to the American Speech-Language Hearing Association, speech disorders can result from hearing impairment, cerebral palsy, Down syndrome, learning disabilities, problems related to traumatic brain injury or stroke, and unknown causes. For children with these conditions, speech therapy is an essential part of the treatment for the underlying condition.

The speech fluency developed by such a child depends upon the condition. Children with hearing impairment may learn to communicate via American Sign Language rather than learning to use their voices. Traumatic brain injury in children is a special situation. Because a child's brain is still developing, a child with this type of injury may be able to recover faster and more completely than an adult by "rerouting" around the problem areas. However, there may be residual difficulties with memory. It is necessary to be alert for residual effects of mild concussions, which may turn up as subtle difficulties, such as an inability to follow instructions. Alexa Kratze of the Speech Hearing and Neurosensory Center in San Diego recommends monitoring a child's behavior and academic performance for a year after a mild concussion.

down the speech. If the child is visibly struggling and is self-conscious about it, the therapist may reassure the child that stuttering is nothing to be ashamed of. The therapist might then work with the child to devise ways to make speech come easier, at the same time determining what parts of speech cause more stress for the child. In more severe cases, the therapist may also focus on easing the child's fear of talking, and help the child find ways of not working so hard at talking. "So much of stuttering is that you have learned to be afraid of it," says Guitar.

Articulation errors are more obvious when the child starts nursery school, particularly to teachers who are not used to how the child speaks. For articulation errors, treatment depends on the type of error. In general the therapist will teach the child how to properly shape the sound, and then apply it to words. The parent plays an important part in the program by helping the child practice at home.

Parents who are concerned that their child may have a speech disability can get more information from the American Speech-Language Hearing Association, 10801 Rockville Pike, Rockville, MD 20852, or call their HELPLINE at 1-800-638-8255. The Stuttering Foundation of America also has information on speech disfluencies, and can be reached at 1-800-992-9392 or in Washington, D.C. at 202-363-3199.

The Challenge of Relieving Pain

by Dori Stehlin

The lucky among us have only an occasional headache. For others, pain is a constant, though unwelcome, companion. Relieving pain is sometimes simple, sometimes impossible. It depends on the source of the pain, and it may also depend on the person.

Everyday Aches and Pains

There are three main nonprescription choices for pain relief—aspirin, acetaminophen (Datril, Tylenol, and others), and ibuprofen (Motrin IB, Advil, Nuprin, and others). All three block the production of chemicals called prostaglandins, which the body usually releases when cells are injured. Prostaglandins are believed to play an important role in the pain, heat, redness, and swelling that occur following tissue damage due to disease or injury.

When it comes to mild, nonspecific pain, headaches, or menstrual discomfort, "all three [nonprescription pain relievers] are quite useful," says Patricia Love, M.D., a rheumatologist with the Food and Drug Administration's (FDA's) Center for Drug Evaluation and Research. "There are probably persons who are not able to detect a difference in the effectiveness of the OTC [over the counter] products."

It has been suggested, Love says, that aspirin or ibuprofen may be more effective than acetaminophen for pain caused by inflammation or mild menstrual discomfort because they have more prostaglandin-blocking effects. "Our best advice at present is that, for mild pain, individuals may use what works best and is safe for them," says Love.

In other words, what doesn't cause them problems. Because prostaglandins play a role in protecting the stomach lining from being attacked by the acid of digestive fluid, aspirin, ibuprofen, and—apparently to a lesser extent, according to Love—acetaminophen may cause stomach irritation, ulcers, or bleeding.

For some people who take aspirin, stomach irritation may be decreased by taking either enteric-coated aspirin, buffered aspirin, or other modified aspirin derivatives such as choline salicylate or magnesium salicylate.

Buffered aspirin contains an ingredient that neutralizes some of the digestive system's acid, and therefore may produce less irritation than plain aspirin.

Coated aspirin dissolves mainly in the intestine. (Uncoated aspirin dissolves in the stomach.) In theory, that difference may mean less stomach irritation, says Love. But, she adds, it still depends on an individual's metabolism. For example, some people can't digest the coating, so while they don't get any stomach irritation, they don't get any benefit either. The aspirin passes out of the body undigested and unabsorbed.

People who can't take aspirin because of allergic reactions (e.g., rash, asthma, anaphylaxis) generally can't take ibuprofen either. For them, acetaminophen may be the only nonprescription choice.

All three drugs have the potential to cause liver damage, although liver toxicity is much less common than gastric ulcers or bleeding.

The FDA is reviewing recent studies that suggest an association between use of all three nonprescription pain relievers and kidney disease. But the agency says that not enough is known yet about these possible associations to make any changes in current recommendations for use by healthy individuals.

"I think one of the important safety issues in choosing a medication is it's not just whether or not you have minor pain, but what is your medical history on top of the minor pain," says Love. "People who have specific disorders—kidney disease, heart disease, bleeding problems, liver disorders, medication allergies—should talk to their physicians."

Americans spend over $2.1 billion on nonprescription pain relievers each year.

Acute Pain from Injury or Surgery

When the pain becomes too much to bear, or is the result of a serious injury or surgery, relief requires stronger medicine and a doctor's prescription. One class of frequently prescribed pain relievers is nonsteroidal anti-inflammatory drugs, often abbreviated NSAIDs. (The three nonprescription pain relievers are also NSAIDs, according to Love, although acetaminophen is not commonly referred to by that term.)

Prescription NSAIDs are given at higher doses than the nonprescription types, but the mechanism for pain relief is the same—blocking the production of prostaglandins.

Opiate drugs are another class of pain-relieving prescription drugs. Commonly prescribed opiates include morphine, codeine, hydromorphone (Dilaudid), and me-

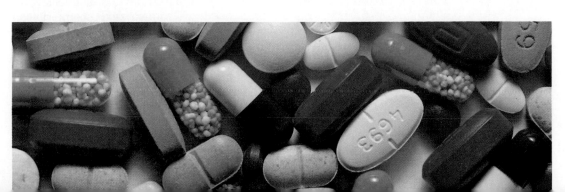

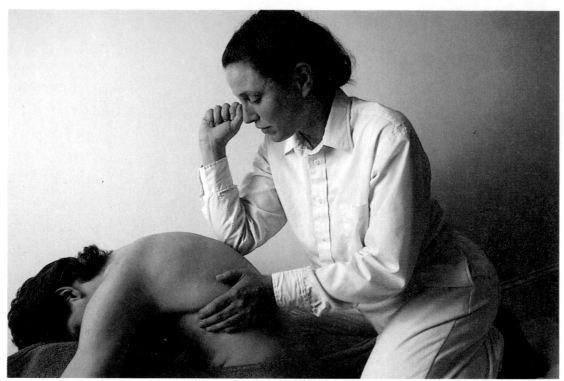

When orthodox medicine fails, pain sufferers often seek relief in alternative medical techniques. Rolfing (above) is a systematic deep-muscle therapy that is intended to provide both physical and emotional benefits.

peridine (Demerol). Most of these drugs are derived from opium, the juice of the poppy flower.

Opiate drugs work by altering the transmission of pain messages in the brain and spinal cord, blocking pain messages or altering their character.

The pain-blocking action of the opiates can be enhanced by taking aspirin, ibuprofen, or acetaminophen at the same time as the opiate. This hits pain with a "double whammy." The NSAIDs block the pain at the site of injury, while the opiates suppress in the brain any remaining pain.

Unfortunately, the effect of opiates on the brain isn't limited to pain control. Opiates can cause drowsiness, nausea, weakness, dry mouth, constipation, and unpleasant mood changes in some people. However, sometimes simply trying a different opiate may be all that's needed to reduce these side effects.

> *People who are truly seeking help for their pain and who are in good medical hands do not have drug-addiction problems.*

Tolerance and Addiction

Because doctors are afraid patients may become dependent on opiate drugs, they sometimes hold back on the amount or number of doses, even if this means the patient doesn't get sufficient pain relief.

Ronald Dubner, D.D.S., chief of the neurobiology and anesthesiology branch of the National Institute of Dental Research, says those fears are unfounded. But, he explains, "One needs to be very clear about making the distinction between tolerance and addiction." Tolerance occurs when the body no longer responds as well to the opiate's pain-relieving properties at the current dose. For example, some cancer patients with severe pain may need increasing amounts of morphine to maintain the same level of pain relief.

Addiction, on the other hand, is an overwhelming compulsion to continue use of the drug even when pain relief is no longer needed. While some of the addiction is physical, it is mainly considered a psychological dependence.

Addiction is "really a red herring in the field of pain control," says Dubner. The fear that giving patients opiates will turn them

Common Pain-Relief Medications

Drug	Benefits	Possible Side Effects
NON-PRESCRIPTION DRUGS		
Aspirin (Bayer, Anacin)	Relieves mild to moderate pain, including headache, muscle pain, and menstrual cramps; reduces inflammation and fever; higher doses, under a doctor's supervision, may prevent blood clotting and heart attacks.	Stomach irritation, heartburn, nausea, vomiting, skin rash; Reye's Syndrome if taken by children with flu or chicken pox.
Acetaminophen (Tylenol)	Relieves mild to moderate pain, including headaches and muscle pain; reduces fever.	Prolonged use in excessive doses can cause anemia, liver and kidney damage.
Ibuprofen (Advil)	Relieves mild to moderate pain, including headache, muscle pain, and menstrual cramps; reduces inflammation and fever; higher doses, under a doctor's supervision, may reduce swelling associated with arthritis.	Stomach irritation, heartburn, cramping, nausea, vomiting; prolonged use may cause kidney damage in people with liver, heart, or kidney disease.
NON-STEROIDAL ANTI-INFLAMMATORY DRUGS (NSAIDs)	Relieve moderate pain caused by rheumatoid arthritis, osteoarthritis, menstrual cramps, dental problems, gout, tendinitis, bursitis, sprains, and strains.	Nausea, cramps, indigestion, headache, drowsiness; occasionally, stomach ulcers, anaphylaxis, exacerbation of underlying heart or kidney disease.
NARCOTICS		
Codeine	Relieves mild to moderate pain.	Drowsiness, lightheadedness, constipation, skin rash, nausea.
Meperidine (Demerol)	Relieves moderate to severe pain.	Side effects of meperidine, methadone, and morphine include drowsiness, lightheadedness, weakness, euphoria, dryness of mouth, constipation; extended use may lead to drug dependence.
Methadone	Relieves moderate to severe pain.	
Morphine	Relieves severe chronic pain, usually in cancer patients.	

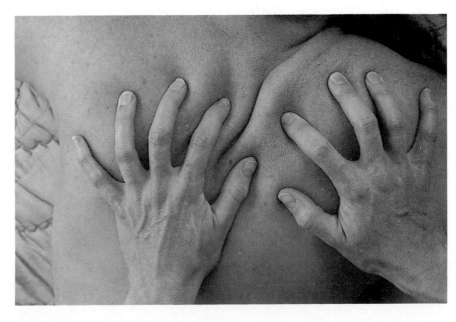

Long considered a luxury for the health-spa crowd, massage is gaining more general acceptance as a legitimate way to alleviate pain. When properly performed by a trained massage therapist, massage can reduce fluid accumulation and swelling around an injury.

How You Know That You Stubbed Your Toe

1. Nociceptors are specialized nerve endings in the skin and other peripheral tissues that respond exclusively to tissue-damaging stimuli. Prostaglandins sensitize these nerve endings, and the pain message starts on its way to the brain. (The drugs aspirin, ibuprofen, and, to a lesser extent, acetaminophen can block prostaglandin production at this point.)

2. Pain travels along special nerve fibers.

3. The message of pain arrives at the part of the spinal cord called the dorsal horn. (Tricyclic antidepressant drugs act there by enhancing the effects of the body's own natural painkillers. Or, if opiates are given, they cause the brain to suppress pain messages before they leave the dorsal horn.)

4. If untreated, the pain ascends to the thalamus and then to the cerebral cortex.

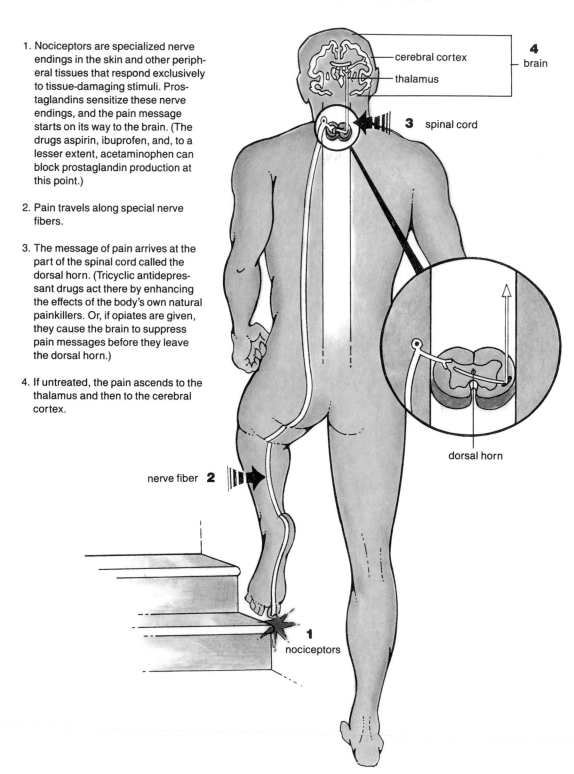

cerebral cortex

thalamus

4 brain

3 spinal cord

dorsal horn

nerve fiber **2**

1 nociceptors

into addicts craving the drugs long after the pain has ended is unfounded, says Dubner.

"People who are truly seeking help for their pain and who are in good hands do not have addiction problems," he explains.

In any case, Dubner says, it is very rare for a patient to reach a point where no amount of an opiate will relieve pain, and that should never be used as a reason for not increasing the drug's dose.

Anesthesiologist Francis Balestrieri agrees. "There's no reason to hold back the drug dose for people in acute pain," says Balestrieri, who is the director of the Woodburn Surgery Center at Fairfax Hospital in Falls Church, Virginia.

However, the FDA's Curtis Wright, M.D., warns that the pain relief from higher doses of opiates must be weighed against the side effects these drugs can cause.

"It's a balancing act," says Wright. "The amount of pain relief must be weighed against the effects of adverse reactions such as agitation, nausea, confusion, and potentially lethal respiratory depression."

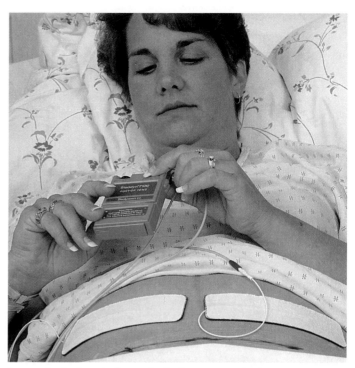

Increasingly, hospitals are designing new methods that permit patients to have a larger role in their own pain control.

Patients in Control

Frequently, however, the doses of narcotics that physicians prescribe are too low, not too high, and the time between doses is too long. One solution to inadequate doses of pain relievers is patient-controlled intravenous analgesia (PCA), which is usually used in hospitals for acute pain following surgery. In PCA the patient is connected to a machine called a PCA pump. When the patient pushes a control button, the machine delivers a dose of narcotic or other pain reliever intravenously. The doses are smaller than what would be given by injection, but because the drug goes directly into the bloodstream, relief can occur within seconds. A patient receiving traditional administration with an injection in the muscle or under the skin may have to wait anywhere from 5 to 30 minutes for pain relief.

Although the pain relief with PCA's small doses may last only 10 to 15 minutes, the patient can get another dose the second pain begins to return. Injections, on the other hand, may last up to two hours, but since the

usual dosage schedule is three to four hours, the pain returns long before the nurse does.

"PCA matches the patients' relief to their pain," says Balestrieri. "It also relieves patients of the worry over their pain relief in the majority of cases."

It also helps patients deal with the side effects opiates can cause, says FDA's Wright. "A substantial portion of patients don't want complete pain relief," says Wright. "They want as much pain relief as they can get without bad side effects."

The undesirable side effects of narcotics can be avoided completely with another form of continuous administration—epidural therapy. Epidurals, which inject the narcotics into the membrane surrounding the spinal cord, have been used for many years to block the pain of labor. Now this is being adapted to control pain after some major surgery, especially abdominal.

Drugs injected into the epidural space don't travel to the brain like other types of injections, explains Sherry Fisher, R.N., pain-management coordinator at Fairfax Hospital. Therefore, complications such as nausea and respiratory depression don't occur.

With epidurals, "patients can talk to me, take deep breaths, cough, and even be up and walking around, sometimes 24 hours after surgery," says Fisher. Normally, after the type of major surgery that requires the kind of pain control epidural therapy provides, "the patient would still be on a ventilator after 24 hours," she says.

However, epidurals aren't effective for every type of pain. Besides pain from abdominal surgeries, epidurals are best used for pain following major chest and urologic surgery, according to Fisher.

The ancient Chinese technique of acupuncture is still used today to treat the pain from such ailments as arthritis and headaches.

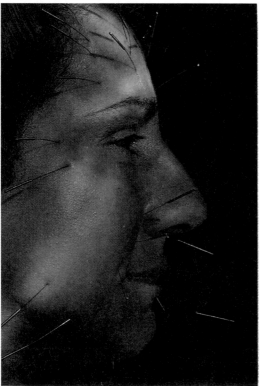

Chronic Pain

Unfortunately, "when it comes to chronic pain, there are situations where pain cannot be controlled as well with the approaches that are available to us today," says Dubner. Opiate drugs are usually avoided in chronic-pain management because of the potential for tolerance.

Some types of chronic pain that are difficult to control include:
• pain from nerve damage caused by diabetes or shingles;
• lower-back pain that continues long after the initial injury has healed;
• arthritis;
• migraine and other chronic headaches.

There is some hope, though. Tricyclic antidepressants, especially amitriptyline, have been found to relieve pain in patients with nerve damage. These drugs aid the body's own defenses by trapping serotonin, a pain-blocking chemical, at its point of production in the nerve endings in the dorsal horn of the spinal cord. An excess of serotonin builds up and suppresses pain signals longer than usual.

Although the FDA has not approved tricyclic antidepressants for pain control, these drugs are gaining wide acceptance for this purpose. (The practice of medicine commonly may include the prescribing of approved drugs for unapproved uses that are supported by clinical research and not otherwise contraindicated.)

Treatment of chronic and migraine headache pain may include two drugs approved for heart problems—calcium channel blockers and beta-blockers.

Treatment for mild arthritis pain, on the other hand, often begins with aspirin. If the patient can't tolerate aspirin, ibuprofen is a reasonable substitute, says Love. She warns, however, that even though people can buy aspirin and ibuprofen without a prescription, the doses required to treat arthritis pain are too high to be taken without a physician's care.

"The treatment of chronic arthritis, regardless of severity, requires an adequate diagnosis and possible use of many different types of medications, physical therapy, or surgery," says Love.

TENS applies electrical impulses at the pain site. These impulses travel to nerve endings and block pain signals from reaching the brain.

TENS

Another potential source of relief for chronic pain is transcutaneous electrical nerve stimulation (TENS). Through the use of the TENS device—a battery-powered generator that could be mistaken for a Walkman portable radio or a beeper—electrical impulses are transmitted to the site of pain through electrodes placed on the skin. These impulses travel to nerve endings and block pain signals from reaching the brain.

With the most common course of treatment, the physician or physical therapist sets the TENS device to deliver 80 to 100 impulses a second for 45 minutes, three times a day.

But there are a wide variety of parameter ranges, and what works for one person may have no effect on another. Determining the most effective settings "is a real art," says Stephen M. Hinckley, from the FDA's Center for Devices and Radiological Health.

Pain can be very subjective, explains Hinckley. Two people whose pain is caused by the same problem may need very different settings to achieve relief.

If a patient doesn't require hospital care, he or she can use the TENS device, preset to the proper level, at home. The device does not interfere with normal activities.

Although it isn't clear why TENS works, there are two plausible theories, according to the *Harvard Medical School Health Letter*. The first holds that nerves can easily carry only one message at a time. The electrical pulses from TENS overload the nerves, and the pain message shuts down. A second theory hypothesizes that the electrical pulses stimulate the body to release its own painkilling molecules, called endorphins, into the fluid bathing the spinal cord.

Behavior-modification techniques help many chronic pain sufferers focus on their quality of life instead of their pain.

Focus on Life

Sometimes, though, none of these therapies will completely relieve the pain for chronic sufferers. They don't have to give up hope, though. For many in chronic pain, behavior-modification techniques such as biofeedback, meditation, and relaxation training may offer some relief. These treatment approaches are designed to alter a patient's reactions and behavior in response to pain.

"They learn that they can deal with their pain effectively if they focus on improving their quality of life instead of focusing on their pain," says Dubner.

Seymour Rubin, 67, who has suffered with chronic back pain for 40 years, agrees. "If I focus on the pain, it just gets worse," he says. Instead, Rubin keeps busy with walking, reading, and running errands with his wife.

"Singing helps; talking helps," adds Rubin. "And I've just learned to accept the fact that I have pain."

Housecalls

By George Valko, MD, a physician on the active medical staff at Thomas Jefferson University Hospital and the Jefferson Family Medicine Office in Philadelphia, PA.

Q *I sometimes have trouble sleeping. I have heard of various sleep disorders that can be evaluated at sleep clinics. What kind of sleep problems are most common, and when should they be checked out?*

A Lots of things can keep a person from sleeping, including many types of physical discomforts as well as anxiety or emotional problems, or various combinations of the two.

Heavy snoring can be a manifestation of a sleep disorder called sleep apnea, in which a person does not breathe properly at night. Another disorder is narcolepsy, which is marked by uncontrollable bouts of sleep. Both should be checked by a physician, who may recommend overnight testing at a sleep clinic.

In our busy society, when tiredness from disrupted sleep interferes significantly with daytime activities, it's often the result of disrupted "sleep hygiene," a term that simply refers to the practice of allowing yourself a *regular* adequate amount of sleep.

Here are some hints for achieving good sleep hygiene:
• Use your bedroom as exclusively as possible for sleeping;
• Avoid caffeine in the evening and night, including that which comes from chocolate, soft drinks, and medications;
• Make sure your environment is comfortable, not too hot, too stuffy, or too noisy;
• Have a light snack at bedtime;
• After 20 minutes, if you can't sleep, go into another room and read or otherwise relax until you feel sleepy again.

Q *Are there any new means of male contraception currently available that don't involve surgery?*

A No, there are not. The barrier method, i.e., condom use, is the only nonsurgical method of contraception that can be used specifically by the male.

Under development is a pill that decreases the number of sperm cells by blocking the production of testosterone. Unfortunately, this pill has significant side effects. Also under investigation is an antisperm vaccine that would give a man antibodies that attack and kill his own sperm; however, to develop such a vaccine in a safe form will take many years.

Q *Magic Johnson says he contracted the AIDS virus through unsafe sexual practices. Apparently, if he had used a condom, he would have protected himself against this virus and against other diseases that have received a lot of attention over the years, such as herpes and venereal diseases. Are there other, less-well-known sexually transmitted diseases that one must now protect against as well?*

A The environment for sexual activity has changed in the past decade with the increase in prevalence and danger from sexually transmitted diseases (STDs). In addition to herpes and AIDS, which are caused by viruses, other sources of STDs are of great concern:

In a sleep clinic, electrodes attached to the patient transmit readouts of vital signs to a physician or other specialist, who monitors the data for signs of a sleep disorder.

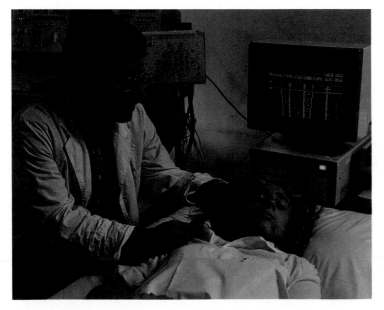

• Bacteria, such as those that cause gonorrhea and chlamydia, which have few symptoms in the female, but can lead to serious infections and can permanently damage fertility; syphilis, which causes organ and brain damage if not diagnosed early; chancroid, a painful ulceration; and others.

• Parasites such as *Trichomonas,* which can cause irritation to the mucous membranes of the vagina or urethra or both.

• Other viruses, such as human papilloma virus, which causes genital warts and is implicated in cancers of the female genital tract.

Hepatitis—which is caused by a virus and can also be transmitted by blood—and yeast-infection vaginitis—which can be brought on by antibiotics, birth-control pills, and douches—can be sexually transmitted, but are not strictly considered STDs.

Those having sex in other than a monogamous, long-term relationship can take several common-sense (albeit inconvenient) precautions to avoid contracting STDs. They should find out all they can about their partner's sexual history, physically check the partner, and always use a condom. Condoms, however, do nothing against oral-to-oral contact, and do not cover the testicles and groin, areas in which some STDs can either be contracted or transmitted.

Q *I've heard that there is good cholesterol and bad cholesterol. What's the difference, and how can you get more of the good and less of the bad?*

A There are actually several subtypes of cholesterol, but the most important are the low-density lipoproteins (LDL), commonly known as the bad cholesterol, and high density lipoproteins (HDL), or good cholesterol. The two differ in biochemical makeup and effect, but both are essential to the body.

LDL, in essence, delivers dietary cholesterol to the cells of the body, including the cells that line blood-vessel walls. Over the years, cholesterol forms layers on vessels, which contributes to blockages of blood flow. This is particularly dangerous when cholesterol builds up in the vessels of the heart. HDL does the opposite, taking cholesterol from the blood-vessel walls and delivering it back to the liver for processing.

You can lower your bad cholesterol by following a low-fat diet. If the diet fails, medications available through your doctor can help. These steps may also increase good cholesterol, though this is a more difficult step to achieve.

Remember, regular exercise, healthy diet, and quitting smoking will improve your cholesterol profile.

Q *Sometimes after I've been to a noisy party or loud concert, my ears ring. Should I be alarmed? Could this be a sign of a hearing problem?*

A Called *tinnitus,* such ringing is a sign that damage may have been done to your hearing. There are a number of causes of tinnitus, but a common reason is acoustic trauma from exposure to loud noise.

Usually the ringing will go away, leaving only mild, imperceptible damage to the nerves that help to change sound waves into audible sound. However, take the tinnitus as a warning to protect your hearing from further such loud sounds.

A recent study showed that most men over 30 in this country have some hearing deficit. The baby-boom generation has been exposed to music and industrial sounds at volumes never encountered before, and this is thought to be a culprit in an epidemic of hearing loss that may have only just begun and the extent of which is still impossible to calculate.

Sound above 80 or 90 decibels for an hour or so can cause damage; rock concerts and headphones, including the personal, portable kind, can expose ears to as much as 120 to 150 decibels. People who work in heavy industrial and other noisy environments without any ear protection are also at risk. Your doctor can help screen you for hearing loss, but the damage cannot be repaired.

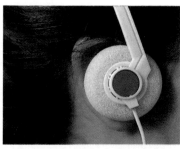

Even tiny headphones can expose the ears to damaging levels of sound. Just a brief exposure can result in permanent hearing loss.

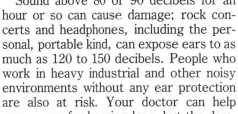

Do you have a medical question?
Send it to Editor, Health and Medicine Annual, P.O. Box 90, Hawleyville, CT 06440-9990

Nutrition

See also:
Individual articles in the second half of this book, arranged in alphabetical order, for additional information.

Scientists continue to produce evidence that supports the old adage "You are what you eat." And many people are eager to follow nutritional practices that will help ensure good health. Unfortunately, this isn't always as simple as it seems.

The public is often confused about what constitutes a healthy, well-balanced diet. Take salt intake, for example. After years of being told to limit salt intake to prevent hypertension, people now learn that some recent studies indicate that salt-restrictive diets may have few if any benefits in fighting hypertension. As some nutritionists are dismissing salt's role as a culprit in hypertension, they are focusing on calcium and magnesium. A study by Harvard University researchers found that people whose diet was very low in calcium or magnesium had a 23 percent greater risk of becoming hypertensive.

Not everyone agrees. Malcolm Law of the University of London's St. Bartholomew's Hospital Medical College directed an analysis of 78 studies on blood pressure and diet, which indicated that the link between salt and hypertension was even greater than previous studies had indicated. "Everyone, even if their doctor didn't tell them they were at high risk for heart disease, should reduce the amount of salt in their diets by at least [half a teaspoon] a day," commented Law.

One of the hottest areas of cancer research is the study of natural dietary substances that may inhibit the development of cancer. Large amounts of green and yellow vegetables are known to have protective effects against cancer. Garlic, citrus fruits, and herbs such as rosemary and oregano also appear to be beneficial. In 1991, several teams of scientists reported that green tea, a popular drink in Japan and several other Far Eastern countries, had potent anticancer properties in tests conducted with mice. The scientists indicated that the growth of skin, stomach, small-intestine, liver, and lung cancers was significantly reduced in mice that were given green-tea extracts compared with those given water. It was also noted that Japanese people who are heavy drinkers of green tea have lower death rates from cancer of all types and especially stomach cancer, a major killer in Japan.

It has long been known that processed meats like bacon and ham, which contain nitrosamines, can increase the risk of cancer. Now even certain cooking methods have become suspect. For example, grilling, frying, and broiling meats produce substances called heterocyclic aromatic amines (HAAs), some of which have been shown to cause cancer in laboratory animals, including primates. The longer the meats are cooked, the greater the amounts of HAAs produced.

According to the Calorie Control Council, some 48 million Americans will try to lose weight this year. Many will be repeaters—people who have lost weight in the past, then regained it. Yale University weight specialist Kelly Brownell discovered that such yo-yo dieters are at greater risk of developing heart disease, and have a higher overall death rate, than people whose weight remains stable. Other researchers learned that obese yo-yo dieters are more likely than other people to crave fatty, sugary foods.

A survey released in 1991 indicated that Americans are much better informed about cholesterol and its effect on heart disease than they were in the early 1980s. At the same time, however, the survey indicated that there has been almost no increase in the percentage of people who say they are trying to lower their cholesterol levels by changing their diets.

Wine lovers received welcome news when French scientists reported that drinking red wine appears to lower cholesterol levels. Now Cornell University researchers have isolated resveratrol, the chemical in grapes that they believe is the cholesterol-lowering substance. No health professionals recommend wine drinking as a substitute for a low-fat diet, however.

A new study confirmed that oat bran helps lower blood-cholesterol levels. Chemists at the U.S. Department of Agriculture (USDA) have developed a concentrated form of the active ingredient, beta-glucan. Adding a fraction of an ounce of beta-glucan to breads and other foods would give these foods the healthful attributes of an entire bowl of oatmeal.

What's on a label? Not enough, say many health experts. But in 1993, when new USDA regulations take effect, Americans will face fewer misleading claims on supermarket shelves. They'll find it easier to determine the nutritional value of foods. And they'll find it harder to lie to themselves about what they eat.

Confusion continues over what constitutes a well-balanced diet.

Today's fast-food restaurants offer an expanded menu of nutritionally balanced meals. Even classic fast-food fare—burger, fries, and soft drink—now carries less grease, fat, salt, and calories than before.

The New Fast Food

by Robert Barnett

There was always something quintessentially American about fast food. For decades the term somehow embodied the dynamism of life in the United States—fast, sporty, unpretentious, fun-loving. Grab a burger; jump in the car; take off! It's no wonder that fast-food chains hit so big in foreign markets.

And though the chains continue to thrive abroad, times have changed back here in the United States. Suddenly, it seemed, health experts began equating the nutritional value of fast food with the on-the-road safety record of drunk drivers. Things got even direr: the newly health-conscious dared to malign the cheeseburger, the staple of fast food, and far and away the most popular American

sandwich, blaming it for clogging arteries and causing heart disease. Jayne Hurley, a registered dietitian at the Center for Science in the Public Interest (CSPI), minced no words when she described the state of the fast-food restaurant a half-decade ago as "a mine field of grease and salt."

Hurley was right. Five years ago, fast food included just about every edible entity now known to be nutritionally undesirable. High in fat, saturated fat, and cholesterol, and low in fiber, fast-food fare delivered a combination that many doctors believe can increase the risk of colon cancer and other diseases, even possibly breast cancer. A high-saturated-fat diet can raise blood cholesterol, increasing the risk of heart attacks. Even the potatoes that are made into french fries, a plant food with no cholesterol, were fried in highly saturated beef fat! Virtually every fast-food item also contained enough salt to raise blood pressure in some people.

What fast food lacked was even worse. Restaurants provided very few whole grains or fresh fruits and vegetables, the cornerstone of a healthy diet. Nutritionists tell us that eating at least five small servings of fruits and vegetables a day could reduce our risk of developing certain cancers by half. Until recently, however, finding an apple or a bell pepper at a McDonald's or a Wendy's was a wild-goose chase.

Fortunately, that's all changed. In the past five years, and especially in the past year, the nation's fast-food establishments have cleaned up their nutritional act. Nearly every major chain—McDonald's, Burger King, Wendy's, Taco Bell, Arby's, Roy Rogers, Jack-in-the-Box—now offers a wide choice of low-fat foods. It's now possible to get your fast-food day off to a healthy start with cereal and low-fat milk; have a low-fat bean burrito and a salad for lunch; and enjoy a dinner of a low-fat hamburger, a baked potato, and a yogurt. "It's getting easier to eat healthfully at fast-food restaurants," says San Diego nutritionist Mary Donkersloot, R.D. "Now people need to take advantage of these lower-fat options."

Who Is Serving What

McDonald's, an industry leader, now also leads the pack in improved nutritional products. The spring of 1991 saw the introduction of the McLean Deluxe, the first truly low-fat hamburger available to American consumers. With very low-fat beef and a little carageenan, a seaweed derivative, to hold in the moisture, the new burger, bun, and trimmings carry only about 10 grams of fat and 320 calories. The Big Mac, by contrast, has nearly 42 grams of fat and 500 calories.

The McLean Deluxe derives about 28 percent of its calories from fat, not a "nutrition-buster" by any means, considering that nutritionists suggest that no more than 30 percent of our calories should derive from fat over the course of a few days. Amazingly, the McLean Deluxe rates even lower in fat than most "lean" hamburger meat from a supermarket, which can actually be pretty fatty (up to 60 percent of its calories are from fat). McDonald's also sells low-fat shakes, salads, low-fat cholesterol-free apple-bran muffins, cereal, low-fat milk, frozen yogurt, and, in some locations, snack-packs of sweet carrot sticks and stringless celery.

Catering to better nutrition is hardly a McDonald's patent. "Today every fast-food restaurant has lower-fat items," says Donkersloot. Burger King offers bagels, salads (including their Chunky Chicken salad), and

McDonald's and other American fast-food chains have expanded overseas rapidly. For some foreign patrons, particularly in Asia, fast food represents their first exposure to American cuisine.

Wendy's (above) and other fast-food restaurants have established salad bars for the health-conscious diner. Taco Bell offers bean burritos (left) and other nutritious Mexican-style entrees.

the BK Broiler, a chicken-breast sandwich on an oat-bran bun. Wendy's offers the ultimate low-fat entrée: a plain baked potato, not to mention a garden salad, low-fat chili, and its own grilled chicken sandwich. Taco Bell now lets its customers choose a bean burrito, pinto beans and cheese, or a tostada with green or red sauce, all relatively low-fat dishes. A two-slice serving of Domino's cheese pizza has 376 calories and only 10 grams of fat. In addition to its grilled chicken sandwich, Hardee's menu now offers a

Chicken 'n' Pasta salad, which, with 1 tablespoon of low-cal dressing, has 239 calories and only 4 grams of fat.

These days the fast-food aficionado can design a reasonably healthy diet around fast-food meals. Indeed, that's exactly what Mary Donkersloot has done. Her new book, *The Fast Food Diet: Quick and Healthy Eating at Home and On The Go* (Simon & Schuster, 1991), provides menu plans built around the lowest-fat fast foods. A typical day might include a low-fat breakfast at home, a grilled chicken sandwich or *fajita* or lower-fat burger at a fast-food restaurant, and a dinner such as a pasta with vegetables, or a Chinese-vegetable stir-fry. Donkersloot, a careful eater herself, enjoys fast food. "I'll often get the bean burrito at Taco Bell for lunch," she says.

Nutrition Knowledge a Must

Fast food may have improved, but it's still a far cry from perfect. Regardless of their gimmicky names, many of the so-called lower-fat dishes register high in the fat department. This fact is driven home when you actually calculate fat content, a process that requires some basic arithmetic.

Let's say you consume 1,800 calories a day. No more than 30 percent of those calories, or 540, should come from fat. Since 1 gram of fat contains 9 calories, your daily fat allotment should be 60 grams of fat.

An old-fashioned chicken sandwich at Burger King, the fried variety, delivers a whopping 40 grams of fat—two-thirds of the maximum allowed for an entire day! Add an order of french fries, and you've already topped 50 grams from one meal.

With 18 grams of fat, the new grilled chicken is a better bet, but it is not really a low-fat food. An order of french fries added to that as a side dish means you've already eaten two-thirds of your day's fat allowance in just one meal. Although the "lower-fat" choice is better than the old sandwich, it's still not so easy to eat a fast-food entrée every day and stay slim. By contrast, a homemade chicken-breast sandwich, with low-fat or even nonfat mayonnaise, would deliver just a few grams of fat—probably less than 5.

In many fast foods, fat works its way in deceptively. Take salads, for instance. Everyone knows that salads are healthy, right? Certainly it's important to consume salad greens and vegetables. But as every dieter knows, the downfall comes with the salad dressings, which often carry incredibly high levels of fat.

Kentucky Fried Chicken even changed its logo to KFC to avoid the bad connotations of the forbidden "fried" word. Its recent introduction—Skin-free Crispy chicken—has the skin removed before frying. Skin is fatty, but then again, so is frying. The Skin-free Crispy may have fewer calories and less fat than does the Extra Crispy variety, but that's due only to smaller portions—3 ounces of the "lighter" chicken versus 5 ounces of the original. Each has about 4 grams of fat per ounce, and each derives about 50 percent of its calories from fat.

The fast-food industry has finally taken steps to clean up its nutritional act.

French fries present another good example of hidden fat. This mainstay of fast-food restaurants was one of the first products to be lightened up. Wendy's, Burger King, and, ultimately, McDonald's all agreed to stop frying their fries in saturated beef fat and, instead, switch to healthier vegetable oils. But all that really changed was the *kind* of fat, not the amount. Our dietary aim is to cut our total fat, while reducing our intake of the saturated fats found in whole-milk dairy foods and fatty red meats and poultry with the skin. So, while a medium order of McDonald's french fries now has only 3.5 grams of saturated fat versus 7.2 before, both orders serve up a hefty 17.1 grams of total fat. At Wendy's the saturated fat dropped from 6 grams to 2.5, but the total fat fell only from 15 to 12 grams.

Sodium is also a concern. Many fast foods, even the low-fat ones, still contain high levels of sodium. Too much sodium can make you feel bloated by increasing water retention, and, if you have high blood pressure, too much can elevate it further.

Clues for Low-fat Cuisine

The trick with fast food is to order the low-fat items more often, while balancing the rest of the day's foods. "Try to eat animal protein once a day rather than twice," suggests Donkersloot. "If Mom is cooking chicken for dinner, get a pizza with less cheese and lots of vegetables for lunch. If you had a burger for lunch, try making a cheeseless pita-bread pizza, with tomato sauce and veggies and fresh basil, for dinner."

That's the approach taken by Mindy Herman-Zaidins, a registered dietitian who works just outside New York City, when she counseled a high-school wrestler recently. "He had a terrible diet," she recalls. "He'd

them. I made him have some juice or a piece of fruit at breakfast, and I had him drink a glass of milk."

That single healthy breakfast gave the young wrestler fiber-rich carbohydrates (in the bagel and fruit), vitamins A and C (in the juice or fruit), and calcium (in the low-fat milk).

"Calcium requirements are very high for teens," Herman-Zaidins notes. "It's four servings a day. If you're not conscientious about getting enough low-fat dairy products, it can be a problem." Indeed, young growing bones need calcium. The daily calcium requirement for teens is fully 50 percent greater than that for adults. Young bodies

More healthy fast food: Wendy's low-fat chili (above) and its chicken sandwich (facing page) have proved to be enormously popular entrees. McDonald's (right) and several other chains now offer nutritionally balanced breakfasts.

have breakfast at a fast-food restaurant, skip lunch, have fries in the afternoon, and maybe a slice of pizza for dinner.

"We worked around changing meals that didn't have a great social impact. With teens, it's important to work around their social life, rather than disrupt it. If your circle of friends is eating cheeseburgers and french fries, you're going to be less likely to order a low-fat burger.

"So we worked on breakfast. I convinced him he could get by without meeting his friend for breakfast at a fast-food restaurant. Instead, I suggested a bagel with some low-fat or even regular cream cheese, or some microwaveable pancakes, which are pretty nutritious if you don't slather butter all over

also enjoy the unique ability to store extra calcium in the bones, thus furnishing the body with a calcium reserve that can help prevent osteoporosis, the "brittle-bone" disease, later in life.

Many fast-food restaurants now offer calcium via low-fat milk or frozen yogurt. Fast-food patrons who routinely limit themselves to salad, fries, and a diet soda may, in the long run, weaken their bones.

After a good breakfast, the wrestler was free to have a fast-food lunch with his friends. But instead of a double cheeseburger, he ordered a grilled-chicken sandwich, or a single hamburger, and perhaps a side salad. Rather than large fries, he opted for a small order.

With all the new choices—and the potential pitfalls—it's more important than ever to know the nutritional profile of fast foods. Many chains offer brochures with nutritional information. Unfortunately, such pamphlets are often not available, and when they are, they can be confusing. "It's still a problem," says CSPI's Hurley. "We did a survey of nine states where nutritional brochures were supposed to be available, but Jack-in-the-Box was the only one that consistently had them. McDonald's has a poster, but it's confusing, with weights in grams, and all sorts of information about vitamins and minerals, when what people are really interested in is calories, fat, and sodium."

What Hurley would like to see is information posted immediately beside the item on the menu or the menu board. "If you're ordering, and you see that a Big Mac has 500 calories, but a McLean Deluxe has 320, you might decide to order a McLean," she says.

New Thinking

There's more to a healthy diet than avoiding fat: what you eat matters, too. Perhaps the most dramatic change in nutrition science has been the growing consensus that the healthiest diet to follow is one with more vegetables. That doesn't mean everyone should be a vegetarian, although vegetarianism represents a healthy choice, as long as iron and calcium intake do not suffer.

The emphasis on vegetables does mean that the centerpiece of most meals should be plant foods, not animal foods. We should increase our intake of whole grains, beans, fruits, and vegetables, and decrease the amount of red meat and dairy foods, the two greatest sources of saturated fat in the American diet. Concern has also grown about excess protein. Most Americans eat 1.5 times as much protein as they need, levels that may strain the kidneys, increase the risk of osteoporosis, and perhaps raise the risk of certain cancers.

These simple yet profound changes to the American diet haven't come easy to fast-food restaurants. "They're still pushing a meat-based diet," says Hurley. "Vegetarians still don't really have much choice. There's the salad bar and the baked potato, and that's it. I'd like to see a vegetarian chili, for example."

There's an indirect environmental concern as well. Raising cattle puts more of a strain on the land than does growing grains, for the simple reason that grains are fed to cattle. If grains or vegetables represent your own main source of calories, it's much more ecologically efficient.

Then there's the question of packaging. McDonald's, for one, has made great strides in minimizing the waste it generates. Working with an activist group called the Environmental Defense Fund, McDonald's in 1990 switched from styrofoam packaging to paper wrapping. Nonetheless, fast-food meals still create a tremendous amount of waste—just take a look at what gets thrown out by a typ-

ical party of four, and then multiply that amount by millions every day.

When it comes to nutrition, and increasingly to environmental concerns, fast-food restaurants are doing a praiseworthy job of responding to critics and cleaning up their acts. Fast foods can now fit quite comfortably into a healthy life-style for a customer equipped with a little knowledge and the wisdom to make good choices. But consumers need to understand that while fast food is better than it once was, it's still not ideal. On precisely this point, New York City nutritionist Mona Sue Boyd, R.D., offers a worthy adage to remember: "Fast food should be a complement to your diet, rather than a mainstay."

In the U.S., milk production per cow averages over 14,000 pounds a year. Lactation, or the production of milk, begins when the cow bears a calf, and lasts about 305 days.

Dairy and your Diet

by Ruth Papazian

"Finish your milk!"

That familiar command punctuated many a meal during our formative years. Back then everyone seemed to understand the essential role that dairy products played in a balanced diet. Dairy foods meant strong bones, good teeth, and healthy growth. Then, at some undefinable moment a few years ago, dairy products seemed to become the bane of good health. These days some people even get sick when they consume dairy products! Were our mothers misled all these years?

Not exactly. Dairy products still serve as an important source of calcium. And while, yes, certain dairy products carry high levels of fat and cholesterol, there's no reason why dairy foods cannot be incorporated into a healthy, low-fat and low-cholesterol diet. And for those people who lack the enzyme needed to digest dairy foods properly, enzyme supplements can change their lives (and diets). For everybody, today's wide selection of dairy products, available at virtually every supermarket around the country, offers us unprecedented choices in planning a healthy, nutritious, and delicious food regimen.

Dairy Definitions

Not long ago, shopping for dairy products was an uncomplicated affair: milk, butter, cheese, eggnog during the holidays. Things have changed. Today's grocery shopper is confronted with a bewildering array of products in the dairy case: whole milk, 1-percent milk, 2-percent milk, skim milk, milk substitutes—and those are just the milks! Confusion reigns again at the butter counter: salted butter, unsalted butter, corn-oil margarine, safflower-oil margarine, butter-margarine blends, you-name-it breakfast spreads. And then there are the wide varieties of yogurts . . . and cheeses . . . and creams. . . .

Dizzying though these dairy choices may seem, consumers need only familiarize themselves with the standards set by the Food and Drug Administration (FDA) to find out what ingredients and nutrients each food contains. For dairy products, the emphasis lies with fat content. For a product to be labeled ice cream, for instance, the FDA demands that it have a minimum of 10 percent butterfat. "Ice cream" with less butterfat carries the label "ice milk." The FDA sets similar standards for other dairy foods. New government regulations concerning misleading claims should also help clear up the confusion on supermarket shelves.

Dairy-deficiency Diseases

As noted before, dairy products are the primary source for calcium. In addition to this essential nutrient, yogurt, cheese, and other dairy foods are also rich in a number of other vitamins and minerals, including vitamins A, K, and the various Bs, phosphorus, and magnesium—substances crucial to maintaining good health. The table on page 79 describes how the body uses the various nutrients found in dairy foods.

Without the nutrients provided by dairy products, serious diseases can develop. *Os-*

teoporosis most commonly results from calcium deficiency. As many as 24 million Americans (80 percent of them women) suffer from this debilitating condition. More than a million osteoporosis-related fractures of the wrist, hip, and spine occur each year, primarily among those aged 45 and older.

The body stores calcium in the bones and teeth. Whenever dietary intake is insufficient to meet the body's needs, these reserves are

Dairy products, including milk, cheese, and ice cream, are nutrient-laden foods high in calcium, phosphorus, vitamin A, and riboflavin.

drawn upon. To release stored calcium, the body breaks down bone tissue. The bone tissue is then rebuilt, and a fresh supply of calcium is deposited.

From birth until the mid-30s, bone is rebuilt at a faster rate than it is broken down, so bones continue to grow in strength and size. If osteoporosis develops, however, the balance shifts, and bones gradually lose density, becoming thin and brittle.

Some researchers differentiate between two types of osteoporosis. Type I occurs in some women during the years immediately following menopause. The decline in estrogen production in a menopausal woman impairs her ability to absorb calcium and incorporate it into bone. At greatest risk for Type-I osteoporosis are thin, small-boned, Caucasian or Asian women who have had a hysterectomy or have reached menopause before age 45, and who have a family history of the condition.

Type-II osteoporosis is bone loss that occurs in both sexes as part of the aging process. It affects nearly half of all people over the age of 75. Though men are also at risk, this type of osteoporosis is still twice as common among women.

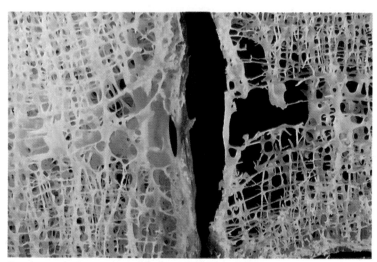

In osteoporosis, the absorption of old bone exceeds deposition of new bone, enlarging the spaces within the bone structure to produce bone fragility.

There is no cure for osteoporosis, but bone loss can be arrested in postmenopausal women with estrogen-replacement therapy. However, since estrogen cannot undo the damage caused by a hip or compression fracture that has already occurred, prevention is still the best approach. The risk of osteoporosis can be minimized by eating dairy foods rich in calcium during the crucial bone-forming years between adolescence and young adulthood. A consensus statement issued in October 1990 at the Third International Symposium on Osteoporosis held in Copenhagen, Denmark, recommended a daily minimum intake of 800 milligrams (mg) of calcium for all adults. The RDA for those between the ages of 11 and 14 is 1,200 mg. These numbers may sound high, but fulfilling them is relatively easy with dairy products when you consider that 1 cup of 1-percent milk contains 300 mg of calcium, 1 ounce of cheddar cheese contains 203 mg, and 1 cup of nonfat plain yogurt contains 452 mg.

Another disease that affects the bones is *rickets*. Although not technically a dairy-deficiency disease, rickets afflicts infants who lack vitamin D, which is catalyzed in the body by exposure to the Sun. Vitamin D helps the body absorb the calcium and phosphorus provided by dairy foods, which help the bones to grow and harden properly. Without the vitamin, bones become pliable and malformed, a condition that can ultimately lead to bowlegs, pigeon chest, and other deformities. Vitamin D also plays an important role in dental development; a child who lacks the vitamin may experience some delay in the teething process.

Prolonged deficiency of vitamin D in adults can cause *osteomalacia*, a disease that, like rickets, leads to poor bone calcification and subsequent deformities of the limbs, spine, or pelvis. Other symptoms of osteomalacia include rheumaticlike joint pain, facial twitching, and a waddling gait.

Some people develop osteomalacia because their bodies have much higher vitamin-D demands than normal. Most at risk are women who have had successive pregnancies within a year of each other, particularly if they breast-feed, and elderly people who do not venture outdoors, where sunlight triggers vitamin D production in the body.

Dairy Intolerance

As nutritious as this food group is, dairy foods cannot be tolerated by some people. Many have difficulty digesting milk products, and those who are troubled by kidney stones, high cholesterol, and other chronic conditions may need to curtail their intake.

Lactose intolerance makes some 30 million Americans wary of dairy. People with this

How Safe Is Milk?

Milk, the very symbol of wholesomeness and purity, isn't what it used to be, according to critics of modern farming techniques. Two of the most controversial practices are the use of antibiotics, to treat infections in cows, and hormone injections, to get cows to produce more milk. But do antibiotics and hormones get into the milk we drink? If so, in amounts that are harmful? The answers to these questions depend on whom you ask.

Residues of penicillin, streptomycin, tetracycline (which can all cause allergic reactions), and sulfa drugs (some of which have been associated with cancer in mice and rats) were present in a significant percentage of milk samples collected in the Washington, D.C., area in an independent test conducted by a consumer group in 1989. Even more troubling, the activists alleged that use of drugs banned by the FDA in milk cows was also widespread. At the same time, *The Wall Street Journal* conducted its own tests on samples from 10 cities around the country and came to the same conclusions.

In response to the ensuing criticism from Congress and consumer groups, the FDA implemented a new testing program in February 1991. Milk from 250 of the nation's largest milk-processing plants is now randomly tested for eight types of sulfa drugs and three types of tetracycline. This program supplements testing already implemented at the state level, which is concerned with detecting penicillin and related antibiotics.

Most experts agree that the concentration of drugs present in milk is too small to cause a health risk to anyone except those who are highly allergic to antibiotics. But consumer groups argue that even though the risk is small, it is entirely unnecessary and should be eliminated.

The latest shake-up over milk concerns the safety of recombinant bovine somatotropin (rBST), an experimental synthetic growth hormone that can increase a cow's milk production by 10 to 15 percent. Critics claim that milk from cows treated with rBST has a higher-than-normal level of the hormone, which may have a physiological effect on people who drink the milk (especially infants).

These arguments may not be scientifically valid, claim proponents. The synthetic hormone is virtually identical in molecular structure and composition to bovine somatropin (BST), the hormone produced naturally by the cow's pituitary gland. Small amounts of BST are present in milk even when cows are untreated, and the concentration of the synthetic hormone in milk does not exceed naturally occurring levels. And since BST is a protein-based hormone, whatever traces exist in milk (whether natural or synthetic) are destroyed by the human digestive system. Furthermore, there is no scientific documentation that rBST or BST has any effect on human growth. In fact, in the 1950s, researchers studied BST to treat growth disorders in children, but abandoned the effort because the hormone had no effect.

A 1991 report published in the *Journal of the American Medical Association* concluded that the "composition and nutritional value of milk from rBST-treated cows is essentially the same as that of milk from untreated cows." However, the panel did recommend further research into the health effects of a secondary hormone associated with rBST use known as insulin-like growth factor I (IGF-I), which is present in higher concentrations in the milk of treated cows. But it is unlikely that IGF-I will pose a health risk to humans, since the hormone naturally occurs at equally high levels in breast milk and in saliva.

Currently rBST is still experimental, and the FDA has not approved the hormone for commercial use.

Residues of certain chemicals fed to cows are sparking concern over milk's safety.

The dizzying array of milk products now available poses a daily dairy dilemma for consumers interested in including such foods as part of a healthy diet.

condition are deficient in lactase, an enzyme that enables the small intestine to break down milk sugar (lactose) into its constituent simple sugars (glucose and galactose). Certain ethnic and racial groups—among them Asians, Africans, Eastern Europeans, North and South American Indians, and those of Mediterranean descent—are especially prone to this problem.

Though most newborns produce ample amounts of lactase, many people, for some unknown reason, lose the ability to make sufficient quantities of the enzyme by the time they reach adulthood. Secondary (or transient) lactose intolerance can occur as a side effect of antibiotics, ibuprofen, and chemotherapy, all of which may destroy lactase in the small intestine.

Symptoms of lactose intolerance—often mistakenly attributed to stress or other causes—include abdominal pain, gas, bloating, and diarrhea. Depending on the amount of lactase that a person has in his or her intestine and the amount of dairy food actually consumed, symptoms can develop within 10 minutes or up to 20 hours after ingesting dairy foods.

There is no cure for lactose intolerance, but symptoms can be controlled. While it is not necessary to give up dairy foods entirely, the unpleasant aftereffects can be avoided by limiting portion size and by making a dairy food one component of a larger meal. For example, if you're going to have ice cream for dessert, eat it directly after the meal rather than a couple of hours later.

Some lactose-intolerant people can handle whole milk better than low-fat varieties. Whole milk takes longer to digest because of its higher fat content; thus, the intestine has more time to deal with the lactose. Chocolate milk may also go down easily, because cocoa reduces gas and bloating. Aged and ripened cheeses are comparatively low in lactose, and yogurt contains active cultures that have already broken down some of the lactose, making these products easier to digest.

Food manufacturers have introduced a variety of lactose-reduced products, including milk (both whole and low-fat), cottage cheese, and ice cream. If a lactose-reduced version of a particular dairy food is not available, an over-the-counter lactase pill taken before a meal can prevent symptoms from occurring.

The Cholesterol Question

According to health experts, 28 percent of Americans have *serum cholesterol* levels above 240 milligrams per deciliter (mg/dl), putting them at serious risk of suffering a heart attack. The continued good health of another 30 percent is threatened by cholesterol levels higher than 200 mg/dl.

Cholesterol deposits in the inner lining of the arteries, leading to atherosclerosis, or hardening of the arteries. Eventually, the resulting buildup, called plaque, partially or totally blocks the blood's flow, which may cause a heart attack. In general, however, if most cholesterol in the blood is in the form of high-density lipoproteins (HDLs), it seems to protect against arterial disease; but if most blood cholesterol consists of low-density lipoproteins (LDLs), the risk of disease developing is increased.

For the past few years, nutritionists have advised Americans to cut back on whole-milk dairy products, including rich creams and butter sauces. These foods are high in saturated fat, which elevates blood cholesterol in the body.

Fortunately for dairy lovers, diet is not always the main culprit leading to high cholesterol. The liver produces about 800 to 1,500 mg of cholesterol a day for use in such processes as digestion and the synthesis of cortisone, estrogen, and other hormones. The body usually adjusts its cholesterol output whenever dietary intake is high. But in some people, a genetic flaw in the liver's regulatory mechanism causes cholesterol to be pumped out at the same rate, regardless of diet. If the liver's output isn't too high, cutting back on foods containing cholesterol and saturated fat can compensate.

Health experts advocate limiting daily dietary cholesterol consumption to 300 mg and trimming dietary fat intake to 30 percent of calories (with only a third of these coming from saturated fat). If diet changes alone are unsuccessful, drug therapy is needed to control the amount of cholesterol produced by the body itself.

Is it possible to enjoy dairy products while keeping cholesterol levels low? Whole milk, dairy products made with whole milk, and ice cream are all relatively high in cholesterol and saturated fat. But low- (and even no-) cholesterol-and-fat versions of each of these foods are available on supermarket shelves. For instance, 1 cup of whole milk contains 5 grams (g) of saturated fat and 33 mg of cholesterol, while 1 cup of 1-percent milk con-

Dairy Food Nutrients and What They Do

Nutrient	How the Body Uses It
Vitamin A	Aids night vision; assists in the formation of bones and teeth; needed for healthy reproduction.
Vitamin D	Fosters absorption and use of calcium and phosphorus for proper bone-growth maintenance.
Vitamin K	Aids blood clotting; helps maintain normal bone metabolism.
Thiamine (B$_1$)	Helps the body convert glucose into energy; keeps the nervous system healthy.
Riboflavin (B$_2$)	Helps release energy from carbohydrates, proteins, and fats; helps maintain mucous membranes.
Vitamin B$_{12}$	Aids in the formation of red blood cells; keeps the nervous system healthy.
Calcium	Builds bones and teeth; maintains bone strength; aids muscle contraction and blood clotting.
Phosphorus	Maintains bones and teeth; aids food metabolism; acts in formation of genetic material, cell membranes, and many enzymes.
Magnesium	Aids in enzyme activation, nerve and muscle function, and regulation of heartbeat.

Salmonella

While technically a part of the meat and meat-products food group, eggs are still closely associated with the dairy foods. Both the dairy industry and public-health officials became alarmed when eggs recently became a major cause of food poisoning from the *Salmonella* bacteria. Each year about 40,000 cases of *salmonellosis* are traced to raw or undercooked eggs or foods that contain uncooked eggs, such as Caesar salad, hollandaise sauce, homemade mayonnaise, meringue, and eggnog.

Each year about 40,000 cases of salmonella poisoning are traced to eggs or egg-based foods.

The symptoms of salmonella poisoning include diarrhea, vomiting, abdominal pain, chills, fever, and headache. Symptoms typically develop between 12 to 48 hours after eating contaminated food; it usually takes from four to seven days for the illness to run its course. The elderly, infants, and those with weakened immune systems—such as AIDS patients or people undergoing chemotherapy—are at the highest risk of salmonella poisoning. In these high-risk groups, serious complications can occur if salmonella bacteria enter the bloodstream and invade organs outside the gastrointestinal tract.

In the past, salmonella outbreaks were caused by cracked eggs or eggs that had been contaminated by chicken droppings. Since the early 1970s, the U.S. Department of Agriculture (USDA) has required egg distributors to wash eggs with disinfectants to minimize risk. What alarms officials this time is that the salmonella epidemic involves uncracked, sanitized eggs that are infected on the inside before they are laid. Agricultural experts now believe that the eggs somehow become infected with salmonella bacteria harbored in the hens' ovaries before the shell is fully formed. By some estimates, 1 in 10,000 eggs in the New England states, New York, and Pennsylvania (the areas where the problem is most widespread) are contaminated. As a result, each year 1 in 50 people in these areas will eat a contaminated egg. The epidemic can't be eradicated until scientists figure out exactly how infection is occurring. But to minimize risk of illness, experts recommend these precautions:

• Store eggs in their original carton at a temperature no higher than 40° F (eggs stored in the egg bin in the refrigerator door deteriorate more quickly because of temperature changes that occur each time the door is opened).

• Discard cracked eggs or eggs that are older than five weeks.

• Don't allow raw or cooked eggs to remain out of the refrigerator for more than two hours (including preparation and serving time).

• Avoid eating raw eggs or foods that contain raw eggs, such as homemade hollandaise sauce and homemade ice cream (commercial preparations of such foods are safe because they are made with pasteurized eggs).

• Cook eggs until both the white and yolk are firm, not runny. Hard-boiled and scrambled eggs are less likely to contain viable bacteria than those cooked sunny-side up. Here are some recommended cooking times:

Scrambled—1 minute at 250° F;
Sunny-side up—7 minutes at 250° F;
Fried, over easy—3 minutes at 250° F on one side, one minute on other side.

tains 1.6 g of saturated fat and 10 mg of cholesterol. Similarly, sour cream has 2 g of saturated fat and 10 mg of cholesterol per tablespoon; its low-fat counterpart has only half as much saturated fat and cholesterol.

Eggs, while not technically a dairy product, are closely associated with foods made with dairy products. Eggs are relatively low in saturated fat (about 1.5 g each). Unfortunately, they pose quite a cholesterol quandary, since one egg supplies about two-thirds of the daily cholesterol quota (213 mg on average). As yet, no one has figured out how to get hens to lay reduced-cholesterol eggs, but not from lack of trying. In one experiment, researchers fed hens lovastatin (a drug prescribed for people with high cholesterol levels), and a number of farmers have claimed that special regimens, such as stress-free environments or adding iodine-rich seaweed to the feed, can cut cholesterol levels in eggs significantly.

There are only two tried-and-true ways to reduce the cholesterol content of an egg—to eat the white only (the yolk contains all the cholesterol) or to use a liquid egg substitute, which is made of egg whites to which yellow food coloring and vegetable fat have been added. In cooking and baking, two egg whites or 1/4 cup of egg substitute equals a whole egg.

When to Restrict Dairy Products
Dairy products are by and large a healthy, nutritious part of the well-balanced diet. Still, people suffering from various conditions—inflammatory-bowel disease and kidney stones most notably—should restrict dairy products, as their consumption will aggravate an already uncomfortable situation.

Inflammatory-bowel disease, a chronic condition often accompanied by lactose intolerance, afflicts 2 million Americans. Symptoms include abdominal pain and cramping, persistent diarrhea, blood in the stool, high fever, and weight loss; joint inflammation and skin rashes may also occur. The disease takes one of two forms: Crohn's disease (ulcers and inflammation that can occur in any part of the gastrointestinal tract) and ulcerative colitis (which affects only the large intestine).

While no one knows the exact underlying causes of inflammatory-bowel disease, the immune system may be involved. The condition may be associated with stress, anxiety, and depression. Those who have a family history of the disease are also at increased risk.

Inflammatory-bowel disease is treated with symptom-specific medications such as sulfasalazine, an anti-inflammatory drug. Doctors may also recommend restricting milk and milk products. Lactose-reduced products and lactase pills are often helpful to avoid discomfort.

Certain types of *kidney stones* may be caused by excess calcium in the urine. Ironically, this condition can sometimes result from a diet that overemphasizes calcium and vitamin D. Other causes include a problem in the parathyroid gland, which affects calcium metabolism, or a blockage in the urinary tract that interferes with urination.

By one estimate, as many as 1.4 million Americans over the age of 30 have kidney stones; men are three times more likely to be affected than women. Risk factors include a family history of the problem, chronic dehydration (lack of fluid causes the urine to become concentrated), high alcohol intake, and prolonged confinement to bed.

Kidney stones—as tiny as a grain of sand or as large as a golf ball—can form in one or both kidneys. Large stones usually stay in the kidney and are thus asymptomatic. Stones small enough to pass through the ureter—but too big to pass easily—cause excruciating pain. The pain usually occurs first in the back (below the ribs), and then follows the course of the stone through the ureter toward the groin, where the bladder is located. The pain may be accompanied by nausea, and there may be traces of blood in the urine. It can take anywhere from several hours to several days to pass the stone.

To prevent kidney-stone development, doctors advise drinking plenty of fluids to keep the urine diluted, and, in some cases, avoiding milk and milk products. Once kidney stones have developed, however, an ultrasound technique called lithotripsy, which crushes small stones so that they can pass easily through the ureter, can successfully resolve the problem.

A single bad habit can greatly offset the benefits of a well-balanced diet. Smokers, for instance, have lower levels of several essential vitamins in their bodies compared to nonsmokers.

NUTRIENT THIEVES

by Marilynn Larkin

When it comes to your health, even virtues can become vices if carried to extremes. Despite your efforts to exercise regularly and eat a balanced diet, other life-style habits can rob your body of important nutrients and sabotage your health. Here are some examples.

Cigarettes

Smoking has such detrimental system-wide effects that giving it up is the *single most important* thing you can do to improve your health. In addition to causing heart disease and cancer, smoking can have negative nutritional consequences. Numerous studies have found that, on average, the level of vitamin C is 30 percent lower in smokers than in non-smokers. Researchers believe that nicotine and other active chemicals in cigarettes may interfere with vitamin C absorption. According to another theory, nicotine speeds up the metabolism, so the vitamin is used up at a faster rate. Either way the National Research Council has raised the recommended dietary allowance (RDA) of vitamin C for smokers to approximately 90 mg daily, as opposed to 60 mg for nonsmokers. Not only is vitamin C important in collagen formation and maintenance of capillaries, bones, and teeth, but it may neutralize nitric oxide and other free radicals (highly reactive molecules that attack the fat-containing portion of cells —particularly in the lungs—causing mutations that could lead to cancer) found in cigarette smoke. To get adequate amounts of vitamin C, your diet should include plenty of citrus fruits, tomatoes, green peppers, and potatoes.

Another important nutrient for smokers is vitamin E, even better at counteracting the damaging effect of free radicals than is vitamin C, says Karen Owens, R.D., a San Diego-based nutritional biochemist. "Smokers have very low levels of vitamin E in lung cells and in the blood because they use it up so quickly," she says. Ongoing research suggests that smokers may need to take in 400 to 800 international units (IU) of vitamin E daily; the RDA is 15 IU.

Smokers also lose folic acid, a B vitamin necessary for normal division and repair of DNA, the genetic material found in every cell. According to a 1988 study at the University of Alabama in Birmingham, 36 smokers given 10 mg of folic acid and 500 micrograms (μg) of vitamin B_{12} (the RDAs for these nutrients are 180 to 200 μg, and 2 μg, respectively) over a four-month period had significantly fewer precancerous cells in their phlegm than did a control group of 37 smokers who received a placebo. To increase folic acid in your diet, choose dark-green leafy vegetables, oranges, whole-wheat products, low-fat dairy products, lean meat, and shellfish.

Alcohol

Like smoking, drinking poses myriad consequences to your health. Heavy drinkers (more than two drinks daily, counting 12 ounces of beer, 5 ounces of wine, or 1 to $1\frac{1}{2}$ ounces of distilled spirits as one drink) risk cirrhosis of the liver as well as cancer of the mouth and esophagus. Since alcohol contains high amounts of sugar, heavy drinking increases the body's need for B-complex vitamins, which are necessary for carbohydrate metabolism, explains Allison Boomer, R.D., chief research dietitian at Wayne State University School of Medicine in Michigan, and

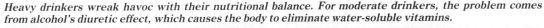

Heavy drinkers wreak havoc with their nutritional balance. For moderate drinkers, the problem comes from alcohol's diuretic effect, which causes the body to eliminate water-soluble vitamins.

a spokesperson for the American Dietetic Association. Exacerbating the problem, alcohol can damage absorption sites for thiamine and folic acid in the small intestine. The National Research Council has not recommended raising the RDA of thiamine (1 g), niacin (20 mg), vitamin B (1.6 to 2 g), or folic acid for heavy drinkers, says Boomer, but she recommends that if you do drink, be certain to take in adequate amounts of the B-complex vitamins.

Even moderate drinking can affect your nutrient balance, because alcohol has a diuretic effect, causing you to lose lots of water —and at the same time, the water-soluble vitamins, such as B complex and C—when you drink. To counteract these effects, eat such foods as cod, pork, brown rice, and spinach, which are rich in vitamin B, and make sure your intake of vitamin C meets the RDA.

Perhaps the biggest nutritional danger of drinking too much is that alcohol not only displaces nourishing calories with "empty" calories, but it also depresses the appetite, making it all the more difficult to take in adequate important nutrients.

Over-the-Counter Medications

The antacid tablet you take after a dietary indiscretion may prevent your body from utilizing the iron, calcium, and vitamin A in your meal, notes David Rush, Ph.D., professor of medicine and clinical pharmacology at the University of Missouri in Kansas City. Due to a process called adsorption, these nutrients adhere to the surface particles of magnesium- or aluminum-containing antacids and are not absorbed by the body. "Women with osteoporosis can sidestep detrimental effects of calcium adsorption by using a calcium-based antacid," Rush suggests. However, "As all types of antacids act to raise the pH (alkalinity) of stomach acid, iron absorption is hampered by all formulations," he adds. To counteract these nutritional effects, it's best to allow at least a couple of hours after eating before taking an antacid. If you can't wait, and suffer from heartburn only occasionally, your health probably won't suffer. But if you have chronic heartburn or an ulcer, consult your physician for other treatment options.

Strenuous exercise increases the body's need for certain vitamins. Athletic women should be especially careful to get enough iron.

"Laxatives containing mineral oil can lead to loss of vitamins A, D, and E because these fat-soluble vitamins dissolve in the oil and pass from the body without being absorbed," says Rush. "Phenolphthalein-based laxatives cause significant contractions in the colon and upper intestine, and food passes through so quickly, there's no chance for nutrients to be absorbed." These laxatives are associated with potassium loss in particular. To prevent nutritional deficiencies, take laxatives only occasionally (it's better to up your fiber intake to prevent constipation) on an empty stomach, and don't eat for at least two hours afterward.

Rheumatoid arthritis sufferers and others who need to take aspirin for an extended period are susceptible to acidosis (excessive acidity of urine and other body fluids), which causes potassium loss, particularly in those who take diuretics, says Rush. Chronic aspirin users should include such potassium-rich foods as oranges, cantaloupes, broccoli, and potatoes in their diets.

Exercise

Although exercise is good for you, even a moderate aerobic workout performed three times a week can increase your need for specific vitamins and minerals—especially if you're a "weekend warrior" or have to contend with smog.

Heavy exercise (training past your target heart rate) causes some iron loss. This is of particular concern to women, since menstruation depletes the iron supply to begin with. The RDA for adult women is 15 mg. Trying to increase intake by eating more iron-rich foods isn't easy from a nutritional standpoint, because the best sources—meat and eggs—are high in fat and cholesterol. However, fish and enriched grain products also provide iron. If you exercise strenuously, consult your doctor about the possibility of taking an iron supplement.

Studies conducted by Daphne Roe, M.D., professor of nutrition, division of nutrition science at Cornell University in Ithaca, New York, suggest that regular exercisers should include at least 2.8 mg of riboflavin (a B-complex vitamin) in their diets (the RDA is 1.2 mg). "Riboflavin is required for energy utilization and goes to active muscle, so you need more of it when you exercise," she explains. To meet your body's riboflavin requirements, eat low-fat dairy products, mushrooms, and broccoli.

According to a number of studies at the University of California at Berkeley, stren-uous exercise raises the need for vitamin E. During exercise the body takes in 10 to 20 times more oxygen, increasing the production of free radicals (in addition to being a component of cigarette smoke, they are generated with every breath we take as a part of normal body metabolism; air pollutants add to the problem). Normally, a well-balanced diet supplies adequate vitamin E to counteract the degenerative effects of free radicals, but exercisers use up their supplies more quickly because of increased oxygen consumption during exertion, and may need to take in more than the RDA of 8 to 10 mg. Vitamin E-rich foods include vegetable oil, almonds, and sunflower seeds.

Poor Eating Habits

"Wolfing down coffee and doughnuts instead of a healthful breakfast, or skipping meals altogether until late evening, can put tremendous stress on the body," says nutritional biochemist Owens. Normally, your body fuels itself on carbohydrates taken in at meals. If you skip meals, you are operating on "deficit energy"—your body raids its fat stores for energy. This can lead to depletion of vitamins A and E, which are stored in fat. Also, you are unlikely to take in the full complement of required nutrients if you eat only one meal a day, Owens adds.

A varied diet of healthful foods will provide all the nutrients you need, and cover the occasional overindulgence, says research dietitian Boomer. If you want the extra protection of a supplement, rather than gulping a fistful of pills, take a multivitamin and mineral supplement that contains no more than 100 percent of the RDA of each nutrient—higher concentrations will be excreted unused from the body, and you'll have wasted your money.

Fresh-from-the-garden herbs add a healthy zest to almost any dish. Most herbs are grown for their leaves; one exception is coriander (above), for which recipes usually call for seeds, either whole or crushed.

Growing Herbs for Healthier Cooking

by Erin Hynes

Most likely you've been eating herbs since you were a kid. Maybe your first experience with herbs was losing half your potato chip in the dill dip at a family party. Or watching a pizza maker sprinkle oregano on your pie in progress. Or maybe just laughing at the third-grade groaner, "What's green and sings?" (Elvis Parsley, of course).

No matter how you were introduced to herbs, you're one of millions of people throughout history who have used herbs in cooking, medicine, dyeing, and for fragrance. With the growing concern about nutrition, cultivating herbs and cooking with them are enjoying new popularity.

A Quick Herbal History

According to Connie Moore, coauthor of *Natural Insect Repellents for Pets, Plants, and People* (Herb Bar, 1991, Austin, Texas), Chinese Emperor Shen Nung wrote the first herbal—a book describing herbs and their medicinal uses—in about 3000 B.C. The Greek physician Hippocrates, writing in the 5th century B.C., mentioned 400 or so herbal medicines. And in the 1st century A.D., another Greek physician, Dioscorides, named and described the healing properties of about 600 herbs.

Most herbs are native to the Mediterranean region. With the northern expansion of the Roman Empire into Britain in the 1st century A.D., Roman settlers introduced herbs tolerant of the cooler climate, including dill, mint, rosemary, parsley, and garlic. These herbs, and others, found their way to North America when Europeans colonized the continent in the 1600s and 1700s. Conversely, the colonists added to the herbal inventory when they sent to their homelands plants native to North America.

Over the centuries, folklore has evolved concerning the uses and power of herbs. The ancient Greeks, for example, believed rosemary strengthened the memory. Romans wore parsley wreaths to absorb wine fumes and, they thought, to prevent intoxication. In the Middle Ages, the superstitious believed dill provided protection against witchcraft, and that evil spirits could be kept out of the house if fennel was stuffed into the keyholes.

Today these beliefs seem silly. Yet not all herbal remedies have turned out to be nonsense. Digitalis, which is derived from foxglove, is used to treat heart ailments. Thymol, an essential oil in thyme, is an antiseptic. Ginger helps control motion sickness. And, as even Peter Rabbit knows, there's nothing like a soothing cup of chamomile tea when you've had a bad day.

Using Culinary Herbs

Little is known about the nutritional value of most herbs used in cooking. "There haven't been a lot of studies done," explains author Connie Moore. "The nutritional value of herbs just hasn't been documented." She adds that, since culinary herbs are used in such small quantities, any vitamin and mineral nutrients they have don't have much of an impact on a dish.

However, the main nutritional value of culinary herbs is not what they add to the diet, but what they let you take away—salt and fat. "Both salt and fat bring out the flavor in foods," explains Jeannine Pfau, a registered

Chive pasta with lobster derives its nutritional value not from the herbs it includes but from the spice the dish leaves out: salt. Using herbs, health-conscious cooks can draw out the flavor of food without resorting to salt or fat.

dietitian with Good Samaritan Hospital in Downers Grove, Illinois. "By making food tastier, herbs make it easier for people to stick with low-salt or low-fat eating plans, whether their doctor puts them on the diet or they just want to eat more healthfully." Pfau stresses that people should adopt good eating habits early in life, since that's when health problems, such as blocked arteries, begin developing.

Cooking with Herbs

Herbs have 101 uses in cooking. You should always remember, however, that dried herbs have concentrated essential oils. If a recipe calls for fresh herbs, cut the recommended amount by two-thirds if using dried herbs (i.e., $1^1/_2$ cups fresh versus $^1/_2$ cup dried). In either case, herbs should be added at the end of cooking so the heat doesn't destroy their flavor. Here are a sample of some easy herb delights.

Herb Mixes: Blending herbs can create a flavor that's more than the sum of its parts. *Bouquet garni* has many variations. One is to put a bundle of parsley stalks, two sprigs each of marjoram and thyme, and one bay leaf in a cloth pouch. Add the pouch to a stew or broth while cooking, and remove before serving.

Fines herbes combines $^1/_2$ cup chopped parsley and $^1/_2$ cup chervil, $^1/_4$ cup chives, and a few chopped tarragon leaves. Use in egg dishes and with white fish.

Mixing herb vinegars (below) with olive oil creates a delicious, low-fat salad dressing.

Herb Vinegars: Use thyme, tarragon, basil, savory, mint, chervil, dill, or fennel to flavor wine or cider vinegar. Crush $^1/_2$ cup of fresh, flawless herb leaves in a glass bowl, then add 1 pint of vinegar. Cover and set aside for three to five days. Strain to remove the leaves, then heat the vinegar until it starts boiling. Pour the boiling vinegar into hot, sterilized bottles. Add a flawless sprig of the herb, then close with an airtight, nonmetallic seal. Store in a cool, dark, dry place.

Herb Butters: Let $^1/_2$ cup of butter soften, then mix in 2 tablespoons dry or 6 tablespoons chopped fresh herbs. Refrigerate and use, on bread and vegetables, within a few days.

Growing Herbs

An herb garden doesn't demand much space, since a few plants of each herb usually produce as much as you need. The ideal spot for an herb garden is just outside the kitchen, so you don't have to trot across the yard to pick the basil sprig for your tomato sauce. If your yard is little more than a sunny patio or balcony, you can grow herbs in containers—they'll just need more water than their ground-grown counterparts.

Most herbs like a well-drained soil that's not too fertile; an overly fertile soil will produce lush plants with little flavor. Almost all herbs, except the mints, need at least six hours of full sunlight per day.

Most herbs can be grown in the garden directly from seed. To grow herbs outdoors from seed, plant in the spring, after the danger of frost has passed (ask your county extension agent for the date in your area). Follow the instructions on the seed packet for how far apart and how deep to plant the seeds. The packet also tells how far apart to thin the seedlings, which will be too crowded once they emerge from the soil.

To keep the soil moist while waiting for the seedlings to emerge, you might want to

Outdoor herb gardening has become a popular pastime. Except for the mints, most herbs need a sunny spot in order to thrive.

cover the row with a board or newspaper to slow evaporation from the soil. Once the seedlings appear, remove any covering, and water the small plants every day or two to keep them from withering.

For a head start on the season, you can start herbs indoors about six weeks before the frost-free date. Sow them in a shallow seed tray, using a store-bought soilless potting mix instead of soil. To speed up seed germination and early growth, you can set the seed tray on a warm (not hot!) surface, such as a gas stove with a pilot light. Or buy commercially available heating cables from a garden center. Keep the soilless mix moist.

After the seedlings emerge, they will need plenty of light, from either the Sun or fluorescent lights. If the young plants are pale and spindly, they're getting too little light. Your herbs are ready to transplant outdoors when they're sturdy and have several leaves.

If you don't want to start plants from seed, you can buy transplants at a garden center and treat them as you would transplants you'd grown yourself. You'll pay more per plant, of course, since convenience has its price.

As the plants grow, they'll become more tolerant of dry spells. Mature plants need about an inch of water each week, depending upon such factors as your soil type, the relative humidity, and how windy it is. If the plants droop, water them. As with any garden, you'll need to water less if you spread a three-inch layer of mulch, such as grass clippings or bark chips, on the soil surface.

Herbs are fairly free of pests, so don't even consider using pesticides. And since they thrive in poor soil, you don't need to fertilize them, either. About the only thing you should do, other than watering, is pluck off the flowers as they begin to form. Removing the flowers will keep your plants producing flavorful leaves longer. If you're growing the plant for its seed, you'll need to leave the flower so the seeds can develop.

Many herbs—such as basil, chervil, coriander, dill, parsley, rosemary, sweet marjoram, and summer savory—are easy to grow indoors. Use a flowerpot with a drainage hole in the bottom and obtain some good-quality potting soil. To keep the soil from running out with the draining water, cover the hole with a thin layer of gravel, a few small rocks, or pieces of a broken clay pot.

Indoor herbs need plenty of light, so set them in a south-facing window if possible. Pinch off stem tips to encourage bushy, compact growth. Water the plants only after the soil has dried to a depth of about 1 inch below the surface. Keep in mind that more plants die from overwatering than underwatering.

For fresh herbs year-round, an indoor garden might be the best bet. A sunny, south-facing window makes an ideal location.

A Cook's Dozen

You can choose from hundreds of culinary herbs to jazz up your meals. This chart covers a dozen of the most common. It gives their mature height and their life cycle — whether they're annuals that must be replanted each year, or perennials that come back year after year. The table also includes special pointers about growing the herbs, and lists some of their more common uses. Most grow easily from seed; the exceptions are noted.

Basil
Annual, 2 feet
Keep seeds moist after planting. Pinch tops off plants for bushy, compact growth. Does well indoors. Purple-leaved varieties available. Use in pesto, Italian dishes.

Parsley
Biennial, grown as an annual, 6-10 inches
Soak seed overnight before planting. Takes a long time to germinate, so plant early. Doesn't transplant well. Likes moist soil. Curly and flat-leafed types available.

Chives
Perennial, 6-10 inches
Grow from bulbs divided from existing plants. Tolerates light shade. Does well indoors. Use oniony leaves in dips, salads, soups, egg dishes.

Rosemary
Tender perennial, 3-6 feet
Freezes in cold climates if not brought indoors. Buy transplants. Upright and spreading types available. Pungent, piney flavor goes well with meat.

Dill
Annual, 3 feet
Doesn't transplant well, so plant it where you want it. Reseeds itself. Tolerates light shade. Leaves ready in two months, seeds in three. Use in dips, fish, vinegars, pickling.

Sage
Perennial, 2-3 feet
Likes dry soil. Need only one or two plants. Gold and purple varieties available. Does well indoors. Use to flavor meat, poultry, and cheese.

Marjoram
Perennial, 8-12 inches
Needs winter protection in northern climates. Tolerates light shade; doesn't like wet areas. Freezes well. Does well indoors. Use with red meats.

Savory
12-18 inches
Summer savory annual, winter savory perennial. Propagated from seeds or root division. Peppery flavor. Use in fish, poultry, or egg dishes.

Mints
Perennial, 2-3 feet
Many types, including spearmint, peppermint. Start from root division. Spreads aggressively, so plant in a bottomless pot set in the soil. Needs moist soil. Use in teas, Middle Eastern cooking, jellies.

Tarragon
Tender perennial, 3 feet
Grow French type, not Russian. Buy transplant. Cut back a few times during season to encourage bushiness. Use in vinegars, with fish, in sauces. Good with tomatoes.

Oregano
Perennial, 2 feet
Prefers dry soil. Best propagated from root division. Does well indoors. Use in Italian cooking, stews, and soups.

Thyme
Perennial, 6-8 inches
Dozens of types, can be used as a ground cover. Tolerates drought, hates weeds. Use as ingredient in bouquet garni, stuffings, stews.

Harvesting and Storing Herbs

For maximum flavor, pick leaves when the flowers are just beginning to open. Flavor is strongest in the midmorning, after the dew has dried.

If you want a few leaves for cooking, just cut or pick off the leaves as you need them. If you plan to dry or freeze leaves for later use, cut the stems off near the ground, then strip off the leaves. Rinse them in cool water and pat dry. If handling several cups of leaves, roll them in a bath towel, unroll, and let them air-dry for an hour or two.

Some herbs—such as dill, mustard, caraway, anise, and sesame—are grown for their seeds. Harvest the seed heads when the seeds are brown, but before the seeds begin dropping off the plant.

If you plan to use the herbs shortly after harvesting, wrap them in damp towels, place them in a plastic bag, and refrigerate. They will keep for a day or two. Beyond that, you'll need to freeze or dry the herbs. To freeze them, place cleaned herbs in a sealable plastic bag, label them, and place them in the freezer. Frozen herbs keep for months.

The entire dill plant can be used for seasoning, although the seeds contain the highest concentration of aromatic dill oil.

Herbs are most flavorful when cut in midmorning. If not used within a few days, the freshly cut herbs should be dried or frozen.

Herbs can also be air-dried or dried in an oven or microwave. With any drying technique, the herbs are ready to be stored when a test sample of leaves crumbles easily. To best preserve their flavor, store the leaves whole, in airtight containers away from light.

One air-drying method involves spreading the leaves thinly on a tray or screen. Place the tray in a warm (not hot), dry, well-ventilated room away from sunlight, stirring every so often to ensure even drying. Another method is to put a dozen or so stalks of a long-stemmed herb upside down in a paper bag. Scrunch the bag's top around the stem ends, and tie with a string. Punch a few holes in the bag for ventilation, and hang the bag in a dry, warm room.

To oven-dry herbs in two to four hours, arrange the leaves one layer thick on a cookie sheet. Place in a 120° F oven with the door propped open for ventilation.

To dry herbs in a microwave oven, place three or four stalks between several sheets of paper toweling. Zap at medium power for two to three minutes. If the leaves aren't dry yet, microwave them for additional 30-second intervals.

You can use the same drying methods for seed heads. To loosen the dried seeds, roll the seed heads between your palms. Store seed in an airtight container away from light.

Americans are confronted daily with "food news"—sometimes important, frequently meaningless. We all must learn to distinguish the food news of genuine concern from the half-baked findings and wild advice.

FOOD NEWS BLUES

by Anthony Schmitz

Not long ago I set a coffee cup on the table and opened the newspaper to a piece of good news. "New Study Finds Coffee Unlikely to Cause Heart Ills," read the headline. One less thing to worry about, I thought, until I remembered a story from a few weeks before. That morning the headline warned, "Study: Heart Risk Rises on 4, More Cups Coffee Daily." My paper—yours, too, most likely—does this all the time. Concerning the latest dietary findings, it flips and flops like a fish thrown to shore.

"Medical research," it declared one Wednesday, "repeatedly has linked the solu-ble fiber in oats with reductions in serum cholesterol." By Thursday of the next week, all that had changed. "Studies Cast Doubt on Benefits From Oat Bran," the headline cried. Once again the paper offered its readers a familiar choice. Which story to believe? This week's, last week's, or none at all?

The paper in question is the *St. Paul Pioneer Press*. It's a respectable provincial daily, not unlike the papers in Houston, Detroit, and dozens of other cities. One day recently the news editor, Mike Peluso, said he'd take a crack at explaining his paper's flip-flops.

Peluso is compact, graying, more grave than jocular. He meets me at the newsroom door. "You want a cup of coffee?" he asks, pointing at a vending machine. No, I say, trying to recall whether this week, coffee is supposed to be good or bad. Peluso shrugs and heads for his cluttered cubicle. Beyond its flimsy walls, reporters jabber into phones.

I arrange the coffee and oat-bran clippings on a paper-strewn table. Peluso examines them one by one. He grimaces. He sighs. He swallows black coffee from a paper cup.

"How do you reconcile the conflicting claims?" he asks himself. "One month, coffee can't hurt you; the next month, quit coffee, and your heart will tick forever."

Exactly.

Peluso shakes his head. "I don't know. I don't have any answers for that. You've got to talk about the real world here."

For Peluso the real world looks something like this: news of a hot nutrition study gets beamed into the newsroom from wire services such as the Associated Press (AP), *The New York Times,* or the *Baltimore Sun.* Peluso and his staff poke at the story, trying to find flaws that argue against putting it in the paper. By and large, it's a hamstrung effort. Never mind that the reporter who wrote the piece is thousands of miles away. She'd defend the story anyway. The paper's own health reporter is scant help; he's been on the beat two months.

Meanwhile, Peluso knows that his competitors—another daily paper, plus radio and television news—won't spend a week analyzing the study. They'll run it today. Which is to say, Peluso will, too. But the story the reader sees won't be as detailed as the piece that came over the wire. Compared to *The New York Times,* the *Washington Post,* or the *Los Angeles Times,* the *Pioneer Press* is something of a dwarf. Stories get trimmed to fit. Subtleties and equivocations—the messy business of research—don't always make the cut.

"Look," says Peluso, "we're not medical authorities. We're just your normal skeptics. And it's not like we're inventing this research. We're simply reporting on it. We present what's there, and let people draw their own conclusions."

"So what should readers make of all the contradictory advice you offer them?"

SHOULD ICE CREAM CARTONS CARRY WARNING LABELS?
And Other Questions from a Gallup Poll

No matter what you read in the news on food these days, it always comes down to one word. One boring, irritating word. If you want to eat right and stay healthy, just remember: *moderation* is the key word. It is certainly easy to preach, but in practice we all seem more at home with that other pesky word: *excess.*

There's a reason: most of us still take our mealtime eating cues from our taste buds. And we've formed very strong opinions about the kinds of nutrition advice we will and will not accept. The following new national Gallup poll reveals the wide range of Americans' understandings and misunderstandings about sitting down to eat in this great age of moderation.

Americans don't know what really causes cancer.
"Which one of the following factors do you think the National Cancer Institute says causes the largest number of cancer deaths?"

SMOKING	72%
DIET	8%
GENETICS	6%
POLLUTION	5%
ALCOHOL	2%
PESTICIDES	2%
SEXUAL BEHAVIOR	1%
DON'T KNOW	4%

Diet is linked to at least a third of all cancer deaths, says the National Cancer Institute. But a mere 8 percent have learned that our

Peluso sighs again. "I don't know," he says. "You've got to take everything with a grain of salt until the last word comes in. I hate to tell people I don't believe everything I read, but the fact is, anybody who believes everything they read is nuts."

Researchers whose work makes news soon learn that the match between science and journalism wasn't made in heaven. Richard Greenberg, a microbiologist who directs the office of scientific and public affairs at the Institute of Food Technologists, has watched what happens when the scientific method collides with journalistic technique.

"The first thing you've got to remember," says Greenberg, "is that science is not fact. It is not truth. It is not Holy Scripture. It's a compendium of information. You try to put all the research together and come to a consensus. Just because somebody runs a study that comes to a particular conclusion doesn't change everything that's gone before."

Scientists don't generally reach consensus in time for the next deadline. After 30 years

How do you separate the sense from the nonsense?

of study, coffee's link to heart disease remains an open question. Four-plus cups a day may slightly increase the risk, though some research suggests only decaf is linked to heart problems. Similarly, a decade's worth of oat-bran experiments have served only to get a good argument going. Some studies suggest oat bran isn't any better at lowering cholesterol than white bread. If you eat enough of either, the message goes, you won't have room for fatty food. Others say oat bran has innate—though so far inexplicable—cholesterol-lowering properties.

While on their way to answering the big questions about fat or cholesterol or fiber, researchers often pause and dicker merrily about the design flaws in one study or the dicey statistical analysis in another. "Among ourselves," says one epidemiologist, "we're more interested in the detail of how things are done than in saying right now whether oat bran's good for you."

For journalists, it's exactly the opposite. The arcana of statistical analysis and re-

---

taste for fat and our distaste for fruits and vegetables are putting us at risk.

Too many of us still haven't heard the most important health message of our time.
"The surgeon general has singled out the chief health problem in the diet of Americans. It contains too much . . ."

FAT	39%
CHOLESTEROL	32%
PESTICIDES	11%
SALT	9%
SUGAR	5%
FIBER	0%
DON'T KNOW	4%

A modest 39 percent know that the most dangerous thing in our food is fat, linked to both heart disease and cancer. Six out of 10 Americans remain in the dark.

We pick the most difficult and risky ways to cut fat from our diets, ways that are sure to result in failure.
"Health experts often give the advice, 'Cut your fat intake to 30 percent of calories.' What's the best way for you to do that?"

TRY TO BE SURE EVERY MEAL YOU EAT IS LOW FAT	36%
TRY TO BE SURE EVERY ITEM YOU EAT IS LOW FAT	21%
AVOID RED MEAT AND DAIRY PRODUCTS	20%
EAT SOME LOW-FAT MEALS SO THAT YOU'LL BE BELOW THE FAT LIMIT BY THE END OF EACH DAY	15%
EAT SOME LOW-FAT MEALS SO THAT YOU'LL BE BELOW THE FAT LIMIT BY THE END OF EACH WEEK	5%
DON'T KNOW	3%

We're all going to splurge sometimes, health experts say, so there's no point in trying to make every item or meal low in fat. A full 95 search design are boring at best, baffling at worst. The big question is whether oat bran will keep your heart ticking.

"The reporter and headline writer are trying to distill the meaning of the latest piece of research," says Greenberg. "They're trying to grab the eye of the reader. They're searching for absolutes where there are no absolutes. And this is what happens: one day you read caffeine is bad. Then you read that if you take caffeine out, coffee is O.K. Then you hear the solvent that takes out the caffeine is dangerous. Then you find out the caffeine isn't dangerous after all. It so confuses the public, they don't know who to believe. And the truth is, there wasn't really any news in any of these studies. Each of them was just another micromillimeter step toward scientific consensus."

For Greenberg, news exists in those rare moments when scientists weigh the evidence and agree to agree—when the American Heart Association (AHA), the National Cancer Institute (NCI), or the National Academy

Reporters search for absolutes where there are no absolutes.

of Sciences (NAS) pronounces that you ought to eat less fat, or more vegetables.

But by the terms of journalism, scientific consensus is a dead-letter file. If everybody agrees, there's no conflict. If there's no conflict, there's no news. In comparison, debates such as those about coffee or oat bran are a newsroom gold mine. Contradictions and conflict abound. Better still, almost everyone has oatmeal or coffee in the cupboard.

"You can't convince an editor not to run this stuff," says Howard Lewis, editor of the newsletter *Science Writers*. "My advice is that they do it for the same reason they run the comic strips and the astrology columns. But I feel it's all a hoax. Usually they're not accomplishing anything except sowing panic or crying wolf."

A Purdue communications professor raised a stir a few years back, when he suggested that research news might be more harmful than helpful. Writing in the journal *Science, Technology, and Human Values,*

---

percent of Americans haven't heard, or choose to ignore, the experts' more palatable advice: just try to reach a reasonable fat balance by the end of each week.

We don't know the best way to lower our cholesterol.

"If you learned that you have a high blood cholesterol level that put you at heightened risk of heart disease, which would you say was the single most important dietary change you should make?"

LOWER IN CHOLESTEROL 34%
LOWER IN FAT 23%
LOWER IN SATURATED FAT 21%
HIGHER IN FIBER 20%
DON'T KNOW 2%

Less than a quarter of Americans have grasped the message from health experts that saturated fat—prevalent in meat and

dairy products—is most likely to raise cholesterol and prompt heart disease. The cholesterol in food *can* raise blood cholesterol. But in most people, for reasons researchers don't wholly understand, saturated fat has a stronger effect.

We know what foods can help prevent cancer.

"Which one of the following groups of fruits and vegetables would be best to add to your diet to cut your risk of cancer?"

BRUSSELS SPROUTS, CAULIFLOWER, AND
BROCCOLI 47%
APPLES, PLUMS, AND PEARS 22%
ONIONS AND GARLIC 11%
PRUNES, DATES, AND FIGS 9%
ALFALFA SPROUTS AND SOYBEANS 4%
NONE OF THE ABOVE 1%
DON'T KNOW 6%

Leon Trachtman observed that some 90 percent of the new drugs touted in newspaper reports never reached the market or were driven from it because they were ineffective, too toxic, or both. Readers relying on this information would have made wrong choices 9 times out of 10.

So who's served, Trachtman asked, by publicizing these drugs before there's a scientific consensus on them? "When there's no consensus, why broadcast contradictory reports?" Ultimately, he said, readers are paralyzed by the pros and cons. He asked whether the result will be contempt for research, followed by demands to stop wasting money on it.

Not surprisingly, Leon Trachtman got blasted for implying that a scholastic elite ought to be making decisions for us. Among the critics was David Perlman, science editor for the *San Francisco Chronicle,* who writes regularly about health and nutrition. Often, Perlman says, research leads to public de-

Readers are becoming very contemptuous of much of today's scientific research.

bates. Will avoiding fatty foods really lengthen your life? Should government experts try convincing people to change their eating habits? It's debatable. But citizens can hardly take part if they're capable of nothing more than numbly accepting expert advice. "To abdicate an interest in science," says Perlman, citing mathematician Jacob Bronowski, "is to walk with open eyes toward slavery." Perlman trusts people's ability to sort through well-written news.

"It's not just the masses who are confused," says Trachtman. "It's the same for well-trained scientists once they're out of their field. I think people ought to establish a sensible, moderate course of action and then not be deflected from it every morning by what they read in the paper."

But let's face facts: do you have the resolve to ignore a headline that declares, "Sugar, Alzheimer's Linked?" If you can't help but play the game, you can at least try

We may turn a deaf ear to any warnings about risky foods, but we listen most eagerly to good news. For years now, word has been spreading from the nation's research laboratories that cruciferous vegetables—broccoli, cabbage, and their kin—contain potent chemicals that seem to fight many kinds of cancer.

We want the government to save lives by discouraging smoking.
"As you may know, smoking causes lung cancer. As a result, the U.S. government currently bans cigarette advertising on television. Do you think the government should continue to ban ads for cigarettes on television or should they lift the ban?"

CONTINUE THE BAN 77%
LIFT THE BAN 20%
DON'T KNOW 3%

But we don't want it to defend us from fatty foods.
"As you may know, eating foods high in saturated fat, such as ice cream, causes heart disease and cancer. Do you think the government should start banning ads for ice cream on television?"

A BAN IS NOT NECESSARY 88%
START BANNING 10%
DON'T KNOW 2%

There *is* a clear parallel: smokers and lovers of foods rich in saturated fat both run an added risk of heart disease and cancer. But Americans' attitudes plainly clash when it comes to the government's role in curtailing those risks. Three out of four condone efforts to protect us from the potential harm of ads that promote smoking. Almost 9 of 10 would oppose such shielding were it applied to fatty foods.

to defend yourself from non-sense by following these rules:

Count the Legs. First ask if the group studied bears any relation to you. Don't let research done only on four-legged subjects worry you. Pregnant rats, for instance, are more likely to bear offspring with missing toes after getting extremely high jolts of caffeine. What does this mean for humans? Probably nothing. There's no evidence that drinking moderate amounts of caffeine causes human birth defects.

If research subjects have two legs, read closely to see if they're anything like you. Early research that helped launch the oat-bran fad involved only men, most of whom were middle-aged. All had dangerously high blood cholesterol, which reportedly fell after they ate a daily cup-plus of oat bran—enough for a half-dozen muffins. Fine, unless you're female, have low cholesterol already, or can't stand the thought

Studies done on pregnant rats do not necessarily apply to humans.

of eating half a dozen bran muffins every day.

Check for Perspective. Even if you're a match for the group being studied, don't assume the results are significant. "Check if the journalist gets the perspective of other people in the field," says Harvard epidemiologist Walter Willett. "People who've watched the overall flow of information are in a good position to say, 'Well, this really nails it down,' or, 'That's interesting, but it needs confirmation.'"

Ask How Many Guinea Pigs. Quaker Oats research manager Steven Ink, who's written a guide to nutrition studies, says the best research uses at least 50 subjects. By this standard, we should look askance at the recent study showing that eating 17 tiny meals a day lowers cholesterol: only seven people took part. But rules of thumb don't always work. A small number *can* be meaningful if the effect observed is large and consistent.

We'd cut back on salt to help other people's health.
"Suppose you had the option of voting to lower the salt in all food. Would you vote for it or against it if you knew it would not improve your own health but would improve the health of other people?"

VOTE FOR IT 83%
VOTE AGAINST IT 14%
DON'T KNOW 3%
Only about 5 or 10 percent of the 60 million Americans with high blood pressure would benefit directly from avoiding salt. Still, if citizens call for low-salt foods, manufacturers and restaurants will start cooking with less salt, and everyone will end up eating less of it. The outcome: many people who are unaware they have high blood pressure will benefit. It's a roundabout but economical way to treat a nationwide health problem.

We want more information so *we* can decide what's safe.
"Which of the following do you think health agencies should do?"

REQUIRE THAT ALL FOODS SHOW THE
EXACT FAT CONTENT SOMEWHERE
ON THE LABEL 69%
REQUIRE THAT FATTY FOODS, LIKE
ICE CREAM, ANNOUNCE THE EXACT
FAT CONTENT IN LARGE, BRIGHT LETTERS
ON THE LABEL 15%
PERMIT ALL FOOD LABELS TO MENTION
OR NOT MENTION FAT AS THE
MANUFACTURER SEES FIT 8%
REQUIRE THAT FATTY FOODS, LIKE
ICE CREAM, CARRY A MESSAGE FROM
THE SURGEON GENERAL DECLARING THEM
HAZARDOUS TO YOUR HEALTH 5%
DON'T KNOW 3%
Our call for improved labeling information seems finally to have reached Washington policymakers. The new federal rules to

You don't need to feed 50 people cyanide to figure out that it's going to be bad for everyone.

What's more, Ink advises, subjects shouldn't be fed quantities of food that no one in his right mind would eat. One example is the recent study showing that trans-fatty acids such as those in margarine may be bad for your heart. Subjects ate three times more trans-fatty acids than the average American.

Finally, any group tested should be compared to a similar group. Early studies that linked coffee to heart disease were skewed because coffee drinkers differed greatly from the control group: the coffee drinkers were more likely to smoke and to eat a high-fat, high-cholesterol diet. Both habits carry bigger heart risks than does drinking coffee.

Wait for Confirmation. "Don't let one study change your life," says Jane Brody, *The New York Times'* health writer. She generally

One editor's advice: "One study does not a finding make."

waits for three types of food-research studies to have agreeing conclusions before she will consider changing her eating habits.

First she looks for studies of large groups that show a link between a food and good or bad health—Italy's big appetite for olive oil, and that country's low rate of heart disease, for instance. Then she watches for laboratory evidence in test animals that suggests how the food causes its effect in people. Finally she considers human experiments in which two groups are compared—one eating the food, and the other not eating it, with neither group knowing which is which.

Applying this rule to her own meals, Brody skimps on the saturated fats contained in butter and favors olive oil. She eats plenty of fruits and vegetables, lots of potatoes, rice, beans, and pasta, and modest amounts of lean meat. "This plan won't make you sick, has a good chance of keeping you well, and is immune to these fads that are here today and gone tomorrow," Brody says.

take effect by the end of 1992 require food makers to present detailed nutrient data on packaging—including fat, saturated fat, cholesterol, sodium, sugar, complex carbohydrates, and fiber.

We wait for a second opinion when food news seems too good to be true.

"If a major producer of peanut oil paid for research that found peanut oil greatly lowered your risk of heart disease, which one of the following statements best describes how you would react? Would you . . ."

WAIT UNTIL FURTHER RESEARCH
BACKED UP THE STUDY BEFORE
USING PEANUT OIL MORE OFTEN 36%

WAIT UNTIL THE SURGEON GENERAL
OR SOME NATIONAL HEALTH AGENCY
ADVISED ALL AMERICANS TO USE MORE
PEANUT OIL BEFORE USING IT MORE OFTEN . 35%

START USING PEANUT OIL MORE OFTEN 15%

IGNORE THE STUDY BECAUSE THE RESEARCH
WAS PAID FOR BY A PEANUT OIL COMPANY . . . 8%
DON'T KNOW 6%

In this hypothetical example, only 8 percent of Americans would assume the very worst: that the peanut-oil company would use its influential dollars to make sure the scientific researchers ended up with good health news about its product. Remarkably, more than 70 percent of Americans reveal a mild but healthy skepticism of such a study. They'd prudently wait for confirmation from other, perhaps more objective studies before using peanut oil more often.

In fact, peanut oil (like most other vegetable oils) appears to cause neither good nor bad effects when it comes to heart disease. If it's eaten moderately (mentioned earlier as the key word for all nutrition news) *instead* of butter or other saturated animal fats, peanut oil can help lower heart-disease risk.

Hunt for Holes. No matter how carefully you read, you'll have to rely on the information your newspaper chooses to supply. If the big mattress ad on an inside page gets dropped at the last minute, the editors may suddenly have room for an exhaustive treatment of the latest coffee study. But if a candidate for national office gets caught with his pants down, the space required for a thorough exposé may mean the coffee piece gets gutted.

When editors at the *St. Paul Pioneer Press* got hold of a wire-service report debunking oat bran, they found room for the first two-thirds of the report. The third that didn't fit held a stern critique by other experts. They charged that the study contained too few people (20 female dietitians), didn't adequately control the rest of what they ate, and started with subjects who had unusually low cholesterol to begin with.

"The reader really has to be skeptical," says Frank Sacks, the Harvard researcher whose oat-bran study was under attack. "Take my case, for instance. The reporter really ought to say that this is a new finding, that it needs to be replicated. This is a warning sign that you have to wait awhile. Reporters hate that when you say it. They call it waffling. But the truth is, your hot new finding might not be confirmed down the line. You hate it when that happens, but it happens time and again.

"The real conservative advice is not to take any of this stuff in the newspaper with a whole lot of credence," says Sacks. "You could just wait for the conservative health organizations like the American Heart Association to make their recommendations, and then follow their advice."

"We don't have an opinion," says John Weeks, somewhat plaintively. I'm calling the American Heart Association to get its line on oat bran and coffee.

"We get calls every day from the media," says Weeks. "They want to know what we think about every new study that comes out. And we don't have an opinion. We don't try to assimilate every new study. Our dietary guidelines would be bouncing all over the place if we did. Once the evidence is there, we move on it. Until then, we don't."

Food studies using animals may not directly apply to humans. A reader should ask if the test animals ate an amount that would be reasonably eaten by that animal, or by a human for that matter.

The American Heart Association is sticking with the same dietary advice it has dispensed since 1988, when it last revised its model diet recommendations. It suggests that Americans should eat less fat and eat more grains, vegetables, and fruits. The evidence that oat bran lowers cholesterol is so limited that the heart association makes no specific recommendation about it. Concerning coffee, the group has absolutely nothing to say.

Weeks's advice for whipsawed newspaper readers has a familiar ring. "What people need to keep in mind," he says, "is that one study does not a finding make."

"You mean," I ask, quoting Mike Peluso's newsroom wisdom, "I'm nuts to believe everything I read?"

Says Weeks: "That's exactly correct."

Housecalls

Mona Sutnick, R.D., Ed.D., is a lecturer in nutrition in the department of community and preventive medicine at the Medical College of Pennsylvania in Philadelphia.

Q *Are the liquid-diet programs of today safer than they used to be? How long will I be able to keep off the weight that I've lost on such programs?*

A Yes, they are safer, partly because the liquid supplements now have a better protein and mineral balance. However, these programs are appropriate only for people at least 30 to 40 percent overweight, or whose obesity is causing or complicating medical problems.

Liquid-diet programs are expensive. Because many are considered a "very-low-cal diet," they *must be administered under medical supervision.* Owing to pressure from consumer groups and the Food and Drug Administration (FDA), the companies that sell liquid weight-loss diets have now agreed to scale down their advertising to the general public.

Most people fail to keep off the weight they lose on these programs, Oprah Winfrey's case being the most publicized example of this. Those who must lose a lot of weight usually need to revamp their lifestyle with regard to exercising and eating. Liquid diets have not been shown to prompt such change in habits to date, although some programs have begun to integrate behavior modification.

Like most liquid dieters, Oprah Winfrey gained back what she had lost during her much-publicized weight-reduction program.

Q *Will taking a vitamin pill provide the same benefit as eating food that has a lot of that vitamin in it?*

A No. The actual vitamin itself, as a molecule, is the same regardless of the source; however, when you get vitamins from the food you're eating, a lot of other good things come your way as well, like fiber and trace minerals. Some of these substances help the body take advantage of vitamins, and there are probably many interactions in a balanced diet that we just don't know about yet.

One-a-day multivitamins are not the real problem in vitamin use. The actual culprit is single-vitamin supplements from which a person can ingest an excess of a particular vitamin. Toxicities, for example, are known to arise from high levels of vitamins D, A, and B_6, and new findings are suggesting risks from long-term iron supplements.

Vitamin supplements can be appropriate for certain groups, such as for pregnant women and some older people. However, humans have evolved so as to efficiently derive nutrients from food sources. Vitamin supplements are pricey, are of questionable benefit, and can simply be an excuse for not eating well.

Q *Is there any evidence that sugar and fat substitutes help you lose weight?*

A There is no such evidence, and here's an illustration why: many of us go to a party and eat some of the vegetables available and then use the vegetable consumption as a justification for eating potato chips. The same thing happens with sugar and fat substitutes. Studies have shown that they reduce calorie intake only if substituted into a person's diet without the person knowing it. Unfortunately, people controlling their own diet compensate for substitutes. The classic example is the person who uses artificial sweetener in coffee and then sees this as a justification for eating a doughnut.

Sugar substitutes have been around for a while, and obesity has continued to increase demographically. Fake fats are newer, and many are still under development. Again, though, the concern is that people will compensate by simply eating more of the ice cream and frozen desserts that incorporate these "foods."

In general, substituting "lite" products in your diet is a good thing, and fat substitutes may have some impact if they become an ingredient in a much wider range of snack foods. However, all this ducks the real goal of good eating, which takes advantage of fruits and other healthful, natural foods as snacks.

Q *I understand that reducing red meat in your diet is a way to cut down on fat and cholesterol. Are dairy products a good source of supplementary protein in your diet when cutting down on meat?*

A The answer is: it depends. Most people making this substitution will reach first for cheese. Unfortunately, most cheeses actually have a *higher* ratio of saturated to unsaturated fats than meats do, and so are actually *worse* in terms of fat intake.

Dairy products are a source of protein, and the key here, if you are going to have dairy products in your diet, is to get versions of these products made from low-fat or skim milk. (See the article "Dairy and Your Diet" on page 74 for more information.) Other sources of protein are legumes (beans) and whole-grain products.

You can almost certainly benefit from reducing the amount of red meat you eat. Most Americans have more than enough protein in their diet, and so can reduce it without a problem. High meat intake may do double dubious duty: the risks of high-fat diets are well established, and research suggests that high-protein diets may have unhealthy ramifications in the long run.

Q *I've been interested in buying more organic produce, but can't seem to find it in supermarkets. Why is organic produce so difficult to find?*

A There are a number of reasons. For one thing, organic produce is more perishable than conventionally grown produce; thus, supermarkets find it hard to handle, because speed of delivery and sale is important. Much organic produce is still grown by small or specialty farmers, and supply usually falls short of demand. As a result, organic produce is expensive. Some people are not willing to pay the extra amount, especially for produce that may not look as perfect as what we're used to seeing in grocery stores.

National and many state standards for certifying produce as organic are still under development. In addition, it will take time for more farmers to convert to organic-farming methods and for demand to reach levels where supermarkets respond—*if this is going to happen at all.*

People will also have to start to change their sense of aesthetics enough to recognize that an apple with a blemish on it is just as nutritious as one without.

Q *How does a person know if she or he is at the right weight?*

A There are many different ways of judging the "right weight." The most commonly accepted are weight ranges based on a person's height and sex, such as those published by the United States Department of Agriculture and United States Department of Health and Human Services (see the table). This body-mass index is a suggested normal, healthy range for adults. Different charts are needed for children, and depend on variable growth rates.

Other frequent indexes of correct weight are lean-to-fat measures, which may be performed by pinching the skin with calipers, and by hydromeasures that involve weighing a person in water. It's not just total body fat, but its distribution, that is important. We now know that fat can have different effects depending on its position in the body; abdominal fat, for example, is of more concern than fat in the hips or buttocks.

HEIGHT without shoes	WEIGHT without clothes	
	AGE 19 TO 34*	35 AND UP*
5'0"	97–128	108–138
5'1"	101–132	111–143
5'2"	104–137	115–148
5'3"	107–141	119–152
5'4"	111–146	122–157
5'5"	114–150	126–162
5'6"	118–155	130–167
5'7"	121–160	134–172
5'8"	125–164	138–178
5'9"	129–169	142–183
5'10"	132–174	146–188
5'11"	136–179	151–194
6'0"	140–184	155–199
6'1"	144–189	159–205
6'2"	148–195	164–210
6'3"	152–200	168–216
BODY MASS INDEX	19–25	21–27
* Women or men		

Our society rewards thinness to an inordinate extent. There are too many people trying to get to a body weight that is unnatural for them. Weighing too little is not good; the medical disadvantages of spending life underweight are becoming increasingly clearer.

Genetics is a critical factor. So, too, are learned eating habits that "push" someone to one end or the other of their normal, "chart" range.

Do you have a nutrition question?
Send it to Editor, Health and Medicine Annual, P.O. Box 90, Hawleyville, CT 06440-9990

Fitness and Health

See also:
Individual articles in the second half of this book, arranged in alphabetical order, for additional information.

One of the central components of a healthy life is regular physical exercise. Some people keep fit with traditional forms of exercise, such as walking, swimming, skiing, and tennis. Others regularly go to gyms for aerobics classes and workouts on high-tech machines. Still others enliven their exercise routines by adding such comparatively esoteric activities as rock climbing and tandem bicycling.

Physical fitness is a worthy goal for everyone, from young children and teenagers to baby boomers and senior citizens. It is a goal for those who want to stay healthy and those with weight problems, diseases, and disabilities. Being fit means feeling better, looking better, living better.

Regardless of the form of exercise, a growing body of evidence indicates that people who exercise regularly lower their risk of becoming ill. California epidemiologists reported in 1991 that middle-aged men who exercise regularly have a significantly lower risk of developing adult diabetes, a disease that afflicts some 10 million Americans. The study found that every 500 calories burned during weekly exercising reduced the men's risk by about 6 percent. The researchers suggested that exercise helps prevent diabetes by keeping weight down and improving the body's ability to metabolize sugar.

Other new studies demonstrate the positive effects of exercise on the circulatory system. Scientists at the University of Washington in Seattle found that older men who follow a regimen of vigorous exercise experience an increase in the activity of tissue plasminogen activator (t-PA), an enzyme that dissolves blood clots.

A study by Harvard University researchers found that people can reduce their risk of colon cancer by up to 50 percent by engaging in regular exercise. And research conducted by Robert Dustman at the Veterans Administration Medical Center in Salt Lake City showed that sedentary people age 55 to 70 who exercised vigorously improved their memory, mental flexibility, and other neuropsychological skills.

Unfortunately, in their pursuit of physical fitness, some people resort to dangerous practices. Millions of athletes, both amateur and professional, continue to illegally take steroids to develop increased muscle mass. Efforts to ban athletes who use steroids from competitions, coupled with widespread publicity of the medical dangers of steroid use, has not ended misuse of the drugs. However, some athletes have switched to genetically engineered human growth hormone, which also increases muscle mass but which cannot be detected by screening tests. The problem received renewed attention in 1991 when it was announced that Lyle Alzado, a former defensive lineman for the Los Angeles Raiders, was suffering from inoperable brain cancer, which Alzado attributed to his use of steroids and human growth hormone during his two decades in college and professional football.

A study of 49 men who frequently lifted weights and abused steroids demonstrated that steroids can indeed be addictive and lead to such drug-dependent problems as withdrawal symptoms. The researchers suggested that addiction may only occur in people who use steroids primarily to enhance physical appearance rather than athletic ability. They suggested that those people who abuse steroids for purely cosmetic reasons have a psychological vulnerability to the drugs.

For many, the image of fitness includes a tanned skin. But tanning, whether by sunbathing or using artificial sunlamps, is the primary cause of skin cancer. Citing the annual incidence in the U.S. of over 600,000 new cases of skin cancer, the Skin Cancer Foundation called for dramatic changes in public attitudes about sun exposure and stressed the importance of a wide range of year-round sun-protection practices, starting in infancy. These practices include avoiding unnecessary sun exposure, wearing protective clothing and sunglasses when outdoors, and the liberal use of sunscreens. Commented one expert: "Think of the Sun as a giant nuclear reactor: how much time would [you] want to bask in the glow of a nuclear power plant?"

Melanoma, a potentially fatal form of skin cancer, continues to increase at an alarming rate. According to Darrell S. Rigel, clinical assistant professor of dermatology at New York University School of Medicine, the lifetime risk of an individual in the U.S. developing malignant melanoma reached 1 in 105 in 1991. If the current rate of increase continues, he predicted, the lifetime risk in the year 2000 will be 1 in 75.

Being fit means feeling better, looking better, living better.

BETWEEN A ROCK AND A HARD PLACE

by Linda J. Brown

The smooth rock wall of awesome proportions juts sharply toward the sky. About 50 feet up, a lean, muscular figure is perched on the wall, seemingly defying gravity as he slowly progresses up the rock face. What appears as a mentally (if not physically) unbalanced person is just a rock climber out having some fun.

Long thought to be the domain of mavericks, daredevils, and thrill seekers, rock climbing has recently gone mainstream, gaining popularity nationwide. Michael Kennedy, editor and publisher of *Climbing* magazine, estimates that there are currently 125,000 to 150,000 technical rock climbers in the United States. And this number seems to be increasing at a rate of 15 to 20 percent each year.

Rock climbing belongs to the broad field of mountaineering that encompasses hiking, snow and ice climbing, and wilderness survival. Historically, when humans began climbing mountains for sport in Europe in the mid-1700s, the sole goal was to reach the summit. It wasn't until the 1930s that rock climbing just for the challenge of the climb itself started to have merit. A climber earned respect for tackling a tough cliff or face, regardless of whether it led to the top of the mountain. American rock climbing lagged behind the European sport earlier in this century, but by the 1960s rock climbing in the U.S. had gained respectability as a specialized sport.

As equipment and climbing techniques improved, participants gained the freedom to try new and more challenging feats. As a result, several branches of rock climbing developed. First, a distinction is made between free and direct-aid climbing. In free climbing, hands and feet make progress over the rock, while rope and equipment

Rock climbing can be risky business. Climbing routes are rated for climbers to gauge if their skills will be challenged, or overwhelmed, by a particular rock face.

come into play only as a safety feature in case of a fall. In direct-aid climbing, the equipment is used to progress up a rock or to rest on. Specialized areas of climbing include big-wall climbing and sport climbing, a highly athletic, gymnastic style of ascent. Bouldering —climbing on smaller rocks without a safety rope—is usually used as a warm-up for bigger ascents or as a training exercise. Some enthusiasts feel that indoor rock climbing has almost developed into another branch of rock climbing.

To help climbers gauge if their ability will match a particular rock face, routes are rated for their degree of difficulty. Different rating systems exist around the world. In the American system, technical rock climbing starts at a 5.0 rating. The scale originally went up by decimal points to 5.9, but as climbers continued to push the limits, the ratings rose as well, and the system became open-ended. Once you get past a 5.9, the scale extends to 5.10, 5.11, 5.12, 5.13; 5.14 is currently the highest rating. To further classify climbs, those at a 5.10 or higher are also assigned the letters *a, b, c,* or *d.* The easiest level at any given number is *a,* going up to *d* for the most extreme. Direct-aid climbs are scaled differently, and these climbs are grouped from A1 to A5. In addition, climbs are also graded from I to VI to tell how much time an experienced climber should need to complete a route. Grade I takes one to three hours, while Grade VI means climb of two or more days.

Getting Physical

Climbing offers a good all-around workout that calls on muscles in both the lower and upper body. In correct climbing technique, the aim is to keep your weight over your feet, since supporting body weight with leg

strength comes much more easily to most than doing so with the arms.

On the flip side, the upper-body muscles of the arms, shoulders, and back, and of the fingers and forearms are also essential in rock climbing. "The real link is the fingers," says Dan Cauthorn, co-owner of the Vertical Club, an indoor rock-climbing facility in Seattle. "You're constantly grabbing onto holds with your fingers and fitting them into cracks. Since they are tendons and ligaments, not muscle, they take about twice as long to develop as do big muscles like your biceps."

You can be a tower of strength, but if you're not flexible, you'll probably find the going tough on the more difficult moves. "Flexibility is key," says Steve Young, executive director of the American Mountain Guides Association. "Climbing can be likened to ascending a ladder, except that the rungs are spaced variably, and they aren't always straight up and down. That means you've got to figure out how to move around on the rock. When you first start, you feel like a monkey."

Rock climbing's popularity has triggered international competitions. Contenders climb up specially designed walls to test their skill and agility.

Brute strength may not be as useful to a climber as flexibility and digital strength. Climbers use fingerboards to build fingertip agility.

While there is no perfect body type for rock climbing, most of the top climbers are flexible and thin.

What's more important in rock climbing: endurance or strength? It all depends on what type of climbing you do. On very hard, technical routes, power and strength matter a great deal. On less technical and perhaps longer climbs, endurance may be more crucial. "Overall, I would say, for most people, endurance is probably a little more important than power," says Kennedy. But you can certainly benefit from both.

How can you train, apart from climbing? Activities such as jogging, biking, or swimming will give you a solid aerobic base to start with. Weight training is becoming popular as a way to build strength and prevent injuries. Since rock climbers do not need to pump up and build bulk, lifting lower weights with high repetitions is generally the rule. Some specialized equipment often found in health clubs may also help a climber train. Versa Climber machines mimic the movement of rock climbing and work the whole body. Many people use fingerboards, which have different finger holds that you pull up on to build digital strength.

No matter how much you train and prepare, injury is always a possibility. There were 100 reported injuries in 1989 among rock climbers, according to the American Alpine Club; a very small number of these injuries were fatalities. The most obvious accident, injury from a fall, can result in anything from scrapes to sprained ankles to death. Acute injuries can occur when climbers try moves that are beyond their

Rock Rap

Rock climbers have a lingo all their own to describe their sport. Here's a sampling of climber jargon:

Bombproof: when an anchor or piece of protection cannot come loose.
Chickenhead: a rounded knob of rock.
Chimneys: rock cracks large enough so they can be entered.
Edging: using the sides of your boots to stand on thin rock edges.
Fist Jam: the technique of placing your fist in a fist-sized crack so you can climb up the crack.
Pocket: a shallow hole in the rock.
Protection: anchors used to safeguard a climber.
Rack: a climber's gear sling and all the equipment he or she plans to carry with him or her.
Redpoint: to lead a climb without resting on any aid or falling.
Smear: a climbing technique with the feet in which friction holds your boots to the rock.

The rubber toes and heels of climbing shoes help the climber above edge on a bombproof chickenhead.

physical or technical ability or climb without warming up, resulting in strained or dislocated shoulders or knee injuries from extreme stepping motions. Overuse problems, which can produce tendinitis in the fingers, elbows, or shoulders, can come from climbing too much or too aggressively.

"The best cure for injuries is prevention," says Kevin Brown, director of Orthopedic and Sports Physical Therapy in Portola Valley, California. "People need to listen to their bodies. If you don't listen to the language of your body, you're bound to get hurt." In other words, don't ignore that nagging pain in your shoulder or knee. Know your limitations and your body.

Gearing Up

In rock climbing, having good equipment and knowing how to use it properly is essential—in fact, your life may depend upon it. Today's climbers have come a long way from the early mountaineers who had little more than hemp ropes and clunky boots. "As gear evolves, so does rock-climbing technique," says John Long, author of *How to Rock Climb*. Better gear allows people to try new moves, to ascend tougher walls. The amount of money you spend on equipment—or your "rack," as it's called in rock-climbing lingo—can vary

Great advances have been made in climbing equipment. As a result, climbers are able to try more challenging feats and ascend tougher walls.

widely. Basic climbing gear includes:
• *Ropes* are perhaps the most important piece of gear, and your lifeline. Use them to climb up and rappel down rocks. Since 1945 almost all climbing ropes have been made of nylon, a cut above natural blends in elasticity, strength, and durability. Ropes today are made of kernmantle, a woven nylon sheath over a braided core. The standard climbing rope is 165 feet long.
• *Harnesses* consist of a waist strap and leg loops sewn together. You tie your rope into the harness as part of the safety setup. They've been around for about 20 years, but early models were of questionable quality. These days, harnesses are light, strong, and well-fitting.
• *Carabiners* are metal looplike snaplinks used to connect two pieces of gear. Also called *biners* or *krabs,* they come in different sizes and strengths, and are most often made of aluminum alloy. Until the mid-1970s, biners did not consistently meet the highest manufacturing standards. But as climbing's popularity increased, so did the quality of this vital piece of gear.
• *Chocks,* or *nuts,* are metal wedges of different sizes and shapes used with slings or cable to fit into cracks and crevices in the rock. They form another link in your chain of protection that safeguards against falling. Chocks are a British invention, but have been in widespread use in the U.S. since the 1970s.
• *Spring-loaded camming devices* (SLCDs) came onto the market in the late 1970s under the name Friends. They work similarly to nuts, but can be used in parallel-sized cracks, where they expand to fit perfectly. They operate on the same principle as a wedge under a door. In his book, Long writes: "Friends work so well that when they first came out many past rock masters thought they were a means of cheating."
• *Pitons* are spike-shaped steel devices hammered into cracks to clip to carabiners as protection. Prior to World War II, they

> *Traditionally the domain of mavericks and daredevils, rock climbing is gaining popularity nationwide.*

Rock climbing is popular with people of all ages. But novices are strongly recommended to take lessons (above) from seasoned professionals before striking out on their own.

were made of soft iron and were left in place, since removal could damage them. By the 1960s space-age metal alloy pitons were widely available. They were strong enough to be removed and replaced again and again. That seemed like an advantage, until rocks started scarring from repeated use of pitons, making them environmentally undesirable. As chocks came on the scene, piton use dropped dramatically. They are still used today, but not as often. In his classic book *Basic Rockcraft,* author Royal Robbins writes: "Chocks have the great virtue of being removable points of protection which do not damage the rock."

• *Bolts* provide secure protection, but their use sparks controversy. These thin metal rods can be drilled into rock where no cracks exist for nuts or pitons. One reason for the fuss: bolts create a visual impact because they are permanent anchors. Robbins writes: ". . . bolts are at once a blessing and a curse. They make possible some of the finest rock climbs on Earth by opening up stretches of blank and otherwise unclimbable rock. But they also diminish the value of climbing by making it possible for anyone to go anywhere if they are willing to drill."

On the positive side, bolts have really opened up the whole field of sport climbing. Climbers can spend more energy tackling tough moves because they spend less time working with their equipment.

• *Shoes* these days are far removed from the heavy, clunky boots that early mountaineers wore. The biggest advance may have come in 1982 with the introduction of sticky rubber soles that make it easier to grip rock. The rubber portion on many climbing shoes covers the toes and heels, and runs along the sides of the foot. They are lightweight and flexible to allow feet to feel the rock.

While there are many good all-around climbing boots on the market for the less advanced climber, the evolution of shoes has reached the point that, for the more advanced climber, shoes can be designed to fit certain rock conditions and climbing techniques. For instance, stiffer shoes are better for standing on small edges, while softer soles fit better into narrow cracks.

Mind Over Matter

The best gear in the world means very little if you don't have the proper skills and the right mental attitude. Rock climbing is a thinking person's sport—state of mind is critical. Young, who has been climbing for almost 20 years, believes that rock climbers depend far more on brains than on brawn—perhaps up to 80 or 90 percent.

The mental stimulation and interplay between physical prowess and brainpower may well be what hooks rock climbers. "To exercise normally is pretty boring. In climbing, you get consumed into it to where time just sort of doesn't exist. You could spend hours at it a day," says Mike Donahue, director and owner of the Colorado Mountain School in Estes Park.

The primary mental challenge of rock climbing is to stay relaxed and focused, which is easier said than done when you're 100 feet up on a steep cliff wall. Climbers use many methods to stay calm and move well, from basic breathing exercises to sophisticated mental imagery.

One of the keys to staying relaxed is keeping fear under wraps. "New climbers are

either afraid of falling or afraid of failing, not being able to do the climb," says Patricia McClung, longtime climber and director of safety and programs at Outward Bound, a wilderness-skills educational program. To conquer that fear, you must win the constant battle between the positive and negative in your mind. The negative says, "You're crazy; you can't do this; you might fall." And the positive says, "You can do it; you're protected, and you'll be O.K."

"You can't climb if your negative is in control," Donahue says. However, a little bit of fear is healthy. "True climbers never lose all their fear," says McClung. "They just learn to listen to it, and know when they can work with it, and know when the fear is justified enough that they need to back off."

The obvious mental teaser climbers face is figuring out how to get up the rock. Nothing substitutes for experience, but many people also use methods such as visualization, in which they plan the next few moves in their mind and picture themselves going through them successfully before they actually try anything.

An added bonus is that some find that problem-solving techniques learned in climbing carry over into other areas of their lives.

Planning efficient climbing strategy and conquering fear and fatigue while 100 feet up a steep cliff wall demand enormous mental strength.

Indoor Action

You're raring to climb, but the weather's nasty. What should you do? Head indoors to the nearest indoor climbing wall. More and more indoor walls are springing up nationwide to provide sites for off-season or supplementary training time. Constructed with both permanent and movable panel walls, they can provide a workout for any level, from beginner to expert. Some are built within health clubs; others stand on their own as a climbing facility. Membership may be required, or you may be able to pay a use fee.

Indoor walls are now the overwhelming choice for competitions, and are used almost exclusively for world and national contests. Difficulty of the climb can be varied and controlled on artificial walls; not so with real rock. There also isn't the danger of delicate vegetation being damaged by spectators and other climbers milling around the base of an outdoor route. By and large, the only time people compete on real rock is in bouldering competitions.

Used for training or in indoor climbing competition, this patchwork artificial wall can be easily rearranged to design climbing routes of varying difficulties.

McClung notices that her approach to climbing helps her focus on the immediate tasks at hand every day. "When I look up at a 400-foot cliff and realize I have 400 feet to go, I get totally psyched out. But if I focus on the 2 or 3 feet in front of me, I can do that. That's a skill that often gets me through the rest of my life." Young finds that when faced by mundane problems, he's able to keep negative feelings at bay and evaluate the situation objectively, much as he would do on a climb. These skills are invaluable both in business and in personal relationships.

As John Long wrote in *How to Rock Climb,* "The airy exposed routes, the spectacle of ascent, the physical and mental demands—

they all give a rush to your blood. In a flash, mundane life is forgotten; your world focused to a scant toehold."

So if you enjoy the outdoors, crave adventure, and want to give both your mind and body a workout, rock climbing may be just the sport for you. Your best bet is to seek instruction from a respected guide service or climbing school. Rates range from $160 to $250 a day for private lessons. Group rates, depending on the size of the group, average from $80 to $150 a day. For a list of skilled guides and reputable schools in your area, contact American Mountain Guides Association, P.O. Box 2128, Estes Park, CO 80517; (303) 586–0571.

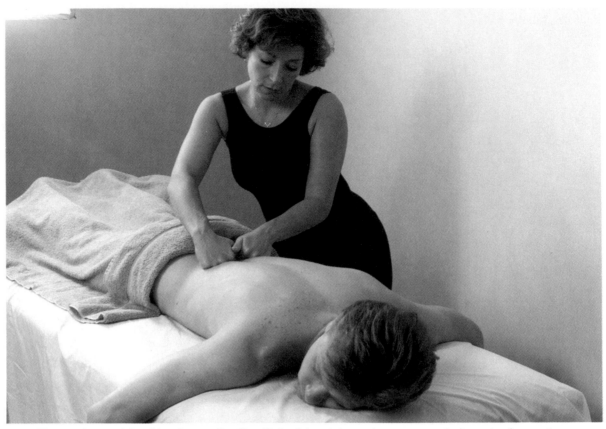

Massage is one of the oldest forms of healing. Today it is gaining mainstream popularity, not only as a stress reducer, but also as a physical therapy to improve mobility of painful or stiff muscles and joints.

Massage: A Hands-On Therapy

by Carole F. Gan

Chuck Galante, a train engineer, hadn't thought much about massage before one fateful day in August disrupted his life. After eight years on the job, the high-speed commuter train he was driving couldn't stop in time to avoid hitting a car that had illegally crossed the tracks. Passengers in the car were killed.

While judged not his fault, the accident left Chuck with physical and emotional injury. "I had muscle spasms that began in my neck and radiated down my arms," he says. "And even though I was not consciously thinking about the accident, I felt constantly on edge and couldn't sleep without having nightmares." He found relief after his doctor referred him

to a massage therapist. "The idea of getting a massage seemed a bit unusual to me at first because I had never gone before, but the sessions really helped relieve the painful spasms and calmed me down. I still go back every now and then when I need to relax."

Like Chuck, many Americans are increasingly calling on massage therapists and other alternative-medicine practitioners to treat ills caused by stress, injury, and disease. Encouraged by patients who have visited massage therapists on their own and have benefited from the therapy, more and more physicians are willing to refer others for this simple treatment. While massage is not a replacement for conventional medical practices, this hands-on approach offers a means of easing a multitude of physical and emotional ills, from arthritis and whiplash to on-the-job stress and emotional trauma.

Many civilizations through the ages valued the use of touch to heal and soothe. The earliest written records mentioning massage date back 3,000 years to the Chinese, who treated constipation with abdominal massages and created wooden rollers to deliver uniform pressure to the body. Julius Caesar was pinched daily to ease the severe stabbing pains of a nervous-system disorder; Pliny, the great Roman naturalist, received massages to relieve chronic asthma.

Considered a "good" word throughout the ages, massage fell by the wayside in the United States after World War I. Back then, red-light districts touted the charms of massage and emphasized the erogenous possibilities. Moreover, people became infatuated with high-tech medicine and no longer regarded massage as an effective healing tool.

"We've learned to look for quick fixes and wonder drugs," says L. Victoria Ross, a professional massage therapist since the early 1970s, and an instructor of advanced techniques at the Pennsylvania School of Muscle Therapy in suburban Philadelphia. "But now that's changing. People are much more interested in taking responsibility for their health, and are more readily accepting massage as a legitimate route to ease muscular ills and achieve wellness."

Membership in professional massage organizations has grown dramatically in recent years, reflecting the explosive interest in the technique. Since 1986 the American Massage Therapy Association (AMTA), the oldest and largest of these groups, has tripled its membership to more than 13,000. Likewise, the number of accredited schools approved by AMTA has grown dramatically, from only 12 in 1983 to 57 in 1991. The association is striving to increase the acceptability of therapeutic massage nationwide; already, 15 states currently license massage therapists. Today's massage therapists can be found in a variety of health-oriented settings, from health clubs and private-practice clinics, to on-site therapy in the workplace and in private homes.

How Massage Works

Massage works directly on the skin and skeletal muscles to produce physical and psychological benefits. Although scientific evidence documenting the underlying cause of these benefits is scanty, massage is thought to help relieve muscle stiffness by removing excessive fluid buildup, and to reduce pain by stimulating sensory receptors.

Each muscle is composed of a group of fibers that runs the entire length of the muscle. Surrounding each fiber is a tough, connective-tissue layer that binds fibers together and attaches them to bone. As muscles contract, metabolic wastes are "milked" from muscle fibers. The wastes pass into the fluid-filled spaces between cells and migrate into capillary beds of the circulatory and lymphatic systems to be carried away. Extreme muscular activity or injury disrupts this natural process, contributing to pain and stiffness. Overexertion loads the muscles with metabolic waste products that cannot be removed fast enough, and inactivity doesn't provide sufficient contractile force to pump them away.

Massage relaxes the body and reduces pain through its effects on the nervous system. Superficial stroking stretches the skin

The stroking techniques used in massage stretch the skin and activate its sensory receptors. These receptors then promote muscle relaxation.

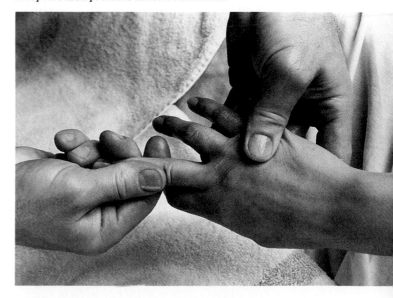

and activates its sensory receptors. Deep massage, which applies more pressure to reach tissues below the skin surface, activates sensory receptors scattered throughout muscles. "These mechanoreceptors, especially the free nerve endings found in muscle, trigger a cascade of physiological responses that promote muscle relaxation," explains William Rymer, M.D., Ph.D., director of research at the Rehabilitation Institute of Chicago. "When these established reflex pathways become activated, they act on the spinal cord and are capable of shutting off muscle contraction, which reduces pain."

Sports-Medicine Link

Massage owes a great deal of its increasing popularity to the practice of sports medicine. This highly visible medical specialty elevated sports training and the treatment of athletic injuries to a science. As medical specialists looked for ways to enhance athletic performance and to alleviate pain from injury, massage found an important niche.

"Athletes use massage before exercise to prepare muscles for more-intense activity, lessening the chance of injury from muscle tears," says Phillip J. Marone, M.D., team physician for the Philadelphia Phillies, and director of Thomas Jefferson University's

Acupressure applies specific pressure to points along "energy pathways" in the body to release blocked energy and rebalance its flow.

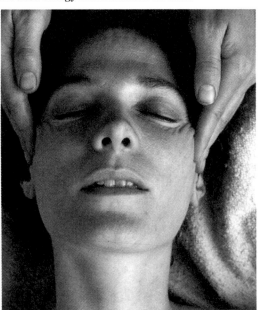

The Mechanics of Massage: what to expect from the many manipulative modalities

For the uninitiated, massage may conjure up images of celluloid prizefighters receiving a series of brisk, alternating blows to the back. While this approach worked in Hollywood, it is rarely a part of routine massages.

Typical full-body massage sessions last about an hour, and comprise a variety of strokes. Long, gliding motions, known as *effleurage,* soothe and relax the body. They are used throughout a massage session to begin and end treatment and to progress from one body area to another. As this manipulation identifies areas of spasm and soreness, therapists then apply a little more pressure, using a kneading motion to loosen muscles and stimulate circulation. Depending on the extent of muscle damage, the kneading action, known as *petrissage,* may be followed by more vigorous strokes that penetrate deep within the muscle to break up tension. Although massages often consist of only these light, superficial strokes, more vigorous techniques employing friction and finger pressure are commonly used to correct muscles damaged by serious injury, overuse, or disease.

"Therapeutic massage is not the same as a cosmetic massage," says Jeffrey Bresnahan, a physical therapist specializing in the treatment of sports-related injuries at Thomas Jefferson University in Philadelphia. "While a feeling of well-being is important, not all massages feel soothing while they are occurring, especially if there is some injury. Massages designed to obtain results deep within the tissue to break up scar tissue, for example, require more than light pressure to penetrate the muscle more deeply. This can cause some temporary discomfort. While the beneficial feelings do occur, they surface about 20 minutes after the massage."

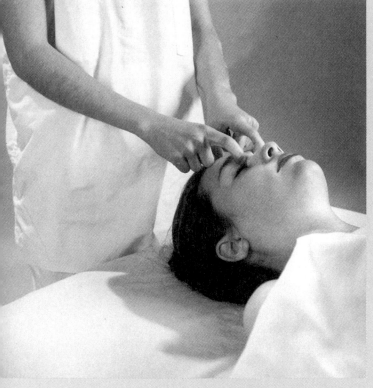

While both physical therapists and massage therapists perform massages, there is a distinction between the two professionals. Physical therapy encompasses a wide variety of modalities. Designed to be case managers for physicians, physical therapists create exercise programs, use electrostimulative devices to relieve pain, and have more training in pathology and in postsurgery rehabilitation. Massage therapists have training in anatomy and in how to manipulate soft tissue. As a result, massage therapists only help treat muscles, tendons, connective tissue, and skin through massage.

The following chart provides a quick summary of a few approaches to massage. While some massage therapists focus on applying one or two approaches, others combine techniques as needed.

Some massages consist of only light, superficial strokes; more vigorous techniques apply friction and finger pressure for deep-muscle therapy.

Massage Type	Strokes	Purpose
Swedish	Gliding, kneading, and friction	To relax, improve circulation and flexibility, and to relieve muscle tension
Deep Muscle	Slow strokes and deep finger pressure applied with the grain of the muscle or connective tissues	To relieve pain and improve circulation in deep muscle
Pfrimmer	Deep-muscle massage applied 90 degrees against the grain of the muscle or connective tissue	To improve flexibility and correct muscle damaged by injury or disease
Trigger Point	Concentrated finger pressure to painful, irritated areas in muscles	To treat pain
Shiatsu and Acupressure	Finger pressure applied at special points along the body	To release blocked energy that this Oriental healing art sees as the cause of disease and discomfort
Reflexology	Finger pressure applied to the hands and feet at specific points	To release blocked energy, as in shiatsu

Sports Medicine Center. "It's also used to relieve muscle spasms, to remove fluids caused by inflammation, and to help stretch or break up scar tissue caused by injury."

Muscles become sore when waste products build up at capillary beds. "One of the benefits of massage is that it loosens muscles and increases blood and lymph flow to the massaged area, speeding the removal of debris and the delivery of more oxygen and nutrients to muscle tissues," Marone says.

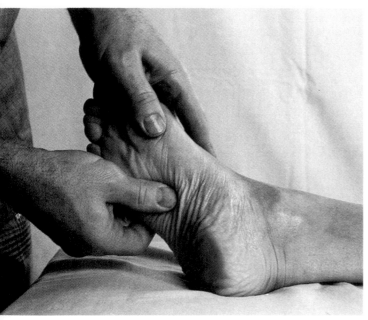

While massage can relieve pain, it can not arrest the underlying cause of disease, and it should only be used as a complement to medical therapy.

"The more quickly you get rid of the waste products, the faster the recovery."

While massage enhances muscle performance, it does not give athletes "superpowers or serve as a cure-all," he warns. "At times, massage can relieve the pain of arthritis by keeping muscles around the joint flexible, but it does nothing to arrest the underlying cause of the disease. It can't prevent the loss of muscle tone following permanent nerve damage, and doesn't increase metabolism, remove cellulite, shrink tumors, or treat infectious disease. And while almost everyone can benefit from a massage, people with acute injuries, broken bones, or circulatory problems should avoid it."

Benefits for Chronic Disease

Because massage helps to relax the body and increase the flexibility of muscles, individuals plagued by chronic disease also benefit from massage. "There is no question that massage works to help relieve a variety of aches and pains that are muscular in origin," says Joel Press, M.D., director of the Sports Rehabilitation Program at the Rehabilitation Institute of Chicago. "It may be useful in treating inflexibility, pain, and other secondary complications caused by chronic disorders such as arthritis, muscular sclerosis, and lupus. However, because it is a passive modality, patients need to do stretching exercises at home to maintain the flexibility gained through massage."

Diagnosed with chronic progressive multiple sclerosis 15 years ago, Linda Lasky has watched her ability to get around on her own power dwindle. Because the disease disrupts the conduction of nerve impulses throughout the body, muscles receive partial or no signals to contract. As a result, affected muscles produce jerky movements or are paralyzed.

Linda has been getting massaged for the past seven years. Although she is mostly wheelchair-bound, massage helps Linda lead an active life. "Because I have less mobility, my muscles, tendons, and ligaments can get tight," she says. "Massage helps to identify and loosen problem areas, which I then focus on during my daily stretching exercises for the rest of the week. Without massage and daily stretching, I would lose function in my muscles more quickly. It's either use it or lose it."

Massage for the Psyche

Massage may also touch a more fundamental human need. Just as intuition leads us to rub an area that aches, and compassion guides us to comfort another in pain, the need to touch and be touched, to care and be cared for, lies deep within the human psyche. So essential is touch to the human body that babies deprived of it fail to thrive. Many who have experienced the benefits of massage feel the need to keep returning for more.

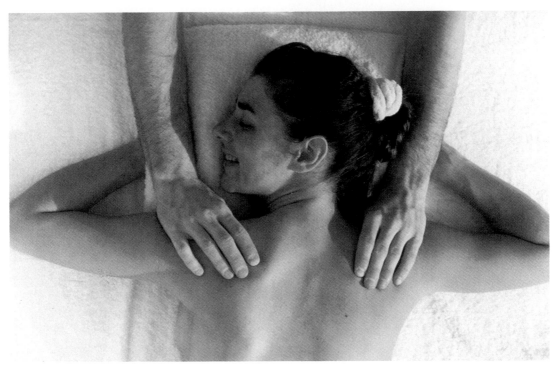

Massage touches a fundamental need within the human psyche to touch and be touched, to care and be cared for. Massage rejuvenates, reducing stress while improving mental alertness.

Burt Hollen got hooked on massage three months after an automobile mishap left him with serious neck pain. "I remember seeing the sign offering therapeutic massage, and thought I had nothing to lose," he says. "That was four years ago, and I've been going weekly ever since."

Burt finds that the sessions relieve recurring stiffness in his neck and shoulders, thus relieving his chronic pain. What he really enjoys, however, is the "floating" feeling he gets from massage—a sensation he compares to the effects of drinking a glass of wine. "I feel deeply relaxed but mentally alert," he says. "I notice the difference for several days after the massage, and can't wait to go back. It's addictive."

For others, massage helps them reduce stress so they can better cope with difficult situations. "Reducing stress helps people think more clearly," says Karen Wrigley, a clinical therapist in private practice in Norristown, Pennsylvania, who is also certified as a massage therapist. "It lets them stand back from overwhelming situations, allowing them to get a better perspective."

Thomas Cadwaller tried massage after a series of tragedies struck his life. After losing his sister and a close colleague to cancer, he found himself in the midst of a divorce. Feeling tense and restless, he tried an hour-long session four months ago at a local wellness center. Now it's become a part of his weekly routine. "I found massage to be so relaxing that I go weekly," he says. "It relieves job-related stress and increases my level of awareness, which helps me work through the more emotional aspects of my life."

Although combining counseling with massage is frowned upon by her colleagues, Wrigley sees it as an effective tool. "It helps build trust in the counselor-client relationship, and helps people communicate personal trauma," she says. "Patients don't always feel like diving right into heavy issues. It is emotionally draining. I let them choose whether they want to have a massage or need to talk. The choice is theirs."

Massage helps patients who are experiencing difficult issues in their life rejuvenate themselves before having to address the stressful situation again. But even for those not going through a crisis, massage is beneficial. "Massage helps the body come down to a level that it wants to be at, but can't reach on its own," says Wrigley. "It makes us feel loved and nurtured. And who couldn't use a little more of that in their lives?"

FLEXING CORPORATE MUSCLE

by Susan Randel

Albert grunts and sweats, pushing his legs to go yet another mile on the stationary bicycle. He moves on next to the Nautilus equipment, working to build the muscles in his legs and upper body. The workout complete, he goes to the locker room, grabs a towel from the attendant, showers off, and gets dressed. He runs into his boss, Lauren, after her aerobics class; together they head back to their offices at a Fortune 500 company.

A health club in midtown Manhattan? Perhaps a few years ago. These days, Albert and Lauren's health club could just as easily be owned by their employer as part of their company's suburban office complex.

Corporate fitness programs, including on-site health clubs at many companies, have spread like wildfire in the past decade. According to the Association for Fitness in Business, there were 30 such fitness programs in the United States in the mid-1970s; now 56 percent of businesses with more than 500 employees have fitness programs.

Corporate fitness began as a perk for top executives, an incentive to keep the people in charge in good health. Then, throughout the 1970s and 1980s, medical studies began linking physical fitness with a decline in heart disease, cholesterol levels, and blood pressure. Companies soon were opening their fitness programs to all employees. Before long, fitness centers appeared at the headquarters office. Many companies inaugurated screenings for conditions like high cholesterol or high blood pressure.

The theory behind setting up what amounts to a health club in the office is simple: healthy employees are more-productive employees. It follows that an on-site fitness center makes it easier for employees to work out and stay fit. Early results from corporate fitness centers back up this theory. Companies with full-scale fitness facilities report happier, healthier employees and an overall higher morale.

The term "corporate fitness program" covers rather broad territory. A corporate fitness program can include a separate building on the office grounds with the equipment, facilities, classes, and personnel of a fancy health club or a top-of-the-line YMCA. At the other end of the spectrum, it may simply involve recreational softball and some annual health screenings. Many programs fall somewhere between these extremes, offering discounts at nearby health clubs or monthly newsletters on a variety of health- and fitness-related issues.

At the top end of the scale are programs and facilities like those found at PepsiCo Inc.'s headquarters in suburban Purchase, New York. PepsiCo has a 12,000-square-foot facility that rivals any health club. The facility is open to all employees, their immediate families, retirees and their families, and employees visiting from other divisions and locations around the country.

As in most health clubs, a wide array of exercise machines is available, including treadmills, stairclimbers, stationary bicycles, rowing machines, and both resistance and free weights. A multipurpose exercise room houses aerobics classes of all kinds: high- and low-impact, step aerobics, even special exercises for pregnant women. At other times, this same room is used for classes in self-defense and yoga. For joggers, PepsiCo also has indoor and outdoor tracks for year-round running. The outdoor pool is a prime summertime attraction.

An employee who wants to work on his or her skills in recreational sports can choose to use the company's basketball courts and softball diamonds, or seek easy access to local tennis, racquetball, and volleyball courts. PepsiCo will supply needed equipment for anyone who wants to play these sports. Also available are bicycles for anyone who wants to pedal around the grounds, and personal cassette players for those who like to work out to music. And of course, there are full locker-room facilities.

A wide variety of health programs is offered in conjunction with the exercise programs. Those seeking to diet can join classes in weight loss; other classes help workers quit smoking; still others teach stress-reduction techniques. A series of programs that screen for high cholesterol or blood-pressure levels completes the picture.

Running the show at PepsiCo are two health and fitness coordinators, a massage therapist, and administrative personnel. These folks get input from departmental representatives throughout the company's headquarters staff, including suggestions for new programs. Frank LoCastro, PepsiCo's manager for corporate health and fitness, notes that the company has been active in fitness for its employees since its days on

Joining a Corporate Fitness Program

A corporate fitness program is like any other exercise program, albeit with a more personal touch. A person who signs up must get a basic medical examination, including blood-pressure and cholesterol checks. If any of these readings are high, the exerciser should get a full physical examination or clearance from his or her physician to begin an exercise program.

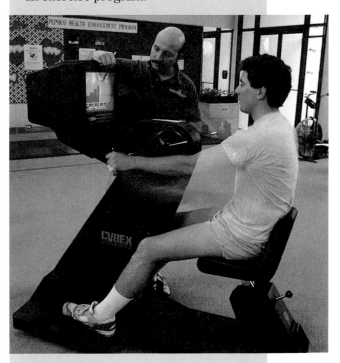

The next step is the fitness evaluation. The exerciser's body-fat content, muscle tone, flexibility, and endurance are measured, and a program is designed around the person's needs and abilities. As these abilities develop, more-challenging programs are used. One person may start very slowly, and work her way up to more aerobically challenging exercises; another may have developed his aerobic capacity more quickly and can do more-strenuous exercise sooner.

While a relatively new trend in the American business world, corporate fitness programs have long been a mandatory tradition in many of Japan's most prestigious companies.

Park Avenue in Manhattan. "The multipurpose fitness facility in Purchase celebrates its 10th anniversary this year," he says.

A program this old can boast quite a few success stories. PepsiCo employees have lost weight, lowered blood pressure, and generally grown fitter, thanks to easy access to health facilities. Roger King, senior vice president of personnel, has been part of the corporate fitness program for about 15 years; he now runs about 20 miles a week. He attributes his feeling of vitality—and the stamina to work long hours—to the fact that he is physically fit.

Are PepsiCo's employees happy with their facility and programs? Apparently so, judging from the fact that 70 percent of the approximately 700 people at the Purchase site make use of some aspect of the corporate fitness program. Most other companies with on-site fitness centers and recreation programs report that an average of 20 to 40 percent of the employees regularly use the facilities.

Many corporate fitness centers are similar to PepsiCo's, with full locker-room facilities,

state-of-the-art exercise equipment, aerobics classes, and an indoor track. At some companies the classes are specially tailored to the needs of the employees.

• Dow Chemical Company's fitness center at its headquarters in Midland, Michigan, includes a lending library, classroom, and a teaching kitchen where an on-site dietitian can show employees how to cook food in healthier ways.

• Air Products and Chemicals Inc., in Allentown, Pennsylvania, starts its ski-conditioning classes in the fall, so skiers will be in shape when winter arrives.

• Olin Corporation's Lake Charles, Louisiana, plant, which has the company's only fitness center at this time (its Stamford, Connecticut, headquarters will pay 50 percent of the membership fee if an employee joins the local YMCA), offers classes in circadian rhythms for its shift workers.

An important function of a fitness center is to keep hours that suit the workers. Most on-site fitness facilities are open from the early morning to the early evening, five days a week, so employees can take advantage of the hours before and after work and during lunchtime. Some remain open on weekends for shorter hours. A few, including PepsiCo's center and, in the near future, Olin's Lake Charles facility, are open 24 hours a day, seven days a week. This is particularly important for Olin's workers, many of whom work rotating shifts.

Most fitness programs start at corporate headquarters. As its popularity and success become apparent, the program is spread in varying degrees to other sites around the country. A large office or manufacturing plant may end up with facilities and programs similar to those at headquarters, complete with fitness coordinators. Smaller sites may receive occasional visits from the head of the corporation's health and fitness program or from volunteer coordinators who initiate programs. Even the smallest subsidiary receives video or written information on activities.

Some companies that have decided to start a corporate fitness program utilize fitness consultants to set up and run the facility. One such consulting firm is Fitness Systems, which includes Gannett News Service among its clients. For Gannett, a Fitness Systems representative worked with the architects of

the fitness center, chose the equipment to be purchased, and now runs the entire program. The firm arranges for professionals, such as exercise physiologists, to work with Gannett employees. Fitness Systems also takes care of the recreational programming—activities like the softball teams and golf.

In terms of actual exercise programs, the differences between a company fitness program and joining a health club are for the most part insignificant. The key factors seem to be convenience—the on-site club does not re-

Corporate fitness centers strive to meet the exercise needs of people of all ages and athletic ability. Most on-site fitness facilities keep hours that suit the schedules of their employees.

Success Stories

Sue, a 49-year-old employee of Chevron Corporation in San Francisco, has been overweight since she was a child. "Initially, I signed up with Chevron's HealthQuest to try and get more mobility —I'm 5 feet 2 inches, and at the time weighed 300 pounds. I was having trouble getting around; my feet hurt when I walked." She signed up when the center opened in May 1991, but "I didn't use it regularly, until I gained weight on my vacation in September." In October, Sue began patronizing HealthQuest regularly, walking on the treadmill. Gradually she has built up her stamina, and is now walking on a 4-degree grade for 20 minutes at 2 miles per hour three times a week. So far, Sue has lost 40 pounds.

Sue has found that as she loses weight and builds muscle, she can do more. The trainer at HealthQuest has started her on a weight machine (to build upper-body and leg strength), and she has started walking the 1.8 miles to work. Although she works with the trainer at the center, they have not set any specific weight-loss goals. "The trainers tell me not to worry about what the scale says, and just keep going. They say, 'See how you feel and how your clothes fit.'" So far, she feels great. Even her coworkers have noticed. They sense a different attitude about her, and many have told her so.

The only goal she has in mind is to change the route she walks to work. "I plotted a route that is relatively flat," but it takes her right through San Francisco's notorious Tenderloin district. "If I could walk some hills, I could go through some nicer neighborhoods."

Ernie Espiritu knew he wanted to get rid of his big waistline when he joined Chevron's HealthQuest fitness program, so he signed up for a fitness evaluation. The 46-year-old was not significantly overweight (227 pounds on a 6-foot 3-inch frame), but the evaluation said, "I was in no shape! I didn't like the results." He started on a treadmill and weight machine, but saw little progress, so, with the advice of a trainer, he began a more aerobic program. Now Ernie works out for 45 minutes to an hour most days of the week, using the stairclimber, stationary bicycle, and weight machines. "I've lost 24 pounds, and my waist has gone from a 42 to a 36."

The difference in his appearance is very noticeable, Ernie says, since his waist is no longer big and his face is not puffed out. He feels better, too. "I don't get tired as much walking up those hills in San Francisco. When I walk those hills, I just pretend I'm on the Stairmaster, and I'm there."

quire travel time—and the more personal approach that is taken. PepsiCo's Frank LoCastro feels that this personal touch helps give exercisers support, and keeps them coming back regularly.

Perhaps the most significant difference between a company-subsidized facility and a private health club is the cost: most corporate facilities charge a minimal fee, something along the lines of Gannett's $10 per month; a YMCA might charge $30 or more, with additional charges for special classes; and more exclusive health clubs charge even higher fees.

It is still too early to evaluate what kind of effect on-site fitness centers are having on the workers who use them. A study commissioned by the Association for Fitness in Business reports that over the short term, employees who take advantage of on-site health facilities have fewer absences and a moderate reduction in health-care costs. And while these savings are significant, they don't come close to telling the whole story. For many companies, the cost of building and maintaining on-site fitness centers is a small price to pay for happier, healthier, and more-productive employees.

Tandem bicycles have come a long way since their introduction in 1884. Today racing enthusiasts and leisurely pedalers alike are jumping at the chance to take a whirl on a bicycle built for two.

TANDEMONIUM!

by Susan Nielsen

On May 6, 1884, a Mr. J. Rucker obtained a U.S. patent for a contraption consisting of two seats atop two enormous wheels, with a bar between them. But not too many people were willing to risk their necks to hop up onto his Kangaroo tandem. Little did the inventor know at the time, but the next century would find enthusiasts jumping at the chance to ride the redesigned descendants of his two-seated cycle.

Manufacturers estimate that tandem sales have tripled in the past three years and continue to grow at the phenomenal rate of 15 to 20 percent annually. Tandems have been virtually unaffected by the recession   it's the only segment of the bicycle market that has

grown in the past two years. Indeed, membership in the Tandem Club of America has taken off, from a mere 11 teams in 1976 to more than 2,000 in 1991, with enthusiasts from every state and even a few foreign countries, reports Jack Goertz, editor of the club's newsletter and owner of Tandems Limited in Birmingham, Alabama. Why the renewed interest? Some industry experts say the tandem offers a taste of simpler times and a chance for couples to be together and work out together—in a noncompetitive way. "Here's a way for couples to recreate without competing," says Jim Leis, general manager of Santana Cycles, Inc., in Clare mont, California. "In other sports, there's always a winner and loser, or someone who can go faster or play harder. Here you're going at the same speed for the same goal: an enjoyable time together."

Santana Cycles, Inc., which makes only tandems, is located in the same state where, according to the Tandem Club's files, two-seated cycles are the most popular—365 teams at last count. One of those teams is California couple Bill and Lois Weast of Carmichael. The two semiretirees have taken their tandem bicycling all the way to France, where rides in the countryside on their custom-made red Ritchey bike were greeted with smiles and waves. Bill, 61, and Lois, 54, belong to the Bay Area Roaming Tandems, otherwise known as BART. They and the other 100 or so members meet a few times a month to cycle and just talk tandems, says Bill Weast. "We share the same language," he explains.

Synchronized Cadence

Tandem riders talk of centuries, or cycling 100 miles a day, and of the pleasures of being the captain or stoker. The captain, at the helm of the two-seated "ship," controls the bike's gears, brakes, steering, and keeps the bike steady when stopped. Goertz sums it up: "The job of the captain," he says, "is to keep the stoker happy." Not that the stoker is a passive passenger by any means. The backseat rider must lean with the captain in the turns while making the proper hand signal and watching for road hazards, like cars approaching from the rear. "The stoker's view is like that of a passenger on a train looking out the window at all the scenery," says Goertz. Whether captain or stoker, the tandem team must get used to riding a bike together. What they find out quickly is that communication is key. They must continually keep each other informed of what they see or are about to do—all the while pedaling in "tandem" to keep the bike cruising.

The synchronized cadence the couple creates while pedaling is good for the heart and soul. Bicycling is a low-impact aerobic exercise, so it's easy on the hips, knees, and other joints. That's why former joggers are some of the most enthusiastic converts to the sport. Plus, like running, it's a great way to keep the vasti, recti, sartorii, gastrocnemii, and glutii in shape. When toned, these thigh, calf, and buttocks muscles make the legs shapelier and more defined. And dieters take note: bicyclists can burn up to 2,000 calories in as little as two hours! Best of all, nearly anyone, at any age, can ride a bike. There are many cyclists, like the Weasts, who are

Tandem rallies bring cycling twosomes together for noncompetitive bike tours. The renewed popularity of tandem bicycling may rest with the opportunity it gives couples to spend quality time together.

over 50 and ride regularly. As a matter of fact, tandem cycling has always been most popular with the 40-plus set, and now interest is growing among younger adults, observes Goertz, who finds the first fun-seekers of a new generation in the club, on the road, and at tandem rallies.

While strengthening their legs, a couple, whether young or old, can strengthen their relationship, too. Exercising on a bicycle built for two has practically twice the motivation built into it. Not only is it a pleasure to exercise with someone else, but, unlike riding two solo bikes, couples can talk and be heard more easily on a tandem. "My wife, Susan, and I use riding time as our talking time," says Goertz. "After all, you're only 25 to 28 inches apart." Words are rarely lost on the wind, and, best of all, says Goertz, "You're only a touching distance away." He wholeheartedly believes in the romance of the two-seated sport. For his first date with Susan, "I asked her to ride my tandem with me," he recalls. They've been married more than 11 years, and continue to ride together.

A Family Affair

But tandem biking isn't just for couples. As more parents take their children for a ride on their tandems, it has become a family affair. Besides the typical bike safety seat, there are other ways to bring the kids along. "Trailers are becoming more and more popular," says Russell Morton, an administrator at Burley Design Cooperative in Eugene, Oregon. The trailers look like squared-off pup tents with windows and two big wheels. Trailers seem to offer more stability than a safety seat, especially for the superlong, eight-foot frame of a tandem. The "baby buggies" come with a roll bar, seat- and shoulder-belt harness, and hold up to two kids. Even if the tandem should take a tumble, the trailer probably won't topple, due to the trailer's low center

of gravity and its special safety attachment to the bicycle. Trailers range in price from $250 to $350, with collapsible models at the higher prices. Bike safety seats, on the other hand, are often under $100. For older children—the four- to nine-year-old set, too big for a trailer, but too small to reach the pedals—a

While most tandem bicycles are built for road travel, tandem enthusiasts are increasingly using mountain-bike tandems for off-road spins through wilder, more challenging terrain.

child stoker conversion kit ($200 to $350) is the answer. This allows the pedals to be brought up higher, and also comes with a replacement stoker stem designed for a child's reach. "It only takes about 20 minutes to do the conversion," claims Goertz.

Couples and families alike show up for tandem bike rallies. Industry experts say attendance has grown from just a few tandems a few years ago to more than 300 at some events. Most riders prefer to stay on pavement, as opposed to taking to the hills on a tandem. And sales reflect this. While the

Taking a Backseat

More often than not, when a couple rides a tandem, the man will sit up front as the captain, and his wife or girlfriend becomes the stoker in the back. Does this seating arrangement reflect the thinking of the turn of the century, when women would automatically take a backseat to their husbands—on and off a two-seated cycle?

Most industry experts say no, claiming that the reason the frame of a tandem is larger in the front than in the back is strictly ergonomics—not sexism. They explain that since the captain is responsible for the bike's operations, the larger, stronger person is often in front. Indeed, a smaller person can be captain, but then it is often difficult for a larger person to get the proper fit in the stoker's seat. "For one thing," says Jack Goertz, owner of Tandems Limited in Birmingham, Alabama, "there's only so far up the stoker's handlebars will go to accommodate a larger person, since they're attached to the stem of the captain's seat." To remedy this, some manufacturers will custom-make what is called a backward tandem. Goertz says he gets only a few requests a year for one. Sexism issues aside, there's no denying physics: greater speeds can be achieved when the stoker's smaller body frame is tucked behind the captain's larger one—a position called drafting. Still, many couples—both racers and slow pacers—do switch seats once in a while. In making the switch himself, Goertz found that he'd actually prefer to be the stoker *all* the time. "Stokers actually have a better view," he says. "The captain is too busy watching the road straight ahead to check out the scenery." He pauses and sighs: "We captains find out about what we missed after the trip is over."

trend in solo bicycling has been toward hybrid bikes with slightly knobby tires for on- as well as off-road use, most tandem riders, on the other hand, still prefer the smoother on-road tires. One reason is the speed factor. Generally, two cyclists on a tandem can ride faster than a solo bicyclist. The additional weight of a tandem, plus the doubled energy of its riders, make it sail along more quickly than a solo bike. Also, the stoker's position in the captain's shadow, called drafting, makes a tandem aerodynamically superb for high speeds—except uphill. Here its weight works against it, as the tandem fights gravity to climb hilly terrain. "That's why a typical tandem has higher high gears and lower low gears than a solo bike," says Leis of Santana Cycles. "They are usually made in 21 or 24 speeds." The added low gears allow the cyclists to get all the help they can in climbing hills. And higher high gears are needed for cruising at high speeds on flat and downhill terrain.

If you and a partner are thinking of trying a two-seated cycle, a tandems-only retailer is your best bet. If one is not located nearby, your search should start at a local bike shop. Although most local shops do not carry tandems, a dealer should be able to tell you whom to contact, whether a club, manufacturer, or another dealer. And some dealers who do not carry tandems still may be able to special order one for you. If a tandem is not available for a test ride or rental, a dealer may be able to hook you up with local enthusiasts or tandem-club members who may be willing to let you try their bikes before you invest in one. Tandems range in price from about $1,000 to $4,000, with models made with aluminum and lighter metal-alloy frames and components at the higher end. More manufacturers than ever are making tandems today, including these 18 companies competing for a share of the ever-growing market: Burley, Bushnell, Cannondale, Co-Motion, Davidson, Dawes, Fisher, Giant, Ibis, Miyata, Moots, Rodriguez, Santana, Schwinn, Sterling, and Yokota; Specialized and Trek are scheduled to release their first tandems in the spring of 1992.

ADVENTURE TRAVEL
for the disabled

by Elizabeth McGowan

Tom Whittaker's friends didn't pull any punches. Whittaker, they made it quite clear, was no longer welcome to join them on a kayaking trip they had been planning together for a year. He had recently lost a foot in an automobile accident, and the rest of the group didn't want to "take responsibility" for him.

"To hell with that," thought the British outdoorsman, angry and hurt. "I can take responsibility for myself." The next morning he bandaged his stump, stuck it in a Prince Albert cigar can, limped to a put-in point on Idaho's Snake River, and solo-kayaked the roughest stretch of white water he could find.

That day, Whittaker learned a lesson that has influenced his life ever since—he might have lost a foot, but he hadn't lost the ability to enjoy or participate in the wilderness he has loved since childhood.

The pain of rejection and the exhilaration of triumph proved to be a personal psychological turning point for Whittaker. It also was a catalyst for his formation in 1981 of what

A disability need not disqualify one from skiing. A single-leg amputee fitted with a prosthesis and endowed with good balance can often handle the slopes as well as an able-bodied skier using conventional equipment. A few single-legged skiers have succeeded without a prosthesis.

many considered a radical new enterprise: the Cooperative Wilderness Handicapped Outdoor Group (C.W. Hog), an outdoor-activities program geared to people with disabilities, one of a small but growing number of disability-friendly programs across the United States.

Today C.W. Hog, based at the Pocatello campus of Idaho State University, includes courses in whitewater rafting, rock climbing, kayaking, skiing, sailing, waterskiing, and dogsledding for people with disabilities ranging from cerebral palsy and spinal-cord injuries to visual impairments and developmental problems. Most courses are open to the able-bodied as well, and can be taken for college credit or just for fun.

Common-Adventurer Principle

C.W. Hog also offers multiday skiing, rafting, kayaking, and horseback-riding expeditions based on what is known as a "common-adventurer" principle, a legal condition under which participants agree to cooperate in a joint enterprise. There are no paid guides on C.W. Hog trips, and expenses are shared by all participants. Accordingly, any instruction and advice provided are given in the spirit of cooperation rather than as a guide/client obligation, and the activity stays within the safety bounds of the collective experience of the group.

"In our planning meetings, the difficulty of the trip is evaluated, and each person will say, 'Well, what about me? What are the rest room facilities like?,' for example, and we discuss what everyone needs, as well as potential medical problems," explains Jim Wise, the director of C.W. Hog.

If necessary, the program supplies adaptive equipment, such as flexion mitts, which enhance the grip abilities of quadriplegics, and rafts designed with adjustable seats for people with the balance problems typical of cerebral palsy or high-leg amputations.

By all reports, both the equipment and the common-adventurer concept work. Though C.W. Hog expeditions have traveled to some of the most pristine wilderness areas in the United States and have included some participants paralyzed from the neck down and others who are totally blind, the organization has confronted few insolvable problems. The trips succeed because participants make them succeed, according to Steve DeRoche, a bilateral below-the-knee amputee and a self-described "original Hog," who makes his living fighting forest fires. He explains, "We have a four-wheel-drive mentality. If we can't sidestep it, we'll get over it, whether it's with adaptive equipment or moral support or somebody has to carry you."

A Spiritual and Emotional High

Wilderness Inquiry, a Minnesota-based outdoor-adventure company, shares C.W. Hog's can-do philosophy, if not its modus operandi. A more traditional guide/participant-style organization, Wilderness Inquiry was started by environmentalist Greg Lais as a political statement of sorts. "There was a fight going on in 1976 about allowing motorboats in the Boundary Waters area," he says. "The pro-motor constituency argued that motors were necessary to provide access for women, the handicapped, and the elderly."

Lais disagreed. He decided to test his hypothesis by taking a group, including two people in wheelchairs and two people with hearing impairments, into the contested area. Lais remembers the trip as being "the most physically uncomfortable, disastrous journey ever made. It rained every day. It was the worst weather I've ever seen."

And one of the best times he's ever had. "It was a spiritual and emotional high," he continues. "We were all sleeping in a tent with 4 inches of water. I was blown away seeing how well these people coped."

In 1978 Lais turned his political statement into a business plan, incorporating Wilderness Inquiry. The company made four trips into the wilderness with a total of 34 participants in its first year of operation. In 1991 Wilderness Inquiry took 2,700 people rafting, canoeing, sea kayaking, and dogsledding in destinations as far-flung as Alaska and the Everglades.

Lais attributes the business boom to an increase in the general population's interest in adventure travel, as well as a greater awareness among people with disabilities that outdoor activity is something within their capabilities. As Lais puts it, "It's like bungee jumping. Imagine what people would have thought about that 20 years ago. Now everybody wants to do it."

Wilderness Inquiry tries its best to make sure everybody *can* do it. In planning trips, leaders weigh group strength rather than individual ability, and they encourage team effort. A typical group may include one hearing-impaired person, one or two people in a wheelchair, a person with cerebral palsy, another with a cognitive disability, and several able-bodied folks. "We would never do a trip with five quadriplegics, for example, because we couldn't pull it off," explains Lais. "There would be too much lifting. And if someone needs help with hygiene, we require that they bring a companion."

In such a mix-and-match crowd, the abilities of each individual contribute to the overall success of the group. A blind person might push a paraplegic in a wheelchair, for example, who in turn provides the sight necessary for the blind person to negotiate uneven terrain. Or a mentally retarded person might carry the pack of someone with multiple sclerosis, who in turn describes the scenery to someone who can't see.

Wilderness Inquiry also stresses the value of nonphysical accomplishment. "Nobody likes to be a sack of potatoes," says Lais. "Someone might not be able to contribute a lot physically, but be really good at group processing or able to share knowledge about things like botany or geology that makes the trip more interesting to other participants. We once had a guy who had studied navigation and was quite accomplished at it. He couldn't paddle, but he was, in fact, the navigator on that trip."

Does Wilderness Inquiry ever turn anyone down? Rarely, answers Lais. "We do a lot of careful screening. There are a million medical

Specialized outdoor-activities programs have opened a wide range of sports to people with disabilities. With special adaptive equipment, just about anybody can savor the thrill of whitewater rafting.

issues with quadriplegics, for example, so we need to know details so we can be prepared." There are also ongoing medical problems like kidney dialysis that the company can't handle on long trips. And they won't take someone with open pressure sores because of the risk of infection.

"But overall, our general policy is to try to accommodate everybody," says Lais. "People sometimes fib about their disability because they think we won't take them if we know the truth. That is a lot less true than they think."

Part of a Day's Work

In reality, however, people with disabilities have good reason to fear rejection. Most mainstream outdoor-adventure companies have neither the resources nor the inclination to handle their needs, as Steve Schwab found

out after a skiing accident, when he joined the ranks of the 43 million Americans with disabilities.

Seven years ago, the pharmacy student was carving turns down an icy slope. The next thing Schwab remembers is waking up in a hospital bed from an 11-day coma. The head injury he sustained left him with a permanent weakness in his left side and a multitude of problems including aphasia and a transient inability to register the correct emotional response to stimuli.

Though he relearned how to walk and talk, Schwab was sure his skiing days were over —until he was introduced by a therapist to Shared Outdoor Adventure Recreation (SOAR), a Portland, Oregon, organization operated along the same lines as Wilderness Inquiry. Now the veteran of 50 SOAR trips, Schwab has learned how to ski again, and has taken up the sports of rafting, backpacking, and biking for the first time. "Nothing like this was offered in the real world," says Schwab. "An ordinary outdoor company doesn't understand where someone like me is coming from." To illustrate his point, Schwab tells of a day a couple of years ago when he had a seizure while cross-country skiing. "The SOAR people knew how to take care of me," he says. "It wasn't a big deal."

Like Schwab, Dolly Nickerson was delighted to discover that her disability was just all part of a day's work to instructors at Shake-A-Leg, an adaptive sailing program with operations in Newport, Rhode Island, and Miami, Florida. A 54-year-old mother of two, Nickerson had been an athlete before

By and large, most wilderness-adventure groups are organized in terms of collective strength rather than individual ability. On a typical trip, participants confined to a wheelchair (above) might scout out the perfect campsite. Neither paralysis nor visual impairment interferes with one's ability to help erect a tent (right).

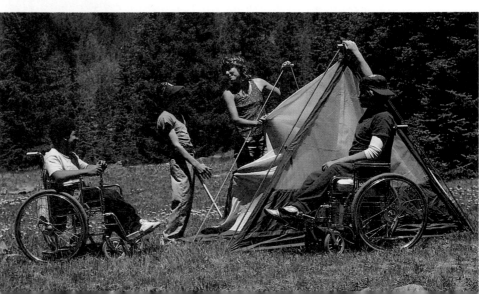

she lost the use of her legs in an automobile accident 26 years ago. Accustomed to having her wheelchair greeted with less than enthusiasm, Nickerson had resigned herself to the idea that her outdoor options were limited to little more than outings in the city park.

With her children grown and on their own, and her insurance-company job predictable and dull, Nickerson was ripe for a change. Then she spotted an ad in the paper last year for Shake-A-Leg, announcing the opening of its Miami branch. Nickerson, who had sailed before her accident and says she's always felt a kinship with the sea, rushed to the phone to arrange for a lesson. "Essentially I had been waiting for this for 25 years. I was probably their first customer," she laughs.

When she rolled onto the Shake-A-Leg dock, Nickerson was nervous but determined. "The instructors asked if anybody had ever sailed before, and I tentatively raised my hand. They said, 'O.K., you take the helm.' And here I thought I was just going on a little boat ride!"

A transfer seat enabled Nickerson to move easily from her wheelchair into a special seat in the cockpit designed to swivel from side to side so the boat can be tacked properly by sailors who can't stand. Shake-A-Leg boats are also built for maximum stability to accommodate individuals with balance problems, and knots in the lines serve as a sailor's braille for the visually impaired.

Nickerson, who liked Shake-A-Leg so much she now works for the company, says sailing gave her "a chance to be in control of a situation where our community [people with disabilities] is often viewed as being out of control. Now I can take able-bodied friends and family out sailing, and it is my treat."

A Great Equalizer

Nickerson's experience illustrates a truism that is almost a cliché among people with disabilities: water is a great equalizer. Legs, eyesight, hearing, and good balance are not necessary to sail, canoe, raft, or kayak. And, "as long as you can move your arms some, you can propel yourself forward," adds Wilderness Inquiry's Greg Lais. "You may not be able to win a race, but you can paddle and you can be a good swimmer."

Or a good skier, if you prefer colder climes. Advances in adaptive equipment have made it possible for almost anyone to get downhill on snow. The great majority of ski areas now provide instruction for skiers with disabilities, and permit adaptive equipment such as monoskis on their lifts.

Three organizations also provide free clinics for skiers with disabilities, supplying equipment, lift tickets, and instruction. New York's 52 Association for the Handicapped works with amputees and the visually impaired; Colorado-based Aspen Blind Outdoor Leisure Development (BOLD) specializes in the visually impaired; and National Handicapped Sports, headquartered in Rockville, Maryland, with chapters all over the country, deals with the visually impaired, amputees, those with spinal-cord injuries, and people with neuromuscular problems.

The type of equipment necessary to ski depends, of course, on the disability. A single-leg amputee who has been fitted with a prosthesis and has good balance can whiz down the slope as well as an able-bodied skier using regular skis and poles. A paraplegic or double amputee would probably require a monoski, a seatlike device mounted on a single ski and suspension system, working in concert with outriggers (basically shortened skis connected to poles). Visually impaired skiers have no need for special equipment, but are guided downhill by instructors who have skied blindfolded as part of their training, and thus understand what their students are experiencing. Whatever the disability, the medium of snow allows the thrill of self-propelled speed and fluidity of motion that is often impossible on dry land.

Freedom of movement also attracts many people with disabilities to the sport of scuba diving. "Along with the beauty of the undersea world, there's an incredible sense of weightlessness in the water," explains Patricia Gatacre, public-relations director for the Handicapped Scuba Association, an organization based in San Clemente, California, that sponsors a network of disability-oriented instruction programs through dive shops across the United States and in 17 other countries. The organization also evaluates dive resorts for accessibility to the handicapped.

According to Gatacre, the Handicapped Scuba Association certifies divers on three levels: an A-level diver is required to dive with one buddy; a B-level diver is required to dive with two buddies; a C-level diver is required to dive with two buddies who are either instructors or trained in diver rescue.

As the two-buddy system implies, a C-level diver is unable to function alone: one buddy tows the diver; the other regulates his or her oxygen. Certification depends on degree of independence, not type of disability.

"Contrary to popular belief," says Gatacre, "people who are quadriplegics are not necessarily C divers. Someone with an incomplete high-spinal lesion may be classified as quadriplegic, but still have a great degree of motion in their arms. The term *quadriplegia* is often misunderstood."

Indeed, if a general statement about people with disabilities can be made, it's that their abilities are misunderstood and invariably underestimated. "Ninety-nine times out of 100, the limitations are not where we thought they would be," says Mark Chandler, program director for Colorado's Breckenridge Outdoor Education Center (BOEC). BOEC offers downhill-skiing courses and outdoor-adventure trips for individuals with physical and developmental disabilities. The

Many people with disabilities are drawn to scuba diving and other aquatic sports from which they derive great freedom of movement.

center also offers wilderness programs at a 39-acre retreat for groups as diverse as children with cancer, mental-retardation organizations, and Youth at Risk, a group Chandler describes as "perhaps too able-bodied."

BOEC custom-designs its programs to fit the group. "We try to size up who needs what," Chandler explains. "In our ski program, for example, we have had people who have been in wheelchairs for 20 years. They've gone through the whole shock and the therapy. They're comfortable with their disability and don't need hand-holding. They come to BOEC for the same reasons as anyone else—to learn a new sport for fun and excitement."

Therapy for the Recently Disabled

At the other end of the spectrum are people with a recent disability who are trying to cope with new circumstances. In these cases, outdoor recreation can serve as a continuum of rehabilitation. The groups brought to BOEC two times a year by Joanne Pearson fall into this category. A nurse practitioner for the oncology department of Denver's Children's Hospital, Pearson strongly advocates the therapeutic value of a wilderness environment and outdoor recreation.

"We have some kids who have brain tumors who are scared, others who have lost limbs, still others who have leukemia and are scheduled for a bone-marrow transplant and are worrying, 'It's my last chance; what if it doesn't work?' " Pearson explains. "We try to provide opportunities at BOEC for the kids to talk to one another about problems they are having. What is it like to deal with an amputation or limb salvage? What is it like to get on a school bus with the other kids after you've lost your hair to chemotherapy? Some of these kids are very frightened; some are very angry."

The outdoor activities offered by BOEC provide a nonthreatening testing ground and supportive context for children to discover the extent of their abilities. A child who has recently lost a leg, for example, can try rock climbing or cross-country skiing and discover that he or she has a lot more dexterity than imagined. It also helps, says Pearson, for the kids to see other kids in the same boat.

Whether the participant is a child or an adult, at ease with their disability or still trying to cope, the ultimate goal of BOEC—indeed, of all outdoor-adventure programs surveyed—is the achievement of confidence and independence. As David Espeseth, executive director of SOAR, puts it, "We want people to do it on their own. We don't want people to depend on our meager schedules and resources. We want people to graduate from our courses."

Darrel Von, a 40-year-old logging-company vice president and SOAR alumnus, should have graduated summa cum laude. Paralyzed from the chest down, Von originally signed up for a skiing class with SOAR because he "always likes to go fast and find out about ways to get around and have fun without a wheelchair." Today Von is adept at a roster of sports that would put Bo Jackson to shame: basketball, hunting, fishing, bicycling, hiking, and skiing. For the past two years he's run his own whitewater-rafting company, guiding clients, most able-bodied, down the Class IV rapids of the Deschutes and MacKenzie rivers. In his spare time, he also volunteers as an instructor for SOAR.

Von says his outdoor adventures have taught him that there's nothing he can't do, except, he admits with a grin, "maybe the long jump."

But who knows? Give him another couple of years, and he'll probably figure out that one, too.

CROSS OVER TO CROSS-TRAINING

Cross-training adds fun and variety to the fitness routine. Rotating activities throughout the year helps work all the muscles while avoiding the aches and pains that come from overdoing a single type of exercise.

by Hal Higdon

Is your exercise bike gathering dust? Maybe it's time you took a page from Bo Jackson's book and expanded your horizons. Doing more than one sport, or cross-training, is the new wave in exercise, and even the most dedicated single-sport purists are getting caught up in the tide. Several years before Bo knew anything about it, cross-training was born in the form of the Ironman Triathlon, a daylong swim-bike-run affair in Hawaii that begins with a 2.4-mile swim in the ocean, moves on to a 112-mile bicycle ride, and concludes with a 26.2-mile run. Not everyone wants to swim, cycle, and run for a day through the choppy surf and arid lava fields of the Big Island, of course—but cross-training turns out to be just as good for ordinary folks as for world-class athletes. When you've got a limited amount of time to put into exercise, dividing it into different activities is a way to make sure you're working all your muscles while avoiding the aches and pains that come from overdoing any single kind of exercise. It can also add fun and variety to your fitness routine. Who wouldn't mind exchanging running shoes for a pair of rollerblade skates once in a while, or going for a refreshing swim instead of automatically jumping onto a stationary bicycle?

"Among our members who exercise regularly," says Neil Sol, general manager of the Houstonian Health and Fitness Center in Houston, "there's hardly anyone who doesn't cross-train in some fashion." At the Aerobics Center in Dallas, exercise physiologist John Duncan sees a great surge in the number of multiple-sport athletes, particularly women. "A lot of women who started as aerobic dancers have blossomed into walkers, swimmers, or cyclists as well," says Duncan.

Cross-training can actually accelerate your development. "A novice runner or cyclist isn't going to be able to train hard every day," says Jim Bolster, head swim coach at Columbia University and a competitive triathlete himself. "Doing another form of exercise is a great way to recover from a workout without being idle." While you ponder what sports to add to your cross-training menu, keep these tips in mind:

Pick sports you enjoy. The point of cross-training is to have fun—so use your imagination. This is your chance to rekindle your tennis or golf game or to satisfy your secret desire to buy a fast bicycle and tear up the pavement. Remember, in cross-training, almost every physical activity is fair game.

Move into a new sport gradually. Always warm up carefully, and keep the initial workout short. This conservative approach will give your muscles and tendons a chance to adjust to the new movements you're asking them to do.

"Even if you're already fit, you should approach a new sport as if it were a long-distance event the first few times," says

Bolster. "Start out slowly, and learn as you go." If you want to try a sport unfamiliar to you, whether it's bicycling or swimming, it's a good idea to start off with some lessons. Or do your first few workouts in the company of someone more experienced.

Invest in the appropriate gear. Well-made shoes are the most important piece of equipment in any exercise involving running, walking, or jumping. While you may feel decadent

Cross-country skiing provides a low-impact full-body workout of all the major muscle groups while at the same time increasing aerobic capacity.

having several pairs of sports shoes in your closet, you're better off with a shoe designed specifically for running or walking rather than with so-called cross-training footwear. Ditto for aerobic dancing and basketball. If you decide to take up cycling, purchase a bike from a reputable shop, and don't forget to buy a helmet while you're at it.

Mix-and-Match Training Menu

	Aerobic Units	Body benefits	Training key
RUNNING (high-impact)	6 per hour.	Excellent for leg strength, aerobic fitness, and weight control.	Run at a pace that feels comfortable to you, and walk should you feel the need. Whenever possible, seek out a soft training surface such as grass, dirt, or a track made of cinder or rubberized material.
SWIMMING (low-impact)	6 per hour.	Excellent for developing arms and shoulders and great for aerobic endurance. Also good for overall flexibility and fair for weight control. It's a good stress reducer as well.	When doing the crawl, keep the waterline even with the bridge of your nose.
BICYCLING (low-impact)	6 per hour.	Excellent for aerobic endurance and weight control. Develops strong legs and thighs without pounding the feet, knees, and ankles.	Find riding partners to reduce wind resistance; learn to maintain a high pedal tempo (80 to 100 revolutions per minute).
ROWING (low-impact)	6 per hour.	Excellent for upper-body and leg strength and for aerobic fitness.	Learn to maintain a smooth, even rhythm.
AEROBIC DANCING/ STEP AEROBICS (low- to high-impact)	6 per hour (high-impact); 6 per hour (step); 4 per hour (low-impact).	Excellent for cardiovascular health and overall body toning.	Find an instructor who works in a style and tempo you feel comfortable with.
WALKING (medium-impact)	4 per hour (fast); 2 per hour (slow).	Good for leg strength and cardiovascular health. New research shows walking is also an effective way to control your weight.	Pump your arms faster, and your legs will follow suit. Try to fit walking into your daily commute to work or errand running. Even better, find a friend to walk with you.
YOGA (low-impact)	2 per hour.	Excellent for flexibility, relaxation, and stress reduction.	Find a good instructor who can modify yoga to suit your individual needs, rather than someone who insists on "classical" yoga positions.
WEIGHT TRAINING (medium-impact)	3 per hour.	Excellent for overall muscle, tendon, and bone strength; mildly beneficial for the heart. Done properly, weight training can improve your performance in virtually any sport.	Work your legs first, then your arms. Do between 8 and 12 repetitions of each exercise.
GOLF (low-impact)	2 per hour (walking the course).	Excellent for eye-hand coordination. If you walk the course, golf also enhances cardiovascular health and aids in leg toning and weight control.	Beginners tend to retain early habits, so start off with a few lessons from a certified instructor.
TENNIS/ RACQUETBALL (medium-impact)	4 per hour.	Excellent for eye-hand coordination, balance, and leg and arm toning. Moderately good for aerobic fitness and weight loss.	Work on developing a smooth, consistent swing. Lessons will help your game improve more rapidly.
STATIONARY BICYCLING (low-impact)	6 per hour (strenuous effort); 4 per hour (moderate effort).	Excellent for cardiovascular fitness, weight control, and leg strength. Because it develops the quadriceps, it's a good complement to running.	Varying the effort helps combat boredom. New bikes offer computerized workouts, which add spice to the session.
STAIR CLIMBING (low-impact)	6 per hour (strenuous); 4 per hour (moderate).	Excellent for aerobic fitness, leg and buttock strength, and overall toning.	Short, quick steps work best.

Essential gear	Caution	Calories burned in 30 minutes
A comfortable, well-made pair of running shoes ($50 to $80).	Running is a high-impact activity. If you feel any aches or pains in your hips, knees, legs, feet, or ankles, stop immediately and take several days off before resuming. If the pain lasts more than a week, see a doctor.	450 (six-minute miles); 355 (10-minute miles).
A tight-fitting one-piece bathing suit ($20 and up) and a swimming cap (for people with long hair). If you don't have access to a lake or private pool, check with your local YM/YWCA or school board to locate a public facility.	Swimming skills take time to perfect. If yours are rusty, start off with a few lessons. Novice swimmers should always swim with a partner or under a lifeguard's supervision.	320 (50 yards per minute); 150 (20 yards per minute).
A well-made 10- or 12-speed bicycle ($300 and up; $400 and up for mountain bikes) and a helmet ($60).	Beginners should learn hand signals and rules of the road, and should ride in a traffic-free setting. Local cycling clubs offer courses on proper signaling and road etiquette.	325 (13 miles an hour); 225 (10 miles an hour).
A shell and oars ($1,500) or a rowing machine ($700 for the most popular model).	Rowing puts pressure on the lower back; if you have a history of back problems, stay away.	530 (strenuous effort); 200 (moderate effort).
A pair of well-cushioned shoes with good lateral support ($50 to $60).	High-impact aerobics can strain the knees, hips, and ankles. Step aerobics is lower-impact, but should be avoided by anyone with knee problems. The use of hand weights in any form of aerobics is being discouraged by many experts.	400 (strenuous effort); 300 (moderate effort).
A well-made pair of walking shoes ($50 to $70).	Make sure your shoes fit and are broken in before trying any long excursions.	300 (12-minute miles); 200 (16-minute miles).
A mat and comfortable, loose-fitting clothing.	Don't push. Develop your skills slowly, and yoga will give you a lifetime of satisfaction.	100.
A weight machine ($900 to $5,000 for a multistation machine), or free weights (dumbbells or barbells, $10 to $100).	Don't overdo it! If you use barbells, always have a friend spot you. Take at least two days to recover between weight-training sessions.	250.
Clubs ($250 to $2,000 for a full set of woods and irons).	Stretch your shoulders and upper body before you play, to improve your swing and prevent injury.	130.
A racket (for tennis, $100 to $300; for racquetball, $65 to $100); and shoes ($50 to $100).	Wear shoes with good lateral support to prevent foot and ankle injuries.	370 (strenuous effort); 210 (moderate effort).
A smoothly operating bike ergometer with calibrated, variable resistance ($200 to $2,000).	The exercise bike is most effective when supplemented with other activities.	325 (strenuous effort); 225 (moderate effort).
A quality stair-climbing machine ($1,500 to $5,000).	Overstriding can strain your knees.	350.

Figure out your goals, and then try to stay on a consistent, balanced schedule. Planning where and when to work out is half the battle, especially when you're doing more than one sport. Use the variety to your advantage. Try to avoid doing any high-impact activity two days in a row.

If your legs get tired or sore, switch to an upper-body activity for a few days. If your arms are fatigued, do the reverse. Feeling bored or unmotivated? That's a sure sign you need a change: go to our "Mix-and-Match Menu" on page 136 and pick a new activity!

There are several general approaches to mix-and-match sports, one of which may apply to you:

Short Addition

This is for people who have a hard time getting in three 20-minute aerobic workouts a week (the minimum recommended dose of aerobic exercise). To reach this goal, simply add a day or two of a new aerobic activity to

Walkers can complement their lower-body workout with an activity that works the upper body. Golfing makes a good substitute—walking the course provides the same benefits without the boredom.

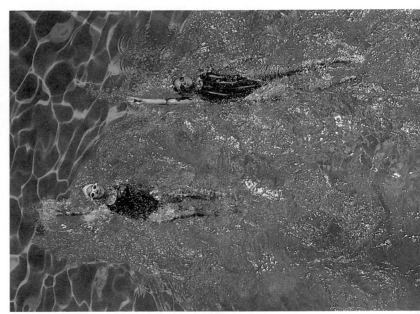

The right combination of activities will reinforce each other. By weight training or swimming laps, runners and walkers can improve upper-arm strength and raise their aerobic power, without damaging their joints.

what you're already doing, until you've got your three weekly sessions. Even if the activity is mild, the extra workout will still boost your overall health and fitness.

If you're looking for a way to improve in your primary sport, add a matched activity (preferably something low-impact) that works similar muscle groups. If you want to improve your overall fitness, add a sport that emphasizes different muscle groups, or a weekly strength-training session. Looking for mental refreshment? Consider adding a skill-oriented activity, yoga, or a stretching workout to your schedule.

Long Addition
Here's one for the seasonal athlete—the person who does a lot of aerobic dancing or tennis in the winter, for instance, but lounges on the beach all summer; or who turns into a couch potato as soon as the winter winds begin to blow. Find an additional sport or sports to do in your off-season, and then pencil them into your calendar accordingly.

Substitution
If you've been faithfully doing the same sport, week in and week out, try this approach. Begin by taking one day a week and substituting a completely different aerobic activity for your usual pursuit, and then expand from there. After these respites from your routine, you should find yourself feeling fresher as a result, since cross-training tends to raise overall fitness without tiring one particular part of the body.

Multiplication
This is the advanced philosophy of cross-training. If you carefully choose the right combination of activities, they will begin to reinforce each other. By pedaling an exercise bike or working out on a stair-climbing machine, runners and walkers can raise their aerobic power while protecting their joints. Dry-land exercisers can increase their flexibility and upper-arm strength by swimming once a week. Swimmers can get stronger by lifting weights, while weight lifters can reduce body fat and improve their cardiovascular fitness by doing aerobic exercise. And on it goes—each sport multiplying the effects of the other, until you eventually find yourself in such great shape that you're ready to tackle anything. Now, about that Ironman competition. . . .

Housecalls

Jennifer Kennedy, M.S., is a health-fitness specialist experienced in fitness testing and counseling. She has a Master of Science in Health Fitness Management and has taught aerobic dance and health fitness.

Q *I've heard that walking can burn up as many calories as running. How can that be?*

A Since walking and running both burn calories, a given walk *can* burn calories equivalent to a run. The rate at which these exercises burn calories depends on their intensity and the person's level of fitness.

A heavier, less fit person will burn more calories in the effort of walking; those in better shape may not find it as easy to burn off significant calories through a moderate walk. The person in better shape exercises more efficiently, and may need more-vigorous exercise than walking to achieve the same results.

Maximum calories can be burned while walking by pumping hand-held weights with a bent arm swing.

The number of calories burned per mile may be similar in these two exercises, but the calories burned per minute is greater in running. To burn equivalent calories in a walk, the walk must last longer.

Q *Exercise causes me to perspire a great deal. I worry that I'm losing an excessive amount of salt through sweat. Should I take a salt pill before or after exercising?*

A No. Salt pills are rarely used these days. As a rule, Americans have more sodium in their diets than they need. Our salt comes from three places: natural sources in food, added salt in commercially processed foods, and salt that we use for seasoning. For most people under most conditions, a balanced diet provides sodium and other electrolytes and minerals in amounts more than adequate for rigorous exercise. Stores of these nutrients will replenish themselves by normal routes after exercise.

Salt pills might be called for under extreme conditions, but normally they will make water absorption by tissue more difficult. During and after heavy sweating, water replacement is the most important issue. Normal thirst and hunger for salt, both mediated by hormones, will readjust your balance of sodium and water. If you feel that you've lost a great deal of salt, eating lightly salted food may help.

Q *Is it true that women will bulk up if they participate in a strength-training program?*

A No. Women don't produce enough of the hormone testosterone to bulk up significantly. They can gain as much strength proportionally as men, but have much greater limits on increases in muscle-fiber size.

Women can still build muscle mass, but they will achieve a leaner and more toned look. Keep in mind that leading women bodybuilders are probably genetically predisposed to have large, highly defined muscle groups. Further, such female physiques are achieved only through extremely intense workouts.

Most strength-training programs are based on weight lifting of some type. With a sensible program along these lines, strength training, done properly, will help condition muscles in a way that contributes to general health and helps avoid orthopedic problems later in life.

Weight lifting takes a variety of forms: free weight, including aerobic classes using hand weights, and programs based on equipment from such companies as Cybex, Keiser, Universal, and Nautilus.

Many women avoid weight training for fear of becoming muscle-bound. But such "bulking up" requires many hours of very intense workouts each day.

Q *Many of my friends and younger family members don't exercise very much. How do you go about getting someone more physically active? Is enrollment in an organized sports program the answer for such a person?*

A Depending upon whom you are talking about, the answer can be as different as people are. The first—and by far most important—thing to find out is what the person's interests are. Very few people will stick with an exercise program that is not enjoyable to them. Some like to exercise with others; some don't. Some like to compete; some don't. Some like conventional "sports" activities; some prefer active "chores" around the home.

Today there are an infinite variety of organized programs and other outlets for physical activity. The key is to find something that works over the long term. The no-pain, no-gain concept does not always hold; gardening, for example, does well at burning calories and improving cardiovascular rates. In fact, extended periods of more moderate activity may actually be a more natural form of exercise.

Childhood fitness in this country is a significant problem. An alarming percentage of American children are either obese or carry some other cardiovascular-risk problem. Family activities, with parents setting a role, are the best way to break kids away from a life-style of passive pastimes.

Q *The city in which I live has poor air quality. Would it be healthier for me to stay home and not jog, or do the beneficial effects of exercise outweigh any harmful effects from air pollution?*

A This is a difficult question for which there is no simple answer. Long-term, controlled studies of the effects of running in metro areas have not been done. Clearly, there are risks associated with this practice. In a study done in New York City, blood carbon monoxide levels were higher in runners than in nonexercising individuals; indeed, the runners had carbon monoxide levels one would expect if these individuals smoked half a pack of cigarettes a day!

Carbon monoxide is dangerous because it inhibits the body's ability to oxygenate its tissue, and so can bring on shortness of breath, coughing, or worse. In addition, some components of air pollution, such as ozone and hydrocarbons, are known to be carcinogenic.

Conversely, though, these findings should not be an excuse for couch-potato would-be runners to continue their ways. Lack of exercise is a risk factor for cardiovascular disease and other conditions. When pitting pollutants against a sedentary life-style, the question of which is worse depends in part on the person and on his or her risk factors for such diseases.

Urban runners should avoid exercising during peak traffic hours, and should watch for air-quality alerts. As with many health questions, moderation may be the key here: don't exercise in smoggy areas every day. Cross-train by participating in other types of exercise activities.

Have a fitness question? Send it to Editor, Health and Medicine Annual, P.O. Box 90, Hawleyville, CT 06440-9990.

Psychology

See also:
Individual articles in the second half of this book, arranged in alphabetical order, for additional information.

Hope, learning, depression, stress, motivation, self-esteem, group psychology, drug abuse—these are just a few of the many facets of human behavior. As professionals better understand the biological, social, and other variables that determine behavior, they give us the tools needed to lead happier, healthier lives. The value of a positive mental attitude was emphasized by a study conducted by psychologists at the University of Kansas. They found that students with high hopes of success set higher goals for themselves. Indeed, a freshman's level of hope appears to be a more accurate predictor of college grades than his or her SAT scores or high-school grades. Other researchers report that people with high hopes have less depression, are more optimistic and more flexible, and can cope better with setbacks.

New studies showed for the first time that stress can increase a person's chances of contracting an infectious disease. Researchers reported that high levels of stress can lower a person's resistance to five different respiratory viruses, nearly doubling the risk of catching a cold.

Psychiatrists at the University of Minnesota found that people suffering from severe depression often show signs of anxiety, such as periodic panic attacks. Furthermore, severely anxious depressed people responded to treatment much more slowly than did other depressed people.

Sadly, attitudes toward people suffering from mental illnesses have not kept pace with scientific findings. A poll of 1,022 American adults found that 43 percent considered depression "a sign of personal or emotional weakness" rather than a health problem. The importance of the biological aspects of psychology was reinforced in 1991, when it was reported that researchers had found the gene that causes fragile-X syndrome, a cause of mental retardation. Other researchers have reported a genetic aspect of alcoholism. Alcoholics who have a dopamine-receptor gene may suffer more severe symptoms of alcoholism than do alcoholics who lack the gene.

Neurobiologist Simon LeVay at the Salk Institute reported finding distinct structural differences in the brains of homosexual and heterosexual men. In homosexual men a region of the hypothalamus, a structure in the forebrain that develops at a very young age, averages less than half the size of the same region in heterosexual men. LeVay's discovery lent support to the possibility that biological factors underlie sexual orientation. Additional support came from a study of twin brothers of homosexual men. The scientists who conducted this study found that 52 percent of the identical twin brothers were homosexual, as compared to 22 percent of nonidentical twins.

More and more parents put their infants in day-care programs. New studies suggest that infants placed in high-quality programs do very well when they enter elementary school. They are more likely to be assertive, display well-being, and participate in programs for the gifted.

Studies suggest that the failure of American students to do as well on math-achievement tests as their counterparts in Japan and Taiwan may be due at least in part to parental behavior. Psychologists at the University of Michigan found that parents of elementary-school students in the U.S. generally provide less help to their children, have lower achievement standards, and evaluate their children's math skills less critically than do Asian parents.

Undesirable behaviors create serious problems in our society. Homicide records continue to be set in U.S. cities, including Washington, D.C., which has the nation's highest per-capita murder rate. And the drug problem continues unabated. "Doing drugs" means doing damage, whether those drugs are tobacco, alcohol, or illicit substances such as cocaine. Government officials announced at the end of 1991 that cocaine and heroin use were again increasing. LSD (lysergic acid diethylamide), a drug popular in the 1960s, also appears to be making a comeback; according to a University of Michigan survey, 5.4 percent of the nation's high-school seniors said they used LSD.

A study led by Mark Zimmerman of the Medical College of Philadelphia found that cigarette smokers experience more severe depression, anxiety disorders, personality disorders, and substance abuse than do nonsmokers. This may indicate a biological predisposition to both smoking and psychiatric problems. It may also result from a tendency for people with certain problems to engage in behaviors, including smoking, that are condemned by society.

A positive mental attitude makes coping with setbacks and adversity easier.

143

THE MALADY OF THE MALADROIT

by Lee Galway

D ee Lentchner thought she was doing something terrible. Whenever her first-grade teacher saw her writing with her left hand, she'd smack Dee's fingers with a ruler. Ashamed, Dee would switch her pencil to her right hand and arduously continue her work. Then she'd forget and unconsciously switch the pencil back to the hand in which it felt more natural, inviting yet another crack of the ruler.

Around the same time—the early 1950s—that Dee was suffering through grade school in a small town in Indiana, John Heymann was experiencing only minor difficulties at his school near Milwaukee. His teacher allowed him to write with his left hand, but didn't particularly like the way John hooked that hand around the top of the paper when he wrote. On one occasion the teacher tried to hold John's hand down in the "correct" position during handwriting practice. She soon gave it up as a lost cause.

Left-handed children in the United States faced even worse "cures" 100 years ago. Having the left hand tied to the back of a chair was not uncommon, nor were beatings. Some parents even resorted to scalding the offending hand.

No one really knows how far back this maltreatment of the maladroit goes. By the way, *maladroit,* or "bad at the right," is one of two French words for left-handed; the other is *gauche.* From the Latin word for left-handed, we get *sinister.* In fact, in virtually every language, the word for left-handed has negative connotations. Moreover, a left-handed compliment implies a rebuke of some sort, a left-handed oath reeks of insincerity, and a left-handed marriage is no proper marriage at all.

Most female apes hold their baby on the left side of their body, regardless of whether they are left- or right-handed. This suggests that the brains of apes are similar to humans', with the left and right side carrying out specialized functions.

Linguistic snubbery aside, left-handedness has been disparaged in the verses of the Bible and the Koran, as well as in Egyptian hieroglyphics. Early Christian art nearly always depicted God as right-handed and Satan as left-handed. In medieval times, left-handedness was seen as a sign of witchcraft. In Moslem societies throughout history, the right hand has been reserved for greeting and eating, and the left has been relegated to unclean tasks.

But, for all this concerted and long-standing prejudice, left-handers abound. Estimates vary, but most experts agree that about 10 percent of the population the world over are natural left-handers, slightly more of them male. Surveys in the United States around the turn of the century estimated the left-handed population at 2 percent, this smaller number attributed to the fact that most left-handers back then were forced to be right-handers.

In fact, indirect evidence suggests that the percentage of left-handers has not changed much since the days of the Cro-Magnons some 30,000 years ago. Cro-Magnon artists traced outlines of their hands on cave walls, and almost 20 percent of these outlines are of their right hands, which, of course, had to have been painted with their left hands.

Brain Laterality

Generally, although there are exceptions, motor skills are controlled by the side of the brain opposite from a person's dominant side. Neurologists use the term "laterality" when speaking of the phenomenon, because a left-handed person is also often left-eyed, left-eared, and left-footed.

What causes laterality is unknown, but a number of theories have been proposed. Laterality may have genetic origins involving one or more gene markers. Another theory posits that birth trauma inhibits the growth of the usual hemisphere used for motor control. Yet another theory suggests that an abundance of steroids in an infant's system will lead to left-handedness.

Scientists once believed that animals other than humans do not use a preferred hand (or paw); rather, they will use either for a task, depending upon the situation. More-recent experiments suggest, however, that this may not be the case. Monkeys presented with an immobile object may pick it up with either hand, but when trying to grab at food floating in water, most of them will use their left hand. And the majority of female chimpanzees and gorillas cradle their babies against the left side of their bodies, regardless of whether they are left- or right-handed. This behavior suggests that the brains of the great apes are organized in a similar way to those of humans, with the left and right side carrying out specialized jobs. Evolutionarily speaking, the question might have to be reframed from "When did dominant laterality emerge?" to "When did our ancestors switch hand preference from the left to the right?"

Port-Paw Ramifications

Suzan Ireland, managing editor of *Lefthanders Magazine,* a Topeka, Kansas-based bimonthly with a circulation of 30,000, talks about left-handedness being a "marker" that may someday lead doctors to look for medical problems in an individual. Some studies have shown that left-handers have a higher-than-average incidence of diabetes, dyslexia, schizophrenia, allergies, autoimmune disorders, and neurological disorders. They also seem to suffer a higher amount of birth trauma and a slower maturation rate. However, not all of these findings are universally accepted.

More controversial are three studies carried out by Stanley Coren of the University of British Columbia and Diane Halpern of California State University that indicate left-handers are more accident-prone or have a higher mortality rate than right-handers.

Using statistics from *The Baseball Encyclopedia,* Halpern and Coren analyzed the mortality rates of 1,472 right-handers and 236 left-handers. They found that southpaws lived an average of 63.97 years, while their right-handed counterparts lived 64.64 years, a difference of about eight months.

Celebrity Southpaws

"Left-handers are overrepresented at both ends of the spectrum," says Suzan Ireland of *Lefthanders Magazine.* "Many mathematical geniuses are left-handed, but so are many of the severely mentally retarded." Some of our most celebrated artists, politicians, great thinkers, and entertainers have been left-handed. Here are just a handful (no pun intended):

Artists: Johann Sebastian Bach, Leonardo da Vinci, Michelangelo, Raphael, Pablo Picasso, Paul Klee

World Leaders: Alexander the Great, Julius Caesar, Charlemagne, Napoleon, Queen Victoria, Ronald Reagan, George Bush

Thinkers and tinkerers: Benjamin Franklin, Thomas Edison, Albert Einstein

Entertainers: Charlie Chaplin, W. C. Fields, Harpo Marx, Marilyn Monroe, Jimi Hendrix, Paul McCartney

Sports figures: Babe Ruth, Lou Gehrig, Reggie Jackson, Sandy Koufax, Pelé, Jimmy Connors, John McEnroe, Martina Navratilova

Criminals: Jack the Ripper, Billy the Kid, the Boston Strangler

In the past, many a child faced punishment if caught writing with the left hand. Today, however, lefties are free to enjoy their distinctiveness.

They published their results in a letter in the May 1988 issue of the prestigious British science journal *Nature*. Baseball fanatics and scientists on both sides of the Atlantic vehemently responded to the study. In subsequent letters, a fan from Vienna, Austria, and a professor from Cambridge University in Great Britain both pointed out that the statistics would have to be adjusted because many of the older right-handers (the survey included ballplayers whose careers dated back to the 1890s) could have been left-handers who were forced to convert to right-handers.

Then Elizabeth Wood of Pasadena, California, weighed in with her analysis. She used a more recent edition of *The Baseball Encyclopedia,* a much larger sample, and a different method of statistical analysis to come up with an average life span of 66.7 years for lefties and 66.8 for righties, a minuscule advantage. Hers was not the last letter in *Nature* on the subject, either, proving that in academics, as in baseball, the game ain't over till it's over.

Coren and Halpern dropped a bigger bombshell in 1989 in *The American Journal of Public Health.* Based on 987 deaths in two California counties, they came to the conclusion that, on average, right-handers lived nine years longer than left-handers—75 years compared to 66 years.

Loren Harris, professor of psychology at Michigan State University and author of some 70 journal articles on left-handedness, finds much to criticize in this latter study. First, he points out that nine years is such a large difference that the data begs to be scrutinized more carefully.

One problem Harris and other critics see with the study has to do with methodology, or how the study was done. Coren and Halpern gathered information from obituary columns on almost 3,000 deaths. They then sent postcard questionnaires to the next of kin of the deceased (except for the survivors of murder and suicide victims, who were eliminated from the study). They asked questions about which hand the deceased had written with, drawn with, or thrown a ball with. The results of their survey were derived from a 34 percent response rate to the cards.

Being a southpaw has hardly inhibited Atlanta Braves' pitcher Steve Avery, the most valuable player of the 1991 National League play-offs.

Harris wonders about the 66 percent who did not respond. Is there a reason why a left-hander's next of kin would be less likely to cooperate? He is also concerned about how well the next of kin remembered details about the deceased. Then there is the problem of anomalies. Perhaps, in this particular sampling, a greater-than-average number of left-handers who died very young was included. And what about left-handers who died in automobile accidents? No distinction was made between drivers and passengers in such deaths. Then there are those natural left-handers who were trained to be right-handers.

In short, Harris says of the study, "I'd want to make darned sure that I'd eliminated as many of these variables as possible."

A third study by Coren questioned 1,696 college students to find out the percentage of left-handers and right-handers who had had injury-causing accidents in the previous few years. The study showed that left-handers are about 15 percent more accident-prone than right-handers.

Harris likes the methodology of this study better, but says that, as yet, no one has replicated it. He thinks that much more research is needed to prove that lefties have a higher mortality rate or are more accident-prone than righties.

Editor Ireland makes another valid point: "If left-handed people have a higher mortality rate, why haven't life insurance companies raised their life insurance rates?"

The study of accident-proneness appeals to common sense. The safety cutoff switch on heavy machinery is most often located on the right side. Lefties have to reach across cutting blades or grinding gears to turn off such a machine. Automobiles and road systems are set up to be easiest for right-handers to use, so one might assume that lefties would be in car accidents more often. Ireland might argue that no one has proven that right-handed drivers have more accidents on England's left-leaning roadways.

Makers of scissors, calculators, and other products have finally recognized that left-handers comprise a significant share of the buying public.

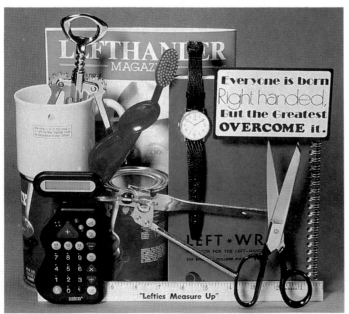

Many other differences exist for the left-hander in a right-handed world, as can be attested by John Heymann and Dee Lentchner, who have outgrown their early handwriting challenges to take on the bigger world.

Heymann is a photojournalist in the Boston area. He uses his right hand to operate his camera and, in fact, has learned how to do many things with that hand.

"I find that if I learn how to do something with my right hand, I can't learn how to do it with my left hand," Heymann says. (His experience is not unusual—many left-handers use their right hand exclusively and quite well for specific tasks.)

"Once in a while," Heymann says, "I'll find that a simple task is more challenging than it should be. Then I realize that it's difficult because I'm left-handed."

Heymann likes these surprises, though. "People find my being left-handed to be unusual. I always felt it made me more distinctive, more unusual. I enjoy being a lefty."

Heymann regrets only that he never got to play shortstop or second base, positions in baseball never assigned to lefties. But it helps him in pickup games of basketball. "The other players never expect me to be as good as I am shooting with my left hand."

Lentchner, who runs an engraving business at a mall near Philadelphia, used to have a shop that sold only left-handed items—left-handed clocks and wristwatches, left-handed oven mitts, pens with nonsmearing ink, novelty T-shirts, and the like.

A favorite item for her was a pencil with the adage "Great thoughts from a left-handed genius" printed upside down on it—that is, upside-down to a right-handed person. (Try this experiment: Take a pencil with a message on it, and hold it in your left hand as if you were going to write with it. You'll see that the print is upside down.)

One final note: Lentchner's mother eventually did find out about that teacher taking a ruler to her daughter, and she put a stop to it. This didn't get the little girl completely out of hot water, though. When the teacher asked the class to "line up on the right side of the room, you know, *the side you write with,*" the little girl did what any left-handed first grader would do. With predictable results.

SUICIDE IN CHANGING TIMES

by Marcy O'Koon

"Richard Cory, one calm summer night, went home and put a bullet through his head."

So ended the life of a man long the envy of his friends and neighbors. A man whose good looks and friendly manner made him popular with men and women alike. A man of wealth and good taste. A man who showed no sign of suicidal tendencies. A man whose self-inflicted death left his family and friends struggling to answer the universal postsuicide questions: "Why?" "How could we have prevented it?" "What can we do now?"

The circumstances surrounding Richard Cory's suicide are remarkably true to life, even though Richard Cory is a fictional character created by poet Edwin Arlington Robinson. Robinson penned his poem in 1896, the year before French sociologist Émile Durkheim published the first scholarly study of suicide. At that time, suicide was considered to be a tragedy, but one that could hardly be fathomed, much less prevented. Today, almost 100 years later, suicidology has developed into a full-fledged field of study, with prevention of suicide as its practical purpose.

Suicide Through the Ages

People were not always interested in preventing suicide. Various cultures throughout history have condoned suicide, even finding it praiseworthy in certain situations. In an-

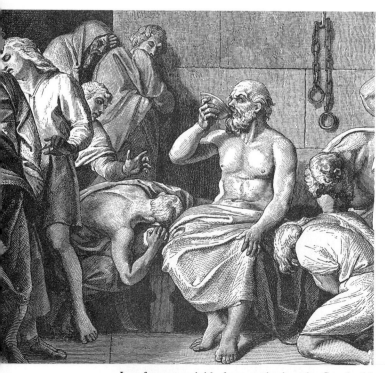

In a famous suicide from antiquity, the Greek philosopher Socrates took his own life by drinking hemlock after being unjustly sentenced to death.

cient Greece, convicted criminals were allowed to end their own lives. Early Christians glorified martyrs who committed suicide, sometimes elevating their status to sainthood. Japanese noblemen were required to kill themselves in a ritual death (called *seppuku*) by means of *hara-kiri* (suicide by abdominal stabbing), as a means to escape humiliation. The Brahmans of India expected a widow to undergo *suttee* and join her husband in death by throwing herself onto his funeral pyre.

The attitudes that encouraged self-destruction in these cultures have for the most part been reversed. The Romans changed their position and declared that suicide among slaves was forbidden, primarily because it deprived the owner of property. During the Middle Ages, church leaders shifted their opinion of suicide to one of disapproval, going so far as to deny Christian burial for those who they now said had sinned and would face eternal damnation. In 1868 compulsory *seppuku* was prohibited in Japan, even though the practice did not become extinct until after World War II. And the British colonial authorities outlawed *suttee* in India in 1828, although there are some pockets of the country where a widow is still expected to follow this tradition.

In the Western world, the changing attitudes toward suicide brought with them a harsher attitude toward those who attempted suicide as well as toward their families. A person who tried to kill himself was considered a criminal in Europe until 1789. Great Britain and the United States did not drop criminal charges against attempted suicide until recent decades. While most U.S. laws against suicide have been abolished, many states have added statutes forbidding anyone to assist a person in the act.

Legal punishments aside, society in general has attached a certain stigma to suicide. This adds a further burden to the troubled survivor of a suicide attempt as well as to the family.

Who Commits Suicide

Each year at least 30,000 people in the United States take their own lives—that's an astounding rate of one person every 17.3

Despair leads many people to contemplate or commit suicide. Often the suicide attempt represents a cry for help. In such cases, timely intervention can sometimes avert a tragedy.

minutes. The majority of suicides are committed by white men over 35 years old. Even though women attempt to kill themselves three times more often than men, men succeed four times more often than women. Minorities of both sexes account for relatively few suicides, about 10 percent of the total, although the suicide rates for specific racial and ethnic minorities are quite variable. For instance, certain native American tribes have the highest suicide rates for all racial and ethnic groups.

People over age 65 are at greatest risk of suicide. The current rate of 21 of every 100,000 older adults is more than 50 percent higher than the national rate of 12 per 100,000 Americans.

A common misperception, possibly due to media coverage, is that teenagers have the highest rate of suicide. Ironically, the intentional death rate among young people between the ages of 15 and 24 is 13 per 100,000 people. This rate is the lowest rate of any age group, with the exception of those 5 to 14 years of age.

These numbers, however, grossly understate the problem, according to John McIntosh, Ph.D., an Indiana University suicide expert. "There are some wild estimates claiming that there are 100 times as many suicides as are reported. That's impossible. But I'd say as much as 50 percent underre-

porting is a more plausible ballpark estimate."

Such underreporting may arise from variations in reporting guidelines among states. As a result, some suicides are not officially acknowledged. A coroner must identify the type of death on the death certificate as natural (illness or old age), homicide, accident, or suicide. But in certain cases it is unclear whether a death is an accident or intentional. The 1962 death of film star Marilyn Monroe is a famous case in point. Because no note or other definitive sign proved that she intended to kill herself, some people think that her barbiturate overdose was an accident, not an intentionally lethal act. One-person fatal car crashes or pedestrian-auto deaths can raise similar doubts. In the absence of a note or some other sign that the death was intentional, it is virtually impossible to know what really happened at the time of death.

Such accident-suicides are just one way in which self-inflicted deaths go unrecognized. Another falls under what is called the indirect suicide. On one level, these deaths seem clearly the result of natural causes or homicide. But a second look might reveal that a victim knowingly put him- or herself in a situation that would likely result in his or her own death. How should one classify the death of someone with emphysema who smoked several packs of cigarettes daily despite doc-

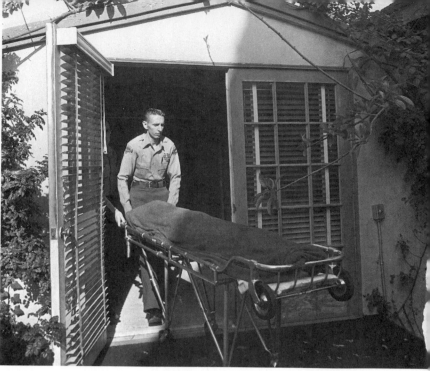

Suicide or accident? That's a puzzle that often confronts coroners after an untimely death. Mystery still surrounds the death of actress Marilyn Monroe (above left), who died in 1962 from a drug overdose.

tor's orders? What about the shooting death of a person who provoked a fight, knowing that his opponent was a gang leader who tolerated no threats? And what about Death Row inmates who try to expedite their executions? One infamous case of indirect suicide occurred in 1977, when convicted murderer Gary Mark Gilmore urged the state of Utah to carry out its death sentence. While the state delayed his execution, Gilmore made an attempt on his own life and failed. Eventually the state executed him by firing squad.

Beyond Surviving: Suggestions for Survivors

Hundreds of books have been written about loss and grief. Few have addressed the aftermath of suicide for survivors. Here again, there are no answers; only suggestions from those who have lived through and beyond the event.

1. Know you can survive. You may not think so, but you can.
2. Struggle with "why" it happened until you no longer need to know "why" or until you are satisfied with partial answers.
3. Know you may feel overwhelmed by the intensity of your feelings, but all your feelings are normal.
4. Be aware that you may feel appropriate anger at the person, at the world, at God, at yourself. It's okay to express your anger.
5. You may feel guilty for what you think you did or did not do. Guilt can turn into regret, through forgiveness.
6. Find a good listener with whom to share. Call someone if you need to talk.
7. Don't be afraid to cry.
8. Remember, the choice was not yours. No one is the sole influence in another's life.
9. Expect setbacks. If emotions return like a tidal wave, you may only be experiencing a remnant of grief, an unfinished piece.
10. Know that you will never be the same again, but you can survive and even go beyond just surviving.

by Iris M. Bolton

Adapted from *Suicide and Its Aftermath*, Edward J. Dunne, John L. McIntosh, Karen Dunne-Maxim, eds. (W.W. Norton and Company, New York, 1987).

Overall, though, it seems that the most common cause of underreporting is societal stigma. Many families hide pertinent evidence in order to avoid the repercussions of a suicide. And sometimes a sympathetic coroner will find the cause of death an accident if there is the least bit of doubt. While gathering data for a suicide study on another subject, McIntosh privately asked all the coroners he met if there had been suicides or probable suicides in their district that were not on the records as suicides. They all agreed that there were. "I'd suspected as much. That just confirmed my hunch," McIntosh says.

The Danger Years

In 1984, four New Jersey high-school students 16 to 19 years old sat inside a closed garage with an idling car engine in order to asphyxiate themselves. This tragedy drew the nation's attention to the phenomenon of teenage suicide. The deaths triggered concern among parents and educators about suicide pacts and copycat (or cluster) suicides among teenagers.

Suicide pacts—agreements by two or more people to kill themselves together—are actually quite rare, usually involving two lovers who feel life is hopeless without each other. A study of 68 pacts in a three-year period revealed that 77 percent occurred between spouses and between lovers.

Copycat suicides, or clusters, occur when two or more suicides happen in such quick succession that it seems a suicide victim's awareness of a previous suicide prompted him or her to take his or her own life. The second victim may have known the first suicide victim as a friend or an acquaintance. In one instance of copycat suicides in 1986, three students from the same Omaha, Nebraska, school—later called "Suicide High"—killed themselves within a five-day period.

Media coverage of a suicide or even a fictional version of a suicide in a television movie can have the same effect as when the victim is known firsthand. The apparent suicides of actress Marilyn Monroe and comedian Freddie Prinze touched off a rash of copycat suicides nationwide. While adults are definitely susceptible to the copycat syndrome, teenagers seem particularly vulnera-

The Right to Life, Liberty . . . and Suicide?

The suicide-prevention movement has its counterpart in the suicide-advocacy groups. These groups, such as the Hemlock Society, want the right to what they call "assisted suicide" for the terminally ill. In the early 1980s, Alain Moreau published a best-selling 276-page book in France titled *Suicide: Operating Instructions,* which boldly told readers how to commit suicide with fatal doses of poisons and pills. In 1991 a similar book, *Final Exit,* by Derek Humphry, the executive director of the Hemlock Society, shot up the best-seller list.

Assisted suicide has created a raging controversy in the medical community. Should physicians aid terminally ill patients who request their help in dying? One doctor, pathologist Jack Kevorkian, provided a solution to the problem. A woman who had been diagnosed with Alzheimer's disease and could not bear to live through the consequences asked Dr. Kevorkian to help her kill herself. He created a "suicide machine"

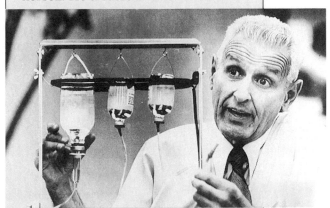

(above) that allowed the patient to flip a lever herself, allowing fatal potassium chloride into her bloodstream. A poll after her death found that 64 percent of Americans favor legal physician-assisted suicide.

A Heavy Rap for Heavy Metal

When a teenager kills himself, his parents inevitably search the universe for the answer to "Why?" Some parents decided that the answer was their children's taste for the heavy-metal music of Ozzy Osbourne (below) and Judas Priest. In separate lawsuits, most asking for millions of dollars in damages, these parents and their lawyers took the rockers to court.

The lawyers in the first case to reach the bench cited Osbourne's song "Suicide Solution" as the culprit. But the judge supported the defendant's claim to First Amendment rights of freedom of speech. Subsequent cases then charged that the rock songs contained "masked lyrics," or subliminal messages, hidden within the music, encouraging the teenagers to take their own lives.

Does the music really contain words that direct listeners to "shoot, shoot, shoot" or "do it, do it, do it," as the plaintiffs claimed? The judges decided there was no proof of masked lyrics and dismissed the suits.

ble to imitation, being so quick to pick up on the very latest dress, slang, or music fads.

The domino effect of copycat suicides may lead some school officials to conclude that a student suicide should be hushed up, so it won't give others ideas. Yet covering up is "the polar opposite of what they should be doing," says Alan Berman, Ph.D., director of the National Center for the Study and Prevention of Suicide at the Washington School of Psychiatry in Washington, D.C.

Suicide, whether it occurs in reaction to another one or not, happens when someone is headed down that tragic road anyway. "There's an imitation effect," explains Berman. "The second kid—who was already predisposed to be suicidal—essentially sees the first incident as covert permission to follow through. The idea has already occurred to him." Berman, author of the American Psychiatric Association's *Adolescent Suicide: Assessment and Prevention,* says parents and teachers need to go on heightened alert after any suicide for any telltale signs of a possible imitation suicide by other students.

Even though those under 25 account for the fewest suicides, that group's rate has seen an alarming increase in recent years. The rate for people between 15 and 24 years old has doubled—some experts say it has tripled—since the 1950s. A nationwide survey of teenagers found that 25 percent of adolescent boys and 42 percent of adolescent girls report having seriously considered suicide at one time in their lives. Even more alarming, 11 percent of the boys and 18 percent of the girls reported having actually attempted suicide.

Dozens of factors are blamed for this sharp rise. The teen years have always been a tough time of life, with perennial adolescent problems—low self-esteem, depression, inability to communicate, desire for instant gratification, difficulty in controlling impulses, and inadequate coping skills. But the past few decades have seen an increase in peer pressure to attain the "right" status and image. Drugs and alcohol are commonplace in the adolescent world. So, too, are divorce and remarriage among parents. The number of two-income households has limited the time parents have to spend with their teen.

In a notorious 1990 suicide, Charles Stuart jumped from a bridge after learning that he was wanted for the cover-up murder of his pregnant wife Carol (left). At right, Boston police retrieve his body.

In addition, genetic research increasingly implicates the makeup of a person's brain chemistry as a key in predicting suicidal tendencies.

Experts agree, however, that each case of suicide is unique, having at its root a number of causes. The above factors, and sometimes a specific triggering event such as a failed romance, make a person who is genetically prone to depression (and perhaps suicide) a higher risk for taking his or her own life.

Lessons Learned

Nearly 100 years after suicide became a subject of study, mental-health workers, crisis counselors, and schoolteachers and administrators continue striving to define the complex forces that lead a person to contemplate or commit suicide. Experts in the field have been able to identify major warning signs. Some of the more common ones are included in the following list:
• Mentioning feelings of hopelessness, helplessness, and worthlessness;
• Preoccupation with death;
• Talking, discussing at length, even joking, about suicide. The widely held belief that people who say they are going to kill themselves never do is a myth, experts insist;
• Sudden changes in mood or behavior that

last for an extended period of time, such as a shy person becoming outgoing or a normally friendly person becoming withdrawn;
• Loss of interest in people, activities, and things normally treasured;
• A sudden calm (indicating the decision to die has been made);
• Getting in touch one last time with special friends;
• Making a will, declaring burial wishes, generally getting affairs in order;
• Giving away prized possessions.

If you notice any of these signs in a family member or friend, do not hesitate to seek advice from a local mental-health professional. To find professional help or a suicide prevention center near you, contact the American Association of Suicidology at 2459 S. Ash Street, Denver, Colorado 80222 (or call them at 303-692-0985).

The sad fact remains, though, that even the most aggressive prevention techniques will not entirely eliminate suicide as a cause of death. Although therapy methods are often quite successful in resolving suicidal crises, in some cases all the love, attention, concern, and professional help in the world won't stop a person from seeking what he or she perceives to be the only answer: self-inflicted death.

ALTERNATIVES TO TRADITIONAL SCHOOLS

by Andrea Mallozzi

The future of our country is in the hands of our children. Unfortunately, the quality of their education is considered by most experts to be in deep decline. Our students lag behind those in other countries in math and science. Illiteracy is widespread. A recent study by the National Assessment of Educational Progress (NEP) even claimed that academic achievement for U.S. students has shown no significant improvement over the past 20 years.

Experts attribute educational decline to a variety of factors. The lack of cohesive fami-

lies places an emotional burden on children that hinders learning. Budget cuts have led to understaffed schools and overcrowded classrooms. Few educational systems cater to the learning styles and abilities of individual students. Overall, our educational system is in need of major reform.

In response to the sad state of education, alternatives to traditional public schools are becoming more popular. Some of these schools explore new philosophies that challenge traditional views of how children learn. Others emphasize traditional educational programs, but provide more individualized attention to the student. Hardly available on a grand scale as yet, alternative schools by their very existence strongly suggest that the United States is finally inching its way back to educational excellence.

Home Schooling

School begins at 8:00 A.M. for Nels and Seth Nelson, ages 13 and 11, of San Antonio, Texas. But the boys don't have to board a bus or walk far for their lessons—their school is in the living room of their own home.

"We usually work straight through to lunchtime," says their mother and teacher, Lynn Nelson. During that time the boys' lessons might include learning about the planet Mars, delving into a language exercise, such as spelling or grammar, discussing Native American history, or practicing multiplication problems. Some days feature a field trip to a local museum. After lunch the boys are free to read, work on projects or hobbies, and play.

This educational concept—called home school in modern parlance—is actually an old practice revived. Some of the nation's most illustrious citizens—George Washington, Thomas Jefferson, and Margaret Mead, to name a few—were taught at home. In recent years the idea has really caught on. Today over one-quarter of a million U.S. families educate their children at home, according to research conducted by the National Association for Legal Support of Alternative Schools.

Why Teach at Home? Reasons for schooling children at home vary among parents. Many are disenchanted by the poor academic standards and difficult social situations that characterize many public schools. Others want a more influential hand in what their children are learning. Still others see it as a wonderful opportunity to spend time with their children.

Lynn Nelson began teaching her children at home when the family moved to the Philippines several years ago. "American schools were virtually unavailable, so there was really no other choice," she explains. The family is now back in the U.S. and she continues to instruct the boys, primarily because

the whole family enjoys it. "I've asked my sons if they want to attend a traditional school, but so far, they'd rather stay here."

Surprisingly, almost anyone can teach at home—usually without formal training or credentials—though the laws in every state vary. Some states monitor the progress of home-schooled children by having them take standardized tests at regular intervals. Often students must keep weekly logs detailing what they have learned. Other states require the parent to be a certified teacher; still others insist that the parent follow rigorous, state-mandated teaching guidelines. In most cases, parents are free to structure the school day any way they like. Most spend at least four hours a day on lessons. Some parents even give their schools a name, and institute such traditions as pledging allegiance to the flag and issuing report cards.

The Home-School Advantage. Advocates claim that individualized attention and the ability to structure lessons according to a child's progress make home-school education superior to classes available in traditional schools. Cheryl Gorder, author of *Home Schools: An Alternative* (Blue Bird Publishing, Tempe, Arizona), and teacher to her

Children educated at home by their parents often develop a strong self-image and a marked resistance to peer pressure.

own kids, has collected statistics that show that children taught at home generally test a grade or two higher than their age level. It should also be noted that home-schooled students have been accepted to Harvard, Yale, and other prestigious universities.

Opponents of home schooling claim that teaching a child at home, away from regular interaction with peers, can't help but put a child at a disadvantage socially. Gorder feels, however, that schools can actually hinder a child's social abilities. For starters, conventional classrooms, out of necessity, separate children by age. Home-schooled children, she points out, are able to socialize with people of all ages. Perhaps more important, the home-schooled student, away from the pressure of his or her peers, often develops a much stronger self-image and learns to make decisions free from peer influence.

To foster a well-rounded environment, many parents involve their children in community activities, such as the Scouts, or have them take music and other lessons outside the home. In some communities, local school systems even permit home-educated students to participate in their sports programs and other extracurricular activities.

Despite the positive aspects of being schooled at home, both Gorder and Nelson concede that the method is not for everyone. "It's a big responsibility, and requires a strong commitment and good communication from both the parents and the children," says Gorder.

For parents interested in educating their children at home, help is available. "I advise anyone starting out to get help and ideas by joining a support group," says Gorder. Lynn Nelson relies on a correspondence course. These programs, sent through the mail, provide parents with work materials, exercises, and teaching manuals that help structure the school day. The *Home Education Resource Guide* (Blue Bird Publishing, Tempe, Arizona) lists a number of national and local organizations that assist in all areas of home schooling—from legal aspects to purchasing educational materials and locating support groups in your area.

Montessori Method

Back in the late 19th century, Maria Montessori, an Italian physician, theorized that children experience "periods of sensitivity"— different developmental stages corresponding to certain ages. In each of these stages, Montessori noticed that a child's interests and mental capacity are particularly ripe for learning specific skills, such as language. To

Self-motivation is the cornerstone of the Montessori schools. Students are able to enjoy an enormous amount of freedom in deciding what they work on and when. Much of the learning takes place in small groups.

test her theories, Montessori established a school (preschool through sixth grade) that nurtures these stages and encourages self-motivation and independence.

Montessori's vision was beyond the conventional classroom style, in which "children, like butterflies mounted on pins, are fastened each to his place." Consequently, Montessori classrooms do not have desks lined in straight rows facing a blackboard. Instead, learning materials are placed in various corners of the room, and children work at small, child-sized tables or on floor mats. Group learning is encouraged, and the younger children often go to the older ones for help before asking the teacher. Students at all grade levels choose what they want to work on and when. The teacher acts primarily as a guide to steer students toward specific learning activities, and then allows each to learn in his or her own unique style. Self-motivated learning is the core of this method, which strives to develop a lively, questioning intellect in a child, while promoting self-discipline and self-confidence.

Classes are arranged with mixed-age groups (ages 3 to 6, 6 to 9, and 9 to 12); children have the same teacher for three years. This mixed-age grouping follows the developmental stages that Montessori believed children experience. For example, she noted that three- to six-year-olds have an absorbent mind and take in their environment with ease. They are very tactile and have good aptitude for movement, order, and handling small objects. In the Montessori method, children in this age group are offered a variety of hand-held materials and exercises that nourish these aspects of a child's personality.

Montessori schools rarely use tests or give homework. And while the schools do not issue report cards, "children learn to be accountable for their work," says Virginia McHugh, executive director of the Association Montessori International—U.S.A., in Rochester, N.Y. "Students meet with their teacher each week to discuss their progress."

Parents of children in Montessori schools seem very happy with the teaching method. Both daughters of Ralph Horton, an attorney in Irondequoit, N.Y., attended Montessori school from preschool through sixth grade. He and his wife chose this type of education because "we wanted independent children, children who know the joy of learning."

Parental belief in and commitment to the Montessori philosophy is paramount to the educational process, stresses McHugh. The Montessori approach encourages independence and responsibility, and many of the methods need to be continued at home, an often time-consuming endeavor. After a long day, many parents find it difficult to continue to educate their children. "Montessori is not for every family," admits McHugh.

Since the Montessori experience usually ends by the sixth grade (some schools do go on to eighth grade), its graduates must necessarily transfer into a more traditional educational setting. According to Horton, his girls, now in public school, were at the same educational level as their public-school classmates, but have much better study habits. Though he does admit the girls needed to adjust to such practices as homework, tests, and multiple teachers, he says the self-confidence they learned in Montessori helped ease the transition to conventional schooling.

Parochial Schools

About 80 percent of students outside the public-school system attend parochial schools—schools run by various religious groups. Of these students, fully half attend schools affiliated with the Roman Catholic Church. Catholic schools are renowned for their rigorous academics and strict discipline. At an ever-increasing rate, Catholic-school students outperform their public-school peers in reading, mathematics, and science. Catholic schools have a lower dropout rate than either public or private schools, and a large number of students (83 percent) go on to college.

Catholic and other parochial schools often lack the facilities to handle learning-disabled students. Like other private schools, paro-

Privately and publicly, the U.S. is inching its way toward educational excellence.

A New "Key" to Learning

The Key School, a small public elementary school in Indianapolis, Indiana, has become the focus of national attention by educators and parents due to its innovative approach to schooling. At this school, physical education, music, art, science, history, and citizenship classes are given as much emphasis as the traditional three Rs—reading, writing, and arithmetic.

The school, founded in 1987, is patterned on the philosophy of Harvard education professor Howard Gardner. In his theory of multiple intelligences, Gardner proposes that intelligence extends beyond language and logical-thinking skills, the areas tested in traditional IQ (intelligence quotient) tests. He believes that intelligence is reflected in seven areas, called intelligences:
- Linguistic: sensitivity to word meaning and order;
- Logical-mathematical: ability to reason and recognize patterns and order;
- Musical: sensitivity to pitch, melody, and rhythm;
- Bodily-kinesthetic: ability to use the body skillfully;
- Spatial: perceptivity to the visual world and ability to re-create aspects of that world, as in artwork;
- Interpersonal: understanding people and developing relationships;
- Intrapersonal: developing a self-understanding.

Gardner believes that not everyone is born with strengths in each of these areas, but everyone is capable of developing greater proficiency in all areas.

The Key School provides a unique environment that promotes learning in these seven areas, no matter what the class. For instance, to emphasize spatial learning, a history lesson may be conducted solely with the use of photographs and geography rather than just using a textbook. A Spanish lesson may teach a Spanish song, to enhance musical ability as well as linguistics. Each child also chooses a "pod" —a class in his or her special interest (such as space exploration), which he or she takes for a year.

"Our system allows a child to excel in his or her area of strength," says The Key School's Yvonne Donatto. The benefits of this arrangement are many. For example, children usually excel in at least one subject area, such as physical education. Since The Key School curriculum places equal emphasis on all intelligences, children are able to develop confidence in themselves in this area. This confidence is carried over into other subject areas, such as science. As a result the students are less fearful of making mistakes or failing. School becomes a friendly, exciting, and rewarding environment that children don't readily want to miss.

Some critics contend that a person deficient in bodily-kinesthetics or in musical skills will not be impaired in the way a person lacking in verbal or reasoning skills will be. Naysayers think that perhaps equal emphasis on all intelligences may be unnecessary. But for the most part, response to The Key School has been overwhelmingly positive. Parents and children are pleased with the school's methods, and educators will continue to look at this school as an example of what could be in store for education in the 21st century.

Private (above) and parochial schools owe their success to their rigorous academic programs and to the expectations they place upon their students.

chial schools have selective admission policies, and can therefore weed out the chronic troublemakers that plague the public-school systems, or can expel a student for serious misbehavior. In Catholic schools the majority of the students adhere to Catholicism, although children of other religious affiliations can, and frequently do, attend, especially in urban areas. Many of the schools have a great ethnic diversity and high minority enrollment.

The Parochial-School Difference. What makes this type of school so special? According to Barbara Keebler of the National Catholic Educational Association in Washington, D.C., Catholic schools place high expectations on their students. "We believe that everyone has potential," she says. Many psychologists believe that this philosophy breeds success. "If you approach students with the idea that they are capable of more than they think—within reason—they'll often perform well," says Jane Zimmerman, Ph.D., a New York City psychologist.

Demanding academics also play a role. Whereas most public-high-school curricula are focused primarily on helping the students earn a diploma, Catholic high schools focus their learning programs on preparing students for the demands of jobs or college after graduation. Few electives are offered, and Latin and religious studies are frequently part of the students' agenda.

Catholic schools maintain strict discipline and foster respect for others. In most schools, all students wear uniforms to set a more serious tone. "Students are here to learn, not compete with each other about fashion," says Keebler.

Catholic-school administrators have more authority and less constraints than those in the public-school system, who have to work within the confines of state and federal regulations, unions, and voters. A principal of a parochial school has much more latitude to formulate a school's vision, and is instrumental in getting faculty, students, and parents involved in school programs.

Perhaps as a direct result of this involvement, Catholic schools provide a sense of community unparalleled in most public schools. Catholic-school administrators, parents, and students share similar values, along with a commitment to education. It's this sense of community, proponents claim, that makes these schools such a strong environment for learning.

Other Alternatives
Alternative-schooling possibilities go far beyond these three examples. Most states run technical high schools that combine training for a trade with conventional secondary-school studies. Private preparatory schools, their student bodies traditionally made up of the children of the wealthy, have in recent years opened their doors to the less affluent, largely through financial-aid packages and scholarships. Some large American cities operate specialized high schools for students gifted in the sciences or the arts. Competition for admission to these institutions, such as New York City's famed High School for the Performing Arts, is usually quite rigorous. Finally, a number of experimental schools—those whose teaching methods incorporate specific nontraditional educational theories—are flourishing in many communities across the country. Some of these schools, including The Key School in Indianapolis (see the sidebar on page 160), have met with great success.

MENTAL GYMNASTICS

by Gina Kolata

At age 55, Ronald L. Graham, a leading mathematician and an administrator at AT&T Bell Laboratories in Murray Hill, New Jersey, is taking up Japanese and golf. He juggles, does handstands, and works out on a trampoline in his backyard. He has learned to speak Chinese, throw a boomerang, play the piano, and beat most comers at table tennis.

When you ask Graham what possesses him to master one skill after another, he says he wants to keep his brain active and capable of finding solutions to thorny mathematical problems. His belief is that the more he uses his brain, the better it will perform, and the more he develops diverse mental skills, the more likely it is that he will have a flash of intuition that links seemingly disparate findings. Learning Chinese, he says, "stretches your brain in dramatically different directions." Even his latest juggling challenge—simultaneously juggling four or five balls at three different heights—"is really amazingly tough mentally," he says. It makes him concentrate every second, which is the sort of mental stimulation he is after.

It's the use-it-or-lose-it idea carried into the sphere of the mind—a principle whose proponents include an increasing number of neuroscientists and psychiatrists. Not that these researchers recommend that everyone become a Ron Graham. But evidence is growing that a mind challenged by reading or an engrossing hobby or paid or volunteer work is a mind likely to remain vigorous and able to learn and create. Not all researchers are convinced by the data, yet even the skeptics admit that people of all ages who continue to use their brains tend to be happier.

Although the brain does change with age, scientists are not sure what bearing this has on the ability to think and reason. Dr. Gene Cohen, acting director of the National Institute on Aging (NIA), a federal research organization in Bethesda, Maryland, says it is no longer a foregone conclusion that old people will suffer mental deterioration. "Many of the changes that were said to be related to aging," says the 47-year-old psychiatrist, "are now thought to be due to illness." A decrease in mental acuity, for example, has often been considered an inevitable part of the aging process, partly because average test scores of older people are pulled down by the low scores of those who have diseases like Alzheimer's or whose alertness has been affected by medication.

As many as 20 percent of the elderly lose none of their mental faculties as they age. Until recently, however, researchers did not ask whether that was because the 20 percent were healthy or because they continually challenged themselves. That is why a study published last year by Dr. John Stirling Meyer, a 67-year-old neurologist at Baylor College of Medicine in Houston, and his colleagues was unusual in the annals of aging research. It followed a group of *healthy* older

The more the brain is used, the better it performs.

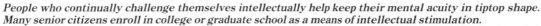

People who continually challenge themselves intellectually help keep their mental acuity in tiptop shape. Many senior citizens enroll in college or graduate school as a means of intellectual stimulation.

The natural vivaciousness of a child can be a stimulating experience for an older person accustomed to a subdued environment.

people for four years, and tried to determine if the members of the group who allowed themselves to stagnate experienced any decline in their mental abilities compared to those who remained active.

The 94 people in the study were about 65 years old and employed when Dr. Meyer and his colleagues began following them. A third of them continued to hold a job. Another third retired but remained mentally and physically active. They walked or bicycled regularly, for example, or were avid gardeners. Some of them did volunteer work. The rest of the participants were inactive after they retired. Basically, they sat around their houses and did nothing.

At the beginning of the study, the researchers gave the participants standard neurological and psychological tests and measured the blood flow to their brains. At this point in the experiment, all the subjects were determined to be at normal levels for their age. Four years later, however, the same battery of tests indicated that the inactive people had less blood flowing to their brains and did significantly worse on I.Q. tests than did the subjects in the other two groups.

"I would definitely say this is cause and effect," Dr. Meyer says. "The study was un-

Cerebral Workout

The following exercises from "Brain Fitness" by Monique Le Poncin are part of a program developed from her work at the French National Institute for Research on the Prevention of Cerebral Aging. They are not easy. According to the book, "brain exercises can condition your mind to an optimum level of fitness, no matter what your age."

Perceptive Ability

Observe this figure for 10 seconds; then try to determine in less than 20 seconds how many squares, rectangles and triangles it contains.

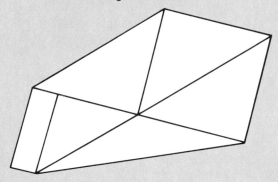

One square, one rectangle, seven triangles.

Logical Thinking

The clock faces in each of the three rows are arranged in a logical sequence. Try to find the sequence in each row, and draw the missing hands on the three blank faces, in less than 15 seconds.

The first blank face should show 5:00 (four and a half hours added each time); the second one, 4:30 (45 minutes subtracted each time); the third one, 7:40 (50 minutes added each time).

Le Brain Jogging

What do a ship and a broom have in common? What synonyms are there for *poet*? And what antonyms for *reality*? How many heads of government do you know? There are no right or wrong answers, for the questions are designed solely to prod the mind, and they are plucked from the repertoire of a new French interest nicknamed "le brain jogging."

France has long had a special infatuation with the intellect, so it seems fitting that the French are quickly taking to new programs that exercise the brain and stimulate imagination and memory. The techniques may vary, but they are all anchored in the growing conviction that the more you oblige the brain to work as you age, the better your chances of staying alert and keeping or even creating an efficient memory. The different brain-jogging options, developed in the past three years, are all ways of stretching and otherwise provoking and stimulating the minds of the elderly and the middle-aged who want to stay in peak form. French gerontologists say that people are particularly bothered by what they see as one main result of aging: a failing memory. But specialists say that memory gaps appear to be a result of anxiety, depression, or just slackening off as people retire.

Le brain jogging takes place in private clubs and clinics. Companies invite specialists to give in-house seminars. Some homes and hospitals for the aged also offer training sessions. By far the largest network of courses has been organized by a pension fund, the Mutualité Sociale Agricole, which in two years' time has trained counselors and started workshops in more than 120 towns and villages. Each of its courses consists of 15 weekly sessions, usually lasting two hours. The program is called Eureka.

At a typical Eureka session, some 20 to 25 "joggers" between 55 and 70 years of age sit around a large table and start off with a quick review of the week's news.

"This is to stimulate curiosity and communication with others," says Jocelyn de Rotrou, a psychologist who designed the Eureka program. Then she projects unrelated images on a screen —a suitcase and a belt, a comb next to a fork. She asks people to remember the pairs. When few can, she asks them to establish a connection between the objects through a phrase, or through size, use, or material. "We cannot remember, if we associate badly or not at all," she says.

But "memory is only the tip of the iceberg," de Rotrou adds. "The exercises involve all the mental faculties: perception, concentration, reasoning, speech, imagination." For example, the group searches for synonyms and antonyms, and classifies words to stimulate verbal fluency. "People complain that they lose their vocabulary as they age," de Rotrou says. "But they may really be hampered by not using it because they isolate themselves."

The problems are less or more challenging depending on the educational level of the group. Participants may be asked to copy a geometric design they have seen only briefly, and then to draw it in reverse. The purpose of the exercise is to learn to memorize and visualize spaces, which, de Rotrou says, is something that intimidates many people, especially women.

"Ever since antiquity, people have done exercises to improve their memory," she says, "but today we understand much more about the functioning of the brain." One of the program's primary objectives is to teach people how memory works, so that they can use it more effectively.

Experience has taught her, de Rotrou says, that in older people who have no se-

rious physical ailments, memory lapses frequently are not so much a consequence of age as they are the result of being less active, less motivated. "People often register poorly; they do not focus or concentrate. But some training can restore those abilities." For example, participants are taught to photograph mentally the context of an object so they can more easily recall where it is.

Françoise Forette, director of the Fondation Nationale de Gérontologie, says that 60 percent of people in France over 60 years of age complain about their memory. But she says that mental stimulation, with an emphasis on memory training, has shown positive results. "We have found," she adds, "that older people gain on other terrain: in reasoning, in judgment, in analysis."

At the Hôpital Broca in Paris, Dr. Forette has started a program for people with serious nervous and memory disorders. During a recent session, the questions and points of discussion for the group—seven patients between 70 and 90 years old—were simple: What images were shown just a moment ago? What are the names of the people around the table? The participants seemed to become livelier and more involved as the hour went by. The purpose of the sessions, a specialist explained, was not to restore badly hampered memories, but to stop them from quickly getting worse.

Three years ago, two physicians and two psychologists in Lyons formed a group called Agora, which takes its name from the ancient Greek marketplace where people gathered to exchange ideas as well as wares. The group started out by running memory workshops for the retired, but soon found that companies were interested in "cerebral-fitness" training for employees. Agora now offers three- and five-day intensive courses to employee groups. These include memory workshops and counseling sessions on ways of dealing with stress, which, the Agora doctors believe, can affect brain efficiency. Invariably, counselors recommend homework, which may include going shopping without a list or memorizing a train schedule. They exhort the elderly to play bridge, chess, and other games.

Participants in one Eureka group cite a benefit that may be as important to the life of the mind as the training itself. Belonging to the group, they say, has given them new confidence, new interests. Some say they have made friends; others say they are doing more reading. "It's not like a competition," says one woman. "Everyone in the group has something different to give. It is exhilarating."

Marlise Simons

like any other. We had controlled for them being healthy and well at the beginning, and they remained in good health," he says of the experiment's participants. The only parameter that varied during the study was the level of activity of the participants.

Other studies that differentiate between active and inactive healthy old people are now in progress, but the results may take years to confirm. In the meantime the idea that people can maintain their mental skills by continually using them remains controversial, grounded for the most part in animal experiments. Most of the research undertaken so far on humans does not indicate conclusively whether people lose some of their mental ability because they do not challenge their minds, or whether they do not challenge their minds because their minds have become dull as a result of aging.

But those who believe in the use-it-or-lose-it idea say they are acting on the hunch that what has proved true for animals will prove true for humans. Carl W. Cotman, a 51-year-old neurobiologist at the University of California at Irvine, cites a number of studies that have convinced him that the brain continues to function well only if it is used. In one study, rats that were stimulated by treadmills and other gadgets in their cages as well as by the company of other rats had 26 percent more connections between their brain cells than did rats raised alone in bare cages. The rats in the enriched environment had an average of 4,546 connections in a cubic thousandth of a millimeter of brain tissue, while those raised in the tedious and solitary environment of an empty cage had an average of 3,596 connections. The study also showed that the rats raised in the dull environment gained brain-cell connections when they were given greater stimulation, while the rats raised in the enriched environment suffered a loss of connections when the stimulation was taken away. This evidence of the value of stimulating the brain, says Cotman, "is very, very solid."

Cotman adds that scientists have learned from laboratory studies that nerve cells stay healthier if they are kept active and firing electrical impulses. The refinement and direction of connections between cells depend on stimulation, he says, and "activity influences how and where connections are made." When investigators blocked nerve receptors from responding to incoming impulses by treating them with toxins, the nerves never made appropriate connections to other nerves.

Scientists have also shown that if an injury destroys brain cells or lops off some of their branches, new branches grow to fill in the

The challenged mind remains vigorous and creative.

The demands of an acting role provide a great deal of mental stimulation. Since making her stage debut in 1929, actress Jessica Tandy (born 1909) has appeared in countless plays and films, and has won a best actress Tony Award (Foxfire, 1983) and Oscar (Driving Miss Daisy, 1989). Fried Green Tomatoes, a 1991 film in which she stars, is doing well at the box office.

Now 96 years old, entertainer George Burns began his show-business career at the turn of the century. His early days in vaudeville were followed by a starring role (with his wife, Gracie Allen) in a comedy radio program of the 1930s and 1940s, and a popular television show in the 1950s. He starred in several films of the 1970s, and remains to this day a nightclub entertainer and television guest star.

gaps. This same process may contribute to a stroke patient's recovery, and help compensate for brain-cell loss during normal aging. Even people with Alzheimer's disease, in which there is a constant death of brain cells, sprout new cell connections before the disease is too far advanced, Cotman says.

Mental stimulation need not depend on input from other people. Pursuits that are individually challenging can often serve the same function.

Remodeling Strategy

The brain uses a remodeling strategy, explains Zaven Khachaturian, associate director for the neuroscience and neuropsychology of aging at the NIA: "It keeps the nerve cells intact, but changes their components." As for the use-it-or-lose-it concept, the 54-year-old scientist says there is no "specific and direct human evidence," but he keeps different parts of his own mind stimulated by practicing a variety of skills.

While studying activity in the cat brain, Khachaturian discovered that when he gave the animal something to look at, not only its visual, but also its auditory, cortex was stimulated. The brain is not strictly compartmentalized, he says, which is one reason that there are not firm data indicating it is better for people to do several different activities than to work on just one task, like reading something challenging every day. Nonetheless, it is his best guess that by using different parts of the brain, people can coax nerve cells to make connections they might not have made otherwise. This, he says, can only be beneficial.

But Dr. Thomas Chase, a 59-year-old neurologist at the National Institute of Neurological Disorders and Strokes, says he is very skeptical of claims that suggest that using the brain makes it perform better. "It is not clear that this really occurs in human beings," he says. "I don't know of any evidence that humans sprout new connections except under conditions of injury, and I don't know of any evidence that physiological use confers any advantage." Dr. Chase cautions that "you can't always extrapolate from a rat to a man."

Herbert Weingartner, chief of the section on cognition at the National Institute on Aging, says it may not even be necessary to postulate on the basis of animal studies that the human brain makes more connections in response to stimulation. Researchers already know that when people are mentally engaged, there are biochemical changes occurring in the brain that allow it to function more efficiently in cognitive areas such as attention and memory. This is true in the elderly and middle-aged as well as in young people, says the 56-year-old Weingartner. People will be alert and receptive if they "are confronted with information that gets them to think about things because they're interested in them."

It makes sense. "An elderly alert individual," Weingartner continues, "will do a heck of a lot better than someone who is sleepy. And someone with a history of doing more rather than less will go into old age looking more cognitively intact than someone who has not had an activated mind."

Many experts are so convinced of the benefits of challenging the brain that they are putting the theory to work in their own everyday lives. The idea, says James Fozard, the associate scientific director of the National Institute on Aging, is *not* to learn to memorize long lists of items. Memory training may, in fact, be a worthless exercise in terms of challenging one's brain. "There are lots of books on how to improve your memory, but most of us don't need those kinds of skills, because we don't have to run between two Greek cities and get the message right," Fozard says. "That kind of specific training is of less interest than being able to maintain a mental alertness."

Cerebral calisthenics can take a number of forms. All the experts agree that any given brain workout should be fun. Fozard and others say they try to use different mental skills as they challenge their brains, both because they enjoy the activities they have chosen and because they are betting that the range of activities will enhance the way their brains work. Fozard, who is 61, plays the trombone in his spare time and leads a jazz band. Khachaturian tries to keep different parts of his mind stimulated by studying languages, playing mental games, woodworking, welding, and repairing machines. Cotman does landscape paintings as well as aerobics and calisthenics. He also builds rock walls. "When I do that," he says, "I definitely feel sharper."

Devise a Plan

Dr. Cohen of the National Institute on Aging suggests that people should use their minds in their old age by devising a plan that includes both mental and physical activities done alone, like reading, walking, or swimming, and those done in group situations, like dancing or playing bridge or tennis. He says that people are always being advised to keep physically active as they age, but that studies have shown that older people who keep mentally active are most likely to maintain their intellectual abilities and to be generally happier and better adjusted. "The point is, you need to do

> *Intellectual and physical activity influences brain-cell health and size.*

Regular exercise does much more than keep the body physically fit: it provides a mental stimulation that carries over into other activities.

both," he says. "Intellectual activity is a very important stimulus to the brain. It actually influences brain-cell health and size."

Even Dr. Chase, who questions the use-it-or-lose-it concept, says that "if this idea makes people work harder and use their brains more, that's all to the good." He encourages people to stay mentally active. "Most human beings function far below their capacity," he says. "Reasoning and judgment are well preserved into old age."

No one has to tell that to Ronald Graham, the mathematician. "The essence of learning is that you learn how to learn and continue learning," he says. "Once you stop learning, you start to die."

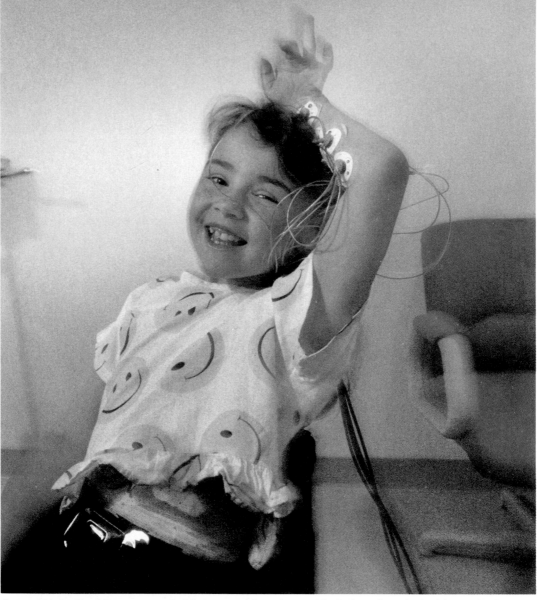

Some of biofeedback's most remarkable successes have been with victims of paralysis. After 20 biofeedback sessions, Cheryl Lietner (above) can move her fingers. Her hands had been paralyzed since birth.

BIOFEEDBACK: WIRED FOR A MIRACLE

by J. Morrow, Ph.D., and Rick Wolff

On a June evening in 1985, Tammy DeMichael and her fiancé were cruising along the New York State Thruway when he fell asleep at the wheel. The car slammed into the guardrail and flipped, leaving DeMichael with what the doctors called a "splattered C-6,7"—a broken neck and crushed spinal cord.

After a year of exhaustive medical treatment, she still had no function or feeling in her arms and legs. "The experts said I'd be a quadriplegic for the rest of my life," she recalls.

DeMichael proved the experts wrong. Today sensation has returned to her limbs, and her arm strength is normal or better. She has rid herself of a wheelchair. "I can walk about 60 feet with just a cane, and I can go almost anywhere with crutches," she says. "I can bench-press 100 pounds, and I ride 4 miles daily on a stationary bike." In fact, she works out so fervently in her rehabilitation program—spending entire days at the gym —that she shocks the very person who put her back in action. "Dr. Brucker says I work out as hard as a professional athlete," she says.

"Dr. Brucker" is psychologist Bernard Brucker, Ph.D., director of a nationally renowned facility at the University of Miami/ Jackson Memorial Medical Center in Florida that develops revolutionary treatments for victims of stroke and spinal-cord damage. Oddly, the central strategy used by Brucker —and the key reason for DeMichael's astonishing recovery—is a technique that at first might not sound revolutionary in the slightest: biofeedback.

Brucker's potent version of the technique is a far cry from the "psychedelic-age" experimental tool of the 1960s. Thanks to major advances in electronics and computer technology, biofeedback now offers a host of important benefits. Brucker is one of many respected health-care professionals who is successfully using biofeedback for a startling variety of purposes—from reducing stress-related illness and enhancing sports performance to treating hyperactivity, addiction, incontinence, and paralysis.

Biofeedback has emerged as a legitimate technique for treating conditions that defy conventional therapy.

Cheryl is connected to equipment which uses blue lines to show the electrical activity in the muscles of her wrist (top half of screen) and fingers (bottom half). Her dexterity improves with each session.

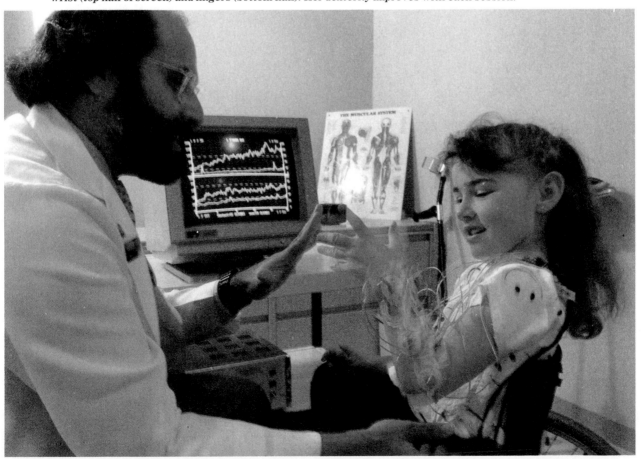

Hard-won Respect

Back in the 1940s and 1950s, Yale psychologist Neal Miller, Ph.D., found that rats could purposely alter their heart rate and blood pressure through positive reinforcement, i.e., to gain food rewards. The idea of controlling one's involuntary (autonomic) systems—the foundation for biofeedback—derives from the behavior-modification principle of *operant conditioning*: when a particular behavior rewards us or is reinforced, it tends to be repeated. If the payoff increases, so, too, does the effort to continue the rewarded behavior.

By the 1960s, Miller and other psychologists had devised ways of testing these tenets. People were wired to electronic equipment (such as heart- and brain-wave monitors) that gave visual or auditory signals —essentially indications of the subjects' internal workings. These early biofeedback subjects focused on altering these signals, i.e., making a dial that indicated their heart rate "move" in the desired direction, or making a tone become higher or deeper. They thus changed their physiological response through sheer concentration, with the signals serving as reinforcing cues. By making unconscious processes perceptible, this method of biological feedback trained the subjects to manipulate the involuntary via conscious mental control.

Unfortunately, the early work was not taken very seriously. Health professionals viewed the method as "fringe" mechanical gimmickry, and all but labeled the subjects thrill-seeking guinea pigs. "Biofeedback in the 1960s was considered a consciousness-raising tool, and that was about the extent of it," explains Brucker.

But with the help of high-tech electronics and modern computer systems, biofeedback's reputation has soared in recent years. State-of-the-art equipment can now continuously store data on almost any measurable body function, including skin temperature, heart rate, brain waves, and muscular activity. Patients can thus compare their results against normal standards and against their own results from previous sessions. The equipment also draws much finer distinctions, so patients can perceive immediately every tiny effect that their efforts are having. Two of the most important biofeedback tools are the *electromyograph* (EMG), which shows the electrical activity of specific muscles, and the *electroencephalograph* (EEG), which reveals the electrical activity in different areas of the brain. Years of refinement have made these machines much more precise: they can now measure down to 1/100 of a microvolt (a millionth of a volt). As Brucker puts it, "We can now detect a single neuron firing.

"How biofeedback learning occurs is still highly theoretical, but we know that it works," adds Brucker. "When learning new behaviors, the brain fires away until it finds the right cells to do them. In biofeedback, you vary your responses and stay attentive to those variations; when you make a hit on a cell that works, your brain sees it and knows you did the right thing. Over time the probability of wrong cells being activated keeps dropping, and the probability of the right cells firing increases."

Microscope to the Emotions

To grasp the extent of what Brucker accomplished with Tammy DeMichael, it helps to understand the earlier treatments upon which Brucker built his strategies. All new biofeedback therapies borrowed from the technique's initial success in stress management during the 1970s. Today experts such as psychologist Stephen Walker, Ph.D., director of the Rocky Mountain Institute for Health and Performance in Boulder, Colorado, are using biofeedback to relieve many stress-related (psychosomatic) ailments.

As Walker explains it, "The mind continually mediates our neurological and glandular functions." When stress besets our mind, it can interfere with these functions, leading to a wide variety of psychosomatic ills. By producing excessive muscular tension and raising blood pressure, for example, it can

> *Computers have helped biofeedback finally shed its image as a psychedelic consciousness-raising tool straight from the '60s.*

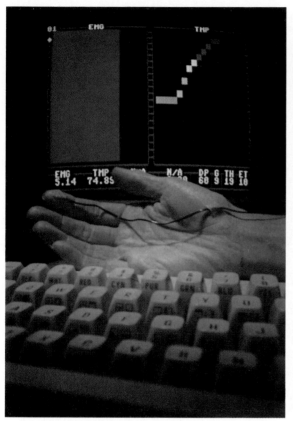

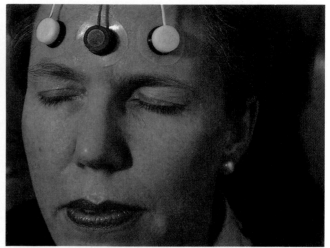

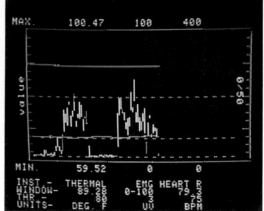

In a typical biofeedback session, electrodes monitor electrical activity in a subject's muscles or brain and transmit the information to an EMG or EEG machine, which displays the information.

cause symptoms running the gamut from simple pains to angina. Deep-breathing and relaxation techniques combined with biofeedback can teach us to master this stress and tension more safely and effectively than, for instance, resorting to muscle-relaxant drugs.

Last year, Walker worked with Mona Gilliam, a marketing executive who suffered from debilitating stress-induced asthma attacks. The prescription asthma medications she had taken most of her life left her weak and nauseated. Walker first had Gilliam keep a daily log to determine what stressful situations caused shortness of breath. After a few weeks, a strong correlation emerged between family conflicts and episodes of wheezing and gasping.

Back in the lab, Walker taught Gilliam *progressive muscle relaxation* (PMR)—the grad-
ual tensing and releasing of all of one's muscles from head to toe. Once she mastered PMR, Walker attached a skin-temperature sensor to her finger, and electrodes from an EMG machine to her forehead and the top of a shoulder (major muscle-tension sites). Then he asked her to close her eyes and visualize a typical stressful situation she had recorded in her log.

Since her eyes were closed, Gilliam received only audio cues in her training. As she imagined a violent argument with her mother, the EMG's computer produced rapid, high-pitched sounds, alerting her to overwhelming muscular tightness. Because stress reduces blood flow to the extremities, the separate skin-temperature monitor produced its own high-pitched sounds, indicating cold and clammy hands.

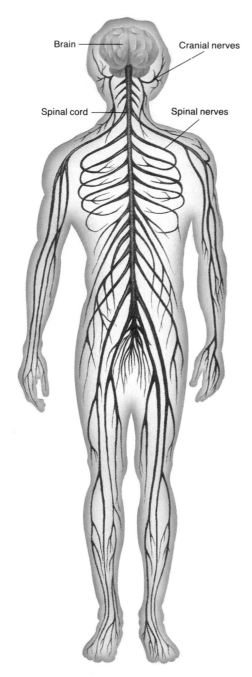

Then Gilliam began PMR. As she relaxed, the tones from each monitor became slower and deeper, signals that revealed lowering muscle tension and rising skin temperature. Thus, by changing her focus from the stressor to the relaxation technique, she was overcoming the stress reaction. Walker subsequently taught Gilliam even simpler relaxation methods that she could use instantly in everyday life.

After only six one-hour sessions, Gilliam had significantly reduced the severity of her asthma episodes and cut down her absences from work by more than 75 percent. "It was the first time she'd ever felt she could do something on her own, without being dependent on medication," says Walker.

Power Source

Walker, Brucker, and others also use EMG training to build strength, power, and mobility in nonfunctioning or insufficiently functioning muscles.

Walker, for example, helps shore up muscular deficiencies in high-level athletes through an EMG method similar to the stress-management technique. One beneficiary, shot-putter Karl Otto Kriger, had always relied on Nautilus weight training to build up his arm and chest muscles. Frustrated because his performance was improving only gradually, Kriger sought out Walker, who used EMG to reveal excessive tension in Kriger's jaw. Kriger was apparently clenching the masseter muscles in his jaw each time he lifted. This exertion was draining energy from the muscles he really needed to develop for shot-putting.

Next Walker wired up Kriger's masseter muscles to the EMG and guided him through relaxation training. During a typical Nautilus session, the audio signal rose in pitch whenever Kriger clenched his jaw, and lowered in pitch whenever he relaxed it. After a few sessions, his jaw tension had vanished during lifts, letting Kriger channel that extra energy into building up his arm and chest muscles. Kriger could soon lift far heavier weights and throw the shot greater distances.

At the Olympic training facility in Colorado Springs, Colorado, Shane Murphy, Ph.D., head of psychological services, has found that

During infancy, certain brain and spinal nerves are responsible for us learning how to use our arms and legs. Should these nerves be damaged, the established command pathway from the brain to a limb or limbs may be broken, and voluntary control of the limb is compromised. Many of biofeedback's benefits derive from the therapy's capacity to "retrain" motor nerve cells. A person using biofeedback may be able to regenerate motor nerve cells. Biofeedback can also help to establish "alternate routes" from the brain to the limb.

athletes in many sports benefit from such EMG training. Endurance runners and swimmers, for example, learn to decrease muscular tension so they can move more fluidly, saving energy.

Hope for Paralysis

Since 1981 some 2,000 people with paralysis and other motion disabilities have been through Brucker's Biofeedback Laboratories: 90 percent have left with improved function. More than a dozen patients as incapacitated as Tammy DeMichael—with no limb use whatsoever and supposedly no medical hope—have regained most of their mobility.

In infancy, certain brain and spinal nerves are responsible for our learning to use our arms and legs. When DeMichael came to

Biofeedback has many applications outside of rehabilitation. Some people seek biofeedback therapy as a means through which to correct posture.

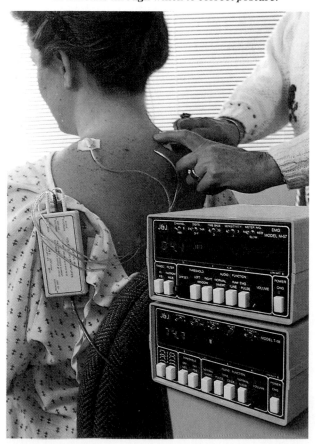

Brucker a year after her accident, most of these crucial nerves in her spine were believed to have been destroyed, so she wasn't expected to ever walk or move her arms again. Then Brucker performed an EMG test on her triceps muscle.

"When Dr. Brucker asked me to raise my arm, microvolt capacity [the percentage of electrical neuromuscular message arriving from the brain] was about 14 percent of normal," DeMichael remembers. Brucker was jubilant. "It wasn't nearly enough to create motion, but it offered hope," says DeMichael. Brucker believed that at least the nuclei of some motor-nerve cells were intact, which meant that these cells could fully regenerate when the brain was properly retrained.

At this session, with electrodes attached to her arm, DeMichael was instructed to watch a blue horizontal line move across a graph on the EMG's computer monitor; the line represented impulses traveling from her brain through the spine to her arm muscles every tenth of a second.

DeMichael's single task was to attempt to move her arm, thereby making the line climb. Though the limb never budged, by the end of the session, the line was moving closer to vertical. "I can't explain it," DeMichael says. "I just concentrated on watching the screen, sometimes thinking about raising my arm, and the line kept going higher."

Biofeedback has been found effective for everything from reducing stress-related illnesses to improving athletic performance.

Within eight sessions, she was making the line go nearly vertical—achieving *80 percent* of normal microvolt capacity. But still there was no motion. The reason, Brucker felt convinced, was simply that the muscles had atrophied during her year of paralysis. "We had reconnected the brain to the muscle, and now we had to develop strength."

In the next year, DeMichael began rehabilitation exercises—essentially "passive" exercise such as icing, massage, and electrical stimulation. At the same time, she kept up her biofeedback training with a vengeance. Session after session after session, DeMichael sat in front of the monitor, concentrating on making the line climb. The process was a tedious, painfully gradual one, and DeMichael credits Brucker's irrepressible enthusiasm for getting her through the slow periods. "Whenever I moved the line, he would scream and jump and get so excited," she recalls.

The day she finally moved her arm, everyone in the room broke out in celebration. The relearning process quickly accelerated from there; as she grew able to move and exercise her arms on her own, the biofeedback sessions emphasized other muscles around her body, especially those in her legs. DeMichael was unrelenting in the regimen year after year, spending almost every waking moment either at the gym working out or at the EMG monitor making that line climb still farther.

Five years later she is a summa cum laude graduate of biofeedback. "Tammy's upper body is so powerful that she looks like a weight lifter, and her triceps are stronger than mine," Brucker declares. Her walking ability keeps improving, and he can foresee a day when she'll throw away her crutches and cane.

More biofeedback applications include treating urinary incontinence, ending drug addiction, and controlling hyperactivity in children.

Taming the Brain
The successes achieved through such muscular retraining are being matched in other patients through brainwave retraining. EEG biofeedback helps patients with psychological disturbances solve problems by controlling their own brain rhythms. At the University of Tennessee in Knoxville, for example, professor of psychology Joel F. Lubar, Ph.D., is treating attention deficit hyperactivity disorder (ADHD) in children.

In school, youngsters must focus on specific tasks, but ADHD kids' interest keeps shifting. They can't concentrate, so they can't learn. "Children with this maladaptive behavior are often bright and creative, but, confronted by academic material, they become frustrated," Lubar explains. This frustration compounds the problem and frequently leads to disruptive behavior.

Extremely slow brain rhythms called theta waves are often associated with daydreaming and unfocused attention; the fastest rhythms, called beta waves, arise from concentrated, complex mental endeavor. Lubar's EEG studies show that almost all ADHD kids have high theta waves and diminished beta waves. Their brains are overly relaxed, says Lubar, so their minds wander, and they have difficulty completing projects. Psychiatrists use amphetamines such as Dexedrine and Ritalin to try to increase their patients' attention span, essentially by speeding their brain waves up to beta levels. Unfortunately, the drugs produce adverse side effects ranging from sleep disturbances and inhibited growth to depression. Biofeedback training is often just as effective, with none of the side effects that make drug therapy so undesirable.

Johnny Williams, a junior-high-school student who had ADHD, was brought to Lubar with a history of inattention and hyperactive episodes in class. Johnny had above-average intelligence, an attribute not reflected in his academic performance: his grades stayed between C and F. An initial EEG profile showed high theta waves and extremely low beta waves when doing focused tasks like reading or drawing.

Lubar began biofeedback training by attaching EEG sensors to Johnny's scalp at sites of beta- and theta-wave activity; an EMG electrode on the scalp simultaneously monitored muscle tension. A solid green circle on the computer screen expanded when his beta activity increased, and shrank when activity went down; meanwhile, a flute tone rose or dropped as beta activity went up or down. Johnny had to attempt, through unwavering concentration on the circle and sounds, to expand the circle and thus turn the flute tones higher. At the same time, he had to be aware of three small red lights that loomed above the green circle. One indicated theta waves; one, muscular tension; and one, head motion. If any of these lights came on,

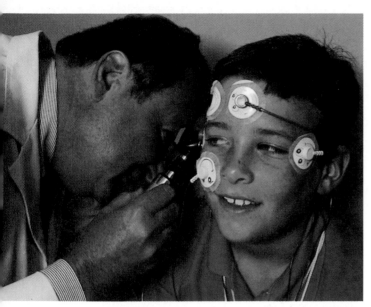

Biofeedback has proved to be quite successful in helping children with attention deficit hyperactivity disorder focus themselves.

the beta biofeedback stopped. Johnny then had to turn the light off by concentrating harder, relaxing his muscles, or holding his head still. "We were trying to teach him to be focused and alert, yet calm," Lubar explains. "We wanted a type-A mind in a type-B body."

The whole procedure was presented to Johnny as an entertaining video game that he could win simply with his mind; in reality, he was learning concentration skills that would prove invaluable. When he completed training four months later (40 to 60 one-hour sessions are the average, says Lubar), Johnny had learned to stay focused. His grades improved to A's and B's; his teachers stopped complaining about inattention and bursts of hyperactivity; his classmates became friendlier toward him.

Follow-up studies since 1986 show that EEG-trained ADHD kids earn far better grades and improve on intelligence tests and behavior scales. Lubar claims that his patients leap an average *two and a half years* in grade-level achievement and have IQ increases of as much as 20 points. What's more, as their frustration wanes, they become better adjusted at home, at school, and in the community.

Infinite Potential

The same professionals who have seen such success with biofeedback say its promise is nowhere near fully explored, even though the range of its therapeutic uses is already staggering. At the University of Illinois at Chicago, for example, occupational therapist Mary Plummer is using EMG biofeedback to retrain vital muscles in people with incontinence. In experimental studies with alcoholics and cocaine addicts, Eugene G. Peniston, a clinical psychologist at the Department of Veterans Affairs Medical Center in Fort Lyon, Colorado, and psychologist Paul J. Kulkosky, Ph.D., at the University of Southern Colorado in Pueblo, have shown that auditory EEG biofeedback works well in lieu of traditional talk therapies and hypnosis. By teaching substance abusers to lower their beta rhythms and increase their alpha and theta rhythms (the brain waves associated with relaxation), the EEG training helps relieve the inner stress and depression that drives them to addiction. The researchers also treat posttraumatic stress disorder in war veterans.

The uses of biofeedback may expand as fast as technology allows. Someday soon, lightweight portable units may become widely available, freeing patients of the wiring that keeps training sessions laboratory-bound. Executives suffering from stress migraines could cop some quick biofeedback before a critical boardroom session; former drug abusers and alcoholics could use a biofeedback "booster" to squelch the stress reactions that lead to sudden cravings and possible relapse.

Indeed, the possibilities are nearly limitless. "Biofeedback offers us intimate evidence of what the brain can accomplish," says Brucker. "In effect, we are looking into our own brains, and watching them encode new information into a few cells based on what we think and do. It's opened up a whole new era in human learning."

For more information concerning new research and clinical applications of biofeedback, contact the Association for Applied Psychophysiology and Biofeedback, 10200 W. 44th Avenue, #304, Wheat Ridge, CO 80033; 303-422-8436.

I've Got a Hunch

by Barbara J. Berg

Since childhood, most of us have learned to investigate a problem piece by piece and apply our reason to hard data, rather than try to grasp the solution all at once. Never give in to intuition, we were taught. Considered "flaky" and unreliable, intuition has long been the stepchild of decision making. Over the past few years, however, what we call intuition or a gut feeling or hunch has gained a place alongside logic as a way to solve a problem or come to a decision.

There's nothing magical about intuition; Webster defines it as "immediate apprehension or cognition," that is, a way of knowing something without knowing how we know it. Intuition is a natural mental ability, strongly associated with experience, that proves to be valuable both at work and at home.

Although conventional wisdom has credited women with a greater capacity for intuition, most experts agree that both men and women have the ability to develop such insights. Age, however, does appear to be an important factor. In a recent interview, Roy Rowan, author of *The Intuitive Manager,* says he believes that these powers improve through our 50s and 60s. By that age we've accumulated a lot of life experience, a knowledge of other people, a sense of ourselves. Most important, says Rowan, we have both the wisdom and the courage to act on our instincts.

Laurie Nadel, coauthor of *Sixth Sense: The Whole Brain Book of Intuition, Hunches, Gut Feelings and Their Place in Your Everyday Life,* explains it this way: "All of us absorb information—we look, we see, we hear. The older we get, the greater the data bank of knowledge our intuition has to draw on."

Intuition can present itself as a picture, an inner voice, or a physical sensation; some people experience it in only one form, others in all three. The process can occur spontaneously. Paul McLean, M.D., chief of brain evolution and behavior at the National Institutes of Health (NIH), says that intuition is "what the brain knows how to do when you leave it alone."

Just what does that mean? Consider the question of retirement, for example. You've planned for it and looked forward to it, but you have some concerns. Have you really saved enough money? You could live more economically if you were to relocate, but then you would be far away from your children and grandchildren. You could work a few years longer, but if either you or your spouse were to become ill, you would never forgive yourselves for not retiring sooner.

Like so many crucial questions in our lives, these have no clear-cut answers. But some experts say that we can reach personally valid conclusions more quickly if we allow our minds to float for a while instead of making a list of pros and cons.

The flashes of insight that may present themselves as solutions, however, do not actually "pop out of the blue." Instead, says Robert Chard-Yaron, Ph.D., a San Diego psychologist, "They are cooked in the preconscious level first." Put another way, hunches are really the end product of thousands of hours of immersion in a particular world. They are based on years of acquired knowledge, much as the automatic responses and judgments of a baseball pitcher whose gut feeling tells him the runner on second will try for third, or a police officer whose inner voice tells her that one man in a crowd is carrying a gun, or a scientist who dreams of the chemical makeup of a drug after months of trying to synthesize it in the laboratory.

Ironically enough, the first wave of interest in this ability came from the traditionally logical business community. The rise of the information society, rapid shifts in the world marketplace, and vigorous economic competition from global rivals showed the inadequacy of the rational management approach that dominated our business schools. "Analysis paralysis" was stifling American corporations.

To remedy this problem, business schools across the nation adopted books on intuitive management while professors held seminars on how to hone and utilize this skill. Weston Agor, Ph.D., professor of public administration at the University of Texas at El Paso, notes that intuition can be useful when you need an unprecedented or imaginative decision, or when data alone can't help because there's either too little information or too much information to be absorbed in a short time.

As books and articles flourished on the value of intuition at work, new research showed its use in our personal lives. Most studies on intuition involve unscrambling pictures, words, and nonsense sentences. According to Dr. Chard-Yaron, results show that intuitive people will probably do better than those attempting a systematic approach when asked to resolve an ambiguous situation. For instance, in one experiment a psychologist asked two groups to figure out arbitrary patterns of grammar from sentences made up of nonsense words. Those who tackled the problem intuitively were able to grasp the rules better than those who tried a methodical approach.

The key to making use of intuition is becoming comfortable listening to that silent information in your daily life. To feel more at ease trusting your "inner radar," try the following:

• First, think back to the times in your life when you followed your instincts with good results, or didn't follow them and wish you had. What made the difference? Why didn't you let yourself listen to your hunch?

• Try gaining confidence in your own intuition. For example, you have some time on your hands and either want to take a part-time sales position or to volunteer your time at a local hospital. You could use the income from working, but the job is tedious and would not provide the satisfactions that volunteering would. Close your eyes and ask yourself which decision is the right one for you. Conjure up a picture of yourself in the setting you feel you should be in. Do you have an order pad in front of you, or are you helping a patient get settled in a hospital room? Now try envisioning yourself in the other position. Do you feel disappointed with your choice? Chances are, you've already made your decision.

• You can use some other tricks to sharpen your intuitive powers. For one thing, try not to make decisions immediately. Take a creative pause before you answer, giving yourself time to become attuned to your feelings as well as your thoughts. Allow ideas to grow freely in an uncluttered mind. Let your thoughts wander for a specific period each day. You're not wasting time when you gaze out a window, close your eyes at your desk, listen to music, or go for a walk.

• Your intuition isn't limited to waking hours only. Think about a problem before you go to bed at night. Even during sleep, the unconscious mind deals with perplexing issues. But once you have a flash of insight, write it down. Inspiration comes quickly—and can vanish just as fast.

Finally, remember that the more comfortable you become relying on your intuition, the more you will feel you can trust yourself.

Housecalls

Michael Silver, M.D., is the director of the Hospital Division at Philadelphia Child Guidance Center, and a clinical assistant professor in the department of psychiatry at the University of Pennsylvania.

Q *My mother seems very depressed recently. Are there certain symptoms that can help me determine if she should seek medical help?*

A Yes, there are signs you can use. One must try to distinguish between mood changes considered within the normal up-and-down range, and more-serious depressions that require treatment.

Short-term variations in mood are of less concern than are episodes in which the person gets "stuck" in a low mood for weeks or longer. Extremes outside the normal pattern—and outside of brief "reactive" depressions to specific events such as a death or job loss—are the key symptoms to watch for. Often a person who is depressed will, in addition to obvious mood symptoms, show these signs:
• Appetite changes
• Sleep disruption
• Loss of interest in work, socializing, hobbies, and other interests

Aside from being in a "low mood," depressed people usually exhibit a number of other classic symptoms.

If the person stops relating to others and is withdrawn, apathetic, and noncommunicative about the problem, you should be additionally concerned. It sometimes helps to talk to other close adult friends or relatives of the person to see if they, too, have noticed the problem.

Q *What role does a woman's state of mind play in premenstrual syndrome (PMS)?*

A Most women do experience premenstrual changes in their bodies and mood states, which they come to know and expect as normal variations. These variations can be highly individualized, but most women are able to detect the physical and emotional fluctuations and are able to function fully despite them. A smaller percentage of women may experience changes that significantly interfere with their normal activities. Similarly, some women experience "postpartum blues" after the birth of a baby. These are serious mood changes that may require treatment.

Doctors and researchers are currently trying, through research, to understand the complex relationship between monthly hormonal changes and mood variations or disorders. They are really only just beginning to understand this interplay of hormones and mood.

Q *I've heard about a new way of looking at psychological problems in individuals and families called "family-systems theory." What is the idea behind this?*

A The guiding principle of family-systems theory is that psychological problems occur within the context of relationships. This approach contrasts with the view of a psychological problem as something that arises out of an individual's own mind—that is, that problems somehow arise outside the context of others and the person's environment. There are already many different schools of family-systems therapy.

This approach in no way should be understood to mean that families are the *cause* of problems; "blaming" is not the meaning or the intention of this concept.

Instead, family-systems theory offers a different way of thinking about emotional problems, by looking at each person as part of a network of interconnected relationships.

Thus, in a family where a child is having a problem, the traditional approach might be to look at the child rather than to also examine how people within his or her family system relate to one another. Often, problems that appear in one person are connected to a process involving others.

Family-systems therapists will frequently ask an entire family to come to counseling to see if the symptoms relate to some process in which stresses or other problems tend to be shared back and forth in a less-than-ideal way. One advantage of this approach is that it offers many more means and points of intervention than do approaches that focus solely on the manifestation of the problem in one person.

Q *Is there such a thing as a "psychosis" linked to marijuana use?*

A The answer depends to some extent on whether you are referring to a single dose of marijuana or to ongoing regular use. In either case, though, it's very unusual for this drug to lead to either acute or chronic psychiatric symptoms of this severity.

Drugs more commonly associated with "breakdowns" are cocaine, amphetamines, and crack. And, of course, true hallucinogens such as LSD, by definition, cause a person to lose touch with reality to some extent—which is usually what is meant by "psychosis." As a psychoactive drug, marijuana certainly shifts a person's view of reality in some ways, whether this shift be with regard to sensations, passage of time, or whatever.

For a normal person to develop schizophrenia or a major mood disorder as a result of marijuana use would be highly unusual. For someone predisposed to these problems, though, using this or any drug *could* push the person over the edge, owing to the shift in reality or the stress added to the person's life. There are certainly drug abusers who suffer from schizophrenia or other psychiatric problems.

In addition, heavy marijuana use can result in what is referred to as *amotivational*

syndrome, in which a person loses energy and interest in other activities. High levels of daily use can also cause a person to become somewhat withdrawn or irrationally suspicious of others. These effects, however, are similar to those seen in other forms of addictive behavior, when the psychological or physical habit becomes consuming. In many cases, it's not clear how clinically observable these effects are in substance abusers after the drug wears off, *i.e.,* in between highs.

Although frequent marijuana use is not known to cause severe psychiatric problems, it has been implicated in the development of a strong "antimotivational syndrome."

Q *I am a busy student, and I've noticed that I am forgetful of small things lately. I worry—do diseases that affect memory, such as Alzheimer's disease, ever affect young people?*

A Generally, chronic brain disorders like Alzheimer's don't affect people until middle age or older. They very rarely occur below this age range.

But here are a few situations where your forgetfulness *might* need medical evaluation:
• If it is associated with other neurological symptoms, such as tingling numbness, loss of sensation, or problems with movement of limbs or difficulty walking;
• If it coincides with something else wrong with your general health or with a recent illness;
• If other people agree that you are acting significantly different than usual because of your forgetfulness.

In general, people with chronic brain disorders have more widespread difficulties than just forgetting "small things," which, in contrast, is exactly the type of problem that happens to people who simply have too much on their minds. If forgetting things is creating problems for you, you may need to step back and assess whether or not you are just overdoing it.

Have a mental-health question?
Send it to Editor, Health and Medicine Annual, P.O. Box 90, Hawleyville, CT 06440−9990.

Practical News to Use

It's easy to ignore your health as long as you're feeling healthy. But many illnesses develop slowly, and treatment prior to the onset of noticeable symptoms can be valuable. Regular dental checkups, mammograms, immunization against communicable diseases, and other standard procedures can prevent great distress—and great costs—later on.

The benefits of preventive medicine were starkly evident last November, when Earvin "Magic" Johnson announced that he had been infected by the virus that causes AIDS. Johnson's infection was discovered during a routine physical exam. The early diagnosis was valuable because it allowed physicians to begin treatment that may delay the onset of symptoms and prolong Johnson's life. Following Johnson's announcement, the number of people being tested for the virus rose sharply; in New York City, tests were up almost 60 percent. Health professionals hoped that sexually active people would also use condoms and be more cautious in choosing sexual partners.

Every 10 minutes, two people are killed and about 170 are disabled in accidents in the United States. The costs incurred from accidents total almost $150 billion annually —for medical care, property damage, fire loss, lost wages, and so on. To prevent deaths and reduce the severity of injuries among motorcyclists, some states have required the use of helmets. An analysis of 49 studies by the U.S. General Accounting Office (GAO) found that helmet-usage laws resulted in both safety and economic benefits: "The studies showed that helmeted riders experienced fatality rates that were 28 to 73 percent lower than for nonhelmeted riders. For helmeted riders, the incidence of head injuries rated 'severe' or worse was 46 to 85 percent lower than for nonhelmeted riders."

The GAO also reviewed 85 auto-safety-belt studies, and reported that "belted occupants tended to survive crashes 50 to 75 percent more frequently than unbelted occupants," and that "belted occupants on average were seriously injured 44 to 66

See also:
Individual articles in the second half of this book, arranged in alphabetical order, for additional information.

182

percent less frequently than were unbelted occupants."

An unsafe behavior common among young people is listening to loud music. It doesn't cause accidents, but it can cause significant disability. According to hearings conducted by a U.S. House of Representatives committee, of the 28 million Americans who suffer from hearing loss, 10 million are victims of exposure to loud sounds. Studies show that live and amplified music are a main cause of hearing loss in adolescents and young adults. Such hearing loss, noted James B. Snow, Jr., director of the National Institute on Deafness, is irreversible.

Certain medical procedures may also prove to be unsafe. Halcion, the world's biggest-selling prescription sleeping pill, was banned in Britain after newly disclosed data supported earlier evidence that the drug may cause memory loss, depression, and other behavioral problems.

More than 2 million American women have received silicone breast implants, mostly for cosmetic reasons. Not until 1991, however, were manufacturers of the implants required to submit safety data. The government rejected the manufacturers' data, saying they were inadequate and did not prove that the implants are safe. Testimony presented at hearings held by the Food and Drug Administration (FDA) indicated that risks of breast implants in-

clude allergic reactions; hardening or lumping of tissues around the implant; and rupturing of the implant with subsequent leakage of silicone, which may increase the risk of cancer. In early 1992 the FDA called for a voluntary moratorium on use of the implants while questions about their safety are resolved.

The cost of medical care continues to skyrocket, increasing much faster than the general inflation rate. There are many contributory factors, including the rapidly increasing elderly population; more-sophisticated, higher-priced medicine and equipment; costly treatments for AIDS and other ailments; and services needed by victims of drugs, crime, and accidents. Some high-cost practices are questionable, however. A study of the three leading drugs used to dissolve blood clots in coronary arteries found that the drugs were equally effective in saving lives. But the drugs' costs were far from equal. Streptokinase, the oldest drug, costs $200 per treatment; Eminase costs $1,700 per treatment; and t-PA (tissue plasminogen activator) costs $2,200 to $2,700 per treatment.

The cost of medical care is rising faster than the inflation rate.

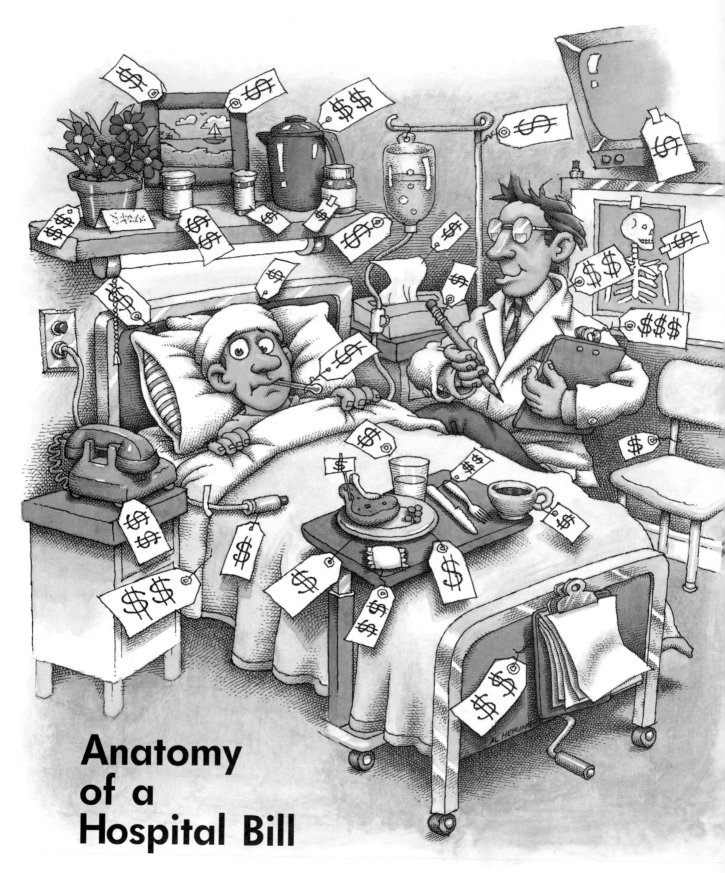

Anatomy of a Hospital Bill

by Joseph Anthony

itch Leventhal was one lucky guy. Rushed to a Maryland hospital emergency room after his motorcycle collided with a pickup truck, Leventhal, miraculously, was slightly battered but in no way broken. Doctors at Shady Grove Hospital in Rockville examined him, asked for a urine sample, and X-rayed his right foot. They put an elastic bandage on what turned out to be just a bad bruise, gave him a pair of crutches, and sent him on his way.

As emergency-room cases go, Leventhal's damage to both body and budget was minor. Still, he was shocked when he got his bill.

"They called the bandage a 'soft foot cast,' and charged me $11.10 for it," Leventhal recalls. "They called the plastic cup they gave me a 'urinal,' and charged $5.06. And they didn't ask me if I wanted to rent crutches. They just handed me a pair and billed me $31.10. I couldn't believe it."

Just as surprised was Sue Horton of Los Angeles, who gave birth by cesarean section to a healthy baby boy at Cedars-Sinai Medical Center. When Horton scanned her lengthy bill, one of the things that caught her attention was a charge for a pacifier.

"The nurse asked me if I wanted a pacifier," she recalls, "and I said sure, even though I didn't need it. I figured she was giving it to me, right?" Wrong. The bit of plastic and rubber that Horton popped into her baby's mouth came to $16.

It's the footwear that patient Beverly Voran remembers from her stay at Cedars-Sinai. "The hospital charged me $15 for a pair of disposable paper slippers," she says.

For Lee Strom, who has a heart condition and was kept overnight for observation in the coronary-care unit at Saint Francis Memorial Hospital in San Francisco, the shock came not only from the overall size of the bill ($2,881.96) for a one-night stay, but from such relatively inexpensive surprises as an $8.85 paper "linen saver" and a charge of $6.00 for six acetaminophen tablets (better known to you and me as Tylenol).

Outraged consumers wonder how a 20-cent plastic cup becomes a five-dollar "urinal."

Plastic cups billed as five-dollar urinals and buck-a-tablet Tylenol are mere dust on the paperwork of America's $500 billion-plus annual health-care budget. But when consumers scan a long and complicated hospital bill, sometimes it's the relatively small and simple charges that jump off the page—because at least they're recognizable everyday items. It's easier, after all, to wonder why "toothpaste" costs $4.50 than to question why "Ifex inj 1 gram" has come to $502.55 or why "Cisplatin 50 mg" has been billed at $478.35.

When it comes to hospital bills, it's no surprise to most of us that nothing comes free, but *does* a Tylenol tablet cost a dollar or more when it's handed to you by someone wearing a white uniform and orthopedic shoes? When asked about everything from pricey plastic pacifiers to $10,000 intensive-care charges, hospital administrators usually have a one-word answer handy: "Overhead."

Overhead—the cost of the hospital building itself, plus expenses of utilities, staff, medical equipment, insurance, and so on—makes its way into every hospital bill, but just how you end up paying for it is up to the accounting department.

That's one reason costs for goods and services can vary tremendously from institution to institution. A recent survey of Chicago hospitals alone revealed that the cost of a CT scan (a highly advanced, three-dimensional X-ray image) ranged from $60 to more than $600, and a simple tonsillectomy ran from a rock-bottom $125 to a whopping $3,000 plus.

Usually a hospital's general overhead is figured into the charge for a bed, and the costs of running individual units, such as the emergency room or the pharmacy, are rolled into the prices of those services. But the delegation isn't uniform. To make itself attractive to consumers, a hospital can rejigger its departmental fees to make one division—say, outpatient surgery—more competitive with other area facilities.

But even in places where hospitals are competing fiercely for business, the customer doesn't necessarily get a break. In an attempt to lure patients, each hospital may add more and more expensive equipment and services—from the latest scanning technology to gourmet meals. Such expenditures mean higher costs passed on to the consumer.

Staff salaries, including paying for the time it takes for a nurse to pick up an individually packaged acetaminophen tablet from the hospital pharmacy and deliver it to your bedside, account for a good chunk of a hospital's expenses. And even previously unpaid bills can also be folded back into overhead, meaning that new patients may be billed more because former patients didn't pay up.

To find out how overhead costs are distributed, you might as well talk to a mystery writer!

"To find out how overhead costs are distributed, you might as well talk to a mystery writer," says Samuel X. Kaplan, chairman of U.S. Administrators, a Los Angeles company that runs corporate health programs.

Adding to the confusion are the billing systems themselves. Geared to the insurance companies who pay most of the bills, the coding and terminology can range from head-scratching to incomprehensible to the average consumer.

What you might call a hospital gown, for example, turns into "Admission kit—custom." And that's the easy stuff. Once you get into the more complex medical jargon, translation can seem next to impossible. Faced with such charges as "Isotope: Indium III Leukocyte, $360" or "Handheld Neb CKT change & TX, $39.75," most of us will be left guessing. Since a single hospital can have as many as 12,000 line items in its computer billing system, familiarizing yourself with the terminology is no small undertaking. Some hospitals these days issue summary bills, which merely list a total for departmental charges—"Medical/Surgical, 5th flr., $2,450," or "Pharmacy, $10,168.10"—making it even harder to know what you've been billed for.

Then again, if you're insured, you're probably not the one doing the complaining —at least not initially. The hard questions most likely are coming from the health-insurance companies and employers, who pay 85 percent or more of the total cost of hospital care in this country, and who are increasingly critical of hospital charges. From the insurer's point of view, the problem isn't just high overhead, or quirky coding and terminology, but some questionable billing strategies aimed at maximizing revenue.

Enter the Auditors

For a decade or more, insurance companies have attempted to keep costs down by ferreting out overcharges. Their auditors take a magnifying glass to doctors' and nurses' notes, patients' charts, and the billing system as a whole. They often find the excesses that they're looking for.

"There is a disappointingly large number of physicians and hospitals overcharging for services or charging for what they don't do," says Laurens P. White, a professor of medicine at the University of California at San Francisco, and a past president of the California Medical Association. "I just saw the case of an oncologist who charged $8,000 to administer a drug that costs $120 and doesn't work well anyway," says White. "I'd like to break his neck, but I plan to discuss with him the joys of honest living instead."

Insurance-company auditors go where the big money is, and that usually means bills of $10,000 or more. The auditors aren't there to argue about overhead; they know how expensive it is to run a hospital these days, and why a patient might be charged $15 for disposable slippers. What they are more likely to question is why someone hospitalized overnight has been billed for a dozen pairs, for example, or for services and supplies that seem unrelated to the patient's illness or injury.

Hospitals, facing diminishing profits, have fought back, beefing up their own auditing departments, or hiring outside guns—"revenue-recovery" firms—to go after *under*-charges.

The revenue-recovery firms—part of an industry that grosses close to $1 billion a year—have gained a reputation for cutthroat tactics, and were in fact the subject of a 1990 U.S. Senate subcommittee hearing on health-care fraud. The investigation documented instances in which these firms, working on a percentage of the money they recovered, encouraged employees to zealously seek out undercharges, while ignoring instances in which the hospital had *over*-charged.

Not that the insurance-company auditors are working overtime to find the undercharges. It is the excesses they're after, and here are the ones they say pop up most often—problem areas you'd undoubtedly do well to examine on your own hospital bill. Even if your insurance company is picking up some of the tab, catching such errors ultimately can save you money as well.

"Ghost" Services. After his daughter was born, Charles Inlander got a bill for $3,000—including about $1,000 for vitamins, predelivery and postdelivery IVs, well-baby care, and other services the Inlanders did not receive. And even though his wife gave birth in the labor room and never used the delivery room, says Inlander, they were still charged a delivery-room fee. Inlander, who is now president of the People's Medical Society, a Pennsylvania-based consumers' advocacy group, later found out that the excess charges were for services that the hospital usually provides during childbirth. As it was explained to him, hospitals often have a standard list of items and services for such routine procedures—and they'll bill for the entire list unless a staff member checks off an item as not having been provided.

"It's like the Book-of-the-Month Club," says Inlander, "where you get the product and get billed for it unless you specifically say you don't want it."

Service Duplication. If communication is poor or lines of command are faulty, patients may get more attention than they need—and be charged for it. An electrocardiogram, for example, may be administered in the morning. "If it's not properly noted, your physician could order another, needless one in the afternoon," says Robert Becker, chairman of the managed-care company Health-Care Compare Corporation.

Patients can also be charged for a hospital's out-and-out mistakes. William Rial of Chicago needed two blood tests a day when he was in the hospital and on an anticoagulant drug. "Twice the medical technician didn't draw the right amount of blood and had to repeat the test," says Rial, director of provider relations for the Blue Cross/Blue Shield Association. Rial was billed for the botched tests as well as for the successful ones.

Multiple Billings. Two different hospital departments can sometimes each generate a bill for the same service, or one department may issue two bills. "Patients in one department of a hospital we've dealt with are routinely double-billed for any services from that department," says Steven Assael, a former account executive with American Claims Evaluations. "The attitude at that department is that the mistake is built into the system, and since 1 or 2 percent of their bills are audited, they'll correct only for those bills."

At another hospital, a Mutual of Omaha audit revealed that one patient was charged for 22 cultures at $74 each, although only 11 cultures were noted on the patient's medical chart. The response of the hospital's billing department, according to an insurance official: "Oh gee, are we still billing twice on those?"

Inflated Services. Faced with a ceiling on how much an insurance company or government agency will actually pay for a particular procedure, some hospitals simply turn to intentional number-juggling, say the auditors. Through a billing sleight of hand called upcoding, the facts of a treatment can be altered ever so slightly to result in a higher fee, noted the Senate report on health-care fraud. A mole that's been removed can be described as a bit larger than it actually was, for instance, thereby adding a couple of hundred dollars to the bill.

Similarly, according to the Senate investigation, through billing tricks called fragmentation or unbundling, a series of charges can be milked out of what is usually a single, less expensive charge. An operation that routinely includes several steps and is usually billed as one procedure may instead be broken down into individual steps and billed as a much more expensive series of procedures, for instance. If the cost of an operating room usually includes certain supplies, these may be "unbundled" and billed separately, greatly boosting the total cost.

> *Hospitals use a billing sleight of hand to inflate the price of certain services.*

Human Error. Some errors are undoubtedly simple misinterpretations; information on the medical chart, for example, may be transferred inaccurately to the patient's bill. Other errors are of the keypunch variety, whereby numbers are transposed or otherwise entered incorrectly. Former Secretary of Health, Education, and Welfare Joseph Califano cites the example of a patient at a Virginia hospital who received a single $56 unit of albumin, but was billed for 111 units ($6,216!). Such mistakes could conceivably be the result of a heavy finger on the keyboard.

"The medical world sees all these things as honest mistakes," says Inlander. "But they're not doing anything to really control or reduce their mistakes."

"Patients, unlike other consumers who can check their bills by comparing what they received to what they ordered, frequently cannot tell if their hospital bills are flawed," points out the report of the Senate hearing on health-care fraud. "This is because patients are often unaware of exactly what hospital services are provided to them, and the only record of what happened [the patient's chart, or medical record] is in the hospital's hands." The report also noted: "If a patient requests his chart, as he is entitled to, he would need a medical background to understand its terminology."

Hospitals can offer a spirited defense. "I know all about those error rates," says Dan Hogan at Monongahela General Hospital in Morgantown, West Virginia. "The average five-day stay here produces a bill with 3,500 line items, and inevitably some of the documentation for a procedure is not going to get done properly, so we're told our bills are inaccurate. A lot of what are called errors are just documentation gaps."

Whatever they're called, such mistakes cost time and money. Unfortunately, when insurance companies and hospitals collide, it is often the consumer who gets bruised. Doctors and hospitals, for instance, can sue patients for the remainder of a bill that an insurance company has refused to pay.

But even if the insurance company picks up all or most of the bill, overcharges drive up insurance premiums, costing employers —and ultimately you—more money. So, in the long run, it pays to examine your hospital bill, right down to the minor charges. Even the small surprises can add up.

"We got a doozy through here the other day," says a California auditor. "A patient was charged $1.81 for 'drinking water.' I'd never seen that one before."

Hospital Patience: Recovering What You Can

If you're like most people, you'll probably worry about your hospital bill after you get it. Comparison shopping before you enter the hospital is just about impossible. For one thing, you won't know in advance all the services you'll require, and even if you did, one hospital may charge more for blood tests but less for drugs, while another has pricier medication and cheaper lab work. Furthermore, your doctor's privileges may limit your choice of institutions. But once you're in the hospital and the meter starts ticking, you might try some of these strategies to keep the costs as reasonable as possible.

If you can, keep a log. Assuming you're at all up to it, you—or a family member—might attempt a daily record of the services, medications, and other supplies you receive. The People's Medical Society in Allentown, Pennsylvania, has forms for logging tests and medication in its publication *Take This Book to the Hospital With You.*

Don't assume anything's free. Ask "How much?" before you accept any optional supplies—even bottled drinking water or tissues. That advice also applies to anything you're offered on the way out of the hospital, particularly drugs. They'll be cheaper at your local pharmacy.

Make sure you see an itemized bill. If you get a summary bill—listing only lump sums from departments—ask the billing office to break down the charges. Under many state laws, you have a right to an itemized accounting. In states without such legislation, some hospitals may be uncooperative. If so, you may have to call the state consumer-protection agency or your state attorney general's office.

Be prepared to spend some time. If the bill is presented as you leave the hospital,

don't pay it or sign any agreements to pay until you've had time to look it over—either on the spot, if it's short and straightforward enough, or later at home if it's long and involved. Even if you're insured, you should scrutinize your bill. If the hospital seems unwilling to let you take the time you need, remind them of the American Hospital Association's "Patient's Bill of Rights": "The patient has the right to examine and receive an explanation of his bill, regardless of source of payment."

To make sure you got what you've been charged for, start with the obvious: the room rate and the number of days, plus charges for major procedures, operating room, recovery room, etc. Then compare the remaining itemized charges against the medical records for your stay. First you'll have to get copies of your records. Hospitals or doctors may tell you that it's illegal, but a number of states (Alaska, California, Colorado, Connecticut, Florida, Georgia, Hawaii, Illinois, Michigan, Minnesota, Nevada, New York, Oklahoma, Virginia, West Virginia, Wisconsin) have passed laws that guarantee your right to copies. And even where there's no law supporting your right, in most cases there's no law prohibiting you from having copies, either.

If your doctor refuses to give you copies, you can have the records sent to a more cooperative physician. If all else fails, you may have to consult a lawyer and possibly obtain a court order.

Examine every bill you receive. After you're home, you'll undoubtedly receive lots of hospital paperwork. Even if subsequent bills look like copies of those you've already seen, read them carefully. Sometimes what looks like a duplicate bill is really an amended bill; after conducting their own audits, some hospitals send updates with added charges.

Ask the hospital to document and clarify any questionable charges. If your insurance company is picking up a substantial chunk of the bill and the total is over $10,000, they may choose to conduct an audit themselves. If you're insured and the bill is smaller, the insurance company's review department may help you. If you're uninsured, start with the hospital's billing office.

If proof isn't forthcoming, ask to have the charges removed. If the hospital refuses, you can turn to your state consumer-protection agency, or, in rare instances where outright fraud may be suspected, the health-care-fraud division of the state attorney general's office. If, in the course of a dispute, a provider threatens you with legal action, or turns your bill over to a collection agency, ask your state consumer-protection agency for advice.

How to Decode the Bill

The bottom line on your hospital bill may be shocking enough. But once you try to decipher the terminology, you may find the document to be as mysterious as it is hair-raising.

What, for example, is one to make of this: "Microstryker/Ergo/Zimm, $93?" To find out, we went right to the source—the hospital that generated the bill (for foot surgery) on which this charge recently appeared. First we talked to the billing department. No one there could clue us in. We were referred to the hospital accounting office—again, no luck—and from there to the department where the surgery took place. That department had to locate a doctor who could finally explain. The $93, he said, was the charge for the cleaning of a particular kind of bone saw used by an orthopedic surgeon.

Another bill showed these itemized charges: "Electrode (3), $13.98" and "Cannula, $4.98." Translation? The electrode charge was for a sort of bandage (three of them, billed at $4.66 each) used to attach wires from a monitoring device to the patient. The cannula charge was for a clip used to connect an oxygen tube to the patient's nose.

The lesson in all this, unfortunately, seems to be that many charges, like these examples, will have to be sorted out one by one. Unfortunately, there's no universal "hospital-bill dictionary" to help you translate all the items on a bill. For one thing, some may be coded numerically. For another, there are no uniform descriptions. There are thousands of medical abbreviations, and what something is called is largely up to the particular hospital's billing department. To make matters worse, a given abbreviation can stand for a number of things, depending on who's using it. Although the Joint Commission on Accreditation of Healthcare Organizations

requires the abbreviations a hospital uses to be consistent within that institution, the rule isn't always followed.

As Neil M. Davis, professor of pharmacology at Temple University in Philadelphia, and author of the booklet *Medical Abbreviations: 7,000 Conveniences at the Expense of Communications and Safety*, points out, the abbreviation "s/p" can mean semiprivate, serum protein, or spinal, depending on the institution. "PE" can stand for physical examination, pulmonary embolism, pulmonary edema, pol-

yethylene, or physical exercise. And "AB" can be used to mean either abortion, antibiotic, or Ace bandage. Here are just a few of the abbreviations that can pop up on hospital bills. As the list shows, even some of the more common ones can have multiple meanings. In order to decode your own bill, you'll have to rely on the context of your treatment, help from the hospital or doctor, and, of course, a great deal of patience and persistence.

BX—biopsy
CAP—capsule (can also be used as an abbreviation for several drugs, including cyclophosphamide and chloramphenicol)
CBC—complete blood count or the drug carbenicillin
CCU—coronary or critical care unit
CXR—chest X ray
ECG OR EKG—electrocardiogram
EEG—electroencephalogram
ER—emergency room
FX—fracture or fractional urine (test)
GA—general anesthesia, gastric analysis, or the drug combination glucose/acetone
GI—gastrointestinal
ICCU—intensive or intermediate coronary care unit
ICU—intensive or intermediate care unit
I&D—incision and drainage
INJ—injection or injury
IV—intravenous or the symbol for class four controlled substances
NS—normal saline solution, neurosurgery, or nylon suture
OP—outpatient or operation
OPD—outpatient department
OR—operating room
PO—post operative
RBC—red blood cell (count)
RR—recovery room or retinal reflex
RX—prescription, therapy, or treatment
SDS—same day surgery
SICU—surgical intensive care unit
SPEC—specimen
TX—treatment, therapy, traction, transfuse, or transplant
WBC—white blood cell (count) or well-baby clinic

Tattoo You?

by Russ Allen

The ancient art of tattooing has gained a new popularity in the United States. Americans everywhere are going under the needle, acquiring tattoos ranging from the subdued to the vainglorious (above).

So you want to look as radical as Axl Rose? Or maybe as chic as Cher? Have you considered a tattoo? At least among some trendsetters, permanent body ink has emerged as a fashionable theme, tying together a disparate group of celebrities. Their decision to acquire tattoos is driving a new wave of popularity for indelible body art. From Prince to Mark Gastineau, from Melanie Griffith to Roseanne Barr Arnold, the current tattoo trend seems to have gone beyond the traditional clientele and has now also trickled down to the general public, where even the more upscale types are going under the tattooer's needle. But getting a tattoo—a brand that can mean so many things to so many people—is a major decision, one that comes with its own set of discomforts and risks.

Colorful History

Strictly speaking, tattooing means introducing colors into the skin through punctures, a step that gets pigment under a person's skin, so to speak, for good. Devices that early societies used to prick the skin included sharpened bones, thorns, and knives.

Tattooing dates to prehistoric times. Back then, everyone from ornately scarified African tribesmen to war-painted American Indians sported tattoos. In fact, the 4,000-year-old corpse discovered in 1991 frozen in the Austrian Alps still had tattoos intact.

Ancient Egyptians, Greeks, Germans, and Britons wore tattoos. The ancient Romans saw tattoos as barbarian, and thus reserved them for criminals and slaves. With the advent of Christianity, tattooing was forbidden in Europe.

As an art, tattooing continued to flourish, mainly in the South Pacific and Japan. James Cook's 1769 expedition to Tahiti introduced the word *tattoo* to the language via the Tahitian *tatau*. Captain Cook noted that the Tahitians were considerably more interested in their elaborate tattoos than in what little clothes they wore. Sailors of the 1700s and 1800s were fascinated by tattoos among the people of Oceania, and thus began the enduring association of tattooing and seamen.

In some primitive societies, body markings such as tattoos were a sign of social or religious rank. Tattooing also served as an initiation rite for young men and women coming of age. Sometimes these occasions were also rituals of endurance, as in Samoan custom, where all or most of the body was covered with tattoos.

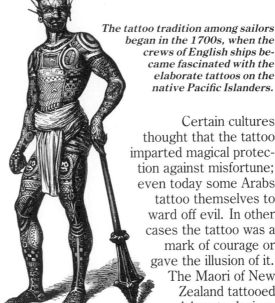

The tattoo tradition among sailors began in the 1700s, when the crews of English ships became fascinated with the elaborate tattoos on the native Pacific Islanders.

Certain cultures thought that the tattoo imparted magical protection against misfortune; even today some Arabs tattoo themselves to ward off evil. In other cases the tattoo was a mark of courage or gave the illusion of it. The Maori of New Zealand tattooed elaborate designs on their faces to disguise expressions of fear. Complex tattooed spirals on their faces and buttocks were also considered a sign of good breeding.

During the late 19th century, tattooing enjoyed a short rage among English upper classes, and it has seen periodic resurgences in this century. The meaning of tattoos, however, has changed somewhat over the centuries. It is enough to say that tattoos rarely reflect high social, educational, or professional status in our own society.

Judging by the instruments (left), tattoo acquisition in the Maori culture was not a comfortable undertaking. In Japan, tattoos often reflect the country's distinctive traditions (right).

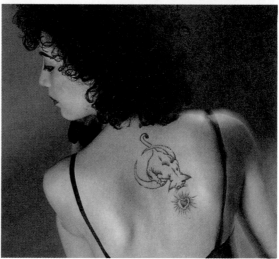

Actor Johnny Depp (at top) sports a traditional tattoo in a traditional place. Women are often more daring, opting to have a leg or back—or a less-mentionable site—tattooed.

Revitalized Interest

Tattoo studios have long been stereotyped as the turf of sailors, bikers, and fraternity men, although military personnel and sectors of working-class, blue-collar groups have consistently been the primary patrons. These latter groups remain the mainstay of the tattoo parlor, despite what University of Connecticut sociologist Clinton Sanders calls "a flurry of interest" surrounding tattooing among the more affluent.

"In the last five years, major figures—including actors and especially musicians in heavy-metal and punk bands—have been a significant force in the renewed interest in tattooing," explains Sanders, whose conclusions about the tattooing trend have been published in the book *Customizing the Body.* "More middle class and upper-middle class individuals—often managerial types—are now getting tattooed."

Why is this? Sanders, who got his first of many tattoos while visiting the Museum of Tattooing Art in San Francisco, maintains that "Tattooing has always been countercultural. Those in the counterculture often alter their bodies or their look as a way of saying, 'I identify with a different set of values.' Getting a tattoo is a sure way to bug adults if you're young, or to get the attention of your contemporaries if you're an adult."

The number of tattoo shops and the sales of tattoo equipment have taken off in recent years. At the same time, more and more yuppies are "getting inked." This group has revived interest in an earlier practice: symbolizing your livelihood in your tattoo.

Previously, men of the trades—metalworkers, carpenters, and others—had the specific insignia of their trades tattooed on their arms (or elsewhere). Now comes—you guessed it—the professional and white-collar version. "We've done doctors, who get medical symbols on their arm, and policeman, who get replicas of their badges," says tattooist Rich Amwake of Jersey Devil Tattooing in Blackwood, New Jersey. Other tattooers tell of a pharmacist who had an R_x tattooed on her shoulder and a salesman who sports an icon of his product on his arm.

An Hour, Tops

What's it like to get a tattoo? Depends. Anyone with a needle and some ink can give themselves or someone else a tattoo, however crudely. (Tattooists often cover up such tattoos, a tricky undertaking in which the old tattoo must be carefully integrated with the new one.) But modern electric needles have refined the tattooing process.

The first step is deciding on a design. If you don't already know, step into a tattoo joint and review the "flash"—the colorful sketches of tattoos that cover the walls of many tattoo parlors. Some people bring their own designs, which most tattooists can redraw and render for an additional cost.

Reputable tattoo artists, however, won't tattoo just any body. Knowing that the tattoo is a significant step, many insist that it not be an impulse purchase. Most claim they will not tattoo anyone under age 18. Others ask potential patrons who have been drinking or seem unsure about a tattoo to think it over and come back another day.

The tattooing process itself is painful. A vibrating needle works in and out of the skin at high speed. Typical tattoos take from 30 minutes to an hour to complete. The cost:

Though painful, the tattooing procedure itself is relatively short. Sixteen states regulate tattoo studios to protect customers' health.

Artsy perhaps, but collecting "Flash" may be wiser

Tattooing is one of the longest-surviving professions. Many tattooers enter the field through an apprenticeship to an established tattoo artist, just as in a traditional craft. Others begin by tattooing themselves: mail-order tattoo equipment is not difficult to get, and one's own skin is a tempting target.

Tattoo artists, like any tradespeople, vary in their level of talent. (Interestingly, "jailhouse" tattoos—tattoos done covertly within the prison system—are said to be of some of the highest quality today.) In the past decade or so, however, a handful of individuals extensively trained in the fine arts have turned to tattooing as a living, and are producing expensive, artistic work. At the better tattoo "studios," such artists wonder whether tattooing will ever achieve fine-art status, as urban graffiti did not long ago.

Tattooing, however, cannot be collected without permanently sacrificing one's own skin. Nor can it be resold, since the goods forever accompany the bearer. However, antique tattoo "flash"—the reference illustrations that tattooists show their customers—has become collectible.

roughly $50 to $150. The site is bandaged and sore for a few days. In a week or so, the scab will fall off, revealing the tattoo in its full, vibrant splendor.

Tattooing is not without significant medical risks. Many parlors create tattoos using reused needles. Some tattoo shops advertise "hospital sterilization," a misleading claim since hospitals use disposable equipment for all procedures involving blood. While there are no clear statistics linking tattooing with such diseases as hepatitis and AIDS, people who patronize such establishments may be putting themselves in danger of contracting these infectious diseases. Bacterial infection is also a possibility. Due to such concerns, 16 states regulate tattooing in some way, and three states have banned it outright.

Perhaps a more common drawback is a possible allergic reaction from tattoo ink. Tamala Bradford, a data-entry clerk for a billing company, summarizes her experience: "I had two cherries tattooed on my ankle. To me, it was great—like permanent jewelry— until I developed an allergic reaction and had to have my tattoo removed."

Every Picture Tells a Story

In 1990 an article in *American Family Physician* said that "finding a tattoo on physical examination should alert the physician to the possibility of an underlying psychiatric condition." Many people experienced in giving, getting, studying, or seeing tattoos would call this statement an outmoded, ludicrous, and perhaps dangerous generalization. Be that as it may, many others judge a person negatively based on the mere existence of a tattoo. So why get one?

Some tattoo parlors rely almost entirely on business from military personnel. Operation Desert Storm produced thousands of new clients.

For many, tattoos have an erotic appeal, a fact supported by the type and placement of many tattoos. For others, tattoos can express devotion to someone (known in tattoo parlance as a "vow" tattoo). A newer type of tattoo furnishes a realistic portrait of friends and family, a kind of snapshot of your honey or of junior that you'll never lose. In still other cases, peer pressure plays a role: the tattooee's objective is to be part of a group. U.S. Marines, for example, are notorious for their USMC tattoos.

In almost all cases, the desire to get a tattoo is passed through personal networks. Amy Buecher, for instance, a certificate writer at an insurance company, had a boyfriend with a number of tattoos and had always wanted one herself. She went to a parlor and had a unicorn tattooed on her back.

"I get a lot of dirty looks, and I have problems with my family about it, but I don't care," she says. Amy is also a confessed victim of "tattoo fever," a condition that can be summarized in a nutshell: once you get one, you have to get another. She now has a heart on her toe, a lion cub on her right thigh, a rose on her arm, a bird on her other arm, another unicorn on her shoulder, and a rose with the word "Harley" on the other shoulder. Tattoo number eight is in the planning stage.

Sonny Tufts, a tattoo artist at South Street Tattoo in Philadelphia, is also well inked. Before switching to the world of tattoos, he studied drawing and painting at a well-known art school. "I've got a picture ID wherever I go," kids Sonny, flashing a forearm on which his name is emblazoned amid an ornate design. "Doesn't work for cashing checks, though," he cautions wryly.

Tufts got his first tattoo—an eagle on his biceps—to match the tattoo that his deceased father had had. He is, nonetheless, skeptical about the "meaning" that tattoos can hold for others. "Basically, tattoos are weird things, and I don't understand why people get them," he says. "If I can talk someone out of a tattoo, I figure they shouldn't have one. If they're on the fence, I'll tell them to come back another day. I never try to talk someone into it."

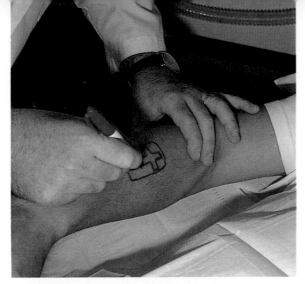

Lasers can remove tattoos with little pain or scarring. Above, the area to be lasered is outlined.

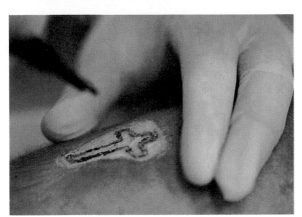

The laser disrupts the pigment molecules in the tattoo, erasing the tattoo but leaving a burn.

Tattoo Removal

What happens on that inevitable day when the tattooed person grows tired of his or her "body art"? Fortunately for them, there's good news. "Tattoo removal has evolved rapidly in recent years," says Stephen Greenbaum, M.D., a dermatologic surgeon at Thomas Jefferson University Hospital. "Unfortunately, the patient will still be trading his tattoo for a scar or a similar mark."

Dermatologists approach tattoo removal in three ways:

• *Surgery.* Doctors can cut out the tattoo, leaving a linear scar. As with any removal procedure, the severity of the scar will be partly determined by the tattoo's location.

• *Dermabrasion.* The doctor will literally sand away the skin over the tattoo. The sanding procedure is sometimes followed with an application of acid, special gauze, or salt to lift the pigment out of the dermis.

• *Laser treatment.* This strategy, which entails less pain and scarring, is rapidly over-taking the first two. The carbon dioxide (CO_2) laser is the most commonly used. It works best for shallower tattoos, although it leaves a burn. The laser that dermasurgeons consider a breakthrough is the Q-switched ruby laser, which can effectively disrupt pigment molecules and remove most tattoos. It works well against navy blue and black pigments and other darker colors, but is not as effective for yellows and oranges.

"We've had great results with the Q-switched ruby laser," says Javier Ruiz-Esparza, M.D., an associate clinical professor of dermatology at the University of California at San Diego. "We are now researching lasers that will be specific for certain tattoo colors."

Tattoo Alternatives

There *are* other options when it comes to body art. Transfer decals, for example—available through certain beauty shops, costume stores, and magazine ads—look just like tattoos, but can be washed off. Many tattoo shops also offer them, in some cases to help customers decide whether or not they want to commit their precious dermal areas to the real thing.

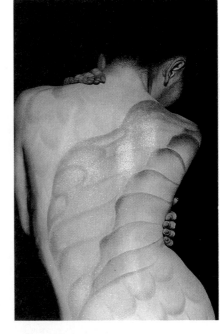

Another safe, non-permanent alternative is the use of makeup pencils to carefully execute body images. This kind of surrogate tattoo can go virtually anywhere on the body (see photo at right) and, for that special, flirtatious occasion, can be placed for maximum dramatic impact. Makeup pencils that lend themselves to this work come in every imaginable color, from such well-known sources as Lancôme, Christian Dior, and Estée Lauder. It's essentially a do-it-yourself project, and, best of all, the designs come off easily with skin cleanser and water.

Contact Lenses: are they for you?

by Janet C. Tate

Imagine throwing away your eyeglasses once and for all and gaining sharper, clearer vision in the bargain. Imagine such unencumbered eyesight without the hassle of cleansing, disinfecting, or storing contact lenses ever again. Imagine having the blue (or green or brown) eyes you've always wanted —with nothing more than a slip of a disk.

Welcome to the brave new world of contact lenses, where modern technology has turned the age-old problem of vision correction into a quick-change, disposable commodity. These small disks, made of special plastics or flexible, gel-like substances, float on the surface of the cornea (the clear eye tissue that covers the iris and pupil), on a thin layer of tears. Contacts provide a vision-correction option that many people find more cosmetically appealing. And with contacts, there is no eyeglass frame to interfere with peripheral vision. If you've tried contact lenses in the past and gave them up because of infection, inconvenience, or just discomfort, now may be the time to give them another try. And if you've never tried contacts before, your options—and chances for success—have never been greater.

Before switching to contacts, it is essential to see a qualified, licensed ophthalmologist or optometrist who specializes in contact lenses and who can give you the best fit and individualized recommendations. Here are some of your contact-lens choices:

Hard Lenses

Besides their cosmetic advantage over eyeglasses and, at the time, the sheer novelty of it all, the original hard-plastic contact lenses introduced to consumers in the 1950s and

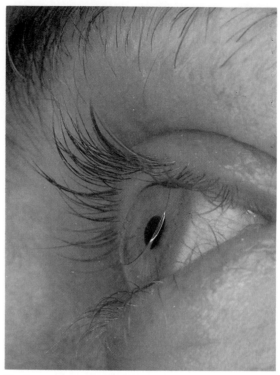

Each year, thousands of Americans abandon traditional eyeglasses for the superior vision and cosmetic appeal offered by contact lenses.

1960s had two advantages that are still highly valued today: they were durable, and they were fairly easy to maintain. Composed of a Plexiglas-type material, these contacts lasted as long as 10 years and required only minimal care and cleaning. But they were easily dislodged, and the scenario of adults crawling around on all fours searching for lost lenses was an all-too-familiar sight.

Perhaps the primary disadvantage of these impermeable plastic lenses was that they hindered oxygen flow to the cornea, making them uncomfortable for many wearers. The cornea is avascular, so no blood vessels bathe the area with nutritive oxygen. As a result the cornea "must get its oxygen from the atmosphere, and waste products, such as carbon dioxide, must be released to the air," says Larry J. Davis, O.D., a contact-lens specialist at the Bethesda Eye Institute in St. Louis, Missouri. "When we place a piece of plastic over the cornea, we interfere with its ability to exchange vital gases."

The discomfort of hard lenses, as well as the common problem of corneal swelling and of temporarily blurred vision when switching to eyeglasses, eventually drove many users away. Hard-plastic lenses are rarely prescribed anymore—usually just for severe cases of astigmatism (a misshapen cornea), or for patients who have thoroughly acclimated to them and don't want to switch to the newer varieties.

A new generation of hard contacts, known as rigid gas permeable lenses (RGPs), is now forging a renaissance in hard-lens popularity. Introduced in 1978, these new hard lenses contain silicone, which permits oxygen to reach the cornea more easily than occurs with the old hard lenses. RGPs retain their predecessor's durability and ease of maintenance, and many ophthalmologists believe they provide sharper vision correction than even soft contact lenses. Davis adds, "They

Hard Lens

also provide a more normal environment for the [cornea] epithelial cells, and thus don't interfere as much with the normal physiology of the front of the eye."

Soft Lenses

The advent of soft contact lenses in 1971 was heralded as an end to the vexations of hard contacts. They quickly became quite popular, and today nearly three-fourths of the contact lenses being worn in the United States are soft lenses.

Unlike the rigid plastic in RGPs, soft lenses are composed of a gel-like, flexible plastic that is between 40 and 80 percent water. This composition permits better oxygen flow to the cornea to provide a considerably more comfortable fit and sustained relief from dryness and tearing, common problems for some hard-contact-lens and RGP wearers.

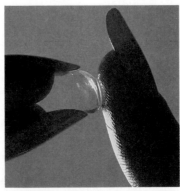

Soft Lens

But soft lenses are not without their drawbacks. While their initial cost may be less than that of RGPs, they require a costly cleaning-and-disinfection regimen, and they must be replaced more often. So the cash outlay in the long run may match or even exceed the cost of RGPs.

The vision correction of soft lenses is frequently not as acute as with hard and RGP lenses, and their water-based composition makes them more susceptible to bacteria and protein deposits from eye fluids. "In order to be soft and water-absorbent, soft lenses have a lot of microscopic pores within the polymer. It's easy for bacteria to get stuck to one of those holes," says H. Kaz Soong, M.D., associate professor of ophthalmology at the W. K. Kellogg Eye Center at the University of Michigan in Ann Arbor. Protein-deposit formation depends upon an individual's eye chemistry and how frequently the wearer blinks, as well as the dryness of the daily environment. Some relief from this problem may be in sight, however. New types of soft lenses are being developed that feature a thin polymer coating that helps shed protein deposits more easily, thus reducing the risk of contamination of the contact-lens surface.

Extended-Wear and Disposable Lenses

The chores of daily cleaning and disinfecting that accompany soft contact lenses are eliminated with extended-wear lenses. These soft lenses are even thinner and more oxygen-permeable than regular soft lenses, and they were originally prescribed for wearing periods of up to 30 days. However, recent studies indicate a sharp increase in the incidence of infections associated with soft-contact-lens wear, and especially with extended-wear lenses. The Food and

Drug Administration (FDA) now requires labels on extended-wear contact lenses that warn against wearing the lenses for more than seven continuous days, and this is now the recommendation of most eye-care practitioners as well.

"It's really the closed eyelid that provides an environment to develop many of the complications associated with oxygen deprivation," explains Davis. He advises extended-wear users to leave the lenses in for up to six nights, then remove them for cleansing and overnight disinfection, just as with daily-wear lenses, before inserting them again for another continuous period of time.

Perhaps the ultimate in contact-lens freedom is the relatively new disposable soft lenses, which are actually extended-wear lenses that are simply thrown away after a week of wear. A year's supply of disposable lenses does cost more up-front, but they can be as economical as any other type of contact lens in the long run, since there is no investment in cleaning materials or other maintenance products.

Contact Lenses for Special Cases

After about age 40, many people develop presbyopia, a form of farsightedness requiring bifocal correction. Traditionally, those

Wearer Beware

Contact lenses can broaden your vision options, but they can also lead to a variety of problems—some potentially serious. Especially with soft-contact-lens wear, it is essential to follow cleansing and prescribed wearing times scrupulously to avoid lens contamination and eye infections. At the first sign of any irritation, sudden intolerance of the lenses, redness, itching, or excessive tearing or eye discharge, the lenses should be removed immediately, and the symptoms reported to your eye-care practitioner. Here are some eye problems commonly associated with contact-lens wearers:

Giant papillary conjunctivitis is typified by tearing, redness, irritation, itchiness, and increased eye secretions. Irritation of the upper eyelid from the lens, usually as the result of overwearing the lenses, may be the culprit, although the condition can also develop when deposits on contacts set up an allergic reaction on the inner eyelid.

Acanthamoeba keratitis is on the rise. Often the result of using unsterilized homemade saline solutions with soft lenses, this difficult-to-treat disease produces irritation, blurred vision, and light sensitivity, and can lead to blindness. The risk of contamination of the lenses from the *Acanthamoeba* microorganism greatly increases when lenses are worn while swimming.

Ulcerative keratitis is an ulcer and inflammation of the cornea that can lead to permanent vision loss. The number of reported cases is increasing, especially among wearers of extended-wear lenses.

While serious corneal damage usually results from infection, "an ill-fitting contact lens can damage the cornea and cause scarring in the long run. It is relatively rare, but it can occur," says Soong.

Other musts to avoid for contact-lens wearers: hair spray; cigarette smoke; and dust, pollen, and other airborne allergens. Lens wearers should also forgo using regular eye drops (those not specifically intended as contact-lens rewetting drops). These drops may "get the red out," but they may also permeate the lens and irritate the eye. It is also a good idea to let the contact-lens case air-dry after use to reduce the chance of infection.

In addition, some wearers may become allergic or sensitive to certain chemicals found in many contact-lens care and cleaning products. The preservative *thimerosal*, often found in saline rinsing solutions, can cause redness and irritation for many users. Ask your eye-care practitioner to recommend a preservative-free alternative.

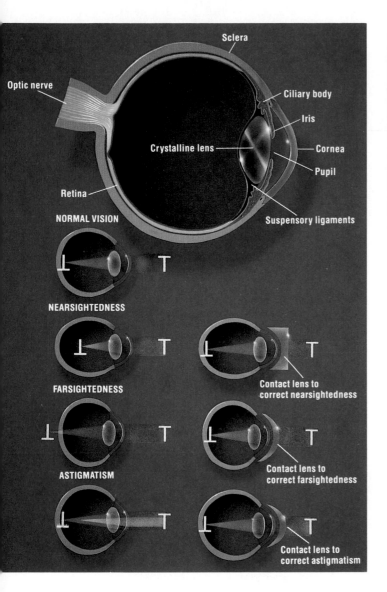

Sclera

Optic nerve

Ciliary body

Iris

Crystalline lens

Cornea

Pupil

Retina

Suspensory ligaments

NORMAL VISION

NEARSIGHTEDNESS

FARSIGHTEDNESS

Contact lens to
correct nearsightedness

ASTIGMATISM

Contact lens to
correct farsightedness

Contact lens to
correct astigmatism

Aside from correcting ordinary vision problems (left), contact lenses can also have such purely cosmetic functions as changing eye color (above).

with presbyopia who were interested in contact lenses were prescribed a near-vision lens for one eye and a far-vision lens for the other, with only limited success. New types of *bifocal lenses* are now replacing that awkward solution. One type of bifocal lens, called a "translating" lens, must be positioned on the cornea precisely, because the lens's top half carries the far-vision prescription, and the bottom half the near-vision prescription. Another lens, the "simultaneous-vision" lens, combines the two prescriptions and lets the brain decide which focus to use.

Some wearers find that their vision isn't as sharp with bifocal contact lenses, but new designs in development may help improve vision quality. Fitting for bifocal contact lenses can be arduous, often requiring appointments over several weeks.

Toric lenses are for patients with misshapen corneas, or astigmatism. "With astigmatism, instead of the cornea being round or spherical, it is warped," explains Soong. "You frequently have astigmatism occurring with far-sightedness and nearsightedness. But toric lenses, which are usually soft, are prescribed for those with moderately severe to severe astigmatism."

Tinted lenses can transform light-colored eyes to dark, and vice versa. It is not uncommon for patients requiring no vision correction whatsoever to wear tinted lenses merely for the cosmetic effect. Some wearers of tinted lenses report a decrease in their peripheral vision. But a good fit, which means as little movement of the lens on the eye as possible, may alleviate the problem.

Unfortunately, not everyone who wants contacts can wear them. Tears are critical for contact-lens success, and some people don't produce enough. Other people suffer from chronic allergies that irritate the eyes. And in some cases, pregnancy may interfere with lens wear by swelling the cornea. Still, some 24 million Americans claim that contacts are far superior to eyeglasses.

Without quick medical attention, a person attacked by a swarm of bees could easily die from the stings.

About Bites and Stings

by Gode Davis

While traveling on various international medical assignments, physician Rose Anderson had run-ins with many of the world's most menacing "creepy crawlies." She'd been stung by a lethal scorpion, survived an attack from a swarm of giant Indian bees, and been bitten by a vicious funnel-web spider.

She died while picnicking in Maine—succumbing within an hour after being stung by a yellow jacket, an ordinary American wasp.

Since wasp venom has only a low toxicity, multiple stings are usually required to produce symptoms more serious than slight pain and localized swelling. In Dr. Anderson's case, her previous stings and bites had sensitized her to any additional stings. Her past stings had caused her body to produce certain antibodies. When she was stung again, the new infusion of antigen (the wasp venom) combined with antibodies, causing the release of histamines, the same body chemical that causes the nasal symptoms of a mild cold. In this case, though, histamines were released in amounts massive enough to generate an overwhelming reaction called *anaphylaxis*. She experienced facial and airway edema, a virulent skin rash, severe muscle cramps, and breathing difficulty. Ultimately her blood pressure dropped and she experienced respiratory failure, and an hour after being stung, Dr. Anderson died.

Of 15,803 Hymenoptera (bee, wasp, or ant) stings reported in the United States during 1990, 128 stung persons experienced serious allergic reactions. Each year, hypersensitivity to insect stings claims dozens of American lives.

As if the Hymenoptera aren't enough to worry about, several prominent arachnids common to North America possess even more-potent venoms. Dangerous examples include the black widow and brown recluse spiders, the bark scorpion, and the giant desert centipede. All the creatures have an alarming potential for delivering poisonous stings and bites. Fortunately, many insect or arachnid stings and bites are preventable, most are treatable, and, if prompt and correct first-aid and medical measures are administered, adverse symptoms can be reduced and recovery is virtually certain.

Generic Facts about Stingers/Biters
The venom of any insect/arachnid stinger or biter is produced in special glands. In stinging creatures, these reservoirs are usually located inside the abdomen, with tubes leading to tail-situated stingers. In venomous biters, special glands inside the creature's head deliver venom to efficient fanglike structures. Venoms consist of naturally occurring substances, such as proteins and enzymes, that are toxic when injected in high doses or concentrations; thus, in the worst cases, the effects of envenomation (the delivery of venom through a bite or sting) can be reversed only by using antivenins (antidotes to venoms).

Bees, Wasps, Ants and Their Stings
Bee, wasp, and ant stingers are really modified egg-laying organs (ovipositors). So only the females are capable of stinging. Bees and ants are not usually carnivorous. Their stinging apparatus has evolved primarily for self- and social-defense purposes. Wasps, however, sting not only in self-defense, but also to put their prey into a state of suspended animation; the prey then become food for parasitic larvae.

Stinging occurs when the stinger's structural components, lancets and stylets, are thrust into the victim's tissue. In bees and wasps, the venom comes from two glands within the abdomen that are attached to the base of the sting shaft: the poison gland and its reservoir, and the Dufour's gland.

Most stinging ants have similar venom-producing glands. The worst example, the fire ant *(Solenopsis invicta),* is a red ant native to the Southeastern states. Its sting can produce a welt, intense pain, and, finally, a pustule that may form a small scarred area. While the venom itself is not considered a high-grade toxin, components of the venom can cause serious and occasionally fatal allergic reactions in sensitive persons.

Swarms of aggressive, social bees (such as the much-feared African "killer" bee now migrating over the U.S. border from Mexico) and disturbed nests of swarming wasps are capable of delivering hundreds of envenomations during a single sting episode. Whenever bees, wasps, or hornets attack in a swarm, the initial sting triggers an alarm pheromone, or scent, that is deposited on the victim. The pheromone continues to elicit attack behavior from the other insects in the hive or nest. (Stinging ants are also capable of depositing alarm pheromones.) Because the venom from multiple stings possesses a cumulative potency, serious, even fatal, systemic reactions sometimes result.

Literally thousands of venomous insect species are indigenous to North America, but only the histamine-loaded venom injected by honeybees *(Apis mellifera),* yellow-jacket wasps of the genus *Vespula,* hornets of the genera *Dolichovespula* and *Vespa, Polistes* genus paper wasps, and the alkaloid-

▲ Honeybee

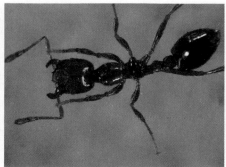

▲ Fire Ant

▲ Yellow Jacket

Stinger/Biter	Range (where prevalent)	Symptoms (serious)	Treatment (most common)
Honeybee	Entire U.S. and southern Canada	difficult breathing	epinephrinc or antihistamine
Fire Ant	Southeast U.S.	burning pain	anti-alkaloid or antihistamine
Yellow Jacket	Eastern U.S. Far West	difficult breathing	antihistamine
Black Widow	Western U.S.	rigid abdomen	antivenin
Brown Recluse	Midwest U.S.	tissue necrosis	clean wound
Bark Scorpion	Southwest U.S.	extreme pain, neurologic anxiety	antivenin
Giant Desert Centipede	Southwest U.S.	tissue necrosis, ulceration	clean wound

Accurate statistics on the number of persons stung or bitten each year by insects and arachnids are virtually impossible to compile. It is fair to say that most bites and stings go unreported. Generally, only serious allergic reactions require hospitalization.

▲ Brown Recluse   Black Widow ▼   ▼ Bark Scorpion   ▼ Giant Desert Centipede

rich venom of fire ants carry a strong potential to produce hypersensitivity. Wasp venoms also contain tiny amounts of enzymes capable of producing tissue and blood-cell breakdown (hemolysis). Hymenoptera venoms generally consist of a complex mixture of polypeptides, and contain only enough histamines and other irritants to cause painful local reactions during a single sting.

Honeybees have barbed stingers. When inserted into a mammal's flesh, this stinger becomes too tightly secured for the bee to remove it. When the stinging apparatus is left behind, the resultant trauma kills the bee shortly thereafter. Removing a honeybee's stinger can also be traumatic for humans: if the stinger is squeezed while it's being taken out, additional venom can be pumped into the skin. To avoid compressing the sting sac, the sting site should be inspected for the presence of the stinger, which should be removed by scraping. Once the stinger is removed, treatment should include applying cold compresses to the sting site and perhaps taking over-the-counter antihistamines.

In more-serious cases of multiple stings or apparent allergic reaction, a physician or emergency paramedic team should be immediately contacted. It should be noted that up to 80 percent of allergic reactions occur in persons without previous allergic histories, and most deaths from insect stings occur within the first 60 minutes after envenomation.

Spider Bites

All spiders are venomous. Spiders lack mandibles or jaws. Instead, they bite their prey with fanglike *chelicerae,* which have venom glands attached to their bases. Spider chelicerae vary greatly from species to species: some jab down; some move laterally. Whatever the case, the design of the chelicerae's tip is well-suited for maximum envenomation of a spider's natural prey. To bite human beings, spiders require a set of powerful "fangs" able to effectively inject extremely toxic venoms. Fortunately, only eight or nine spider genera (out of 30,000 species) have the requisite fangs and venom.

One notorious example so equipped is the black widow. Naturalist Roger Caras once

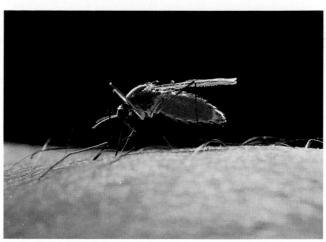

In the United States, mosquito bites usually only cause mild discomfort. Tropical mosquitos are much more dangerous to humans.

helped treat a man who was bitten by a black widow on the penis while using an outdoor privy. "It was some hours before an ambulance reached us. During that time the doctor feared for the man's life. He suffered all the symptoms of extreme shock; and the terrible board-like rigidity of his abdomen, the agonizing 'charley horses' in his arms and legs, and his sobbing are not easy to forget," Caras remembers.

The sharp fang part of a mature black widow's chelicerae is tiny as spider fangs go, about 0.0345 inch long, but, drop for drop, its venom is about 15 times more potent than a prairie rattlesnake's. Several of the *Latrodectus* species, including the female black widow, a coal-black bulbous spider 0.75 to 1.5 inches long with a bright red hourglass marking on its abdomen, are among the deadliest of spiders. Black widows are most prevalent in the western states, but they are also indigenous to the East and Southeast. Males of *L. mactans mactans* possess the toxic venom, but can't envenomate people—their fangs are too small. (Even in females the amount of venom injected varies—three to five seconds are needed for maximum envenomation.) Black widows prefer damp locations to spin their irregular webs—basement windowsills or the underside of toilet seats, for instance, are ideal habitats.

Their venom is a polypeptide mixture that appears to act on nerve terminals to produce an excessive motor "twitch" response. If a black-widow bite is suspected, a physician or paramedic team should be contacted immediately. Less severe envenomations produce only local pain and muscle spasms. These can be treated with analgesics and resolved within a 24-hour period. More serious bites might require general anesthesia, and can involve the use of black widow spider antivenin, a horse-serum product. Without the use of antivenin, symptoms may persist from 48 to 72 hours. Mortality for untreated black-widow bites can be as high as 20 percent for serious envenomations. If a pregnant woman is bitten, the venom may induce a spontaneous abortion.

Equally dangerous are the *Loxosceles* spiders, including *L. reclusa*—the dreaded brown recluse. Such spiders with tissue-killing, or necrotizing, venoms are most prevalent in the Midwest, but are found throughout the United States. Rather common-looking, they are rarely identified because most persons don't realize they've been bitten until a hardened area with a small raised center develops. The painful vesicle quickly ruptures and becomes a small, dark, target-shaped necrotic lesion that slowly increases in size for several weeks. In the worst untreated cases, permanent scarring, gangrenous infections, and even death can result. Treatment entails a physician's careful removal of dead tissue, careful cleaning of the wound area, and tetanus shots. A specific brown recluse spider antivenin is being developed.

Bites from the tarantula and wolf spider species can be painful, although they are rarely serious. Antiseptics to prevent infection and the use of a cold compress are usually sufficient treatment.

Scorpion Stings

The bark scorpion *(Centruroides exilicauda)*, found primarily in Arizona and several other states of the U.S. Southwest, belongs to a potentially lethal North American genus. Other species found in the southwestern desert regions and the southeastern states are capable of producing painful, but not life-threatening, stings. Like spiders, scorpions possess chelicerae, but these are just pincers without venom glands. The venom glands are located in the final abdominal section closest to the animal's stinging tail. After a serious scorpion sting, a rather painful tingling sensation begins in the envenomated area, followed by spreading excruciating pain radiating from the sting site. Other symptoms include high fevers, extreme agitation, and inconsolability. In the worst instances, death may result. The more potent scorpion venom contains polypeptides, which can affect both parasympathetic and sympathetic nerve endings.

Arizona's "bark" scorpions derive their name from their light color and a tendency to favor woody material, such as fallen trees, as a hiding place. They frequently are discovered clinging to the bottom of things upside down. An antivenin derived from goat serum is available for treating the most serious U.S. cases. Up to 10,000 Americans are stung each year, but most are mild envenomations. Scorpion stings are considered a more serious threat in Mexico, where six deadly species kill thousands each year—despite available antivenins.

Centipedes

Indigenous to the Southwest is another dangerous arachnid, *Scolopendra heros,* or the giant desert centipede. A comparatively large creature often attaining a length of 6 to 8 inches, it possesses a powerful biting apparatus for injecting venom. The bite comes from a centipede's single pair of maxillipeds in the rear of its mouth; each maxilliped ends in a curved, needle-like, medially turned-in venom fang. A centipede's venom gland is a whitish, cylindrical sac containing an as-yet poorly analyzed yellowish fluid; in fact, little is known about the properties of centipede venom. Bites from large centipedes can cause intense local pain, ulceration, and induce a tissue necrosis that is slow to heal. With no antivenin for centipede bites yet available in the United States, victims must apply immediate antiseptic into the fang punctures and soak the wound in Epsom salts to relieve discomfort.

Insect and arachnid stings and bites are certainly a potential American hazard. The U.S. is home to many other insects capable of producing mild symptoms, from ticks, lice, and mites to the conenose bug, which can produce an inflamed area around the bite site up to a foot in diameter.

FIRE SAFETY IN THE HOME

by Kenneth E. Isman

Fire can sweep through a home in minutes, killing or injuring the occupants and causing great property damage. Most such tragedies could be averted if the residents had invested in smoke alarms.

During 1990 a startling 5,195 fire deaths occurred in the United States. Another 28,600 people were injured due to fire, and $8 billion worth of property was destroyed. These numbers are particularly devastating in light of the fact that more than 77 percent of these losses occurred in homes —apartments, condominiums, or single-family dwellings.

Americans continue to insist that fires "can't happen to them," yet fire struck 461,000 homes last year alone. These kinds of losses happen every year, yet the technology exists to install in homes devices that would inexpensively and drastically reduce casualties and damage due to home fires.

Such devices, along with simple common sense, would virtually eliminate America's fire problem. A report issued by the National Fire Protection Association in September 1991 concluded that "Residential fire-safety initiatives remain the key to any reduction in the overall fire death toll."

Smoke Detectors

The majority of deadly fires begin between midnight and 6:00 A.M. Most human casualties go to sleep thinking everything is fine, and never wake up again. A properly installed and maintained smoke detector will awaken sleeping occupants and alert them to the danger while the fire is still small—and while a chance for escape still exists.

A variety of smoke detectors are on the market. Some derive their power solely from batteries; others draw their power directly from the home's electrical system. The most reliable smoke detectors from an operational standpoint have a dual power source: their primary power comes from the home's electricity; should the power go out, a battery backup kicks in. The battery-operated variety, although the least expensive smoke detector to purchase, does require regular changing of the battery.

The International Association of Fire Chiefs, using the slogan "Change your clock, change your battery!", urges everyone with battery-operated detectors to change the batteries twice each year. This twice-yearly procedure (going to and from daylight saving time) will ensure that a smoke detector is always functional. Vacuuming the detectors once each year will also help by cutting down the amount of dust buildup around the detector itself.

Smoke detectors in a home should be installed on every floor where there are bedrooms. The optimal location for the detectors is just outside these rooms. Some building and fire codes also require smoke detectors within sleeping rooms in certain circumstances.

Residential Fire-Sprinkler Systems

Unfortunately, all a smoke detector can do is warn building occupants that a fire is in progress. Smoke detectors cannot put out a fire,

Tips for a fire-safe home

A few commonsense tips will go a long way toward preventing home fires from occurring.
• Keep matches and lighters well out of reach of children, and teach children never to play with fire.
• Never smoke in bed, or anywhere else when tired.
• Never put cigarette ashes into the garbage.
• Put fireplace ashes in a noncombustible container, and keep it outside.
• Keep cooking areas clear, and never leave cooking foods unattended.
• Use candles carefully; never walk with a lit candle.
• Keep combustibles away from fixed and portable heaters.
• Never plug too many appliances into a single electrical socket.
• Never run extension cords under rugs.
• Never store or use flammable liquids indoors.
• Practice emergency-exit drills with the family; agree on a place to meet outside to make sure everyone is O.K.
• If you should need to escape from a fire, crawl low under the smoke. The cleanest air is inches off the floor.
• If your clothes catch fire, do not run. Stop, drop, and roll.

so occupants should leave the building as soon as the smoke alarm goes off. However, all too often, people stay to fight the fire and end up as casualties. In the early 1980s, a sprinkler device was developed that detected fires while they were still small, and operated to control or extinguish the blazes while providing time for occupants to escape. These residential fire-sprinkler systems are relatively inexpensive, and hold the promise for drastically reducing our nation's fire losses in the years to come.

Fire-sprinkler systems have, of course, been utilized in business, factory, and stor-

Every home's kitchen should have a fire extinguisher. An extinguisher should only be used to put out small, contained fires.

age facilities to provide life safety and property protection for more than 100 years. But only recently has the technology been refined to the point where a fire can be detected and controlled in a residential structure before it grows into a life-threatening conflagration.

Residential fire-sprinkler systems consist of a series of water-filled pipes and heat-sensitive sprinkler devices carefully spaced throughout specific rooms in a home. When a fire is detected, only those sprinklers closest to the fire open up and discharge water to control the fire. It is a myth that every sprinkler in a system is activated during a fire, causing excessive water damage to a home. In fact, in the overwhelming majority of real fires in sprinkler-equipped homes, only one or two sprinklers have opened and extinguished the fire.

Residential sprinklers are much more aesthetically attractive than are their commercial counterparts. They are chrome- or brass-colored, with heat-sensing elements about the size of a dime. The rest of the sprinkler remains hidden above a ceiling or behind a wall. When the heat sensor detects a fire, it drops away, allowing a small deflector to swing into place while opening a waterway to the pipe. Water then flows from the open sprinkler to put out the fire.

Residential sprinkler systems require relatively small supplies of water. For homes on public-water systems, a common line can be run into the home for both the sprinkler and the domestic water. For homes with their own wells, or where the public supply is insufficient, there are inexpensive stored-water-supply packages that can feed the sprinkler system. These packages take up very little space and can be installed readily in a basement or closet.

Residential fire-sprinkler systems cost about $1.50 per square foot of space to design and install. A system for a typical 2,000-square-foot home would cost about $3,000 (less than the cost of wall-to-wall carpeting). It is best to have the sprinkler system installed while a home is being built. Installation of a system in an existing home presents a greater challenge. The difficulty involved in placing pipes and sprinklers properly can increase the cost as much as 50 percent.

Fire Extinguishers

Three types of fires tend to occur in the home. Class A fires involve ordinary combustibles, such as paper and wood. Class B fires involve flammable or combustible liquids. Class C fires involve electrical equipment.

The best kind of fire extinguisher to have in the home is one designed to combat all three kinds of fire. Fire extinguishers should be placed close to the kitchen and living room, since these are the places where most fires in the home start.

Family members should learn how to use a fire extinguisher *before* a fire occurs. The manufacturer's instructions should be followed carefully. In general, a pin needs to be removed before a lever is pulled to release the chemical. The nozzle should be pointed toward the base of the fire. Care should be taken not to start discharging the extinguisher too early, since the discharge typically lasts only 8 to 12 seconds.

Fire extinguishers should be used only on very small fires (no larger than a trash-can fire) that are confined, or not spreading. Sadly, too many people are injured or killed each year because they choose to fight a fire that can no longer be put out with a fire extinguisher.

GENETIC COUNSELING

Parents who want to know the risk of passing certain inherited conditions on to their children can benefit from genetic counseling. One commonly used prenatal test is ultrasound (above), which helps identify potential health problems of a fetus.

by Jenny Tesar

Carol and Ted are a newly married couple in good health. Although eager to raise a family, they are worried because Carol's sister gave birth to a child with severe mental disabilities. Are they also at risk of bearing a retarded child?

Another couple, Steve and Kathy, know they are carriers of recessive genes that cause an inherited disease. Steve and Kathy each have only one of the genes, and therefore they are both healthy. But if their child inherits the gene from both of them, then he or she will have the disease. What are the chances of this happening?

Not too long ago, only limited answers were available to questions concerning inherited diseases. Many couples accepted this with equanimity, knowing they would love and provide for their children regardless of any problems they might have. Other couples, unwilling or unable to care for children afflicted with severe untreatable disorders, decided not to chance pregnancy. Still others worried through nine months of pregnancy, only to breathe sighs of relief upon the birth of a healthy child, or cries of dismay upon learning that their newborn had a life-threatening genetic disease.

Over the past two decades, however, dramatic advances have been made in identifying the genes that cause certain inherited disorders. More than 200 of the approximately 3,000 inherited disorders can be detected during the early weeks of pregnancy. By diagnosing a problem, doctors may create opportunities for early treatment, thereby preventing or slowing the disorder's progress. In addition, there is the growing possibility that some inherited diseases may soon be cured by implanting healthy genes into afflicted patients.

A New Health Profession

Today families who may be at risk for certain inherited conditions or who have members with birth defects or genetic disorders can obtain information and support from genetic counselors. These health professionals have graduate degrees in genetic counseling or a closely related field, such as medical genetics. For certification by the American Board of Medical Genetics, they also need a year of clinical experience.

Only 20 years old, the field of genetic counseling is a rapidly growing profession. The first class of master's-degree genetic counselors graduated from Sarah Lawrence College in 1971. Today 14 schools in the United States and one in Canada offer master's-level programs in genetic counseling.

Bea Leopold, executive director of the National Society of Genetic Counselors, estimates that there are approximately 1,000 counselors in the United States. The counselors work predominantly in major medical centers and hospitals, although a growing number are establishing private practices. Frequently they are part of a team that includes obstetricians, pediatricians, nurses, social workers, and other specialists.

The Counseling Process

The genetic counselor's first concern is to determine if there is a genetic problem, and, if so, how that problem is inherited. Is it a sex-linked disorder inherited from only the mother? Is it a disorder that develops only if defective genes are inherited from both parents? Is it a disorder caused by a combination of hereditary and environmental factors?

Is Genetic Counseling for You?

Individuals and couples who are most likely to benefit from genetic counseling fall into one of the following 10 categories:

1. People or families with a history of genetic or chromosomal disorders, such as hemophilia, Down syndrome, sickle-cell disease, Tay-Sachs disease, or Huntington's chorea.

2. People or families with physical birth defects, such as spina bifida, congenital heart defects, vision loss, or clubfoot.

3. People or families with learning disabilities or mental retardation, which may have a genetic cause.

4. People or families with a history of multiple miscarriages, stillbirths, or early infant deaths.

5. People with family members who died under the age of 50 from disease.

6. People from an ethnic group with a high risk for certain genetic diseases (for example, people of Mediterranean heritage have a higher-than-average risk of beta thalassemia; Eastern European Jews are at higher-than-average risk of Tay-Sachs disease).

7. People who have been exposed to radiation, chemicals, drugs, or working conditions that they fear may cause genetic abnormalities.

8. Couples who are close blood relatives.

9. Women in their mid-30s or older who are pregnant or planning a pregnancy.

10. Pregnant women whose sonograms indicate the possibility of fetal abnormality.

In general, most people are referred to counselors by their family physicians. State departments of health and local hospitals can also provide referrals, as can the Alliance of Genetic Support Groups in Washington, D.C. (1–800–336-GENE).

Prepregnancy Counseling. The counselor generally obtains a family history, which provides important clues for which diseases to investigate. The counselor asks for health information on the couple, their parents, siblings, first cousins, aunts and uncles, nieces and nephews, and grandparents. Based on this history, the counselor may order certain tests. For example, the blood of a woman from a family with a history of frequent miscarriages may be examined for a chromosomal abnormality known as a *balanced translocation*. This abnormality often leads to miscarriage or birth defects. The blood of an Italian couple may be examined for a gene that causes beta thalassemia, a red-blood-cell disorder that most often affects children of Mediterranean descent. The blood of a couple with family histories of sickle-cell disease will be checked for the sickle-cell gene.

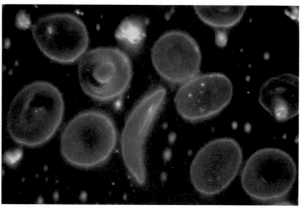

In sickle-cell disease, red blood cells distort into sicklelike shapes, resulting in impeded blood flow. The disease primarily affects blacks and those of Mediterranean and Middle Eastern descent.

Armed with the test results, the genetic counselor is able to discuss the clients' risks and options. If both parents carry one Tay-Sachs gene, then there is a 25 percent risk that their child will inherit two Tay-Sachs genes (one from each parent) and develop the disease. But if only one parent has a Tay-Sachs gene, then there is no possibility that their child will have the disease (though it may inherit that one gene).

Often couples have ruled out pregnancy for fear of a genetic problem that does not exist. For them, testing alleviates anxiety. For couples at risk, the counselor can discuss other reproductive options, including adoption or artificial insemination. The counselor never tells clients what choice to make; rather, he or she provides the information the clients need to make informed decisions.

Prenatal Counseling. If a woman is pregnant and concerned that her fetus may have a genetic flaw, analysis of fetal material is conducted. The two most commonly used diagnostic techniques are *amniocentesis* and *chorionic villus sampling* (CVS). In amniocentesis a hollow needle is inserted through the abdominal wall into the mother's womb, and a small amount of amniotic fluid surrounding the fetus is withdrawn. Fetal cells and other substances in this fluid are studied for abnormalities that may indicate the presence of certain disorders. In CVS a narrow tube is inserted into the womb to suction extra-embryonic fetal cells, which are then analyzed.

For many women the test results are negative, indicating an absence of genetic defects. For clients with a positive diagnosis, the counselor discusses the disorder, its severity, and available treatments, plus the clients' options, which range from abortion to arranging to have the child born in a medical center that specializes in the disorder, to ensure the best possible treatment.

For some disorders the prospects for survival are bleak. But for others the prognosis has greatly improved. Early treatment can dramatically reduce death and illness among children with sickle-cell disease. Improved medical practices, early intervention, and special-education programs enable many children with Down syndrome to lead more normal and productive lives in the community.

The future looks even brighter. Among the latest reasons for hope is gene therapy: curing inherited disease by implanting healthy genes. In 1990 a four-year-old girl became the first person

The future looks bright for treating certain disorders, especially with the emergence of gene therapy.

Prior to World War II, children with Down syndrome rarely grew to adulthood. But with improved medical intervention from birth and better special-education programs, their life expectancy is longer and their quality of life greatly improved.

Down syndrome most commonly results from a chromosomal abnormality in which there is an extra chromosome 21 (below). The syndrome may also occur when part of one chromosome (usually number 21) breaks off and joins another (usually number 14).

ever to receive gene therapy. She suffered from ADA deficiency, a genetic disease caused by the lack of the gene needed to produce adenosine deaminase (ADA), an enzyme essential for normal functioning of the immune system. Using sophisticated laboratory techniques, ADA genes were transfused into the girl's blood. If the procedure is successful, the genes will cause the girl's white blood cells to make ADA, enabling her to build resistance to disease.

Postnatal Counseling. Counseling is also available for couples who have given birth to a child with mental retardation or a birth defect, or who have had miscarriages or stillbirths. "These families comprise a large portion of the people seen by counselors," says Joan Scott, a genetic counselor with Perinatal Associates of Northern California in Sacramento, and president of the National Society of Genetic Counselors. "They're asking what is the problem, what caused it, what can be done about it, and what are the chances of its happening again."

The Cost of Genetic Counseling. Costs of genetic counseling vary significantly, depending on the amount of counseling and on what testing is required. According to Scott,

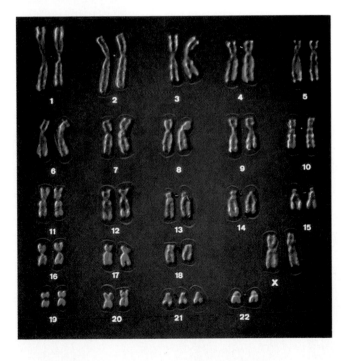

an initial visit with a genetic counselor generally ranges from $60 to $200. Blood-chromosome studies average $350 to $500. Specialized DNA studies to learn a family's genetic history may cost several hundred dollars per family member. Prenatal amniocentesis or CVS averages $1,200 to $1,500.

Most insurance policies cover genetic services, but it is wise for people to check with their insurance carriers concerning their own coverage. "We had a woman today who is 35—an indication for amniocentesis," recalls Scott. "Ninety-five percent of all insurance policies cover this procedure, but hers doesn't unless ultrasound has detected an abnormality."

Difficult Ethical Questions

While offering families valuable help and hope that were heretofore unavailable, genetic testing can also pose worrisome questions. If fetal tests indicate genetic abnormalities, the parents may have to choose between having a child with a disability or aborting the fetus. For some people, including many parents who have previously given birth to a disabled child, this is an agonizing ethical quandary.

Difficult questions also arise for individuals who have a family history of Huntington's chorea. This disease is caused by a dominant gene. That is, anyone who inherits the gene from only one parent will get the disease, which destroys brain cells and causes severe mental deterioration and death in middle age.

Amniocentesis can detect such problems as Down syndrome, hemophilia, and malformations of the brain and spinal cord.

Screening programs to identify people at risk for genetic diseases have a checkered history— they may be helpful, or greatly abused.

Should a person with a family history of Huntington's chorea be tested? Imagine the emotional impact of being told that you have the gene and face ever-worsening debilitation and an early death. On the other hand, the knowledge provided by the test would enable you to decide whether to have children and face the risk of giving them the dread disease. Society might also benefit. By identifying people with the gene and helping them to avoid passing it on to the next generation, it may be possible to gradually wipe out Huntington's chorea.

This leads to another extremely difficult ethical issue: should mass screening programs be conducted to identify people at risk of genetic diseases—or of having children who may be at risk? Screening programs have a checkered history, indicating that the concept may be very helpful, or greatly abused.

In many places, screening of newborn infants for phenylketonuria (PKU) is mandatory. This inherited disorder results in high blood levels of the amino acid phenylalanine because of the absence of a controlling enzyme. Without treatment, severe mental retardation ensues. Screening of a newborn's blood can detect the disease, however. Then, by restricting dietary intake of phenylalanine among affected children, the severity of the disease can be greatly reduced, and the children can function as healthy and productive individuals.

On the Mediterranean islands of Cyprus and Sardinia, voluntary prenatal screening and abortion have almost entirely eliminated beta thalassemia. In the United States, California became the first state to institute mass prenatal screening. In 1986 the state ordered that pregnant women be tested for neural-tube defects, a common class of birth defects including spina bifida and anencephaly. Women can refuse to have the test, but they must then sign a waiver of liability.

In the 1970s many U.S. states had compulsory screening programs for sickle-cell

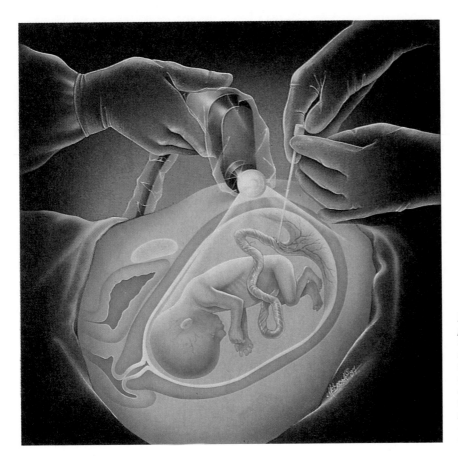

In amniocentesis, a sample of the amniotic fluid that bathes the fetus is removed from the mother's uterus by suction, using a very fine needle. Fetal cells suspended in the fluid can then be grown in the lab and studied to detect genetic disorders.

disease, which is characterized by distorted blood cells that impede blood flow. Though conceived to ensure prompt medical attention for people with the disease, the programs quickly became highly discriminatory. Blacks, who are most at risk of sickle-cell disease, were the only group required to have the tests, even though the gene occurs in many other ethnic groups, particularly those of Mediterranean and Middle Eastern descent. People found to have a single sickle-cell gene, which is not at all harmful, were banned from certain jobs. Many insurance companies charged these people higher insurance premiums or refused to give them any coverage at all. The U.S. Air Force even prohibited them from attending the Air Force Academy.

Today some companies have used genetic tests to screen employees and job applicants. There is concern that this practice may increase as companies seek to reduce health-care costs by refusing to hire people at risk

of chronic illness. Similarly, insurance companies are looking at the possibility of screening people for genetic risk of chronic diseases such as hypertension, cancer, and Alzheimer's disease, as well as for behavioral conditions such as schizophrenia and alcoholism. Who would have access to such data? Might the companies refuse to insure people at risk?

As our knowledge of genetics and heredity grows, and as researchers continue to translate this knowledge into practical technologies, opportunities to misuse these advances will grow. Genetic testing, accompanied by appropriate counseling, has proven to be of great medical value. But it also has raised ethical, legal, and economic issues that will not be quickly or easily resolved. Without care, the rights of individuals could be restricted, or considered secondary to the rights and interests of institutions, governments, and society as a whole.

Orthodontics
for the New Age

by Diana Reese

I f you picture a teenager with a mouthful of metal when you think of braces, you're behind the times. Smaller brackets, new bonding techniques, and space-age wires have substantially reduced the amount of metal in braces. As for teens having a monopoly on tin grins: not at all. Over 25 percent of the 4 million-plus Americans sporting braces today are over age 18, and treatment can start as young as age 4 or as old as 70-something.

Experts stress the importance of correcting bite problems: dental and even general health may be adversely affected, speech can be difficult, and the appearance of the smile can influence a person's self-esteem. "An adult or child who feels unattractive because of crooked teeth or misaligned jaws may become self-conscious and preoccupied with his or her appearance," says psychologist Dr.

Joyce Brothers. "He or she may cover the mouth when speaking or laughing, hesitate to smile, or insist on sitting in a corner to hide his or her profile."

What Braces Fix

The desire to straighten crooked or crowded teeth dates back to ancient history. References to fixing such dental problems can be found in the medical writings of ancient Rome and Greece. But modern orthodontics, as this field of dentistry is called (from Greek words meaning "right" or "correct" and "tooth"), didn't begin until the late 1800s, when St. Louis dentist Dr. Edward Angle developed a system for classifying the different types of dental irregularities, a system still in use today.

Today the range of problems that orthodontists treat extends far beyond just straightening crooked or crowded teeth. The orthodontist considers both dental and facial irregularities, examining the patient's profile and facial harmony and how the teeth relate to each other, as well as how the jaws fit together. When the teeth don't fit together correctly, dentists call the condition a "malocclusion," meaning a bad bite.

Orthodontic problems fall into two categories: skeletal or dental. An example of a bite problem that is skeletal in origin is when one jaw has not grown in alignment with the other. If the condition is dental, the teeth may be crooked, crowded, turned, out-of-line, or even spread out. Sometimes the patient is born having extra teeth or missing certain ones. Both skeletal and dental problems can coexist in the same patient. "Two-thirds of the orthodontic conditions treated in

Today people want to show off their braces! The tin grins of yesterday are being replaced by glow-in-the-dark neon-colored elastic bands (left), ceramic and plastic brackets, and even stylishly designed retainers.

Orthodontics does more than improve dental health—it can influence one's self-esteem. Someone who feels unattractive because of crooked teeth may become overly preoccupied with his or her appearance.

still-growing patients are skeletal," says Lee Graber, D.D.S., Ph.D., a research scientist with the Kenilworth Dental Research Foundation in Illinois, and author of *Orthodontics: State of the Art.*

Here's a rundown of common orthodontic terms and problems:

• **Overbite.** This is the vertical overlap of the upper front teeth over the lower teeth. The front incisors normally fit over the lowers, but in an excessive overbite, they extend down farther than they should. Sometimes the overlap is so great that the lower incisors push into the roof of the mouth. Excessive overbite is also referred to as a closed, or deep, bite.

• **Overjet.** This is the horizontal overlap of the upper front teeth over the lower teeth, and can be measured by the distance between the lower and upper incisors. When the teeth stick out too far, most of us call this problem buck teeth.

• **Crossbite.** In this case, one or more upper teeth actually fit inside the lower teeth.

• **Open bite.** In this less common condition, the teeth don't overlap or even meet at all, leaving an open space between them.

Many of the problems that braces correct are inherited. Some experts believe evolution is to blame: we've still got the same number and size of teeth as our caveman ancestors, but our brains are larger and our jaws are smaller, leaving less room and crowding teeth.

Thumb-sucking—the bane of many parents—can change growth patterns and the way teeth fit together if the habit continues after the permanent teeth start to erupt into the mouth. Other habits like mouth-breathing and tongue-thrusting may also produce bite problems. And, obviously, a traumatic injury to the mouth area, such as a car accident or premature tooth loss, can seriously damage the bite.

Problem Teeth

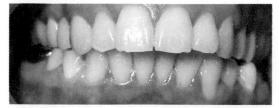

Protruding front teeth caused by the lower jaw being too small or set back too far.

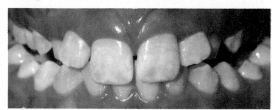

Posterior crossbite in which the upper teeth in the back fit inside the lower teeth.

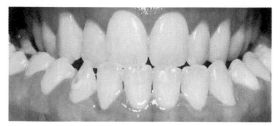

Crossbite is usually caused by an overgrowth of the lower jaw or undergrowth of the upper jaw.

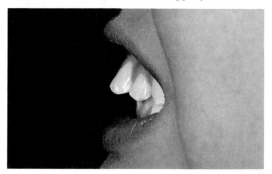

In overjet, or more commonly, buck teeth, the upper front teeth greatly overlap the lower teeth.

Kids and Braces

"The World Health Organization [WHO] reports that 50 percent of children could benefit from orthodontic treatment," Dr. Graber says. To find out if your child is one of them, take him or her to an orthodontist at age 7, recommends the American Association of Orthodontists. Go earlier if you or your child's dentist notice any problems such as chewing difficulties, overlapping or crowding of erupting permanent teeth, a developing problem, like buck teeth or underbite, or jaws that click or pop. Habits like open-mouth breathing or thumb-sucking may also require an earlier visit.

"There's a saying that growth is an angel on the shoulder of the orthodontist. You can work with a growing child and use that growth potential to work to your benefit," says Barton H. Tayer, D.M.D., M.Sc.D., assistant professor of orthodontics at Harvard University School of Dental Medicine. "A four-and-a-half-year-old whose upper jaw is too narrow, preventing the upper teeth from relating normally to the lower teeth, can have the problem corrected relatively simply." But once the jaws and face have completed growing, early growth guidance treatment may no longer be possible.

Show-off Braces

Ironically, many of the improvements in the field of orthodontics have made braces less noticeable. But the latest trend? Neon colors.

"We've gone from people saying, 'I want to hide my braces,' to, 'Look, everybody; see my braces,' " says Jeffrey L. Schauder, D.D.S., from Green Bay, Wisconsin. "The adults behave just like the kids."

Elastic ties, elastics and rubber bands, ceramic and plastic brackets, neck straps on headgear, and even retainers now come in glow-in-the-dark neon colors. Orthodontists across the country report that patients change their elastics with the seasons and the holidays, to match school colors or those of their favorite team. Some girls match their dresses for the prom!

The orthodontists appreciate the craze—anything to encourage patient cooperation. "If only Reebok or Nike would put out braces," sighs Patrick K. Turley, D.D.S., of the UCLA School of Dentistry.

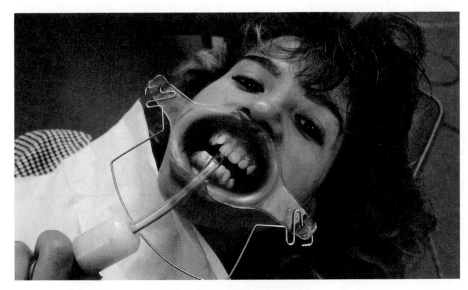

Most kids start wearing braces around ages 11 to 14. Orthodontists use a child's growth potential to rearrange the bones of the jaw and improve the position of the teeth.

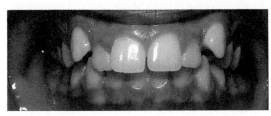

Before orthodontic therapy, this patient had a noticeably bad bite and crowded teeth.

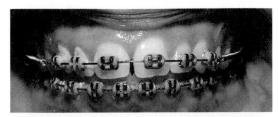

On average, orthodontic treatment takes anywhere from 18 to 30 months.

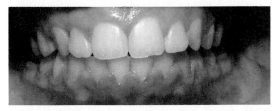

After treatment, the patient has a prettier smile and also a better chance to prevent gum disease.

This is considered the orthopedic phase of orthodontics, where bones are moved, explains Patrick K. Turley, D.D.S., associate professor of orthodontics at the University of California-Los Angeles School of Dentistry. "You set the jaws in the correct position, then braces finalize the position of the teeth."

Most kids won't start wearing braces, though, until age 11 to 12 for girls and 13 to 14 for boys, says Jeffrey L. Schauder, D.D.S., an orthodontist in private practice in Green Bay, Wisconsin. Orthodontic treatment takes anywhere from one to three years, although the average is 18 to 30 months.

Adults and Braces

Dr. Joyce Brothers had braces at age 22 to correct an overbite. Cher also had braces as an adult. More and more adults are opting for orthodontic treatment to improve their smiles. The American Association of Orthodontists reports that 29 percent of people with braces are over age 18, compared to 16 percent in 1979.

It's so acceptable for adults to wear braces that some "yuppies" demand treatment when they don't need it, reports Dr. Graber.

This surge in popularity is due to several factors. People want to look their best. They'll spend money on cosmetic surgery, so why not get their teeth fixed as well?

Furthermore, "it's a lot easier to keep gums and teeth clean when crowding and overlapping are eliminated," says Dr. Robert J. Bray, D.D.S., an orthodontist in the Atlantic City, New Jersey area. And that makes it easier to prevent gum disease, a leading cause of tooth loss in adults.

Adults also find that their teeth shift with age. "There's a tendency for the teeth to drift forward," explains Dr. Graber. Even those who went through orthodontic treatment

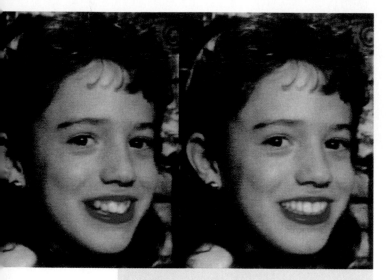

The Smile Bank

What will you look like after braces? Can't wait to see the results? Not sure you want to go through the hassles and expense of orthodontic treatment for a new smile?

Computer imaging—the same high-tech procedure used to help plastic-surgery patients choose a new nose—can let you peek into the future. Now the American Association of Orthodontists is using computer-imaging technology to show how you'll look after orthodontic treatment.

Just send a color photograph that's a clear, close-up frontal shot with a wide "toothy" smile to SMILES, American Association of Orthodontists, 460 N. Lindbergh Boulevard, St. Louis, MO 63141, and include your name, address, and phone number. You'll get an "after" photo returned (like the one above), showing a corrected smile.

during their teen years may find their teeth changing position in mid-life.

Are you ever too old for braces? "You do have to consider the health of the supporting structures," Dr. Tayer says. "The patient must have adequate bony support, but I have a 74-year-old patient right now."

"Adults aren't as healthy as children, either," Dr. Schauder cautions. Gum disease, bone loss, restorations like large fillings and crowns, and diseases like diabetes that make tissue healing more difficult can all interfere with orthodontic treatment. These problems can alter the way bone and gum tissue cells respond to orthodontic brace pressures. "The tissues are less forgiving in an adult, so you may see some gum recession," Dr. Turley says.

Further complicating orthodontics in adults is the simple fact that adults have stopped growing. That leaves surgery as the only option to correct skeletal defects. "Ten to 20 percent of my adult patients do have surgery," points out Dr. Turley. Most dental problems, however, can still be improved with braces.

Most orthodontists agree that treatment may take slightly longer in adults, but Dr. Tayer believes the cooperation from adult patients often compensates for their physical limitations. "You don't have to motivate them."

How Braces Work

What actually happens during orthodontic treatment? The root of the tooth sits in a socket lined with nutrient-providing periodontal fibers in the jawbone. When a gentle force is exerted to move the teeth, the bone is stimulated to produce "osteoclasts," cells that resorb bone, creating space. As the tooth moves, "osteoblasts" are generated to form new bone to fill the now-empty space on the other side of the tooth. "The tooth is always developing a new socket," explains Tayer. "Cells are breaking down bone on one side of the tooth and building bone on the other side."

Braces are used to exert pressure on the teeth. Brackets (usually of metal or ceramic) are bonded, or glued, to the surface of each tooth. Arch wires are fastened to the bracket; miniature wires or tiny elastics actually fasten the main arch wire to the bracket. "The bracket is a handle on the tooth so force can be used to move it in any of the three planes of space," explains Dr. Tayer. "It's like a handle on a suitcase." The arch wire provides the pressure.

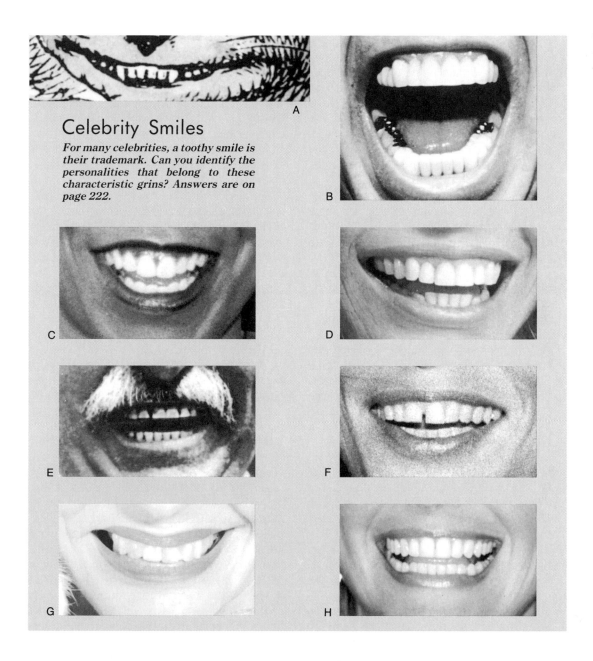

Celebrity Smiles

For many celebrities, a toothy smile is their trademark. Can you identify the personalities that belong to these characteristic grins? Answers are on page 222.

A

B

C

D

E

F

G

H

The correct amount of force has to be used, says Dr. Graber. "Too much, and the cells respond by slowing down; not enough, and the cells don't act at all."

Alternative Orthodontic Tricks

But traditional glued-on braces are just one of the orthodontist's arsenal of tools. Spacers or springs may be placed between teeth to create spaces, sometimes before braces are even put on. An appliance called a tooth positioner may move the teeth if only minor correction is needed, or it may be used to intermesh the teeth after glued-on braces.

Some skeletal problems can be treated by changing the child's growth pattern. Numerous appliances have been developed to do this. Something called a functional appliance may be worn before braces or with them. It may be cemented in place or be removable, but it is designed to help you bite with your jaws in the proper position and to retrain the muscles. Another appliance is called the palatal expander, which helps widen the upper jaw.

Headgear is also designed to help align the jaws. This device, which varies according to the problem being treated, uses your neck or head as an anchor, and can slow down the growth of the upper jaw or pull back the upper teeth that protrude.

Elastics, or rubber bands, may place pressure to move teeth together in a particular position as part of treatment or they may help move teeth closer together when spaces are present.

Surgery is another option. In fact, for adults whose growth is completed, it's the only way to correct skeletal defects.

Once braces come off, treatment isn't finished. Teeth can potentially drift back toward their original position unless an appliance known as a retainer is worn. In fact, some orthodontists are recommending "semipermanent" retainers to be worn two or three times a week "indefinitely," Dr. Graber says.

Advances in Braces

"Everything I use now, I didn't use five years ago when I started my practice," says Jeff Collins, D.D.S., M.S.D., an orthodontist in private practice in the Denver area. "The brackets, the glue, the wires—everything's changed."

There's been a quiet revolution occurring in the materials used in orthodontics, and, as a result, braces are less conspicuous, more comfortable, and even more effective.

Dr. Turley estimates that one-third as much metal is used in today's braces as 20 years ago. It used to be that a metal band was used to wrap completely around the sides of each tooth. "You had to slide them around every tooth, using pliers, and then tap them into position," he explains. Not anymore. Because of their added strength, the bands are often still used on molars (the back teeth used for chewing), but today brackets alone are usually fastened directly onto the front teeth.

Those brackets are even smaller, and they're bonded, or glued, to the tooth's front surface. One type of glue material,

called glass ionomer cement, slowly releases fluoride to help prevent decay around braces.

Brackets made of ceramic materials are translucent and allow the tooth color to show through, making braces even less noticeable. The ceramic brackets are an improvement over the plastic, tooth-colored brackets in vogue several years ago, which stained easily and were weak.

Arch wires were originally made of gold, then stainless steel. They are now made out of space-age materials like nickel-titanium alloy—materials that are much more flexible and elastic, providing just the right amount of force to move teeth, says Dr. Graber. One type is even activated by the heat generated in the mouth. New metals are also used in tiny metal springs, "with permanent memory," he adds, that can create space or pull teeth closer together.

Miniature elastic ties can replace the wire ties that fasten arch wires to brackets. Other elastics, used between bands and brackets, are now made out of specialized plastic instead of rubber bands.

These improvements mean that adjusting braces is easier. "Appointment times are shorter," says Dr. Bray.

And finally, if you're really determined to hide your braces, you can. Lingual braces, introduced in the early 1980s, are placed on the tongue side of the teeth so that they are invisible to the outside world. But these braces take a lot longer for the dentist to position, they may be difficult to adjust to (your tongue feels all that metal), and they may not always work as well. They also cost two to three times more than conventional braces, although some people find them worth it. Lingual braces are not as popular as they were once expected to become, possibly because regular braces, with their aesthetic changes, are more acceptable to adults, says Dr. Graber.

FOOD UNDER SCRUTINY

Food in the U.S. is inspected repeatedly from the time it leaves its point of origin until it is served at a restaurant or sold at the market.

by Abigail W. Grissom

Jack and Marion have a weekly routine: every Wednesday night after their racquetball game they grab a bite to eat at an upscale, homey coffee shop a few blocks from their health club. One evening, after returning home from their meal, Jack got quite sick. Marion, certain that Jack's shrimp dinner from earlier that evening was to blame, contacted the city's department of health. Inspectors paid a surprise visit to the restaurant two days later. They found numerous health-code violations—poorly refrigerated food, dirty sinks, a lax policy for employee cleanliness, even filthy rest rooms. The place was closed down for a month. Since it reopened, officials have inspected the restaurant weekly to monitor compliance.

Although Jack and Marion haven't returned to that establishment again, they never stopped following their Wednesday-night routine. One of their favorite places is a restaurant featuring New Wave food and original live music. Four years ago, local health officials staged a surprise inspection at the restaurant. They gave the establishment a clean bill of health—so clean that they haven't been back for a reinspection since! Unaware of that fact, Jack and Marion still patronize the place, confident that the restaurant is inspected every six months, as dictated by guidelines published by the Food and Drug Administration (FDA).

Should Jack and Marion and other restaurant-goers across America think twice about dining out?

According to Sharon Sachs, the chief of information at the Food Safety and Inspection Service (FSIS) of the U.S. Department of Agriculture (USDA), "Retail exemption laws often allow customers to judge whether a food-service establishment is fit to buy food in—in spite of strict government guidelines that dictate how food *should* be prepared." This means that local governments, who are responsible for carrying out restaurant inspections, may focus their efforts on inspecting known health-code offenders rather than visiting every restaurant in their jurisdiction.

History of Food Protection

To many, the health-inspection system as now practiced may seem unduly lax. Fortunately, however, the consumer food supply is protected by law from the time it leaves its point of origin (barn, field, fishery, etc.) until it is served in a restaurant or sold at the local market. This blanket of protection is a comparatively recent phenomenon. At the beginning of this century, Upton Sinclair's novel *The Jungle,* a thinly fictionalized but well-researched account of life in the Chicago stockyards, raised the first serious concerns about what Americans eat—specifically meat. The book, referred to as "a stomach-turning exposé of unsanitary conditions and deceitful practices in the meat packing industry," caused an uproar that resulted in the Meat Inspection Act of 1906. This measure was one of the first enacted by the government to protect the food supply of consumers. It required the inspection of slaughter of cattle, hogs, sheep, and goats intended for interstate and foreign commerce. The law further mandated that the products processed from these animals be checked for additives, and that the processing plants themselves meet strict sanitation requirements.

Poultry was not subjected to the same government-mandated scrutiny until the 1950s, when its popularity began to soar. The Poultry Products Inspection Act of 1957 required producers of chicken, turkey, and other poultry products to follow the same guidelines as those that are imposed on slaughterhouses and food-processing plants.

Federal Inspection Guidelines

These guidelines currently encompass three phases of inspection that all meat or poultry must pass before being approved by the USDA: (1) animal inspection by USDA veterinarians before slaughter for disease or abnormalities, (2) inspection after slaughter by USDA inspectors of the carcass and internal organs for disease or contamination, and (3) inspection by USDA inspectors, supervised by veterinarians, during processing of the procedures and recipes used and the labels attached to processed products. The initial phase of inspection not only includes a physical examination of the animal, but also entails rapid testing of blood and urine samples from randomly picked animals in the same herd or flock. "Rapid testing," according to Sachs, "is an important development that quickly detects the presence of substances (such as antibiotics and pesticides), but not their precise levels. It's kind of like a home pregnancy test," she says. Samples that contain residues are sent to a laboratory for further analysis to see if the levels are over those set as acceptable by the FDA for animal drugs or by the Environmental Protection Agency (EPA) for pesticides.

The government also inspects a variety of other food products, such as fish and eggs, although meat and poultry are the most strictly monitored.

State and Local Inspections

Health inspections of processed foods other than meat or poultry are monitored by each individual state as long as the products are not sold out-of-state. In addition, states can inspect meat- and poultry-processing plants for in-state sales if the inspectors follow USDA guidelines.

Local governments are responsible for monitoring food that is sold directly to the consumer either in retail food shops or in establishments that sell prepared food. Such establishments are generally divided into three categories: public places (e.g. restaurants, fast-food outlets, taverns, bars, hotels, and street vendors); places that offer semipublic food service

Meat carrying the USDA stamp has been inspected and approved by the U.S. Department of Agriculture.

Who's Inspecting Your Food?

The federal government charges a variety of agencies with the protection of the U.S. food supply:

Agricultural Marketing Service (AMS): inspects egg products for domestic and foreign sale.

Department of Agriculture (USDA): conducts voluntary inspections of fresh and processed foods.

Environmental Protection Agency (EPA): sets tolerance levels for pesticide residues in foods marketed in the United States to ensure that consumers are not exposed to unsafe levels.

Food and Drug Administration (FDA) (part of the Department of Health and Human Services): inspects all foods that move in interstate commerce except meat and poultry and some egg products; enforces the Food, Drug, and Cosmetics Act of 1938, prohibiting shipment of adulterated or mislabeled foods; develops standards on nutrition and food safety.

Food Safety and Inspection Service (FSIS): inspects all meat- and poultry-processing plants engaged in interstate commerce, and operates a joint federal-state program for inspections of meat- and poultry-processing plants not engaged in interstate commerce, also recalls unsafe products after they've reached the grocery shelf.

National Marine Fisheries Service (part of the Department of Commerce) and the **Department of the Interior:** conduct voluntary fee-for-service inspections of fish and fishery products.

(e.g., hospitals, schools, prisons, and employee cafeterias in office buildings); and places that provide limited food service (e.g., private clubs and churches).

Restaurant Inspections

The monitoring of restaurants is especially important because many people eat out today, and food can easily be contaminated in a restaurant setting, resulting in food poisoning (see sidebar on page 226).

Restaurant inspections therefore emphasize the protection of food from all potential sources of contamination. For example, the following areas are checked: the quality of food and its care; personnel; equipment and utensils and their cleaning, sanitation, and storage; water, sewage, plumbing, and toilet and hand-washing facilities; garbage and refuse disposal; insect, rodent, and animal control; and construction and maintenance of physical facilities.

The inspection of food ranges from determining where a restaurant purchases its supplies (they can be bought only from sources that follow U.S. food laws), to how the restaurant refrigerates and heats food. For example, all food that might spoil must be kept either below 45° F (7° C) or above 140° F (60° C). In addition, food must be stored according to very specific standards—a certain height from the floor, for example, or in covered containers made of nonabsorbent materials. Equipment and utensils used to prepare food must be stored and sanitized according to strict guidelines set by the FDA; in addition, thermometers used to measure the temperature of food must be checked regularly to ensure that they are functioning properly.

Employee health is another issue addressed during health inspections. Restaurants may not employ workers who have communicable diseases that can be transmitted through food; nor can they allow employees with skin infections to work around food, as they may carry bacteria that could contaminate the food during preparation. Health inspectors have the authority to prevent an employee from working at a restaurant if it is suspected that he or she carries an infection or disease.

Possible Causes of Food-borne Illness in Restaurants

Food can be contaminated in numerous ways by different types of bacteria. These bacteria and the toxins they produce don't change the appearance or taste of the foods they infect, which makes it difficult to detect the contaminants until the foods have been eaten. (The bacteria themselves cause food-borne infections because they are alive when ingested; the toxins cause foodborne intoxications or poisoning.) Anyone unlucky enough to eat food containing these bacteria or their products may experience acute gastrointestinal illness, the symptoms of which range from mild discomfort to life-threatening disease.

Salmonellosis food infection is caused by many different types of the salmonella bacteria. Most recently, *Salmonella enteritidis* has been implicated in food infections resulting from eating affected poultry, eggs, and other foods. These bacteria cause headaches, vomiting, diarrhea, and fever within 72 hours of ingestion. It can be quite serious or even fatal in very young children as well as the elderly. To prevent infection, eggs and poultry should be well-cooked, and utensils and cutting surfaces should be thoroughly washed immediately after they come in contact with raw poultry.

Staphylococcal food intoxication is caused by *Staphylococcus aureus* bacteria, which grow on various foods—in particular, moist, high-protein foods such as cooked meat and food containing milk and milk products. This type of food-borne illness causes debilitating nausea, vomiting, abdominal cramps, and diarrhea. Symptoms usually appear within one to five hours and are rarely fatal. The bacteria are often carried by humans in the nasal passages and throat, on the hands and skin, and in skin infections in cuts, burns, and pimples. Improper heating and refrigeration of host foods can encourage growth of this bacteria.

***Clostridium perfringens* food infection/intoxication** is caused by the *Clostridium perfringens* bacteria, and accounts for many mild unreported cases of food poisoning. It is found in soil, dust, and the intestinal tracts of humans and animals, and can cause abdominal pain, diarrhea, nausea, and vomiting within 8 to 22 hours of ingestion. It grows in almost any raw food product that is inadequately heated or refrigerated.

Botulism food intoxication is caused by *Clostridium botulinum* bacteria and can be fatal. The bacteria are found in soil, water, and the intestinal tracts of animals and fish; symptoms, which include vomiting, abdominal pain, headache, double vision, and respiratory paralysis, usually appear within 12 to 36 hours. *Clostridium botulinum* bacteria grow in improperly processed (and usually home-canned) foods low in acid, such as green beans, mushrooms, corn, beets, spinach, and tuna.

Inspectors also examine a restaurant's physical premises, including plumbing, which, if improperly installed or maintained, may cause (for example) backups of dirty water that could then contaminate equipment and utensils. Rest rooms for public use are required by law; in addition, employees must have a place where they can wash their hands regularly to prevent the transmission of bacteria carried on the skin. Health inspectors even check the walls, floors, carpets, and ceilings of restaurants to ensure that they can be easily cleaned and do not harbor dirt and other debris that might attract bacteria, insects, or rodents.

To pass inspection and receive the permit or license required to operate, a restaurant must satisfy all local health-inspection codes.

Restaurants and other vendors of prepared food come under especially intense scrutiny from their local health departments. Health codes often require that people handling food wear gloves and hats. Inspectors have the authority to shut down an eating establishment if it does not meet the minimum requirements set forth in the municipality's health codes.

To stay in business, a restaurant must maintain these health-code standards between inspections.

What happens when an inspector finds a violation at a restaurant? Usually the owner is given a reasonable amount of time to fix the problem, depending on its source. If the situation endangers the health of patrons, the establishment must close until it resolves the problem. Owners who refuse to comply with a health inspector's findings can be fined and, if necessary, jailed.

Although the FDA publishes guidelines that detail the thorough inspection of restaurants, there is no one standard set of rules that *must* be followed. Accordingly, local enforcement varies from city to city, depending on the local problems and needs.

A High-Tech Future

The future of health inspections looks bright, especially with the introduction of new methods designed to protect food early in the process. For example, a rigorous inspection procedure known as the Hazard Analysis and Critical Control Point (HACCP) system, developed in the 1960s for the National Aeronautics and Space Administration (NASA) to

ensure that the astronaut food supply wasn't contaminated, is now being adapted by FSIS for meat and poultry inspections. According to veterinarian Dr. Lester Crawford, former head of FSIS, "HACCP is a careful, systematic approach to food safety. You simply do a careful, step-by-step analysis of how a certain food will be processed. Then you designate the steps—the critical control points—where, should something go wrong, the product could become unfit to eat. Finally you set up systems to monitor and quickly correct any problems at those control points."

New noninvasive technologies such as ultrasound, computer imaging, and nuclear magnetic resonance may also someday be used by food inspectors to ensure the quality of food. To detect microbial organisms such as bacteria, gene or DNA probes may also be used, along with monoclonal antibodies. Scientists are also working on breeding salmonella resistance in chickens. Sharon Sachs of FSIS cautions, however, that "these methods are 10 to 15 years down the road. It's very interesting to use science and technology to do a better job [of testing]. We're real excited about things like that, but they're not going to be available tomorrow."

Housecalls

Steven Meixel, M.D., is board-certified in family practice, and practices general medicine as an associate professor in the department of family medicine at the University of Virginia in Charlottesville.

Q *I've read that there has been an increase in the number of rabies cases recently. Why is this? How is rabies spread, and what should I look for?*

A There has been an increase in rabies, but not from the sources you might think. Rabies is almost nonexistent in dogs in this country, due to widespread vaccination. The cat is the most common domestic animal to contract this disease, but the animals that pose the greatest problems are wild animals.

Nearly 9 out of 10 cases are a result of contact with wild animals. Skunks and raccoons are the most common sources, together accounting for over two-thirds of the cases. Bats and foxes can also be a problem. In certain mid-Atlantic and Southeastern states, there have been significant outbreaks of rabies recently in wild animals.

Unfortunately, it's difficult to tell when wild animals have this disease, partly because they don't get as sick as rabies-infected pets do, and partly because we have trouble gauging what "normal" behavior for such animals should be. In addition, there is a "mad" form of rabies as well as a "dumb" form, the latter having no outward symptoms.

The rabies virus comes from animal saliva, and is contracted by people through a bite or scratch that breaks the skin. The virus spreads through nerve cells to the brain and then to muscles and other organs.

The reported incubation period of the disease in humans ranges from 10 days to a year or longer, but once the per-

son has the disease, it is too late. If you are bitten or clawed by a potentially rabid animal, wash the wound with soap and water and seek medical care immediately. The human vaccine is no longer the ordeal it once was, now involving fewer shots injected in the shoulder or thigh.

Rabies has spread at an alarming rate in eastern states. Raccoons appear to be the main source of the disease.

Q *I understand that one can be infected with Lyme disease by a tick and not show any symptoms for years, until the disease arises in a serious form. Is there any way to test for this infection if you think you might have it?*

A Yes, there is. It should first be noted that the disease appears to be spreading. In 1989 there was a 62 percent increase in the number of cases over the previous year. The problem has worsened since then. Most cases are in states along the northeastern seaboard, although Lyme disease also occurs in the Midwest and on the West Coast.

Initially, experts thought that Lyme disease was transmitted only by deer ticks; however, new evidence suggests that it can be spread by five or six different kinds of ticks.

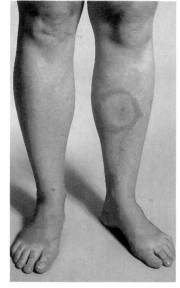

There is far less chance of an infected tick transmitting the disease if the tick is removed from the skin within 24 hours.

If the initial bite goes unnoticed, the disease will usually progress in these stages:
• In most people a small red bump becomes a slowly enlarging red ring (the hallmark of contracting this disease). In about half of all cases, the ring is preceded or accompanied by a headache, fever, and joint pain.
• Weeks to months later, an infection develops in about 80 percent of untreated individuals, with the bacteria affecting muscles, joints, the heart, or the nerves. The disease may stop at this stage.

• Persistent infection may become apparent months to years later. The disease often affects the knees, among other joints. Memory disruptions and other serious neurological problems may ensue.

The blood test for the bacteria is much more accurate the further along the disease has advanced. Some variability in test results exists from one lab to another. Antibiotic treatment can arrest the disease and eliminate the bacteria at any stage, but damage that is significant may continue to linger for years.

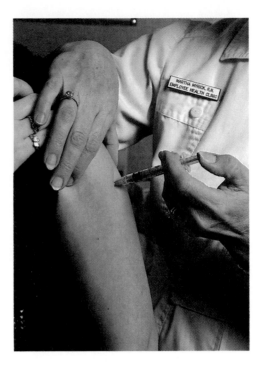

Young people who have not been vaccinated against measles since before 1976 should see their doctors to determine whether revaccination is necessary.

Q *I was vaccinated against measles as a child, but never had a booster shot. Now my college is requiring that I show proof of revaccination against measles in order to be admitted. Why is a second shot needed? Are there other vaccinations that adults need?*

A Measles has declined dramatically since immunizations began, but has now reemerged, mostly in inner-city preschool kids and in high-school- and college-age individuals who were immunized prior to 1976. The latter group received vaccine that was inadequate for granting lifelong protection.

Current recommendations are that people born after the year 1957 (when exposure to measles began to decrease significantly) who have not been vaccinated against measles, mumps, and rubella (German measles) since 1976 should discuss the necessity of immunization with their physicians to try to determine if they have already had the disease or should be revaccinated.

Here are some other adult vaccinations to be aware of:
• Tetanus and diphtheria vaccine is a shot that everyone should have every 10 years;
• Influenza vaccine is recommended for people over 65, anyone at increased risk for influenza or complications from it, and individuals interested in reducing their chances of getting the flu;
• Hepatitis B vaccine is recommended for homosexual males, health-care workers, anyone who has repeatedly contracted sexually transmitted diseases, and anyone in contact with a known carrier of the virus. In general, the more sexual

contacts you have, the wiser it is to get this vaccination.

Q *Is it true that childhood sexual abuse is more common than once thought? How common is it? And what should victims do about it?*

A Sexual abuse of children is defined by a wide range of behaviors, from inappropriate exposure of the adult's or child's body, to genital fondling, penile penetration, or use of children in pornography and prostitution. Females are the primary victims of sexual abuse.

Over the past few years, studies of the prevalence of this problem have produced varied conclusions. Finally, last year a rigorous survey of the data using strict criteria was published in the journal *Pediatrics*. This important report concluded that the incidence of sexual abuse of girls under 14 has not increased but remains at the 10 to 12 percent level that was previously estimated. Nevertheless, this is an extremely high figure, leaving little doubt that there are hundreds of thousands of girls who have been victimized.

The dramatic difference now is that more cases are being reported, and more of the abused are seeking treatment, even decades after the abuse occurred. However, the number of cases reported remains less than 10 percent.

Children often blame themselves for abuse they received. Other victims block out much of the experience. Nonetheless, the trauma lasts long after the event, and can manifest itself in problems ranging from low self-esteem to symptoms of post-traumatic disorder.

Victims must feel free to seek help. Recovery means facing the memories, learning the truth, and being honest about your feelings. Often the best recourse is to find a good counselor to help with this process.

Q *I exercise outdoors during the winter. What are the best clothes to wear when one sweats in the cold weather?*

A Ideally, you should wear material that is breathable and that doesn't hold moisture. Examples of such materials now used for athletic wear are polypropylene, Gor-tex, Capilene, wool, and spandex.

Much athletic wear is still made of cotton. However, cotton holds moisture against the skin, and so, by itself, is not ideal for very cold temperatures. Other suggested guidelines for dressing for cold-weather exercise:
• Dress in layers to trap the heat;
• Don't wear clothing that fits too loosely or too tightly;

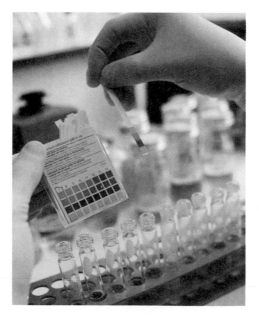

At many companies, the job-application process regularly includes a urine test to determine whether the applicant uses illicit drugs.

• Wear a hat (50 percent of heat loss occurs from the head).

Q *How reliable are home pregnancy tests? Do medications, menstruation, or any other common factors influence the test result?*

A Home pregnancy tests have been used since the 1970s, and the current versions are all basically equivalent and accurate. Taken as a whole, they detect pregnancy 75 to 99 percent of the time, at two days after the missed period. The accuracy is even higher if you wait a few more days.

This accuracy level, though, assumes that you *follow all the instructions correctly*. There are a number of steps that women may not perform properly, including collecting the urine or interpreting the result.

Choose a test kit that gives results quickly, with the fewest number of steps. Most tests provide a toll-free number for you to call if you have any questions.

There are a number of medical reasons why the test might be "tricked" into giving a false positive result, including: conditions that cause you to have protein or blood in your urine, thyroid disease, and menopause. The test can give you a false negative result if done too early or if your pregnancy is ectopic. Medicines that can affect the results include those given for psychiatric conditions or for seizures.

Home pregnancy tests aren't foolproof, so the results should be used with caution. If you think you are pregnant see your doctor, who may retest you and—if you are pregnant—date your pregnancy.

Q *What is the most effective way for employers or others to test for illicit drug use? By a blood test or urine test?*

A Urine tests are most effective. They are standardized and the causes for false positives are clearly defined. Dependable follow-up tests are also available for ambiguous results.

Have a practical question?
Send it to Editor, Health and Medicine Annual, P.O. Box 90, Hawleyville, CT 06440–9990.

Health and Medicine: Reports '92

Aging

▶ Immunization—Not Just for Kids Anymore

Children continue to receive immunization shots to protect them against infectious diseases such as tetanus, diphtheria, and whooping cough. Interestingly, however, as commonplace as immunization is in pediatric practice, it is a subject rarely dealt with in geriatric practice. This is a particularly disconcerting phenomenon considering that all adults who have been immunized with tetanus and diphtheria need a booster immunization every 10 years. Furthermore, all persons over 65 years old should receive an influenza vaccine annually, preferably between mid-October and mid-December before the flu season gets under way. Persons over 65 years of age should also receive a pneumococcal polysaccharide vaccine every five to six years. This recommendation is made in light of a recent study suggesting that the pneumococcal vaccine is more effective in persons less than 65 years of age, both with respect to the percentage of immunized persons protected and the duration of protection. Eighty-five percent of individuals less than 55 years of age were protected for more than five years. In contrast, only 58 percent of individuals 65 to 74 years of age—and just 32 percent of individuals 75 to 85 years old—were protected for more than five years. In view of these results, experts therefore

People over 65 years of age should receive an influenza vaccine annually, preferably between mid-October and mid-December, before the flu season gets under way.

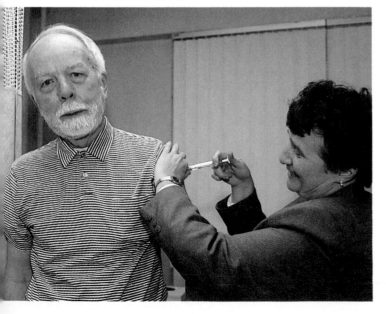

suggest that persons over 65 years of age should be reimmunized every five to six years after their primary immunization with pneumococcal vaccine.

▶ High-Blood-Pressure Treatment in the Elderly

The number of individuals with hypertension increases with age. Physicians divide hypertension into two types: the less serious systolic hypertension, in which the pressure within the arteries is high when the heart is pumping blood; and the more serious diastolic hypertension, in which the pressure within the arteries is high when the heart is not pumping blood. Both types of hypertension increase with age, so that more than 50 percent of persons between 65 and 89 years of age are affected. Systolic hypertension is, almost exclusively, a problem of older adults—it occurs in 6 percent of individuals between 60 and 69 years of age and increases to 18 percent in individuals over 80 years of age.

Both types of hypertension are associated with an increased risk of strokes and heart attacks. Antihypertensive therapy for young patients has been shown to reduce cardiovascular disease. It was never clear if persons over 60 years of age with hypertension would benefit from therapy. In the last two years, however, it has been established that antihypertensive therapy is not only feasible in persons over 60 years of age, but also beneficial.

In 1990 the European Working Party on Hypertension in the Elderly reported that treatment of diastolic hypertension in patients between 60 and 80 years of age reduced their risk of strokes by 50 percent. These results were confirmed and extended by a larger 1991 American study of the benefits of treating systolic hypertension in older adults. Hypertension was easily controlled with a low dose of inexpensive diuretic medication in nearly half of the patients. Two-thirds of patients had their blood pressure controlled with a single medication. Treatment reduced the risk of stroke in all patients over 60 years of age, including those over 80 years of age, by 35 percent. Furthermore, as had been previously reported, the treated patients in this study tended to have fewer heart attacks. There were no significant toxic side effects of the therapy. Thus, in the absence of compelling contraindications, all elderly hypertensive patients should be considered good candidates for diuretic therapy to reduce hypertension and lessen the risk of cardiovascular disease.

▶ Hormone Therapy Effect in Rebuilding Bones

Osteoporosis is characterized by a loss of calcium from bones and ultimately leads to an increased risk of bone fractures. Vertebral collapse leads to loss

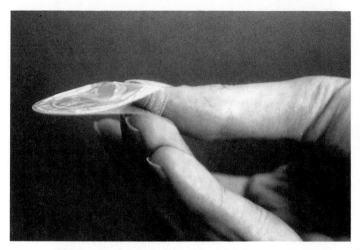

The transparent estrogen skin patch is worn anywhere on the lower body, usually on the abdomen. The silver-dollar-sized device releases a continuous dose of estrogen through the skin, offsetting menopausal side effects.

of height and bent posture in many older women. Hip fractures are also a very common complication of this disease. Although calcium loss occurs in both men and women with age, Caucasian women, especially those of Northern European ancestry, have the lowest peak bone density and are at greatest risk. Bone-calcium loss becomes particularly problematic at menopause, when estrogen levels fall. For this reason, hormone therapy has been suggested as a means to prevent osteoporosis. In 1991 a study on the prevention of osteoporosis by exercise, calcium supplementation, and hormone replacement in postmenopausal women with low bone density was reported in *The New England Journal of Medicine*. Although the loss of bone density was less in women who received calcium supplements in addition to modest exercise, the study indicated that only women who received a combined supplement of estrogen and progestin and who exercised had an increase in bone density. Furthermore, other postmenopausal symptoms—hot flashes, sleeplessness, and painful sex—were reduced in hormone-treated women.

Another benefit of hormone treatment of postmenopausal women is the reduction of cardiovascular disease, the leading cause of mortality among postmenopausal women. A recent study reports that hormonal treatment of postmenopausal women decreased LDL cholesterol (associated with increased risk of cardiovascular disease) and increased HDL cholesterol (associated with lower risk). One significant side effect of hormone therapy was an increase in triglycerides in the blood. Thus, in addition to the relief of postmenopausal symptoms, women should discuss the appropriateness of hormone therapy with their physician, especially if there is a family history of osteoporosis or cardiovascular disease. Whether the increasingly popular transdermal estrogen patch will have the same effects on osteoporosis and cardiovascular disease as oral hormone therapy is not presently known.

▶ Studies on Aging Women

Disability in later life is a serious health problem for women, threatening their independence and resulting in significant health-care needs and expenditures. More than 4 million women aged 65 years and older are moderately to severely disabled, a figure representing about two-thirds of all disabled older adults. Health-care costs associated with disability for older Americans are currently about $65 billion and could top $100 billion annually within 40 years if nothing is done to reduce disability in the rapidly growing older population.

In August 1991, the National Institute on Aging (NIA) announced plans for a $7.9 million Women's Aging Study. This study will be one of the first major efforts to determine what diseases and other events cause and influence disability in older women. The Johns Hopkins University School of Medicine will design and conduct the seven-year study, which will include about 1,000 women. Data will be collected on the presence, severity, and impact on physical disability of nearly 20 major diseases, including coronary heart disease, congestive heart failure, stroke, Parkinson's disease, chronic obstructive pulmonary disease, cancer, diabetes, osteoarthritis, hip fracture, visual impairment, and hearing loss.

The study group will undergo an initial comprehensive evaluation. Researchers will follow up with visits to the women in their homes every six months for three years to assess changes in physical function and to monitor for hospitalization, nursing-home admissions, and use of home health care.

Marc E. Weksler, M.D.

AIDS

Acquired immune deficiency syndrome (AIDS) is now officially a decade old. Although it was first reported as a distinct condition in 1981, evidence has accumulated that a few cases meeting the criteria for the disease existed as early as the late 1950s. Last year was one of mixed hope and setbacks for those seeking to fight the spread of the disease. In the U.S. alone, there have been over 200,000 cases of AIDS reported, with over 120,000 deaths ascribed to the disease. AIDS became the second-leading cause of death among men 25 to 44 years of age, and in 1992 AIDS may become one of the five leading causes of death for women in the same age group.

The World Health Organization (WHO) estimates that 1 million children and 8 million to 10 million adults around the world are infected with the human immunodeficiency virus (HIV), and that this number is likely to increase to about 40 million persons by the year 2000. WHO also believes that during the 1990s, the mother or both parents of more than 10 million children will have died from AIDS, making it one of the leading causes of orphaned children. The Centers for Disease Control (CDC) estimates that at least 1 million persons in the U.S. are infected with HIV.

In Africa and other developing nations, most of the HIV transmission seems to come from heterosexual activity, whereas in the industrialized countries, the majority of cases arise from male homosexual and bisexual activity, and from sharing needles during intravenous drug use. To date, most of those infected with HIV and ill with AIDS have been men. The number of infected men continues to grow. That, coupled with the increasing number of female drug users, will inevitably lead to a higher number of AIDS-infected women.

Magic Johnson. The most riveting AIDS-related event of 1991 was the disclosure by basketball superstar Magic Johnson of the Los Angeles Lakers that he had acquired the HIV virus through heterosexual activity. He announced his retirement from basketball and his intention to dedicate his life to fighting the disease. Some educators were ecstatic that he was willing to acknowledge his infection and enlist in the battle against AIDS, but others doubted that he would really be able to convince many young people (and older people as well) to change their sexual practices. Continued promiscuity is evidenced by the estimated 12 million cases of sexually transmitted diseases (STDs) each year. If other STDs are transmitted by sexual activity, there is a

Since announcing that he had tested HIV-positive, Magic Johnson has retired from professional basketball and is devoting much time to AIDS public awareness.

good opportunity for AIDS to be transmitted also. And having another STD makes transmitting AIDS considerably more likely.

There is no evidence that the message of sexual abstinence or monogamy has been widely effective, and, as some have indicated, Magic Johnson is not the most credible advocate for abstinence. Because of continued widespread sexual activity, the second line of defense has been the use of condoms. This year has seen the introduction of condom-distribution programs in public schools in New York City, and an increase in public messages encouraging the use of condoms. Despite all of the messages for behavior change, the only group that has unquestionably moved toward condom use and safe sexual behavior is middle-class homosexual men who are not addicted to drugs. Even younger homosexual men do not appear to be practicing "safe sex" as much as are their older counterparts who suffered through the early lessons of the AIDS epidemic. The result is that infection with HIV continues to spread in the U.S., both by sexual activity and by the sharing of the "works" of intravenous drug use: needles, syringes, cotton, water, and cookers.

Women More Easily Infected with HIV. A new study confirmed previous research suggesting that women are much more easily infected with HIV during sex with infected men than vice versa. The study used couples in which one of the partners was known to be infected and the other partner was deemed low risk for acquiring the disease. Among such pairings, 18 times as many women as men were found to be HIV-positive.

Kimberly Bergalis Dies. Last year provided another milestone in the AIDS saga with the death of 23-year-old Kimberly Bergalis. The young Florida woman was the first person known to have been infected by a medical-care provider, in this case her dentist (who also died from AIDS). This incident triggered the CDC to establish a new set of guidelines recommending the testing of all medical-care personnel, the informing of patients of those providers who are HIV-positive, and proposing that HIV-positive health-care workers be forbidden to perform certain medical procedures because of the possible danger of transmitting HIV to patients.

Medical-care workers, however, strongly resisted the new rules. They cited doubts about the scientific validity of the rules proposed; the possible stigmatizing of physicians, nurses, and other medical-care providers; and concern that focusing on a few infected persons would lessen providers' belief in the need to hold to the standard precautionary procedures that should be taken with every patient.

Health professionals emphasize that Kimberly Bergalis's dentist used woefully inadequate sterile technique, and that he would have been dangerous even if he had not had HIV himself. The same dentist also managed to infect four other persons with the HIV virus. But no other HIV-positive health-care worker has ever been found to have transmitted the virus to a patient, despite the careful monitoring of over 9,000 patients of infected professionals.

Many health professionals fear, among other things, that accepting the CDC guidelines would open the door to huge liability verdicts, whether or not they were justified on the basis of evidence. In fact, some hospitals have begun to dismiss HIV-infected health-care workers, regardless of the kinds of procedures they perform, in order to reduce their potential liability. The fear of political action in this area is reasonable, based on a congressional resolution in October 1991 urging that all providers be regularly tested for antibodies to HIV.

Fearing just this kind of witch-hunt, the New York State Health Department refused to accept the proposed CDC guidelines, believing that the evidence of risk did not require such drastic measures. In general the New York guidelines are similar to those from the CDC, except that the patients would not have to be informed of the HIV status of their doctors and nurses.

Because of the opposition of organized health professionals, the CDC withdrew its original guidelines and is now preparing a new set of guidelines that will give local medical panels the authority to decide what procedures a given provider should be allowed to perform, taking into account his or her history of infection-control practices, mental state, and stamina. Such authority would require that decisions be made on an individual-case basis, rather than creating broad guidelines that could be applied in lawsuits against medical-care institutions and professionals.

Intravenous-Needle/Syringe-Exchange Programs Seen as Effective. The first detailed evaluation of the effect of a needle-exchange program was made in New Haven, Connecticut, by an investigator from Yale University. The report indicated a clear reduction in the prevalence of infection among intravenous drug users who participated in the needle/syringe-exchange program. These data support the efforts of other groups, such as the National AIDS Brigade, who for years have been seeking to get laws changed to permit needle/syringe-exchange programs to take place.

Influenza Vaccine Produces False-Positive Readings for HIV Antibodies. Perhaps the strangest HIV-related event of the year was the discovery that many blood donors who had received influenza vaccine this fall produced *false positive* tests for antibodies to HIV. These people tested positive on the initial screening test, which, though very sensitive, often produces false positives. Fortunately, those people tested negative on the more costly follow-up test, which has few, if any, false positives. These people had no risk factors for AIDS, but did have a common history of a recent dose of this year's flu vaccine. This second test

In 1991, Kimberly Bergalis died from AIDS. She was the first person known to have been infected with AIDS by a health-care worker (her dentist).

confirmed that these flu-vaccine recipients are *not* infected with the deadly AIDS virus, and it is expected that their blood would be perfectly safe to use for donation. But strict blood-bank rules require that the blood must be discarded if the screening test is positive, even if the follow-up test is negative. This requirement threatened the already precarious blood-donor supply in the United States. Because all of the initially reported false positives came from one influenza-vaccine manufacturer, scientists were looking to see if one of the materials that the manufacturer used in the formulation of the vaccine might cause a reaction with the AIDS-screening tests.

HIV Infection and the Detection of Tuberculosis.
Oddly, HIV has been found to have the opposite effect on the detection of tuberculosis (TB): in a person infected with both HIV and TB, the standard skin test for TB infection can turn out *false negative.* This is because the immune system must be healthy in order to produce the tuberculosis antibodies detected by the skin test. Persons with advanced HIV infection, even if they do not yet have full-blown AIDS, may not produce enough antibodies against the TB germ to enable the skin test to be positive. In this situation, chest X rays can be used to diagnose advanced lung infections, as can sputum cultures for the organism. The X rays, however, are seldom absolutely diagnostic, and the sputum cultures take six to eight weeks to become positive—and still many false negatives occur. Thus, the use of the standard TB skin test in prisons, homeless shelters, and other institutions where the risk of HIV infection is high is no longer

adequate; unfortunately, there is no really satisfactory alternative method to screen for tuberculosis infection. Complicating this situation is the fact that an increasing proportion of the TB germs cultured are resistant to the usual antibiotics used to kill them.

New National Infection-Control Rules Issued.
Although the CDC guidelines for limiting the practice of HIV-infected medical-care workers were rejected, a new set of guidelines regarding infection-control procedures by employers and employees was issued by the federal government, and it carries the force of law. These guidelines are aimed at protecting medical-care workers, police, and other workers who might come into contact with blood or other body fluids that could contain a variety of infections, including AIDS and hepatitis.

The standards require such precautions as wearing gowns, face masks, gloves, and using proper needle-disposal containers when working with patients in a situation where there might be exposure to blood or other body fluids. Employers are required to provide the necessary equipment to all employees who may need it. There are heavy fines for employers who fail to provide the necessary equipment, and for employees who fail to use it.

Unfortunately, these rules do not apply to public employees in the 27 states that lack state occupational safety and health plans, and therefore do not fall under the Federal Occupational, Safety, and Health Administration (OSHA) laws. The governors in these states are being encouraged to extend these protective measures to public workers.

HIV-Infected Employees May Have Health Insurance Limited.
The U.S. Fifth Circuit Court of Appeals has ruled that employers who are self-insured for medical-care benefits may significantly reduce their coverage for workers who develop illnesses like AIDS, which can result in astronomical medical costs. This ruling triggered a great deal of concern on the part of AIDS activists, who see the progressive isolation of HIV-positive patients from insurance mechanisms if this decision is upheld on higher appeal. Hospitals are worried because an increasing proportion of AIDS patients might become non-paying patients.

Didanosine (DDI) Approved for Use in AIDS.
The Food and Drug Administration (FDA) approved the drug Didanosine (dideoxyinosine, or DDI) for use in the approximately 50 percent of AIDS patients who cannot tolerate Zidovudine (azidothymidine, or AZT), the only other drug currently FDA-approved for treating AIDS.

DDI interferes with the reproduction of the AIDS virus and boosts the number of helper T-cells, the

Well over 200,000 cases of AIDS have been reported in the United States and its territories. Despite advances in treatment that help to postpone the full onset of symptoms, over one-half of all people with AIDS die within two years of their diagnosis.

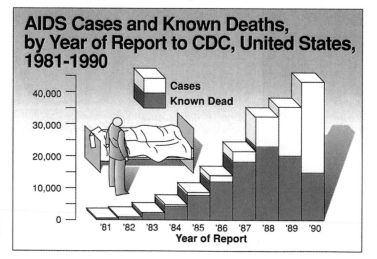

AIDS Cases and Known Deaths, by Year of Report to CDC, United States, 1981-1990

cells of the immune system that are selectively destroyed by HIV. DDI has not yet, however, been shown to lengthen the life of patients.

The FDA approved DDI under its new temporary-use approval method, which allows experimental drug use in limited cases while more-definitive studies are still going on. Many medical scientists are opposed to this hurried procedure, and claim that the FDA has yielded to pressure from AIDS activists. The FDA counters that AIDS represents a special and urgent situation, and that the need for a new drug justifies the action. The biggest concern of the scientists is the potentially serious side effects sometimes caused by DDI, including inflammation of the pancreas.

Presumably the drug company that markets the drug, Squibb, is happy with DDI's new status. Squibb will now be paid for much of the drug distributed (companies are not paid for drugs still considered experimental). Concerns that the drug might not be available to all who need it were countered when Squibb promised to provide DDI free to those who could not otherwise pay for it.

Using AIDS as Revenge. A woman claiming to have AIDS told a Dallas, Texas, talk-show host that she was trying to infect other men with the AIDS virus in order to get revenge on the man who had infected her with HIV. The call followed a request by the talk-show host for the woman to call, after her letter with the same message appeared in *Ebony* magazine. She claimed that she picks up men at nightclubs in the Dallas and Fort Worth areas and has unprotected sex with them.

Although some consider the incident a hoax, the affair has stirred community concern about AIDS. Some nightclub owners have even noted that their clientele seem more cautious. According to Texas law, trying to transmit HIV is a third-degree felony, which could bring up to a $5,000 fine and 10 years in prison. It is uncertain if these penalties would restrain someone with AIDS, who may have a short life expectancy anyway.

New Jersey Begins a Register of HIV-Infected Persons. The New Jersey Health Department now officially requires the registration of persons who test positive for HIV. This new procedure has caused much debate; many fear it will reduce the number of persons willing to be tested. Actually, the state still allows people to have their blood tested anonymously for HIV antibodies at the 17 state testing centers. The state wants to use the names to allow contact tracing and warning. Opponents of the requirement are especially fearful that intravenous drug users will avoid testing for fear of identification.

James F. Jekel, M.D., M.P.H.

Arthritis and Rheumatism

▶ Osteoarthritis

Osteoarthritis is the result of irregular loss and degeneration of joint cartilage. This is not simply a passive process of wearing out of the joint. Studies of the chemistry of the cartilage in osteoarthritis show a highly active process in which enzymes released from cartilage cells degrade the surrounding matrix of protein-rich carbohydrates. Rates of cartilage-cell growth and of synthesis of new matrix proteins are, in fact, increased.

A study published in late 1990 on a family with unusually severe early-onset osteoarthritis provided the first clear evidence that at least some forms of osteoarthritis have a genetic basis. Scientists isolated and determined the structure of the gene for Type II collagen, a structural protein that imports tensile strength to cartilage. The authors reported an inherited change in the substitution of a single amino acid in Type II collagen in every family member affected by osteoarthritis and in none of the unaffected family members. Subsequent studies in 1991 suggest that a proportion of patients who develop osteoarthritis without unusual joint stress or trauma may have this or another genetic defect in a structural protein of cartilage.

Osteoarthritis treatment generally involves a combination of physical measures including rest, joint protection, muscle-strengthening exercises, and joint-stress reduction combined with medication to relieve pain and inflammation. Inflammation occurring secondarily to release of cartilage debris in the joint contributes to both pain and joint injury. Nonsteroidal anti-inflammatory drugs (NSAIDs) have become the most frequently used drugs for the treatment of osteoarthritis. Several recent articles have addressed concerns about the relative effectiveness and toxicity of these agents. A study published in the *New England Journal of Medicine* last year compared acetaminophen, an analgesic without anti-inflammatory activity, to the NSAID ibuprofen. Administered in low doses, ibuprofen would be expected to have only painkilling effect; in higher doses, it would be expected to be anti-inflammatory. The study found no added benefit from the NSAID, even when given in higher doses. Many physicians believe that, for selected patients where inflammation plays an important role, NSAIDs are of value. However, several articles suggest that NSAID toxicity may be a significant concern.

An article published in the August 1991 *Annals of Internal Medicine* reported that regular use of

The discomfort of arthritis and rheumatism makes many forms of exercise impossible. Sufferers often get some relief—and a good workout—by swimming.

NSAIDs may increase the risk of chronic kidney disease. An accompanying editorial in the same journal reviewed the evidence that chronic NSAID use is a risk factor for the development of chronic kidney disease, and suggested that although the association was unproven, there is sufficient evidence for concern.

In November 1991, the *Annals of Internal Medicine* published a review article reporting that users of NSAIDs were at three times greater risk for developing serious gastrointestinal side effects. These studies are causing physicians to show greater caution in the use of NSAIDs in the treatment of osteoarthritis. Unfortunately, for millions of patients with severe pain from osteoarthritis, there is no effective alternative for the pain relief and functional improvement provided by NSAID treatment.

▶ Eosinophilia-Myalgia Syndrome

Many so-called health-food products are widely available in health-food stores, supermarkets, and over the counter in pharmacies. The public generally assumes that because these are *natural* products, they are safe. Unfortunately, this is not always the case. In early 1990 many reports appeared of an unusual illness that included muscle pain, marked fatigue, hair loss, joint pain, tightening and thickening of the skin, shortness of breath, cough, and numbness and tingling. Involvement of other organs, including the heart, also occurred.

Almost all of the patients developed the disease after ingestion of L-tryptophan preparations from a manufacturer whose product has recently been reported to contain a specific contaminant thought to be responsible for this syndrome. As of July 1991, the Centers for Disease Control (CDC) had received reports of 1,543 cases of the disorder, with 31 deaths. Most of these patients had initial onset of the disease between July and December of 1989. New cases are no longer occurring.

A report in September 1991 in the *New England Journal of Medicine* described the natural history of this disease in order to characterize long-term outcome. Patients showed progressive improvement over the first six months after onset of the disease, followed by a very protracted phase of slower improvement. While treatment with drugs such as corticosteroids produced some initial symptomatic improvement, it did not appear to affect the long-term course of the disease. Only 13 percent of the patients had recovered completely after five months; the majority remained symptomatic.

▶ Rheumatoid Arthritis

Several recent reports have suggested that the long-term clinical outcome of rheumatoid arthritis is poorer than had previously been believed. Discouragingly, these reports also suggest that various forms of treatment, which are effective in controlling disease symptoms and progression in short-term clinical studies, do not alter outcome over 20 to 25 years. One 1991 report in the *Journal of Rheumatology* looked at 561 patients with rheumatoid arthritis followed for various periods up to 22 years. It found that loss of function developed very early during the course of rheumatoid arthritis, and worsened steadily over the 22-year period. Although treatment produced improvement in many measures of disease activity, functional loss progressed for the span of the study independent of any treatment. Another 1991 report looked at X-ray evidence of joint erosion and cartilage damage in 292 patients over a 25-year period. Joint injury was most rapid in the early years of the disease, and slightly slower in later years. However, progression of joint injury continued unabated over the 25-year period. There was little evidence that treatment altered this clinical course. These studies and other recent studies—all suggesting that rheumatoid arthritis is associated with a shortened life span —provide a discouraging view of the present prognosis of the disease and of available treatment.

This discouraging news for sufferers of rheumatoid arthritis and their families and friends may be countered somewhat by the general sense that we are on the threshold of a new era in the treatment of the disease as a result of advances in biotechnology. New products that inhibit specific components of the immune response, important in the inflammation of rheumatoid arthritis, hold great promise. For example, helper lymphocytes are necessary to sustain an immune response in rheumatoid arthritis. A recent report describes the use of an antibody specifically directed against CD-4, a protein found on these cells. The use of the antibody to reduce the number of helper lymphocytes results in striking improvement in the disease.

Herbert S. Diamond, M.D.

Bioethics

▶ Assisted Suicide: The Right to Die

Publicly announcing his actions in a *New England Journal of Medicine* article, Dr. Timothy Quill of Rochester, New York, described his anguished decision to write a prescription for a lethal dosage of medication for his longtime patient "Diane." The patient, who previously had overcome significant health problems and other difficulties in her life, was diagnosed as having a severe form of leukemia, from which recovery was considered unlikely (a one in four chance, provided she underwent a grueling course of chemotherapy). The patient chose not to fight her illness, and wished to live out her remaining days in comfort with her family at her side. She also asked Dr. Quill that, if her condition became unbearable, he provide her with a prescription that would painlessly end her life.

Reluctantly, after determining the strength of her decision and requesting that she undergo psychological evaluation, Dr. Quill agreed, although he was not entirely certain that she would actually use the sleeping pills to commit suicide. In fact, the patient did take her own life in this way, and, after arriving at her home, Dr. Quill declared to authorities that she had died of her terminal illness, rather than by her own hand.

This public account led to a grand-jury investigation of Dr. Quill. The question before the jury was whether Dr. Quill should be criminally indicted for assisting a suicide, a rarely prosecuted crime. The jury chose not to indict Dr. Quill, and, in fact, the New York State Department of Health also chose not to formally charge Dr. Quill with professional misconduct.

Dr. Quill's actions and the resulting lack of prosecution fueled the public debate regarding physician-assisted suicide that was started last year by the widely condemned actions of Detroit pathologist Jack Kevorkian. His public promotion of his "suicide machine" led to the suicide death of one early Alzheimer's patient (followed this year by the death of two additional chronically ill individuals). While the Kevorkian-assisted deaths were nearly universally opposed by ethicists (the assistance was given to virtual strangers, and the motives of Dr. Kevorkian were highly suspect), the actions of Dr. Quill were greeted much more ambivalently. The intimacy between patient and doctor, the safeguards brought to bear on the decision, and the strength and resolve of the patient and her family all created a more compelling picture in support of Dr. Quill's assistance, at least to many observers. The essence of the debate concerns the role of the physician: should a physician do all within his or her power to relieve suffering, or are there limits on physician activities, based on the historic role of the physician as trusted healer and promoter of patient well-being?

Underscoring significant public interest in the right of individuals to end their suffering in the face of intolerable illness, a suicide "self-help" book titled *Final Exit* rose to the top of best-seller lists this year. Written by Derek Humphry (photo, below left), the founder of the suicide-promotion group the Hemlock Society, the book describes in graphic detail a variety of methods and mechanisms available for ending one's life. The unprecedented interest in the book led many to oppose its publication, citing concern that the book made it too easy for depressed individuals or those facing other pressures to choose suicide before exploring other options. Conversely, others cited the sometimes tortured medical procedures that extend life regardless of its poor quality, necessitating the need for this kind of manual.

Another end-of-life decision-making case also gained national attention this year, as Minnesota physicians sought court approval to remove the life-sustaining interventions that kept 87-year-old Helga Wanglie alive but permanently comatose in a Minnesota hospital. The court action was initiated despite the wishes of the patient's family. Months of discussion with the patient's husband failed to produce his approval to remove the life support from this patient who had virtually no hope of recovery. Physicians and hospital administrators pushed forward with their legal action because they believed the interventions sustaining Mrs. Wanglie were "medically futile."

The court decision avoided direct discussion of the question of futility, but ruled that the appropriate role of surrogate decision making on behalf of this patient belonged to the patient's husband, who stated that neither he nor his wife would want treatment withdrawn in this circumstance. The hospital was thus legally obliged to follow the husband's wishes that treatment be continued. Three days following the ruling, the patient died despite the interventions sustaining her. The case was of national interest because it marked the first time that judicial intervention was sought to withdraw care *against* familial wishes. The debate over what constitutes "futile" treatment remains unsettled, and is likely to continue as we move into an era of ever-decreasing health-care resources.

New federal legislation came into effect at the end of this year, obligating health-care facilities to educate their patients and surrounding communities about end-of-life decision making. The Patient Self-Determination Act requires that all health-care facilities receiving federal funds must develop policies and inform patients about the mechanisms available in their particular state for planning in advance about end-of-life decisions. Such mechanisms include living wills, health-care powers of attorney, and resuscitation orders. Facilities must now inquire whether an individual has a living will when entering the facility, and must provide patients with information so that they may execute such a document if they wish. Advanced planning not only increases patient control and autonomy during the dying process, but also ensures that patients, families, and institutions can avoid many of the ethical dilemmas that develop when decisions about end-of-life care must be made on behalf of an incapacitated patient.

▶ HIV-Infected Health-Care Workers

As the number of persons infected with the human immunodeficiency virus (HIV) continues to mount, and efforts to find cures or vaccines for AIDS continue to prove unsuccessful, attention began to focus on the risk posed to patients due to HIV-infected health-care providers. In particular, this attention was dramatized by the plight of 23-year-old Kimberly Bergalis, a Florida woman who, along with several other patients, acquired the HIV virus during the course of dental work performed by Dr. David Acer. While these patients are the only known persons to have acquired the virus from their health-care provider, public sentiment nonetheless triggered support for strict legislation prohibiting infected workers from having patient contact, and requiring them to disclose their illness to their patient population. Ms. Bergalis personally lobbied for such legislation just before her death from AIDS.

The desire to restrict infected workers highlighted the conflict between assuring the confidentiality of HIV-infected individuals (who also happen to be health-care providers), and assuring the safety of the general public who may, during the course of care, be exposed to the infected bodily fluids of their health-care providers, particularly during the course of certain types of surgery. The debate mounted as the Centers for Disease Control (CDC) demanded that professional-provider organizations draw up lists of "risk-prone procedures" so that the CDC could determine which types of practices might have to be prohibited for

HIV-infected providers. Most professional provider organizations refused to cooperate with the request, citing the lack of scientific data to support the likelihood of risk, and underscoring that health-care providers are much more likely to acquire the virus from HIV-infected patients, who have the right to refuse to be tested for HIV infection. As the provider protest mounted, the CDC eventually dropped its request, and instead supported the notion that increased attention to infection-control procedures and to the fitness of individual infected health-care workers is all that is required to maintain public safety.

▶ Supreme Court Decision on Abortion Counseling

The United States Supreme Court, in the decision of *Rust v. Sullivan,* voted to uphold federal regulations that prohibit employees of federally funded family-planning clinics from discussing the option of abortion with clinic patients. Physician groups voiced angry opposition to the decision, which was viewed as permitting the government to prohibit the free flow of information between a doctor and patient. To offset this criticism, in March 1992 the Bush administration revised the ruling to permit physicians in federally funded clinics to provide abortion counseling.

According to the revised federal regulations, nurses or counselors who work in clinics that receive federal funding cannot discuss with clinic patients the option of selecting an abortion or provide information about abortion procedures, despite the patient's legal right to obtain an abortion in most circumstances. While the Supreme Court described the regulations as leaving the patient in no worse a position than if no federal funding existed, critics argued that the decision was unjust, particularly for low-income women who often depend on health professionals other than physicans for their health care.

Those opposing the ruling stated that poor women would now be forced into a certain type of care without knowing the range of options available to them. The restriction is considered in violation of the informed-consent process, which supports voluntary patient choice after a full discussion of the patient's options. Many clinics restricted under this ruling are now preparing to seek alternate methods of funding rather than abide by the limitations upheld by the Supreme Court.

▶ Reproductive Rights

The Johnson Controls Decision. In another controversial ruling, the United States Supreme Court struck down a corporation's policy of excluding fertile women from certain aspects of the work environment, for fear of harm to potential or unborn offspring. In its *Automobile Workers v. Johnson Controls* decision, the Supreme Court upheld the right of women to equal access in the workplace, and underscored the right of women to determine which risks they are willing to incur for themselves or their unborn children for the benefit of certain employment advantages.

The Johnson Controls policy was designed to exclude from the company's battery-manufacturing plants all women with the potential to bear children, due to the known risk to fetuses from lead exposure. Women who wished to work in such factories were thus required to become sterile to compete for positions in that workplace. The Supreme Court ruling compels the company to abandon the policy, and leaves the decision to take such risk up to the individual worker.

While critics of the company were pleased with the court decision, some questioned the obligation of the company to create a safe work environment for *all* employees. There is data to suggest that lead exposure in male employees can also lead to fetal damage. Thus, while the court ruling underscored the right of women employees to voluntarily make choices that may affect reproductive health, it did little to address the large public-health concern of occupational hazards to the health of employees in the work environment.

Coercive Use of Norplant. The introduction of a new method of birth control has enhanced the reproductive choices of women, but has also opened up the possibility of coercive interventions to curtail the reproductive decisions of certain women. When using the Norplant contraceptive, a woman has small capsules that inhibit fertility surgically implanted in her arm. The device offers women protection from pregnancy for up to five years.

The ease of this new method has, however, become the subject of potential coercion. For example, legislation is pending in some states to increase the welfare payments of women who use the Norplant method of contraception. There is also legislative consideration in one state supporting the use of Norplant as a condition of probation for certain criminal offenses.

These potential legislative impositions concerning Norplant again raise fundamental questions about the right of women to freely make reproductive choices. As well, such initiatives may force certain women to involuntarily take certain health risks in order to obtain significant benefits for either themselves or their families. Additionally, critics argue that it is unjust to only curtail the reproductive rights of women, particularly minority women, when concerns about welfare payments or child abuse motivate these initiatives.

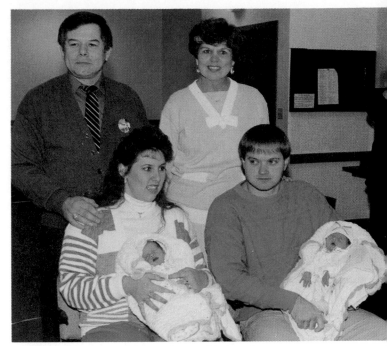

Arlette Schweitzer (right rear) gave birth to her own grandchildren after being implanted with eggs provided by her daughter and fertilized by her son-in-law.

▶ A Mother as Surrogate Mother

A novel case of surrogate mothering surfaced this year with news of the decision of 42-year-old Arlette Schweitzer to become surrogate mother to her *daughter's* child. Mrs. Schweitzer's 22-year-old daughter, Christa Uchytil, was born without a uterus and could not bear children herself. She and her mother therefore arrived at the decision to have Mrs. Schweitzer artificially impregnated with her daughter's eggs fertilized in a laboratory by her son-in-law's sperm. As a result, Mrs. Schweitzer became pregnant with her daughter's twins.

Many applauded Mrs. Schweitzer's actions, citing the altruistic and loving reasons motivating her decision, the lack of monetary incentive, and the slim possibility of any postpregnancy custody battle. However, some commentators worried about the future psychological well-being of a child who, in effect, was the product of his or her *grandmother,* rather than his or her "mother." As with other technological innovations, this case raises the question as to whether there should be limits to certain innovations, due to uncertainty about the ethical propriety and future consequences of the activity. Only one previous case of such grandmother surrogacy has ever been reported.

▶ Organ-Transplantation Dilemmas

The ever-increasing shortage of available transplant organs has led clinicians to devise ever-more-controversial methods to obtain necessary organs for patients in need. A Minnesota case involving the transplantation of live lung tissue from both parents of a dying girl amply illustrated the dilemmas involved in such cases.

When nine-year-old Alyssa Plum became in dire need of a lung transplant after both of her lungs were struck down by a rare virus, her doctors struggled to determine how best to save her life. Efforts to obtain a cadaver organ failed, and the decision was made to transplant a small portion of her father's lung to replace her own. However, this effort proved unsuccessful, and, in a last-ditch effort, lung tissue from the girl's mother was also transplanted, although the patient died during the course of this second operation.

Critics questioned the propriety of this situation, despite the technical possibility of its accomplishment. In particular, given the urgency of the situation, there is concern that both parents in this case placed themselves at some risk under circumstances where their voluntary informed consent was unlikely. Many experts have suggested that in such a case it is virtually impossible for parents to make an informed, voluntary decision, as the fundamental tenets of the informed-consent process require. This may be one more example where the possibility to clinically intervene needs to be re-evaluated in light of the inherent ethical dilemmas.

▶ Growing Inequality in Access to Health Care

Public-policy debates openly surfaced this year regarding our country's system of health-care-financing reimbursement, and the growing disparity between classes of patient categories.

Public-opinion polls now show that health-care costs and access to care are of great concern to consumers. As health-care costs continue to rise, and certain providers are now openly designing systems to limit or ration care for certain segments of the population, there are increasing public calls to universalize access to at least a minimum amount of care for all citizens, perhaps in a system similar to Canada's. The new system of rationing in the Oregon Medicaid program is just one example of singling out an already vulnerable population for measures that further restrict access to care.

Experts estimate that 34 million Americans lack basic health insurance that allows them to buy into our system of health care. Additionally, new data have been produced to demonstrate the inordinate difficulty that most Medicaid patients have in finding willing providers, and the increased morbidity and mortality that they suffer as a result of this unequal access to care. Increasing public demands are calling for an overhaul of our system that will provide a universally available basic level of care, so that opportunities that inevitably rest on good health and well-being will be afforded to all.

Connie Zuckerman, J.D.

Blood and Lymphatic System

There are three major types of cells that circulate in our bloodstreams—red cells, which carry oxygen; white cells, which fight infection; and platelets, which help the blood clot normally. None of these cells can survive indefinitely in the bloodstream—they are either used up or worn out after circulating for a period ranging from a few days to about four months. The lost cells must constantly be replaced. New blood cells are produced by *stem cells,* which are manufactured in the bone marrow. These stem cells have not yet differentiated into red cells, white cells, or platelets. Various types of specialized protein molecules, called *growth factors,* cause the stem cells to differentiate into the proper type of blood cell. For example, erythropoietin is the growth factor that instructs the stem cells to proliferate and differentiate into red blood cells. Another growth factor, Granulocyte Colony Stimulating Factor (GCSF), instructs stem cells to differentiate into a particular type of white blood cell. This complicated but beautifully regulated system ensures that the supply of blood cells is constantly replenished and maintained at the proper level.

In aplastic anemia, the bone-marrow cells fail to grow at all or are destroyed. In other circumstances, one or more of the stem cells can become cancerous, proliferating without regard to growth-factor signals. These cells usually fail to differentiate, resulting in leukemias—diseases in which the primitive undifferentiated cells take over the blood and the bone marrow.

Until recently, physicians had very little control over the function of the bone marrow or the differentiation behavior of stem cells. During the past year, however, several new developments have offered promise for improved ways to control the bone marrow and therefore to treat leukemia and other cancers.

▶ Genetically Engineered Growth Factors

Over the past 10 years, scientists have identified many growth factors that control the production of specific types of blood cells. Using genetic-engineering methods, scientists have isolated the genes for these growth factors and inserted the genes into cells that act as factories to produce large quantities of highly purified growth factors for clinical use.

These genetically engineered growth factors are particularly useful in chemotherapy. Chemotherapeutic drugs work by preferentially attacking cells that are proliferating. Unfortunately, although the drugs kill tumor cells, they also destroy normal blood cells (which, as noted earlier, must continuously proliferate in order to replace worn-out blood cells). In patients undergoing chemotherapy, the loss of blood cells results in severe anemia, low platelet counts and white counts, and, consequently, heightened risks of infection and bleeding.

Patients receiving chemotherapy can now be given growth factors, such as erythropoietin and GCSF, immediately after the course of chemotherapy drugs is completed. This treatment allows the bone marrow to recover much more quickly, and restores normal blood counts before major complications occur. The growth factors can also be used in kidney failure, which causes reduced red-cell production (erythropoietin is normally made by the kidneys), and to counteract anemia and low white-blood-cell counts found in patients with AIDS.

During the past year GCSF has gained prominence as an important tool to help chemotherapy patients who suffer from a prolonged period of low white-cell counts and are thus at high risk of infection. GCSF has been used successfully after radiation and chemotherapy for treatment of lymphomas, ovarian cancers, and certain forms of leukemia. In bone-marrow-transplant procedures GCSF is also showing great promise as a means to stimulate the newly transplanted bone marrow, thus shortening the danger period following transplantation.

▶ Chronic Myelogenous Leukemia

Chronic myelogenous leukemia (CML) is one of the most difficult forms of leukemia to treat. Patients with CML often do well for two to three years, but then develop an aggressive form of acute leukemia called *blast crisis*. Once this occurs, it is very difficult to treat patients effectively. CML cells can be destroyed if the patient is given a high enough dose of chemotherapy. Unfortunately, a dose high enough to kill CML cells will also destroy the patient's healthy bone marrow. Bone-marrow transplantation from a healthy donor could be used to rescue the patient; CML patients who meet requirements for such a transplant are usually encouraged to undergo the procedure at an early point in the disease, before blast crisis begins.

Unfortunately, many patients with CML do not have a compatible donor available. For these individuals, an alternative strategy called *autologous transplantation* may be recommended. In this treatment a sample of the patient's own bone marrow is removed, after which the patient is treated with very high doses of chemotherapy. The bone-marrow sample is then reinfused into the patient. During the past year, a promising new strategy, called *marrow purging*, has been developed in which the

CML cells are removed from the bone-marrow specimen in a manner that does not kill the normal stem cells. Clinical trials are due to begin shortly.

This new strategy takes advantage of recent developments in molecular biology called *antisense* technology. Antisense DNA molecules can be synthesized to have a sequence of nucleotide bases that is the opposite, or complement, of a specific gene within the cell. When these DNA molecules are introduced into the cells, they bind to the target gene or its products and inactivate the expression of that gene. This selectively eliminates the function of that specific gene from the cell.

Thanks to molecular-biology methods to identify specific gene and chromosome abnormalities, this general strategy can be potentially applied to many forms of leukemia or solid tumors.

▶ Treating Acute Leukemia

Leukemia constitutes only one of a small number of cancers that can be successfully treated with chemotherapy. Although the brute force of pharmaceutically *killing* the leukemic cells works in many cases, hematologists have long sought alternative and more subtle methods that would persuade these cells to differentiate into healthy white cells that might then function normally as infection fighters. More importantly, the differentiated cells would eventually die like their normal counterparts, so that the leukemia would not accumulate in the body. During the past year one unusual form of leukemia has been successfully treated with this strategy of *differentiation therapy*. In patients with the form of leukemia called *acute promyelocytic leukemia* (APL), chromosomes 15 and 17 fuse with each other. One consequence of this fusion is disruption of a specific gene coding for a protein called the retinoic acid receptor (RAR). The deranged RAR receptor prevents the normal response to naturally occurring forms of retinoic acid, which is part of the vitamin A complex. However, it was discovered that a form of retinoic acid, called all-trans-retinoic acid, was capable of binding to this abnormal receptor and causing the leukemia cells to differentiate into normal cells. As a result, patients with this unusual form of leukemia can be treated without highly toxic chemotherapy regimens. In one large trial, the vast majority of patients responded well to this agent. Although they may require intensive chemotherapy at a later date in order to effect a cure, the trans-retinoic acid has allowed them to eliminate the bulk of the leukemia cells from the body. Chemotherapy will not need to be as intensive, and will be better tolerated by the patient. This new treatment strategy illustrates the importance of understanding the basic cell and molecular-biology mechanisms that produce disease.

Edward J. Benz, Jr., M.D.

Bones, Muscles, and Joints

The magnificent architecture of the human body is subject to the external forces and internal frailties inherent in each individual. Each year, injury, disease, and aging of the bones, muscles, and joints disable millions of Americans and cost billions of dollars in health care. With about 206 bones and more than 600 muscles constructing our two-legged frames, physical breakdown is all too often inevitable.

▶ Preventing Degeneration

Arthritis encompasses more than 100 conditions that vary greatly in causes, symptoms, and treatments, but it is generally recognized by its characteristic painful swelling of joints and degeneration of bone. The Arthritis Foundation estimates that 37 million Americans are afflicted with some form of arthritis.

Much research has focused on trying to determine not only the cause of the various bone and joint diseases, but the best ways to try to prevent them. While aging has long been thought to be the primary cause of most degenerative conditions, past studies have identified a variety of risk factors for developing some forms of arthritis. Factors contributing to osteoarthritis include obesity, repetitive movements on the job, injury to a joint, or genetic defects. While osteoarthritis is often characterized as "wear-and-tear" arthritis, a study from the Boston

In an arthritic joint, the cartilage that acts as a cushion between two bones has worn away. The bones fuse, and the joint becomes stiffened and inflamed.

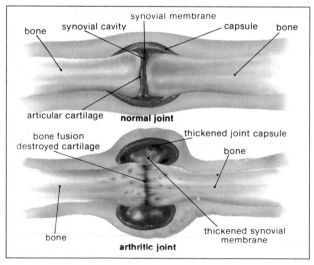

University Arthritis Center found that exercise is not associated with an increased risk for developing the disease later in life. Physical activity of moderate to heavy levels was found to increase the formation of nonpainful bone spurs in knee joints. There was no relationship found, however, between the level of general physical activity a person performs regularly and the later development of knee osteoarthritis.

The loss of estrogen in women who reach menopause has already been linked to osteoporosis, a brittling of bones that affects 25 million older Americans. A 1991 study by a team of researchers at Tufts University in Boston found that women lower their osteoporosis risk by increasing their exercise and their calcium intake "at the earliest possible age." Eighteen of the 36 postmenopausal women who participated in the study were put on a vigorous, supervised 50-minute walk and given 800 milligrams (mg) of calcium per day. The other 18 women remained sedentary and were also given 800 mg of calcium a day. Half the women in each of these groups were randomly selected to receive an additional daily milk-based supplement with 831 mg of calcium. All the women in the yearlong study showed a decreased amount of bone loss, but surprisingly, calcium and exercise each were found to bolster different bones.

Similarly, a 1991 study published in the *New England Journal of Medicine* also showed that bone loss can be slowed or prevented by exercise plus calcium supplementation or exercise plus estrogen-progesterone replacement. This study divided a group of 130 postmenopausal women into segments of exercise, exercise and calcium, and exercise plus continuous replacement of estrogen and progesterone for two years. The exercise-and-estrogen regimen was more effective than exercise and calcium supplementation in increasing bone mass, although this regime caused more side effects.

Fluoride plus calcium is another combination that often has been prescribed to help women restore some of the bone mass lost in osteoporosis. Some researchers have speculated, however, that the new bone growth triggered by this regimen may be abnormally brittle. A report in the *American Journal of Epidemiology* fueled that hypothesis. Research from the University of Michigan in Ann Arbor found that women over 55 who drink highly fluoridated water are more prone to fractures. Over the course of five years, 800 women aged 20 to 80, who came from three different communities with different levels of fluoride and calcium in their water, were measured for bone density. Calcium made no difference in fracture risk, but postmenopausal women drinking the more-fluoridated water faced more than double the fracture risk of their counterparts in the comparison community.

▶ Genetic Links to Rheumatics

While experts suggest diet and life-style alterations to deter the onset of bone, muscle, and joint degeneration, scientists continue to search for genetic causes of such conditions. In 1991 genetic mutation was linked for the first time to osteoporosis. A woman who suffered a broken back was discovered to have osteoporosis. From a sample of her tissue, scientists at Thomas Jefferson University in Philadelphia were able to identify the defective gene that gave her the disease. This discovery may make it possible to develop tests that can predict who is likely to suffer from the illness, decades before symptoms show up. Studies are continuing to find just how common the gene defect is among the general population. This particular mutation has been seen in a few cases in children who suffer from a severe form of brittle-bone disease called osteogenesis imperfecta.

▶ Best Prescribed Therapies

Laboratory science is dealing with the day-to-day management of bone and joint disease by formulating the best therapies to combat pain and inflammation. Rheumatologists are now more often looking to the most aggressive approach to handle the insidious nature of arthritis when first-line treatments prove ineffective. Typical disease-modifying therapies usually lose efficacy within two years, leading physicians to more-potent approaches with disease-modifying anti-rheumatic drugs (DMARDs). An article in the January 1991 *Journal of Rheumatology* studied long-term cyclosporine therapy in rheumatoid arthritis (RA) sufferers. Cyclosporine is a potent drug with selective immunosuppressive action, but a halting side effect for this drug is its destructiveness to the kidneys. The study suggests that doses should "go low, go slow" by not exceeding 10 mg a day for not more than six months. They found the low doses effective when given in conjunction with prostaglandin or fish oil.

An effective short-term therapy for most forms of arthritis has yet to be developed. Non-steroidal anti-inflammatory drugs (NSAIDs) are commonly prescribed to relieve the discomfort of arthritis, particularly osteoarthritis. In the *New England Journal of Medicine,* researchers at the Indiana University School of Medicine compared the NSAID ibuprofen with acetaminophen, a pure analgesic, to treat osteoarthritis of the knee. A higher dose of ibuprofen (2,400 mg per day) was not found to be superior to either the dose of acetaminophen (4,000 mg per day) or a lower dose of ibuprofen (1,200 mg per day) for pain relief or improvement of knee function. Both drugs have significant side effects when used over the long term. Acetaminophen causes a small but significant decrease in kidney function, while NSAIDs in persistent quantities may cause gastrointestinal bleeding, hypertension, congestive heart failure, and kidney trouble.

People who don't respond to therapy for the pain of osteoarthritis often must resort to artificial hip, shoulder, or knee implants. The surgery to replace these joints has been available for several years. But the process of osseointegration, the generation of cell growth around an implant so that the natural tissue will adhere to the artificial surface, has become more clearly understood only over the past year. Researchers at the Washington University School of Medicine in St. Louis, Missouri, investigated the possibility of transforming readily available muscle flaps into vascular bone grafts to use as skeletal replacement parts. The results, published in the October 1991 *Journal of the American Medical Association,* show that it can be done—on a cellular level. Orthopedic researchers at Thomas Jefferson University in Philadelphia have found that adhesion of the implant into the tissue site is improved by coating a coarsened titanium surface with hydroxyapatite (HA), a calcium-based mineral. Existing methods to replace joints have a success rate of anywhere from five to 20 years. The procedure incorporating HA may extend that time span.

▶ Backing into Muscle Pain

The muscles work in conjunction to lift the bones and make them move. Like bones, muscles are susceptible to wear, tear, and disease. Muscles and ligaments play a primary role in the great majority of back injuries that occur in this country. Each year, at least 2 percent of the work force, or 450,000 people, sustain back injuries. Thirty-one million Americans suffer lower-back pain at any given time, and 13 million of these are functionally impaired. A machine developed in Boston measures lumbar muscle endurance and may give physicians their first objective means of assessing patients with low-back pain. The Back Analysis System (BAS) was developed by biomedical engineer Carlos J. DeLuca and his associates at Boston University's NeuroMuscular Research Center. The machine is able to distinguish people with chronic low-back pain from those with healthy backs. Researchers recently have begun to use the machine to study the effects of physical therapy and work-hardening programs on patients with back pain. Back machines have been used since the late 1980s, but the new breed may show whether exercise is helping or if other therapy is needed.

Exercise is currently in favor to help people recover from back pain. Traditionally, bed rest was prescribed for lower-back pain, and surgery was suggested if pain persisted. Several studies this year document the beneficial effects of exercise programs for people with back injuries. Studies from the University of Miami Comprehensive Pain and Rehabilitation Center propose that 90 percent of all back pain is the result of weakened muscles, ligaments, and connective tissue around the spine, hips, buttocks, and stomach. Supervised rehabilitative exercises are suggested to strengthen those muscles as an alternative to rest or surgery.

▶ Combating Muscular Disease

Research into therapies to combat muscle diseases this year achieved favorable results for some children with cerebral palsy. Cerebral palsy results from brain damage before or during birth, and results in muscle incoordination and speech disturbances. Two-thirds of the children who have cerebral palsy also suffer from spasticity—involuntary movements controlled by abnormally tightened muscles. Neurosurgeons at the University of Pittsburgh injected 17 patients who had congenital spastic cerebral palsy and six patients with other forms of spasticity with doses of a drug called baclofen. The results showed that the baclofen effectively reduces spasticity in children with cerebral palsy, as it has previously in adults with spinal-cord injury and multiple sclerosis.

Muscular dystrophy leads to a wasting of muscles. Scientists this year have continued their quest to find how the protein dystrophin functions. The lack of dystrophin causes Duchenne's muscular dystrophy, while a defect in the same protein causes the somewhat milder Becker's muscular dystrophy. Researchers at the University of Iowa in Iowa City proposed a theory to explain how the absence of dystrophin may allow the destruction of glycoproteins by other elements. Researchers still need to determine why the glycoproteins are diminished, but the findings suggest that defects on the glycoproteins are responsible for other forms of muscular dystrophy. Treatment still lies far in the future, but understanding the dystrophin complex may help researchers develop new therapeutic strategies.

Another approach toward a genetic cure for Duchenne's muscular dystrophy was reported in *Nature* (4/29/91). The researchers at the University of Wisconsin-Madison injected the dystrophin gene into mouse models. One percent of the population developed dystrophin in its proper position on the cells' membranes. Meanwhile, neurologists from Vanderbilt University in Nashville proved that prednisone, a powerful steroid, slowed progressive muscle weakening in youngsters with Duchenne's. Because of the serious side effects of prednisone, the Muscular Dystrophy Association does not recommend its use. The scientists from Vanderbilt also acknowledge that it is not a cure, but the secret of the steroid's dystrophy-fighting effect may lead to less-toxic drug treatments.

K. F. McDonnell

Brain and Nervous System

▶ Cerebrovascular Disease

Several landmark studies on treatment of stroke were published in 1991. For the first time neurologists have developed scientifically based guidelines for the prevention of further strokes in certain high-risk individuals. Two of the studies investigated surgical treatment, while the third investigated drug therapy. Although both surgery and medicines have been used extensively, physicians have never been able to reliably determine which treatment was best for an individual patient.

▶ Stroke

Stroke is permanent brain damage resulting from blockage or rupture of a blood vessel supplying the brain. In the United States alone it strikes 500,000 people yearly. About 30 percent of strokes are lethal, making cerebrovascular disease the third-most-common cause of death in North America. The effects of stroke vary from mild to severe, depending on which blood vessel in the brain is compromised and for how long. Blockage of a blood vessel supplying the left half of the brain can cause paralysis of the right side of the body and the inability to speak or understand language. Strokes on the right side of the brain cause paralysis of the left half of the body and, often, spatial disorientation resulting in an inability to dress or find one's way in previously familiar surroundings. Strokes affecting smaller brain regions can selectively impair vision, equilibrium, or personality without any obvious paralysis.

Strokes can develop in two fundamentally different ways. Rupture of a brain blood vessel causes a bloody, or *hemorrhagic,* stroke. Blockage, or *occlusion,* of a blood vessel, depriving brain tissue of blood, causes an *ischemic* stroke. Ischemic strokes are the most common, and it was their treatment that was addressed by the recent landmark studies. Blockage can occur either in large arteries or in arterioles, small blood vessels that branch off from trunklike arteries. Reduction in the internal diameter of arteries or arterioles reduces blood flow through the affected segment, depriving the underlying brain tissue of oxygen and nutrients.

Brain tissue is highly dependent on constant nutrition. Deprivation for more than a few seconds causes a shutdown of activity, producing symptoms that can persist for several minutes after the circulation is restored. Such brief *transient ischemic attacks,* or *TIAs,* provide a useful warning that cerebral circulation is marginal and that preventive measures are needed. Deprivation of circulation for more than a few minutes results in permanent damage in the brain area served by the narrowed vessel —an ischemic stroke or, alternatively, a *cerebral infarction.*

Arterial occlusion can arise in several ways, each requiring a different form of treatment. By far the most common occlusion is atherosclerosis, which results from cholesterol deposits in the walls of arteries. These deposits thicken the arterial wall, reducing the internal diameter of the hollow blood vessel. An arterial wall damaged by atherosclerosis exposes previously hidden tissues, which trigger an explosive chemical cascade that converts freely flowing blood into a solid clot. In a superficial cut of, say, the finger, this coagulation cascade by blood vessels is a useful adaptation that prevents excessive bleeding after injury. But triggering the same cascade in internal blood vessels damaged by atherosclerosis can be devastating. If sufficiently large, the adherent blood clot, or *mural thrombus,* will further reduce the size of the channel inside the atherosclerotic vessel. Alternatively, a piece of the mural thrombus can break off to form an *embolus,* a sort of "floating" blood clot that will be carried downstream until it lodges in a narrower vessel farther down in the arterial tree.

▶ Surgical Treatment of Atherosclerosis
The most common cause of large-vessel atherothrombotic stroke is a deposit in the *bifurcation* of the carotid artery, the point where the artery divides into two branches: the external branch that supplies superficial structures of the head and the internal branch that supplies a large portion of the brain. Because the carotid bifurcation is located in the neck, it can be easily approached by surgeons. In 1954 surgeons developed the technique of carotid endarterectomy—opening the artery to remove atherosclerotic deposits within its inner wall. By 1985, 107,000 endarterectomies were performed annually. Since that time, however, the enthusiasm for this costly procedure has dampened, for a variety of reasons. Many individuals suffered strokes either during the operation or shortly thereafter. Depending on the expertise of the surgeon and supportive staff, this complication varied from less than 3 percent to almost 20 percent. Furthermore, the overall risk of stroke in unoperated individuals had declined, in part from cessation of smoking, avoidance of dietary cholesterol, and from control of high blood pressure. Finally, drug treatments, which reduced the blood's tendency to clot, were also found to be useful. As a result, neurologists were no longer certain which patients would benefit from carotid endarterectomy.

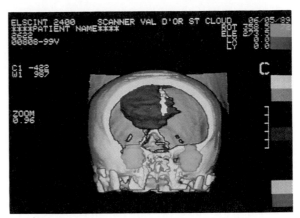

In computerized tomography (CT), revolving X rays create multiple-angled views of the brain, which a computer then processes into a vivid cross-sectional image.

Two independent studies found that individuals who had already had warning symptoms of cerebrovascular disease (either TIAs or previous strokes) and who also had severe atherosclerotic narrowing of the carotid bifurcation did much better if they underwent carotid endarterectomies as well as drug therapy, compared to those individuals given medical treatment alone. The risk of stroke was markedly lower in the surgical group for 30 months after the operation. In stark contrast, it was found that any potential benefits of endarterectomy for those individuals with less than 30 percent occlusion of the carotid bifurcation were greatly outweighed by the immediate risks of surgery.

▶ Medical Treatment of Strokes
Physicians have been treating stroke with drugs aimed at reducing the clotting tendency of the blood. The most powerful of these drugs—heparin and coumadin—inhibit the activity of enzymes that participate in the formation of blood clots. In high doses these drugs can lead to fatal bleeding. Aspirin typifies another class of drugs, acting primarily by preventing the activation of small blood cells called platelets, which also trigger the formation of blood clots. Although the effect is not as severe, antiplatelet drugs such as aspirin also increase the tendency for bleeding, especially at high doses.

Thus, as in the case of surgery, the use of these potentially useful drugs was clouded by uncertainty. In previous years studies demonstrated that the risk of stroke or heart attack in individuals who had already experienced a warning TIA was reduced some 20 to 25 percent by taking one to four adult-strength aspirin tablets daily. However, this benefit was offset by an increased risk of bleeding complications. In 1991 a large controlled study based in the Netherlands reported that taking one 30-mg child dose of aspirin daily offered the same degree of protection from ischemic strokes as did higher doses, but with considerably fewer side effects.

▶ Alzheimer's Disease

In the last decade much research has focused on identifying which nerve cells are preferentially affected by the Alzheimer's process. Much excitement was raised by reports that the disease preferentially affects cholinergic nerve cells in a brain region known as the *substantia innominata;* these cells use acetylcholine as a neurotransmitter. Champions of the "cholinergic hypothesis" of Alzheimer's disease suggested that the key to understanding the disease lay in deciphering the likelihood of these cholinergic neurons to degenerate. Furthermore, they suggested that giving drugs to stimulate the activity of the acetylcholine system might mitigate some of the mental deterioration resulting from Alzheimer's.

However, hopes were soon dashed when more extensive studies showed that the damage does not only affect acetylcholine-releasing cells from the substantia innominata. Furthermore, administration of drugs to bolster the activity of acetylcholine were disappointing.

Other researchers concentrated on the microscopic structures found in Alzheimer's brains. The deposition in brain tissue of *amyloid,* a fragment of beta-amyloid precursor protein, appears to precede the development of *neurofibrillary tangles,* twisted helical structures found in degenerating nerve cells. In the past scientists could not determine whether the amyloid was the cause of degeneration or simply the consequence of nerve-cell damage resulting from as yet undetermined causes.

Genetic studies in 1991 suggest, however, that accumulation of amyloid can cause Alzheimer's disease. Scientists determined that the gene encoding beta-amyloid precursor protein is on chromosome 21. This gene was found to be inherited in certain families with "presenile Alzheimer's disease." Certain variants of the beta-amyloid precursor protein gene have thus far been found only in Alzheimer's individuals. These studies imply that at least some cases of Alzheimer's disease result directly from abnormal accumulation of amyloid. This view has been reinforced by other types of studies, in which investigators were able to damage nerve cells by injecting amyloid into brain tissue. The toxic effect of injected amyloid can be blunted by a small molecule, substance P, normally found in brain tissue.

As always in fast-breaking research, caution is still needed. Many individuals with Alzheimer's disease do not have this variant precursor gene. Alzheimer's may yet prove to have more than a single cause. Despite these reservations, a buoyant optimism has developed in Alzheimer's research.

Orest Hurko, M.D.

Cancer

▶ The Treatment of Cancer

Taxol, derived from the bark of the Pacific yew tree, was originally identified more than 20 years ago during a search for natural products with antitumor activity. But the clinical evaluation of taxol was delayed until recently due to its short supply and poor solubility in water. Now that these problems have been effectively addressed—if not fully resolved—taxol is demonstrating antitumor activity against some very difficult, drug-resistant tumors. Several clinical trials have confirmed that taxol can cause significant tumor shrinkage in 30 to 35 percent of women with recurrent ovarian cancer. Most impressive has been the 25 percent response rate seen in women whose tumors were resistant to cisplatin (the most effective drug currently in use for treatment of ovarian cancer). More recently, 14 of 25 women with recurrent breast cancer had a 50 percent or greater shrinkage of their tumors after receiving taxol. Studies such as these suggest that taxol has a broad range of activity against solid tumors.

Taxol exerts its effect upon cancer cells in a way unlike any other commercially available cancer drugs. It binds to microtubules, the cellular proteins that allow the cell to move, maintain its shape, and transport essential substances into and out of the cell. Microtubules are also key elements in the process of cell division. Taxol interferes with these essential functions, leading to the death of the cell.

Despite its promise as a cancer drug, taxol development has been stymied by its extremely limited supply. The Pacific yew tree is the only current source of taxol, and it takes the bark of one to two trees to extract sufficient quantities to produce a single dose. Since the Pacific yew tree was never cultivated in any coordinated manner (it was considered a weed and routinely destroyed to make room for hardwood forests), and the tree takes up to 100 years to mature, scientists must for the present rely on existing forests for the supply of taxol.

Environmental activists have voiced concern over the large-scale harvesting of the Pacific yew. The old-growth forests most abundant in Pacific yew trees are also the same forests that house the endangered spotted owl. Environmentalists have lobbied for a moratorium on further harvesting of the yew tree until the ecological impact of large-scale harvesting can be assessed. These concerns have prompted the creation of a working group comprised of representatives from the National Cancer Institute (NCI), the U.S. Departments of Agriculture and the Interior, and Bristol-Myers

Squibb (the company that will market the drug). It is hoped that through this collaboration, the supply of taxol may be maintained while protecting this precious environmental resource. Intense efforts are under way to identify ways in which taxol may be produced from renewable resources, such as the needles of the Pacific yew tree, so that the tree would not have to be sacrificed to obtain the drug.

▶ Treatment of Acute Promyelocytic Leukemia

Leukemia is the abnormal and uncontrolled growth of immature white blood cells in the body. Acute promyelocytic leukemia (APL) is distinguished from other types of leukemia by its tendency to cause severe bleeding and life-threatening hemorrhage. APL is also characterized by a unique genetic defect in which there is an exchange, or translocation, of genetic material between the long arms of chromosomes 15 and 17.

The standard approach to the treatment of APL has been similar to the treatment of other forms of acute leukemias: high-dose, intensive chemotherapy. This has proven to be effective therapy for APL; more than 70 percent of patients have all evidence of their leukemia go away, and then enter "complete remission." Unfortunately, half of these patients eventually suffer a relapse. Intensive efforts have focused on the development of therapies that can lead to more-durable remissions with a higher likelihood of cure.

One line of research has explored ways to induce these excess immature white blood cells to develop, or differentiate, into mature normal cells. There is now convincing evidence that a form of vitamin A called all-trans-retinoic acid (tRA) can do just that. Following preliminary reports from investigators in China and France, researchers at Memorial Sloan-Kettering Cancer Center in New York

City recently reported results using tRA to treat 11 patients with APL. Of these 11, nine had complete remission of their leukemia.

Laboratory studies performed on the blood cells obtained from these patients have shed light on the way in which tRA works. These studies demonstrated that the translocation between chromosomes 15 and 17 actually creates a unique receptor to tRA that is not typically found in blood cells. tRA can bind to this receptor and trigger the abnormal leukemic blood cell to complete its development into a fully mature white blood cell. Studies are now under way to determine the best way doctors can use tRA to help people with this form of leukemia. Meanwhile, the vitamin A derivative is available on a compassionate-use basis from the National Cancer Institute for patients with relapsed APL.

▶ The Timing of Mastectomy for Breast Cancer

Levels of the female hormones, estrogen and progesterone, vary during the course of each menstrual cycle. It is well known that these hormones play an important role in the development of breast cancer. Investigators from several institutions have charted the course of women treated for breast cancer to see if the timing of breast surgery in relation to the menstrual cycle had any effect on the long-term recurrence rate for breast cancer. The results of these studies have been both provocative and controversial.

One recent study from Memorial Sloan-Kettering (MSK) Cancer Center in New York City reported that women with tumor involvement of underarm ("axillary") lymph nodes who had their surgery performed at a late phase in their menstrual cycle (called the luteal phase—when levels of progesterone are highest) had a significantly lower chance of tumor recurrence than those women who had their breast operations performed during the early, or follicular, phase of their cycle, when estrogens predominate. While at least two other centers have reported like results, other trials have failed to demonstrate a similar relationship.

In contrast to the MSK study, scientists at the University of Texas Health Science Center at San Antonio utilized data from 675 breast-cancer patients and performed a computer simulation that assigned each patient an

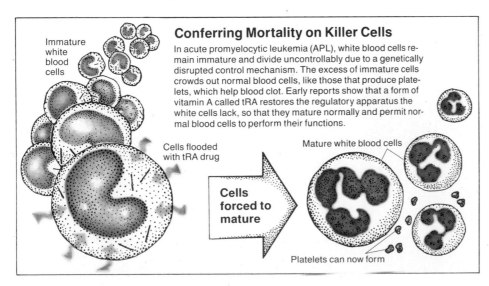

Conferring Mortality on Killer Cells

In acute promyelocytic leukemia (APL), white blood cells remain immature and divide uncontrollably due to a genetically disrupted control mechanism. The excess of immature cells crowds out normal blood cells, like those that produce platelets, which help blood clot. Early reports show that a form of vitamin A called tRA restores the regulatory apparatus the white cells lack, so that they mature normally and permit normal blood cells to perform their functions.

Immature white blood cells

Cells flooded with tRA drug

Cells forced to mature

Mature white blood cells

Platelets can now form

arbitrary day in the menstrual cycle. The researchers found that significant results could be obtained that either supported or refuted the results of the MSK study, suggesting that insufficient information currently exists to determine whether timing of breast surgery in relation to the menstrual cycle has any real impact on the long-term prognosis for women with lymph-node-positive breast cancer. It is hoped that a prospective clinical trial may be able to resolve this controversy.

▶ Reassessing the Danger of Radon

The association of radon with the increased risk of lung cancer has raised the nation's level of awareness of the relationship between environmental risk factors and cancer. Many prospective home buyers have made radon testing a mandatory stipulation in their contracts. But a recent workshop sponsored by the U.S. Department of Energy has brought those concerns into question.

The initial observation that radon might be a risk factor for lung cancer was made in uranium miners, who, chronically exposed to very high radon levels, were noted to have increased rates of lung cancer. There appeared to be a relationship between the level of exposure and risk: the higher the level of exposure, the greater the risk of lung cancer. That association was extended to the levels found in the basements of some homes, and it was theorized that chronic exposures to even low levels of radon could result in an increased incidence of lung

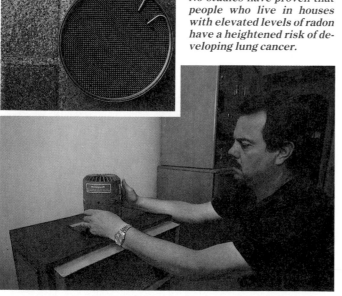

No studies have proven that people who live in houses with elevated levels of radon have a heightened risk of developing lung cancer.

cancer in the general population. However, no studies have ever been performed to prove that people who live in houses with elevated levels of radon developed lung cancer any more frequently than those who were not exposed to such levels. In addition, since most of the miners exposed to high levels of radon also smoked cigarettes, extension of these findings to nonsmokers may not be valid. Until more information is gathered, a relationship cannot be assumed between elevated home levels of radon and increased risk of lung cancer, especially in nonsmokers.

▶ Control of Nausea and Vomiting

One of the most feared and unpleasant side effects of cancer chemotherapy has been nausea and vomiting. The development of some of our most effective drugs, such as cisplatin in the 1970s, was slowed due to the severe nausea and vomiting that accompanied treatment with this drug. The use of multiple antinausea agents ("antiemetics") before, during, and after chemotherapy helped to reduce the incidence and intensity of nausea and vomiting, but the antiemetics themselves could produce unpleasant side effects such as sedation, muscle spasms, restlessness, and low blood pressure.

Recently, the first member of a new family of antinausea drugs was approved for use in the United States. Ondansetron (Zofran) blocks the body's nausea-signaling network more specifically than any of the previously available drugs. As a result, it can be given in doses that are more effective in preventing nausea and vomiting, while minimizing the undesirable side effects seen with other antinausea drugs. Since ondansetron does not cause sedation, it has enabled more patients to receive their chemotherapy in the outpatient setting and then return home or to work to resume their normal daily activities on the day of treatment.

▶ Postchemotherapy Blood Counts

Normally, a tremendous number of blood cells are produced by the body every day. Blood-forming cells are often the hardest hit by cancer therapy, since anticancer drugs are often selected on the basis of their ability to target fast-growing and -dividing cells. This is one reason why low blood counts are a common side effect of cancer chemotherapy. Inadequate blood-cell production increases the risk of infection (due to low white-blood-cell counts) and bleeding (due to low platelet counts).

In the early 1980s, scientists first identified several natural proteins called "hematopoietic growth factors" or "colony-stimulating factors" (CSFs) that promoted the growth of blood cells. Advances in recombinant-DNA technology ("gene cloning") in the late 1980s enabled the genes that coded for

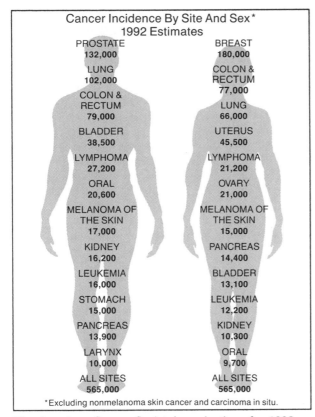

Cancer Incidence By Site And Sex*
1992 Estimates

PROSTATE	BREAST
132,000	180,000
LUNG	COLON & RECTUM
102,000	77,000
COLON & RECTUM	LUNG
79,000	66,000
BLADDER	UTERUS
38,500	45,500
LYMPHOMA	LYMPHOMA
27,200	21,200
ORAL	OVARY
20,600	21,000
MELANOMA OF THE SKIN	MELANOMA OF THE SKIN
17,000	15,000
KIDNEY	PANCREAS
16,200	14,400
LEUKEMIA	BLADDER
16,000	13,100
STOMACH	LEUKEMIA
15,000	12,200
PANCREAS	KIDNEY
13,900	10,300
LARYNX	ORAL
10,000	9,700
ALL SITES	ALL SITES
565,000	565,000

*Excluding nonmelanoma skin cancer and carcinoma in situ.

The American Cancer Society's projections for 1992 suggest that more people will die from lung cancer than from any other form of the disease.

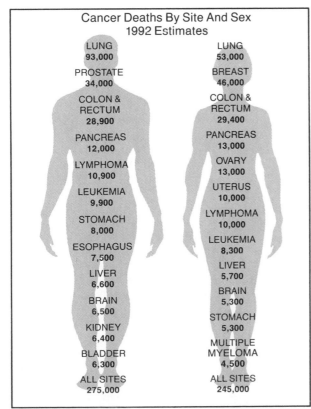

Cancer Deaths By Site And Sex
1992 Estimates

LUNG	LUNG
93,000	53,000
PROSTATE	BREAST
34,000	46,000
COLON & RECTUM	COLON & RECTUM
28,900	29,400
PANCREAS	PANCREAS
12,000	13,000
LYMPHOMA	OVARY
10,900	13,000
LEUKEMIA	UTERUS
9,900	10,000
STOMACH	LYMPHOMA
8,000	10,000
ESOPHAGUS	LEUKEMIA
7,500	8,300
LIVER	LIVER
6,600	5,700
BRAIN	BRAIN
6,500	5,300
KIDNEY	STOMACH
6,400	5,300
BLADDER	MULTIPLE MYELOMA
6,300	4,500
ALL SITES	ALL SITES
275,000	245,000

these proteins to be inserted into bacteria and yeast, which were then able to produce large quantities of pure CSFs. Clinical trials in cancer patients demonstrated that administration of CSFs could limit or entirely prevent low white-blood-cell counts following chemotherapy. Prevention of this side effect also resulted in a reduction in the number of infections and hospitalizations in patients after chemotherapy. Two of these agents, GCSF (Neupogen) and GM-CSF (Leukine), have now been approved by the Food and Drug Administration (FDA). These drugs will help the cancer patient remain active and out of the hospital during treatment.

▶ Tumor-Suppressor Genes

While much of the early work examining the genetic basis for cancer focused on how overactive genes could cause cancer, much progress has been made recently toward understanding how the loss of normally active genes involved in growth regulation can also lead to the development of cancer. The first insights were obtained in this area in the early 1970s, when it was postulated that certain forms of cancer could occur when both copies of a normal gene were damaged or lost. The model for this theory was a childhood tumor of the eye called retinoblastoma that appeared to run in families. It was theorized that this cancer could be due to an inherited defect in one copy of a gene and an acquired defect in the other. But it was not until the mid-1980s that the retinoblastoma gene (Rb) was isolated and identified. In all retinoblastoma samples tested, the Rb gene was noted to be missing or mutated.

Now that the Rb gene has been cloned and its protein product identified, investigators have turned their attention to understanding its normal function in cells. More recently, laboratory researchers have demonstrated that by inserting a normal copy of the Rb gene into cells lacking the gene, the cells lose their cancerous characteristics and behave like normal cells.

The increased incidence of second cancers observed in survivors of childhood retinoblastoma has led clinical investigators to suspect that loss of tumor-suppressor genes may be involved in the development of a number of childhood and adult cancers. Indeed, laboratory analysis of a number of cancers has led to the identification of at least 12 different chromosomal regions that may contain other tumor-suppressor genes. These include the p53 gene, whose loss or mutation appears to play a role in the development of certain forms of lung, breast, and colorectal cancer as well as a bone cancer called osteosarcoma. One of the most exciting fields of cancer research is focusing on the identification of other tumor-suppressor genes and understanding exactly how they function. The ultimate goal would be to replace the genes that are lost or defective, and thereby halt tumor growth. In the not-too-distant future, this approach may be ready for evaluation in people with cancer.

▶ Complications of Breast Implants

Since their introduction 25 years ago, silicone-filled breast implants have been received by more than 2 million American women. Approximately 80 percent of these operations have been performed for purely cosmetic reasons for breast enlargement, while the remaining 20 percent have been performed to reconstruct the breast following mastectomy. Some women experience side effects following the surgery, including scarring and hardening of the breast implant, rupture of the implant leading to local spillage of the silicone gel, and the development of autoimmune disorders, such as rheumatoid arthritis, systemic lupus erythematosus, scleroderma, and Sjögren's syndrome. In addition, breast implants can make the interpretation of mammograms difficult in some women, potentially delaying the early detection of breast cancer, and postponing treatment.

Researchers have found that prolonged exposure to silicone and breakdown products of polyurethane (a material used to coat some breast implants) can affect the immune system and induce cancer in laboratory animals. These findings have led some consumer advocates to call for a ban on silicone breast implants. Others have argued that the cosmetic and psychological benefit of breast reconstruction following mastectomy is so great that banning the implants would deter women from seeking appropriate medical care once diagnosed with breast cancer. In response to these concerns, the FDA now requires manufacturers of breast implants to disclose potential health risks to consumers. Since no central registry has ever been created to assess the full spectrum or severity of side effects from silicone breast implants in humans, the National Cancer Institute recently announced plans to set aside $2.1 million to conduct such a study. Nine thousand women who have had breast-augmentation surgery with silicone-filled implants will be monitored for at least 10 years and compared to a control group of women who have undergone other types of cosmetic surgery. Until the results of this trial are known, the FDA has placed a moratorium on silicone-implant insertions.

▶ Breast-Cancer-Prevention Trials

There were an estimated 180,000 women diagnosed with breast cancer in the United States last year. Nearly 46,000 died from this disease over that same period. About one out of nine women will develop the disease.

For a number of years, tamoxifen has been used to treat women with estrogen-sensitive breast cancers. Tamoxifen is a synthetic hormone that works by blocking the binding of estrogen to its receptor on breast-cancer cells. Large clinical trials have clearly demonstrated the beneficial effects of tamoxifen: it can lead to the shrinkage of breast cancers that have spread to various parts of the body, thereby reducing symptoms and prolonging life; it can delay or prevent the recurrence of breast cancer that has spread to axillary lymph nodes; and it can do the same in women whose tumors appear to be localized to the breast but who are at high risk of relapse. More recently, clinical researchers have noticed that those women treated with tamoxifen after their breast-cancer surgery developed fewer cancers in the remaining breast than those who did not receive tamoxifen, suggesting that tamoxifen may be effective in the prevention of breast cancer.

After extensive consideration, the NCI has embarked upon a clinical trial to determine whether tamoxifen can prevent breast cancer in women who are at increased risk but have never had breast cancer. The study, called the Tamoxifen Prevention Trial, will enroll 16,000 women over the next three to five years. Half the women will receive tamoxifen, and half will receive an identical pill that is inactive. Neither they nor their physicians will know the true identity of the pills until after the trial is completed. Only in this way will researchers be able to determine whether tamoxifen can prevent the occurrence of breast cancer in women at risk.

Two welcome side effects of tamoxifen appear to be a slight lowering of the blood-cholesterol level and a slowing of calcium loss from the bones in postmenopausal women. Since changes in these measures could result in a reduction of cardiovascular and bone diseases, this trial will also monitor these women for the incidence of heart attacks and the occurrence of compression fractures of the spine.

▶ The Women's Health Initiative

Last April, newly-appointed National Institutes of Health (NIH) Director Bernadine Healy, M.D., announced plans to launch the largest study of women's health ever undertaken in this country. The study will involve more than 140,000 women and will target heart disease, cancer, diabetes, and osteoporosis, four of the leading causes of death and disability in older women. This study, termed the "Women's Health Initiative," will study if changes in diet, exercise, vitamin D and calcium supplementation, and hormone-replacement therapy can prevent or delay the onset of these maladies. The trial, scheduled to begin in 1993, will be conducted through dozens of clinics and medical centers throughout the country.

Mace Rothenberg, M.D.

Child Development and Psychology

▶ Childhood Obesity and Dieting Attitudes

Childhood obesity, long recognized as a health risk factor, has also been associated with a child's emotional and social development. Although our society is becoming aware of the factors that lead to obesity, the number of obese children and children with eating disorders continues to climb. Three studies published in 1991 on birth weight, self-concept, and dieting attitudes significantly contributed to the existing body of medical research concerning childhood weight problems.

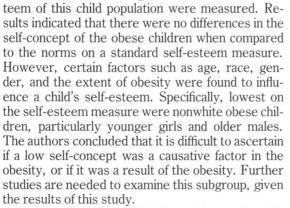

Surprisingly, few studies have found substantial differences in self-esteem between obese and nonobese children. In a study published in February 1991, Sue Y. S. Kimm, of the University of Pittsburgh School of Medicine, and colleagues investigated 130 obese children who were enrolled in an outpatient obesity clinic. The study group was tested using a standard self-esteem scale. In addition, the effects that age, gender, race, degree of obesity, and other factors might have on the self-esteem of this child population were measured. Results indicated that there were no differences in the self-concept of the obese children when compared to the norms on a standard self-esteem measure. However, certain factors such as age, race, gender, and the extent of obesity were found to influence a child's self-esteem. Specifically, lowest on the self-esteem measure were nonwhite obese children, particularly younger girls and older males. The authors concluded that it is difficult to ascertain if a low self-concept was a causative factor in the obesity, or if it was a result of the obesity. Further studies are needed to examine this subgroup, given the results of this study.

A longitudinal study of birth weights and weight problems in late adolescence was published in July 1991. Researchers in Jerusalem followed a study group of 33,413 children born between 1964 and 1971. Birth weights were obtained from files from three major hospitals. Height and weight measurements when the child turned 17 years of age were gathered from the Israel Defense Forces medical examination. The results showed that higher birth weight was a common risk factor for obesity at 17 years of age. A relationship was also found between birth weight and maternal prepregnant body weight. The authors suggest that overweight mothers may have a tendency to overfeed their infants, possibly predisposing the child to obesity in later childhood and adulthood.

Adolescent female concerns about weight and dieting have been documented in several recent studies. In a study of 206 sixth-grade girls, Elissa Koff and Jill Rierdan from Wellesley College in Massachusetts found that weight concerns tend to emerge between the ages of 9 and 11. Girls of this age appeared to have already adopted a "dieting mentality" that included the avoidance of fat, counting calories, thinking often about food, feeling guilty after overeating or even eating normally, and exercising. These practices were found even in girls who described themselves as not being overweight or who were happy with the way they looked. Such results emphasize that a thin self-image, common for women in our society, is now becoming a normal desire for preadolescents. The "dieting mentality" is being adopted even by girls who do not perceive themselves as being above ideal weight. This may cause young girls to become underweight, possibly jeopardizing the health and further physical potential of these youngsters.

▶ Environmental Variables and Temper Tantrums

Temper tantrums are part of the rite of passage experienced by parents as their child progresses through childhood. They occur frequently, are usually short-lived, and eventually decrease over time. However, some tantrums may be more intense and may be accompanied by severe behavioral problems. A study published in April 1991 in *Developmental and Behavioral Pediatrics* was designed to examine the psychosocial correlates of tantrums. The subjects in this study consisted of 502 mothers of three-year-olds in London. The mothers were asked to complete a standardized behavior-problem questionnaire and were given a semi-

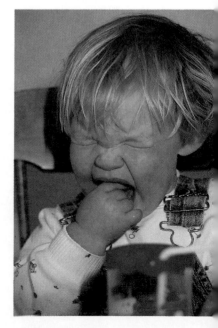

structured interview. Tantrums were operationally defined as occurring three or more times per day or lasting at least 15 minutes. Severe tantrums were reported in 6.8 percent of the children, of whom over one-half had multiple behavior problems. The factors associated with tantrums included maternal depression, marital stress, poor child health, maternal irritability, and corporal punishment. However, tantrums were not related to maternal employment, little social support, or single parenting. As with any study, the authors cautioned the reader before generalizing the results to other subgroups. However, the results of the study force us to examine environmental variables that may be inadvertently or adversely affecting child behavior.

▶ Childhood Stress and Coping Abilities

Current research is beginning to examine the effect of stressful events on a child's social and behavioral skills. A study published in 1991 assessed the effects of stressful life events on two types of resourcefulness skills: the perceived level of social support (a child's perception of being liked and cared for) and social problem-solving skills. These skill levels were observed to see how they contribute to a child's behavioral and academic adjustment across time. The subjects, 361 children, completed measures that evaluated their social-support system and problem-solving skills. The children's parents completed a measure of social position (economic level) and stressful life events, and reported on behavior problems commonly observed in their child. The children's teachers also completed a behavior-problem checklist and calculated grade-point averages based on grades in English, math, spelling, and reading.

Children with a strong sense of social security and good problem-solving skills adjust well behaviorally and academically.

In general the authors found that increases over time in social support and social problem-solving skills were accompanied by an improvement in behavioral and academic adjustment. However, no cause-and-effect role could be found for stressful life events and later adjustment problems.

▶ Planned Parental Absences

Parents often wonder what effect their absences may have on their children—particularly mothers who have to work and must be repeatedly separated from their children. According to a 1991 study by Tiffany M. Field from the University of Miami Medical School, infants and children appear to adapt well to repeated separation from their mothers. The study sample consisted of 80 children ranging in age from 12 months to 62 months, with a mean age of 34 months. In half the sample, children were recruited just prior to being separated from their mothers on one occasion, while the other half of the study sample included children who would be separated from their mothers on multiple occasions (trips lasting an average of 4.1 days). Play behavior and child naptime behavior was observed two days before the mother's departure, the first two days of the separation, and the two days following the mother's return. Field concluded that the children appeared to adapt to repeated separations after an initial stressful response to the first separation. The study found that there were no adverse effects on play behaviors (activity level, cooperative play, verbal interaction) and sleep behaviors (active sleep, wakeful fussiness) as a result of being separated from their mothers.

Although animal studies have found opposite results, the author notes that the child's environment remained constant, whereas, in the animal world, the social structure typically changes in the absence of the mother. Because these children attended day care, the author suggests that the consistency of the day care may have protected the child from any stress caused by repeated separations.

▶ Understanding AIDS and HIV Infection in Childhood

Acquired immune deficiency syndrome (AIDS) has become a perplexing dilemma for parents and educators of young children. In a 1991 study in the *Journal of Pediatric Psychology,* researchers investigated the level of understanding about AIDS in different age groups in order to design better, more effective educational programs. Sixty subjects were recruited representing varying stages of cognitive development: 5- to 7-year-olds (prelogical), 8- to 10-year-olds (concrete logical thinking), and 11- to 13-year-olds (formal logical thinking). Children were asked specific questions about the definition, cause, treatment, and prevention of AIDS. Examiners were allowed to use specified probes if necessary to have the child expand on initial answers. The data revealed a parallel between a child's causal thinking about AIDS and thinking about illness. Younger children perceived little difference between AIDS and an illness, and usually associated the illness with an event that had recently occurred. Older children explained AIDS more as a distinct group of symptoms that were internal. The authors suggest that parents and educators can apply these results by remembering that information must be presented to match appropriate developmental levels. More important, parents and teachers cannot assume that children understand all the issues involving AIDS just because information about the disease has been presented to them.

A child's understanding of AIDS and its transmission increases as the child's ability to understand cause and effect increases. Thus, educational programs should be designed to cater to this developmental process.

An increasing concern among parents and early educators is the presence of the HIV-infected child in the classroom, particularly with younger children and infants. Researchers evaluated the knowledge and attitudes of parents and day-care teachers regarding the transmission of the human immunodeficiency virus (HIV) in a 1991 study published in *Pediatrics*. The study also focused on the willingness of the parents to have their child continue in a day-care setting when there was a child infected with HIV present. Twelve day-care centers were included in the survey; four of these centers were used to conduct the study. The questionnaires administered to the parents and teachers included demographic questions and an evaluation of knowledge about HIV transmission. Altogether, 176 day-care staff members and 219 parents participated in the study. Ninety-eight percent of the parents and day-care staff knew about the proven modes of transmission: sexual intercourse and needle sharing. There was broader uncertainty about HIV transmission through common contacts such as tears, vomiting, coughing, and hand-holding.

While 63 percent of the parents reported that they would permit their child to stay in school with an infected child, only 43 percent of parents would permit their child in the same classroom with an infected child, stating a fear that an HIV-infected child endangers the health of noninfected children. Ninety-five percent of the day-care staff reported they should be informed if a child infected with HIV was enrolled in their class. The authors concluded that there is a significant degree of fear among parents and day-care workers regarding AIDS. They stress the need for educational intervention on attitudes toward children infected with HIV and their ability to integrate into the child-care system.

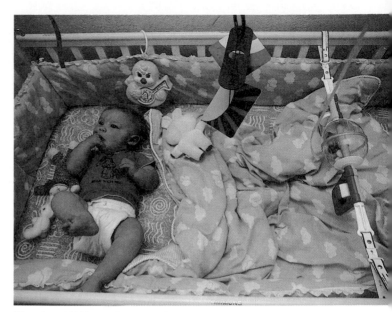

To solve childhood sleep problems, parents try practical solutions before consulting a doctor. Many parents place favorite toys or blankets in the crib.

▶ Parents and their Child's Sleep Problems

Childhood sleep problems include difficulty in going to sleep and night wakings. An interesting study published in April 1991 found that parents usually attempt to solve the problems using common practices before consulting a professional. A telephone survey to determine the prevalence of sleep problems was conducted of all the families in a small midwestern community having children between the ages of 12 and 35 months. Parents were questioned on child resistance to going to bed, night awakenings, and crying episodes during the night. The data gathered revealed that various interventions often used with sleep problems included diet modification, sleeping with parents, background "white" noise, and pacifiers or bottles in the crib. When asked if the children had a problem awakening during the night, 38 percent of parents of infants responded yes, while 62 percent said no. Thirty-three percent of parents of toddlers responded yes, while 65 percent said no. Most parents put their children to bed with toys or blankets, and thought it helped prevent sleep problems. Pacifiers were used often, particularly by parents of infant night wakers. Most parents had tried letting their child "cry it out," with favorable results, but did not like this procedure. Parents obtained most of their information from family or relatives, friends, or books when their child had sleep problems. The author notes that sleep problems may be more common than once thought, and that attitudes of parents may contribute significantly to healthy sleep habits in children.

Cynthia P. Rickert, Ph.D.

Digestive System

For researchers and clinicians who study digestive diseases, 1991 was an exciting year. A possible genetic cause for colon cancer was discovered and may lead to new types of treatment for this often fatal disease. Surgeons have made great strides in performing small-intestine transplants, suggesting that this surgery may soon become as common as other types of transplants. Less dramatic, but with a higher potential to save human lives, researchers have found a simple bacterium to be a leading suspect in causing stomach cancer.

▶ Bacteria/Stomach-Cancer Link Discovered

Mounting evidence has shown that *Helicobacter pylori,* a bacterium commonly found in the gut of half of all Americans and up to 90 percent of people in the world's poorer regions, is intricately linked to stomach cancer. Two studies published in October 1991, one involving 130,000 people by Stanford University and one of 6,000 people by the Kuakini Medical Center in Honolulu, show that carriers of the bacterium are three to six times more likely to develop stomach cancer. Moreover, *H. pylori* was found to be present in 90 percent of patients undergoing surgery for intestinal-type stomach cancer.

H. pylori, which can be picked up through human contact or through dirty water, has long been known for its role as a contributor to peptic ulcers and stomach inflammations. Even so, most researchers don't regard *H. pylori* as the sole cause of stomach cancer, but see it as a strong contributing factor. In response to this demonstrated link, several medical-equipment manufacturers have been rushing *H. pylori* in-office diagnostic tests to market. These enzyme-linked immunosorbent assay (ELISA) devices can process a blood-serum sample in as little as seven minutes, and are better then 90 percent accurate. With the ELISA devices, gastroenterologists have a way to quickly diagnose and treat the bacterial infections. In many cases, *H. pylori* can be treated with common antibiotics.

▶ Fighting Colon Cancer

Of all the cancers that plague the human body, cancer of the colon is one of the deadliest, killing nearly 60,000 Americans per year. Another 156,000 Americans yearly are diagnosed with the disease. Because it has distinct phases of development, colon cancer is also one of the easiest of the cancers for research scientists to study. In a process that occurs over the course of many years or even decades, small masses of polyps will appear on the colon, later to develop into malignant tumors, and then—in the disease's final stages—to spread cancerous growth to other parts of the body.

Researchers have long suspected that some people might be predisposed to the disease by nature of their genetic makeup. Indeed, genetic "markers" (defective genes) associated with some phases of colon cancer were uncovered in the late 1980s. But these markers did not appear to be the "trigger" that started the disease; rather, they were "switches" that turned on new phases of the disease. In August 1991, two research groups jointly announced that they may have uncovered the genetic trigger of colon cancer.

Colon cancer comes in two varieties: the inherited familial adenomatous polyposis (FAP), and the noninherited nonfamilial type. FAP, by far the rarer of the two, accounts for less than 1 percent of reported cases. But because it runs in families, researchers have an opportunity to study a population with a high risk for colon cancer. Raymond White and colleagues from the University of Utah in Salt Lake City discovered that damaged copies of the adenomatous polyposis coli (APC) gene are present in the DNA of all FAP sufferers they tested. Taking a different tack, Ray Vogelstein and his research team at Johns Hopkins University in Baltimore, Maryland, tested samples of damaged colon tissue from victims of the nonfamilial type. They found the corrupted APC genes in many of the samples. Vogelstein has speculated that the APC genes in these patients may have been normal at one time, but had mutated to cause colon cancer.

FAP sufferers develop symptoms early in life, and most have to have their colons removed by age 30. In contrast, the nonfamilial variety surfaces later in life, has environmental causes—radiation, carcinogenic-chemical exposure, or damage accrued from the aging process—and can be treated successfully if caught early. Former President Ronald Reagan put a national spotlight on colon cancer when doctors removed benign polyps from his colon in 1985. For cases where the colon cancer has progressed further, treatment options include surgically removing the colon, or partially destroying it through chemotherapy or through radiation therapy.

The discovery of the gene trigger, besides providing

clues for other cancer researchers to follow, might lead to the development of preventive medicines and earlier diagnoses. Before the APC discovery, FAP expert Malcolm Dunlap of Scotland had developed a way of finding traces of the colon-cancer-switch genes in blood tests. As he pointed out in a February 1991 journal article, this technique enabled him to accurately predict which of his patients with FAP would develop cancer in two-thirds of the cases. The isolation of the APC trigger gene will make advance diagnosis possible in many of the other cases.

There are some ethical issues to consider, however. Could insurance companies use advance diagnostic information to deny health benefits to people at risk for colon cancer? Also, some doctors worry about the dilemma posed by testing fetuses for the presence of the trigger gene, giving prospective mothers the option to abort if the fetus tests positive. Still, doctors feel that the therapeutic benefits of better treatment alternatives far outweigh these possible problems.

▶ Dramatic Transplant Successes

Surgeons from the University of Pittsburgh announced at a June 1991 meeting of the American Society of Transplant Surgeons that they had successfully performed five small-intestine transplants —a first—in the previous year. In the past, this type of transplant has proven difficult to accomplish because it has been nearly impossible to control the body's rejection of the transplanted injection. A Canadian surgeon performed the first successful small-intestine transplant in 1988, and only a few other surgeons have tried the experimental procedure. Drs. Jorge Reye and Satoru Todo, who made the Chicago presentation, attributed their success to FK-506, a new immunosuppressant drug.

The Pittsburgh surgeons performed the transplants, three on children and two on adults, beginning in May 1990. All five suffered from short-gut syndrome, which is the lack of a small intestine. Without a small intestine, the patients had no ability to absorb food into their bloodstream, and had to be intravenously fed. Four of the five patients also received a transplanted liver, but one, a 31-year-old man, received only a small intestine. Plagued by severe rejection, infection, and a kidney failure, his recovery has proven the most difficult of the five. He eventually was released, but requires regular hemodialysis to purge toxins from his blood. A four-year-old boy also required a long hospital stay but has recovered well. The remaining three—a two-year-old boy, a two-year-old girl, and a 27-year-old woman—recovered quickly and are fully active. All five patients could eat normally a month after their respective operations, and had fully functional small intestines after another month.

Ear, Nose, and Throat

▶ Improving Surgical Techniques

Refinements in endoscopic approaches to surgery are making it possible to treat some disorders of the nose, airway, sinuses, and ear with less-invasive procedures than have traditionally been used.

The endoscopy technique uses a thin, fiber-optic tube called an endoscope, which is inserted through the nostril, mouth, or a small incision to inspect and treat areas that before required more-extensive surgery. By looking through the scope itself or at images transmitted to a video screen (see photo), the surgeon can view internal structures, including the paranasal sinuses, Eustachian tube, and middle ear. If surgery is necessary, the surgeon passes small instruments through the scope to carefully scrape away or remove damaged tissue.

Endoscopes are being used to diagnose and treat sinusitis—the num-
ber-one chronic illness in the U.S. The National Center for Disease Statistics estimates that over 31 million Americans, roughly one in eight, suffer from sinusitis at some time.

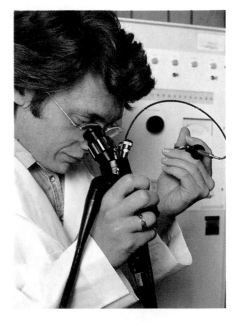

The sinuses are actually only air spaces in the bones behind the nose. When the sinuses or their drainage pathways become blocked, sinusitis results. Symptoms include facial pain and pressure, nasal congestion, headaches, and postnasal drip. In the past, when antihistamines, decongestants, or topical steroid sprays could not improve nasal airflow and sinus drainage, major surgery was available as a last resort. Now endoscopic sinus surgery provides a safer and effective means of clearing obstructions. Initial long-term studies show that endoscopic-surgery patients remained symptom-free for up to 42 months after treatment and experienced few problems. While rare, complications of the procedure may include visual problems and the development of a leak between the sinuses and the fluid around the brain.

► Middle-Ear Infection Therapy

Acute middle-ear infections, most common during childhood, are caused by viruses or bacteria that inflame the cells lining the middle-ear cavity. A liquid discharge thought (but not proven) to be secondary to bacterial infection commonly follows acute episodes. When left untreated, these infections can lead to hearing loss. Amoxicillin, the most widely used antimicrobial agent, kills the majority of organisms known to cause these acute infections.

Disagreements over the effectiveness of amoxicillin resurfaced in December 1991 with the publication of an article in the *Journal of the American Medical Association (JAMA)*. This article, which ignited a dispute about scientific misconduct, contradicted a 1987 article in the *New England Journal of Medicine (NEJM)*.

The 1987 *NEJM* study by researchers at the Otitis Media Research Center in Pittsburgh, Pennsylvania, maintained that amoxicillin was effective in treating middle-ear infection with discharge, and was somewhat effective in treating instances of discharge after infection. One of the cochief investigators of this group, Erdem I. Cantekin, Ph.D., disagreed with the analysis and conclusions of the *NEJM* paper, and wrote his own article reanalyzing the same data. His conclusions: amoxicillin was no better than a placebo in treating both acute middle-ear infections with discharge and asymptomatic discharge. The editors of *JAMA* published Cantekin's paper because they wanted readers to review both sets of data and then decide for themselves.

► A New Hearing Organ?

Researchers found that normal, hearing-impaired, and profoundly deaf people can hear words spoken at high ultrasonic ranges long believed inaudible.

While most sounds are perceived as a result of being carried through the air and converted to nerve impulses by the cochlea, other sounds are sensed as vibrations conducted through the bones of the skull to the inner ear. The cavernous structure and porous consistency of bone make it a good conductor of sound. Individuals hear the sound of their own voices through this kind of hearing.

In the study, ultrasonic speech was conducted through the bones of the skull using a device placed next to a subject's head. The device transmitted ultrasonic sound by vibrating extremely rapidly. While scientists thought these ultrasonic noises would be perceived as nothing more than tones, distinct words were discernible.

The research suggests that people may have a second organ of hearing in addition to the cochlea of the inner ear. This organ may be developed as a means of communicating sound to people with varying degrees of hearing loss.

Carole F. Gan

Endocrinology

► Presidential Malady

President George Bush's hospitalization for Graves' disease in 1991 focused national attention on this thyroid-gland disorder. Located at the base of the neck, the thyroid is part of the body's complex endocrine system that includes the hypothalamus, pituitary, parathyroid, thymus, pancreas, adrenal, testis, and ovary. All these glands secrete and then release hormones into the bloodstream. Hormones are chemicals that regulate a variety of bodily functions. Hormones produced by the thyroid, for instance, regulate the rate at which the body burns carbohydrates, proteins, and fats. Problems develop when endocrine glands produce too little or too much of their respective hormones.

President Bush, a man reputedly in excellent physical condition, returned from jogging around Camp David in early May 1991, uncharacteristically fatigued and out of breath. When a White House doctor noted that Bush also had a fast, irregular heartbeat, a condition known as *atrial fibrillation,* he ordered the president hospitalized. A few days later, Bush was diagnosed with Graves' disease, a condition that may afflict as many as 1 million Americans (including, coincidentally, the president's wife, Barbara Bush, who was diagnosed with the problem in 1989).

Graves' disease causes the thyroid to produce too much of the hormone thyroxine, although the disease's exact cause is poorly understood. In healthy individuals, another gland, the hypothalamus, monitors the level of thyroxine in the body. When that level drops below normal, the hypothalamus chemically signals the pituitary gland to release thyroid-stimulating hormone (TSH) into the bloodstream, which, in turn, chemically signals the thyroid to produce more thyroxine. In Graves' disease the body's autoimmune system attacks the thyroid with antibodies that mimic the hormone TSH, tricking the thyroid into producing more thyroxine. This overabundance of thyroxine in the system can, if unchecked, cause the development of severe heart problems. But what triggers the autoimmune system to produce such antibodies is unknown.

Treatment may involve the surgical removal of the thyroid or destroying it with radioactive iodine. Patients so treated must then take replacement thyroid hormones for the rest of their lives. In some cases, drugs are used to regulate the thyroid; however, since the thyroid remains abnormal, these drugs must be used for a long time and may produce unwanted side effects.

Researchers at the Veterans Administration Medical Center in San Francisco announced in July 1991 that they had identified the areas on thyroid cells to which the TSH and the TSH-mimicking antibodies attach. Scientists have been able to detect these antibodies for many years, but they have not, until this recent breakthrough, been able to observe how the antibodies bind with the thyroid cells. Although any new treatments stemming from this discovery are many years off, researchers hope that it will generate new approaches to uncovering a cure for Graves' disease.

▶ The Homosexual Hypothalamus

In perhaps the most controversial study to emerge from the annals of endocrine research in 1991, Simon LeVay, a neurobiologist at the Salk Institute in San Diego, announced that the hypothalamus of homosexual men is, on average, half the size of that of heterosexual men. LeVay based his findings on autopsies he performed on the brains of 19 homosexual men, 16 heterosexual men, and 6 women. LeVay considers the finding important because many sexual characteristics that define males and females are apparently controlled by hormones produced by the hypothalamus (in fact, a woman's hypothalamus, like those of the homosexual men in LeVay's study, is half the size of a heterosexual male's hypothalamus).

LeVay's work, however, is not without its detractors. Some researchers think that the hypothalamus is just too small (about the size of a grain of sand) to meaningfully study. Others criticize the fact that all 19 of the homosexual men in the study had died of AIDS, and that their hypothalamuses might have been damaged by the disease. LeVay downplays this criticism by pointing out that six of the heterosexual males, as well as one of the females, had died of AIDS. Still other researchers claim that a small hypothalamus might be the *result* of homosexuality, not the cause. LeVay plans to expand his study by performing more autopsies on a larger selection of brains.

▶ New Hope for Diabetics

Diabetes, a disease that afflicts 12 million Americans, is one of the most widespread and dangerous of the endocrine-system disorders. Improperly managed, the disease can lead to such complications as stroke, heart attack, kidney failure, blindness, impotence, and the amputation of limbs. Diabetes is the seventh-leading cause of death in the United States. In Type I diabetes, which usually strikes children, the pancreas gland fails to produce insulin, a hormone that enables fat, muscle, and liver cells to absorb glucose, an essential sugar. Like the mechanism involved in Graves' disease, Type I diabetes is caused by antibodies attacking the pan-

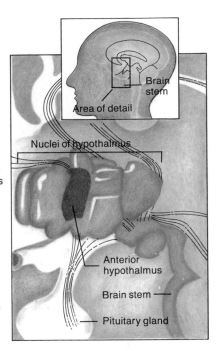

Brain Structure and Sexuality

The hypothalmus is a structure of the brain involved in sexual behavior and emotions. A researcher studying the brains of a small sample of homosexual men says that one tiny region of the hypothalmus, called the third interstitial nucleus of the anterior hypothalmus, is much smaller in homosexual men than in heterosexual men. More research is needed before it can be definitely stated that the size difference plays a role in sexual orientation.

creas. In Type II diabetes, which strikes adults, cells in the body become resistant to insulin, calling on the pancreas to produce more insulin than it can manage.

A Genetic Link. Researchers from three American universities announced in February 1991 that they had determined the general location of a gene that may cause Type II diabetes. When scientists refine their search and zero in on the actual genes involved, this type of diabetes may become a preventable disease. Stefan Fajans of the University of Michigan provided the impetus for the research. For 32 years, Fajans collected data from one family spanning five generations and including 275 members. More than 40 members of this family had developed Type II diabetes, and in each case, the same genetic abnormality was present. Critics of the research—and the researchers themselves—caution that the genetic abnormality may apply to just that one family, and that other families need to be studied before firm conclusions are reached.

A Possible Preventive Measure. Although doctors have been successfully treating the symptoms of diabetes for many years, preventive measures have eluded them. For potential Type I diabetics, a drug called Imuran may provide relief. In 1983, Peggy Polopolus, then 13 years old, was diagnosed in the early stages of diabetes. Her doctors at the University of Florida Health Center prescribed the experimental treatment of daily doses of Imuran, a drug usually used to suppress the immune system of organ-transplant recipients. After an eight-year trial concluded in 1991, Polopolus showed no symptoms of diabetes. Her pancreas, which at one time produced only 1 percent of the insulin a normal pancreas secretes, now produces 25 percent. Since a normal pancreas generally produces an overabundance of insulin, Polopolus's one-quarter production is still three times more insulin than her body needs. While proponents of the study believe that it may be possible to stop Type I diabetes in its tracks, other researchers worry that suppressing the immune system might make diabetic patients more susceptible to infections and higher cancer risks.

Implants and Artificial Pancreases. In May 1991, researchers at BioHybrid Technologies in Massachusetts announced successful trials of an artificial pancreas in diabetic dogs. The plastic device contains transplanted pancreatic cells and is permeable to the tiny blood cells that provide nourishment to the pancreatic cells. But the plastic casing is not permeable to the much larger autoimmune cells that would destroy the transplanted cells. Human trials of the device are expected in less than two years. Paul E. Lacy of the Washington University School of Medicine in St. Louis announced in December 1991 that he had achieved similar results on a much smaller scale by implanting tiny pancreatic-cell-filled tubes no wider than a toothpick under the skin of laboratory mice. Either approach, if successfully applied to humans, would preclude the need for daily shots of insulin in Type I diabetics.

Help for Type II Diabetics. Doctors who treat Type II diabetics advise their patients, who are often overweight, to exercise in order to reduce the disease's symptoms. A study published in July 1991 demonstrates that regular exercise may even help prevent Type II diabetes. Based on a statistical analysis of the exercise habits of 5,990 men over time, epidemiologist Susan E. Heimrich of the University of California at Berkeley found that individuals could reduce the risk of diabetes 6 percent for every 500 calories they worked off weekly.

Some Type II sufferers have to take large doses of insulin to maintain health. An ongoing study in Alberta, Canada, seems to indicate that the taking of insulin itself leads to a higher risk of damage to the retina of the eye. For this reason, stricter diet and exercise management—which can cut down on the need for high insulin ingestion—is important to Type II diabetics.

Meanwhile, researchers may have found a substitute for insulin for Type II diabetics. In two independent studies reported in August 1991 by researchers at the University of Wisconsin and at the University of Zurich, Switzerland, a synthetic hormone called IGF-I may deliver all the benefits but none of the side effects of insulin.

Environment and Health

▶ Persian Gulf War Pollution

The war in the Persian Gulf, from August 1990 through February 1991, triggered many atrocities —including some deliberate, malicious acts against the environment. This environmental terrorism may have both short- and long-term implications for human health, stemming from the polluting effects of hundreds of oil fires in Kuwait and millions of gallons of oil spilled into the Gulf.

The damage started in January 1991, when Iraqi forces began discharging oil into the waters of the Persian Gulf. Estimates from the Environmental Protection Agency (EPA) on the amount released range from 6 million to 8 million barrels—up to 30 times the size of the 1989 *Exxon Valdez* oil spill in Alaska's Prince William Sound. Then, in February 1991, the retreating Iraqi army damaged or set fire to some 749 oil wells, storage tanks, and refineries in Kuwait. Huge plumes of black smoke filled the air for months. Efforts to put out the fires began soon after the war ended. The last fire was finally extinguished on November 6, 1991.

Worldwide response to these environmental affronts came in the form of the United Nations International Action Plan. The Intergovernmental Oceanographic Commission, coordinated under this plan, was put in charge of immediate and long-term cleanup, remediation, and restoration work in oil-spill areas. Great effort was made to protect the desalination plants from oil-spill contamination, in order to safeguard drinking water.

During the Persian Gulf War, Iraqis set fire to hundreds of Kuwaiti oil wells. The long-term health effects of the resultant air pollution are still not known.

But the devastation suffered by wildlife and aquatic creatures is still not fully understood. Thousands of birds became war casualties as the oil reached wetlands, salt marshes, and mangrove swamps, the homes and nesting areas to many migratory and native birds.

From a human-health standpoint, however, the oil fires posed the greatest concern to medical experts. As part of the U.N. plan, the U.S. Interagency Air Assessment Team Response—consisting of representatives from EPA, the National Oceanic and Atmospheric Administration (NOAA), and the Centers for Disease Control (CDC)—was assembled and deployed to Kuwait on March 10, 1991, to determine the potential health threats from the smoke. The group was particularly anxious to learn if hydrogen sulfide, sulfur dioxide, and particulate matter, three toxic pollutants commonly spewed into the air from burning oil wells, were posing an acute health problem.

Atmospheric sampling did not find high concentrations of sulfur dioxide or hydrogen sulfide, although high levels of particulate matter were found in the air. Experts worried that these elevated levels of particulates may have caused health problems during calm periods when winds were not dispersing the pollutants, especially from September through December 1991.

Luckily, surveys of the local hospitals did not reveal increased admission rates for respiratory complaints. Preliminary findings, however, showed that those with asthma and pre-existing pulmonary disease (such as chronic bronchitis or chronic obstructive lung disease) may have their symptoms aggravated; infants, children, and the elderly were particularly susceptible to respiratory irritation. People in the areas most affected by the smoke plumes were advised to limit outdoor activities and keep their windows shut.

Many unanswered questions regarding the health effects of the war zone's devastated environment remain. Medical experts are particularly concerned about the long-term health effects. Only time and more studies will tell, however. In addition to efforts by the U.N. and the governments of the Gulf countries, the United States plans to provide scientific and technical expertise as needed and as resources allow.

▶ Lawn Herbicide May Pose Cancer Risk

A study published in the September 1991 *Journal of the National Cancer Institute* showed that dogs whose owners used lawn herbicide containing the chemical 2,4-dichlorophenoxyacetic acid (2,4-D) were twice as likely to develop lymphatic cancer. Based on this finding, the authors concluded that "human health implications of 2,4-D exposure in the

Dogs whose owners sprayed their lawns with herbicides containing the weed killer 2,4-D have an elevated cancer risk. The risk to humans has not been determined.

home environment should receive further investigation."

Specifically, the study showed that for dogs whose lawns were sprayed or sprinkled once with the weed killer 2,4-D by homeowners or commercial lawn-care companies, the cancer risk was one-third higher than among dogs whose owners did not use the chemical. If the herbicide was applied four times or more a year, that risk increased to twofold.

The findings of this study raise concern for human cancer risk. Other studies have shown that farmers who use this herbicide and often come into contact with it have an elevated risk of contracting non-Hodgkin's lymphoma. This type of cancer has seen the second-fastest increase in incidence rate of all human cancers in the United States over the past 15 years.

With 2,4-D used frequently on public parklands, golf courses, and private lawns, the authors said that "the potential exposure opportunities to people and farm and companion animals continue to be substantial." No formal studies have yet been done on the nonfarming population. The authors said that additional research is needed to determine if dogs and people are equally at risk with home use of 2,4-D herbicide.

▶ Pesticides—New and Old

In a continuing trend toward phasing out harmful pesticides, the EPA and the maker of the pesticide *ethyl parathion* agreed to stop its use on all but nine crops by the end of 1991. This pesticide has been linked to more than 70 deaths and thousands of illnesses among farm workers. The government estimates that 3 million to 6 million pounds of this chemical are used each year in the United States.

The use of the granular pesticide *carbofuran* in certain ecologically sensitive areas was banned by the EPA starting on September 1, 1991. More than 80 bird-kill incidents have been reported to the EPA. Studies in 10 states document carbofuran's high toxicity to birds, including the bald eagle and other birds of prey.

On a more positive note, the EPA gave conditional registration in the summer of 1991 to two pesticides derived from genetically engineered biological organisms. The two products, *M-One Plus* and *MVP,* will be used to control beetles and caterpillars. The EPA found no evidence of harm to people, animals, or birds from these pesticides.

▶ The Pacific Yew Tree
In 1991 a promising new anticancer drug called *taxol,* derived from the bark of the Pacific yew tree, catapulted into a storm of controversy.

Very encouraging clinical trials show that taxol could play a significant role in the treatment of ovarian, breast, lung, and colon cancer. But extracting the drug from the bark of the slow-growing yew tree is time-consuming, expensive, and kills the tree in the process. Environmentalists want to make sure that the supply of yew trees will not be decimated by those wishing to exploit its medical value. They have also tied this tree into the emotion-charged fight to save the old-growth forests in the Pacific Northwest, where the yew trees thrive.

News of taxol splashed across the newspapers and became widely known in 1991, but the drug has a much longer history. The anticancer properties of the yew bark were first discovered in the late 1960s, but scarcity of the material curtailed research for many years. In 1979 interest peaked again when Susan Horwitz from Albert Einstein College of Medicine in New York City discovered

Raymond J. Moshy of Escagenetics Corporation in California is using genetic engineering to make taxol in the lab—and thus spare the Pacific yew tree.

that taxol works by immobilizing cells, thus interrupting the cell-multiplying process gone awry with cancerous cells. Clinical studies began in 1983, and by 1989, in a trial at the Johns Hopkins Oncology Center in Baltimore, patients with advanced ovarian cancer not helped by standard treatment responded to taxol. In over 200 patients, more than 30 percent of the tumors showed a significant response rate.

Although no one has been "cured" by taxol, Dr. Samuel Broder, director of the National Cancer Institute (NCI), has called taxol "the most important new drug to come along within the National Cancer Program in 10 or 15 years." The drug is offered only in clinical trials that are being run by the NCI.

The major hurdle remaining in taxol development is acquiring an adequate supply. Three yew trees must be cut down to treat just one patient because the bark contains only about one-hundredth of 1 percent of taxol by weight. NCI researchers estimate that they will need to harvest a minimum of 750,000 pounds of dried bark (from about 38,000 trees) in 1991, just to yield enough pure drug, about 25 kilograms, to treat 12,000 patients. The drug company, Bristol-Myers Squibb, has signed an agreement with NCI to provide the taxol to them.

To get around the supply problem, scientists are looking into different methods of obtaining taxol. One avenue under investigation is to derive taxol from the tree's needles, although needles have a lower and less stable amount of the drug than does the bark. Other possibilities include synthesis or semisynthesis of the complex chemical structure of taxol, cultivation of the tree in nurseries, or propagation of the yew from branch-tip cuttings.

Pacific yew bark is expected to continue to be the major source of taxol for the next three to five years. After that, scientists hope they will have perfected alternative means of acquiring taxol.

▶ Toxic-Waste-Site Monitoring Inadequate
The National Research Council (NRC) released a report in October 1991 concluding that the EPA Superfund program to clean up hazardous-waste sites is not doing its job. Specifically, the report states that hazardous-waste sites are not being adequately identified or evaluated, and appropriate priorities for cleaning them up are not being set. They believe that these shortcomings may be endangering public health.

Superfund sites are located all over the nation. A recent EPA study disclosed that more than 40 million people live within four miles of a Superfund site. While these people are not necessarily at risk, problems have been documented from several investigations at specific sites. People living near toxic sites have a higher incidence of various symptoms, such as headache, fatigue, low birth weight, heart anomalies, and assorted neurobehavioral problems. Whether hazardous-waste exposure causes long-term medical difficulties is hard to determine, but some studies have shown a high incidence of cancer in people exposed to certain compounds.

The report's authors admit that current health problems from hazardous-waste sites appear to be small, but they feel the future risk might be greater because many of these substances are very persistent. The authors are particularly concerned about the risk of groundwater contamination, which they believe is not being well handled by today's remediation practices.

In conclusion, the NRC report states, "prudent public policy demands that a margin of safety be provided regarding potential health risks from exposures to substances from hazardous waste sites. We do no less in designing bridges and buildings. . . . We must surely do no less when the health and quality of life of Americans is at stake."

▶ Deadly Dioxin Reassessed

The group of chemical compounds known as dioxin is considered to be one of the most potent known carcinogens. But now the high risks of exposure to dioxin are being called into question. New studies have uncovered a better understanding of dioxin's effect as it first enters a cell. On April 10, 1991, EPA chief William Reilly announced that his agency would conduct a scientific reassessment of dioxin now that the human-health and environmental effects of dioxin are better understood.

Dioxin first gained notoriety as the potentially dangerous ingredient in the defoliant Agent Orange, used in the Vietnam War. Veterans' groups claim that military personnel who were exposed to this chemical are now at high risk for debilitating disease. Dioxin made headlines again when dirt roads contaminated with the chemical in Times Beach, Missouri, led to the permanent evacuation of more than 2,000 residents from that town in the early 1980s.

Research for the reevaluation is in progress, but some scientists believe there may be a "safe" dose of dioxin below which no toxic effects will occur. An analysis is not expected to be ready for peer review until June 1992.

▶ Is Electricity a Health Hazard?

A number of scientific studies over the past decade have investigated if electricity can cause cancer, childhood leukemia, or other health effects. Electromagnetic fields (EMFs) are produced by anything electric, from power lines to household appliances. Initially the idea that EMFs could be hazardous seemed farfetched, but now their potential threat is being taken more seriously.

A draft report released in late 1990 from the EPA

Reports continue to implicate electromagnetic fields produced by overhead high-tension wires as a possible cause of childhood leukemia and other disorders.

states that EMFs from power lines and perhaps other sources in the home are a possible, but not proven, cause of cancer in humans. The controversial report is now under review and may be subject to revision.

The whole EMF issue is very confusing because many of the studies are somewhat contradictory or inconclusive. A good case in point is a recent study done in Los Angeles that appeared in the *American Journal of Epidemiology* (11/1/91). The study links increased leukemia risk to children's proximity to high-current power lines, black-and-white television sets, and hair dryers. But they also found that the cancer is not associated with household exposure to EMFs.

In an effort to reach some clearer conclusions, Congress, in the summer of 1991, appointed the Department of Energy (DOE) as the lead agency for research in the EMF area. The DOE expects to develop a strategic plan that will be ready by February 1992.

▶ Lead Safety Threshold Lowered

For years, lead poisoning has been a serious nationwide health problem affecting children. As scientific knowledge about lead has grown, the "threshold of concern," or blood-lead level above which action should be taken, has also dropped. On October 7, 1991, Department of Health and Human Services (HHS) Secretary Louis Sullivan, M.D., announced a new threshold of 10 micrograms per deciliter (μg/dl) of whole blood. That is less than half the level set in 1985 of 25 μg/dl.

Incidences of lead poisoning are widespread and far-reaching. HHS Assistant Secretary for Health James Mason, M.D., said, "lead poisoning is one of the most common pediatric health problems in the U.S. today, and it is entirely preventable. Three to four million children under age six in the U.S. have blood levels greater than 15 μg/dl. This is far greater than the number of children affected by other common childhood illnesses."

Lead affects almost every system in the body. It especially harms the developing brain and nervous system of fetuses and youngsters. Severe lead exposure may result in coma, convulsions, and even death, while levels as low as 10 μg/dl may cause impaired neurobehavioral development, learning disabilities, and decreased stature or growth.

Children come into contact with lead through the air, water, dust, soil, and food that has been contaminated by various sources, including paint, solder, and gasoline. Lead-based paint is the most common source of lead exposure. Currently, 74 percent of privately owned housing units built before 1980 contain lead-based paint. Many cases of lead poisoning come about because owners of homes with lead-based paint don't take precautions when they renovate or remodel.

The government has now decided to put emphasis on lead-poisoning prevention. As part of this campaign, the CDC recommends that universal screening (through blood tests) of young children be phased in, except in communities where large percentages of children have been screened and found not to have lead poisoning.

The CDC has also set up action guidelines to deal with children with various blood-lead-concentration levels. For instance, children with levels of 20 μg/dl or higher should be seen by a doctor, and the source of lead exposure located and removed. For those with blood levels above 45 μg/dl, medical intervention is needed; a new drug to treat lead poisoning was approved by the Food and Drug Administration (FDA) on January 30, 1991. A big advantage of this drug, called *succimer,* is that it is given orally instead of intravenously. Those with blood levels of 15 to 19 μg/dl should undergo more-frequent screenings, and parents should receive nutritional and educational counseling. If the lead level doesn't go down, a home inspection may be required. When many children in a particular locale have blood levels of 10 μg/dl or above, the CDC advises community-wide prevention programs.

Now the challenge is for federal, state, and local governments, along with the private sector, to coordinate their efforts and get these new programs into the communities so they can help children.

Linda J. Brown

Eyes and Vision

▶ Cataracts

With over 50 percent of blindness caused by cataracts, this disease is the largest single cause of blindness in the world. A cataract is a reduction in the clarity, or transparency, of the lens of the eye. With aging, the lens of the eye naturally begins to grow cloudy. The age of onset of clouding is highly variable, occurring anywhere from the 40s to the 90s. The level of vision loss in the eye varies from only minimal to complete blindness.

A variety of studies published during 1991 provided new clues about the cause of cataracts. Cataract development may not only be due to aging, but may also be related to certain environmental factors. Long-term exposure to ultraviolet light, heavy smoking, and multiple episodes of severe diarrhea are all associated with an increased chance of cataract development.

In addition, a 1991 study by Dr. Nancy Isaac and colleagues from the Harvard School of Public Health found that a number of commonly used drugs greatly increased the risk of a patient having to undergo cataract surgery. The study evaluated a group of drugs called phenothiazines, commonly prescribed as sleeping pills, and less often used to treat mental illness. The patients who took phenothiazines to treat mental illness had a significantly increased chance of developing cataracts. The same relationship was not found with the sleeping pills.

A number of studies on possible preventive measures for cataracts were published in 1991. Dr. M. Cristina Lesky and colleagues from the State University of New York at Stony Brook reported on the preventive effect of multivitamin supplements on cataract formation. The authors found that the use of multivitamin supplements at least once a week for one year significantly decreased the chance of cataract development. Multivitamin supplements include large amounts of vitamin A, vitamin C, vitamin E, riboflavin, niacin, thiamine, and iron. These agents reduced the frequency of cataract development by a factor of 2.5. The actual vitamin responsible for this effect is not known. Dr. Lesky also found a number of personal characteristics that were associated with an increased chance of cataract development, including nonwhite race, high-school education or less, nonprofessional occupation, and dark-colored iris of the eye. Further study is still needed before widespread multivitamin supplements to prevent the development of cataracts are recommended. In particular, doctors need to determine which vitamin, or combination of vitamins, is the effective one.

A number of research studies in the past have suggested that aspirin may reduce the chance of cataract development. Dr. Isaac's study, as well as another recent study by Dr. Johanna Seddon and colleagues from the Massachusetts Eye and Ear Infirmary, confirmed this benefit.

▶ Laser Surgery

The cornea is the clear portion of the front of the eye through which all visual information must pass. Nearly a decade ago, Dr. Stephen Trokel of New York suggested that a number of corneal conditions that had previously been treated with surgery or spectacle lenses might be amenable to treatment with laser. He suggested that the excimer laser, which emits ultraviolet radiation, might be able to remove scars and other types of corneal disease to improve vision. The laser works by focusing an intense beam on the abnormal tissue, vaporizing it while leaving the surrounding normal healthy tissue untouched.

In 1991 a number of studies were published supporting the efficacy of laser surgery. Dr. Neal Sher and colleagues from four different institutions in the United States successfully used the laser in the treatment of scarred corneas. In a study of 33 pa-

Laser eye surgery has made great advances in the last decade. In 1991, lasers were used to remove corneal scar tissue and thereby eliminate the need for corneal transplants. Ophthalmologists are investigating the use of lasers to correct nearsightedness and astigmatism.

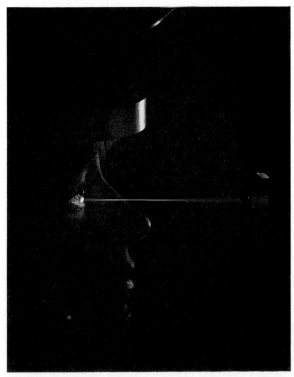

tients with scarred corneas, the laser successfully removed scar tissue and improved patients' vision, and also eliminated the need for a number of more-invasive surgeries like corneal transplant. Laser surgery also improved the comfort of some patients. The results of this early study must be confirmed with a larger group of patients before the technique can be widely used.

One of the most promising and wide-reaching uses of the excimer laser may be in the correction of nearsightedness, a refractive error in which the patient cannot see far away. Roughly one-third of all Americans are nearsighted. A patient characteristically uses contact lenses or eyeglasses to improve vision. But preliminary studies published in 1989 and 1990 have shown that the problem of nearsightedness can also be successfully treated with laser surgery.

Another type of refractive error that may be improved by laser surgery is astigmatism. Astigmatism occurs when the cornea is shaped unevenly. Rather than being shaped like a sphere, as a basketball is, it is shaped like the surface of a football, producing an out-of-focus image. In late 1991 Dr. Peter McDonnell from the University of Southern California reported that lasers could remove varying quantities of corneal tissue from different areas to smooth the corneal surface. In each case, laser surgery reduced the amount of astigmatism, providing the patient with a properly focused image. However, further testing is still needed before this procedure becomes widely available.

▶ Diabetic Retinopathy

A large number of reports appeared in 1991 regarding the value of therapy for diabetic retinopathy. Diabetic retinopathy is the leading cause of blindness among working Americans. Diabetes mellitus is a condition in which a patient has poor control over blood sugar, thus a patient's blood-sugar level is unusually high. Elevated blood sugar is treated successfully with insulin. However, the eye of a diabetic patient may develop certain abnormalities, including loss of normal capillary blood vessels in the retina; leakage of fluid, protein, and fat from the existing blood vessels into the retina; and abnormal blood-vessel development. The latter condition is called neovascularization. Each of these ocular complications of diabetes may lead to loss of vision.

Physicians have long speculated that improved control of blood sugar may reduce the complications of diabetes in the eye and in other organs as well, particularly the kidney and brain. Dr. Per Reichard and his colleagues from the Stockholm Diabetes Innervation Study reported on the results of a five-year study in which some patients were treated aggressively to control blood sugar, while others were given conventional treatment. The intensified therapy consisted of education, tutoring, blood-glucose testing at home, and three to six insulin injections daily. Conventional treatment usually includes only one or two injections. These doctors had previously reported that renal and neurologic complications of diabetes were markedly reduced by such an approach. As a result of this more aggressive therapy, there was a remarkable slowing of diabetic-retinopathy development. The study's authors noted that these techniques were well within the range of every diabetic patient. Their patients did not use an insulin pump, one of the more sophisticated, expensive, and invasive techniques being evaluated today. Slowing development of visual loss will reduce the duration of disability faced by diabetic patients, and hopefully reduce the cost of their medical care.

Once a patient develops diabetic retinopathy, particularly the complications of excessive fluid in the retina or new abnormal blood vessels, laser therapy is necessary. But unlike the excimer laser, which vaporizes tissue, the laser used to treat retinopathy heats the retina. Numerous studies have shown that laser treatment of the retina improves visual acuity and prevents progressive vision loss in most cases. But some studies suggest that diabetic-retinopathy treatment administered as early as possible after development of high-risk characteristics is advantageous. In a study by Dr. James Vander and colleagues from the Wills Eye Hospital in Philadelphia, patients who were treated early and responded immediately to treatment had excellent long-term vision. Fifty-two percent of their patients maintained visual acuity of 20/20 or better.

Since early treatment appears to be crucial in preventing the blinding complications of diabetic retinopathy, considerable discussion has occurred regarding the most appropriate means of screening. Current recommendations from the American Academy of Ophthalmology suggest annual ophthalmologic examinations beginning five years after the diagnosis of diabetes. A study by Dr. Jonathan Javitt and colleagues from the Johns Hopkins University suggests that screening during the first five years after diagnosis of diabetes could save money. In their analysis the authors found that it was less costly for the federal government to fund screening eye examinations to detect diabetic retinopathy earlier, when it is most responsive to treatment. Their report suggested that performing examinations even one year earlier might cause savings of $17.4 million and 5,961 person-years of sight. This analysis is based on what the patient's cost of disability would be, his or her loss of wages, and the loss of income-tax revenues. Such studies bring home the significance of preventive medical care in terms of the long-term impact.

Michael X. Repka, M.D.

Genetics and Genetic Engineering

In 1991, scientists continued their remarkable progress toward identifying the causes of a variety of inherited disorders and gaining a better understanding of the genetic mechanisms by which the human body functions.

▶ Alzheimer's Disease
Alzheimer's—characterized by memory loss, disorientation, depression, and deterioration of body functions—affects about 4 million Americans, mostly over the age of 65. But the inherited form of the disease, which accounts for 15 to 20 percent of Alzheimer's cases, strikes earlier, between the ages of 35 and 45, and is usually fatal within seven years.

In October 1991, molecular geneticist Merrill D. Benson and his colleagues at the Indiana University Medical Center reported that they had associated a genetic defect with an inherited form of Alzheimer's disease in three generations of a large family. Benson and his colleagues found that each of five Alzheimer's patients in the family had a defect in the gene that serves as the blueprint for a protein called *amyloid precursor protein* (APP). Defective APP breaks down into a protein called beta-amyloid, which accumulates in the brains of Alzheimer's victims. Other researchers had demonstrated earlier in the year that beta-amyloid can cause the death of cells important in controlling body motions, and that it interferes with learning. The discovery of the gene will make it possible to identify many individuals who are at risk of developing hereditary Alzheimer's. It may also lead to new ways to simplify diagnosis and treatment of the more common form of the disorder.

▶ Deafness
Also in October, researchers from the University of California at Berkeley and the University of Costa Rica reported the discovery of the first gene known to cause primary inherited deafness—that is, deafness not associated with some other disorder. About one in 1,000 Americans is born deaf, and perhaps half of those cases have genetic causes. The researchers studied 500 descendants of a prosperous 18th-century Costa Rican landowner named Felix Monge, who, like his descendants, was deaf but could speak, indicating that the deafness began long after birth. The gene, which has not been precisely identified, is located on chromosome 5, one of the 23 pairs of chromosomes that serve as the

blueprint for the human body. Researchers hope identification of the gene will provide clues about how and why deafness arises.

▶ Charcot-Marie-Tooth Disease

In July 1991, Texas and Belgian researchers discovered the defective gene that causes Charcot-Marie-Tooth (CMT) disease, an inherited disease of the peripheral nerves. CMT affects about 125,000 Americans; symptoms include foot and hand deformities and loss of sensation resulting from the wasting of muscles. Molecular biologists James R. Lupski and his colleagues at the Baylor College of Medicine in Houston, and Christine Van Broeckhoven of the University of Antwerp in Belgium, independently reported that the defect was caused by the duplication of a small segment of chromosome 17. The researchers have developed a simple, painless diagnosis for the disorder, which now is diagnosed by either a surgical biopsy of nerve tissues or a procedure in which electrical voltage is applied to nerves and the speed of its transmission measured. No therapy exists for the disorder as yet, although early identification will allow victims to redirect their lives toward occupations that do not require manual dexterity.

▶ Marfan's Syndrome

In July 1991, two teams of researchers independently reported that they had identified the genetic defect that causes Marfan's syndrome, a potentially fatal disorder that affects one in 10,000 people worldwide and as many as 40,000 Americans. Marfan's is a disorder of the connective tissue that holds together skin, muscles, and organs, and is marked by impaired vision, weakened arteries, a lanky appearance, and enlarged hands and feet—traits often found in athletes. Many athletes have been sidelined by the disease. Olympic volleyball player Flo Hyman and University of Maryland basketball star Chris Patton are two athletes who died during competition when their Marfan's-weakened coronary arteries burst.

A team headed by cardiologist Harry C. Dietz of the Johns Hopkins School of Medicine and molecular biologist Lynn Y. Sakai of the Shriners Hospital for Crippled Children in Portland, Oregon, and a second group led by molecular biologist Francesco Ramirez of the Mt. Sinai School of Medicine in New York City found that the defective gene was the blueprint for a protein called *fibrillin*. Fibrillin is especially important in the aorta, bones, and the suspensory ligament of the eye lens—all sites most affected by Marfan's syndrome. Now that researchers have identified the gene for Marfan's, they hope to test preserved tissues from President Abraham Lincoln to determine whether he suffered from the disorder (see the box on page 269).

▶ Fragile-X Syndrome

In May 1991, U.S. and Dutch researchers reported that they had identified the genetic defect that causes fragile-X syndrome, the most common form of inherited mental retardation. The syndrome affects one in every 1,250 males and one in every 2,000 females. It produces symptoms ranging from subtle learning disabilities to behavior problems such as hyperactivity, violent outbursts, and hand biting, to severe mental retardation. Males with the disorder are usually infertile.

A team headed by geneticist Stephen T. Warren of Emory University in Atlanta reported that the disorder is caused by a defect in a gene they named FMR-1. The gene is the blueprint for a protein that is "completely unlike any protein ever seen before," Warren said. The discovery will make possible prenatal screening for the disorder and may lead to the first therapies for it. Perhaps even more important, the discovery is the first of a gene thought to play a direct role in intelligence. The discovery may thus provide new insight into mental function.

▶ Lou Gehrig's Disease

Researchers identified the approximate location of the gene that causes the devastating paralytic disorder *amyotrophic lateral sclerosis*, better known as Lou Gehrig's disease. The April 1991 discovery marks the first major advance in determining the cause of the disorder since it was first diagnosed 122 years ago, according to neurologist Teepu Siddique of Northwestern University Medical School, leader of the team that made the discovery.

The disorder strikes about 5,000 Americans each year; an estimated 300,000 Americans now alive will thus develop it. It results in a degeneration of the brain and spinal-cord cells that control muscle function, which leads to generalized and progressive weakness and wasting of skeletal muscles and paralysis. It typically develops between the ages of 40 and 70; 90 percent of victims die within five years of diagnosis. The research team studied members of 23 families with a history of the disorder. About 60 of the 510 family members either had the disorder or carried the defective gene. Researchers estimate the gene itself will be located within five years.

▶ Smell

A Columbia University team reported in April 1991 that they had identified a family of 18 genes that are the blueprints for the sensitive receptors in the nose that signal the presence of odors. The team's results suggest that as many as 200 more such genes may exist, with their combined functions allowing humans to differentiate among the estimated 10,000 different smells to which they are exposed.

Proteins produced from these genes are located on the exterior of nerve cells high in the nose and are found nowhere else in the body, according to Columbia molecular geneticists Linda Buck and Richard Axel. When these proteins bind odorous molecules from the air, they send a specific signal to the brain, which combines signals from all the receptors to identify the scent. The research is expected to provide new insight, not only into human physiology, but also into the behavior of insects and animals. Animal behaviors are regulated in part by scents, called pheromones, that are transmitted through the air.

▶ Birth Defects and Aging

A new study published in March 1991 demonstrates that the increasing age of a potential mother does not increase the risk of birth defects—with the sole exception of Down syndrome, which has long been known to have a higher incidence among children of older mothers. Patricia A. Baird and her colleagues at the University of British Columbia in Vancouver studied the records of more than 500,000 live births occurring in British Columbia between 1966 and 1981. They identified more than 27,000 children with birth defects of unknown cause. They found no increase in incidence of birth defects with the age of the mother. This discovery, they said, should be "very reassuring" to older women contemplating pregnancies.

▶ Premature Delivery

California researchers have developed a new test that may be able to predict which women are more likely to deliver their fetuses before the pregnancy has proceeded to full term. Premature delivery is the leading cause of illness and death among newborns in the United States. About 400,000 babies are delivered prematurely each year, and nearly 30,000 of them die. Researchers from the University of California at Irvine, Adeza Biomedical in Sunnyvale, California, and the Mt. Sinai School of Medicine in New York City have linked premature delivery to a protein called *fetal fibronectin,* which they believe is released as a result of damage to the fetal membrane in the womb. The protein can be identified in the mother's vaginal and cervical secretions by a test similar to the Pap smear. They found that the presence of the protein indicated with 80 percent accuracy which women would deliver prematurely. The researchers hope that they can eventually use the test to identify women at high risk of premature delivery, and then take steps to delay the birth.

▶ Gene Therapy

Human gene therapy took several steps forward in 1991 after the first approved test of the technique

occurred in late 1990. That first case involved a four-year-old girl with *adenosine deaminase deficiency* (ADD), an inherited condition that left her without a functioning immune system. Molecular biologist W. French Anderson of the National Heart, Lung and Blood Institute in Bethesda, Maryland, removed white blood cells from the girl's body and inserted a healthy gene for the missing enzyme, adenosine deaminase, before infusing the cells back into her. Anderson reported in July 1991 that the unidentified girl was making good progress, and that, for the first time, she had successfully responded to a tetanus test. Anderson treated a second girl with the disorder in early 1991.

Biologist Steven A. Rosenberg of the National Cancer Institute conducted two gene-therapy experiments last year. In January 1991, he removed white blood cells called tumor-infiltrating lymphocytes (TILs) from two patients with advanced melanoma—a highly lethal form of skin cancer—and inserted into them the gene for a cancer-fighting protein called tumor necrosis factor (TNF). TNF kills cancer cells, but is too potent to be injected directly into humans. Rosenberg's plan was to have the altered TILs, which are infused back into the patient, release TNF only at the tumor site.

In October 1991, Rosenberg performed a different form of gene therapy on another melanoma patient. In this case, he removed cancer cells from the patient, inserted the TNF gene, and infused the cells back into the patient. Three months later, he planned to remove some of the patient's white blood cells, which had been stimulated by the TNF to attack the cancer cells. Rosenberg intended to grow large quantities of these white blood cells and inject them back into the patient in a kind of vaccination against cancer. By the end of the year, he was still unable to report on the effectiveness of the technique, but he had determined that the patients were not harmed by it. He has permission to treat 14 other patients. By the end of the year, the National Institutes of Health (NIH) had given permission to three other groups of researchers for human-gene-therapy experiments, but none had been attempted yet.

▶ Blood

In June 1991, researchers at DNAX Corporation of Princeton, New Jersey, reported that they had created a strain of pigs that produce human hemoglobin in their blood. Hemoglobin, the primary component of red blood cells, is the protein that actually carries oxygen throughout the body. The researchers said they had also developed a simple method for breaking open the pig blood cells and separating the human hemoglobin from the pig's own. The researchers hope that the human hemoglobin can eventually be used in a blood-replacement product.

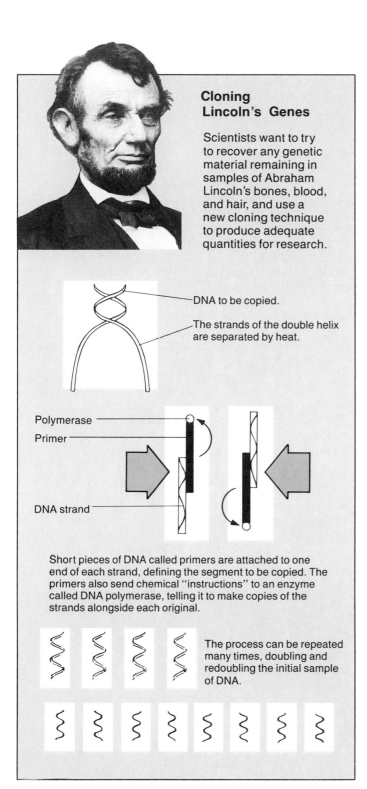

Cloning Lincoln's Genes

Scientists want to try to recover any genetic material remaining in samples of Abraham Lincoln's bones, blood, and hair, and use a new cloning technique to produce adequate quantities for research.

DNA to be copied.

The strands of the double helix are separated by heat.

Polymerase

Primer

DNA strand

Short pieces of DNA called primers are attached to one end of each strand, defining the segment to be copied. The primers also send chemical "instructions" to an enzyme called DNA polymerase, telling it to make copies of the strands alongside each original.

The process can be repeated many times, doubling and redoubling the initial sample of DNA.

▶ Genetic "Pharming"

In August 1991, two groups of researchers independently reported development of techniques for using farm animals to produce genetically engineered pharmaceuticals. Virtually all genetically engineered drugs are now produced in altered bacteria, yeast, and animal cells grown in the laboratory. As a consequence, the desired products are present in the organisms only in very low quantities, so that complex procedures are required to harvest the cells and purify the drugs. Molecular biologists have long hoped to engineer larger animals, such as cows, goats, and sheep, so that they would secrete the desired products into their milk. The animals could then be milked every day, and the drugs readily separated from the milk.

That dream has proved elusive because of the inherent difficulties of genetically engineering large animals. Researchers from Genzyme Corporation in Cambridge, Massachusetts, and Pharmaceutical Proteins Ltd. in Edinburgh, Scotland, now report that they have succeeded in goats. The Genzyme researchers inserted the gene for a protein called tissue plasminogen activator (t-PA), which is now used to dissolve blood clots. They found that the t-PA concentration in milk was 100 to 1,000 times as high as the concentration in bacterial cultures. The Scottish researchers did the same thing with the gene for a protein called *alpha-1-antitrypsin*. That protein, which is now isolated from human blood plasma, is used to treat emphysema. They found that alpha-1-antitrypsin accounted for more than half of the proteins in the goats' milk.

▶ Genetically Engineered Mice

In July 1991, three research groups independently reported that they had used genetic-engineering techniques to produce mice that develop Alzheimer's disease. The researchers inserted extra copies of the gene that codes for beta-amyloid, and found that the protein accumulated in the animals' brains as they aged, just as it does in humans. The feat gave researchers the first animal model of Alzheimer's. They can now use the animals both to study the mechanisms of Alzheimer's development and to test potential new forms of therapy.

▶ Vaccines

A major step toward the development of a single, inexpensive vaccine that could protect Third World children against a variety of life-threatening diseases was reported in June by researchers from the Albert Einstein College of Medicine in New York City. Molecular biologist Barry Bloom and his colleagues reported that they had made a genetically engineered form of the tuberculosis vaccine that also stimulated immunity (in mice) against tetanus. The vaccine is a prototype of an eventual product that would protect against 6 to 10 diseases simultaneously. Modification of the tuberculosis vaccine is important because vaccinations of more than 2.5 billion people have shown it to be extremely safe. Furthermore, it is cheap, does not require refrigeration (an important trait in the tropics), and provides long-lasting immunity with just one injection.

Thomas H. Maugh II

Government Policies and Programs

The spiraling cost of health care focused heated attention on government health-care policy this past year. The United States comptroller general, Charles A. Bowsher, announced that more than 12 percent of U.S. national income is used for health care. He warned that by the end of this century, if current trends continue, the United States would spend nearly 15 percent of its national income on health care. While everyone agrees that reforms are needed, what constitutes reform remains a source of contention among public officials.

The debate on health care under way in 1991 was the third such national debate since World War II. The first occurred during the administration of Harry Truman, in which the medical community successfully defeated a proposal for national health insurance. The second debate, during Lyndon Johnson's administration, resulted in the creation of the Medicare and Medicaid programs in 1965. These two programs extended health care to millions of Americans, but they did not change the fundamental essence of the health-delivery system. Instead, the federal government committed itself to pay the health-care industry for medical care provided to Medicaid and Medicare patients. For most of the history of these programs, the federal government paid the health-care industry the same way it pays contractors for military weapons: the actual cost plus a reasonable profit margin.

In November 1991, Harris Wofford won the Pennsylvania senatorial race, an upset victory attributed to his campaign emphasis on the need for health-care reform.

The current debate on health-care reform has produced two schools of thought—advocates of incremental reform and proponents of comprehensive reform.

▶ Incremental Reform

Incremental reform, which makes the health-care system respond to the market forces of supply and demand, has substantial support from the Bush administration. For most of 1991, however, the administration took the position that a proposal should be developed only after careful study. Then, in the November 1991 elections, Harris Wofford defeated Bush's former attorney general, Dick Thornburgh, in the Pennsylvania senatorial race, a victory attributed to Wofford's campaign emphasis on the need for health-care reform. Two days later the president ordered his advisers to develop a market-based health-care-reform proposal.

The way the federal system operates gives advocates of incremental reform a significant advantage over those who support comprehensive reform. The elaborate constitutional system of checks and balances within the federal government and between the states and the federal government, together with the diffusion of power in the U.S. Congress, make comprehensive changes difficult to achieve.

▶ Comprehensive Reform

Proponents of comprehensive reform argue, however, that changes in just one part of the health-care sector simply result in increased spending in another. "Pressing the balloon of health-care spending in one spot results in the balloon bulging out elsewhere," comptroller general Bowsher claimed.

The balloon analogy is a metaphor for what economists call a "zero-sum" game: one person's gain is another's loss. Yet the economic reality is that cost reduction would require health-care providers to take one or more of the following actions: earn less, become more efficient, or reduce the quality of health care. In addition, currently there are incentives for health-care providers and various levels of government to shift costs to someone else. The way it stands now, health-care financing is to some extent a form of musical chairs.

The Prospective Payment Assessment Commission, a government commission that monitors health-care costs, issued a preliminary report in October 1991 documenting what many health experts had long suspected. Faced with insufficient reimbursement of their expenses by Medicaid and Medicare programs, hospitals shift costs onto private health insurers. The commission found that the average hospital lost $3.2 million in 1989 from treating Medicare and Medicaid patients and those without any health insurance. To make up for these losses, the average hospital charged private insurers 28 to 40 percent more than the actual cost of patient treatment.

▶ Single-Payer System

Two leading candidates for comprehensive reform emerged during 1991. One popular proposal was to adapt the Canadian national health-care system to the United States. Under this approach the government would administer all health insurance. This approach spawned yet another Washington bureaucratic appellation, the "single-payer" system. The federal government would become the single payer, substituting one organization for the complex combination of employer-based insurance, individual health insurance, and various government programs, such as Medicare, Medicaid, federal employee health insurance, and Department of Veterans Affairs health care.

Two members of the House Committee on Ways and Means, Jim Moody (D-Wis.) and Marty Russo (D-Ill.), were prominent supporters of the single-payer approach. Russo introduced legislation (H.R. 1300) to impose a new 6 percent payroll tax on employers to finance the single-payer system. Russo also proposed to increase federal income taxes to make up for any shortfall in funding.

A big question remains with the single-payer approach: would the American public tolerate tax increases to finance the program? Congressman Dan Rostenkowski (D-Ill.), the chairman of the House Committee on Ways and Means, skeptically remarked that "people are disappointed with the health-care system, but when you talk about paying for it, there is a deafening silence."

The Bush administration opposes the single-payer approach as too costly and too much of an intrusion by government into the private sector. Advocates believe that the single-payer system would reduce paperwork and administrative costs. To demonstrate his belief that simplified procedures could be achieved within the current health-care system, President Bush proposed three major administrative reforms: a single health-care insurance claim for the entire public and private health-care system; an insurance card for every American that would identify what his or her public or private health insurance covers and what costs the policyholder would pay; and the computerization of every American's medical history so that a hospital or physician could access key medical information on their patients through a computer network, rather than having patients repeat their medical histories every time they saw a new physician.

Health and Human Services (HHS) Secretary Louis Sullivan estimated that these three administrative simplifications, when eventually implemented, would save $20 billion to $50 billion.

▶ Play-or-Pay System

The second comprehensive approach to health-care reform addresses employer health insurance. Currently, 80 percent of working Americans obtain their health insurance through their employer; on the average, employers pay 70 percent of the cost of this coverage. For the other 20 percent, many public officials support an approach known as "play or pay." Employers that do not "play" by providing health insurance for their workers would "pay" a tax to help finance government health insurance for people without private coverage.

Politicians in Congress introduced comprehensive health-care-reform legislation based on the play-or-pay concept in 1991. The Senate majority leader, George Mitchell (D-Maine), introduced S. 1227, *HealthAmerica: Affordable Health Care for All Americans.* Joining Mitchell were Senators Ted Kennedy (D-Mass.), Jay Rockefeller (D-W.Va.), and Donald Riegle (D-Mich.).

S. 1227 has a play-or-pay provision that goes into effect if fewer than 75 percent of workers are covered by health insurance after a five-year phase-in period. The pay requirement would come in the form of an employer payroll-tax contribution. The secretary of Health and Human Services would set the rate. The tax is described as a contribution, in an attempt to avoid the constitutional crisis that would arise if Congress were to delegate to the executive branch its authority to set a tax rate.

S. 1227 also addresses the special problems that small businesses face in providing health insurance for their workers. First, in a small business, if one of its workers has a costly illness or accident, the business is placed in a high-risk pool and must therefore pay high premiums. Firms with many employees have a larger risk pool. This makes their premiums relatively lower for the same amount of coverage. Second, small businesses often provide lower wages and benefits than large firms. The cost of providing health insurance to low-wage employees can push up compensation costs dramatically. Average health-care spending by employers is $1,722 per employee per year. To encourage small businesses to provide health-care coverage for employees, S. 1227 proposes that small businesses be provided with a 25 percent tax credit for the cost of insurance provided to lower-income employees.

S. 1227 would also set up procedures for the government and the private sector to negotiate rates for hospitals, physicians, and other health-care providers. A new agency, the Federal Expenditure Board, would be created to host negotiations between providers and purchasers of health care. If negotiations on reimbursement rates are successful, the agreed-upon rates would be binding. Otherwise, the Federal Expenditure Board would publish recommended rates.

Another play-or-pay bill was introduced by Congressman Dan Rostenkowski. Under Rostenkowski's bill (H.R. 3205), all employers would have to either provide health insurance by January 1, 1996, or pay an excise tax equal to 9 percent of the Medicare wage base (the amount of annual earnings on which the Medicare tax is levied). The Medicare wage base in 1991 was $125,000. It normally increases each year as average wages increase. Under Rostenkowski's bill, the wage base would rise to $200,000 starting January 1, 1993.

Employers who elect to play rather than pay would have to offer a health-insurance package equal to Medicare with certain liberalizations in coverage. Employers would receive some relief from rising health-care costs, however, because the eligibility age for Medicare would fall to age 60.

Rostenkowski also proposed national limits on public and employer health expenditures similar to the expenditure limitations used in Canada.

If the taxes paid under the play-or-pay provisions do not cover the cost of H.R. 3205, a universal health surtax on individual and corporate taxes, as well as increases in the Medicare payroll tax, would make up the difference.

In contrast to the single-payer approach, the burden of play-or-pay proposals would fall on employers. For that reason, the Bush administration opposed this approach as a mandate on employers. But in November 1991, an impressive group of business and union leaders, as well as two former presidents of the United States, endorsed the play-or-pay approach. The National Leadership Coalition for Health Reform announced a plan very similar to Senator Mitchell's proposal, which former Presidents Ford and Carter, the Chrysler Corporation, Bethlehem Steel Corporation and six other steel companies, Xerox, Westinghouse, and a number of other leading corporations all endorsed. Also meeting in November was the AFL-CIO in Detroit, Michigan. The AFL-CIO went on record in support of a single-payer system as an ultimate goal, but play or pay as a first step toward that goal.

▶ Fights over Money

The most important issue in overall health-care reform is who will pay the cost. During 1991 a nagging bone of contention among the federal government, states, private insurers, and the medical profession focused on who should bear the burden of holding down medical costs in the current system.

Faced with rising Medicaid costs, states have developed ingenious ways to leverage funds from the federal government. The states administer the Medicaid program, but the federal government helps finance the costs. Federal payments vary state by state based on a complicated formula. Nationwide the federal government pays 57 percent of Medicaid costs. By the fall of 1991, 37 states started leveraging more money from the federal government by levying taxes on hospitals and other health-care providers or by accepting donations from them.

The federal Medicaid program director, Gail Wilensky, described how this procedure works. She used as an example a hypothetical state that increased its payment to a hospital from the $100 normal cost of a medical procedure to $200. The state told the federal government that the service cost $200, but then taxed the hospital or accepted a donation from the hospital for $100. Thus, the state actually paid $100 for the procedure, while the federal government was told it cost $200.

The Bush administration objected strongly to this practice, estimating that these creative-financing schemes had cost the federal government $3 billion over the past year. On the other hand, state officials privately believed that this was a form of poetic justice. For years the federal government has imposed mandates directing increased Medicaid coverage that in turn increased state spending.

In the fall of 1991, the Department of Health and Human Services issued regulations to stop this creative financing. Legislation began to move in both the House and the Senate, however, to prevent these regulations from going into effect. Faced with a combination of strenuous congressional and state opposition to these regulations, the HHS offered a compromise in November 1991. States could continue levying the special taxes, but they no longer could accept the donations.

Another money fight involved the HHS and the medical profession. In 1989 Congress enacted legislation directing the HHS to develop fee schedules by medical specialty for the reimbursement of physicians for treatment of Medicare patients. The goal was to reduce reimbursement to some high-priced specialists and to increase reimbursement for lower-paid specialists. (Congress has been reducing reimbursement to hospitals and physicians since the early 1980s.)

When HHS instituted this fee schedule, there was an uproar from the medical community. The reimbursement rates assumed what the HHS called "behavioral changes" by physicians. The HHS predicted that doctors would offset their income loss from reimbursement reductions by increasing the number of procedures and tests they ordered. In anticipation of this assumed behavioral response, the fee schedule proposed to reduce reimbursement to physicians overall by 3 percent. Opponents of this schedule argued that HHS was simply trying to cut spending.

Late in 1991 Congress seemed likely to side with the physicians on this issue. The chairman of the Senate subcommittee with jurisdiction over Medicare, Jay Rockefeller (D-W.Va.), introduced legislation to make sure that the adjustment for behavioral response was fair to physicians. Rockefeller claimed that the HHS proposal was inconsistent with what Congress intended. He also told the medical profession that the offset was "a basic attack on your profession and personal dignity." As 1991 drew to a close, the Bush administration continued to resist any changes to this fee schedule.

▶ Federal Anti-Cholesterol Program

The program to encourage Americans to reduce their cholesterol levels with changes in eating patterns and, when necessary, prescription drugs, came under attack in 1991. Criticism focused on the National Cholesterol Program, a set of guidelines developed by a panel of physicians appointed by the federal government. The guidelines called for periodic cholesterol testing of all Americans age 20 or older. Medical intervention or a change in diet was recommended for all those with cholesterol counts above 200 milligrams per deciliter (mg/dl). Economists criticized these guidelines because they forced many people at low risk for heart problems into cholesterol-reduction treatment. One study found that 973 out of 1,000 men treated with cholesterol-lowering drugs for five years did not have a heart attack during that period. In that same study, among a control group of 1,000 who received a placebo, 959 did not have a heart attack for five years. The authors concluded that the risks associated with these powerful, costly drugs were larger than their heart-attack-preventive benefits.

In an editorial on cholesterol lowering in the *New England Journal of Medicine,* Dr. Alan Brett of Boston's Deaconess Hospital wrote: "When a large population undergoes a treatment alleged to benefit only 1 or 2 percent of its members, the balance of burdens and benefits requires close scrutiny."

Findings from this and similar studies did not go unchallenged. Dr. John LaRosa, a Washington, D.C., heart-disease specialist, noted that such studies deal with economic models. These models contain many unverifiable assumptions that cannot be relied upon in dealing with patients.

▶ The Food and Drug Administration

The activist commissioner of the federal Food and Drug Administration (FDA), David A. Kessler, so aggressively used his regulatory powers that he acquired the nickname Eliot Kessler (for the famed government agent, Eliot Ness, who brought down Al Capone). The FDA has the authority to regulate drugs, medical devices, and labels on food products. Its food-labeling authority is shared with the U.S. Department of Agriculture (USDA). In 1991 Kessler took aggressive action in all three areas.

In November, in response to the Nutrition Label-

Newly enacted food-labeling legislation will make it easier for consumers to understand a product's ingredients and to evaluate the food's nutritional value.

ing and Education Act of 1990, the government released proposed regulations that would make the most comprehensive changes in food labeling in the history of the FDA. Currently, only about half of food products have nutrition labeling. The new regulations would increase the number of products requiring such labels. In addition, some misleading types of labeling would be banned. For example, manufacturers will no longer be able to describe a product as having no cholesterol if it is naturally cholesterol-free because it contains no animal fats. This will prevent consumers from being misled that a product naturally cholesterol-free is also free of fat, when it actually contains vegetable fat.

Another reform will standardize serving sizes for 176 kinds of food products. This will prevent manufacturers from claiming that a product is low in sodium or fat based on an unrealistically small serving size. The food industry and other interested groups will have a year to comment on these regulations.

This change in food labeling represented a bureaucratic breakthrough. For the first time, the U.S. Department of Agriculture (USDA) and the FDA are working together on food labeling. For years, these two federal agencies had often worked at cross-purposes.

Also in November, the FDA initiated two steps to speed up the drug-approval process. The first was to contract with outside researchers to evaluate certain drugs. The objective was to reduce the backlog of drug-approval applications awaiting internal FDA review. This initiative triggered some concern that outside review of drugs may create conflicts of interest. The number of qualified scientists in the field of drug evaluation is relatively small, and many academic scientists receive contracts from drug companies.

The second step was to expedite the review process for drugs that will be used to treat certain life-threatening diseases. Pharmaceutical companies seeking approval of this type of drug would have to meet less-stringent requirements to demonstrate the efficacy of a drug and the absence of serious side effects. On an informal basis, the FDA had already been following this expedited procedure (see the artwork on pages 294-295) for drugs to treat AIDS patients. The rationale behind this relaxed drug-approval procedure is that patients with a life-threatening illness can afford to endure what may be a risky treatment, since the alternative is oftentimes death.

The FDA also aggressively asserted its authority to regulate the sale of medical devices. More than 2 million American women have had cosmetic or reconstructive surgery in which silicone-gel implants (photo at left) were used. Experts are concerned about potential implant rupture or leak and about the resultant risk of cancer if silicone gets into the body.

On November 13, 1991, an FDA panel of experts voted nine to one to reject the data on the safety of silicone-gel implants submitted by the Dow Corning Wright Company, one of the implant's manufacturers. The panel's vote was not on the question of whether these devices are safe. Instead, the vote showed that the overwhelming majority of the panel believed that the company's data did not demonstrate the devices to be safe enough to be sold in the United States.

The very next day, however, the panel voted to allow the silicone implants to continue to be sold, while the manufacturers conduct additional research on the long-term effects of the implants. In particular the panel urged the FDA to require the manufacturers to conduct studies on the rate at which the implants rupture and the amount of silicone that seeps out of the implants over time. In January 1992 FDA chief Kessler placed a moratorium on the sale of silicone-gel implants until questions about their safety could be answered.

James A. Rotherham, Ph.D.

Health-Care Costs

In years to come, 1991 may be remembered as the turning point in the nation's health-cost crisis. In that year, growing concerns about soaring expenditures and the increasing failure to meet the health needs of millions of people prompted a cascade of proposed solutions that moved the issue to new prominence on the national agenda. The impact of the health-cost crisis on a troubled economy only intensified the issue.

No consensus emerged on how to solve the problem—only a painful recognition that there was no simple, quick fix. Analysts blamed everything from excessive administrative costs to sheer greed on the part of health-care providers. Most agreed that any solution must touch all parts of the medical-industrial complex, including government programs, private insurers, employers, physicians, hospitals, the drug and medical-technology industries, as well as unrealistic patient expectations.

"Americans have three incompatible basic demands," explained former Surgeon General Dr. C. Everett Koop, who spent much of 1991 studying the health-care crisis. "They expect immediate access, state-of-the-art medicine, and limited price. Any two can be done. All three can't."

Further dampening prospects for a quick halt to ever-spiraling costs was the paradoxical fact that the continued growth of the health-care sector made it the strongest part of a sagging economy. According to *Health Care Financing Review*, 60 percent of net private-sector job growth in 1990 came from health services. The health sector also contributed to the nation's international trade, with drugs and medical products together accounting for $11 billion in exports and a $3.2 billion trade surplus. Tampering with that success, some experts warned, would only add to the nation's overall economic woes.

Stark facts illustrate the dimensions of the health-cost problem:

—The nation spent some $2 billion a day on health care. Projections show that, at current rates of increase, total spending will reach approximately $2 trillion by the end of the century, a staggering 20 percent of the gross national product.

—The government reported that the nation's spending on health reached $666.2 billion in 1990, the most recent year for which complete figures were available. That represented an increase of 10.5 percent over the previous year, and the third consecutive year in which national health expenditures rose in double digits. Spending in 1991 was expected to top the $730 billion mark.

—Total federal health spending reached $195.4 billion in 1990, including Medicare for the elderly, the federal share of Medicaid expenditures for the poor and disabled, as well as Veterans Administration and health care for military dependents. State and local expenditures accounted for another $87.3 billion, including the state share of Medicaid. Medicare spending for the elderly rose by 8.6 percent, while Medicaid grew by nearly 21 percent, largely because of mandated expansion of services to pregnant women and poor children.

—Private insurance accounted for 33 percent of total expenditures; out-of-pocket payments, including deductibles, copayments, and services not covered by insurance, accounted for 20 percent; and other private payments accounted for the remaining 5 percent of health-care spending.

—Thirty-eight percent of the nation's medical bill went to hospital care; 19 percent to physician services; 23 percent to other forms of personal health care, including dental, vision, and home health services; 8 percent to nursing-home care; and 12 percent to such "other" expenditures as administrative costs.

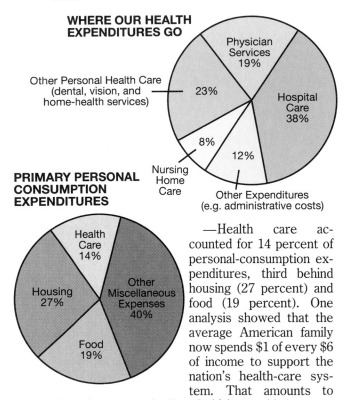

WHERE OUR HEALTH EXPENDITURES GO

Physician Services 19%

Other Personal Health Care (dental, vision, and home-health services) — 23%

Hospital Care 38%

8%

12%

Nursing Home Care

Other Expenditures (e.g. administrative costs)

PRIMARY PERSONAL CONSUMPTION EXPENDITURES

Health Care 14%

Housing 27%

Other Miscellaneous Expenses 40%

Food 19%

—Health care accounted for 14 percent of personal-consumption expenditures, third behind housing (27 percent) and food (19 percent). One analysis showed that the average American family now spends $1 of every $6 of income to support the nation's health-care system. That amounts to about $6,535 per family, of which two-thirds comes from families through insurance premiums, federal and state taxes, and direct payments, while the remaining one-third is paid by businesses.

—An astounding 34 million Americans have no health insurance. Employers provided health insurance for 66 percent of the nonelderly population, while 9 percent of this population purchased private health-insurance coverage on their own. Another 12 percent of the nonelderly population received care through publicly financed programs.

—The United States spends far more of its gross national product for health care than does any other country. Yet workers in other countries have greater access to care through systems that are partially or wholly financed by their governments, and these workers, indeed, were healthier as measured by such indicators as infant mortality, where the United States ranked low among industrialized nations.

—In many parts of the country, there were signs that the quality of care had started to erode as the result of efforts to constrain costs. This was particularly true in rural and inner-city areas, which experience shortages of primary-care physicians and, increasingly, of hospital beds.

▶ Increased Costs, Decreased Care

In a major article in the November 1991 issue of the *Journal of Health Care Benefits,* former Health and Human Services Secretary Dr. Otis Bowen and Thomas R. Burke put the problem in sobering perspective: " . . . Health care has become a lucrative business in this country, and because of the nature of the products and services it is selling, namely health care, it has been allowed to ignore economic principles that restrain virtually every other type of industry in this country. Health care providers can generate their own demand and increase their revenues and profits despite declines in the demand for their services. If prices are fixed or frozen, providers simply increase the number of services they provide in order to maintain or even increase their revenues or income." Such increases are possible, the authors argued, because "the ordinary person is incapable of determining which services are medically necessary and which ones are being delivered primarily for financial reasons."

Other factors helped fuel the cost increase. The population is aging, and older patients consume a disproportionate share of the nation's health expenditures. Both the volume and the intensity of care provided continued to grow, along with use of expensive procedures like magnetic resonance imaging (MRI), about $400; and positron emission tomography (PET), at more than $1,500; as well as new therapies such as drugs called tissue plasminogen activators (t-PA), which lessen the severity of heart attacks, at $2,500 a dose; and treatment with human growth hormone, which can cost more than $10,000.

Studies by the Rand Corporation showed that between 15 and 35 percent of expensive, high-volume procedures were unnecessary, including 14 percent of coronary-bypass operations, 20 percent of

pacemaker insertions, and 32 percent of carotid-artery surgery. A survey by the American Medical Association (AMA) revealed that two-thirds of doctors say they order more tests than necessary to guard against liability claims, and 70 percent admit to ordering excess consultations. Many also said they increased the number of services provided to maintain their incomes as price constraints tightened.

▶ What Can Be Done?

By the end of the year, more than three dozen legislative proposals to correct all or part of the ailing system had been tossed into the congressional hopper. Most of the legislative proposals featured one of three types of major reforms. One is a national health-care system patterned on the Canadian system, in which taxes would support a government-administered health-insurance program for all Americans. Some variations would extend Medicare to everyone. Others would provide patients with insurance cards, much like credit cards, and doctors and hospitals would then bill the government for payment. Under these plans the government would either set fees or set an overall health budget for the nation.

Another popular approach, the so-called "play-or-pay" plans, would build on the current system of employer-provided health-insurance benefits by requiring all employers of three or more workers to either provide insurance or pay taxes into a state-administered insurance pool. The uninsured would be covered by some form of tax-supported government insurance. The self-employed would be required to purchase insurance, but could use premiums as a tax write-off. Small businesses fear that the costs of providing insurance for their workers would force them to lay off workers or go bankrupt.

Insurance reforms are a third approach. Proposals include setting up insurance pools for small companies and requiring insurers to provide coverage for people with preexisting conditions. Many plans now exclude coverage for people with such problems as diabetes or cancer, or impose an extensive waiting period before coverage goes into effect.

Many proposals incorporate a variety of strategies to cut costs. One is to let the government set fees for providing care. Another creates incentives for parties to bargain for the lowest rates. Managed care, through either formal prepaid health-maintenance or preferred-provider organizations, or close outsider scrutiny of the kind of care hospitals and doctors provide, is another popular feature.

Health and Human Services Secretary Dr. Louis Sullivan, among others, would like to streamline the administration of health claims to help cut costs. Currently, health providers must cope with some 1,500 different insurance forms ranging from simple, one-page forms to the 30 pages required by Medicare. Analysts calculate that if the number of forms were trimmed back to several simplified, one-page forms, the costs of administering insurance claims would be cut in half, or by about $120 billion.

Another common reform theme would change the current malpractice system through such mechanisms as imposing binding arbitration before a case can be taken to court, eliminating or capping pain-and-suffering awards, and limiting attorney fees in malpractice suits.

The notion of a basic health-benefit package underlies all reform proposals. This package would cover both primary and catastrophic care. Some emphasize prevention as a key to controlling costs. Creating a better balance between physician supply and patient need is essential to provide universal access and basic health care. Expanding the National Health Service Corps to attract young doctors to underserved areas in exchange for help with the costs of a medical education is one suggestion. Incentives to induce more young doctors to become family physicians is another.

▶ Hospital Health

Overall, the financial performance of hospitals improved slightly, but future prospects were dampened by the recognition that hospitals are increasingly reliant on large government purchasers. As government budgets tighten, health care is a prime target for cuts. Because of low reimbursement rates, Medicaid represents a particular problem for hospitals. Analyses show that hospitals that cared for high numbers of Medicaid patients also had a disproportionate share of bad debts and charity care.

For nine years the government system has reimbursed hospitals for Medicare patients according to diagnosis-related groups (DRGs). Financially stable hospitals tend to have a lower percentage of Medicare patients than do more-troubled hospitals. During that nine-year period, both the number of hospital beds and the average length of stay shrank dramatically, countered by a sharp rise in outpatient use, including same-day surgery, and increases in both the number of surgical procedures and births.

However, the American Hospital Association (AHA) reported "tough times" for both inner-city and rural hospitals. Inner-city hospital emergency rooms treated 104 percent more patients in 1990 than a decade earlier, and the number of community hospitals declined by 446, many of them in rural areas. In the same period, the AHA reported a decline in certified trauma centers, a drop due to high operating expense and reimbursement problems. But there was a dramatic increase in the number of

hospitals offering substance- and alcohol-abuse treatment, home health services, computerized tomography (CT) scans, and outpatient rehabilitation programs.

▶ Medicare and Medicaid Programs

By 1991 nearly half the nation's physicians had agreed to charge Medicare patients no more than 20 percent above what the government would reimburse them. In 1986 only 28 percent of U.S. physicians had agreed to limit their fees for Medicare. Patronizing these "participating physicians" limits the out-of-pocket costs to elderly beneficiaries. Participating physicians account for more than 70 percent of doctor bills paid by Medicare; more than 85 percent of those bills were paid under assignment, which means the physician agrees to accept Medicare as full payment.

On January 1, 1992, the most significant revision in physician-payment procedures in the history of the Medicare program went into effect. The new fee schedule established payment levels for approximately 7,000 different medical services. Those levels take into account relative value of the work involved in the procedure, overhead, and malpractice expense incurred in providing a service.

According to Health and Human Services Secretary Sullivan, "The fee schedule goes far toward correcting long-standing price distortions." Those distortions tended to reward "technical" care provided by surgeons, radiologists, and anesthesiologists over more "cognitive" care from internists and family physicians. Under the new system, primary-care physicians will receive fairer payment from Medicare.

Doctors also came under federal scrutiny for "self-referral" of patients to laboratories in which they had a financial stake. A 1989 AMA study estimated that fewer than 10 percent of the nation's doctors invest in laboratories, diagnostic-imaging centers, or other facilities to which they refer patients. But a more recent study in Florida found that 40 percent of Florida's physicians had invested in such facilities. Under new federal rules designed to eliminate potential conflicts of interest, the facilities that receive referrals from doctors can be no more than 40 percent physician-owned and can depend on the investing physicians for no more than 40 percent of their referrals.

Expenditures under Medicaid rose even more sharply than those under Medicare, contributing to the budget crises of many states and localities, which pay 43 percent of the program's total costs. Between 1988 and 1990, Medicaid spending rose by one-third, to $72.2 billion. Estimated costs for 1991 are $92.7 billion; and for 1992, $105.1 billion.

Despite the dramatic increases, the program fails to cover the nation's poor, the constituency it was

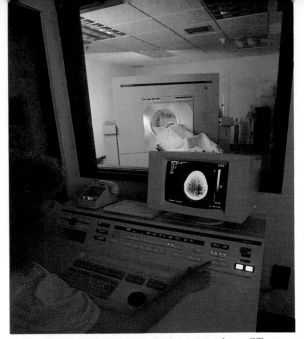

State-of-the-art imaging techniques, such as CT scans (above), MRI, and PET, while highly effective diagnostic tools, add considerably to medical bills.

designed to serve in the first place. The cost increase has been blamed on two factors. The recession prompted more who were eligible to sign up for the program. And new benefits mandated by Congress in 1989 required states to cover pregnant women, infants, and children in families having incomes less than 133 percent of the federal poverty line. In addition, the state governments involved have taken measures to be sure that eligible families are enrolled in Medicaid and receive needed care. The combination of factors has caused Medicaid enrollment to swell from 23.5 million in 1989 to 28.9 million by 1992.

Such growth has created financial problems for the state governments involved. In 1990 almost $1 of every $10 of state tax revenues went to Medicaid, about one-third of the amount states spend on public schools. Health-care spending by the federal government, mostly Medicaid and Medicare, consumed 13.4 percent of the total budget, a figure the Congressional Budget Office estimates could reach 19.5 percent by 1996.

A major factor in Medicaid's growth is that the program pays roughly one-half of the nation's total long-term-care bill for the elderly and disabled, including AIDS patients who are impoverished by their illness. The elderly and disabled represent only 5 percent of the program's recipients, but, according to the Health Care Financing Administration, account for 75 percent of the program's spending.

▶ Private-Insurance Plans

Figures for 1990, reported by the Health Insurance Association of America, showed the average rate of increase in employer-sponsored group-health premiums was 14 percent, down from 24 percent the previous year. As employers tried to check the growth of their costs for providing health-insurance benefits, more turned to plans with some form of managed care. A sharp increase was seen in the conventional group plans with utilization control, like preadmission review, up to 57 percent from 49 percent the previous year. Those offering a health-maintenance organization (HMO) increased slightly, to 20 percent, while the relatively new point-of-service plan, which covers some of the costs of services from providers outside of a designated network, was offered by 5 percent.

Another cost-saving measure for large firms, self-insurance, or partial self-insurance by purchasing stop-loss coverage to cap expenditures, also continued to grow. In 1990, 56 percent of the nation's employees worked for firms that either totally or partially self-insure. Of the rest, 25 percent were covered by conventional plans, and another 18 percent by Blue Cross/Blue Shield plans.

A number of large firms, Goodyear Tire and Rubber and Southern California Edison among them, have started providing in-house health services for workers in order to hold down insurance costs.

Also noted was a slight increase in the proportion of monthly premiums paid by employers, with employers paying, on average, about 85 percent of monthly premiums for individuals and from 70 to 74 percent for family coverage. The most common co-insurance rate remained 80-20, and out-of-pocket maximums ranged from a $500 deductible up to no limit, with 25 percent having a maximum deductible of $2,000 or more.

Employers tried a variety of other cost-saving strategies. More imposed waiting times before covering preexisting conditions, or offered incentives in the form of reduced premiums or rebates to healthy employees who were nonsmokers and/or regular exercisers. Both trends marked a major shift from the traditional insurance principle that everyone should pay the same for coverage, and that the healthy would subsidize the sick. Small insurers especially began to exclude high-risk individuals and waive coverage for certain medical conditions.

Much of the health-cost picture of 1991 was a repeat of past years. The same problems. The same galloping cost escalation. But there was one key difference. By 1991 the middle class was either beginning to hurt, or worried they would be hurt in years to come. When the middle class worries, politicians, at least, listen and speak. Unfortunately, extravagant preelection claims and promises can create the false perception that problems can be fixed overnight. Nothing could be further from the truth.

Mary Hager

Health Personnel and Facilities

▶ AIDS and the Health-Care Worker
Current statistics indicate that the likelihood of a patient contracting the human immunodeficiency virus (HIV) from a physician or health-care worker is remote. The Centers for Disease Control (CDC) have documented only 703 physicians and 5,733 other health-care workers with AIDS since the epidemic began in the early 1980s. The risk of an HIV-infected surgeon transmitting the disease to a patient is calculated at only one in 48,000.

Nevertheless, the fact that a handful of patients have been infected with HIV by a health-care worker (including the late Kimberly Bergalis, who acquired AIDS from her dentist) has ignited a firestorm of debate about how physicians and other health-care professionals should protect patients from the disease. The American Medical Association and the American Dental Association have urged HIV-infected surgeons and dentists to inform patients of their condition even if the health-care professionals lose their practices as a result. The CDC has asked individuals who perform invasive procedures to learn their HIV status and refrain from performing procedures if they test positive. Despite the small risk of infecting their patients with HIV, health-care professionals today are being told they need special precautions to adhere to Hippocrates' dictum to do no harm.

▶ Outpatient Growth
Hospitals are taking advantage of opportunities in the growing outpatient health-care market. According to the American Hospital Association's *Hospital Statistics 1991–1992,* inpatient admissions dropped 14 percent between 1980 and 1990, and inpatient vacancy rates increased from 25 percent to 33 percent. Meanwhile, outpatient visits jumped 49 percent, and outpatient surgeries soared 263 percent. A survey by *Hospitals* magazine disclosed that outpatient services accounted for approximately 30 percent of net patient revenues in 1991.

Freestanding ambulatory facilities also grew rapidly. The total number of ambulatory-care facilities increased 18.2 percent (with the greatest rise occurring with diagnostic-imaging centers), and outpatient surgical centers increased 11.2 percent.

Outpatient care clearly is the wave of the future. Outpatient services may account for as much as half of hospital-net-patient revenues by the year 2000, and ambulatory care as a whole is expected to expand for the next 20 years.

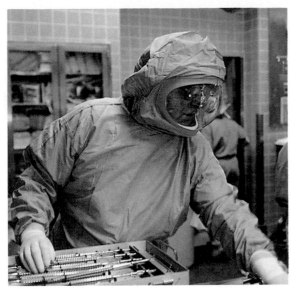

Gloves, masks, and other protective garments have become the everyday hospital apparel for medical personnel worried about AIDS transmission.

► Hospital Industry Shrinks

The 1991 recession in the United States foisted additional burdens on already financially squeezed hospitals. The slowed economic growth, coupled with the steady rise in the federal deficit, caused Congress to bolster its efforts to cut Medicare spending. The sluggish economy also prompted employers and other third-party payers to reduce their health-care outlays. As a result, payments for hospital services dropped, and hospitals saw their profit margins dip dangerously. Hospital profit margins on average fell 10 percent in 1990, and another 8 percent in 1991.

Poor financial performance for a decade has taken a heavy toll on hospitals. *Hospital Statistics 1991–1992* showed that the number of community hospitals nationwide fell nearly 8 percent between 1980 and 1990. The number of urban institutions having six to 24 beds decreased 26 percent, and the number of rural institutions decreased 32.9 percent.

Other hard-core financially "underclass" urban and rural facilities in 1991 came closer to the edge. The Healthcare Financial Management Association (HFMA) has tracked 1,300 hospitals for the past five years, and has identified 236 as touch-and-go. These generally older facilities had an anemic 1.4 percent operating-profit margin in 1986 and a −1.7-percent profit margin in 1990.

Nevertheless, 1991 could still be considered a watershed year. While weak institutions tottered or closed, strong hospitals rebounded. Healthy hospitals improved bottom lines by aggressively managing costs through cost-tracking budgeting systems, improving billing and collections procedures, making group-discount purchasing agreements, streamlining inventories, and renegotiating deals with managed-care organizations.

Many community hospitals, particularly small urban facilities, reduced costs and increased patient volumes by specializing in the types of care they do best, such as open-heart surgery, obstetrics, and sports medicine.

► Focus on the Patient

Perhaps the most welcome movement afoot in health-care facilities has been the growing sensitivity to the needs of patients. Hospitals and ambulatory-care facilities have been altering their environments to become more hospitable. Neutral color schemes, skylights, fish tanks, landscape paintings, and gardens to enhance visual stimulation are often used to soften the institutional setting. Hospitals are camouflaging imposing high-tech equipment by placing it inside cabinets. The hospital clamor is being reduced by acoustically treated walls. Some intensive-care units are even hiding the nursing-control-center display terminals behind an electrically charged window that can readily be turned opaque. Other innovations include sleeping areas and kitchens for family members, playrooms for young patients and visitors, and terraces and roof gardens for patients to meet with friends, relatives, and physicians in private.

Beyond the aesthetic changes, health-care facilities are fundamentally altering the ways in which they interact with patients. Several hospitals are encouraging patients to participate in treatment by making them responsible for taking and charting their own oral medications. Many are assigning the care of each patient to a particular nurse who individualizes therapy and follows the patient from admission to discharge. Some are simplifying registration and accounting procedures to reduce confusion and frustration among patients. Ambulatory facilities are offering extended hours of operation, "express" service for routine follow-up care (such as immunizations), and daylong or half-day subspecialty clinics that deal with a particular treatment area, such as orthopedic problems.

► Work Force Expansion

Although employment in U.S. hospitals declined by 2.3 percent between 1983 and 1986 owing to cost-cutting efforts, it currently is on the rise, having increased by 6.9 percent between 1986 and 1989.

The greatest increase has occurred in managerial and administrative positions. A 20 percent increase in managers and administrators occurred between 1983 and 1989 as hospitals emphasized strategic planning and marketing to withstand competitive pressures. Professional and technical ranks also expanded significantly, rising 10 percent in that time period, as more skilled personnel were needed to care for seriously ill patients and to operate increasingly complex technology.

Even greater numbers of skilled workers will be needed in the health-care field in the future. *America's 50 Fastest Growing Jobs* reported that seven of the top 10 jobs in the next decade will be in health industries, and that jobs in health care will grow by 3.1 million by the year 2000.

However, changes in the U.S. population will profoundly affect the health-care work force. U.S. Labor Department statistics show that 68 percent of the 42.8 million people joining the overall work force between 1989 and 2000 will be minorities: women, blacks, Hispanics, Asians, and Native Americans. Many of these new workers will speak English as a second language and have different attitudes about work and the workplace.

Health-care facilities in 1991 began to prepare for these diverse worker populations by educating managers about the differences in culture, mores, values, and career and instructional needs of minorities, and by using role-playing exercises, videotape examples, and discussion groups to highlight workplace-diversity issues.

▶ Costs Cutting into Physician Practices

In their attempt to keep costs in line, health-care payers and facilities have been exerting tougher controls over physician health-care decision making. Because of a rise of nearly $4 billion in drug spending by the nation's hospitals from 1985 to 1989, health maintenance organizations (HMOs), hospitals, and insurers have established lists of the drugs physicians may order, and they have been substituting generic or cheaper drugs for the ones physicians prescribe.

Reeling from a jump in the mean payment for physician services from approximately $130,000 in 1986 to $155,800 in 1989, hospitals, employers, and insurers have stiffened utilization-review practices. A small but growing number of hospitals have begun to determine which physicians will be allowed to admit patients and which procedures they will be allowed to perform on the basis of the economic consequences of their actions. These institutions are evaluating physician cost-effectiveness according to such measures as patients' length of stay in comparison with state averages, total per-patient charges in comparison with hospital averages, and number of denials of payment by insurers.

Insurers and employers have been examining physician treatment patterns in relation to their own internal guidelines for cost-effective care, and eliminating from their provider networks physicians who consistently exceed the guidelines. They also have been increasing pressure on physicians to obtain approval before ordering surgical or other costly procedures.

Karen M. Sandrick

Heart and Circulatory System

▶ Coronary-Artery Disease: Risk Factors and Treatment

In 1991 coronary-artery disease continued to be the leading cause of death in the United States. But a new Framingham Heart Study report confirms a 30 percent national drop in mortality due to heart disease since 1978. These improved heart statistics were attributed to better blood-pressure and cholesterol control, less smoking, and improved medical and surgical care of chronic angina and heart attacks. However, despite lower death rates, the prevalence of coronary disease, angina, and heart attacks remains unchanged.

Given the continued high incidence of coronary disease, interest in risk factors and effective preventive treatments is intense. Reports from the Physicians' Health Study and the Framingham Heart Study published in 1991 confirmed the predictive value of total cholesterol, particularly beneficial HDL (high-density lipoprotein) cholesterol levels, as a predisposing factor for coronary disease.

A study published in June 1991 extended the known benefits of blood-pressure control to a group not previously studied: patients over age 60 with isolated systolic hypertension (abnormal systolic but normal diastolic blood pressure, a common scenario in older patients). Improved blood-pressure control reduced the stroke rate and the incidence of coronary disease and deaths by 36 percent.

Regarding the role of postmenopausal estrogen treatment in preventing coronary disease, the Nurses' Health Study reported in September 1991 that estrogen reduced the risk of coronary disease (heart attack or death) by 44 percent, death from cardiovascular disease by 28 percent, and death from all causes by 11 percent. Another prospective study of retired women found that estrogen reduced the risk of death from heart disease and stroke as well as from cancer. The preventive value of estrogen will remain controversial until randomized, placebo-controlled studies are performed.

The use of aspirin to prevent death from heart attacks and to prevent second heart attacks and strokes is well established. Two major studies in 1991 added to growing evidence that aspirin can prevent first heart attacks as well. The Physicians' Health Study and the Nurses' Health Study reported that aspirin use reduced the risk of first heart attack in men with angina and in healthy women, respectively. A Dutch study also reported that a 30-milligram (mg) dose of aspirin daily was as effective (and caused fewer side effects) as a 283-mg daily dose in reducing vascular death, strokes, and heart attacks in patients who had had a ministroke.

Both the Physicians' Health Study and the Nurses' Health Study also reported on the possible role of antioxidant vitamins in reducing heart attacks and coronary death. The Physicians' Health Study reported that beta-carotene reduced heart attacks, the need for bypass or angioplasty, and cardiac death by 44 percent in male physicians with angina. The Nurses' Health Study concluded that healthy female nurses with high intakes of beta-carotene, vitamin A, and vitamin E had approximately 30 percent fewer coronary problems.

Finally, two reports from 1991 described reduced rates of coronary disease associated with moderate alcohol use, most likely due to the ability of alcohol to raise levels of beneficial HDL cholesterol. This beneficial effect of alcohol use on coronary disease must be balanced against the known negative effects of alcohol on high blood pressure, heart failure, cerebral hemorrhages, and various noncardiac diseases.

▶ Thrombolytic Therapy

Reported trials of the thrombolytic agents streptokinase or tissue plasminogen activator (t-PA) given late (6 to 24 hours) after the onset of a heart attack have demonstrated no significant benefit of such late treatment. Similarly, the enormous Third International Study of Infarct Survival (ISIS-3) of 46,000 heart-attack patients shows no survival benefit of streptokinase, t-PA, or APSAC (anisoylated plasminogen-streptokinase activator complex) when used 6 to 24 hours into a heart attack.

American physicians have been reluctant to embrace the use of streptokinase, despite studies showing that it prevents mortality at the same rate as t-PA. It is associated with fewer strokes, and is much less expensive than t-PA. To settle the ongoing debate about the relative benefits of the different thrombolytic drugs and heparin regimens, another large trial is under way, comparing the effects of a streptokinase regimen, a streptokinase and t-PA combination, a rapid infusion of t-PA, and different heparin regimens.

Research has been active in the use of combinations of thrombolytics, synthetic thrombolytic "mutants," thrombolytics specially targeted to home in on blood clots, and potent new adjunctive agents.

▶ Angioplasty and Catheter Techniques

The use of balloon angioplasty to dilate coronary arteries blocked by blood clots employs a catheter —a narrow tube that is inserted through the skin. A balloon is inserted through the catheter to the bocked artery. The balloon is then inflated to widen the artery. This technique avoids open-heart sur-

Cardiovascular Operations Performed in the United States

(estimated numbers in thousands)

Operation	Sex		Age			
	Male	Female	<15	15–44	45–64	65+
Valve Replacement Surgery	24	27	—	7	12	30
Balloon Angioplasty	344	155	—	36	258	203
Bypass Surgery	271	97	—	12	165	191
Pacemaker	142	133	—	7	43	221
Cardiac Catheterization	601	357	18	95	425	415

Source: American Heart Association 1992 Heart and Stroke Facts

gery. Reports from several studies published in 1991 provide support for extending the use of angioplasty to new areas.

Angioplasty is very successful in opening the blood-clot-filled arteries of acute-heart-attack victims. It appears to be more effective than thrombolytic therapy in treating heart attacks complicated by shock (the most severe type), and it does not carry the risks of stroke and bleeding often associated with thrombolytic therapy. Ongoing studies are exploring the use of angioplasty in cases where thrombolytic drugs do not open the artery successfully, and the studies are comparing the two treatments for the initial treatment of heart attacks.

Several studies are comparing the benefits of angioplasty versus either medications or bypass surgery for chronic angina. The Angioplasty Compared with Medicine (ACME) trial recently reported that angioplasty treatment is superior for blockages of one artery, but there was no difference in cases where two arteries are blocked.

New generations of catheter devices to treat coronary blockages without surgery continue to be developed. These techniques include laser angioplasty, ultrasonic angioplasty, various types of atherectomy catheters (devices that mechanically cut or grind off plaque from the arterial wall), and coronary-artery stents (devices that provide a scaffold to keep the artery open).

Other innovations developed to avoid open-heart surgery are balloons to treat stenosis (obstruction) of the mitral valve, repair of atrial or ventricular septal defects (abnormal holes between heart chambers), and the delivery of radio-frequency (or higher-energy) waves to correct arrhythmias.

▶ Bypass-Surgery Update

Several recent updates from the large-scale randomized trials of bypass surgery versus medications for chronic angina performed in the 1970s have been reported. The Coronary Artery Surgical Study (CASS) reported that patients with reduced heart-muscle function who underwent bypass surgery had an improved survival rate 10 years later. Those with normal heart function had similar survival rates with either bypass surgery or medication therapy, and therefore could be safely managed without surgery, unless symptoms progress. The rates of heart attacks were similar with either treatment in this study, as well as in a 10-year follow-up from a Veterans Administration study; however, the bypass patients in the VA study who subsequently had heart attacks had improved survival compared to those who had heart attacks that were treated nonsurgically. The CASS group also reported that the quality of life was improved in the bypass group for the first five years, but not by 10 years.

▶ Congestive Heart Failure

Several 1991 studies supported the use of a class of drugs called Angiotensin Converting Enzyme Inhibitors (ACE Inhibitors). One of these drugs, enalapril, had been previously shown to extend survival in patients with severe heart failure. In August 1991, a government-sponsored study of patients with mild to moderate heart failure reported that enalapril reduced five-year mortality by 16 percent, and hospitalizations for heart failure by 26 percent. The same study later reported that in patients with poor heart-muscle function but not yet with any symptoms, preventive treatment with enalapril improved five-year survival rates and reduced the rate of hospitalizations and of fatal and nonfatal heart attacks, as well as the risk of developing the symptoms of heart failure. In August 1991, a VA study compared the use of enalapril versus a combination of hydralazine and isosorbide dinitrate (previously shown to also reduce mortality in mild to moderate heart failure). The study found enalapril to be superior in mortality reduction, but hydralazine and isosorbide dinitrate to be superior in improvements in exercise tests and in heart-muscle function.

A report in November 1991 on the use of the experimental drug milrinone showed that the drug worsened arrhythmias and increased mortality in patients with severe heart failure, without improving any parameter of heart-muscle function. This report is the latest in a series of disappointing results with families of drugs that increase the contractility of the heart. The only exception is digoxin, whose effect on survival is being examined in a new government study.

For end-stage heart failure resistant to medications, research continues into surgically implanted temporary heart-muscle-assist pumps for patients awaiting heart transplant. Recent advances in cardiac transplantation over the past several years have produced five-year survival rates of about 85 percent in a group of patients considered terminally ill before surgery.

▶ Arrhythmias: Drugs, Devices, and Catheters

Several reports from 1991 continue to point out the danger of certain popular drugs commonly used to treat serious ventricular arrhythmia, a condition that can cause sudden death and is usually associated with coronary disease or heart failure. Several analyses of previously reported studies demonstrated that conventional antiarrhythmic drugs such as quinidine, used for either ventricular arrhythmias or less severe conditions, such as atrial fibrillation, are effective in suppressing arrhythmias, but cause serious side effects and increase mortality dramatically. Many other antiarrhythmic drugs with mechanisms of actions similar to quinidine are also now implicated.

A government study had previously shown that the drugs encainide and flecainide caused increased mortality in patients who experience extra heartbeats after a heart attack. The study was terminated in September 1991, as it became clear that the drug moricizine increased mortality over a three-year period, with a clear increase in mortality during the first two weeks of its use.

These discouraging results contrast with the several promising studies reported in the past year concerning the safety and effectiveness of a drug with very different actions. Both a Swiss study and a Polish study of heart-attack patients with extra heartbeats found that amiodarone improved survival after one year. Results of a pilot study of a Canadian trial also show a trend toward improved survival; this study and a VA and European study of amiodarone are ongoing.

A recent report on the automatic implantable defibrillator, a pacemakerlike device that detects serious arrhythmias and treats them with lifesaving electric shocks, showed a 10-year sudden-death rate of only 10 percent. Comparatively, untreated high-risk patients have one-year sudden-death rates of 30 to 40 percent. New prototypes of the defibrillator device, which can be implanted without the need for open-chest surgery, continue to undergo investigation.

An intriguing report published in September 1991 described drug-resistant atrial fibrillation in a small series of patients whose normal heart rhythm was restored by an open-heart surgery called the "maze procedure." Another severe-case option that avoids open-heart surgery is the use of radio-frequency catheters that destroy the normal conduction pathway, followed by implantation of a pacemaker.

Richard Mueller, M.D.

Immunology

▶ AIDS

Acquired Immune Deficiency Syndrome (AIDS) impacts virtually all social, economic, and scientific disciplines with frightening regularity and consequences. It is not possible to discuss current trends in immunology without mentioning AIDS and the human immunodeficiency virus (HIV). Two of the most volatile issues are the public risk from HIV-infected health-care workers (see "Health Personnel and Facilities" on p. 278) and the safety of the current blood supply.

Safe Blood. Transmission of HIV by transfusion of blood products has fostered public concern over the sensitivity of antibody-detection methods and the frequency of HIV-infected blood donors with blood that tests antibody-negative for HIV. These concerns were addressed in a recent study performed on antibody-negative blood obtained from San Francisco, a high-risk metropolitan area. Blood from 76,500 donations previously tested as HIV-negative was screened by two highly sensitive methods to detect infectious virus and the presence of viral DNA. Only one pool tested positive in both additional tests. Thus, the probability that a screened blood sample will be positive for HIV was estimated at only 1 in 61,171 cases, making AIDS transmission via HIV-contaminated blood products a very low risk factor.

AIDS Vaccine. Immunologists are hard at work trying to develop a safe and effective HIV vaccine. Two basic approaches have been followed: active and passive immunization. Several laboratories have reported advances in the use of active immunization, in which modified-HIV or HIV-protein products are used to induce protective immunity. In the past, these efforts have been thwarted by the high degree of molecular variability among HIV isolates. This variability resides predominantly in the envelope glycoprotein gp120, which serves as the attachment site on target cells. A subregion within the gp120 protein has now been identified that contains the principal neutralizing determinant (PND) whereby antibodies block virus infection. Antibodies prepared to fight this PND were capable of inactivating a wide range of HIV isolates, offering promise for a broad-spectrum vaccine.

Passive immunization involves the direct administration of preexisting, purified HIV-reactive antibody to patients. Workers have now successfully developed primate models of AIDS to analyze the protective effects of passively administered anti-body. The results of these models indicate that passive immunization may have potential direct benefits for HIV-infected individuals, and additionally provide a screening mechanism for vaccine-development programs.

▶ Organ Transplantation

The immune system plays a major role in the fate of transplanted tissue. Immune graft rejection occurs when the graft recipient's body recognizes donor graft tissue as foreign. Management of graft rejection requires constant monitoring and lifelong drug therapy. To avoid rejection, researchers have attempted to shield or trick the immune system from responding to transplanted tissue. The most innovative of these techniques have been applied to endocrine transplants, particularly transplantation of pancreatic islets for the maintenance of normal blood-sugar levels in diabetics. Paul E. Lacy of the Washington School of Medicine in St. Louis, Missouri, and coworkers have successfully developed techniques for shielding islets from immune recognition by encapsulating them in hollow synthetic fibers. These fibers enable the transplant to have free access to nutrients while blocking immune recognition. This technique allows long-term survival of rat islets in diabetic mouse recipients with complete restoration of blood-sugar levels. Another promising procedure has been developed by Andrew M. Posset and colleagues of the Hospital at the University of Pennsylvania in Philadelphia. The researchers were able to evade immune recognition of transplanted islets by positioning grafts in the thymus gland. The success of this procedure suggests that since the thymus is a primary site for maturation of lymphocytes, grafted tissue is recognized by developing lymphocytes as self-tissue and is not rejected. Both of these experimental techniques offer tremendous promise for future human clinical trials.

The success of bone-marrow transplantation, which is applied in instances of both immunodeficiency and leukemia, has been greatly augmented by the identification and elimination of offending lymphocyte populations prior to engraftment. The recipient must be purged of all residual lymphocytes to ensure graft acceptance, and, in the case of leukemia, all residual tumor cells must be destroyed. In a like manner, the donor marrow must be purged of all mature lymphocytes, the presence of which results in graft-versus-host disease, where donor cells attack the immunologically depleted tissues of the host. Several recent reports utilized a highly sensitive molecular technique, termed the polymerase chain reaction (PCR). PCR combined with pregraft purging could someday enable the reseeding of self-marrow from leukemic patients, thereby avoiding complications of graft rejection altogether.

►Cancer

The immune system has been shown to play a role in the recognition and destruction of many types of tumors that display unique, or modified, self-proteins. This recognition process recruits several types of lymphocytes to the tumor site; they then act to destroy the tumor cells. The activation of these lymphocytes at tumor sites is largely controlled by a family of lymphocyte hormones termed interleukins. Several laboratories have attempted to enhance antitumor immunity by the administration of interleukins directly to human patients or to isolated lymphocytes, with some limited success reported.

More-sophisticated methods using this technique are now being reported. In the latest wave of experiments, tumor cells themselves are excised, and the gene for the hormone interleukin-4 is added to the tumor. The tumor cells are then reinjected into the experimental animal. The animal rejects the tumor and retains immunity to any further exposure to this tumor. This active tumor immunity represents a promising breakthrough in the management of undetected metastasis.

►Autoimmunity and Self-Tolerance

This year witnessed a major breakthrough in the study of the basic mechanisms whereby self-tolerance and autoimmunity are regulated. Multiple laboratories simultaneously demonstrated that products of murine mammary tumor virus, a distant relative of HIV, could bind to and inactivate a large percentage of the total lymphocyte pool. This lymphocyte deletion is believed to mimic mechanisms that operate during the developmental maturation of all normal lymphocytes in the thymus. That is, the thymus specifically deletes any lymphocytes that would potentially respond to self-tissues in an aggressive manner. These laboratory observations were followed by two reports of large-scale lymphocyte modulation in both AIDS and rheumatoid arthritis.

Depletion of thymus-derived T lymphocytes is a hallmark in the transition of HIV-infected patients to AIDS. Recent studies indicate that deletion of some T lymphocytes in HIV-infected patients may be a direct consequence of HIV proteins that mimic normal deletion processes. The deletion of these lymphocytes is tightly coupled with disease pathogenesis. In the case of rheumatoid arthritis, responding lymphocytes are deleted from the peripheral blood supply and sequestered in synovial sites, where they release inflammatory molecules. This may reflect the presence of an as-yet-unidentified molecule, much like that described for the viruses above, as the causative agent in rheumatoid arthritis.

Glen N. Gaulton, Ph.D.

Kidneys

►Kidney Transplantation

For many Americans with advanced kidney disease, a disabling condition called end-stage renal disease (ESRD), a kidney transplant offers the best chance for full rehabilitation. A successfully transplanted kidney will perform all of the functions of native, healthy kidneys, and with nearly the same efficiency. This is not the case for artificial kidney treatments or dialysis. Currently available dialysis techniques can substitute for only one (albeit the most vital) of the many physiological functions performed by native kidneys, namely the filtration of blood and removal of waste products derived from the diet. Compared with two healthy, native kidneys functioning at 100 percent efficiency, a transplant performs at about 75 percent, and dialysis at only 25 percent.

If a kidney transplant performs so much better than dialysis, it may seem surprising that more than 100,000 Americans with ESRD are sustained by maintenance-dialysis treatments. What are the barriers to transplantation in this large group?

The scarcity of kidneys is clearly the critical factor that prevents more transplantation. In 1990 over 20,000 patients were on waiting lists, and many of these individuals must wait a year before a kidney becomes available. In any given year, nearly 1,000 patients will die on dialysis while waiting for a kidney.

Improving Transplantation. Two new immunosuppressive drugs introduced in the early 1980s have consistently produced transplantation success rates of nearly 80 percent when added to the existing drug regimen. Cyclosporine, derived from a soil fungus, has a fairly selective ability to chemically paralyze T lymphocytes (the major population of cells responsible for immune destruction of transplanted organs) without interfering with any of the other properties of the patient's immune system. The second new drug, OKT3, is an antibody derived from mouse cells by bioengineering techniques. When directed against a surface protein present on almost all T lymphocytes, OKT3 is capable of reversing nearly 95 percent of organ-rejection episodes.

FK-506 and rapamycin are two new experimental drugs currently undergoing clinical trials for use in transplantation. These drugs display relatively selective inhibition of T lymphocytes and may be less-toxic alternatives to cyclosporine, which paradoxically can cause serious, irreversible kidney damage when used for too long or at too high a dose.

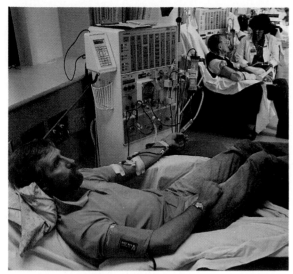

Dialysis (above) removes waste products from the blood, a vital kidney function. Dialysis is no longer necessary after a successful kidney transplant.

Immunotoxin Therapy. The ideal immunosuppressive drug would target only that portion of the immune system that has been specifically activated by the transplanted organ, leaving overall immunity otherwise intact. In recent months a novel experimental approach to this problem has resulted in several drugs that may fulfill the goal of truly selective immunotherapy.

The basis of action for these new drugs is deceptively simple. Activated T lymphocytes, which are called into action by a transplanted kidney and which trigger the cascade of events that eventually destroys the organ, represent only a small fraction of the body's entire complement of lymphocytes. Most lymphocytes are unaffected by the transplant, and are called resting T lymphocytes.

All drugs previously used for transplant immunosuppression are incapable of distinguishing resting from activated lymphocytes, and thus inhibit or destroy them all indiscriminately. However, activated cells betray themselves by expressing newly synthesized proteins on their surfaces, such as the interleukin-2 (IL-2) receptor. Monoclonal antibodies against the IL-2 receptor have been developed, and appear to be promising agents. In a related approach, extremely potent cell toxins such as those derived from the *Diphtheria* or *Pseudomonas* bacteria have been chemically linked to interleukin-2 itself. When injected into a patient undergoing rejection, this toxin-IL-2 complex attaches to the IL-2 receptor on activated lymphocytes. It is internalized, and the toxin is cleaved and released with immediately fatal results for the cell. Approaches such as this will soon lower the medical risk of transplantation enough so that it will be applicable to a much greater proportion of the dialysis population.

J. Douglas Smith, M.D. and Eric Brown, M.D.

Liver

The field of liver diseases, or hepatology, has witnessed extraordinary advances in recent years. Scientists are steadily improving our understanding of liver function at the subcellular level, while elucidating the immunological and virological mechanisms at work in a number of important liver diseases. Clinicians have departed forever from the era in which they could do little for most patients afflicted with liver diseases; today they can offer pharmacological treatments that can arrest the course of some diseases, or even cure them. For patients facing imminent or eventual death from advanced liver disease, liver transplantation offers an excellent chance for a return to normal life.

▶ Viral Hepatitis

There are an estimated 1 million chronic carriers of hepatitis B virus in the United States, and some 200 million around the world. Hepatitis B has been identified as a cause of chronic liver disease. As a result of this infection, liver cancer is a leading cause of death in many areas of the world, particularly in Asia, where carrier rates range up to 10 percent of the population. Enormous strides have been made in understanding the structure of the viral genome and the functions of its protein products. Recently, mutant strains of the virus have been identified, along with the precise portion of the genome that is altered. Several publications during the past year indicate that these mutant strains may be even more pathogenic than "native" hepatitis B virus, conferring a particularly high risk of severe acute or chronic hepatitis B.

Intense interest in the treatment of hepatitis B during the past decade has culminated in recent studies that demonstrate conclusively that *alpha interferon* is effective in 30 to 50 percent of patients. In most studies, efficacy has been measured in terms of elimination of standard markers of viral replication rather than by eradication of all traces of the virus from the liver. A recent exciting study from the National Institutes of Health (NIH), however, indicates that the majority of patients who respond to interferon will eventually (several years following treatment) lose all evidence of chronic carriership. Alpha interferon has already been approved by the Food and Drug Administration (FDA) for chronic hepatitis C; it is hoped that FDA approval of alpha interferon to treat hepatitis B will be forthcoming in the next year.

Tragically, new hepatitis B infections remain common despite the availability during the past decade of a safe and effective vaccine. Targeting of high-risk populations for vaccinations has failed to have the hoped-for impact. Recently, universal vaccination of children was recommended by an advisory committee of the Centers for Disease Control (CDC). Although no large-scale vaccination program has been fully implemented, the means are at hand for eradication of this serious infection within the next one or two generations.

The most important development in all of hepatology during the past decade was the discovery in the late 1980s of the hepatitis C virus, the cause of nearly all hepatitis infections transmitted via transfused blood. Hepatitis C is a common infection in intravenous drug users, and a relatively common cause of chronic liver disease, even in patients without exposure to blood or blood products.

The transmission routes of hepatitis C remain to be fully clarified. The disease is transmitted less efficiently via the sexual route than are other blood-borne viruses, such as hepatitis B virus and human immunodeficiency virus (HIV). Unlike hepatitis B virus, which causes chronic infection in about 5 percent of infected persons, hepatitis C virus causes chronic infection in at least 50 percent of those infected. Although the clinical course may be asymptomatic, cirrhosis is a frequent consequence of long-term infection, occurring in 20 to 50 percent of cases. Recent seroepidemiological studies have established hepatitis C virus-induced liver disease as an important cause of liver cancer, which kills over 12,000 men and women each year.

Recombinant alpha interferon was approved early in 1991 for treatment of chronic hepatitis C. Although about 50 percent of patients respond to treatment, at least half relapse after treatment is stopped. The results of studies evaluating higher doses or longer periods of treatment should be available soon; trials involving other new drugs may also be expected.

Primary Biliary Cirrhosis

A disorder called primary biliary cirrhosis (PBC), in which the immune system attacks the small bile ducts within the liver, is most common in middle-aged women, and slowly leads to cirrhosis in many patients. In advanced cases, liver transplantation has shown excellent results. Still, less radical treatments to cure or at least arrest the disease at an early stage are urgently needed.

Recent interest has centered on *ursodiol* as a treatment for PBC. A bile acid originally introduced for medical dissolution of gallstones, ursodiol is now used infrequently for this purpose because of the recent introduction of laparoscopic cholecystectomy. In this new procedure, the gallstones are removed with a tube inserted through the abdominal wall. Treatment of PBC with ursodiol reduces the abnormally high serum levels of liver enzymes that characterize the disease. A recent French multicenter study also demonstrated that, after a follow-up period, the liver appeared to improve microscopically after treatment when compared with livers of patients in an untreated control group. However, improvement in survival, the ultimate goal of any therapy for chronic liver disease, has not yet been demonstrated. Moreover, it is recognized that even if the drug has beneficial effects, it is not a cure for the underlying disease.

Recently, favorable experience with methotrexate, a powerful anti-inflammatory and anticancer drug used to treat conditions such as psoriasis, rheumatoid arthritis, and certain malignancies, has been tested in patients with PBC. However, more clinical trials will be required before the drug has an accepted role.

Liver Cancer

Malignancy can arise in a number of chronic liver diseases. Chronic viral hepatitis (related to both the hepatitis B and C viruses), alcoholic cirrhosis, and hemochromatosis (genetic iron overload) are particularly notorious causes of liver cancer.

By the time patients with liver cancer develop symptoms, their prognosis is poor. Recent studies, particularly from Asia, suggest that when tumors are detected while small and asymptomatic, the prognosis after surgery may be better. Many clinicians therefore routinely monitor their patients who are at risk for tumor formation. A test measuring blood alpha-fetoprotein levels is used as an indicator of the disease. Elevated levels of this protein characterize 70 to 90 percent of patients with liver disease. Such surveillance is combined with regular ultrasound of the liver.

Liver Transplantation

Pioneered in the 1960s, but not available on a widespread scale until the 1980s, liver transplantation offers a chance for a healthy life in the face of otherwise-certain death from advanced liver disease. In addition to advances in the technique pioneered by Dr. Thomas Starzl, first in Colorado and later in Pittsburgh, the introduction of cyclosporine as an immunosuppressive drug to prevent graft rejection in the early 1980s led to major improvements in patient survival. The operation is now available in a number of large American cities. Many transplant surgeons advocate earlier recognition of, and transplantation for, patients with advanced chronic liver disease so that life-threatening complications that might preclude the chance for a transplant can be avoided. Long-term survival of 80 percent of patients is now the rule. The results may improve still further with the introduction of newer immunosuppressive drugs such as FK-506.

Ira M. Jacobson, M.D.

Medical Technology

▶ Stainless Steel Stents Help Blocked Arteries Remain Clear

Hope arrived for some sufferers of atherosclerosis with the approval of the Palmaz Balloon-Expandable Stent by the Food and Drug Administration (FDA) in September 1991. Atherosclerosis is the narrowing of an artery from the buildup of fat, calcium, cholesterol, and other cell products on the artery's inner layer. These substances tend to accumulate in arterial areas that have been damaged, forming lesions called plaque. (High levels of cholesterol, cigarette smoking, and high blood pressure are believed to play an important role in plaque formation.) When plaque begins to line the arteries that supply blood to the heart, the resulting reduction in blood flow causes chest pains; eventually the artery completely closes, causing acute heart failure. Blockage in arteries leading to other areas of the body can damage the organs and tissue that they supply, as well.

The Palmaz stent, a stainless steel mesh tube manufactured by Johnson & Johnson, Warren, New Jersey, can be implanted in blocked arteries to facilitate the flow of blood and prevent them from closing completely. This device is the first to be approved by the FDA for this purpose.

The new stent is not the appropriate treatment for every patient who suffers from atherosclerosis, however. Physicians have found that it works best when used in conjunction with balloon angioplasty, a noninvasive catheterization procedure first introduced in 1977 to open clogged arteries with an inflated balloon. (Balloon angioplasty was originally developed as a safer alternative to open-heart bypass surgery, which attaches vein grafts to coronary arteries to redirect the flow of blood around a blockage.)

During balloon angioplasty, surgeons typically thread a thin wire (using an X-ray monitor) through the large femoral artery in a patient's thigh up to the affected artery. Once the wire is in place, a flexible catheter (a tube with a circumference about the size of a pencil) is inserted around it and also guided through the artery. A second, more narrow tube is then threaded through the first catheter; this second catheter carries a deflated balloon at its tip. Once the balloon is positioned at the blocked area of the artery, surgeons inflate it, pushing the fatty deposits against the inner artery walls to widen the passageway. The balloon is then deflated and removed along with the catheters and wire.

Since balloon angioplasty was first introduced nearly 15 years ago, the initial success rate has climbed to 90 percent. About one-third of patients treated with this technique, however, experience restenosis, or renarrowing, of the damaged artery within six months. It is these patients who may benefit most from the Palmaz Balloon-Expandable Stent.

The Palmaz stent, named for Dr. Julio C. Palmaz, of the department of radiology at the University of Texas in San Antonio, is implanted in the affected artery using the same method employed in balloon angioplasty. However, before the second catheter is inserted into the patient's body, the mesh stent is collapsed over the deflated balloon attached to the catheter's tip. The stent-encased balloon is then guided to the arterial plaque and inflated, which opens both the stent and the blocked artery. The balloon is then deflated and removed and the stent is left behind to hold the arterial walls open.

From December 1987 to September 1989, Palmaz, Dr. Richard A. Schatz from the Scripps Clinic and Research Foundation in La Jolla, California, and other researchers conducted a multicenter investigation of two variations of the stent (the Palmaz and the Palmaz-Schatz) for use in coronary arteries. All 226 participants were candidates for coronary-artery bypass surgery. Implantation was successful in 213 of these patients. In addition, after three months, 92 percent of the group was still free of the symptoms that led them to initiate care. In a more recent study, Japanese scientists evaluated the Palmaz-Schatz coronary stent in 61 patients; implantation was successful in 59 of the 61.

The Palmaz stent is not without drawbacks. Because it is constructed of stainless steel, a patient's body may react to it unfavorably. One dangerous side effect is the formation of a blood clot, which can cause immediate and complete arterial blockage, resulting in death. Patients implanted with the stent should therefore receive anticoagulants (blood-thinning medications) for at least several months following the procedure. It is also possible that the stented artery will close again—especially if the patient's body responds to the implant procedure as an injury, triggering rapid cellular growth and migration to the treatment site.

For now, the FDA has approved the Palmaz Balloon-Expandable Stent for use in patients who have had unsuccessful balloon angioplasty of the iliac artery, which supplies blood to the upper pelvic area.

▶ New Tests Allow for Quick and Accurate Detection of Gastritis- and Ulcer-Related Bacteria

Researchers recently discovered that the *Helicobacter pylori* bacteria (formerly *Campylobacter pylori*), which is commonly found in low levels in the stomach linings of adults, can cause gastritis, ulcers, and intestinal-type stomach cancer when present in high levels in certain patients. News of this discovery has prompted investigators to develop blood tests that can measure the amounts of this bacteria present in a patient's system. These tests work by detecting the presence of immunoglobulin (IgG) antibodies, which are produced to fight *H. pylori;* previous detection required endoscopy, an invasive procedure that biopsied selected areas of the stomach.

In April 1991 the FDA approved the first serological test for this purpose, the Quidel Helicobacter Pylori Test, manufactured by Quidel, Inc., of San Diego, California. Since then, Whittaker Bioproducts of Walkersville, Maryland, has also received marketing clearance for the Pylori Stat ELISA and Pylori Fiax immunofluorescence assays.

High levels of IgG in a patient with recurrent stomach problems may indicate that *H. pylori* is causing inflammation, rather than other suspected agents, including stress and diet. A patient infected with high levels of the bacteria can be appropriately treated to eradicate it. The enzyme immunoassay test can also be used to monitor the patient's recovery. For example, low levels of IgG after treatment would indicate successful treatment. In addition, recent studies have shown that patients with low levels of IgG after ulcer therapy remain healthy longer than patients with high levels.

H. pylori serological tests are 98 percent accurate; they are also convenient—researchers predict that some form of the test will eventually be available for use in a doctor's office. Endoscopy and biopsy, which require hospitalization, often provide less-accurate results because they measure bacteria levels in only selected areas of the stomach, which may be free of the bacteria, leaving infected areas unidentified.

▶ Smoking-Cessation Aid Gains Approval

An end-of-year FDA approval in 1991 may help smokers stick to their 1992 New Year's resolution to finally quit. Alza Corporation's Nicoderm transdermal nicotine patch was approved in November as the latest smoking-cessation aid available to the hopelessly addicted smoker.

Typically, transdermal patches are attached to an area of the body that is determined by the type of drug involved. For example, the patch to prevent motion sickness is usually worn behind the ear, while the nitroglycerin patch to control angina is applied to the chest. Patches, similar to adhesive strips, consist of several layers of flexible membranes and an adhesive. The top layer is usually an impermeable backing, followed by a layer that holds the drug to be administered; another layer controls the rate at which the drug is released to the body, while the final layer consists of the adhesive agent.

The patch works by releasing the drug through the skin into the bloodstream at a preset rate determined by the manufacturer. Usually, a patch administers the lowest effective level of the drug to prevent adverse effects.

The nicotine patch is attached to the upper arm of the smoker; a new patch is applied each morning and then removed before the user goes to bed. The patch releases a fixed dose of nicotine that cannot be altered by the smoker. It is the user's responsibility to change the patch each day, however, so the smoker still controls his or her compliance rate.

During clinical trials of nicotine patches, a small number of test subjects experienced side effects ranging from nausea, headache, and vertigo, to acute skin irritation in the area of the patch. However, test subjects were still more likely to use the patch despite these drawbacks when the only alternative is nicotine gum, the first nicotine aid approved by the FDA.

▶ Diagnostic Tools Identify Coronary-Artery Disease

Two diagnostic products for identifying heart disease without using invasive procedures were approved by the FDA in December 1990. Cardiolite, manufactured by DuPont Merck Pharmaceutical Company, Wilmington, Delaware, and CardioTec, sold by Bristol-Myers Squibb Company, Princeton, New Jersey, are cardiac-imaging agents that allow technicians to track the flow of blood through the heart and coronary arteries without resorting to catheterization techniques.

Cardiac-imaging products typically consist of specific chemicals tagged with radioisotopes. A technician injects these agents into a patient's bloodstream and then monitors their movement through the heart using a special camera.

CardioTec consists of teboroxime tagged with Technetium-Tc99m, a radioisotope. It allows clinicians to capture images of the heart, including partially obstructed blood flow through coronary arteries, only a few minutes after it is injected, and it washes out of the body very quickly. In addition, CardioTec is not easily absorbed by the lungs.

Cardiolite is composed of the chemical sestamibi, which binds to undamaged heart muscle, and Technetium-Tc99m (the same radioisotope tagged in CardioTec). Because Cardiolite specifically attaches to the heart, photographed images are precise for coronary screening.

Before the FDA approved Cardiolite and CardioTec, one of the more popular cardiac-imaging agents was thallium T1–201. The two new agents offer distinct timing advantages over thallium imaging. Cardiolite allows the heart to be "photographed" for up to four hours—a much longer period of time than that provided by thallium test-

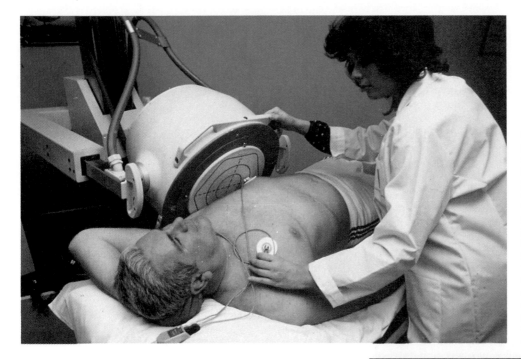

Cardiolite cardiac-imaging agent is used as part of a noninvasive procedure on patients suspected of having heart disease. The substance works by binding specifically to live heart muscle and emitting gamma rays. A gamma camera (left), used in conjunction with a computer, reconstructs images of the heart. A normal heart exhibits blood flow throughout (below); an abnormal heart has diminished blood flow.

ing. CardioTec, conversely, measures heart activity during stress-rest tests in one to two hours, less than half the time required by thallium imaging.

A new tool called Cadkit, which helps physicians diagnose patients at risk for heart attack and stroke, was approved by the FDA in June 1991. Using a monoclonal antibody, Cadkit, manufactured by American Biogenetic Sciences, Notre Dame, Indiana, identifies fibrinogen, a blood protein that interacts with thrombin, an enzyme, to clot blood. Since high levels of fibrinogen can cause coronary-artery disease, early detection of high fibrinogen levels may help physicians prevent or predict heart failure in high-risk patients.

▶ Morphine-Filled Microinfusion Pumps Relieve Chronic Pain

Controlling severe pain in cancer patients requires an intimate understanding of both how the human body reacts to drugs that stop the pain and how the drugs are administered. For example, when pain is controlled by injections and pills, patients often experience significant and sometimes prolonged gaps in pain control, during which time their anxiety levels rise, contributing to their discomfort. Experimental evidence indicates that not only does anxiety increase pain and the amount of the drug needed to relieve it, but pain can also accelerate growth of the tumor that causes it.

One method that can be used to alleviate those windows of pain involves tiny pumps called microinfusion devices. Microinfusion devices are about 3 inches in diameter and contain very small concentrated amounts of a pain-relief drug. They are usu-

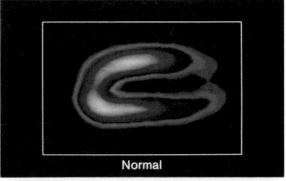

Normal

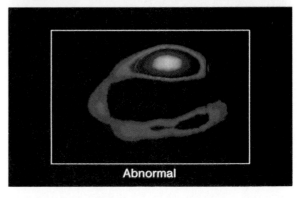

Abnormal

ally implanted under the skin of a patient's abdomen, but they can also be worn outside the body. Before a pump is implanted in the body, it is programmed to dispense a predefined dose of a specific drug and then filled with a concentrated form of that drug. Once in place, the pump delivers a constant supply of the drug to the patient's body to relieve the appropriate symptoms.

In 1991, the FDA asked Elkins-Sinn, Inc., Cherry Hill, New Jersey, to develop a concentrated form of morphine for use in microinfusion devices. Morphine, an opiate, is a strong painkiller and is often used to relieve the pain of cancer patients. In its standard dosages, however, it was ineffective for use in microinfusion devices because they could not hold enough of it to be effective. In July 1991 the FDA approved two highly concentrated dosages of morphine called Infumorph 200 and Infumorph 500 developed by Elkins-Sinn for use in continuous microinfusion devices.

Infumorph 200 and Infumorph 500 have proved to be highly effective in combating chronic pain in cancer patients. Complications with Infumorph can occur, however, if the microinfusion device that dispenses it is programmed to release an inappropriate dose of the drug. These side effects include seizures and respiratory problems. As a result, once a new pump is implanted in a patient, he or she must remain in the hospital for at least 24 hours, until the initial dose from the microinfusion device can be verified as correct. Once it is verified, however, the patient can go home, returning only when the pump needs to be refilled, about once a month. If a pump does need to be reprogrammed, it is not necessary to remove the device from the patient's body; the correct dosage amounts can be beamed through the skin to the pump's control mechanism.

▶ Predicting Premature Labor

One of the more controversial devices approved by the FDA in the last year was the Genesis Home Uterine Activity Monitoring System (HUAM), which was cleared for marketing in late 1990. This prescription device, manufactured by Physiological Diagnostic Services, Inc., Atlanta, Georgia, a division of Tokos Medical Corporation, Santa Ana, California, is designed for use at home by pregnant women who have a history of premature labor. The monitor detects uterine contractions as early as possible so that appropriate action can be taken by a physician. The women use the device twice a day, once in the morning and once at night, and it is prescribed for use after the 24th week and up to the 36th week of pregnancy.

HUAM is simple to operate—a pregnant woman simply places electrodes connected to the monitor onto her abdomen while lying down. She then allows the electrodes to monitor her uterine activity for one to two hours while remaining in a reclined position. Any electrical impulses detected in the uterus are recorded by the monitor as possible contractions. This information is then transmitted by the monitor via telephone lines to a trained technician or nurse on the other end who interprets the data and determines if the woman might be experiencing premature labor. If the contractions exceed a rate of four per hour, the woman is advised to go to the hospital immediately.

Before the device was approved, Tokos Medical Corporation conducted a multicenter randomized clinical trial that compared standard obstetrical care for high-risk pregnant women to the same care plus the use of the HUAM device, with no additional nursing care provided for either group. Three facilities that had never used the HUAM device before and that had no relation to the device's manufacturer were deliberately included in the study for objective purposes. Cervical dilation was used as the end point for the study because it is considered to be the best objective measure of the progress of labor.

The results of the study were then evaluated in terms of gestation, birth weight, and neonatal outcome for 82 women with preterm labor and 252 women experiencing regular labor. For the 252 women with regular labor, there were no differences in the three variables studied. In the women who experienced labor prematurely, the group using the HUAM device had gestations that were 1.7 weeks longer than those of the women in the group not using the HUAM device. In addition, the HUAM group had babies that were on average 21 ounces heavier and that spent 9.3 less days in neonatal intensive care.

From these data, and supporting data that measure the degree of cervical dilation at the time of diagnosing premature labor, the FDA concluded that use of the device without contact with nurses resulted in clinically important early detection of preterm labor. Accordingly, they approved it for sale, but for detection purposes only. The agency was quite clear in stating that the device could not be sold as an aid for reducing the incidence of premature birth, as it had not demonstrated the ability to do so. However, the FDA also indicated that it would be unreasonable to expect that any diagnostic tool should be expected to prevent prematurity— the ability of the HUAM device to alert physicians and nurses to the patient's need for immediate medical attention was itself clinically important enough for its approval by the FDA.

In November 1991, a letter to the *New England Journal of Medicine* challenged the ability of the HUAM device to effectively monitor premature labor. The letter's authors, all physicians at respected hospitals and universities, noted that from 1989 to 1990, the United States had one of the highest infant-mortality rates of the Western industrialized countries, despite many obstetrical advances in the last 20 years. They also noted that the incidence of premature birth in the United States remained the same during this period despite these advances. They went on to state that no evidence is currently on record that indicates

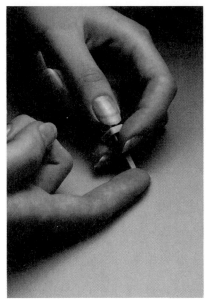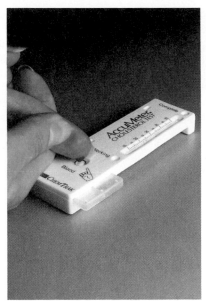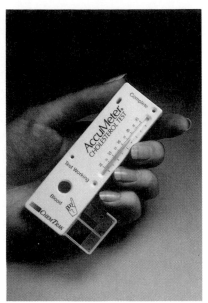

To use the AccuMeter cholesterol-screening kit, the patient (left to right) pricks a finger, puts a few drops of blood into the well, and then waits for the meter to register the blood's cholesterol level.

that uterine activity increases before premature labor begins.

Finally, after reviewing the clinical trials conducted by Tokos Medical Corporation as part of the FDA approval process, and examining data from clinical trials conducted by other researchers (using other experimental home uterine monitoring devices subsequently denied approval by the FDA), the authors disputed the ability of the HUAM device to detect premature labor. They expressed concern that despite the FDA's careful labeling of the HUAM device, some users might use it inappropriately to prevent premature labor rather than simply detect it. This was feasible, they noted, since many physicians are unable to accurately identify women likely to deliver prematurely. The authors concluded that the increased contact of the pregnant women with medical personnel necessitated by using the test twice a day was of more value in diagnosing premature labor than was the information actually recorded by the device.

In the *NEJM* letter, the authors also pointed out that the device is costly—about $5,000 for each user. They further noted that many of the babies born prematurely in the United States are born to socially disadvantaged women who cannot afford and/or do not have access to quality health care. The adoption of devices such as the HUAM increases the cost of health care, they believe, and diverts resources from areas of greater need. In conclusion, they recommended that physicians first meet the goal of providing basic preventative health care for all pregnant women before they endorse unproven and expensive new medical technology.

▶ Cholesterol-Screening Devices

In other diagnostic news, the FDA approved the first disposable cholesterol-screening kit in March 1991. Designed for in-office and at-home use, this kit detects the amount of cholesterol present in the blood with 97 percent of the accuracy delivered by more expensive laboratory techniques—and in only 15 minutes. Chemtrak of Sunnyvale, California, began selling AccuMeter in May 1991 for $6.25. The kit, which is available by prescription through a physician, simply requires that a user prick his or her finger and then deposit several drops of blood into a well built into the kit. The well then filters the blood into red cells and plasma; the plasma is transferred to a pad for temporary storage.

The blood plasma is run through a series of steps that extract and measure cholesterol using chromatographic strips. In the final stage, the chromatographic strip changes color: the greater the amount of the strip that changes, the higher the level of cholesterol in the blood sample. The length of strip that changes color is read like a thermometer. For precise numbers, the kit comes with a chart that converts the length of the colored area on the strip from millimeters to serum cholesterol levels.

A more complex cholesterol-measurement test designed for laboratory use only also received federal approval in 1991. The ICA Plasma HDL and LDL Measurement System is the first approved device that uses proton nuclear magnetic resonance spectroscopy to identify and then simultaneously measure high-density lipoproteins (HDL) and low-density lipoproteins (LDL) in human blood.

Abigail W. Grissom

Medications and Drugs

▶ Advances in Cancer Therapy

Relief for Cancer-Treatment Nausea. Drugs used for treating cancer (antineoplastic agents) may cause severe nausea and vomiting in as many as 70 to 80 percent of patients. Unfortunately, this nausea and vomiting can persist for days or even weeks. The cause of this situation appears to be stimulation by the antineoplastic agents of several different "vomiting centers" located in the brain. There are some drugs, such as antihistamines and anticholinergics, which can be used to provide relief. However, these drugs are also very potent, and they, too, can produce side effects in many patients. A new antinausea agent, called *Zofran* (ondansetron), appears to alleviate side effects caused by chemotherapy. Of particular note, Zofran seems to cause less sedation and fewer muscular spasms than other antinausea medications, although it can cause headache, diarrhea, or constipation. Typically, the drug is given intravenously just prior to administration of the chemotherapy to prevent any instant nausea and vomiting; it is then given every four to eight hours to prevent any delayed effects.

Better Anticancer Drugs. In addition to killing cancerous cells, many antineoplastic drugs also destroy healthy cells, such as white blood cells that fight off infection. This leaves the patient extremely vulnerable to infection. Even a common cold can be life-threatening in a patient who has no defenses.

The only source of taxol, a promising new anticancer drug, is the bark of the rare Pacific yew tree. Until taxol can be produced synthetically, doctors will have to rely on yew-tree nurseries (below) for a steady supply.

Two new agents produced by recombinant-DNA technology have recently been released by the Food and Drug Administration (FDA). Known as colony-stimulating factors (CSFs), these agents stimulate the first steps of cell production in the bone marrow, which is where blood cells are made. *Neupogen* represents a very important advance because it specifically stimulates the production of certain white blood cells called granulocytes—cells needed for fighting infection. With the exception of mild bone pain, patients experience very few side effects from Neupogen treatment. Therapy begins about one day after administration of the chemotherapy, and a single dose is given each day for up to two weeks.

The other new anticancer drug, *Prokine,* is approved for patients who have various lymphomas (cancer of the lymph nodes) or leukemias (cancer of the bone marrow) and who have undergone autologous (self) bone-marrow transplantation. In this kind of transplant, the patient's own marrow is removed and set aside while the patient undergoes antineoplastic drug therapy. Once the therapy is completed, the bone marrow is put back into the patient, thus avoiding destruction of the marrow by the anticancer drug. Prokine enhances granulocyte recovery following bone-marrow transplantation. Patients receive their first Prokine treatment two to four hours after the bone-marrow transplant; treatment is continued until cell counts return to normal levels.

Neupogen and Prokine are also expected to be useful in a number of other diseases. Currently, there are studies under way to assess the ability of these agents to treat patients with other diseases of the bone marrow, as well as AIDS.

▶ Important New Drugs for Women

Ovarian Cancer. Ovarian cancer is a difficult disease to prevent or cure because it commonly develops without any symptoms until it is in its final stages, at which point it is very difficult to treat. A new drug called *Hexalen* (altretamine) has been found effective in treating persistent or recurrent ovarian cancer. This drug represents an important breakthrough because, at the present time, there are very few agents available for treatment or cure of ovarian cancer.

Hexalen use is reserved for patients who have been treated with other anticancer therapies, but still have evidence of active disease. Like many other anticancer drugs, Hexalen kills noncancerous cells along with cancerous ones. As a result, it may cause some serious side effects in patients, including severe nausea and vomiting, decreased white-blood-cell counts, and peripheral neuropathy (numbness or tingling sensations of the hands and/or feet).

Endometriosis. Endometriosis occurs when cells usually located in the lining of the uterus escape and attach themselves elsewhere in the abdomen. Once these cells are outside the uterus, they begin to grow and form a foreign tissue, or lesion. This lesion is responsible for causing the pain associated with the disease. *Synarel* (nafarelin) has been approved for the treatment of endometriosis; it relieves pain and reduces the lesions. Prior to the release of Synarel, which is inhaled as a nasal spray, the only drug available for treatment of endometriosis was Danocrine, which is taken orally. Both drugs work by inhibiting estrogens, which are responsible for causing the abnormal cell growth. Studies comparing Danocrine and Synarel have shown that patients treated with Danocrine had fewer estrogen-type side effects (such as hot flashes), but had more complaints of muscle pain, fatigue, and stomach upset than did patients treated with Synarel.

Synarel has also been shown to be useful in the treatment of uterine fibroids (nonmalignant tumors of the uterus), prostatic cancer, and as a contraceptive.

▶ Nicotine Patch

Although Christopher Columbus is generally credited with the discovery of the New World, little recognition is given to another discovery he made: he observed the natives inhaling the fumes from herbs (tobaccos) that had been wrapped in a large leaf, making what we now call a cigar. He returned to Spain with this herb, which is indigenous to North America, and introduced smoking to Europe. The use of tobacco spread very quickly. Initially, it was smoked as it had been seen by Columbus. The use of snuff originated in Portugal and was imported to France by French ambassador Jean Nicot. From the 17th through the 19th centuries, snuff was the preferred tobacco of the upper classes. The lower classes preferred to chew tobacco. This left their hands free to perform work. In addition, pipes or cigars were smoked. The cigarette has been used for only the past 100 years, gaining great popularity during World War II. Smoking, chewing, and snuffing all permit tobacco or tobacco-smoke contact with mucous membranes of the nose or mouth, and ultimately, contact with surfaces of the lung, permitting easy absorption of nicotine into the bloodstream.

It is interesting to note that there are *no* medicinal uses for nicotine. Nonetheless, its presence in tobacco and its high toxicity make it a medically important drug. The use of tobacco is so widespread and socially accepted that it is not usually considered addictive, even though it fits all of the accepted criteria for drug dependence.

A chewing gum was developed a few years ago that would deliver nicotine through the simple act of

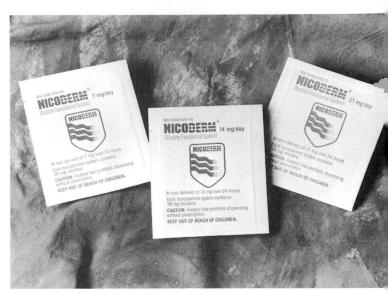

The new nicotine patch supplies a fixed dose of nicotine to the body through the skin, thus reducing the urge to smoke.

chewing *(Nicorette Gum),* so that the user could chew gum instead of smoking. Not only did it provide the nicotine, but chewing in the absence of puffing seems to be a therapeutic activity. As for helping people quit smoking, the gum, when used alone, achieved moderate success. As the blood level of nicotine would rise and fall, not only would craving for nicotine arise, but also the desire to smoke. Smoking is not just a chemical problem, but, as with other addictive substances, it also has a behavioral component.

The pharmaceutical industry has now developed and marketed a new adhesive skin patch that will deliver a continuous, specific dose of nicotine to the bloodstream by direct absorption through the skin, thus maintaining a constant blood level and reducing the temptation to smoke. The success rate of the new patch, without behavioral therapy, is only about 25 percent, which is still a significant improvement over any other product to date. However, there is more work to be done in the area of behavioral change to provide smokers with the ability to quit. The patches are available as *Habitrol* and *Nicoderm.* Side effects of the patch include nausea, sweating, dizziness, and muscle pains, as well as possible itching, swelling, rash, and pain at the site of the patch.

▶ New Sleep Medicine

The benzodiazepine (Valium-type) drugs are a group of antianxiety medications that make people sleepy to varying degrees. Those that cause the least sleepiness often are marketed as anxiolytics (anxiety reducers), and those causing the most

DRUG APPROVAL: The Standard Process and the Fast Track Approaches

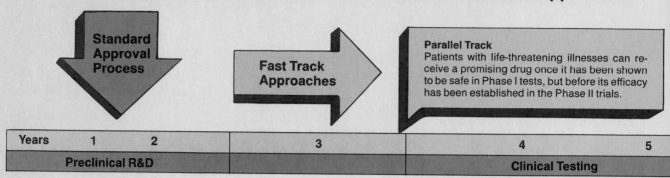

Standard Approval Process

Fast Track Approaches

Parallel Track
Patients with life-threatening illnesses can receive a promising drug once it has been shown to be safe in Phase I tests, but before its efficacy has been established in the Phase II trials.

Years	1	2	3	4	5
Preclinical R&D				Clinical Testing	

Preclinical R&D (Years 1 and 2). The compound is synthesized (left), then tested for biological activity and safety in animals. The drug company then files an Investigational New Drug (IND) application with the FDA. The IND becomes effective if the FDA does not disapprove it in 30 days.

Phase I (Year 3). The drug is tested in usually no more than 100 healthy volunteers (right). Dosages are slowly increased to gauge the drug's safety, evaluate its effects, and to learn more about the way it is metabolized.

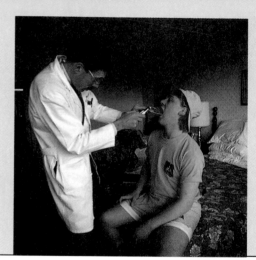

sleepiness as hypnotics (sleep medications). The ideal drug for the treatment of insomnia will not cause dependence, will allow the user to fall asleep quickly, sleep through the night, and awaken refreshed without a hangover (drowsiness due to continued effect of the drug).

The newly approved benzodiazepine *ProSom* acts rapidly, provides natural sleep, and has a low potential for hangover effect. As with other hypnotic drugs, ProSom is indicated only for the *short-term* management of insomnia, usually limited to two weeks, since continual use leads to physical and psychological dependence. Ideally, if a patient obtains a good night's sleep for one or two nights, the drug should be skipped on the third (and possibly fourth) night to see if its use is still necessary.

Pregnant women should not use the benzodiazepines, because the drugs cross the placenta; it is then possible for the fetus to have a higher blood level of drug than the mother. If the mother uses a benzodiazepine up until the day she delivers, her child probably would be physically dependent on the drug and, as it withdrew from the drug, might have

seizures. Also, in nursing mothers the drugs do pass into the milk (and therefore into the baby), and thus should not be used.

▶ Relief After Eye Examination

If you recall the days of going to the eye doctor, having drops put in your eyes to dilate the pupils for an eye examination, and then having to wear sunglasses for the rest of the day to protect yourself from strong sunlight, relief has arrived. Angelini Pharmaceuticals has begun marketing a product called RĒV-EYES (dapiprazole hydrochloride), which reverses the effects of pupil-dilating (mydriatic) agents such as atropine, allowing the eyes to react appropriately to light.

▶ Obsessive-Compulsive Disorder

For many years, psychiatrists have wanted a drug that would treat obsessive-compulsive disorder, an anxiety condition characterized by obsessions (persistent ideas, thoughts, or impulses) followed by compulsive (forced) actions or thoughts to eradicate or neutralize the unwanted thought. For in-

One IND, aerosol pentamidine, is given to some AIDS patients to prevent pneumocystic pneumonia (right).

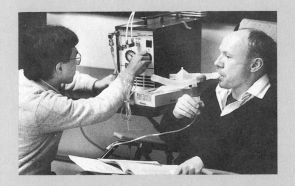

Treatment IND
Under special circumstances, an investigational new drug (IND) can be administered to patients not taking part in Phase III clinical trials and prior to FDA approval. Drug companies may charge patients for the drug.

6	7	8	9	10
			Approval	

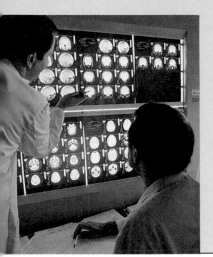

Phase II (Years 4 and 5). The drug is given to about 200 to 300 patients to determine its side effects and to measure its effectiveness against existing treatments or a placebo. Trials are conducted by a university or government medical center.

Phase III (Years 6, 7, and 8). The effectiveness of the drug is tested in 1,000 to 3,000 patients in clinics and hospitals; the results are compared with existing treatments (left). Trials must confirm Phase II studies and yield a low incidence of adverse reactions.

Approval (Years 9 and 10). The drug company files a New Drug Application (NDA) with the FDA, containing reams of laboratory, animal, and clinical data. After extensive review, the FDA may approve the application, in which case full production of the new drug begins (right). The FDA may, however, seek more data before granting approval.

stance, if the obsession is that one might become infected or infect other people by shaking hands, the compulsion might be to wash one's hands continually.

When the obsessive-compulsive person attempts to resist a compulsion, the result is a mounting tension and anxiety that can be relieved only by yielding to the compulsion. The person recognizes that his or her behavior is excessive or unreasonable and that the activity does not produce any pleasure, but this does not relieve the tension. Depression and anxiety are very common in these people.

A variety of drugs have been used for treating this disorder, with only limited success. But recently, the antidepressant *Anafranil* (clomipramine) has been found to be effective against obsessive-compulsive disorders.

▶ New Drugs for Hypertension

Hypertension, or elevated blood pressure, is a disease that affects approximately 60 million Americans. The higher the blood pressure, the greater are risks of cardiovascular disease.

Studies have shown that reduction of blood pressure protects against major cardiovascular disorders such as stroke, kidney failure, and heart failure. Several classes of drugs have been shown to be effective for treating hypertension. Recently, three new ACE inhibitors and two new calcium channel blockers were approved by the FDA for use in treating hypertension.

ACE inhibitors are drugs that prevent angiotensin-converting enzyme from producing angiotensin, a substance that causes blood vessels to constrict and thereby increases blood pressure. Three new ACE inhibitors—*Lotensin* (benzapril), *Monopril* (fosinipril), and *Altace* (ramipril)—are very similar to agents already available. The major advantage of these new products is that they allow once-a-day dosing, whereas the older products all required dosing two or three times daily. Reducing the number of times per day a medication must be taken improves patient compliance. Side effects of these new agents, however, are just like those of their predecessors: headache, dizziness, fatigue, nausea, and cough (usually a dry, tickling hack).

Also, in contrast to other ACE inhibitors that depend mainly on the kidney for elimination of the drug, Monopril is eliminated by both the liver and the kidney. This may be an important feature in selecting the appropriate drug therapy in patients who have kidney impairment.

Calcium channel blockers, as their name implies, block calcium from reaching cells. In order for muscle fibers to contract, they must utilize calcium. Each muscle cell has special channels for pumping calcium ions in and out. If the smooth muscles of our blood vessels contract, they constrict the blood vessels. The heart then has to work harder to pump blood through a narrower pipeline at a higher pressure. If the calcium channels are blocked, the cells cannot obtain calcium, contraction is prevented, and the vessels dilate, lowering the blood pressure. Calcium channel blockers have been in use for the past several years. The new calcium-channel-blocking agents offer very few advantages over the older agents, but they do offer physicians a wider range of choices. This is ideal in cases where a patient is unable to tolerate one drug, but does react favorably to another. The two new agents, *Dynacirc* (isradipine) and *Plendil* (felodipine), are as effective as the older agents and have much the same side effects. Side effects usually consist of headache, swelling of the legs or feet, flushing, and dizziness.

▶ A New Anti-Inflammatory Agent

The anti-inflammatory class of drugs all relieve pain, reduce inflammation, and have a number of other effects on the body. These other effects occur because a pill is taken by mouth and is distributed throughout the body—not just to the site of the problem.

So, for instance, when aspirin or any other type of analgesic is taken for aches and pains, other effects occur that may or may not be desired, such as lowering fever, suppression of the stomach wall's ability to protect itself from acid (leading to ulcers), suppression of the kidney's ability to move sodium ions out of the body (leading to fluid retention), and, in some rare cases, suppression of the ability of the breathing passages to dilate (leading to asthma attacks).

Probably the best-known and least-expensive anti-inflammatory drug is aspirin. Seventy percent of patients with rheumatoid arthritis are able to tolerate aspirin. The others usually are not able to use it because of severe gastric side effects. These 30 percent of patients are usually given newer, more-expensive anti-inflammatory agents, only to find that most of them also cause gastric bleeding and ulcers. Now an exciting new agent called *Lodine* is 2.5 times less likely to cause stomach problems than other anti-inflammatory agents. Furthermore, Lodine is very effective in the treatment of inflam-

mation in osteoarthritis and is the first drug of its class that has been effective in treating anything other than pain in this debilitating disease, which affects over 15 million Americans.

▶ New Drugs for AIDS Victims

Two drugs for use in patients with AIDS have recently been approved by the FDA. The first drug, Didanosine (dideoxyinosine, or DDI), is used for treating patients in the advanced stages of AIDS infections who cannot tolerate the only other FDA-approved AIDS drug, zidovudine (azidothymidine, or AZT), or whose health has significantly deteriorated while on AZT.

Both AZT and DDI interrupt the process by which the AIDS virus reproduces itself. While neither AZT nor DDI is a cure for AIDS, these drugs can slow down the progress of the disease by slowing down the growth of the virus.

Unfortunately, both AZT and DDI can cause serious and debilitating side effects. AZT is known to cause several severe blood-related toxicities; in some patients, DDI is known to cause pancreatitis (inflammation and swelling of the pancreas, an enzyme-producing organ located near the stomach) and peripheral neuropathy (an inflammation of nerves, leading to numbness or tingling of the hands and feet). Although both of these conditions can be treated if discovered early enough, the damage can become permanent if left untreated. Due to their potential for dangerous side effects, it is extremely important that patients on AZT or DDI be carefully monitored.

Since there are very few treatment options available for treating AIDS-related diseases, physicians and patients must weigh the benefits against the risks when selecting drug therapy. Even though the drugs themselves may induce life-threatening side effects, no treatment at all may mean a quicker or more painful death.

Approximately 30 percent of AIDS patients develop cytomegalovirus (CMV) retinitis, a viral infection of the eye that can lead to permanent blindness. The CMV virus circulates within the bloodstream until it reaches the eye, where it causes infection. A newly approved drug, *Foscavir* (foscarnet) slows down the progression of this disease by interfering with the ability of the virus to reproduce itself. The drug is administered intravenously (not as an eyedrop), so that it can reach the virus within the blood, slow down its replication, and thereby cause less of the virus to reach the eye. Like other AIDS drugs, Foscavir is known to cause kidney impairment, and some patients may experience seizures, thus requiring close monitoring of those receiving this drug.

Marvin M. Weisbrot, R.Ph., M.B.A.
and Kimberley L. Adler, Pharm.D.

Mental Health

▶ Psychological Impact of the Persian Gulf War

The intense media coverage of 1991's Persian Gulf conflict brought many powerful and vivid images of war into American homes. Millions of Americans experienced war as never before. They found themselves drawn to the television, watching for hours on end as news teams relayed the sights and sounds of destruction brought on by bombing raids against Iraq and by the Scud missiles launched in retaliation. Media coverage also increased awareness of the pervasive psychological effects of war on people of all ages—even though the battlefield was thousands of miles away.

Psychiatric experts on aggression and violence observed that certain segments of the population were at greater risk for stressful reactions to the war. These included individuals with biological predisposition to anxiety and other psychiatric disorders. People who had experienced traumatic life situations also were particularly vulnerable, as were people living on their own with limited psychosocial support. Veterans of the Vietnam War were prone to anxiety and flashbacks upon being exposed to combat scenes flashed repeatedly across television screens. Anxiety and stress reactions were likely to be more intense in people who had been victimized in the past by child abuse or other means. Traumatized individuals were more likely to develop feelings of helplessness in response to the war as they identified with the vulnerability of both soldiers and civilians near the combat zone. More-generalized anxiety was aroused in the population at large as they saw or heard about how burning oil fields and the enormous oil spill in the Persian Gulf threatened the world's already-fragile ecosystems.

The war had a special psychological impact on certain ethnic groups. Although innocent and not responsible for the war, Arab-Americans experienced a fear of violence toward them and their families or a fear of other forms of retaliation such as business boycotts or even internment. Given the psychology of war, where fear and anger can be linked with paranoia, it is possible that if the war had been prolonged, some individuals in this country would have dealt with their feelings of impotence and rage by becoming even more suspicious and hostile toward Arab-Americans. Jewish-Americans also were prone to developing anxiety and fear of victimization, but for different reasons. They were affected by the threat of specific terrorist attacks against them in America, but even more powerful was their reaction to seeing their historic homeland

The psychological impact of the Persian Gulf conflict on people of all ages, particularly military families, is still being assessed by experts.

of Israel under regular attack by missiles. Knowing the threat to Israel, many Jewish-Americans suffered anxiety or had painful memories associated with their experience or awareness of the Holocaust of World War II.

Individual psychological reactions to the war were often manifested most vividly in people's fantasies and dreams. Commonly reported dreams during the war were of being shot or bombed or of being taken hostage. This highlighted the tendency to identify with victims as well as to fear for one's own safety. In one newspaper article, a psychologist reported that his patients had an increase in dreams after they saw coverage of the pilots who were taken prisoner by Iraq. The war also seemed to trigger more basic anxieties and fantasies not so specifically related to the war itself. Children in particular were more prone to developing fears of loss of loved ones and fears of injury and death. This was true even when they did not have parents or older siblings involved overseas. Being egocentric and unable to understand how far away the war was, young children needed reassurance that their homes would not be bombed and that they and their families would not be hurt.

Fortunately, mental-health programs, schools, and churches across the United States responded quickly and offered support groups and individual counseling to those most directly affected by the war. The strong sense of national identity that developed also provided a powerful buffer against stress and maladaptive reactions. The Persian Gulf conflict nevertheless demonstrated how war has an enormous impact on individual and group psychology. The overall psychological effect of the extensive, high-technology media coverage of the war appears to have been positive for the vast majority of Americans, although vulnerable individuals may have found it too stressful or overstimulating to follow closely.

▶ Antidepressants and Suicidality

Controversy surrounding the antidepressant Prozac (fluoxetine hydrochloride) continued into 1991 as a group known as the Citizens Commission on Human Rights pursued a petition to the Food and Drug Administration (FDA) to have the drug removed from the pharmaceutical market. This followed publication in 1990 of case reports that Prozac appeared to cause an increase in suicidal behavior. The Citizens Commission on Human Rights made allegations that Prozac also induced violent behavior, had serious side effects, and was addictive. In July 1991, the FDA ruled that none of the claims against Prozac were scientifically founded; therefore, Prozac remained available as the most widely prescribed antidepressant in the United States. Both the FDA and the company that manufactures Prozac issued information clarifying concerns about the relationship between depression, suicide, and use of medication. Of central importance was the recognition that depression itself is highly associated with suicide, and that there is no way of distinguishing the role of a patient's underlying medical condition and the role of the drug in causing suicidal events.

When looking at the use of antidepressants in general, it appears that Prozac may have been singled out as the target of a special-interest group. There have been reports in the medical literature of other antidepressants, chemically unrelated to Prozac, causing an increase in suicidal behavior in small numbers of patients. In fact, there are no definite answers to the question of whether any antidepressant actually causes suicidal thinking or behavior in anyone. Research is needed to determine if there are indeed answers.

A recent article in the *Archives of General Psychiatry* reviewed the known facts concerning the emergence of suicidal thoughts and behavior during treatment with antidepressant drugs. The authors report that the appearance or increase of suicidal thinking and behavior in patients taking antidepressant medication has been noted in patients with various psychiatric diagnoses, but has not been proven to be associated with any specific type of medication. The authors also report that it is not known if certain antidepressants produce or aggravate suicidal thoughts in small, at-risk subgroups of psychiatric patients who need the drugs. They recommend that whatever antidepressant is used, the prescribing psychiatrist should monitor the patient for severity of depression and suicidal tendencies, aggressive thoughts or behavior, agitation, and akathesia (uncontrolled restlessness, which can be a side effect of certain medications). It is possible that increases in suicide in patients on antidepressants are more likely to occur in nonresponders, in those who have unrecognized akathesia, and in those with histories of attempted suicide. In any case, the psychiatrist should inform depressed patients who are on antidepressants that depressive symptoms and worsening or emergence of suicidal thoughts may occur occasionally during drug treatment. The patient should inform the psychiatrist as soon as possible if such symptoms develop.

While it must be acknowledged that the potential for antidepressants to induce suicide is unknown, clinical experience shows that the risk is very small. Millions of patients have been treated for depression with many different medications producing good results. The risk of not treating the seriously depressed and suicidal patient is far greater than the risk that might be attributed to the use of antidepressant medication itself.

▶ Advances in Panic Disorder

New research indicates that panic disorder—sudden attacks of absolute terror that trigger a racing heart, tingling hands, dizziness, and breathlessness —may affect as many as one in seven people at some point during their lifetime.

In the past five years, researchers have made significant progress in unraveling the causes of this long misunderstood and misdiagnosed condition. Imaging techniques have revealed that people prone to panic attacks tend to have abnormalities in the brain's limbic system, a network of nerve centers that regulates emotion. Some investigators believe that certain ingrained patterns of thinking play a role in determining the course of panic disorders.

But perhaps the most encouraging advances deal with treatment. Helpful drugs include imipramine and monamine oxidase (MAO) inhibitors, two tricyclic antidepressants that increase norepinephrine and serotonin levels in the brain, which reduces panic. The tranquilizer alprazolam has recently been approved specifically as a treatment for panic disorder. The controversial drug fluoxetine, more commonly called Prozac, increases serotonin levels in the brain and prevents nerve cells from reabsorbing it.

Drug therapy is usually prescribed in combination with psychological therapy. The most successful approach seems to be cognitive therapies, which teach people to recognize destructive thought patterns and change them.

▶ Attention Deficit Hyperactivity Disorder

Attention Deficit Hyperactivity Disorder (ADHD) is one of the most common behavior disorders found in children and adolescents. Psychiatric researchers have estimated that 3 to 5 percent of school-aged children are affected by ADHD. Many of these children continue to show signs of the disorder into adolescence, and it is now recognized that anywhere from 30 to 50 percent of people affected still show some signs of ADHD in adulthood. The chief symptoms of ADHD are lack of attention and concentration, hyperactivity, and impulsivity. These problems often make it difficult for children and adolescents to perform well in school. ADHD also can lead to potentially serious social-adjustment problems, including poor peer relationships, lack of social acceptance, and conduct problems at home and at school. Adults with ADHD often have difficulty holding a job, and they have trouble maintaining personal relationships. A small but still significant percentage of adults with ADHD, perhaps up to 25 percent, are involved in substance abuse and antisocial behavior.

Although ADHD is very common, for a long time there was controversy over its cause and even as to whether it actually existed. Recent research has helped to differentiate ADHD from other psychiatric and developmental disorders with which it might be confused. There is increasing evidence that ADHD has a neurobiological basis, which gives credence to its existence as a true disorder that can be treated with fairly specific approaches.

Important research conducted at the National Institute of Mental Health using a technique called positron emission tomography (PET) has demonstrated that the brains of hyperactive adults who are parents of ADHD children function differently from the brains of adults in a control group that did not show signs of ADHD. These studies measured glucose metabolism in different parts of the brain. The results showed that the brains of ADHD adults had regions of reduced glucose metabolism, indicating lower activity levels and probably decreased function in those regions. Areas of the brain found

Children with ADHD typically have serious social-adjustment problems, often resulting in poor peer relationships. Such children are often aggressive.

to be most affected were the premotor cortex and the superior prefrontal cortex.

These findings are thought to be very significant, since the premotor cortex and the superior prefrontal cortex have been shown previously to control attention and motor activity. Disorders of the prefrontal regions of the brain are known to result in inattentiveness, distractibility, and inability to inhibit inappropriate responses. Problems in the premotor cortex could cause motor restlessness. The researchers conducting these studies concluded that reduced glucose metabolism in the areas of the brain mentioned may play a significant role in the pathophysiology of ADHD.

Evidence that ADHD may have a neurophysiological basis helped to influence a very important decision made by the United States Department of Education in September 1991. The department determined at that time that children with ADHD could qualify for special education and related services solely on the basis of ADHD. Prior to this ruling, it had been very difficult for many ADHD children to obtain educational support services if they were doing poorly in school. Many schools essentially have not recognized ADHD as a unique problem, and they have viewed ADHD children as poorly motivated underachievers or as emotionally disturbed individuals.

Fortunately, the parents of ADHD children have teamed up and developed a strong lobby for them through the organization of support groups such as C.H.A.D.D. (Children with Attention Deficit Disorders) and the Attention Deficit Disorders Association. These groups have helped inform educators and legislators about the critical need to help ADHD children.

Provision of special-education services to ADHD children who need them is an important mental-health measure. Many of the social and emotional problems known to affect ADHD children actually result from their experience of academic failure and of being labeled as behavior problems at school. The ADHD child who receives special-education services, sometimes with the additional help of psychological counseling and medication, is much more likely to function better in adolescence and to go on to enjoy success in a career and family life in adulthood.

▶ Psychiatric Aspects of Chronic Fatigue Syndrome

Chronic fatigue syndrome (CFS) is a condition that was formally defined by the medical community in 1988 to characterize disabling fatigue of uncertain origin and of at least six months' duration. Reports of CFS have occurred worldwide. The disease so far has been found primarily in persons 20 to 50 years of age, with a preponderance in females. More recently, there have been reports of CFS affecting adolescents and even children. Despite the development of research criteria to define who should really be diagnosed as having CFS, there continues to be disagreement over what patient populations to include. This disagreement centers on differing opinions as to whether or not the etiology of CFS is organic or psychiatric.

It is known that many patients with CFS report onset following an infectious illness. There is, however, no convincing evidence linking any known infectious agent to CFS. While many patients show minor immunologic abnormalities on laboratory testing, the findings are inconsistent and of uncertain significance. There also have been no consistent findings pointing to any sort of muscle disease or loss of physical conditioning as part of the disease process.

Fueling the controversy concerning a psychiatric versus organic cause for CFS is that depression is found in from 50 to 70 percent of patients with the disorder. In about half of the depressed patients, the depression preceded the physical symptoms. Anxiety and somatic psychiatric disorders also have been found to occur at higher rates in CFS patients as compared to other patients with physical illnesses. Proponents of a psychiatric cause of CFS point out the fact that the rate of psychiatric disease is indeed higher among CFS patients than it is among those with other medical conditions. They also note that when patients with CFS are systematically interviewed, they often report previous episodes of psychiatric illness. Finally, those who see

CFS as psychiatrically based cite findings that psychological stress itself can lead to disturbances in neurohormonal and immunologic function that may result in illness.

Proponents of an organic cause of CFS note the sudden onset of the malady in patients who had been in good health; findings of sore throat, enlarged lymph nodes, and low-grade fever in some patients; and serological and immunologic abnormalities that accompany fatigue. If CFS is primarily organic, then apparent psychiatric disorders might be secondary to the effects of the acute illness and to the stress of suffering from prolonged disabling fatigue.

Given the diversity and inconsistency of findings in chronic fatigue syndrome, it may be that CFS inadvertently has become a broad label for a heterogeneous group of illnesses, which would include some that are primarily psychiatric and some primarily organic. A recent article in the *American Journal of Psychiatry* addressing the CFS issue notes how cultural factors may influence medical diagnosis and acceptance of the diagnosis by patients. The authors note that in the past several decades, the diagnosis and treatment of infectious diseases and the emerging science of immunology have been at the forefront of advances in medicine, and these facts have shaped opinion as to the causes of syndromes such as CFS. Some patients with CFS may actually have psychiatric disorders, which they do not want to acknowledge. The diagnosis of CFS becomes for them a legitimate "medical" reason for fatigue, emotional distress, and associated psychophysiological symptoms. It allows patients to withdraw from situations they find intolerable on the basis of being sick, rather than by their own volition.

This does not mean that all cases of chronic fatigue syndrome should be linked to this psychological mechanism. It is very likely that some patients diagnosed as having CFS have had an acute illness, possibly viral in nature, that has caused their symptoms. Further research is needed to differentiate the various types of cases now being grouped together under the diagnostic heading of CFS. Eventually the diagnosis may be limited to a specific subgroup, or it may be abandoned altogether.

It should be noted, however, that most chronic-fatigue-syndrome patients as they are now identified do have some form of psychiatric symptoms. Whether the symptoms are primary or secondary, it is important that they be treated, since CFS patients tend to recover better when their psychiatric symptoms are addressed. Treatment generally should be focused on the depression and anxiety which appear to be the most common psychiatric problems in CFS patients.

Stephen G. Underwood, M.D.

Nutrition and Diet

▶ Food-Labeling Legislation

During the past decade, as Americans began to change their diets to meet the U.S. Dietary Guidelines, manufacturers challenged the existing food-labeling regulations by making disease-prevention claims. Vital nutrition information was not available on most products, and shoppers were often deceived into a purchase based on seeing a bold health message (such as "no cholesterol") on the front of a package. Although sodium-content labeling was added in the late 1980s, no major changes have been made in food-labeling regulations by the Food and Drug Administration (FDA) since the early 1970s.

Congress took action in November 1990 by passing the Nutrition Labeling and Education Act (NLEA) to encourage the FDA to propose tighter regulations on food labeling and health claims made by the manufacturers. As a result, on November 6, 1991, the FDA, with the support of the U.S. Department of Agriculture (USDA), announced the most comprehensive set of food-labeling regulations in history. The FDA oversees packaged products, including produce, while the USDA monitors the meat and poultry industries. Although in the past these two agencies did not require the same standards for food labeling, their latest proposal represents a cooperative effort to provide consumers with educational and truthful food packaging.

Nutrition Information. The key components of the regulations require that practically all packaged foods supply nutritional information about the product. Only small packages (no larger than a package of mints), most spices, restaurant food, and products sold by companies with sales of less than $500,000 per year will be exempt. Labeling of nutrients for the 20 most popular varieties of fresh fish, fruits, and vegetables will be encouraged, but initially not mandatory. The USDA will also allow voluntary disclosure of nutrition information for meat and poultry producers until 1995, when their disclosure, too, will become mandatory. Historically, nutrition information was voluntary except for companies that made a nutritional claim, such as "dietetic," or those that fortified a product with vitamins or minerals. The new regulations also require that the 235 standardized foods, such as mayonnaise, which had been exempt, must now list ingredients.

The nutrition information required on labels includes serving size, and the amount per serving of the following: total number of calories, calories de-

rived from fat, total fat, saturated fat, cholesterol, total carbohydrates, complex carbohydrates, all sugars in one number, fiber, protein, sodium, vitamins A and C, calcium, and iron. The FDA will set the standards for serving sizes, eliminating the problem of manufacturers manipulating the portion to make the nutrition appear healthier.

Nine Basic Descriptors. Consumers will find it easier to shop for healthier foods once they learn the new food-labeling vocabulary. The FDA will allow the use of nine core terms to describe foods: *free, low, high, source of, reduced, light, less, more,* and *fresh.* When combined with certain nutrients, these nine descriptors also have precise definitions. For example, if a product is labeled "low-fat," it must contain no more than 3 grams of fat per serving. The consumer will be guaranteed that if he or she purchases a "low-fat" product, he or she isn't buying an impostor. The USDA will have two other terms, *lean* and *extra-lean,* which apply just to meat and poultry. Consumer groups have praised the FDA for banning many misleading terms such as "no-cholesterol." This phrase has been used on vegetable oils, margarines, potato chips, and high-fat crackers and cookies. Since "no-cholesterol" does not mean low-fat, it is deceiving to have this term on vegetable oil, which is 100 percent fat.

Reform on Health Claims. The proposal also addresses what health claims manufacturers may make about the relationships between diet and disease. The FDA will allow the use of just four health claims that are supported by scientific evidence: adequate calcium intake will reduce one's risk of developing osteoporosis; a low sodium intake helps control high blood pressure; a low-fat diet reduces one's risk of developing heart disease; and a low-fat diet may prevent cancer. For example, the manufacturer of a product that meets the FDA's definition of "low-fat" can claim the food lowers one's risk of cancer and/or heart disease. The FDA will continue researching the relationships between a high-fiber diet and cancer, and between a high-fiber diet and heart disease, to decide if they are legitimate health claims.

While there is some concern that the proposed food-labeling terminology may confuse shoppers, the overall response from consumer-advocacy groups has been very positive. Strong public education about the new food-labeling regulations, which is being planned by the FDA, will be a must to ensure consumer understanding. Health professionals must also continue to educate consumers about the U.S. Dietary Guidelines, since the nutrition information will not make sense to individuals who do not know the basis of a healthy diet. While costs to the manufacturers and supermarkets for the labeling proposals have been estimated at $1.6 billion over 20 years, savings in health-care costs could exceed $100 billion over the same period, as consumers improve their eating habits and lower their risk of disease. The FDA and USDA plan to have regulations finalized by November 8, 1992, and effective in supermarkets by 1993.

▶ Cholesterol Guidelines for Children

In April 1991, the National Cholesterol Education Program (NCEP), sponsored by the National Heart, Lung and Blood Institute, released the first recommendations for managing cholesterol levels in children and adolescents. A thorough review of the scientific literature led the expert panel—comprised of pediatricians, cardiologists, nutritionists, and epidemiologists—to conclude that atherosclerosis (hardening of the arteries) begins in childhood and continues into adulthood, often leading to coronary heart disease. Furthermore, children and adolescents in the United States have higher blood cholesterol and higher intakes of saturated fat and cholesterol compared to children in other countries.

The NCEP panel suggests a two-level plan to lower cholesterol levels in our youth. The first is the population-approach, or Step-One Diet, focusing on all healthy children over the age of 2, which recommends that children eat a wide variety of foods that contain sufficient calories for normal growth. In addition, saturated-fat intake should be less than 10 percent of calories, total fat should be no more than 30 percent of daily calories, and dietary cholesterol should be less than 300 milligrams (mg) per day. By switching to skim or low-fat dairy products and by limiting eggs, fatty meats, and all visible fat such as mayonnaise, margarine, and oil, these goals can easily be achieved. Adequate calories may be obtained by increasing intake of fruits, vegetables, and grains, which do not contain cholesterol or saturated fats.

The second level is called an individualized approach, which seeks to identify those children and adolescents who are at the greatest risk of having elevated blood cholesterol as adults. Although routine screening of all children could identify every youth with high cholesterol, the panel, after careful consideration, decided against mass screenings. The panel wanted to avoid the possibility that many children may be labeled as having a "disease," which could cause undue fear for them. Second, the panel had concerns that universal screening might lead to the overuse of cholesterol-lowering medications. Instead, the committee recommends selectively testing those children and teens who have a family history of heart disease or at least one parent with an elevated blood-cholesterol level (adult cholesterol levels above 240 mg per deciliter are considered high).

Many shopping malls and supermarkets are sponsoring cholesterol-testing drives. Patrons can use the results to assess their risk of developing heart disease.

According to the panel, if a young person has a parent with high blood cholesterol, the initial test should simply be for total cholesterol. However, if there is a family history of cardiovascular disease, the first test should be a total lipoprotein analysis. The lipoprotein analysis provides total cholesterol levels, with exact breakdowns of high-density lipoproteins (HDL, which are considered "good" cholesterol), low-density lipoproteins (LDL, which are considered "bad" cholesterol), and triglycerides. When a youth's total cholesterol test results are high, then a more specific lipoprotein analysis should also be done.

Treatment is determined based on the average of two LDL levels. The same dietary guidelines recommended in the population-approach (Step-One Diet) would be used as treatment for children and teenagers with "borderline" or "high" LDL levels. If, after three months, the LDL level has not decreased in a youth with a "high" level, the diet is modified further. This Step-Two Diet limits dietary cholesterol to less than 200 mg per day and saturated fat to less than 7 percent of total calories. The NCEP panel recommends counseling from a registered dietitian to ensure nutritional adequacy from the Step-Two Diet.

The panel advises that drug therapy be used only in youths over age 10 with very high LDL levels that have not responded successfully to diet modification after six months to a year.

The NCEP's cholesterol-lowering guidelines for youths will need strong involvement by parents, schools, health professionals, government, food manufacturers, and the media to effect change in the eating habits of American children.

▶ Television Commercials and Children

In July 1991, the Committee on Communications for the Academy of Pediatrics released a policy statement on the commercialization of children's television, based on their opinion that it exploits young people. Since young children do not understand that advertisements are intended to market products, the committee feels that commercials aimed at kids are unjust.

Foods and toys are the most commonly advertised products. Toys also appear as characters in a program (for example, Smurfs), a common marketing technique known as "program-length commercials." The Academy of Pediatrics defines a "program-length commercial" as a program that promotes a toy based on the program within two years of its commencement. Exempt from this definition are programs such as "Sesame Street" that rely on the marketing of their products to maintain their existence. Since toys are used to promote foods, and foods are often named after toys, there is a rebound effect in which each product promotes sales of the other.

Children's television watching, averaging more than three hours per day, has been linked with obesity and elevated cholesterol levels, both major health problems of the young in this country. During children's programming, the food commercials often featured are for high-fat, high-calorie snacks, and research indicates that regular viewing of these ads leads to a higher consumption of these calorically dense foods. In 1987, 71 percent of all television commercials were for food, with 34 percent for high-fat snacks and almost 30 percent for sugary cereals. Unable to comprehend the relationship between food and health problems, young children are unfairly influenced to make choices that adversely affect their health.

The Committee on Communications recommends that materials be developed to help parents teach children that commercials are intended to sell products. They encourage that pediatricians, parents, and communities closely monitor children's programming to ensure that the programs are following the limits on commercial time set by the Children's Television Act of 1990. The committee further advises that the Academy of Pediatrics continue to push for elimination of "program-length commercials" and support the development of alternative programs for children. Since children are often not well-informed enough to make healthy food choices, the committee also recommends that advertisements of food directed at children be abolished. Finally, they encourage studies that examine how shopping habits begun in childhood affect choices made as adults.

▶ Proposal for Vegetarian Food Groups

On April 8, 1991, the Physicians' Committee for Responsible Medicine (PCRM), a nonprofit organization of physicians, made its recommendations to the USDA for sweeping changes in the "Basic Four" food groups. Since 1956 nutritionists, home-economics teachers, and other health educators have used the "Basic Four" food groups to teach people how to follow a balanced diet. The "Basic Four" graphic, displayed as a wheel or a chart with four equal quadrants, was designed from information from the USDA's "Food for Fitness," a daily food-guide mobile.

The PCRM's new food groups include whole grains, legumes, and vegetables and fruits. Animal protein and dairy products would become optional choices, losing their position as separate food groups. The PCRM encourages consumers to eat a variety of foods from these plant-based groups, and suggests eating only small amounts, if any, of meat, dairy products, sweets, and fats.

The organization bases its recommendations on epidemiological and clinical studies that have shown that people who consume a diet low in fat, high in fiber, and with little or no animal protein have the lowest incidences of heart disease, cancer, and obesity. The PCRM feels that the old "Basic Four" food groups encourage an excessive intake of protein, which is often high in fat and fails to promote a sufficient intake of fiber. Another drawback cited by the PCRM is that the old food groups are not nutritionally adequate, since they were initially designed in 1953 to provide 1,200 calories and 80 percent of the Recommended Daily Allowances (RDAs) for the levels of protein, vitamins A and C, thiamine, riboflavin, niacin, calcium, and iron. Since the 1950s, however, nine nutrients have been added to

Young "couch potatoes" are at heightened risk for developing obesity and elevated cholesterol levels, two widespread health problems in American children.

the RDAs, levels for some nutrients have been changed, and the role of fiber in the diet has been clarified. These changes are not reflected in the "Basic Four" food groups.

While the PCRM should be commended for its efforts to effect dietary changes that may lower disease risk in this country, most nutritionists and physicians feel that its proposal has some weaknesses. While a strict vegetarian diet can be healthy with careful meal planning, the average person would have trouble consuming a balanced diet from just plant-based food groups. Many Americans—especially pregnant women, children, and teenagers—already do not meet the RDAs for calcium, iron, zinc, and important B vitamins. Lean animal protein and skim dairy products are the best sources of these nutrients. The PCRM intends for legumes, including tofu and other soy products, to replace animal sources of protein. While legumes are high in protein and fiber and low in fat, the reality is that most people are not willing to eat them on a daily basis. According to Mary Abbott Hess, M.S., R.D., past president of the American Dietetic Association (ADA), although the ADA continues to promote a diet with emphasis on whole grains, legumes, and fruits and vegetables, the association cannot support the PCRM's recommendations to omit meat and dairy products from the four food groups. For similar reasons, the American Medical Association refused to support the PCRM's vegetarian-food-groups proposal.

▶ USDA's Food Pyramid

The USDA has been conducting research on its own to design a nutrition graphic to replace the "Basic Four" that would teach people how to put the U.S. Dietary Guidelines into action.

In April 1991, the USDA released information about research results being conducted on their new graphic, the "Eating Right Food Pyramid." While the "Basic Four" food groups give nearly equal weight to the protein, dairy, grain, and fruit/vegetable groups, the new pyramid design gives more emphasis to grains, fruits, and vegetables, and less prominence to dairy products and meats. Grains make up the base of the pyramid, fruits and vegetables are the next-highest level, meats and dairy products are in the third and smaller level, and sugars and fats would make up the small apex. Based on our present knowledge of the relationship of a low-fat, high-fiber diet in lowering risk of heart disease and cancer, this updated design would be a progressive guide to educate Americans about implementing a healthy diet.

Shortly after this information from the USDA was made public, articles appeared in several newspapers, including the *Washington Post,* that stated that the food-pyramid design had been shelved.

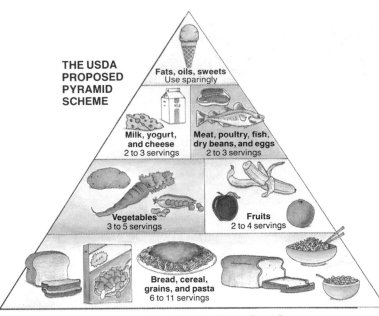

THE USDA PROPOSED PYRAMID SCHEME

Fats, oils, sweets
Use sparingly

Milk, yogurt, and cheese
2 to 3 servings

Meat, poultry, fish, dry beans, and eggs
2 to 3 servings

Vegetables
3 to 5 servings

Fruits
2 to 4 servings

Bread, cereal, grains, and pasta
6 to 11 servings

The USDA has proposed the "Eating Right Food Pyramid" as a replacement for the traditional "Basic Four" food groups to teach how to follow a balanced diet.

Pressure from the meat and dairy industry was given as the reason why the USDA dropped its design. But according to Johna Pierce of the Human Nutrition Information Service of the USDA, the press had been misinformed, and publication of the graphic has been postponed because of concern that the pyramid design may be misunderstood by children and low-literacy adults. The USDA has received letters from teachers and nutritionists across the country, commenting that children may think that fats and sweets are the healthiest foods since they are at the top of the food pyramid.

When the USDA began research on this project, the goal was to design a graphic that would be understood by adults with a high-school education. Under the new USDA chief, Edward Madigan, the focus of the research has shifted to developing a nutritional visual aid that will reach the broadest group of people. According to the USDA's Pierce, this additional research should be finished by January 1992, and one or more new designs will be published during the year.

Nutritionists, registered dietitians, and several professional nutrition associations have strongly supported USDA's food-pyramid graphic. The American Dietetic Association, the American Cancer Society, and the Society of Nutrition Education all sent letters of support for this design to the USDA, requesting that the "Eating Right Food Pyramid" be published.

▶ Pregnancy and Breast-Feeding

Folic-Acid Supplementation. The results of the Medical Research Council (MRC) Vitamin Study, published in July 1991 in the British medical journal *Lancet,* revealed that supplementation with folic acid, a B vitamin, started before pregnancy can prevent neural-tube defects (NTDs), conditions in which there is incomplete closure of the spine. Since these defects occur in the first four weeks after conception, prescription of folic acid at the first prenatal visit is usually too late.

In the study a total of 1,817 women who had previously had an NTD birth were assigned randomly to one of four groups. The first group received only 4 mg of folic acid daily; the second, folic acid plus other vitamins; the third, a multivitamin without folic acid; the fourth group, no vitamin supplements. The prevalence of NTDs in the group of women receiving folic acid was only 1 percent, compared to 3.5 percent in the women in groups that did not receive this vitamin. The researchers ascertained that it was folic acid specifically that provided the protective effect, not other vitamins.

In response to this British study, in August the Centers for Disease Control (CDC) released a report recommending that all women at risk for an NTD birth take folic-acid supplements prior to conception. However, according to Carol Suitor of the Food and Nutrition Board of the National Academy of Sciences (NAS), the Subcommittee on Pregnancy has not made any new recommendations on nutritional supplementation since the release of their publication "Nutrition During Pregnancy" in 1990. That publication recommended that healthy women with balanced diets only need supplementation with 30 mg of iron during the last six months of pregnancy.

The MRC Vitamin Study advises that public-health measures be taken to ensure that all women who become pregnant have an adequate intake of folic acid. The best sources of folic acid are spinach, other leafy green vegetables, legumes, oranges, bananas, and strawberries. Since it is unclear yet whether women who are not at risk for NTDs should take folic-acid supplements, efforts must be made to get adequate amounts from foods. The study also suggests that manufacturers should consider investigating the value of fortifying staple foods with folic acid.

Nutrition During Lactation. In February 1991, the Institute of Medicine and the NAS released new dietary guidelines for women who breast-feed. The publication, *Nutrition During Lactation,* also made important recommendations to health professionals who must educate lactating women.

While many lactating women take a multivitamin and mineral supplement, the publication advises against routine supplementation. Since women who breast-feed are at risk for deficiencies of calcium, magnesium, zinc, folic acid, and vitamin B$_6$, health educators should counsel them to follow a well-balanced diet of at least 1,800 calories per day. Certain groups of lactating women may need supplements to avoid nutritional problems. Low-income women, teenagers, and women on restricted diets—such as those who are trying to lose weight or are vegetarians—need careful assessment.

Another widespread practice by lactating mothers is to eliminate certain foods in the maternal diet in order to treat colic or allergy in the infant. According to *Nutrition During Lactation,* it is unwise to exclude major food sources unless an oral-elimination challenge study reveals that the mother is intolerant of a specific food or that the baby reacts to certain foods eaten by the mother.

The publication also encourages health educators to provide women who plan to breast-feed with information about weight change during lactation. While the average weight loss is 1 to 2 pounds per month after the first month postpartum, some women do not lose weight and may even gain. Dieting women should be advised against losing more than 4.5 pounds per month, since greater losses may decrease their milk supply. The publication also cautions against the use of liquid diets and weight-loss medications during lactation.

Extensive education is available to women about pregnancy and infant care, but less attention is given to counseling women about lactation. According to *Nutrition During Lactation,* health professionals should provide a concrete care plan during

Healthy nursing mothers do not need vitamin supplementation. Instead, these women should follow a well-balanced diet of at least 1,800 calories per day.

the prenatal period for women who plan to breast-feed, a plan that includes nutrition counseling and screening for dietary problems.

▶ Lead Exposure from Wine

Data collected over a two-year period by the Bureau of Alcohol, Tobacco and Firearms (BATF) from analysis of foreign and domestic wines sold in the United States revealed potentially dangerous levels of lead. The source of the contamination is lead-foil wraps, frequently used to cover the tops of wine bottles, not only to protect against insect infestation, but also for decorative purposes.

All wines were analyzed by, first, drawing a direct sample from the bottle without the wine touching the bottle's rim, and, second, by pouring a sample of wine from the bottle. Nearly all the wines analyzed contained traces of lead. However, the 250 poured samples of wine showed higher lead quantities than the wines sampled by the direct method. While imported wines contained more lead than domestic ones, overall the levels ranged from 3 to 180 micrograms per liter (μg/l) of wine. According to the BATF, if wine leaks between the cork and the wrap and the foil seal deteriorates, lead salts may be deposited on the rim, causing contamination of the wine when it is poured into a glass, and, consequently, a potential health risk.

In September 1991, the FDA and the BATF announced their plan to decrease consumers' exposure to lead from table wines. First, the agencies will issue a proposal to eliminate the use of lead-foil wraps to cover the neck and cork of wine bottles. Their second step is to establish a limit on lead residues in wines. An interim lead limit of 300 parts per billion was set by the FDA while the agency evaluates more information. As the BATF continues to randomly retest wines, manufacturers will be notified so they can remove wines that exceed this limit from the marketplace.

According to the FDA, long-term exposure to the lead levels in wine could pose a health risk to consumers, particularly for pregnant and lactating women. Even small amounts of lead may harm a fetus's or nursing infant's brain function and affect the capacity for learning. While pregnant women are advised to avoid alcohol due to other health risks, it is not uncommon for a nursing mother to drink a glass of wine. Both pregnant and lactating women need to be aware of the potential danger that threatens their unborn child or infant from continued exposure to lead in wine.

Consumers who drink lead-foil-wrapped wines can decrease their risk by removing the foil wrap and wiping the neck of the bottle and cork with a cloth, preferably moistened with vinegar or lemon juice, before pouring the wine.

Maria Guglielmino, M.S., R.D.

Occupational Health

▶ Electromagnetic Radiation

Workers concerned about possible reproductive-health problems caused by exposure to the electromagnetic fields (EMFs) generated by video display terminals (VDTs) received some reassurance in 1991. A study of more than 2,000 female telephone operators found "no excess risk of spontaneous abortion among women who used VDTs during the first trimester of pregnancy," according to the report published in the *New England Journal of Medicine* (3/14/91) by researchers from the National Institute for Occupational Safety and Health.

The study found that rates for spontaneous abortion among VDT-exposed pregnant women were 14.8 percent, versus 15.9 percent for unexposed pregnancies. Among women who used VDTs for up to 25 hours per week, the spontaneous-abortion rate of 17.2 percent was slightly, but not significantly, higher than the 15.6 percent found among women not using VDTs.

The study did not address the relationship between spontaneous abortion and physical or psychological stress factors, nor did it examine other adverse reproductive outcomes such as early fetal loss, difficulties in conception, and birth defects.

The possible association between childhood leukemia and exposure to electromagnetic fields has been at issue since 1979. Now a preliminary investigation of telephone lineworkers indicates an association between exposure to low levels of electromagnetic fields in their work and an increased risk of contracting leukemia. At a June 1991 meeting of the Bioelectromagnetic Society, Dr. Genevieve Matanoski of the Johns Hopkins School of Public Health in Baltimore, Maryland, said she and her colleagues studied 124 men who died of leukemia between 1975 and 1980, and 337 controls who were matched for age, year of hire, and company. The Johns Hopkins team found a higher leukemia risk among workers whose EMF exposures were above the median for the study group. The researchers cautioned that the study did not prove a cause-and-effect relationship, and they said that more studies were needed.

In a related development, state troopers around the country are claiming that they contracted cancer from the hand-held radar guns they use to catch speeding motorists. Two California officers who habitually rested the radar guns on their laps developed cancers on their legs. A Connecticut trooper blames his radar gun for testicular cancer. In other states, rare cancers of the eye and eyelid have afflicted state-police officers who use the gun. Al-

Police officers around the country are claiming that they contracted cancer from the hand-held radar guns they use to catch speeding motorists.

though the cancer cases may be coincidental, police departments are not taking any chances. In Connecticut the state police have banned the use of hand-held radar guns altogether.

▶ Shift Work

About 20 percent of American workers do shift work, performing their duties on evenings, at night, or on rotating shifts. In late September 1991, the Congressional Office of Technology Assessment (OTA) drew attention to the health consequences of the hours people work in its study *Biological Rhythms: Implications for the Worker.* OTA warned that "any work schedule that requires people to work when they normally would be sleeping conflicts with and can cause disruption in workers' circadian cycles."

The consequences of shift work cited by the study include decreased well-being, chronic malaise, and poor sleep; in addition, shift workers have a higher rate of cardiovascular disease and negative reproductive outcomes, such as preterm births and babies with low birth weight. However, OTA concluded that there was too little data yet available to draw firm conclusions as to how shift work affects the safety of workers and the public.

▶ Solvents

Approximately 10 million workers in the United States are potentially exposed to solvents, which have been recognized for many years to have an adverse effect on the central nervous system. For example, a study in the September 1991 *American Journal of Industrial Medicine* found that painters who were exposed to low levels of solvents for a period of a week experienced "significantly increased" occurrences of slips, trips, and falls.

Along with neurotoxic effects, researchers in 1991 found further evidence that solvent exposure can result in adverse reproductive outcomes. A study by California researchers in the May 1991 *Journal of Occupational Medicine* reported that women exposed to solvents during their first trimester of pregnancy were three to four times more likely to have a spontaneous abortion than were their nonexposed counterparts. The study also found that women working in electronics assembly were five times more likely than normal to deliver a low-birth-weight baby, though researchers cautioned that other factors, such as exposure to heavy metals and ergonomic stresses, could have contributed to the problem.

A larger study of women exposed to perchloroethylene, trichloroethylene, or paint thinners found that they were twice as likely as unexposed women to suffer spontaneous abortions. The study, published in the August 1991 *American Journal of Industrial Medicine,* did not show a consistent dose-response effect when exposures of more than 10 hours per week were compared to exposures of 10 hours or less. But based on this and other studies, researchers said it seemed "prudent" to recommend that "workplace policies be developed to minimize the potential reproductive risks of solvent exposure."

Reproductive risks stemming from solvent exposure may not be confined to women alone. A study in Finland of the effects of paternal occupational exposure on spontaneous abortion found that there was an increased relative risk of spontaneous abortion among the wives of men exposed to ethylene oxide, chemicals used in rubber production, and solvents used in refineries. The risk of spontaneous abortion also was higher among wives of rubber-products workers than among wives of unexposed men. However, the Finnish researchers, reporting in the August 1991 *American Journal of Public Health,* cautioned that their findings were "only suggestive," given that the rate of spontaneous abortion in the study population (8.8 percent) was nearly the same as among Finnish women as a whole (8.9 percent).

▶ Secondhand Tobacco Smoke

Support for branding environmental (or secondhand) tobacco smoke (ETS) as a significant occupational-health threat continued to accumulate during 1991. In a June *Current Intelligence Bulletin,* the National Institute for Occupational Safety and Health (NIOSH) recommended that ETS be regarded "as a potential occupational carcinogen," and that "exposures to ETS be reduced to the lowest

The National Institute for Occupational Safety and Health has recommended that secondhand smoke be classified as a "potential occupational carcinogen."

feasible concentration." NIOSH noted that non-smokers living with smokers had a 30 percent greater risk of developing lung cancer than nonsmokers living with nonsmokers. Also, NIOSH cited studies indicating a possible association between exposure to ETS and an increased risk of heart disease among nonsmokers.

▶ AIDS And Health-Care Workers

Health-care workers were a focus of concern about possible workplace exposure to the human immunodeficiency virus (HIV), which causes AIDS. In the January 1991 *American Journal of Medicine,* a study of medical residents at three San Francisco hospitals found that approximately 25 percent of first-year interns were pricked by needles contaminated with the AIDS virus. Researchers also reported that 19 percent of the medical residents were exposed to HIV-infected blood, and 36 percent were exposed to blood from patients considered at high risk for having HIV infection. Noting that 12 percent of the needle pricks occurred during recapping, the study's authors concluded that the "best way to decrease health-care workers' exposure rate to infected blood is to redesign blood drawing and intravenous infusion equipment so that workers' hands always remain behind the needle."

In a six-month study of surgical services at an Atlanta, Georgia, hospital, researchers found that one or more operating-room personnel had contact with blood during 30 percent of the procedures monitored by trained observers. The study, published in the *Journal of the American Medical Association* (3/27/91), recorded 147 instances of blood contact, with injuries from sharp objects, and 3 percent resulting from mucous-membrane contacts (in these instances, eye splashes). The authors said

most of the blood contact could have been prevented by better use of barrier precautions such as gloves or face shields.

In 1987 the Centers for Disease Control (CDC) recommended that all hospitals adopt "universal precautions," in which all blood and body fluids are assumed to be infected with blood-borne pathogens. In a study of two Richmond, Virginia, hospitals, researchers found that observing universal precautions decreased the incidence of occupational exposure to blood and body fluids. Physicians were asked to record their daily exposures with blood and body fluids before and after such universal precautions were implemented. The results, published in the *Journal of the American Medical Association* (3/6/91), reported that direct-exposure incidents dropped from 5.07 to 2.66 exposures per physician per patient-care month.

▶ Farm Workers

The use of chemicals to control pests and diseases has become a way of life on most farms. Recent studies now indicate, however, that this chemical dependence may be taking a serious toll on farm workers' health. For instance, farm workers who use herbicides, particularly 2,4-dichlorophenoxyacetic acid, have been linked to higher-than-expected rates of non-Hodgkin's lymphoma.

In July 1991, the U.S. General Accounting Office (GAO) warned that agricultural employees may be suffering from 20,000 to 300,000 acute illnesses and injuries annually as a result of exposures to pesticides. The problem may be particularly serious for children who work on farms, GAO pointed out, because doses are more potent due to their smaller body weight and because their developing systems

Certain chemicals that act as herbicides and pesticides have been linked with a heightened incidence of acute disease in farmers who use them.

may be more susceptible to the toxic effects of pesticides. GAO said farm workers receive little information about chemical hazards, regulations to protect them are inadequate, and enforcement of federal laws regulating pesticides, child labor, and field sanitation is lax.

▶ Cancer in the Workplace

Two studies of well-known occupational-health risks confirmed that they pose a threat to workers. In a study of workers exposed to dioxin at a dozen chemical plants, an increase in cancer deaths was found, though the risk was not as great as previous studies had indicated. For those exposed to high levels of dioxin (approximately 500 times higher than among the general population), researchers from NIOSH found a 46 percent increase in overall cancer deaths and a 42 percent increase in cancers of the respiratory tract. The study, published in the *New England Journal of Medicine* (1/24/91), found that, among the more than 5,000 workers surveyed, there was no significant increase in Hodgkin's disease, non-Hodgkin's lymphoma, or cancers of the stomach, liver, and nose—all cancers associated in earlier studies with dioxin exposure.

Workers exposed to vinyl chloride suffered significantly higher rates of death from cancer of the liver, cancer of the brain and central nervous system, and emphysema and chronic obstructive pulmonary disease. These results, gathered for a mortality study published in the September 1991 *American Journal of Industrial Medicine,* were derived from the records of 10,173 men who had worked for at least one year in jobs in which there was exposure to vinyl chloride. Employment occurred prior to January 1973 in 37 plants in the United States. The study found 37 deaths from cancer of the liver, compared to the 5.8 expected, and 23 deaths involving cancer of the brain and central nervous system, compared to the 12.9 expected.

In March, NIOSH issued an alert, warning that epidemiologic evidence "clearly associates" O-toluidine and aniline, chemicals used in the manufacture of dyes, pharmaceuticals, pesticides, and rubber, with an increased risk of bladder cancer. Chronic exposure to the chemicals has previously been linked to bladder cancer, but other bladder carcinogens were present as well. Over 60,000 workers were exposed to the chemicals during the period from 1981 through 1983. NIOSH recommended that exposures be reduced to the lowest feasible concentrations.

Radiation-exposed workers at the Oak Ridge National Laboratory in Tennessee were found to suffer a 63 percent higher death rate from leukemia than white American males in general. In a *Journal of the American Medical Association* (3/20/91) article, researchers said they examined 8,318 men who

Asbestos removal from buildings continues (above) despite reports suggesting that occupants of well-maintained buildings need not worry about exposure.

worked in different capacities at Oak Ridge from 1943 to 1972. For all but four years, the workers were exposed to an average annual radiation dose of 0.1 rem, significantly below the 5.0-rem standard set by the Nuclear Regulatory Commission (NRC). Some 638 workers were exposed to radiation at a dosage higher than 5.0. Despite uncertainties in the study, such as the role of smoking or exposure to other hazardous materials, some experts said the study could indicate that current radiation-exposure safety limits are too high.

▶ Asbestos

Asbestos has been well-documented as a cause of cancer and pulmonary disease among workers. But in recent years, concerns have been raised about the risk it poses to occupants of public and commercial buildings. On September 25, 1991, the Health Effects Institute-Asbestos Research released a review of current research that found that well-maintained buildings do not pose any greater risk of asbestos exposure than does the outside air. The panel said there was too little risk of asbestos exposure to office workers to justify removing intact asbestos-containing materials. The report warned that custodians and maintenance workers do face a higher potential risk of exposure.

Some asbestos experts criticized the report, claiming it failed to recognize that asbestos levels will inevitably increase in buildings as they age and the asbestos is disturbed.

Stephen G. Minter

Pediatrics

▶ Lead Poisoning

In October 1991, the Centers for Disease Control (CDC) issued its summary statement "Preventing Lead Poisoning in Young Children." This statement addresses current recommendations for both screening and treatment. But perhaps most important, new guidelines were set that significantly lowered the blood-lead level thought to cause lead toxicity.

The CDC statement is quite clear in defining lead poisoning as one of the most common and preventable pediatric-health problems in the United States. One report estimates that 17 percent of all American preschool children have blood-lead levels greater than 15 milligrams per deciliter (mg/dl).

Lead is present throughout the environment as a result of its numerous industrial uses. Previously, airborne lead from the combustion of leaded gasoline was the major source of lead in the United States. Since the Environmental Protection Agency (EPA) ordered the reduction of almost all gasoline lead during the 1970s and 1980s, this airborne source has considerably lessened. The primary sources of lead exposure for children today are lead-based paint, soil contamination (from deposited airborne lead), and drinking water.

Lead has no known biological value, and consequently, all effects of lead on children are adverse. Children are at high risk for lead exposure because they have more hand-to-mouth activity than adults and because gastrointestinal absorption of lead in children is more efficient. The principal effects of lead are on the red blood cells of the bone marrow, the peripheral and central nervous systems, and the kidneys. The deleterious effects of lead on the red-blood-cell system are reversible; however, the effects on the nervous system and kidneys may be permanent.

The acute central-nervous-system effects of lead poisoning have been well recognized. The effects of chronic low-level lead intoxication, however, have not been so well appreciated. Two recently published studies have highlighted what appear to be significant effects of chronically low lead levels in children. In one study on the long-term effects of exposure to low doses of lead, an 11-year follow-up report concluded that even low doses of lead exposure in young children are associated with persistent abnormalities in a number of educational skills. The second study analyzed previous reports relating low-level lead exposure and the IQ of children, and concluded that low-level lead exposure is associated with deficits in measurable intelligence.

Even low levels of lead can have detrimental health effects on children. Children generally acquire lead poisoning through hand-to-mouth activity.

Based on the conclusions that lead is harmful to children at low levels and that lead poisoning is not solely a problem of inner-city and minority children, the CDC report made revised screening recommendations. These include the measuring of blood-lead levels in children who are at greatest risk for high-dose lead exposure at six months of age. Additionally, measuring blood-lead levels in children who are at low risk is recommended at 12 to 15 months of age. Since no socioeconomic group, geographic area, or racial or ethnic population is unexposed to lead, universal screening is recommended. The report also lowered the recommended intervention level from 25 mg/dl to 10 mg/dl. Since the previously used screening test for lead poisoning, erythrocyte protoporphyrin (EP), is not sensitive enough to identify children with blood-lead levels below 25 mg/dl, the screening test of choice is now blood-lead-level measurement.

In January 1991, the Food and Drug Administration (FDA) approved *succimer* for treating children with lead levels above 45 mg/dl. The CDC, however, emphasizes that succimer is not a substitute for effective environmental decontamination.

▶ Surfactant Therapy for Respiratory-Distress Syndrome

Neonatal respiratory-distress syndrome (RDS) is the most common of the acute severe respiratory diseases occurring in the first days after birth. Primarily a disease of prematurely born infants, in RDS the infant's attempts to breathe are impaired by the immaturity of the alveoli, the air cells of the lungs, and by inadequate surfactant, secretions that add to the elasticity of lung tissue. Breathing difficulty and cyanosis, bluish skin due to poor oxygenation of the blood, result as the volume of functional lung decreases.

The previous mortality rates of 50 percent or more have been substantially reduced over the past decade due to technical advances in mechanical-ventilation and drug therapy. Surfactant-replacement therapy has been added to the neonatologists' list of promising therapies for RDS. Current issues concerning the use and benefits of surfactant therapy center around three factors: the optimal timing of the treatment; the comparable efficacy of natural versus synthetic surfactant; and the short- and long-term benefits of treatment with surfactant on related problems, such as bronchopulmonary dysplasia, necrotizing enterocolitis, and intraventricular hemorrhage.

In February 1991, a multicenter controlled trial reported in the *Journal of Pediatrics* investigated the short- and long-term effects on mortality of a single dose of synthetic surfactant (Exosurf) in premature infants. Approximately 500 premature infants were enrolled in this study, with 19 hospitals participating. The administration of surfactant was associated with a significant reduction in mortality. However, the incidence of bronchopulmonary dysplasia was unaffected by the use of surfactant.

In an attempt to clarify the issue of the efficacies of natural and synthetic surfactant, an analysis of 33 reported randomized trials was performed. The

A cheerful playroom incorporated into the pediatric ward can help make the hospital a less-threatening environment for sick children.

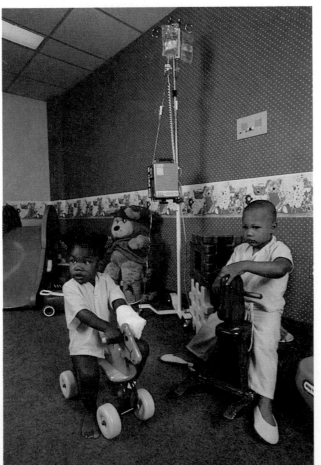

conclusions of this study were that both synthetic and natural surfactants significantly decrease mortality in infants, and that natural surfactants have the most significant effect.

There are two current treatment methods with surfactant: administration of the aerosolized substance into the lungs at the time of delivery, or in rescue therapy or later treatment hours after birth. In March 1991, a collaborative study reported results comparing the two treatment modes. It appears that prophylactic, or early, treatment is superior to later treatment.

And finally, a two-year follow-up study of infants treated with surfactant offers the encouraging news that major long-term side effects do not result from such treatment.

▶ IV Immunoglobulin (IVIG) Therapy

The past three years have witnessed remarkable developments in the use of intravenous immunoglobulins (IVIG), proteins that fight an extensive array of pediatric diseases. A National Institutes of Health (NIH) consensus conference reviewed the currently reported uses of IVIG and published up-to-date recommendations. IVIG has undisputed value for the primary immunodeficiency diseases, including X-linked agammaglobulinemia and immunoglobulin-subclass deficiencies. IVIG continues to show efficacy in reducing the incidence of coronary-artery abnormalities in Kawasaki syndrome. IVIG is also recommended for the treatment of immune thrombocytopenic purpura (ITP). Although data does not support the curative effects of IVIG, the therapy has been demonstrated to increase blood-platelet counts, and may enable postponement of splenectomy, or spleen removal, in chronic ITP.

The NIH conference also addressed the use of IVIG in neonatal medicine. The report did not recommend the use of IVIG as either treatment for low-birth-weight infants or as adjuvant therapy for neonatal infections. In September 1991, a study reported in *Pediatrics* demonstrated that treatment of premature infants with IVIG resulted in no statistically significant reduction in the number or severity of acquired infections.

Clinical trials of IVIG in the treatment of children with AIDS are ongoing. In 1991 the National Institute of Child Health and Human Development Intravenous Immunoglobulin Group published the results of a large multicenter study in the *New England Journal of Medicine*. This study demonstrated a statistically significant reduction in the number of infections in children suffering from AIDS who received monthly IVIG therapy.

Large multicenter trials of IVIG in the coming year should continue to clarify treatment dosing for current uses and, perhaps, add new indications for IVIG therapy.

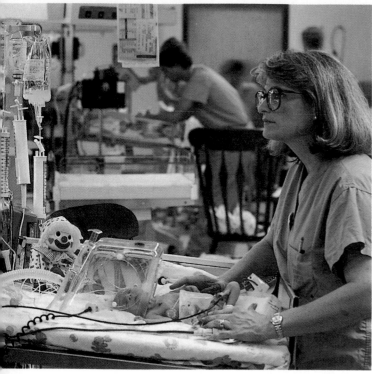

Improved drug therapy has enabled physicians to greatly reduce the mortality of premature children suffering from acute respiratory diseases.

► Child Abuse

Child abuse continues to be an alarming issue. All types of maltreatment syndromes are being recognized with increasing frequency by practitioners in all disciplines of medicine. While child abuse is a sociocultural problem, its health implications are profound. In June 1991, the first North American Conference on Child Abuse and Neglect was convened in Toronto, Canada. Current research and clinical data were presented, addressing many of the most commonly encountered clinical problems seen in maltreatment syndromes.

The Shaken Baby Syndrome (SBS), in which an infant is violently shaken, is one of the most complex clinical problems of child abuse. As a result of the whiplash motion of the head, victims are subject to a variety of internal head injuries, including retinal hemorrhages, cerebral contusions, and subarachnoid and subdural hematomas. In the majority of instances, however, no external injury is present to raise suspicions. The only symptoms may include lethargy, irritability, apnea, and seizures. Among the conclusions of a consensus opinion from the conference were that while computerized tomography (CT) scan is the initial radiological study of choice, magnetic resonance imaging (MRI) may be more sensitive in identifying acute central-nervous-system injury.

The alarming increase in sexually transmitted diseases (STDs) in the United States has been paralleled by an increase in STDs in young children. The Toronto conference set some practical guidelines to assist doctors and social workers in their investigations of sexual abuse in children. Children with culture-confirmed gonorrhea or chlamydia, or with a positive blood test for syphilis, should be considered victims of abuse until proven otherwise. Children with herpesvirus type II and *Trichomonas* infections beyond the neonatal period have a high probability of having been sexually abused. Because of the relatively long latency of *Condyloma acuminata* (the cause of genital warts), an infection acquired during birth may not become evident for two years or more. However, documented *Condyloma acuminata* in toddlers and older children should prompt the suspicion of sexual abuse.

► Pediatric AIDS

Human immunodeficiency virus (HIV) infection is a growing clinical problem. In 1990, 43,339 cases of AIDS were reported. The *Morbidity and Mortality Weekly Report* (MMWR) reported in 1991 that AIDS cases in women of childbearing years are increasing geometrically. Since almost all cases of pediatric AIDS infection are acquired from the mother during birth, the implications are obvious—a similar increase in HIV infection and disease in children can be expected. A 1991 European study in *Lancet* suggested that the transmission of the virus from mother to fetus may range from 13 to 65 percent.

Since it is desirable to diagnose HIV infection as early as possible in infancy, current research is focusing on the development of sensitive diagnostic tests for young infants. Currently available AIDS tests are not recommended for diagnosis of HIV infections in infants below 18 months of age. This is because HIV antibodies from the mother may be present in a newborn for up to 15 to 18 months after delivery. Tests using polymerase chain-reaction (PCR) techniques may offer the possibility of earlier diagnosis. A review study reported in *Pediatric Infectious Disease Journal* in 1991 suggests that a PCR-based test may reach 90 to 100 percent sensitivity by six months of age. Such early detection of the disease is critical if treatment interventions are to have maximum benefit.

In 1991 dideoxyinosine (DDI) was approved for use in children with AIDS. This antiretroviral agent is now added to the previous therapeutic options of IVIG, zidovudine (AZT), and drug therapy for *Pneumocystis carinii* pneumonia. The main toxic side effect of DDI is pancreatic inflammation.

Current clinical trials are in progress to study the efficacy of various combination and sequential therapy.

John M. de Triquet, M.D.

Public Health

During 1991 the AIDS epidemic completed its first decade (see article on AIDS, page 234). Other areas of public-health concern in the United States included the influenza epidemic, inadequate control of vaccine-preventable diseases, and worsening problems with salmonella infections.

▶ Influenza

After two years of relatively low rates of influenza, the infection hit early and hard in 1991. By year's end the hospitals in many states were crowded due to influenza cases, and there were an excess number of deaths due to the disease. Normally in the winter, slightly over 6 percent of the deaths that occur are expected to be due to influenza and pneumonia. By the end of 1991, more than 7 percent of deaths were due to influenza.

This year was atypical because influenza hit early. It is unusual for the disease to become epidemic before December, but in 1991 it started in the fall, and widespread outbreaks were being reported by mid-November. The 1991 outbreak also was unusual because the early epidemic predominated among children and college-age young adults. Normally the type of virus that caused most of the 1991 outbreaks (influenza type A/Beijing/1989-like/H3,N2) produces as much illness in adults as it does in children.

The influenza virus is difficult to control, despite the existence of influenza vaccines, because it constantly changes its structure, and the available vaccines (made from previous years' viruses) may not be sufficiently up-to-date to give protection against the types of virus currently circulating. In most years the active influenza viruses have had only minor changes from the previous year—called *antigenic drift*—but occasionally very new viruses appear—called *antigenic shift*.

The viruses producing illness in the fall of 1991 were seen in 1990, and the structure of the most common 1990 viruses was in the 1991 influenza vaccine. The epidemic, however, hit so early in the season that most people had not yet been vaccinated, so the vaccine had no chance to forestall the epidemic. The hope now is that those people who have been given the vaccine, typically health professionals and the elderly or chronically ill, will be protected.

Americans have used influenza vaccine somewhat cautiously since the unsuccessful "swine flu" vaccine episode in 1976. Because the 1991 influenza outbreak was early and severe, supplies of vaccine were exhausted in many areas of the coun-

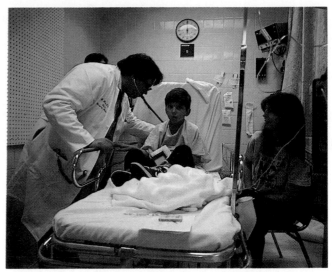

The influenza epidemic of winter 1991–1992 hit children and young people the hardest. Thousands of sufferers sought treatment in local emergency rooms.

try. It takes several weeks for manufacturers to make more vaccine, so additional vaccine supplies were not available by year's end.

In 1991 for the first time, a number of persons without risk factors for AIDS produced a positive screening test for the human immunodeficiency virus (HIV) when they donated blood following influenza-vaccine inoculation. Even though these people were subsequently shown not to have the virus, their blood could not be used, because regulations prohibit anyone who screens HIV-positive from donating, regardless of confirmatory tests. This event has puzzled scientists and has raised special concern about the already low blood supply at blood banks.

▶ Cholera

A total of 25 cases of cholera were reported in the U.S. in 1991, up from six in 1990 and none the year before; none of the cases was fatal. Two-thirds of the cases were associated with the South American cholera epidemic, acquired either during travel there or from fish and other food products imported from cholera-infected areas. However, eight cases came from elsewhere, mostly Asia. Six cases were attributed to imported frozen coconut milk from Thailand. The Food and Drug Administration (FDA) has since stopped the importation of any coconut products from Thailand. The cholera organism, *Vibrio cholera,* has also been found in oysters collected in Mobile Bay, Alabama.

▶ Loss of Critical Tuberculosis Drug

The only two U.S. drug companies that manufacture streptomycin, one of the leading drugs to combat tuberculosis, have discontinued its production. Public-health physicians are outraged at this situation, coming as it does during a time when tuberculosis is on the rise, due to AIDS and increasing resistance to antibiotics by the tuberculosis organism. Streptomycin, which was introduced in the late 1940s, was the first drug effective against tuberculosis, and it provided a powerful tool in the fight against the disease. In time, other antibiotics were added to the tuberculosis armamentarium, but streptomycin has remained an important drug because it is injectable, effective, and relatively inexpensive.

The tuberculosis organisms (there are several subtypes that can cause the disease) have gradually developed resistance to one or more antibiotics, so that the common inexpensive drugs often don't work. This is a double hazard because, if the treatment is ineffective, the person continues to spread the disease, and, even worse, the disease he or she spreads is also resistant to antibiotics. Because the antibiotic-sensitive organisms are eliminated by treatment and the antibiotic-resistant strains are not, gradually the resistant tuberculosis organisms become more common.

Persons with AIDS are especially susceptible to the tuberculosis organism because the kind of immunity most severely damaged by HIV is that which is most important in resisting tuberculosis. Shelters

The number of cases of tuberculosis has risen dramatically, although not to the level earlier this century (below), before streptomycin therapy was introduced.

for the homeless are also a fertile environment for tuberculosis. The homeless, even if they do not have AIDS, may have lowered resistance because of poor nutrition, exposure to the elements, drug use, and/or the loneliness and depression associated with their condition. The twin factors of AIDS and homelessness, both of which contribute to the rise in tuberculosis cases, now have been joined by the growing problem of antibiotic resistance. In this environment the inexpensive and relatively safe streptomycin is an absolutely necessary drug, and yet it is no longer available in the U.S. Many are trying to get the two drug companies involved, Pfizer and Eli Lilly, to reverse this decision.

▶ Vaccine-Preventable Infections

In 1991 the third-worst measles outbreak of the past decade occurred in the U.S., exceeded only by 1990 and 1989. The reason for the measles outbreaks is simple: too many children are not immunized adequately or on time.

In 1991 the U.S. National Vaccine Advisory Committee stated that the U.S. health-care system created " . . . barriers to obtaining immunization and fails to take advantage of many opportunities to provide vaccine to children." Children should receive their first dose of live, attenuated measles vaccine (preferably also combined with mumps and rubella vaccines) at about 15 months of age, followed by a booster dose when they enter school. Often parents delay the vaccination until the children enter school, when a vaccine is part of an admission requirement.

Currently, up to 50 to 70 percent of children in some urban areas are inadequately immunized against measles and other diseases. The unfortunate result is that the younger children—the most important to protect—are unimmunized until they begin school. One of the reasons given for this delay in immunization is that parents struggling with poverty or drug use are unable or unwilling to focus on this parental responsibility.

The medical profession must share some of the blame because it long has been reluctant to allow children with runny noses to be vaccinated, even if the child has no fever. One possible reason for this policy is the fear of malpractice suits. But the Centers for Disease Control (CDC) may soon recommend a change in this policy, because the diseases the vaccine protects against are more of a threat than the possible reaction vaccination may have on a child with a runny nose.

German Measles. Measles is not the only vaccine-preventable disease that was on the increase in 1991. Rubella (German measles) cases showed more than a 50 percent increase since 1990, also due to inadequate immunization.

Pertussis Vaccine. Not all vaccine news was bad, however. A new vaccine against pertussis (whooping cough) was approved by the FDA. The older pertussis vaccine tends to cause more side effects —occasionally severe—than do other childhood vaccines. The new vaccine has fewer and less-severe side effects. Because of the problems with the vaccine, some parents were insisting that their children be given vaccines without pertussis antigen, or they were not completing the basic series of shots. The new vaccine is "acellular," in that it is made just from the important pertussis structures, rather than from the whole cells of the whooping-cough bacteria.

The increased frequency of whooping cough in Europe has demonstrated how important it is for the public to have confidence in a vaccine. In Europe, where the pertussis vaccines used appeared to cause more and more-serious reactions than in the U.S., people began to avoid the vaccine in the 1970s. Within a few years, epidemics of whooping cough began occurring in several countries of Europe and in Japan.

▶ *Salmonella Enteritidis*

In the past decade, an organism called *Salmonella enteritidis* has caused more-frequent outbreaks of salmonellosis in New England and the Middle Atlantic states. The reasons are unclear except that some of the large egg farms in these regions are infected with this strain. Outbreaks involving this organism have also been increasing in other parts of the country, with several outbreaks occurring in the Midwest in 1991.

In a desperate effort to fight off the illnesses caused by salmonella, the state of New Jersey took the unusual step of requiring restaurants to serve only eggs that were "firm." Thus, delicacies that contain raw eggs, such as hollandaise sauce, poached or soft-boiled eggs, or fried eggs over easy, became illegal. Of course, an individual can still eat these foods at home. Public-health officials were dubious about the effectiveness of these measures, because most outbreaks come from foods in which the salmonella organisms have incubated for some time, thus magnifying the number of these organisms many hundredfold.

▶ Rise in Illegal Drug Use

After some years of decline in the use of illegal drugs by young people in the U.S., there now is evidence that the use of cocaine and heroin is on the rise again. Some of the increases came from long-term users, in addition to new drug users. Data came from both a national survey and from a monitoring of a sample of emergency rooms in U.S. hospitals.

James F. Jekel, M.D. M.P.H.

Respiratory System

▶ Asthma

Asthma is characterized by narrowing of the large and small airways, a constriction often (but not always) reversible either spontaneously or with medication. Asthma results in trapping of air within the lungs and impairment of gas exchange, the fundamental job of the lungs. Research over the past several years has emphasized the role of inflammation in the initiation and propagation of asthmatic attacks. This emphasis has led to profound changes in the therapeutic use of inhaled bronchodilators such as beta agonists or oral steroids, both of which may cause undesirable long-term side effects.

Several clinical studies have documented the benefit of early introduction of less-risky anti-inflammatory agents, such as inhaled steroids and/or cromolyn. The latter agent acts to stabilize mast cells, thereby preventing the cascade of events that leads to bronchoconstriction. For some patients with refractory asthma who take oral steroids all the time, the use of a high-dose steroid inhaler (unfortunately not yet available in the United States, but obtainable from abroad) or of other medications—such as troleandomycin, methotrexate, or gold—has proven helpful.

Long-acting inhalers with prolonged effects are being tested. These agents should help in the management of asthmatics who suffer relapses in the early-morning hours, despite the use of currently available agents such as theophylline and inhaled steroids.

The availability of these novel agents, together with improved patient education and participation by patients in their own asthma management, will have an impact on the alarming and increasing morbidity and mortality of this disease.

▶ Smoking and Lung Cancer

Lung cancer is the leading cause of cancer death in adults. The American Cancer Society estimates that in 1991, 161,000 new cases of lung cancer were diagnosed, and that 143,000 individuals will have died of this disease. Because of the long latency in the development of lung cancer, this figure will remain high for many years to come, even as smoking cessation reduces the numbers of new smokers. The encouraging news is that there has been a certain leveling off in lung-cancer mortality. Considering that no major changes are noted in survival rates, this trend must be attributed largely to the vigorous efforts at preventing and decreasing cigarette smoking. According to U.S. Surgeon General Dr. Antonia Novello, 40 percent of U.S. adults were smokers in 1965. By 1987 only 29 percent of the population were smokers.

A number of techniques with varying degrees of success are available to help the smoker quit. Being tested as smoking-cessation aids are medications such as clonidine. And a nicotine transdermal patch has just been approved by the Food and Drug Administration (FDA). These techniques offer the advantage of longer-lasting effect without the need for repeated administration. In conjunction with other techniques—including nicotine gum, behavioral modification, aversive procedures, acupuncture, smoking deterrents, and educational and emotional support by medical staff and family—this will improve the success rate of smoking cessation. Fewer smokers will translate into a decrease in the smoking-related morbidity and mortality of respiratory, as well as nonrespiratory, illness.

Genetic predisposition to lung cancer has recently been recognized. Gene coding for enzymes that transform certain components of cigarette smoke into potent carcinogens was reported in smokers and in patients with lung cancer. Vitamin A derivatives such as beta-carotene have been found to mediate the differentiation of transformed cells. Administration of beta-carotene in patients with premalignant lesions decreased the rate of evolution into fully malignant lesions. When given to patients with head and neck cancer, it proved effective in preventing the emergence of second primary tumors, including lung cancer. A major Italian interventional trial in surgically treated early lung cancer suggests that an analogue of vitamin A may significantly improve survival.

▶ AIDS

The advances in our understanding of the etiology, diagnosis, and treatment of AIDS parallels the magnitude of the epidemic. According to the Centers for Disease Control (CDC), AIDS is the leading cause of death among men and women less than 45 years of age. As of May 1991, 179,136 cases were reported. The World Health Organization (WHO) has estimated that around the world, 8 million to 10 million adults and 1 million children are infected with the human immunodeficiency virus (HIV), the virus that causes AIDS.

The pulmonary complications of AIDS account for the greatest portion of mortality associated with the disease. *Pneumocystis carinii* pneumonia (PCP), tuberculosis, and bacterial and other opportunistic pulmonary infections affect most, if not all, AIDS patients at some point in the course of their illness.

There has been a significant increase in the survival of patients with AIDS. This is the result of the rapid introduction of drugs that slow the replication of HIV, as well as new drugs used to manage the complications. A short course of steroids in patients with AIDS and PCP has been shown to decrease the morbidity and mortality of this common complication. Steroids are now an accepted and recommended adjunctive therapy in the management of PCP to prevent early deterioration and respiratory failure.

▶ Tuberculosis

Tuberculosis (TB) is the most prevalent infection in the world. Up to one-third of the world's population is infected with the tubercle bacillus. Eight million new cases and 3 million deaths are estimated to occur worldwide each year. In the United States, the rate of decline seen up until 1984 has now stopped. The CDC reports an excess of 28,000 cases more than had been anticipated in the six years from 1985 through 1990. More than 20,000 new cases are being reported yearly.

The increased prevalence of this disease is due to multiple factors. There is an association between HIV infection and tuberculosis, and a great proportion of new cases of TB are seen in patients with AIDS. Tuberculosis has been classified as an AIDS-defining disease in patients with HIV infection. Race and ethnicity play a role in the rising morbidity of TB. Of the almost 24,000 cases reported in 1989, 37 percent occurred in blacks, 17 percent in Hispanics, 12 percent in Asian/Pacific Islanders, and 1.5 percent in American Indian/Alaskan natives. The institutionalized elderly and the homeless-shelter population represent another group at substantially increased risk.

Just as alarming is the emergence of multiple-drug-resistant tuberculosis. Until recently, routine testing of the tubercle bacillus for sensitivity to drugs was not necessary except in unusual circumstances. The organism was extremely sensitive to available medications, and testing was considered unnecessary and a poor use of resources. Increasing reports of resistant strains make sensitivity testing essential. It is also important to initiate therapy with at least two agents to which the organism is likely to be susceptible.

These data clearly demonstrate that a plan for the prevention and treatment of tuberculosis needs to be implemented. The Department of Health and Human Services, in collaboration with the CDC and various medical associations, has established a plan to improve surveillance, case prevention, and disease containment. The national goal is elimination of TB by the year 2010.

▶ Lung Transplantation

Lung transplantation has evolved as a treatment option for a variety of end-stage lung diseases. Successful transplantation is the culmination of ongoing research in several disciplines, with the ultimate goal being the continuation of a life with quality and significance. Patients with diseases such as pulmonary fibrosis, emphysema, sarcoidosis, bronchiectasis, cystic fibrosis, pulmonary hypertension, and other end-stage lung diseases have undergone successful transplants. In 1990, 468 lung transplants were performed, as reported to the Registry of the International Society for Heart and Lung Transplantation. Three procedures are available: single-lung, double-lung, and heart-lung transplantation.

Heart-lung transplantation is the oldest and best established procedure, but advances in surgical technique and immunosuppressive therapy have made single- and double-lung transplantation viable alternatives. Single-lung transplantation allows one donor to provide organs to two recipients; the growing list of candidates for lung transplantation makes it likely that this procedure will become increasingly popular. However, the patient's underlying disease will continue to dictate the choice of operation. An illness characterized by infection and secretions, such as bronchiectasis or cystic fibrosis, can be safely treated only with double-lung or heart-lung transplantation.

The use of cyclosporine revolutionized organ transplantation by dramatically decreasing the risk of rejection. Novel approaches to immunosuppression include the use of anti-thymocyte globulin, monoclonal antibodies against T cells, and the investigational drug FK-506. These offer hope for the increased success of lung transplantation.

The major limitation to lung transplantation remains a shortage of donors. Even a short period of mechanical ventilation damages the lungs, and most organ donors have undergone mechanical ventilation, some for many days. The cost of lung transplantation remains very high, but as its therapeutic value is recognized, more third-party payers are assuming responsibility for the expenses.

▶ Diagnosis and Gene Therapy

Diagnostic modalities are in a state of constant evolution. While we still cannot dispense with the traditional chest X ray, new techniques have assumed a major role in the diagnosis and staging of lung disease. Beyond the first-generation CT scanners and magnetic resonance imagers are machines with the contrast and spatial resolution that define the histology of disease.

Basic research in genetic defects has come to the bedside, where gene therapy is being used to treat diseases such as alpha-1-antitrypsin deficiency, and to diagnose and treat others, such as cystic fibrosis. The molecular basis of other pulmonary diseases is being unraveled, heralding an exciting era of prevention and targeted therapy for the illnesses of the respiratory system.

Maria L. Padilla, M.D.

Sexually Transmitted Diseases

With an estimated 12 million new cases of sexually transmitted diseases (STDs) each year, two-thirds of them occurring in people under age 25, STDs continue to be among the most important health problems in the United States. This point was emphatically underscored in the July 1991 Centers for Disease Control (CDC) report, *Sexually Transmitted Disease Surveillance 1990*. Among other issues, the report highlighted the serious implications that STDs have for women. Women who contract gonorrhea and chlamydia infections, for example, often develop pelvic inflammatory disease, which can lead to infertility and ectopic pregnancy. STDs also adversely affect unborn babies, who become infected from their mothers either while in the womb or during delivery.

The CDC reports that there are 30 million Americans infected with the herpes virus; 12 million infected with genital warts, caused by the human papilloma virus (HPV); and 1 million infected with the human immunodeficiency virus (HIV), which causes AIDS (see AIDS, page 234). The fact that these viral STDs still have no cure makes these numbers truly disturbing.

▶ Syphilis

Syphilis cases have been increasing each year since 1986, according to the 1991 CDC report. The 50,000 cases of syphilis reported in 1990 were the most reported in any year for the past 40 years. The greatest increase in syphilis occurred among heterosexual minority populations: in 1990 the rate of infectious syphilis among blacks was more than 56 times higher than the rate among whites! Recent outbreaks of syphilis have also been associated with the use of crack cocaine, which is commonly exchanged for sex.

Doctors have also grown increasingly concerned about the number of cases of neurosyphilis, a central-nervous-system infection occurring in early syphilis cases. J. M. Flood and colleagues at the San Francisco Department of Public Health found that while the number of cases of infectious syphilis declined in San Francisco from 1,200 in 1982 to 373 in 1989, the number of early symptomatic neurosyphilis cases doubled over that same period. The researchers found that 87 percent of the patients with early symptomatic neurosyphilis were also infected with HIV or had a known risk factor for AIDS. Thus, early symptomatic neurosyphilis may be more common in the HIV-infected patient.

▶ New Drug to Treat Chlamydia

The current treatment for *Chlamydia trachomatis* infection requires seven days of antibiotic therapy. A single-dose therapy would have the advantage of improving patient compliance. M. R. Hammerschlag and colleagues at SUNY Health Sciences Center in Brooklyn studied the effect of azithromycin, a new antibiotic, in the treatment of chlamydia infection. Study results found that azithromycin in a 1-gram oral dose was an effective therapy against chlamydia organisms. A single dose of the drug also remains in the body for an extended period of time —its half-life is 68 hours, which means that after 68 hours, one-half of the peak dose is still present in the blood. These positive conclusions were confirmed by a second multicenter trial. Azithromycin appears to represent a major advancement in the treatment of *Chlamydia trachomatis* genital infection. Unfortunately, the antibiotic is not yet available in the United States.

▶ HPV Detection

Certain strains of the human papilloma virus (HPV), which causes genital warts, have been associated with an early form of cervical cancer. Early diagnosis and treatment of this STD is imperative in order to prevent the cancer from progressing. Yet accurate diagnosis of HPV has been stymied because the virus often appears in normal-appearing tissue free of the telltale genital warts. And the diagnostic techniques available were limited to only specific HPV strains. As a result, HPV often went undetected. A recent study by researchers from Cetus Corporation, the University of California, Berkeley, and Roche Biomedical Laboratories found that polymerase chain reaction (PCR), a new, rapid, highly sensitive DNA detection method, is useful in detecting the presence of a broad variety of HPV strains. It is particularly useful in cases where the test sample is of poor quality, or the patient has a low-level infection. Experts hope that this method, not yet in widespread use for STD diagnosis, will improve our understanding of the natural history of HPV infection and its role in cervical disease.

▶ Unsafe Sexual Practices

In recent years, sexual behavior that leads to a higher risk of contracting AIDS and gonorrhea has slightly declined in many cities across the country. Nonetheless, a recent study by Lynda S. Doll of the CDC and collaborators at three urban STD clinics has found an alarmingly large number of homosexual men who continue to engage in unprotected oral and anal sex. In the study, 601 homosexual men who had engaged in these practices with a male partner in the prior four-month period were interviewed regarding their sexual and drug-use practices. One-quarter of the men reported one to two episodes of unprotected anal sex, and another 20 percent admitted that they had engaged in more than 23 episodes of unprotected anal sex. Experts need to identify the types of men prone to high-risk practices, as well as the circumstances associated with varying levels of risk, in order to target effective risk-reduction programs.

▶ Condoms in High Schools

A raging controversy erupted this past year over the policy of handing out condoms in the nation's high schools to reduce the risk of STD transmission, particularly AIDS. Adherents of the policy refer to the escalating AIDS statistics—more than one-fifth of all AIDS victims in the United States are in their 20s. Since the incubation period for this disease can be as long as 10 years, most of the older age group probably became infected as teens. Condoms are, of course, readily available from drugstores; still, many teens do not use them properly or consistently. A school condom program, proponents say, would provide instruction on the importance of safe sex and proper condom use.

Opponents adamantly state that there is no safe sex, and the school's endorsement of condoms will give the students a false sense of security. Condoms have a failure rate of between 10 and 15 percent; thus they hardly represent a foolproof method for STD prevention. And while condoms may reduce the risk of STDs, critics contend that relying on condoms to simply *reduce the risk* of a fatal disease like AIDS, or of incurable infections such as herpes and genital warts, is unacceptable and irresponsible. The better policy would be to encourage abstinence or sex with a mutually faithful, uninfected partner.

▶ Goals for the Future

The U.S. Public Health Service (PHS) has recently published the book *Healthy People 2000: National Health Promotion and Disease Prevention Objectives.* By the year 2000, the PHS hopes to increase to at least 50 percent the proportion of sexually active, unmarried people who use condoms during sexual intercourse. The PHS has based its target on 1988 statistics that showed that only 19 percent of sexually active, unmarried women aged 15 through 44 reported that their partners used a condom during their last sexual intercourse. Also, by the year 2000, the PHS hopes to reduce the proportion of adolescents who have engaged in sexual intercourse to no more than 15 percent by age 15 and no more than 40 percent by age 17. The baseline for this target was data in 1988 indicating that 27 percent of girls and 33 percent of boys by age 15 had engaged in intercourse. By age 17 these figures stood at 50 percent of girls and 66 percent of boys.

Robert C. Noble, M.D.

Skin

▶ Lethal Reactions to Latex Rubber Products Reported

Allergic reactions to products containing latex are now increasing in frequency and severity. Because some of these recently reported reactions have been life-threatening and even fatal, an added degree of urgency exists in the need to understand this new public-health problem. The magnitude of this new problem can be attributed partly to the proven efficacy of the latex material as a barrier against the human immunodeficiency virus (HIV), which causes AIDS. Because of latex's viral-barrier quality, there has been a dramatic increase in the use of latex rubber gloves by physicians and latex rubber condoms by the general public.

Latex is the natural milky sap produced by the rubber tree *Hevea brasiliensis*. This natural substance is widely used in the production of common products like rubber gloves, condoms, rubber bands, balloons, and rubber adhesives. Allergic skin reactions to these products are not new, but past reactions were usually only at the nuisance level, producing itching, scaling skin reactions limited to the area of the skin contact. In these cases, the causative factor was not the latex product, but one of the many chemical additives used in the production of rubber. These mild reactions could be alleviated by simple avoidance of the rubber products that contained the irritating chemical.

In contrast, more-recent cases of allergy to latex products have been severe and fatal. Investigations have revealed that these patients were truly allergic to latex, and they most frequently developed their allergy through the use of latex gloves or latex condoms. Because these latex products involve close chronic skin contact, they appear to frequently lead to the development of allergy. In fact, recent studies have shown that 3 percent of health-care professionals are now allergic to latex. As long as these individuals limit their exposure to skin contact with the offending allergen, they will probably experience only focal hive reactions in the specific area of exposure.

Examples of focal responses include hives on the hands caused by rubber gloves or hives on the lips after blowing up a balloon. If the same allergic individuals are exposed to airborne latex, as can occur from the air in an industrial plant producing latex, they may develop watery eyes, a runny nose, and difficulty breathing. However, if the allergic individuals are exposed to latex through mucous membranes, severe life-threatening allergic-shock reactions can develop.

In recent cases, fatal reactions have resulted when unsuspecting allergic individuals underwent surgical procedures. When they came in contact with the latex contained in the gloves of their surgeon, the lethal allergic-shock reactions occurred. Oral mucosa contact with latex in the form of surgical gloves or latex barrier used during dental procedures was another form of exposure leading to some fatalities.

The early reports of fatal latex reactions have occurred predominantly in health-care professionals. However, because of the increasing exposure of the general public to latex in the form of condoms and other products, additional serious and lethal reactions can be expected in the future. Individuals who suspect they are sensitive to latex can have their allergy confirmed by a simple latex skin test. Once identified, they can take steps to limit casual contact with latex, and to totally avoid use of latex during surgical procedures. Clearly, an urgent need exists for the development of a nonallergenic, latex-free material that creates an effective barrier to the AIDS virus.

▶ Topical Magainins for Skin Infections

In 1987 a simple question about how frogs could possibly heal their skin wounds while living in dirty, bacteria-rich water led to the discovery of a new type of antibacterial agent. The new, naturally occurring antibacterial peptide was isolated from the skin of the African clawed frog *Xenopus laevis* by Michael A. Zasloff from the University of Pennsylvania School of Medicine in Philadelphia. He called it *Magainin,* the Hebrew word for "shield." Subsequent studies have revealed that Magainin has broad-spectrum activity against bacteria, fungi, amoebas, and parasites.

Magainin, an antibacterial agent derived from the African clawed frog (below), may have therapeutic applications for a variety of skin infections.

Preliminary in vivo studies of a synthetic Magainin, MSI-78, were presented by Patricia Mertz and colleagues from the University of Miami in Coral Gables, Florida, during the 1991 American Academy of Dermatology meeting in Dallas, Texas. MSI-78 was applied to surgical wounds in pigs that had been artificially infected with the bacteria *Staphylococcus aureus*. Not only did the synthetic Magainin display an ability to reduce the numbers of staphylococcal organisms, but it also prevented the overgrowth of other normal skin bacteria. Magainin appears to possess broad-spectrum activity against all types of bacterial organisms. In Mertz's study, Magainin prevented the secondary emergence of gram-negative organisms, a frequent side effect of the chronic use of other topical antibiotics. Although preliminary, these studies promise useful therapeutic applications of topical Magainin in the future.

▶ Topical Vitamin C Provides Sun Protection

During the past decade, studies of the effects of topical vitamin applications to the skin surface have yielded interesting results. The application of vitamin A and its derivatives to the skin led to the discovery of tretinoin (Retin-A), a chemical with a wide array of antiacne, antiaging, and antitumor effects. Experiments with the topical application of vitamin D derivatives to the skin have led to the discovery of calcipotriol, a potential treatment for psoriasis. This year, studies on the effects of topical application of vitamin C to the skin of pigs have again yielded fascinating results.

Preliminary studies of Sheldon Pinnel and colleagues from the Duke University Medical Center in Durham, North Carolina, have documented that the topical application of 10 percent L-ascorbic acid (vitamin C) to pigs reduces their sensitivity to ultraviolet light. Topical vitamin C appears to produce a broad-spectrum protection against ultraviolet damage. Unlike sunscreens, which do little against the longer wavelengths of ultraviolet light, vitamin C protects against all wavelengths.

The mechanisms of topical vitamin C photoprotection are different from the mechanisms of sunscreens. Sunscreens work predominantly by absorbing ultraviolet-light energy. In contrast, topical vitamin C appears to interfere with the biochemical mechanism by which ultraviolet light causes damage. When ultraviolet light interacts with normal skin, it leads to the production of oxygen-free radicals. Vitamin C, functioning as an *antioxidant,* is believed to prevent the damaging effects of these oxygen-free radicals. Because oxygen-free radicals are also thought to be important in the development of skin cancer as well as some inflammatory diseases of the skin, vitamin C may have other important effects on skin disease. The photoprotective effect of vitamin C may prove to be merely the first in an array of therapeutic effects of topical vitamin C.

▶ Melanocyte-Stimulating Hormone Produces Skin Pigmentation

The quest continues to find a safe method for tanning. The ability to obtain a tan while avoiding the adverse aging and cancer-producing effects of ultraviolet light would have significant medical and cosmetic benefits. In the past, sunscreens have attempted to obtain this goal, but in order to obtain a tan, it has always been necessary to accept some of the deleterious effects of ultraviolet light. Ingesting large quantities of yellow food dye to impart an artificial tanlike coloring to the skin has also been tested. Unfortunately, these dyes produce a cosmetically undesirable yellow skin color rather than the desired "rich" tan. More-recent efforts to find a safe tan have been experiments with melanocyte-stimulating hormone (MSH) injections.

MSH plays a major role in the control of skin coloration in animals. For example, this hormone has a key function in the ability of amphibians to suddenly change color. MSH and related chemicals can be detected throughout the human brain and body. In humans, there is experimental evidence that MSH functions as a modulator of inflammation, the immune system, the nervous system, and the endocrine system. But the effect on human skin pigmentation remains unclear.

Recent studies by Norman Levine and colleagues from the University of Arizona Health Sciences Center in Tucson have investigated the effects of MSH on human skin pigmentation. They observed skin darkening in 28 healthy Caucasian males following injections of a synthetic form of this hormone. Increased pigmentation was observed in all patients whether or not they were good tanners. Surprisingly, the tanning effect of this hormone was not uniform. The face and neck and, to a lesser extent, the extremities, appeared to darken, while the abdomen and buttocks remained unaffected.

Mild flushing and temporary gastrointestinal upset were the only side effects of the hormone injection. Because MSH has so many varied effects in humans, it is likely that its artificial use in high doses will produce additional side effects, and its long-term safety must still be studied. Despite these concerns, this preliminary study has documented that even in humans, MSH can produce skin darkening without exposure to harmful ultraviolet light. MSH also has the potential to protect fair-skinned individuals from skin cancer, as well as to prove beneficial in the treatment of some forms of hereditary albinism, a disease affecting normal skin pigmentation.

Edward E. Bondi, M.D.

Substance Abuse

▶ Addiction: Just What Is It?

The vocabulary associated with drug addiction is commonly misused in the media, causing great confusion. A review of commonly used terms may provide a better understanding of a drug-abuse victim. Drug *tolerance* describes a condition in which a person no longer gets the same effect from a given dose of drug. It takes larger and larger doses to get the same effect as before. *Cross-tolerance* is a situation in which a person becomes tolerant of a whole group of drugs as a result of using one drug. For example, becoming tolerant of Valium usually means becoming tolerant of the entire class of benzodiazepines, to which Valium belongs.

Dependence is a condition in which a person adapts psychologically or physically to the presence of a drug, and it then becomes necessary to continue to use the drug in order to feel well. *Physical dependence* is evidenced by the need to continue using the drug in order to avoid a withdrawal syndrome. For instance, withdrawal from heroin or other narcotics can cause runny eyes, runny nose, gooseflesh, diarrhea and cramping, increased heart rate and blood pressure, yawning, sweating, or pains in the bones and muscles. *Psychological dependence* is evidenced by a marked craving, or desire, for the drug, either to continue getting pleasure or to avoid withdrawal symptoms.

Finally, *addiction* has been defined as "a behavioral pattern of compulsive drug use characterized by overwhelming involvement with the use of the drug, the securing of its supply and a high tendency to relapse after withdrawal." Associated with addiction are behavioral patterns in which the individual continues to use the substance in spite of known hardships and severe consequences, such as the loss of job or family, or going to jail. Usually, people who are addicted to a substance demonstrate tolerance, physical dependence, psychological dependence, and a withdrawal syndrome if they stop using the drug. The relapse rate for most of the drugs commonly abused in the U.S. appears to be about 98 percent.

In the brain are a number of chemical systems, including the adrenaline system, the serotonin system, the dopamine system, and the endorphin system. In each of these systems, a particular chemical serves as a messenger, or neurotransmitter, to carry an action message from one nerve cell to the next.

In between nerve cells, there is a gap, called the *synapse*. The neurotransmitter is released into the synapse, where it migrates across the gap and car-

ries the message to the next cell. The chemical then attaches to a *receptor*. This attachment is very specific. For instance, only an endorphin neurotransmitter will attach to an endorphin receptor, much like a specific key is needed to fit a certain lock. Morphine and other narcotics and opiates mimic neurotransmitter substances that we produce within our bodies. By connecting with specific receptors in the brain, they are able to produce the unusual mental and physical effects associated with a drug "high." Substance-abuse experts are experimenting with ways to interfere with this messenger system to fight drug addiction.

▶ Alcoholism

In 1990 a controversial study indicated that the susceptibility to at least one type of alcoholism may be linked to the presence of a particular gene on chromosome 11. The gene directs the production of key dopamine receptors on brain cells. But critics pointed out flaws in the study's methodology, putting the dopamine receptor gene in doubt as a cause of alcoholism.

Then, in July 1991, a report in the *Archives of General Psychiatry* provided evidence that the gene may intensify the severity and medical consequences of alcoholism, rather than cause the disorder, by disturbing normal dopamine transmission.

Currently, Indiana University geneticist P. Michael Conneally and seven other investigators are directing the largest-ever study on alcoholism. Conneally and his colleagues hope to learn if certain genes produce a susceptibility to alcoholism or to other compulsive behaviors.

Babies born with fetal alcohol syndrome characteristically have a low birth weight, an abnormally small head, facial deformities, and mental impairment.

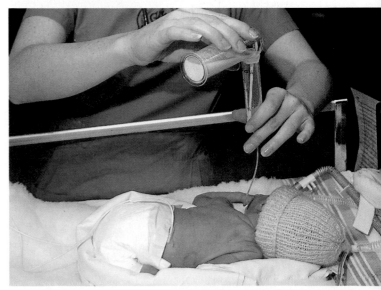

Recovering drug addicts often find that group counseling with people undergoing the same ordeal helps them succeed in staying clean.

In May 1991, the American Society of Addiction Medicine meeting in Boston presented findings that alcoholics fare significantly better when inpatient hospital treatment precedes enrollment in Alcoholics Anonymous (AA) than they do when they depend on AA meetings alone.

And surprisingly, while AA was expected to cost less than inpatient care, there was actually no cost difference between the two groups, since 62 percent of the AA participants were eventually hospitalized due to alcoholism, compared with only 23 percent of those originally treated as inpatients.

As with cocaine addiction, experts are beginning to realize the urgency of improved alcoholism treatment to reduce the number of cases of children born with fetal alcohol syndrome (FAS). FAS is now recognized as the leading cause of mental retardation in the United States, surpassing Down syndrome and spina bifida. Symptoms of FAS include low birth weight, an abnormally small head, facial deformities, and behavioral and cognitive problems. Doctors are just now realizing the long-term implications of this disease—the progression of the disorder continues into adulthood. The resulting maladaptive behaviors will make it difficult for patients to successfully complete job-training programs. The combination of nationwide medical costs, unemployment costs, and mental-health costs of FAS will be astronomical, with conservative estimates ranging from $321 million a year for all FAS cases to $1.4 million across the lifetime of an individual child with FAS.

▶ "Ice"

A year ago, "ice," a smokable form of pure, crystalline methamphetamine, was expected to become the recreational drug of the 1990s. The intense high from ice lasts for hours, making it more appealing to drug users, since the crack-cocaine high lasts only 10 to 30 minutes. Users also tend to become paranoid, psychotic, and violent, making this a very dangerous drug. A year ago, it had already become the leading drug of abuse in Hawaii, surpassing cocaine. An illicit ice laboratory was seized in northern California in January 1990.

But today, for most of the United States, ice seems to be lingering in the wings, while cocaine continues to be the preferred recreational substance. Ice will probably grow in popularity if the cocaine supply dips. This provides drug-enforcement officials with a social dilemma. If, by interdiction, they reduce the supply of cocaine, we may see it replaced by an even more dangerous drug.

"Ice," also called "glass" or "freeze," is a smokable form of methamphetamine. The crystals (below) are heated in a glass pipe and the vapor is inhaled.

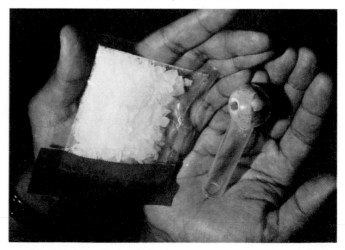

▶ Cocaine

Cocaine abuse has progressed from a relatively minor problem to a major public-health threat over the past 15 years. This drug causes short-term euphoria, excitement, and motor stimulation. Once thought to be nonaddictive, it is now known that these pleasing effects produce a potent positive reinforcement to reuse the drug, leading to addiction. The drug causes profound effects on brain chemistry and a physiological withdrawal state that produces psychotic behavior. Illicit drug use costs America about $60 billion a year. Medical care of cocaine addicts consumes a substantial portion of that money. Cocaine abuse has fueled the AIDS problem through the sharing of contaminated syringes and the tendency of users to pay for their drug with sex. Probably 30 percent of new AIDS cases are due to intravenous drug use.

Several studies have tested the ability of various compounds, some with antidepressant properties, to block craving in cocaine users. The Medications Development Program of the National Institute on Drug Abuse (NIDA) is currently studying bupropion (trade name *Wellbutrin*), a drug approved for use by the Food and Drug Administration (FDA) as an antidepressant. The study will be double-blind and placebo controlled (where neither the doctor nor the patient will know what medication the patient is receiving). Each patient will be evaluated over a 12-week period.

Reduction of craving is one of several medication approaches to treatment of cocaine addiction. Other approaches include treatment for the acute toxic effects of overdose, blocking of euphoric effects, treatment of withdrawal symptoms, and normalization of central-nervous-system disorders. At the present time, there is no antagonist for cocaine that would equate to naloxone (trade name *Narcan*), a drug that blocks narcotics from reaching the brain receptor, or disulfiram (trade name *Antabuse*), a drug that interferes with the metabolism of alcohol and makes people extremely ill if they drink alcohol. Moderate doses of Inderal or of long-acting benzodiazepines (Valium-type drugs) have been recommended for relief of the severe symptoms of cocaine intoxication such as agitation, anxiety, or psychosis. Antipsychotic drugs, such as Haldol, have been tested for efficacy in blocking cocaine euphoria, but they appear to cause depression and severe side effects. A variety of other agents— including bromocriptine, amantadine, Ritalin, and several antidepressants—have been studied for their ability to relieve craving or reduce withdrawal. These agents have been shown to have some benefit, but they also have disadvantages, including tolerance and a gradually diminishing anticraving effect. They also produce another effect called "priming," in which mild stimulation reminds the

Crack—the smokable form of cocaine—was once thought to be nonaddictive. It is now recognized that its use produces a craving to reuse the drug.

patient of cocaine use, and thus increases craving and drug use rather than decreasing them.

The search for remedies for cocaine addiction is becoming ever more crucial as the number of children born to cocaine-using mothers increases. In many cases, these innocent victims are born with severe physical deformities. The damage to other cocaine babies is more subtle—they may have severe developmental and behavioral problems that may sabotage their schooling and social development. In addition to requiring extended medical care resulting in huge medical bills, these children will also put a strain on an educational system already overburdened.

▶ Transcutaneous Electrostimulation

Over the years, there have been a number of attempts to improve sleep or provide pain relief using machines that provide low-frequency currents to the brain by way of transcutaneous cerebral electrostimulation. In the past, however, continuous low-frequency currents often produced pain, burns, and other skin damage, in addition to circulatory and respiratory side effects. It was not until this century that anything beyond marginal success was achieved, although side effects in human subjects still occurred, such as muscle contractures, cere-

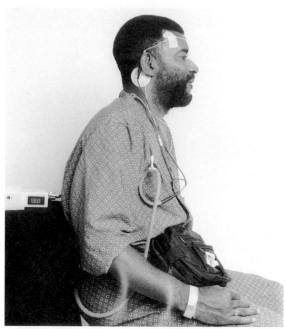

A transcutaneous cranial electrostimulation unit (TCES) is being tested as a possible treatment for rapid detoxification of patients addicted to heroin.

bral shock, cerebral hemorrhage, fever, incontinence, cardiac arrhythmias, apnea, convulsions, and a "nightmarelike state" in which the subject was aware of pain, but could not react to it. Since the 1950s, there has been better success, however, particularly with the transcutaneous electrical nerve stimulation (TENS) unit, a battery-powered generator the size of a portable radio that sends electrical signals through the skin at the site of pain, and electrical acupuncture.

Recently a transcutaneous cranial electrostimulation unit (TCES), designed by a French group headed by Aimé Limoge, has been used to combat drug addiction. The Limoge unit utilizes a complex current composed of alternating high-intensity electrical impulses with negative low-intensity impulses lasting about 3 or 4 milliseconds. The pulses are followed by an off time of about 7 to 10 milliseconds. These wave currents are specially designed so as not to produce skin burns or any other damage. The exact mechanism of action of the electrical current is unknown, but the unit seems to add to the effectiveness of drug analgesia, making it possible to reduce the drug dosage.

Based on these results, Dr. Jean Pierre Daulouede of Bayonne, France, tested the units as a treatment for rapid detoxification of patients addicted to heroin. Over 400 successful opiate-detoxification treatments with Limoge current have been reported, with no side effects. Studies are now being conducted in the United States and France to determine the usefulness of the Limoge unit in detoxification. The study under way at the Department of Veterans Affairs Medical Center in Philadelphia will evaluate the Limoge unit for efficacy in reducing withdrawal symptoms and preventing early relapse after detoxification. It is not expected that the unit will provide any kind of maintenance capability after detoxification.

▶ Methadone Alternatives

Methadone is commonly used as a maintenance drug to wean patients away from heroin and other opiate addictions. A major complaint by patients is their inability to stop taking methadone, which is given once a day. They complain that methadone "gets into their bones," and that they are unable to detoxify from it. L-alpha acetylmethadol (LAAM) is considered to have several advantages over methadone in the treatment of narcotic addiction. Because the body metabolizes it very slowly, LAAM need only be taken three times a week. Most importantly, its slow-release action causes only a mild withdrawal syndrome when the drug is discontinued. NIDA is currently sponsoring a multisite LAAM study to collect enough safety and efficacy evidence to garner FDA approval.

Another major study under way in the NIDA centers focuses on the use of buprenorphine as a substitute for methadone as a maintenance drug in opioid addiction. Buprenorphine is a member of a series of semisynthetic opioid compounds produced from thebaine and oripavine, two compounds that occur naturally in opium. Oripavine has little or no medicinal activity, and thebaine causes severe nausea and vomiting.

One reason for the investigation of buprenorphine as an alternative to methadone is the apparently low level of dependence caused by this drug. Unlike methadone, abrupt discontinuation of buprenorphine after eight weeks results in only a mild withdrawal syndrome.

Experts are worried that buprenorphine will not be acceptable to patients, and they wonder if it will prevent withdrawal as well as methadone. In a study under way in Bayonne, France, Dr. Daulouede has treated over 50 patients with buprenorphine. His preliminary conclusions show that patient acceptance is excellent. It must be pointed out, however, that methadone is not available in France. But some patients have crossed the border from Spain, a country where methadone is available, in order to obtain buprenorphine.

Dr. Daulouede's study will determine the safety and efficacy of 8 milligrams (mg) per day of the drug, as compared to 1 mg per day, in decreasing illicit opiate use. Abuse will be measured by urine testing three times a week.

Marvin M. Weisbrot, R.Ph., M.B.A.

Teeth and Gums

▶ Fluoride Use Given Clean Bill of Health

After a yearlong review of more than 50 epidemiology studies, scientists from the Public Health Service (PHS) concluded in February 1991 that there is no evidence that fluoride causes cancer in humans. "In contrast, the benefits are great and easy to detect," claimed James O. Mason, assistant secretary of Health and Human Services. The report by the PHS concluded that the average child today has decay in three tooth surfaces, as opposed to 10 in prefluoridation days.

But the study also noted that since fluoridation of drinking water began in the mid-1940s, many fluoride-containing oral-health products, such as toothpastes and mouthwashes, have been introduced to the market. These additional fluoride sources make it difficult for scientists to study the effects of fluoridated water alone. Some experts are concerned that exposure to high levels of fluoride has increased the incidence of dental fluorosis—the mottling or discoloration of teeth. And fluoride may augment the incidence of bone fractures associated with osteoporosis.

The report recommended that the PHS sponsor scientific conferences to determine "optimal" levels of fluoride exposure from all sources. It also recommended that the Environmental Protection Agency (EPA) review its standards for natural fluoridation in drinking water.

▶ Clinical Use of Titanium

Smaller dental restorations to replace decayed or broken portions of a tooth are usually made from silver/mercury alloys or composite resins. These materials are flowed into the region and then carved to shape as they solidify. Larger restorations, which must provide more resistance to crushing and shearing forces, are typically constructed from cast metals. Porcelain facings are often attached to the metal's surface to simulate missing tooth structure. Gold has traditionally been the metal of choice for cast restorations, by virtue of its mechanical properties, biocompatibility, and ability to be bonded with porcelain. Cost, however, is a major limiting factor for its selection.

Recently, titanium has gained popularity as a dental-casting metal. Discovered in the late 1700s, titanium is the ninth most abundant element in the Earth's crust. It wasn't until 40 years ago, however, that refining problems were solved and commercial applications of titanium were initiated. It was first used in airplane and spacecraft construction.

Titanium's tendency to quickly form an oxide layer gives the metal immunity to corrosion from air, water, and body fluids. And titanium is nontoxic and nonallergenic, making it remarkably compatible with human soft tissues and bone. These properties led to the use of titanium for prosthetic replacement of knees and hips, and, now, as dental implants.

Titanium-casting techniques were first developed by the aerospace industry in the late 1980s. But casting of titanium is difficult because the metal is highly reactive at its melting temperature and requires an inert atmosphere to control oxidation. In the past few years, dental-casting machines capable of managing the physical properties of titanium have been developed. Trials are now ongoing at several institutions to evaluate the dental restorations produced in these machines and determine if they are capable of becoming durable, aesthetic, and economical replacements for broken teeth or large regions of decay. The outcomes of these trials could have a profound impact upon the future of restorative dentistry.

▶ Developments in Dental Implants

Implant techniques have been used for decades in dentistry to replace missing natural teeth. The introduction of the osseointegrated implant system from Sweden in the early 1980s revolutionized the field and made artificial replacement of teeth with implants truly successful and predictable. Recent modifications of techniques and approaches have expanded the utilization and predictability of osseointegrated dental implants.

Until recently, predictability of dental-implant placement depended upon having sufficient remaining jawbone to completely encapsulate the implant. Thus, areas where the jawbone was extremely narrow or was missing could not receive an implant.

Titanium's growing use in dental implants derives from the metal's immunity to corrosion from air, water, and body fluids and from its nonallergenic properties.

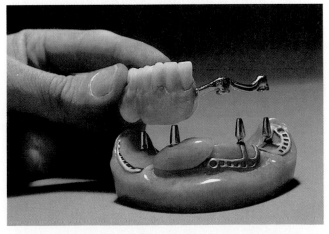

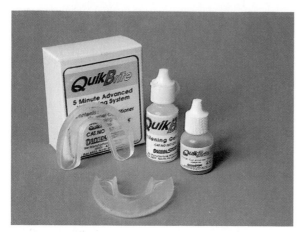
Most tooth-whitening agents require that the user apply a gel solution to a plastic tray similar to a mouth guard and wear the tray for several hours per day.

Work now has been completed showing that implant placement in regions with deficient bone, combined with the placement of an expanded polytetrafluoroethylene membrane (a material similar to that used in athletic apparel), stimulates the regeneration of bone in the region to encase the implant. Following several weeks of healing, during which the membrane material "guides" the migration of healing cells, the membrane is removed, and healing progresses to completion. Recent studies have demonstrated that this technique is successful in over 89 percent of sites previously thought to be poor candidates for implants.

The use of dental implants as fixtures for facial prosthetic rehabilitation has also been recently expanded. Individuals who have lost an eye, nose, ear, or other facial part to cancer or trauma no longer have to receive replacement structures that rely on adhesives to hold them in place. Now prostheses can be securely attached to implant fixtures to provide long-term stability and durability.

▶ Tooth-Whitening Agents

During the past two years, chemical bleaching agents to whiten teeth have been marketed in a very aggressive manner. Most of these agents were designed for home use under the supervision of a dentist, but many were sold over the counter or through mail order.

These whiteners are oxygenating agents, typically containing 10 percent carbomide peroxide. Carbomide peroxide reacts with water to release hydrogen peroxide, which is capable of penetrating through the surface of the tooth enamel coating to produce bleaching. Manufacturers claim that these agents remove staining caused by drugs taken during tooth development, leaching from adjacent filling materials, or "yellowing" caused by aging.

Teeth are bleached with these agents by applying a gel solution of the whitener to the inside of a plastic tray similar to a protective mouth guard. The tray containing the gel is worn several hours a day for several weeks until the desired level of whitening is achieved. In most cases, teeth are slightly "overwhitened," allowing for some rebound.

In September 1991, the Food and Drug Administration (FDA) notified manufacturers of these agents that tooth whiteners had been declared a drug and were subject to the new drug-application process, which requires extensive documentation of research trials to demonstrate safety and efficacy prior to approval for consumer use. Currently, little, if any, data exists proving whitening agents are safe or effective. In fact, some studies suggest that hydrogen peroxide may be potentially cancerous. Intraoral use of hydrogen peroxide may also produce chronic infections from opportunistic bacteria.

▶ Wisdom-Teeth Extraction

It has long been assumed that third molars, commonly known as wisdom teeth, should be extracted in most individuals to prevent oral complications later in life. A growing trend in dental therapy has been to remove wisdom teeth before the development of their root structure is complete, usually in the early teen years. This procedure is thus less traumatic than if it is performed later in life. In addition, surgery on a younger and potentially healthier patient will minimize the healing time.

But a recent study, completed jointly by researchers from Harvard's Schools of Public Health and Dentistry and the University of North Carolina at Chapel Hill's School of Dentistry, has demonstrated that, based upon the risks associated with surgical procedures and the eventual complications and pathology, third molars should not be removed unless pathology is present.

▶ Drug Therapy Controls Thrush

Patients debilitated by disease or aggressive chemotherapy are commonly subject to the opportunistic overgrowth of the fungus *Candida albicans* in the mouth. Commonly called "thrush," this fungal growth is painful and may limit a patient's ability to eat or swallow. If the fungus spreads in a person with a compromised immune system, it may lead to a life-threatening infection.

Antifungal drugs have been utilized for some time in an effort to control thrush. Typically these drugs came in the form of lozenges that the patient dissolved in the mouth five times daily. But a daily, single tablet of a new drug called fluconazole has been found to reduce thrush symptoms in AIDS patients and in patients undergoing chemotherapy. Tablets should improve patient compliance.

Kenneth L. Kalkwarf, D.D.S.

Urology

Advances in urology during the past year include new and promising treatments for prostate problems, bladder and kidney cancer, urinary-tract stones, and impotence.

▶ The Prostate Gland

Prostate problems generally afflict men over 60 years old, and are, in fact, the most common reason for surgery for men in that age group. Recently, much research has focused on the development of alternative prostate treatments that would eliminate the need for the much more costly surgical procedures.

Holding great promise is a new drug called Proscar, now being tested to treat benign prostatic hyperplasia (BPH). In BPH, a condition occurring primarily in older men, the prostate enlarges, causing obstruction of the urinary flow. Proscar inhibits 5-alpha-reductase, the enzyme that helps turn testosterone into the prostatic-growth promoter, dihydrotestosterone. The drug helps "shrink" the prostate, apparently with few side effects, and thus relieves the obstruction. Proscar may win approval by the Food and Drug Administration (FDA) sometime in 1992.

Another family of medications, called alpha-adrenergic-blocking agents, also used to treat hypertension, have proved helpful in managing BPH. These drugs relax the prostatic smooth muscle, thereby relieving the bladder-outlet obstruction caused by an enlarged prostate.

A number of nonsurgical, nonpharmacological treatments for prostate enlargement are being investigated. These include balloon dilatation of the prostate and shrinking the prostate with hyperthermia, coils, stents, and the like.

While these new therapies add to physicians' arsenal against BPH, experts do not believe that any therapy currently available will supplant surgery as the mainstay for treating BPH.

Prostate surgery is the second-most-common procedure reimbursed by Medicare. Some 400,000 men undergo the procedure each year. (See also the article "The Problematic Prostate" on page 24.)

Prostate cancer kills about 30,000 men in the United States each year, in part because 70 percent of all cases go undetected until the malignancy has spread beyond the prostate gland.

Significant progress has also been made toward facilitating the early detection of prostate cancer, particularly through imaging techniques and the development of a blood test to detect a substance called prostate specific antigen. An annual digital rectal examination of the prostate, coupled with the determination of prostate specific antigen, followed by, if indicated, a transrectal ultrasound examination of the prostate, has significantly improved the accuracy with which an early diagnosis of prostate cancer can be established.

The Prostate Cancer Education Council, supported by the American Urological Association, sponsors an annual Prostate Cancer Awareness Week featuring screening clinics throughout the country. Its purpose is to educate men about this very common malignancy, and to encourage examination so that an early diagnosis can be made.

▶ Bladder and Kidney Cancer

Bladder cancer is the fourth-most-common form of cancer in men. New agents are being studied to treat superficial bladder cancer with the specific aim of preserving the bladder. When the bladder must be removed because of advanced cancer, urine must be diverted to a conduit. Advances continue to occur in reconstructive surgery whereby intestinal pouches, or neobladders, are created, and the patient maintains continence. Occasionally, the new bladder can be connected to the urethra, further improving the quality of life.

Doctors have expressed optimism over reports of immunological treatment of advanced kidney cancer. As our knowledge of molecular biology and genetic engineering increases, a breakthrough in treating kidney cancer, as well as other types of cancer, is likely.

▶ Other Urological Problems

The management of urinary-tract-stone disease has changed vastly in just a few years. Open surgical procedures to remove obstructing stones are quite uncommon now. Instead, using technological advances in telescopic, or endoscopic, instrumentation, many stones can now be treated with ultrasound or laser therapy under direct vision—all without resorting to surgical incisions. Extracorporeal-shock-wave stone fragmentation continues to improve as new generations of machines eliminate the need for anesthesia.

A study published in the *New England Journal of Medicine* (1/9/92) suggests that up to 80 percent of the cases of impotence, or erectile dysfunction, in American men derive from a lack of the chemical nitric oxide in the smooth muscles of the penis. This discovery could lead to new treatments for the condition. Research into the causes and pathophysiology of impotence has already resulted in new treatments for the condition. Vacuum devices have been popular with some patients. Also effective are injections of medication, such as prostaglandin E, into the penis.

Brendan M. Fox, M.D.

Women's Health

▶ Chorionic Villus Sampling and Amniocentesis Safety

Chorionic villus sampling (CVS) is a technique for gathering placental cells for genetic studies. It is usually performed during the first trimester of pregnancy, permitting diagnosis of genetic defects at a time when abortion is safer and less emotionally and physically traumatic than when performed later in pregnancy. A large American multicenter study published in 1989 indicated that the risk of miscarriage as a result of CVS was approximately 1 percent above the risk of amniocentesis. Amniocentesis, a test in which amniotic fluid is taken from the sac surrounding the fetus, is typically done at the fourth month of pregnancy and takes two weeks to process, permitting a mid-trimester pregnancy termination when a severe abnormality is detected. Experts estimate that the risk of amniocentesis triggering a miscarriage is approximately 0.5 percent.

A European study published in 1991, however, indicated an increased miscarriage rate due to CVS of 4.6 percent. Due to increasing concerns about the safety of CVS and to consumer pressure to obtain earlier diagnoses, many genetic facilities are starting to offer amniocentesis at earlier stages of pregnancy. Supporters of CVS point out that the European results may have reflected inexperience with the CVS procedure, which is a much riskier method in inexperienced hands. CVS proponents also point out that there have not been any well-designed studies of the safety of amniocentesis when performed during the late first or early second trimester.

There is little question that as educated consumers become aware of the increasing number of genetic disorders that can be diagnosed prenatally, and as more couples are choosing to postpone childbearing to an age at which they have an increased risk of an age-related genetic defect, there will be more demand for genetic studies, and more pressure for safe procedures that provide information on the fetus. Happily, geneticists are also working on ways of testing maternal blood to identify women at increased risk of bearing a child with a genetic disorder, and in the future may be able to culture fetal blood cells directly out of maternal blood.

Unfortunately, so far the major advances in genetics have simply enabled a wider variety of diseases to be diagnosed in utero, and prenatal diagnosis is used primarily to offer the option of pregnancy termination to the parents of affected fetuses. However, technology is being developed to insert healthy genes into individuals with diseases due to genetic defects. It is likely that in the future geneticists will be able to inject healthy genetic material into fetuses or individuals with genetic defects and actually correct the defect.

▶ Genes for Cystic Fibrosis and Fragile X

Cystic fibrosis is a serious genetically transmitted disease that causes chronic lung disease, chronic diarrhea, and growth problems. Historically, affected children usually died in childhood. More recently, many children are surviving into adulthood, but require ongoing intensive medical care. It is an autosomal recessive disease, meaning that the genetic defect that causes it is carried on a matched set of chromosomes. A child must inherit a defective gene from each parent to develop cystic fibrosis. It is one of the most common genetic defects in the Caucasian population, with one in 25 North

In amniocentesis, some of the fluid surrounding the fetus is removed to detect the chromosomal abnormalities that cause Down syndrome, sex-linked disorders (such as Tay-Sachs disease), and developmental disorders (such as spina bifida).

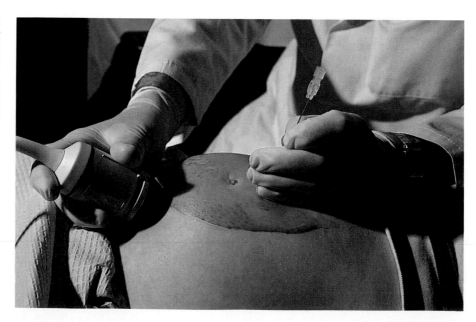

Americans of Caucasian ancestry carrying the gene, and one in 2,500 infants affected.

In recent years the gene sequence responsible for 75 percent of the cases of cystic fibrosis has been identified on chromosome number 7. Families and extended families of affected individuals can now be tested with a high degree of accuracy to see if they are carriers of the defective gene. Pregnant women can be tested with amniocentesis or chorionic villus sampling to see if they are carrying an affected child.

Unfortunately, the screening process is more complicated for the general population. People can try a blood test to see if they are carrying one of the common forms of the cystic fibrosis (CF) gene, but only one-half to two-thirds of couples at risk for an affected child will be identified. The National Institutes of Health (NIH) is funding pilot screening programs for the general population. At present, any individuals who are aware of cystic fibrosis in their families should consult with a genetic counselor and consider having screening tests done.

Another genetic breakthrough occurred in 1991 with the development of a more reliable DNA "probe" for detecting the Fragile-X chromosome. The Fragile-X syndrome is the most commonly inherited form of mental retardation, affecting one in 1,000 males and one in 2,000 females. Tests available to date have been cumbersome and not completely reliable. In late 1991 Dr. François Rousseau of the Centre Nationale de la Recherche Scientifique in France and Dr. Grant Sutherland from Queen Victoria Hospital in Australia reported simultaneously on the development of a more reliable methodology for testing for the gene for Fragile X, which will allow for more accurate prenatal and early-childhood diagnosis.

▶ Improving Research on Women's Health

Recently a variety of studies have highlighted what critics have long contended is a systematic disregard of women in clinical trials. For example, two recent studies on coronary heart disease found that doctors treat women with heart disease less aggressively than they treat men, even though the disease tended to be further advanced in the women. Women are also half as likely as men to undergo cardiac catheterization or bypass surgery to unclog blocked arteries. One reason for these discrepancies is the deplorable ignorance about heart disease in women. Most studies on this disease have had men as subjects.

The research on the effectiveness and safety of antidepressants (drugs used to treat clinical depression) has also been conducted solely on men. This omission of women is particularly alarming in light of new evidence that the effects of some antide-

Bernadine Healy, M.D., director of the National Institutes of Health, is working to close the gender gap in medical research by setting up more clinical trials focused on women's health issues.

pressants vary during the menstrual cycle. This may mean that doses that were found effective for men may be too high or too low for women. Likewise, a recent review of seven major studies concluded that hypertension treatments that work for men may be ineffective, or even harmful, for white women.

At the turn of the century, life expectancy for women was 45 years. Today life expectancy for women is close to 80 years in developed countries. As larger numbers of women can now anticipate living 30 years or more after menopause, and as women assume increasingly important roles in the labor force, there is much interest in women's health issues in the postreproductive years. The NIH, under fire from consumer groups and women congressional leaders for the historic lack of funding for research on women's issues, has launched major new initiatives in women's health research.

Led by director Bernadine Healy, the NIH has established the Office of Research on Women's Health to counteract this scientific sexual bias. Among the programs to improve the women's research agenda is the Women's Health Initiative, a 10-year project that will study the impact of diet, exercise, smoking cessation, and hormone-replacement therapy on cancer, cardiovascular disease, and osteoporosis in American women in all racial and socioeconomic groups.

▶ Women and Menopause: Debate over Estrogen-Replacement Therapy Continues

At the heart of the health care of midlife women is controversy concerning the pros and cons of estrogen-replacement therapy (ERT). A major 10-year study of 48,000 nurses indicated a 50 percent reduction in the rate of major coronary disease in women taking ERT. In addition, ERT has been found to produce dramatic reductions in bone fractures due to osteoporosis. However, these benefits come at the cost of many years of taking medication, as well as prolonged side effects such as vaginal bleeding, which in turn may increase the need for surgical procedures to evaluate and control the bleeding. There is also some evidence that prolonged use of ERT may lead to a small increase in breast-cancer risk.

More research is clearly indicated. While the benefits of ERT can be enormous, many women resist committing themselves to many years of taking medication that may prolong menstrual bleeding and may carry even a very small increased risk of breast cancer. Fortunately, the research community has been sensitized to the increasing need for research targeted at women.

▶ AIDS and Women

Women account for an increasing proportion of individuals affected with the human immunodeficiency virus (HIV). In Rwanda, 32 percent of women in one study carried the virus, while only a small proportion of American women test positive. However, women represent an increasing proportion of AIDS cases in the United States, and one study indicated that 70 percent of AIDS cases acquired by heterosexual intercourse occurred among women, representing 29 percent of the total cases. The death of Kimberly Bergalis, a young woman who had evidently acquired the virus from her dentist, also raised public awareness of the possibility of acquiring the HIV virus from other types of poorly understood transmission routes.

The risk of health-care workers transmitting the AIDS virus is minuscule, but health experts fear this slight risk will obscure the danger of the more common transmission routes: the majority of women contract AIDS through sexual contact with an infected individual or from sharing needles during use of illicit intravenous drugs with an infected person. While the risk of heterosexual transmission is greater to women than to men, ironically it was the news that a male basketball star, Magic Johnson, had evidently acquired the virus through heterosexual sex that has produced greater public awareness of this risk. Those at most risk for heterosexual HIV transmission, namely adolescents and young adults with multiple partners, report irregular use or nonuse of condoms in the majority of encounters. If the United States is to turn around this tragedy, massive public-health changes will need to take place.

Linda Hughey Holt, M.D.

World Health News

The most important new world-health problem of 1991 was the spread of cholera to the Western Hemisphere. AIDS continued its relentless march around the world, and once again the devastating effect of war on health became apparent in Iraq.

▶ Cholera

An epidemic of cholera began in Peru in January 1991, and continued to spread throughout South America. Public-health officials fear the epidemic may be difficult to eradicate, and it has already produced a significant increase in the public-health problems of the Western Hemisphere.

Cholera has existed in the Middle East for thousands of years. Since it began to be monitored in 1817, it has spread around the world seven times in global epidemics known as *pandemics*. The latest pandemic began in the early 1960s and, with its most recent appearance in Peru, now involves both hemispheres.

If not treated quickly, cholera is the most acute and fatal of the diseases that cause dysentery. The organism, one of the *Vibrio* family, contains an enterotoxin that causes the human intestine to pour

Cholera has spread like wildfire through South America (see map). In Peru alone, over 285,000 cases were reported, with 3,000 deaths. Victims (below) mostly lived in rural villages with poor sanitation facilities.

out large quantities of fluids and salts, producing very rapid dehydration and frequently death, if not treated. Antibiotics are relatively ineffective against this threat, and the primary treatment is massive fluid-and-salt replacement, either intravenously or by a technique developed fairly recently called oral-rehydration therapy (ORT). ORT involves having the affected individual drink large quantities of water with the proper amounts of sodium and potassium salts, sugar, and, if possible, some rice extracts. The sugar and the rice extracts activate intestinal mechanisms that reabsorb water and salts; this process alone is sufficient to save the majority of cholera victims, even if intravenous rehydration is not available.

Like some other major epidemic diseases (such as smallpox), cholera can be caused by either of two major varieties of the organism: classic cholera or the *El Tor* ("the bull") variety. El Tor cholera is responsible for the current pandemic. It is clinically less severe than the classic variety, although it is still very serious once symptoms develop. Up to 75 percent of those infected with the El Tor variety of *Vibrio cholera* are without symptoms. Thus, in the absence of a very high level of personal sanitation, the disease can easily spread from person to person without being detected. This greatly complicates control efforts and helps to maintain the disease's presence.

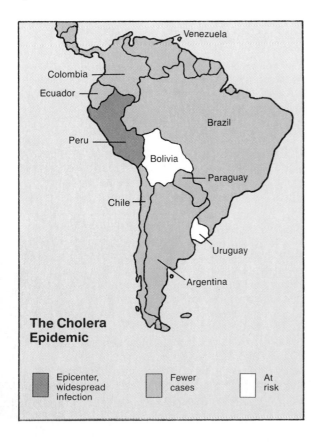

The Cholera Epidemic

■ Epicenter, widespread infection

■ Fewer cases

□ At risk

The poor sanitation in the coastal communities of Peru, where the current pandemic started, has meant that the cholera organism is being returned to the sea. Consequently, increasing numbers of fish and shellfish are being infected and then caught and eaten without adequate cooking in the seacoast towns of Peru, Ecuador, and Chile. Not only has cholera spread up and down the western coast of South America, but it has also spread inland in these countries and into the upper Amazon region of Brazil. In addition, some cases of cholera in New Jersey were traced to infected shellfish from Ecuador. As of December 1991, there have been over 285,000 reported cases of cholera in Peru, and almost 3,000 deaths.

The cholera epidemic has produced both physical devastation of the infected communities and major economic damage to the all-important fishing industries in the shore cities. Western nations have banned the import of uncooked fish and shellfish from the countries along South America's western coast.

The public mostly fears epidemics, the rapid spread and unusually high rate of diseases that come early in the appearance of cholera. The big fear of public-health authorities is that cholera El Tor will become *endemic* in South America, meaning that the disease would persist and be very difficult to eradicate. Endemic cholera may be able to survive almost indefinitely in the poor environmental conditions of the sprawling suburbs around the cities of many poor countries, putting a severe strain on the already limited medical facilities in such places.

Cholera has now been reported in six South American countries. The countries, in descending order by the number of cases, are Peru, Ecuador, Colombia, Brazil, Bolivia, and Chile. A growing number of cases have been reported in Central America in Guatemala, El Salvador, Panama, Honduras, and Nicaragua; and even in North America, mostly from Mexico, which has reported over 2,000 cases. The Pan American Health Organization estimates that more than 600,000 Central Americans will fall victim to the disease.

The U.S. has had 16 cases related to the South and Central American outbreak, but some were related to importation of food from regions other than South America. For example, in August in Maryland, three cases of cholera occurred following consumption of frozen coconut milk imported from Thailand. Canada had no cases of cholera in 1991.

U.S. public-health officials believe that Brazil is most likely underreporting the disease; the country has officially reported 887 cases, but experts believe that the correct number is probably more than 5,000, most of them in the regions along the Amazon River.

Travelers who develop a severe watery diarrhea (with or without vomiting) a week or less after traveling in an infected area should seek care immediately. If they test positive for the disease, it should be reported to local and state health departments.

Cholera continues to be an ongoing health scourge in an increasing number of nations worldwide. It will take its worst toll on nations with poverty and poor sanitation. Like AIDS, part of the danger inherent in cholera is its ability to be spread by people who are infected but have no symptoms.

▶ Ozone Depletion

For years, environmentalists have been decrying the rapid loss of the ozone layer in our atmosphere, which performs the vital function of filtering out most of the ultraviolet rays of the Sun before they reach the Earth's surface. The worst ozone depletion has occurred over Antarctica and the southern part of South America.

The ozone layer is broken down by fluorohydrocarbons, chemicals used in many industrial pro-

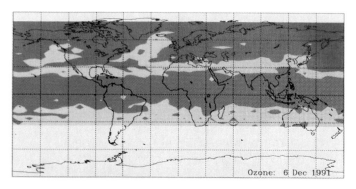

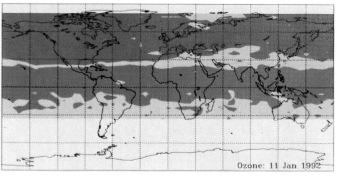

The Earth's ozone layer is rapidly being eaten away by human-made chemicals. In little more than a month, the ozone layer (yellow bands, above) has decreased dramatically over the Northern Hemisphere.

cesses worldwide, from refrigeration and air conditioners to aerosol spray cans. Once in the atmosphere, these chemicals gradually rise and, once at the level of the ozone layer, persist for a long time.

In 1991 some strange and frightening events developed in southern Chile, which, if they prove to be related to the ozone depletion, will show that environmentalists are correct to worry about ozone depletion. There have been reports from southern Chile of blinded salmon, rabbits, and sheep; the latter were noted to have cataracts, which have been shown to be increased by ultraviolet light. People in this region have reported increased photophobia (difficulty with glare and eye sensitivity in bright light), and even severe eye damage. There also have been reports of increased numbers of skin burns, skin blotches, and malignant melanomas of the skin, as well as damage to vegetation and even to the sails of yachts.

It is estimated that the amount of the cancer-producing ultraviolet-B radiation was at least 10 times the normal level in southern Chile on the worst days in 1991. Despite these reports, there are many scientists who remain unconvinced of the danger of ozone depletion. Nobody disputes, however, that the ozone hole in the Arctic is growing much faster than expected, and that there may be unfortunate consequences for people, animals, and the ecosystem in general.

▶ Declining Birthrates

The birthrates fell steeply in some of the former Eastern Bloc countries. The decline has been most severe in what was East Germany, where the birthrate dropped by about one-third in the two years from 1989 to 1991, and in Romania, where the decline has been about one-quarter. However, all of Eastern Europe has had some birthrate decline. Much of the drop is attributed to the lack of stability common during economic upheaval, as well as the recent relaxation of abortion restrictions in Eastern Europe.

▶ Infant Deaths in Iraq

There are few events that have a more destructive effect on the health of infants and children than war. The most vivid example of this during 1991 was the Persian Gulf war. Follow-up public-health studies in Iraq have suggested that this nation's child mortality has at least tripled, and perhaps quadrupled, to about 80 per 1,000 children, compared to a prewar estimate of 20 to 30 deaths per 1,000 children. Results of previous studies based at hospitals have been questioned, so the new study was based on approximately 9,000 home interviews conducted by Arabic-speaking interviewers.

The reasons for the increase in child mortality include the acute shortage of infant formula and powdered milk, an increase in the price of food, and lack of medicines and supplies. Apparently the food supply is sufficient for most children under five years of age to avoid acute starvation, but malnour-

The political upheaval in the former Soviet Union contributed to reduced farm production and a breakdown of distribution networks, resulting in food shortages and long food lines in some areas.

ishment is evident in almost 30 percent of these children. The extreme price inflation for food due to lack of supplies has caused millions of Iraqis to go hungry for the last part of every month, when the monthly government food rations are exhausted. The herds of cattle, goats, and sheep have shrunk by at least one-half as slaughter rates are increased to counteract the hunger.

Sanitation is poor, and millions are drinking contaminated water, which already is supporting high rates of typhoid and may lead to devastating rates of cholera, if that organism is introduced into the country.

Children were particularly hard hit by the Persian Gulf War. In Iraq, child mortality now stands at about 80 per 1,000 children, triple the prewar figure.

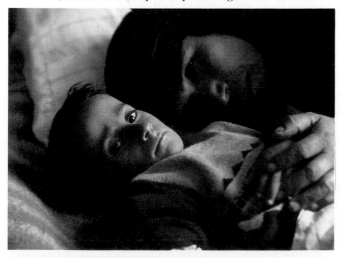

▶ Drop in World Food Supply

At a time when the world population is fast approaching 6 billion persons, the world food supply in 1991 dropped significantly for the first time since 1983. Contributing to this was the political upheaval in the former Soviet Union, where losses in wheat production due to weather and infrastructure chaos reduced production by almost 25 percent. Despite what happened to the Soviet Union, several of the former Eastern Bloc countries had food surpluses this year.

▶ AIDS

In the United States, AIDS is transmitted primarily through the sharing of infected needles or homosexual sex with an infected partner. Less than 6 percent of the 200,000 Americans afflicted with AIDS over the past decade contracted the disease from heterosexual contact. But worldwide, heterosexual transmission is the rule, not the exception—causing over 75 percent of all AIDS cases. Experts fear that this may soon be true in the U.S., as well. The incidence of heterosexually transmitted AIDS is rising dramatically, jumping up over 40 percent between 1989 and 1990.

Hardest hit by AIDS is Africa, where only one-tenth of the world's population lives, but where half the estimated 10 million AIDS infections around the globe occur. Unfortunately, recent research efforts in Zaire have been threatened by political chaos. Because of the growing number of AIDS cases in Africa, such research projects are considered to be critical.

James F. Jekel, M.D., M.P.H.

Index

Main article headings appear in this index as bold-faced capitals; subjects within articles appear as lower-case entries. Both the general references and the subentries should be consulted for maximum usefulness of this index. Cross references are to entries in this index.

Acknowledgements

ALIGNING EYES: STRAIGHTENING OUT STRABISMUS, Page 48
Reprinted from *FDA Consumer.*

ANATOMY OF A HOSPITAL BILL, Page 184
Reprinted from *HEALTH* (formerly *IN HEALTH*) magazine. Copyright © 1991.

BIOFEEDBACK: WIRED FOR A MIRACLE, Page 170
Reprinted with special permission from *HEALTH MAGAZINE,* May 1991. Copyright by Family Media, Inc. All rights reserved.

THE CHALLENGE OF RELIEVING PAIN, Page 56
Reprinted from *FDA Consumer.*

CROSS OVER TO CROSS-TRAINING, Page 134
Reprinted from *American Health Magazine* © 1991 by Hal Higdon.

FOOD NEWS BLUES, Page 92
Excerpted from *HEALTH* (formerly *IN HEALTH*) magazine. Copyright © 1991.

I'VE GOT A HUNCH, Page 178
First published in *NEW CHOICES for the Best Years,* May 1991.

LE BRAIN JOGGING, Page 165
Copyright 1991 by The New York Times Company. Reprinted by permission.

MENTAL GYMNASTICS, Page 162
Copyright 1991 by The New York Times Company. Reprinted by permission.

Illustration Credits

The following list acknowledges, according to page, the sources of illustrations used in this volume. The credits are listed illustration by illustration — top to bottom, left to right. Where necessary, the name of the photographer or artist has been listed with the source, the two separated by a slash. If two or more illustrations appear on the same page, their credits are separated by semicolons.

168 © Carl Purcell/Photo Researchers
169 © Joe Sohm/The Image Works
170 © D. Gorton/Onyx
171 © D. Gorton/Onyx
173 Top photos: © Dan McCoy/Rainbow; © Robert Goldstein/Photo Researchers
175 © Bob Daemmrich/Stock Boston
177 © Griffin/The Image Works
178 © Robbie Marantz/The Image Bank
180 © Louie Psihoyos/Matrix
181 © G. Azar/The Image Works
183 © Werner Bokelberg/The Image Bank
184- Artwork by Al Hering
191
192 © Jon Killen/Rainbow
193 © Culver Pictures; © The Granger Collection; © Photo Researchers
194 © Spider Webb; © Paul Gobel/Outline Press; © Spider Webb
195 © Spider Webb; © Jean-Marc Giboux/Gamma-Liaison
196 © Steve Earley/Gamma-Liaison
197 Upper left photos: © Custom Medical Stock Photo: bottom right: Hideki Fujii/The Image Bank
198 © David Parker/Science Photo Library/Photo Researchers
199 © David Parker/Science Photo Library/Photo Researchers; © Pete Turner/The Image Bank
201 © Edmond Alexander; © Dan McCoy/Rainbow
202 © Richard Hutchings/Photo Researchers
203 © Treat Davidson/National Audubon Society/Photo Researchers
204 Top row photos: © Runk/Schoenberger/Grant Heilman; center photo: © Larry Miller/Photo Researchers; bottom row: © James Castner; © C.K. Lorenz/Photo Researchers; © Dr. Edward S. Ross
205 © Nuridsany et Perennou/Photo Researchers
207 © Steve Webber/Stock Boston
209 © David Frazier/The Stock Market
210 © Howard Sochurek/Medical Images Inc.; © Will & Deni McIntyre/Photo Researchers
212 © Al Lamme/Phototake
213 © Richard Hutchings/Photo Researchers; © CNRI/Science Photo Library/ Photo Researchers
214 © Will & Deni McIntyre/Photo Researchers
215 © Teri J. McDermott/Phototake
216 Masel Company
217 Masel Company
218 Top three photos: American Association of Orthodontists; bottom: © Sylvia R. Miller/Custom Medical Stock Photo
219 Top: © Roberto Valladares/The Image Bank; others: © Stanley R. Gibbs/Peter Arnold
220 American Association of Orthodontists
221 Clockwise from top left: The Granger Collection; Everett Collection; Everett Collection; © UPI/Bettmann; © Peter Borsari/FPG International; © Archive Photos; The Granger Collection; Reuters/Bettmann
223 © Larry LeFever/Grant Heilman
224 © Martin M. Rotker/Photo Researchers
227 © Bachmann/The Image Works
228 Photo: © John Radcliffe/Science Photo Library/Photo Researchers
229 © Will & Deni McIntyre/Photo Researchers
230 © Florence Durand/Sipa
231 © Ted Horowitz/The Stock Market
232 © Frances M. Roberts
233 Both photos: Ciba-Geigy Corporation, Pharmaceuticals Division

234 © Robert Trippett/Sipa
235 © F. Lee Corkran/Sygma
238 © Bob Daemmrich/The Image Works
239 © Steve Slocum/Sipa
241 Reuters/Bettmann
247 © ELSCINT-CNRI/Science Photo Library/Photo Researchers
249 Copyright © 1991 by The New York Times Company. Reprinted by permission.
250 © Dion Ogust/The Image Works; © Cameramann/The Image Works
251 Cancer Facts and Figures—1992, © American Cancer Society
253 © Mike Okoniewski/The Image Works; © James Sugar/Black Star
254 © David Butow/Black Star
255 © James Sugar/Black Star
256 © Susan Leavines/Photo Researchers
257 © NCI/Science Source/Photo Researchers
260 © Reuters/Bettmann
261 © Judith Kramer/The Image Works
262 © Jim Wilson/NYT Pictures
263 © Alon Reininger/Contact Press Images/Woodfin Camp
266 Will & Deni McIntyre/Photo Researchers
269 Photo: Library of Congress; artwork: copyright © 1991 by the New York Times Company. Reprinted by permission.
270 © Todd Buchanan/Black Star
273 © Daemmrich/The Image Works
274 © L. Steinmark/Custom Medical Stock Photo
277 © Terry Qing/FPG International
279 © Pamela Price/Picture Group
285 © Hank Morgan/Rainbow
289 Photos courtesy of DuPont Radiopharmaceuticals
291 Photos courtesy of Chemtrak
292 © Matthew McVay/Saba
293 Edelman Public Relations
294 © Hank Morgan/Photo Researchers; © Charles Archambault
295 Clockwise from top right: NYT Pictures; © Ron Sherman/Uniphoto; © Will & Deni McIntryre/Photo Researchers
297 Gamma-Liaison
299 © Glassman/The Image Works
302 © Spencer Grant/FPG International
303 © Erika Stone/Peter Arnold
305 © Erika Stone/Peter Arnold
307 © David R. Frazier/Photo Researchers
308 © David H. Wells/The Image Works; © Dan Guravich/Photo Researchers
309 © Pat Goudvis/Picture Group
310 © Laura Dwight/Peter Arnold
311 © C.C. Duncan/Medical Images Inc.
312 © Jim Olive/Peter Arnold
313 © C.C. Duncan/Medical Images Inc.
314 UPI/Bettmann
319 © Zig Leszczynski/Animals Animals
321 © Ansell Horn/Phototake
322 © Jim Olive/Peter Arnold; © Dennis Oda/Sipa
323 © Roy Morsch/The Stock Market
324 Courtesy of the Addiction Research Center, VA Medical Center, Philadelphia
325 © Bryce Flynn/Picture Group
326 © Yoav Levy/Phototake
328 © Will & Deni McIntyre/Photo Researchers
329 © Courtesy of the National Institutes of Health
330 © Gustavo Gilabert/JB Pictures
331 Newsweek, May 6, 1991, staff.
332 NASA
333 © East News/Sipa; © Andy Hernandez/Sipa

Acknowledgments

We wish to thank the following for their services:
Typesetting, Dix Type Inc.; Color Separations, Colotone, Inc.;
Text Stock, printed on Champion's 60# Courtland Matte;
Cover Materials provided by Holliston Mills, Inc. and
Decorative Specialties International, Inc.;
Printing and Binding, R. R. Donnelley & Sons Co.